*Dictionary of Bibliographic
Abbreviations Found in the
Scholarship of
Classical Studies and
Related Disciplines*

Dictionary of Bibliographic Abbreviations Found in the Scholarship of Classical Studies and Related Disciplines

COMPILED BY
Jean Susorney Wellington

Greenwood Press
Westport, Connecticut • London, England

ERRATA

The headings "Cyrillic" and "Greek" on pages 101 and 102 were inadvertently transposed. The abbreviations on page 101 are Greek, and those on page 102 are Cyrillic.

For Donald, my Father,
and Celine

483.2
W45d

Library of Congress Cataloging in Publication Data

Wellington, Jean Susorney.
  Dictionary of bibliographic abbreviations found in
the scholarship of classical studies and related
disciplines.

  Bibliography: p.
  Includes index.
  1. Classical philology—Bibliography.   2. Classical
philology—Abbreviations—Dictionaries.   I. Title.
Z7016.W44   1983   [PA95]   483'.1   82-21068
ISBN 0-313-23523-6 (lib. bdg.)

Library of Congress Catalog Card Number: 82-21068
ISBN: 0-313-23523-6

First published in 1983

Greenwood Press
A division of Congressional Information Service, Inc.
88 Post Road West, Westport, Connecticut 06881

Printed in the United States of America

10 9 8 7 6 5 4 3 2 1

Contents

Preface

It is a pity that this dictionary needed to be compiled. The task would not have been required if keys to abbreviations were always provided in books and articles.[1] Since the autumn of 1970, when I became the librarian of the Burnam Classical Library at the University of Cincinnati, I have found that the most frequently recurring reference question has been to help users identify abbreviated bibliographic references. In fact, it seems to me that use of abbreviations is on the increase.[2] This dictionary is a partial answer to this recurrent question. I say partial because I came to realize that I could never hope to collect all the abbreviations that a Classicist might find. I hope that I have compiled a list that is big enough and arranged in such a way that the dictionary will answer most needs.

The work began in 1977, when I started collating lists of abbreviations found in major journals and reference works in Classical Studies such as *L'Année Philologique, Fasti Archaeologici, Archäologische Bibliographie, American Journal of Archaeology, Numismatic Literature, Oxford Classical Dictionary*, and *Lexikon der alten Welt*. I spent the academic term 1979-1980 at London's Institute of Classical Studies carefully going through its collection of journals searching for additional lists and scrutinizing footnotes for additional abbreviations.

Since the same abbreviation might be used for several different titles, and since journals often undergo numerous changes in title, I felt that it was necessary to provide users with full bibliographic descriptions. The descriptions are based on data found in standard reference sources such as the *Union List of Serials, British Union-Catalogue of Periodicals, Catalogue Collectif des Périodiques du Début du XVIIe Siècle à 1939, Gesamtverzeichnis deutschsprachiger Zeitschriften und Serien, Gesamtverzeichnis ausländischer Zeitschriften und Serien*, the *National Union Catalog*, the printed catalogs of the British Museum and the Bibliothèque Nationale, and the OCLC data base. In addition, two special periodical bibliographies were also consulted: J. E. Southan's *A Survey of Classical Periodicals*; *Union*

Catalogue of Periodicals Relevant to Classical Studies in Certain British Libraries (Institute of Classical Studies, London 1962); and G. Bruns's *Zeitschriftenverzeichnis* (Deutsches Archäologisches Institut, Wiesbaden 1964).[3] When possible I tried to secure descriptions from two different sources in order to ensure an accurate description. Whenever discrepancies were found, a third source or the title itself was examined to try to resolve the conflict. Notwithstanding my efforts, I am sure that inaccuracies still exist. I apologize for them, especially for those due to my own error. I will be grateful to any reader who brings them to my attention.

I thank the University of Cincinnati, especially its library system, for granting me a year's leave to work on this project. The following institutions very kindly let me use their library collections: the University of London's Institute of Classical Studies, Institute of Archaeology, and its central collection at Senate House; the British Museum; the University of Chicago; Indiana University; the University of Vermont; and Middlebury College, Vermont. Special gratitude is due the staff at the Institute of Classical Studies who showed me every courtesy during my nine-month stay in London, and I would like especially to thank the head librarian, Ana Healey, who served as a "sounding board" for my ideas about the project and responded with many helpful suggestions. I also want to thank all who have typed, alphabetized, and performed countless other tasks: Mary Lou Bradeen, Melodie Domurad, Rebecca Hanscom, Mark Hewitt, Huey McClellan, Susan Stites, Janet Sullivan, Joyce Sullivan, Theresa Susorney, Ines Torres, Sara Walter, and Hilda Wellington. Juli Peters was especially helpful during the last year of the preparation of the manuscript. She and Mary Luebering typed the final copy. I particularly want to thank Donald for his combined roles of taskmaster, principal research assistant, and patient husband.

Jean Susorney Wellington
University of Cincinnati

NOTES

1. Even in journals that provide lists of abbreviations which should be used, I have found articles in that very issue using different abbreviations.

2. Some journals have even begun to include abbreviations as part of the title or to display them prominently on the title page.

3. I very much regret that I did not become aware of "Sigelschlüssel der archäologischen Literatur" by Müller, Nagel, and Strommenger, *Acta Praehistorica et Archaeologica* (9/10) 1978/79, pp. 167-383, until a few weeks before giving this manuscript to the publisher. Although that work has far fewer abbreviations than mine (a little over half), it would have been an aid in helping me identify some illusive abbreviations.

Introduction

SCOPE

The dictionary is an attempt to bring together in one publication the abbreviations of journals, series, and standard works[1] that Classicists most frequently find in the scholarship of their discipline. Classical Studies is a cross-disciplinary study. While a scholar may specialize in Greek or Latin literature, archaeology, or history, he can never really isolate himself from the other areas of concentration. Researchers eventually learn to recognize the abbreviations to journals and standard works in their own area of concentration, but they often lose much time trying to identify citations to journals and works in other areas of Classical Studies or in allied fields like Byzantine and Ancient Near Eastern Studies.

I have purposely defined Classical Studies broadly in order that this work be of the most assistance to its users. All aspects of the study of the civilization of ancient Greece and Rome have been included. Furthermore, I have tried to include abbreviations likely to be encountered by Classicists working on the perimeters of Greek and Roman civilization. Those working in the Bronze Age and early Greece will find abbreviations used in ancient Near Eastern Studies, prehistoric archaeology, and anthropology. For historians and philologists working in the late antique and the early Christian eras, there are abbreviations used in Medieval and Byzantine studies. One area in which I especially tried to be thorough was in collecting abbreviations to the serial publications of regional archaeological and historical societies and museums. Familiarity with these titles is limited, and the identification of abbreviated references to them can be especially tedious for those working in provincial archaeology and history.

It became obvious during the year in London that I would have to limit this project lest the resulting work be in several volumes. Consequently the inclusion of abbreviations to ancient authors and texts (with a few exceptions) was abandoned as well as thorough coverage of papyrological abbreviations.[2] It was also not feasible to collect all abbreviations formed by the initial syllables of the title; to cope with this problem a special cross-reference and interfiling system was designed for the dictionary.

ARRANGEMENT

The dictionary consists of two parts. The first is a list of abbreviations followed by an alphanumeric code which refers users to bibliographic entries in Part II.

Part I: Abbreviations

Abbreviations formed from initial letters (for example, REA) and those composed of initial syllables (such as, RevEtAnc) are included. These are arranged in strict alphabetical order, with upper case letters filed before the same letter in lower case (for example, BAC, BaC, and BACr). The ampersand files before any letter (for example, A, A&F, and AB). Punctuation, most diacritical marks, and spacing between the elements have been eliminated in order to reduce unnecessary duplication (for example, Rev. Et. Anc. and Rev Et Anc appear as RevEtAnc). A few diacritical marks have been retained when, according to United States library practice, they affect filing: that is, the Swedish Å is filed as if spelled aa, the Scandinavian ø as if spelled oe, and the German ä, ö, and ü as if spelled ae, oe, and ue.[3] Part I also includes some abbreviations of a general nature for which a meaning is provided directly following the abbreviation. The following examples illustrate their varied nature.

Anz: Anzeiger. See also A (followed by the next capitalized letter).
Diss: Dissertation.
NF: Neue Folge.
T: Tidskrift; Travaux; Trudy.

References of the first type may help users identify abbreviations not found in Part I by directing them to check under Anzeiger in Part II or elsewhere in Part I; for example, if an abbreviation AnzÖstAkWiss is not in the list, the user should try AÖ, and so forth.

Although abbreviations of Classical authors and texts have had to be excluded from the work, a few potentially troublesome ones have been included with the meaning provided directly after the abbreviation in Part I. Usually these are cases where letter abbreviations have been used instead of the more common syllabic abbreviations such as in the following cases:

AP: Palatine Anthology
DL: Diogenes Laertius
SHA: Scriptores Historiae Augustae

The list of abbreviations in the Roman alphabet is followed by additional lists in the Greek and Cyrillic alphabets.

Part II: Bibliographic Citations

Since I soon realized that to collect all abbreviations would be an impossibility, Part II was designed to fill the need of users whose particular abbreviation might not be listed in Part I. Bibliographic descriptions are in order by title rather than by author or by sponsoring agency since abbreviations are usually based on title. The entries are not arranged in strict alphabetical order word by word but by key words. Articles, prepositions, and words meaning royal or imperial, for example, are disregarded in filing. The words that determine filing are in upper case; others are in lower case. Similar words, singulars and plurals, variant spellings, and different spellings required by grammar have usually been interfiled, since the abbreviations for them are usually the same.[4] Revue and Revista are both usually abbreviated as R or Rev; archaeological, archéologique, and archäologisches usually appear as Arch, Ar, or A; studi, studia, studies, and Studien invariably become Stud in abbreviations. By interfiling, the user consequently needs only to examine one alphabetic sequence in Part II to identify an unknown abbreviation beginning Stud. Cross-references are provided when the interfiling results in significant relocation in the alphabetic listing.

Transliteration of titles in non-Roman alphabets follows Library of Congress practice.

Entries for journals and other serials include title, place and dates of publication, and notes about any title changes. A subtitle or the name of the institution responsible for publication is included when the title alone does not make clear the topic it covers. If the serial is published as part of another series, this fact is also noted. The entry ends with a list of frequently used abbreviations for the title. The format for the entries is as follows:

TITLE; subtitle (Institution). Place dates (Series).
Notes about title changes. (Abbreviations).

In cases where journals have undergone changes in title, the latest title has usually been chosen for entry if the volume numbering is continuous. When the numbering is completely new, and there is no linking phrase such as "new series vol.," then a separate entry has usually been established for the new title. Cross-references have always been provided for variations in titles.[5]

Entries for monographs include title, author, latest edition statement, place and dates of publication, and series information. Frequently, notes about reprints and the date of the first edition are also provided. The last element again is the most commonly used abbreviations for the title. The format for the entries is as follows:

TITLE / Author. Edition. Place dates (Series).
Notes about reprints, etc. (Abbreviations).

Special mention should be made about the abbreviations provided in the entries. It is not the purpose of this dictionary to promote the use of particular abbreviations, but rather only to collect those already in use. Abbreviations are provided in Part II only when they have been found to be in common use; consequently for many entries no abbreviations are listed.[6]

NOTES REGARDING SPECIAL AREAS OF CLASSICAL SCHOLARSHIP

Ancient Authors and Texts

Identification of most abbreviated references to ancient authors and texts can be made by consulting the very full lists that appear in the following easily obtainable reference sources: *Oxford Classical Dictionary*, Liddell-Scott-Jones's *Greek-English Lexicon*, Lewis & Short's *Latin Dictonary*, and *Lexikon der alten Welt*.

Congresses

Although abbreviations for a few congresses have been included, for the most part this area of scholarship has been excluded. Because of their very complicated bibliographic nature, I am of the opinion that users can only be successfully aided in their identification by a checklist which would list their places and dates and the bibliographic descriptions for those actually published. Until this is compiled, users should consult the sections specifically devoted to congresses in such bibliographies as *L'Année Philologique*, the *Fasti Archaeologici*, and *Archäologische Bibliographie*.

Festschriften

Only general references for Festschriften have been provided in Part I. When users have references such as "Festschrift Robinson" or "Mélanges Murray," they should consult D. Rounds's *Articles on Antiquity in Festschriften: An Index*.[7] There they will find the actual title of the publication and its complete bibliographic description.

Papyrology

Abbreviations of papyrological texts have been a special headache for scholars, since they are often tucked away in serial publications or as part of complicated series. J. F. Oates, R. S. Bagnall, and W. H. Willis's *Checklist of Editions of Greek Papyri and Ostraca*[8] has organized the texts and provided full bibliographic descriptions including detailed information regarding reprint editions. Of special importance is that these prominent papyrologists have provided abbreviations which they urge be adopted as standard usage by scholars. Consequently in entries for papyrological works in Part II, only the abbreviations from the *Checklist* have been listed, and reprint information has not been included. If a user of this dictionary does not find his particular papyrological citation (which usually begin P . . . or Pap . . .) in Part I or Part II, he should certainly consult the *Checklist*.

NOTES

1. The decision not to limit the abbreviations to journals and series, as is often the case with abbreviations dictionaries, is due to the frequent use of abbreviations to works of reference and monographs. This has especially been the case among archaeologists and epigraphers, but philologists and historians are not far behind.

2. For ancient authors and texts several extensive lists already existed, and a checklist for papyri had just appeared. For such abbreviations the user is directed to the special sections at the end of this introduction.

3. Note that the symbol ¨ above vowels in Turkish or Hungarian does not affect filing.

4. This idea was borrowed from the *British Union-Catalogue of Periodicals* after noting how helpful it is in identifying unknown titles.

5. Although this system is not in agreement with the new cataloging rules that require separate entries for each title change, it has been adopted both to save space and because it best serves the user, since an abbreviation that reflects an earlier or later title might have been used by a scholar in order to be consistent with his other references to that journal.

6. I wish to caution writers that journals often publish their own lists of approved abbreviations or refer prospective contributors to already published lists. When they do not, a writer may be guided in his choice by those listed in Part II, but I urge him to provide a key to the abbreviations he has chosen to use.

7. D. Rounds (Cambridge, Mass: Harvard University Press, 1962). *Articles on Antiquity in Festschriften: An Index.* A similar title which may be of use for some Classicists is *Index to Festschriften in Jewish Studies* by C. Berlin (Cambridge, Mass.: Harvard University Press, 1971).

8. Missoula, Montana: Scholars Press, 1978 (*Bulletin of the American Society of Papyrologists. Supplements*, 1).

PART **I**

ABBREVIATIONS

A

Å: This letter is filed as if spelled aa.

A: Abhandlungen; Acta, Actes, etc.;
Analecta; Ancient; Anales, Annales, etc.; Annual, Annuaire; Archaeology, Archéologie, etc.; Archivio, Archives, etc.; Atti.

Ä: This letter is filed as if spelled ae in German words.

A: A352
A&A: A353
A&F: A561
A&R: A626
A&S: A381
AA: A420, A34, A95, A207, A421,
M257
AAA: A469, A224, A31, A36, A39,
A483, A638
AaA: A602
AAAd: A345
AAAH: A34
AAALiv: A224
AAAS: A225
AAASH: A39
AAASzeged: A35
AABordeaux: A32
AAC: A41
AAcMâcon: A218
AACos: A640
AAE: A485
AÄA: A482
AAEC: A220
AAEG: A226
AAegArch: A482
AAel: A420
AAG: A10
AagArch: A482
AAH: A39, A42
AAHG: A395

AAHung: A39
AAJ: A240
AAJord: A240
AAL: A642, M107, N83, R69, T105,
A224, A641
AALig: A641
AAM: A601
AAMz: A15
AAN: A644, A648, R68
AandS: A381
AANT: A34
AAntH: A34
AAntHung: A34
AAntiquaAcadSciHung: A34
AAnZ: A421
AAP: A644
AAPad: A657
AAPal: A646
AAPat: A657
AAPel: A643
AAPN: A644
AAPont: A644
AAPP: A643
AARA: A645
Aarb: A4
AArbKøb: A4
AArbøger: A4
AArch: A38-A39
AArchAcadSciHung: A39
AArchArSyr: A225
AArchCarpathica: A41
AArchHung: A39
AArchLodziensia: A43
AArchMus: I128
AArchSlov: A571
AArchStor: A38
AArchSyr: A225
AArchSyrie: A225
AArh: A603

AARMSI: M134
AARov: A645
ÅrsberättelseLund: A8
AAS: A225, A37, A614
AaS: A381
AASF: A219
AASN: A78
AASO: A222
AASOR: A222
AASP: A646
AASS: A81
AASyr: A225
AAT: A639, A649
AATA: A604
AATC: A659
AAU: A422
Audenaerde: A235
AAustr: A422
AAVV: By a number of authors.
AAW: A395
AAWG: A10
AAWL: A15, A21
AAWM: A15
AAWW: A399
AB: A166, A425, A211, A208, A592,
    A605, A623, G125
ABAI: I153
ABalt-Slav: A44
ABAW: A11
ABeja: A592
ABF: A673
ABFC: A535
ABFL: A672
ABG: A156, A487
Abh: Abhandlungen.
AbhAkadBerlin: A12
AbhAkadMainz: A15
Abhandl: Abhandlungen.
AbhandlHeidelbAkad: A18
AbhandlNaturHistGesNürnberg: A20
AbhandPreussAkadWissBerlPhilHistKl:
    A12
AbhBayAkWiss: A11
AbhBayr: A11
AbhBayerAK: A11
AbhBerl: A12
AbhBerlAkad: A12
AbhBerlin: A12
AbhdlBerlin: A12
AbhdlLeipzig: A21
AbhGött: A10
AbhGöttGes: A10
AbhHeid: A18
AbhHeidelb: A18
AbhHeidelbAk: A18
AbhHeidelberg: A18

AbhKM: A19
AbhL: A21
AbhLeipz: A21
AbhLeipzig: A21
AbhMainz: A15
AbhMünch: A11
AbhMünchen: A11
AbhPreussAk: A12
AbhPreussAkWiss: A12
AbhSächs: A21
AbhSächsAkad: A21
AbhSächGesWiss: A21
AbhsächsGesWiss: A21
AbhThANT: A22
AbhzuGeschdMath: A16
AbhzuGeschdMed: A17
ABI: A27
ABL: A672
ABM: A476
ABME: A476
ABMH: A476
ABoT: A217
ABourgogne: A227
ABPO: A228
ABr: G125
ABret: A427
ABretagne: A228
ABS: A229
ABSA: A229
Abt: Abteilung.
ABull: A605
ABV: A673
AC: A430, A376, A46-A47, A431,
    A26, A354, A428
Acad: A26
ACAM: A236
ACambr: A428
AcAn: A34
ACant: A429
AcArch: A38
AcArchLjub: A571
AcBibl: A27
ACC: A556
Acc: Accedemia.
AccNazLinc: A642, M107, M246, N83,
    R69, T106
ACCV: A146
ACD: A46
ACER: A230
ACF: A239
ACFA: A384
ACh: A354
AChil: A45
ACIAC1: A50
ACiL: A155
ACIO: A52

ACL: A155
AClass: A47
ACM: A383
ACMI: A383
ACMIT: A383
ACMT: A383, A651
ACMTr: A383
AcNazLinc: A642, M107, M246, N83,
   R69, T106
ACO: A49
AcO: A73-A74
AcOr: A73-A74
AcOrB: A73
AcOrH: A73
AcOrL: A74
ACR: A142
Acr: A30
AcRBelg: M95
ACRMI: M134
ACS: A190
Acta: See also A (followed by the
   next capitalized letter).
ActaA: A38
ActaAAcadHung: A39
ActaAArtHist: A40
ActaAbo: A31
ActaAcAbo: A31
ActaAcadHung: A34
ActaACarp: A41
ActaAnt: A35
ActaAntAcHung: A34
ActaAntArch: A35
ActaAntHung: A34
ActaAntiquaetArch: A34
ActaAntSzeged: A34
ActaAr: A38
ActaArch: A38-A39
ActaArchaeolHung: A39
ActaArchBp: A39
ActaArchBudapest: A39
ActaArchCarp: A41
ActaArchCarpathica: A41
ActaArchHung: A39
ActaArchKøbenhaven: A38
ActaArqHisp: A42
ActaAthen: S98
ActaCl: A47
ActaClassDebr: A46
ActaClassDebrecen: A46
ActaClDebrec: A46
ActaClDebrecen: A46
ActaDorpat: A48
ActaEthnHung: A57
ActaEthnogrHung: A57
ActaGH: A88
ActaHA: A62

ActaHistArtHung: A62
ActaHistDac: A61
ActaHistHung: A60
ActaInstRomFin: A64
ActaIRF: A64
ActaIRNov: A40
ActaLing: A67
ActaLitt: A68
ActaLittHung: A68
ActaLund: A86
ActaMN: A71
ActaMusNap: A71
ActaMusNapoca: A71
ActaMusNapocensis: A71
ActaNum: A72
ActaO: A73-A74
ActaOr: A73-A74
ActaOrHung: A73
ActaOrientHung: A73
ActaPhilSocDac: A76
ActaPraehistetArch: A78
ActaPrHistA: A78
ActaRCF: A80
ActArch: A38
ActArchBp: A39
ActaRCRF: A80
ActaRom: S99
ActasMemSocEspAntr: A70
ActaSS: A81
ActaSS(month): A81
ActasyMem: A70
ActaVel: A33
ActesCNSSav: A53
ActMuz: A92
ActSS: A81
ActSS(month): A81
ACUD: A46
ACuerpFac: A384
AcUG: A85
ACUM: A231
ACW: A189
AD: A355, A470
ADA: A396
ADAJ: A240
ADAW: A12
ADelt: A470
AdI: A271
ADIK: A13
ADion: A54
ADLI: A110
AdM: A518
ADN: A238
ADOG: A14
ADSV: A347
AdW: Akademie der Wissenschaften.
AE: A245, A471, A191, A433, A580,

A606, S151
AEA: A490–A491
AEAA: A492
AEAArch: A492
AEArq: A490
AEarq: A490
AEArte: A491
AECO: A494
AEG: A226
AEg: A191
Aeg: A97
ÄgAbh: A95
AEgB: A244
ÄgFo: A96
AegForsch: A96
AegHelv: A93
ÄgM: M191
AegM: M191
ÄgyptolForschgn: A96
ÄgZ: Z19
AegZ: Z19
AEHE: A241
AEHE(IVe sect): A241
AEHE(V^e sect): A242
AEM: A432, A385, A473
AEMausOe: A432
AEMI: A192
AeMitt: A432
AEMO: A432
AEMÖ: A432
AEMOE: A432
AEMOU: A432
AE/NB: N77
AEnghien: A233
AEO: A193
AEp: A245
AEPHE: A241
AEPHEH: A241
AEPHER: A242
AEpigr: A245
AEpigraphique: A245
AeR: A626
AerArch: A98
AErt: A433
AESEE: B265
AESEE(Arch): B261
AEsp: A492
AEspA: A490–A491
AEspAA: A492
AEspArq: A490
AEsph: A56
AEst: A246
AEth: A247
AEthnHung: A57
AEubM: A473
AEuras: A493

Aev: A99
Aevum: A99
ÄZ: Z19
AF: A96, A434, A690
AFA: A58, A484
AFB: A408
AFC: A169
AFD: A634
AFGK: A496
AFH: A495
AFig: A607
AFK: A512
AfK: A523
AFLA: A255
AFLB: A249
AFLC: A248
AFLL: A250
AFLM: A251
AFLN: A252
AFLNice: A252
AFLP: A254
AFLPad: A253
AFLPer: A254
AFLT: A258, H123
AFMB: A259
AFMC: A248
AFML: A260
AFMP: A261
AFO: A523
AfO: A523
AfOBhf: A523
AFP: A497
AfP: A525
AFrH: A495
AFribourg: A264
AfricaItal: A101–A102
AfricaItalianaRiv: A102
AfriI: A101–A102
AfriIt: A101–A102
AfrIt: A101–A102
AG: Aulus Gellius.
AG: A356, A194, A208–A210, A334,
   A500
Ag: A633
AgAbh: A95
AGB: W31
AGb: A139
AGD: A357
AGDS: A357
AGeo: A436
AGf: A114
AgFo: A96
AGG: A466
AGI: A501
AGIt: A501
AGKMW: A358

AG1I: A501
AGM: S267
AgM: M191
AGNM: A397
AGO: A498
Agora: A633
AGP: A499
AGPh: A499
AGPhilos: A499
AGR: A1
AGRL: A619
AGWG: A10
AgyptolForschgn: A96
AgZ: Z19
AH: A173, A438, A564, A590
AHA: A62
AHAM: A171
AHAW: A18
AHC: A268
AHD: A504
AHDE: A388
AHDEsp: A388
AHDLMA: A504
AHDO: A505
AHDo: A505
AHDO-RIDA: A505
AHE: A243
AHES: A506
AHGA: A502
AHHI: A118
AHID: A172
AHistHung: A60
AHMA: A504
AHN: A63
AHP: A507
AHProv: A267
AHR: A143
AHRev: A143
AHuy: A237
AHW: A105
AI: A65, A101-A102, A134, A195,
  A442, A597
AIALux: A270
AIAS: S98
AIASI: A195
AIB: A597, C185
AIBL: C185
AIBS: M118
AICA: A271
AIEC: A389
AIEG: A174
AIEMA: B304
AIFrZagreb: A263
AIFZ: A263
AIGC: A278
AIHS: A511

AIIA: A390-A391
AIIAC: A390
AIIACluj-Napoca: A390
AIIAI: A391
AIIAIasi: A391
AIIAr: A390-A391
AIIC: A390
AIICN: A390
AIIN: A279, A664
AIINum: A279, A664
AIIS: A280
AIJ: A359
AIK: A273
AILC: A169
AIOB: A274
AION: A281
AION(archeol): A281
AION(filol): A281
AION-L: A281
AION(ling): A281
AIPB: A275
AIPH: A275, A509
AIPh: A274
AIPHO: A274
AIPhO: A274
AIPhOr: A274
AIPHOS: A274
AIPO: A274
AIRF: A64
AIRN: A40
AIRRS: S99
AIRSOpArch: O20
AIRSOpRom: O25
AISC: A392
AIStCl: A392
AIug: A442
AIUON: A281
AIV: A647
AIVP: A162
AIZ: A584
AJ: A378, A441, A113, A134
AJA: A145
AJAH: A144
AJArch: A145
AJBA: A694
AJN: A146
AJNum: A146
AJP: A147
AJPH: A147
AJPh: A147
AJPhil: A147
AJSemL: A148
AJSL: A148
AJSLL: A148
AJug: A442
AK: A579, A523, A360, A444

AkadErt: M17
AkAlm: M18
AKB: A443
AKErt: M17
AKF: A523
AKG: A512
Akkadica: A104
AKM: A19
AKMV: A3
AKorrBl: A443
AKut: A66
AL: A86, A283, A514
ALA: A255
al-And: A205
Alb: A109
ALBO: A175
AlbR: A108
AlBrioude: A116
ALex: A513
ALG: A335
ALGHJ: A407
ALGP: A285
ALing: A515
AlingHung: A67
ALKMA: A516
ALL: A513
ALLG: A513
Allg: Allgemein.
ALMA: B273
AlmanachWien: A117
ALMF: A282
ALN: A257
ALorraine: A315
ALOS: A284
ALouviere: A234
AlT: A107
Alt: A127
AltbayerMonatsschr: A121
AlteModKunst: A122
AltO: A123
AltOr: A123
AltOrF: A130
AltschlesBl: A136
AltThür: A119
Alt-Thüringen: A119
ALUOS: A284
Aluta: A138
ALw: A517
AM: A287, A568
AMA: A348
AMAAV: A656
AmAcRome: A110
AMal: A176
AMAMod: A658
AmAn: A141
AMAT: A659

AMBB: A288
AMDMod: A661
AMediev: A445
AmerAcadRome: M110
AMErgH: M192
AmerHistRev: A143
AmericanClR: A142
AmericanJPh: A147
AmerJournArch: A145
AmerNumSocNMon: N116
AMes: A59
AMF: A163
AMGR: A289
AmHistRev: A143
AMI: A446
AMidi: A287
AMIIN: A664
AMIran: A446
AmJ: A145
AmJArch: A145
AmJArchaeol: A145
AmJofarch: A145
AmJournalArch: A145
AmJournArch: A145
AmJournArchaeol: A145
AmJournNum: A146
AmJournofPh: A147
AmJournPhil: A147
AmJournSemLang: A148
AmJPh: A147
AmJPhil: A147
AMMarche: A662
AMMG: A666
AMN: A71
AMNG: A362
AMold: A568
AMons: A236
Amp: A154
AMPlovdiv: G60
AMRB: A288
AMRBB: A288
AMRom: A663
AMS: A69
AMSEAE: A70
AMSEAntr: A70
AMSEAP: A70
AMSEAEP: A70
AMSI: A665
AMSIA: A665
AMSL: A518
AMST: A667
AmStP: A151
AMT: E25
AmtlBer: B65
AmtlBerPrS: B65
AmtsblWien: A157

AMUGS: A361
AMuGS: A361
AMusAPlovdiv: G60
AMusDPlovdiv: A71
AMusNapocensis: A71
AMusPlovdiv: G60
AMVM: A660
AMW: A519
AN: Akademiia Nauk.
AN: A406
An: Anales; Analecta; Anais. <u>See</u>
  <u>also Ann and A (followed by the</u>
  <u>next capitalized letter)</u>.
AnAAS: A225
AnAcRom: M134
AnadoluAras: A160
AnalAcRom: M134
AnalAug: A164
AnalBoll: A169
AnalBolland: A166
AnaleleAcadRom: M134
AnalFran: A170
AnalFranc: A170
AnalFrancisc: A170
AnalO: A178
AnalOr: A178
AnalRom: A179
AnalSacrTarrac: A181
AnalUnivBucuresti: A182
AnalUnivCraiova: A183
ANamur: A310
ANantes: A290
AnArchSyr: A225
AnatolianStud: A186
AnatSt: A186
AnatStud: A186
ANB: A447
AnB: A166
AnBekk: A208
AnBi: A165
AnBib: A165
AnBoll: A166
AncEg: A191
AncInd: A195
ANCL: A332
AnCl: A376
AnColmar: A316
AnComMonTrans: A383
AncSoc: A203
AncW: A204
AnD: A168
AnDambach: A314
AnDobr: A168
AndServSuppl: A304
ANE: A196
AnecdBekk: A208

AnecdGr: A208-A212
AnecdGraec: A208-A212
AnecdGraecOxon: A210
AnecdMedGraec: A213
AnecdOx: A210
AnecdPar: A212
AnecdStud: A214
AnecGrParis: A212
AnEgB: A244
ANEP: A197
AnEp: A245
ANET: A198
AnHE(ScHist): A241
AnHE(ScRel): A242
AnHist: A161
ANice: A320
Anima: A216
AnInstCluj: A390, A392
AnInstIasi: A391
AnnInstIstArhCluj: A390
AnIsl: A277
ANivelles: A309
ANivernais: A293
AnkaraDilDerg: D65
ANL: A449
AnLorraine: A315
ANLR: A642
AnMunster: A319
Ann: Annual, Annuaire; Annals, etc.
  <u>See also An and A (followed by</u>
  <u>the next capitalized letter)</u>.
Ann: A271, A279, A301
AnnAAS: A225
AnnAcEtr: A220
AnnAcFenn: A219
AnnAcTorino: A221
Annales: <u>See also Ann and A (fol-</u>
  <u>lowed by the next capitalized</u>
  <u>letter)</u>.
Annales: A304, A243
AnnalesarchSyrie: A225
Annalesdel'Instarch: A271
AnnalesEcon: A243
AnnalesESC: A243
AnnalesInstitutoum: A276
AnnalesOSB: A177
Annali: A271
AnnaliBari: A249
Annalidell'InstArch: A271
AnnaliIstNumismatica: A279
AnnaliNapoli: A252
AnnalsofAA: A224
AnnAnt: A304
AnnAntJord: A240
AnnArch: A223
AnnArchAnthrLiverpool: A224

AnnArchArSyr: A223
AnnArchArSyri: A223
AnnArchBrux: A307
AnnArchSyrie: A225
AnnASyr: A225
AnnAthen: A469
AnnBari: A249, A259
AnnBrSchAth: A229
AnnBrSchAthens: A229
AnnBruges: H19
AnnBSArchAth: A229
AnnCagliari: A248
AnnClBp: A327
AnnColl: A239
Anndel'InstitutdePhilol: A274
Anndell'Inst: A271
AnndI: A271
AnndInst: A271
AnndIst: A271
AnndRScuolArchAtenMissItalOriente
  A301
AnnduServ: A304
AnnduServicedesant: A304
AnnEcPr: A242
AnnEcPratHEt: A241
AnneeEp: A245
AnneeEpigr: A245
AnnEgBibl: A244
AnnEötvös: A327
AnnEp: A245
AnnEPHE: A241
AnnEPHEt: A241
AnnEpigr: A245
Annepigr: A245
AnnESC: A243
AnnEth: A247
AnnFABelg: A262
AnnFederArchHistBelgique: A262
AnnFogg: A296
AnnGand: H22
AnnGeogr: A265
AnnIEOAlg: A272
AnnInst: A271, A276
AnnInstArchLuxembourg: A270
AnnInstKond: A273
AnnInstPhilHistOrient: A274
AnnION: A281
AnnIst: A271
AnnIstGiapp: A278
AnnIstNum: A279
AnnLecce: A250, A260
AnnLeedsUnOrSoc: A284
AnnLiv: A224
AnnMidi: A287
AnnMusAlex: A289
AnnMusGrRdAlex: A289

AnnMusNatArchPlovdiv: G60
AnnNap: A252
AnnNormandie: A287
AnnOSBM: A177
AnnPal: A261, A303
AnnParis: A329
AnnPerugia: A254
AnnPhil: A294
AnnPhilHist: A274
AnnPisa: A302
AnnPlovdiv: G60, G62
AnnRep: Annual Report. <u>See also</u>
  <u>AR (followed by the next capit-</u>
  <u>alized letter)</u>.
AnnRepCypr: A295
AnnRepFoggArtMus: A296
AnnRepMFA: A234
AnnRScuNormSupPisa: A302
AnnSAE: A304
AnnSAEg: A304
AnnScAt: A301
AnnScAtene: A301
AnnScPisa: A302
AnnScuolIrAt: A301
AnnSemPalermo: A303
AnnServ: A304
AnnServAnt: A304
AnnServAntEg: A304
AnnServAntiqu: A304
AnnServAntiquEgypte: A304
AnnSkopje: G65
AnnSocArchNamur: A310
AnnSocRoyArchBruxelles: A307
AnnSofia: G61
AnnSRABrux: A307
Annstdir: A323
AnnTheol: A325
AnnTriest: A326
AnnualBrScAthens: A229
AnnualDepJordan: A240
Annuario: <u>See also Ann (followed</u>
  <u>by the next capitalized letter)</u>.
Annuario: A301
AnnuarioAccEtrCortona: A220
AnnuarioAcEtr: A220
AnnuarioAt: A301
AnnuarioScArcheolAtene: A301
AnnuarScuolaarchAtene: A301
AnnuBritSchoolAthens: A229
AnnuMusAntiqIstanbul: I128
AnnUnivBesançon: A286
AnnUnivBudapest: A327
AnnUnivPadova: A328
AnnuReportInstArchUnivLondon: A297
AnnuSocArchBruxelles: A308
AnnWorcArtMus: A331

ANOH: A4
AnOr: A178
ANormandie: A291
AnOx: A210
AnPar: A212
AnRom: A179
ANRW: A678
ANRWFestschriftJVogt: A678
ANS: A149, M314, N116, N122
ANSAE: A304
ANSCent: A149
AnSelestat: A305
AnSEV: A311
ANSMN: M314
ANSMusN: M314
ANSMusNotes: M314
ANSN: M314
ANSNNM: N116
ANSNS: N122
ANSP: A302
AnSt: A186
AnSTar: A181
AnStud: A186
Ant: A352
AntAb: A353
AntAf: A374
AntAfr: A374
AnTan: A351
AntAth: A375
AntC: A376
AntChr: A354
AntCl: A376
AntClass: A376
Antclass: A376
AntDenk: A355
AntDenkm: A355
AntH: A377
AnThann: A317
AnthGraec: A334
AnthLyr: A335
AnthLyrGraec: A335
AnthLyrGraeca: A335
AntholPal: Palatine Anthology.
Anthr: Anthropology, Anthropologie,
   etc.
Anthr: A339-A343
AnthrHung: A336
AnthrK: A337
Anthropol: A339-A343
AnthrQ: A338
AntHung: A377
AntikvTidskrSverige: A366
Antiq: A372-A373
AntiqAfr: A374
Antiqclass: A376
AntiqJourn: A378

AntiquAfricaines: A374
AnitquClass: A376
AntiquHung: A377
AntiquitRundsch: A380
AntiquJournal: A378
AntiquNationales: A379
AntJ: A378
AntJourn: A378
AntK: A360
AntKunst: A360
AntNat: A379
AntPal: Palatine Anthology.
AntPis: A346
AntPl: A363
AntR: A368
AntSt: A186
AntTan: A351
AntTidskr: A366
AntWelt: A365
AnuariInst: A389
AnuariInstEstCat: A389
ANum: A72
AnUnivSof: G63
Anz: Anzeiger.
AnzAkadWien: A399
AnzAkWien: A399
AnzAlt: A395
AnzAW: A395, A399
AnzAWW: A399
AnzeigdkbayerAkdWiss: G12
Anzeiger: A421
AnzeigerWien: A399
AnzElsässAltkde: C5
AnzfschweizAK: A400
AnzÖAk: A399
AnzÖsterAkadWissPhilHistKl: A399
AnzSchwAlt: A400
AnzSchweiz: A400-A401
AnzSchweizAK: A400
AnzSchweizAlt: A400
AnzSchweizAltdke: A400
AnzWien: A399
AO: A123, A210, A73-A74, A523,
   A572, A585
AOASH: A73
AOAT: A124
AOATS: A124
AOAW: A399
AOB: A132
AOC: A522
AOChr: A522
AOD: A129
AÖAW: A399
AÖG: A520
AOEG: A520
AOF: A130, A523

AOf: A523
AoF: A130
AOG: A520
AOH: A73
AOKW: A292
AOL: A524
AOP: A521
AOr: A521
AOrientHung: A73
AOS: A150
AOSBM: A177
AOT: A131
AOTU: A133
AP: Palatine Anthology.
AP: A212, A294, A452-A453, A474,
    A525, A569, A586, A591
APA: A78, A12, P110
APAA: A668
APal: Palatine Anthology.
APamKiev: A586
APant: A75
APARA: A668
APAT: T87
APAW: A12
APEF: P20
APF: A525
APf: A525
APh: A294
APhil: A77
ApJ: A404
APL: A522
APl: Anthologia Planudea.
APLev: A522
APM: A393
APN: A293
APol: A452-A453
APolona: A452
APort: A493
APP: A199
AppAnth: E77
APrAW: A12
APregl: A569
AProd: A532
AProt: A79
APS: A188
AQ: A600
AquilN: A406
AquilNost: A406
AR: A626, A454-A457, A201
Ar: A413-A419
ARA: A200
ARAA: A483
ARAB: A200
ARadRaspr: A570
ArAu: A422
ARBB: B243

ArbBlRest: A409
ArbeitsblRestauraturen: A409
ArbeitsuForschberSachsen: A408
ArBerne: A508
Arch: Archaeology, Archéologie,
    etc. See also Arh and Arkh
    (for Slavic titles).
Arch: A413-A419
ArchA: A422
ArchAA: A483
ArchAAd: A483
ArchAegArch: A482
ArchAel: A420
ArchAeliana: A420
Archaeol: A417
ArchaeolBelgica: A424
ArchaeologZeitung: A464
ArchäolZeitung: A464
ArchaiolEphem: A471
ArchAn: A469
ArchAnalekta: A469
ArchAnAth: A469
ArchAnthrop: A484
ArchAntrEtn: A485
ArchAnz: A421
ArchArtiDec: A480
ArchAustr: A422
ArchAustriaca: A422
ArchBegriffsGesch: A487
ArchBelg: A424
ArchBibGBrit: A426
ArchBibl: A425
ArchBLim: A423
ArchBM: A476
ArchByzMnem: A476
ArchCam: A428
ArchCamb: A428
ArchCambrensis: A428
ArchCantiana: A429
ArchCl: A430
ArchClas: A430
ArchClass: A430
ArchDalm: A538
ArchDelt: A470
ArchDeltion: A470
ArchDepRom: A489
ArchEkklHist: A472
Archeocivil: A477
ArcheolgrTriest: A478
ArcheologErtesito: A433
ArchEph: A471
ArchEphem: A471
ArchEphemeris: A471
ArchepigrMitt: A432
ArchEpigrMittÖsterreich: A432
ArchEpMitt: A432

ArchepMitt: A432
ArchErt: A433
ArchErtes: A433
ArchErtesitö: A433
ArchEsp: A490-A492
ArchEspA: A490-A492
ArchEspArch: A490
ArchEspArq: A490
ArchEspArt: A41
ArchEspArte: A491
ArchfAnthr: A484
ArchfAnthrop: A484
ArchfBegriffsgeschichte: A487
ArchfgdPhilos: A499
ArchfGeschdPhilos: A499
ArchfGPhilos: A499
ArchflatLex: A513
ArchfOrient: A523
ArchfPap: A525
ArchfReligionswiss: A528
ArchfRelWiss: A528
ArchfRw: A528
ArchfürPap: A525
ArchfgdPhilos: A499
ArchfGeschdPhilos: A499
ArchGeogr: A436
ArchGeschMed: S267
ArchGiur: A500
ArchGlIt: A501
ArchGlotlIt: A501
ArchHistDO: A505
ArchHom: A437
ArchHung: A438
ArchInf: A439
ArchInstBulg: A577
ArchIntelligenzBlatt: A440
ArchIug: A442
ArchIugoslavica: A442
Archiv: See also Arch (followed by
    the next capitalized letter).
Archiv: A525
ArchivEspanArq: A490
ArchivEspanArte: A491
ArchivesSuissesAnthrGen: A554
ArchivfLatLex: A513
ArchivflatlexuGramm: A513
ArchivHistDrOr: A505
ArchivInstPaléontHumMem: A509
ArchivMiss: A518
ArchivfürlateinLexik: A513
Archivio: See also Arch (followed
    by the next capitalized letter).
ArchivioInternazEtnogrPreist: A510
Archivo: See also Arch (followed
    by the next capitalized letter).
ArchivoEspañolArqu: A490-A491

ArchivoEspArte: A491
ArchivoPrehistLevantina: A527
ArchivoStSiciliano: A549
ArchivPap: A525
ArchivPhilos: A499
ArchivRel: A528
ArchivRom: A529
Archivum: A481
ArchJ: A441
ArchJahrb: J21
ArchJourn: A441
ArchJournal: A46
ArchJug: A442
ArchK: A444
ArchKeil: A523
ArchKözl: A444
ArchKözlemenyek: A444
ArchKorrbl: A443
ArchKorrespondenzbl: A443
ArchKozl: A444
ArchL: A513
ArchlatLex: A513
ArchLiturg: A517
ArchLMA: B273
ArchMed: A445
ArchMiss: A518
ArchMittIran: A446
ArchN: A448
ArchNachrBaden: A447
ArchNews: A448, H2
ArchNL(Br): A449
ArchNL(US): A448
ArchOr: A521
ArchOrient: A521
ArchOtkr: A585
ArchOxon: A451
ArchP: A525
ArchPamjatkiURSR: A586
ArchPap: A525
ArchPapyrusf: A525
ArchperlAntelEtn: A485
ArchPF: A525
ArchPhilos: A526
ArchPol: A452-A453
ArchPolon: A452
ArchPolona: A452
ArchPolski: A453
ArchPont: A474
ArchPort: A591
ArchPortugues: A591
ArchPrehLev: A527
ArchPrHistLev: A527
ArchPrLev: A527
ArchRelig: A528
ArchRelw: A528
ArchRelWiss: A528

ArchRep: A455
ArchReports: A455
ArchRom: A529
ArchRoz: A457
ArchRozhl: A457
ArchRozhledy: A457
ArchRozled: A456
ArchRW: A528
ArchS: A458
ArchScot: A459
ArchSlovFontes: A460
ArchSocRom: A489
ArchSofia: A576
ArchStor: A539
ArchstorCla: A536-A537
ArchStorCalabria: A536-A537
ArchstorCalLuc: A537
ArchStorFilos: A488
ArchStoricoperProvNap: A545
ArchstorItal: A539
ArchstorLomb: A541
ArchStorPatria: A489
ArchstorProvdiSalerno: A544
ArchstorProvNap: A545
ArchStorPugl: A547
ArchstorSic: A549-A550
ArchStorSicilia: A549-A550
ArchStorSiciliaOrient: A550
ArchstorSicor: A550
ArchTess: A475
ArchTriest: A478
ArchVestnik: A571
ArchZeit: A464
ArchZtg: A464
AR: See also AnnRep (Annual Report)
   (followed by the next capitalized
   letter).
ARDA: A295
ARDC: A295
ARdeM: A530-A531
ARE: A201
ARe: A528
ARepLondon: A455
Areth: A563
ArFSchweiz: A435
ARFVP: A675
ArH: A503
Arh: See also Arch and Arkh (follow-
   ed by the next capitalized let-
   ter).
ArhEz: A580
ArHisp: A503
ArhMol: A568
ArhMold: A568
ArhMoldovei: A568
ArhOlt: A572

ArhPam: A586
ArhPamURSR: A586
ArhPr: A569
ArhPreg: A569
ArhPregled: A569
ArhSb: A588
ArhSbornikErm: A588
ArhunEtn: A567
ArhV: A571
ArhVest: A571
ArhVestnik: A571
ARID: A179
ArkDerg: T129, T131
ArKF: A523
Arkh: See also Arch, Arh (followed
   by the next capitalized letter).
Arkh: A578
ArkhEz: A576
ArkhiEtn: A580
ArkhIssl: A582
ArkhIsslUKr: A582
ArkhOtkr: A585
ArkhPam: A586
ArkhRask: A587
ArkhSbor: A588
ArkIsslGruz: A581
ArkKiev: A579
ArkOtkr: A585
ArkPamURSR: A586
ArkUkr: A579
ArLeon: A514
ARLibyanStudies: A299
ARM: A530-A531
ARMSI: M134
ARMT: A530
ArO: A521
ARonse: A266
ArOr: A521, A523
ARoz: A457
ARozhl: A457
ArPap: A525
ArPhil: E14
ArqBeja: A392
ArqPort: A591
ArqueHist: A590
ArquPort: A591
ARR: A570
ArRoz: A457
ARS: A180, A202
ArsAs: A594
Arsberättelse: A8
ArsH: A596
ArsHisp: A595
ArsIsl: A597
ArsIslam: A597
ArsOr: A598

ARSRMmeSectStiintIst: M134
ArtandArch: A602
ARTANES: A103
ArtAsiae: A614
ArtB: A605
ArtBull: A605
ArteLomb: A610
ArteVen: A613
ArTi: A553
ArtiFig: A607
ArtJ: A608-A609
ArtLomb: A610
ArtQ: A611
ArtQuart: A611
ArtS: A612
ArtScript: A615
ArtVen: A613
ARU: A625
ARV: A675
ArVen: A557
ARVinAmMus: A674
ARVP: A675
ARW: A528
ARw: A528
AS: A186, A125, A304, A458, A622
ASA: A301, A304, A400
ASAA: A301
ASAB: A307
ASAE: A304
ASAG: A554
ASAIO: A301
ASAntEg: A304
ASAtene: A301
ASAW: A21
ASAWL,p-h: A21
ASBoll: A81
ASbor: A588
ASCANewsletter: M2
ASCG: A321
Asch: A135
ASCL: A537
AScuolPisa: A302
ASD: M99
ASE: M113
ASFN: A312
ASFNA: A312
ASG: A21
ASGA: A401
ASGP: A303
ASGW: A21
ASHAL: A315
ASHS: A318
ASI: A539
ASIA: A665
ASJE: A84
ASL: A541

ASLig: A654
ASLod: A540
ASM: A461, A542
ASMG: A666
ASN: A545
ASNAP: A302
ASNP: A302
ASNU: A83
ASocArchNamur: A310
ASocSciLittCannes: A321
ASoignies: A232
ASP: A547
ASPA: A670
ASPABA: A670
ASPap: A151
ASParm: A545
ASpr: A125
ASPrat: A543
ASR: A364, A533
ASRS: A489
ASS: A549, A81-A82
ASSard: A548
ASSardo: A548
ASSic: A549-A550
ASSir: A551
ASSO: A550
ASSP: A489
ASSPh: A232
AsSt: A618
AssyriolStud: A622, A624
AssyrS: A622, A624
AST: A181
ASt: A186, A618
ASTarr: A181
AStCal: A537-A538
ASTI: A324
AStIt: A539
ASTL: A552
AStLomb: A541
AStMalo: A313
AstNap: A545
AStPugl: A547
AStSic: A549
AStSicOr: A550
ASV: A534
ASWG: A21
AT: Old Testament.
AT: A107, A181, A351, A478
At: See also Atti (followed by the
    next capitalized letter).
At: A636
AtAccNap: A644, A648, A671
AtAccScPa: A646
ATANT: A22
AteR: A626
ATh: A325

Ath: A631
AThAug: A325
Athen: A629, A631
AthenMitt: M192
AthensAnnArch: A469
AThM: A475
AthMit: M192
AthMitt: M192
AthMitth: M192
ATL: A635
AtRoma: A626
AToulon: A322
Atti: See also A (followed by the
    next capitalized letter).
AttiAccadNapoli: R68
AttiAccadPalermo: A646
AttiAccadPontaniana: A644
AttiAccadScienzediTorino: A649
AttiAccadZelantiAcireale: M133
AttiAccLinc: A642
AttiAccNap: R68, R648
AttiAccNapoli: R68, A648
AttiAccNazLinc: A642, M107, N83,
    R69, T106
AttiAccPont: A668, A644
AttiAccScienzeTorino: A649
AttiAccTorino: A649
AttiAccTosc: A659
AttiAcCos: A640
AttiAcTorino: A647
AttiAcUdine: A647
AttiCeSDIR: A650
AttiCIAC: A50
AttiCItRom: A650
AttiCNStR: A653
AttiComconsMonProvTerLavoro: A652
AttiCongOr: A52
AttiCongrStudRom: A653
AttiCos: A640
AttiCStR: A653
AttidAcPelorPericClletfilbelarti:
    A643
AttieMemIstItalNum: A664
AttieMemItalNum: A664
AttieMemSocMagnaGrecia: A666
AttiGenoa: A641
AttiIstr: A665
AttiIstVeneto: A655
AttiistvenSSLLAA: A655
AttiLinc: A642
AttiMemBologna: M108
AttiMemFirenze: A659
AttiMemIstriana: A665
AttiMemModena: A658, A661
AttiMemRomagna: A663
AttiMemSocIstriana: A665

AttiMemSocMagGr: A666
AttiMemSocMagnaGrecia: A666
AttiMemSocTiburtina: A667
AttiMGr: A666
AttiMGrecia: A666
AttiMod: A667
AttiNapoli: A644, A648, A671
AttiPalermo: A646
AttiPARA: A668
AttiPont: A668, A671
AttiPontAcc: A668
AttiPontRomArch: A668
AttiRIstVen: A655
AttiRoveretana: A645
AttiSMG: A666
AttiSMGraecia: A666
AttiSocIstr: A665
AttiSocLigStorPatria: A654
AttiSocSceLettereGenova: A641
AttiSocTiburtina: A667
AttiTor: A649
AttiTorino: A649
AttiVen: A655
AttiVenezia: A655
AttLinc: A642, M107, N83, R69,
    T106
AttPontAcc: A668
AtVen: A627
AU: A137
Au: A692
AuA: A353
AUB: A182, A327
AUBIst: A182
AuC: A354
AuChr: A354
AUCr: A183
Auct: A677
Auctar: A677
AUD: A48
AUDTCFD: D65
AUF: A556, U28
AUf: A556
AUG: A85
AugStud: A679
AuJBA: A694
AUM: A184
AUMLA: A2
AUnivSofia: G64
AUO: A7
AUPO: A87
AUS: G64
Aus: A692
AusBiR: A693
Ausgr&Funde: A690
AusgrBerlin: A689
AusgrFu: A690

AusgruFunde: A690
AUSS: A206
AUT: A185
AuvergneLitt: A695
AV: A571, A330, A462, A686
AVDAI: A462
AVen: A557
AVes: A571
AViva: A463
AVN: A269
AvP: A126
AVSL: A558
AW: A365
AWaas: A292
AXen: A89
AXer: A90
AyasofiaMüzyil: A696
AyasofyaMuzYil: A696
AZ: A464, Z19
AzerbAkHerberleri: I150
AZog: A91

B

B: Beiheft; Beiträge; Berichte;
  Biblioteca, Bibliotheca, Biblio-
  theque; Boletin; Bollettino;
  Bulletin.
B: P144
B&O: B69
B&TS: B70
B&W: B102
BA: B148, B74, B30, B78, B127,
  B198, B258, R144
BAA: B257
BAAA: B77
BAAlg: B257
BAAlger: B257
BAB: B243, I103, I153
Bab: D22, T86, I103, B2
BABA: B26
BAbbeville: B395
BABESCH: B1
BABesch: B1
Babesch: B1
BABsch: B1
Babyl: B2
BAC: B146, B258
BACA: B450
BAcadRoyBelg: B243
BACAEP: B450
BAcBelg: B243
BAcH: B243
BAClLg: B263
BAcN: B351
BAcNimes: B351
BACopt: B368
BAcPol: B246
BACr: B146
BAcRBelgique: B243
BACrist: B146
BAcSerbe:
BACT: B258

BACTH: B258
BAcZagr: B249
BAD: B244
BadFB: B7
BadFber: B7
BadFuBer: B7
BadFundber: B7
BadN: B6
BaehrPLM:
BAEO: B129
BAF: B361
BAG: G88
BAGB: B264
BaghdaderMitt: B9
BagM: B9
BAH: B80, B245
BAHD: V58
BAHist: B126
BAHR: B253
BAHV: B266
BAIEMA: B304
BAin: B430
Balgezik: B12
BalKanSt: B11
BalkE: B12
BalSt: B11, B13
BaltischeStud: B13
BAM: B260, B41
BaM: B9
BAMaroc: B260
BAMontl: B346
BAmSocP: B253
BAN: B147
BAnalytHistRom: B255
BAnB: B1
BAncLit: B256
BANE: B250
BAngres: B416
BantBeschav: B1

BAntFr: B361
BANVL: B267
BAO: M273
BAOrange: B254
BAPC: B245
BAR: A201, B208
BARB: B243
BArch: B258
BArchAlex: B365
BArchAlg: B257
BArchCTHS: B258
BArte: B148
BAS: B30
BASD: V58
BASE: B133
BASEE: B265
BASEEur: B261
BaslerZs: B20
BASLS: B247
BASM: B149
BASO: B251
BASOR: B251
BASP: B253
BASPR: B252
BASR: I152
BAssBude: B264
BAssMosAnt: B304
BAssProAventico: B264
BAT: B127
BATarr: B127
BathFCP: P191
BAUB: B28
BAug: B198
BAuvergne: B302
BAV: B248
BAVA: B27
BAvalon: B397
BAVF: B262
BAW: B79
BAWb: B31
BayerSitz: S90
BayerSzb: S90
BayerVorgeschbl: B23
BayerVorgeschfreund: B23
BaySitz: S90
BayVBll: B23
BayVgBl: B23
BB: B36, B5, D15, D15, V57
BBA: B61
BBAA:
BBayonne: B440
BBB: B190
BBCS: B270
BBeauvais: B373
BBelfort: B389
BBeucaire: B411

BBF: B269
BBG: B18, B22
BBGG: B150
BBI: B272
Bbl: J74
BBM: B230
BBMB: B131
BBMP: B130
BBMSWK: B59
BBona: B245
BBretagne: B413
BBSAJ: B271
BBude: B264
BBudeSCr: B264
BBudeSuppl: B264
BBur: B138
BBurgos: B138
BBV: B60, B58
BBVF: B60, B58
BByz: B272
BByzI: B272
BC: B159, B151, B237
BCAB: I153
BCAHCo: B274
BCALezoux: B277
BCamunoStPrIstor: B152
BCAN: B279
BCAR: B159
BCASM: B278
BCCR: B162
BCEN: B275
BCerclNum: B275
BCETA: B321
BCH: B284
BCHAM: B282
BChI: B21
BCHist: B281
BChr: V57
BCILL: C26
BCircNumNap: B156
BClevMus: B276
BCLF: B286
BClGrLat: B157
BCMA: B276
BCMB: B138
BCMI: B237
BCMJ: B237
BCML: B132
BCMLugo: B132
BCMO: B133
BCMOr: B133
BCMS: B283
BCO: B81
BCom: B159
BCommArch: B159
BCommSicilia: B158

BComRom: B159
BCorse: B437
BCPdC: B280
BCPE: C255
BCPMBurgos: B138
BCPMLugo: B132
BCPMOrense: B133
BCRF: B281
BCRH: B281
BCSA: B153
BCSF: B154
BCSSA: B155
BCStStorArchit: B155
BCTH: B258
Bd: Band.
BDA: B160
BdA: B148
BDB:
BDelph: B244
BDF:
BdF: B134
BDG: D55
BDI: B167
BdI: B166-B167
BdIDirRom: B167
BDL: B49
BDLG: B114
BDR: G80
BDraguignan: B400
BDrome: B385
BDU: B161
BDVA: B32
BE: B290, B289, B3, B242
BEC: B82
BEcCamCommercRavenna: B162
BECCRavenne: B162
BECh: B82
BedfordArchJ: B25
BEFAR: B83
BEG: B289
BEHEt: B84
Beih: Beiheft.
BeitArch: B29
Beitr: Beiträge.
BeitrAnthruUrgeschBayern: B28
BeitrDeutVolksAlter: B32
BeitRheinKunst: B39
BeitrNamF: B37
BeitSaarlArchKunst: B40
BekesMK: B43
Bel: B45
BelgAcBull: B243
BEO: B291
BEODam: B291
BEOR: B291
BEP: B292

BEp: B290, B289
BEPIF: B292
BEPort: B292
Ber: Berichte.
BerAmersfort: B51
BerAntiquGesZürich: A400
BerBayDenkmPfl: J61
BergensMusÅrbok: A6
BergensMusÅrsberetning: A6
BergensMusSkrifter: U14
BerichteLeipzig: S94, B55
BerichtRom-GermKomm: B52
BerJhb: B62
BerksAJ: B57
BerksBucksOxonAJ: B57
BerkshireArchJ: B57
BerKunsts: B65
BerlAbh: A12
BerlAkAbh: A12
BerlAKSb: S91
BerlBer: M234
BerlBlätterfürVuFg: B60
BerlBLVFrüGesch: B60
Berl: Berliner.
BerLeipz: B55
BerlinerBlVoruFrühgesch: B60
BerlinerJahrVorFrühgesch: B62
BerlinerMus: B65
BerlinerNumismZtschr: B66
BerlinerNumZ: B66
BerlinJahrbfWissKritik: J60
BerListe: B56
BerlJbfVor-uFrühgesch: B62
BerlKlT: B63
BerlMB: M234, M230
BerlMünzbl:
BerlMus: B65
BerlNumZ: B66
BerlNZ: B66
BerlphilolWoch: P114
BerlPhilWoch: P114
BerlphilWoch: P114
BerLS: B56
BerlSitz: S91
BerlSitzb: S91
BerlWPr: W31
BerMus: B65
BerRGK: B52
BerRGKO: B52
BerROB: B51
BerRömGermKom: B52
BerSächsGesell: B55
BerSächsGesWiss: B55
BerStaatDenkmalpfSaarland: B53
BerVerhLeipz: S94
BerwickNFCP: P192

BEtOrient: B291
BezzBeitr: B36
BezzBeiträge: B36
BF: B7
BFAM: B353
BFC: B163
BFChTh: B33
BFilGrPadova: B168
BFilLingSic: B154
BFLL: B86
BfM: B117
BFougeres: B372
BFS: B7, B293
BG: B191
BGA: B87
BGAMac: B295
BGANogent: B296
BGAS: P193
BGASM: B297
BGAST: T91
BGDM: B34
BGeneve: B415
BGHB: B107
BGien: B411
BGL: B76
BgldHb: B446
BGM: B112
BGN: B108
BGRCB: B299
BGrenoble: B244
BGRL: B298
BGrottaf: B150
BGU: A94
BH: B8
BHAcRoum: B352
BHAR: B352
BHautes-Alpes: B398
BHB: B17
BHb: B16, B446
BHBl: B446
BHesbaye-Condroz: B274
BHG: B88
BHH: B92
BHHL: B303
BHipp: B245
BHisp: B300
BHL: B89
BHM: B301
BHO: B90
BHSA: B302
BHTh: B35
BHuningue: B425
BHVG: B192
Bi; B72, I153
BIA: B164
BIAA: B164

BIAB: I153
BIABulg: I153
BIAL: B308-B309
BIALondon: B308
BIALux: B310
BIAO: B314
BIAOr: B314
BIASA: B164
Bib: Bibliothèque, Biblioteca,
    Bibliotheca.
Bib: B72
BibAr: B74
BibArch: B74
Bibl: B72
BiblA: B74
BiblArch: B74
BiblClassOr: B81
BiblClassOrient: B81
Bibld'etudedel'IFAO: B85
BiblEcChartes: B82
BiblEcFranc: B83
BiblH&R:
BiblHistVaudoise: B91
BiblHumHist: B92
BiblIFAO: B85
BiblOr: B97
BiblOrient: B97
BiblOriental: B97
BiblPraehHisp: B98
BiblScriptGrRomTeub: B100
BiblTeubn: B100
BibMes: B96
BibO: B97
BibOr: B97, B69
BibOrPont: B73
BIBR: B315
BIBulg: I153
BibVC: B71
BibZeit: B105
BICA: B166
BICByz: B305
BICentRest: B165
BickelCMN: B106
BiClOr: B81
BICR: B165
BICS: B311
BICSL: B311
BIDR: B167
BIE: B312
BIEA: B135
BIEG: B136
BIEGien: B136
BIEH: B137
BIES: B318
BIFAO: B314, B85
BiFAO: B314, B385

BIFAOr: B314, B85
BIFG: B168, B138
BIH: I153
BIHBulg: I153
BII: B317
BIlle-et-Vilaine: B369
BILPatr: B306
BIME: B171
BIN: B172, B4
BInst: B166
BInstArchBulg: I153
BInstEstHel: B137
BInstHistBelgRom: B315
BInstHistBulg: I157
BiogrGr: B112
BiOr: B97
BIPA: B316
BIranInst: B317
BirmAST: T90
BirmMidlInstT: T90
BISAO: B170
BISI: B171
BISLM: B169
BISS: B139
BIstRest: B165
BiulNum: B113
BiW: B75
BiZ: B105
BJ: "Jerusalem Bible".
BJ: B193, B448
BJb: B193
BJBb: B193
BJbb: B193
BJewPalSoc: B318
BJF: B138
BJFAO: B314
BJPES: B318
BJRL: B319
BJV: B62
BJVF: B62
BK: R263, B103
BKA: B95
BKAT: B103
BKIs: B36
BKM: B455
BKNOB: B340
BKT: B63
BKV: B94
BL: B56, B322
Bl: Blatt, Blätter.
BLA: B308
BLaborMusLouvre: B320
BLAC: B256
BlätfMünzfreunde: B117
BLDeutscheLandesgesch: B114
BLDtePhilos: B115

BldtLandesgesch: B114
BLE: B323
BLePuy: B303
BlfbG: B22
B1H: B116
B1HK: B116
BLimoges: B375
B1MüFreundeF: B117
BLorraine: B247
BLOT: B194
BLR: B119
BLund: A8
BM: Bulletin et Memoires. <u>See
    also Bull and B (followed by
    the next capitalized letter)</u>.
BM: British Museum.
BM: B327, B9, B96, B447, S189
BMA: B227, B325
BMAH: B329
BMAngers: B339
BMAPOrense: B140
BMaroc: B424
BMArqOr: B140
BMArras: B357
BMaurienne: B417
BMAW: B50
BMayenne: B282
BMB: B331
BMb: B236
BMBA: B330
BMBB: B332
BMBeyr: B331
BMBeyrouth: B331
BMBl: D30, B236
BMBll: D30
BMBronzes: B209
BMC: (British Museum Catalogs)
    B209-B227
BMC: (BM Coin Catalogs; often
    followed by place name) B210-
    B213
BMCatC: B209-B227
BMCB: B209
BMCBronzes: B209
BMCByz: B210
BMCCat: B210-B213 (British Museum
    Coin Catalogs)
BMCEmp: B212
BMCG: B214
BMCGC: B211
BMCGr: B211
BMCJ: B218
BMCoins: B210-B213
BMCoinsRomEmp: B212
BMCoinsRomRep: B213
BMCP: B172

BMCR: B223, B175
BMCRE: B212
BMCREmp: B212
BMCRomEmp: B212
BMCRomRep: B213
BMCRR: B213
BMCV: B174
BMCVenezia: B174
BMD: B358
BMDijon: B358
BMemSocArchBordeaux: B366
BMetrMus: B224
BMF: M305-M306, B117
BMFA: B333
BMFAB: B333
BMFEA: B342
BMFerr: B176
BMFr: M305-M306, B117
BMGN: B109
BMGreekCoins: B211
BMGS: B456
BMHB: B336
BMHBA: B336
BMHM: B335
BMI: B217
BMi: B217
BMI&V: B369
BMIi: B237
BMImpR: B177
BMinG: B217
BMInscr: B217
BMIPA: B313
BMIR: B177
BMJewell: B257
BMLamps: B219
BMLyon: B337
BMM: B326
BMMA: B326
BMMANY: B326
BMMarbles: B281
BMMK: B43
BMNB: I158
BMNBurgas: I158
BMNE: B324
BMNEA: B324
BMRings: B223
BMNRuse: I159
BMNSumen: I160
BMNVarna: I161
BMon: B327
BMonIst: B237
BMontbeliard: B396
BMQ: B228
BMQu: B228
BMSAB: B366
BMSAF: B361

BMSculpt: B225
BMSF: B372
BMSPM: B433
BMTerracottas: B226
BMu: B65
BMus: B65
BMusArt: B329
BMusB: B333
BMusBeyr: B331
BMusBeyrouth: B331
BMusCivRom: B177
BMusFA: B333
BMusFr: M305-M306
BMusHong: B336
BMusHongr: B336
BMusImp: B177
BMusInscr: B217
BMusMonaco: B328
BMusMonLyon: B337
BMusMulhouse: B335
BMusNatKolarovgrad: I160
BMusPadova: B172
BMusVars: B338
BMVases: B227
BMVTarnovo: I163
BN: Bibliotheque Nationale.
BN: B37, B113, B457
BNancy: B247
BNC: C82
BNF: B37
BNFAS: N73
BNFC: B15
BNGJ: B458
BNgJb: B458
BNimes: B351, B288, B402
BNJ: B458, B229
BNJb: B458
BNJbb: B458
BNogent: B419
BNum: B113, B341
BNumParis: B406
BNZ: B66
BO: B97, B133
BodDenkmPfMecklenb: B118
BOffInst: B343
BOIA: B343
BOKK: V40
Bol: Boletin. See also Boll, Bull
    and B (followed by the next
    capitalized letter).
BolAcadCordoba: B123
BolAcadHist: B126
BolAcHa: B126
BolAcHist: B126
BolAkHist: B126
BolArq: B127

BolArqTarrac: B127
BolArqu: B127
BolArte: B148
BolArteArqValladolid: B141
BoldelSEAA: B141
BoletRAcadHist: B126
BolInstEstAstur: B135
BolInstEstGiennenses: B136
Boll: Bollettino. See also Bull,
    Bol and B (followed by the next
    capitalized letter).
BollArte: B148
BollAssArchRom: R341
BollAssarchRom: R341
Bollcap: B151
BollCentro: B155
BollCircNumNapoletano: B156
BollClass: B157
BollCom: B157
Bolld'Arte: B148
Bolld'ArteMPI: B148
BolldAssocintStudmedrr: B149
BollFcl: B163
BollFilCl: B163
Bollfilcl: B163
BollFilClass: B163
BollGrott: B150
BollICR: B165
BollIstArchStArte: B164
BollIstNazArcheStArte: B164
BollIstRest: B165
BollIstRestauro: B165
BollMC: B175
BollMuseiComRoma: B175
BollMuseoCivicoPadova: B173
BollN: B178
BollNazDrAnt: D68
BollSocPiemontese: B181
BollStA: B184
BollStArteSalerno: B184
BollStCremonese: B186
BollStM: B149
BollStNovara: B188
BollStorCremonese: B186
BollStPatriaUmbria: B161
BollStPiacentino: B187
BolRACEsp: B124
BolRAH: B126
BonnCorpus: C239
Bonned: C238
BonnerJ: B193
BonnerJahrb: B193
BonnerJh: B193
BonnHeftVg: B192
BonnJ: B193
BonnJahrb: B193

BonnJb: B193
BonnJbb: B193
BonnJhb: B193
BOP: B38
BOran: R95
BOrleans: B377
BOrnes: B420
BoSt: B120
BostonMusBul: B333
BoTU: B121
BPA: B268
BParthenay: B409
BPas-de-Calais:B280
BPC: B183
BPEC: B157
BPh: P114
Bphcl: B448
BPhilW: P114
BphilWoch: P114
BPhM: B427
BPhW: P114
BphW: P114
BPhWschr: P114
BPI: B179
BPiacenza: B187
BPicardie: B364
BPKS: B65
BPM: B345
BpR: B234
BpReg: B234
BPrHistFr: B435
BProvidence: B347
BProvins: B410
BPSR: P3
BpSzle: B235
BPW: P114
BpW: P114
BR: B233-B234
BRAAV: B141
BRABL: B449
BRAC: B123
BracAug: B198
BRACord: B123
BRACordoba: B123
BradfordAnt: B199
BRAE: B124
BRAG: B125
BRAH: B126
BraunH: B200
BraunJ: B201
BrBl: B202
BrBr: D15
BRealAcad: B124, B126
BremABl: B202
BremerArchBl: A209
BreslphilAbh: B204

BRest: B165
BrettJ: B205
BRGK: B52
BrH: B197
BRISD: B347
BritAA: B207
BritArchAbstracts: B207
BritMusInscr: B217
BritMusQ: B228
BritMusQuart: B228
BritMusQuarterly: B228
BritSchAthensAnn: A229
BrJb: B203
BR-KÜRTE: R263
BRL: B319, B104
BRMA: B348
BrMQu: B228
BrMusQ: B228
BrN: B231
BROB: B51
BROM: B344
BROMA: B344
BrooklMQu: B230
BrookMusQ: B230
BRSV: B144
BRSVAP: B144
BS: Bulletin. Société. See also
  BullSoc.
BS: B19, B451
BSA: A229, B240, B359
BSAA: B365, B141
BSAA1: B365
BSAAlex: B365
BSAAube: B353
BSAAV: B141
BSAB: I153, B380, B390
BSABulg: I153
BSAC: B367-B368
BSACopt: B368
BSAE: B350, P241
BSAEL: B370
BSAF: B361
BSAFin: B371
BSAG: B376
BSAHB: B373
BSAHG: B376
BSAHL: B375
BSAHLiege: B388
BSAHNoy: B382
BSAHO: B377
BSAHT: B378
BSAHW: B307
BSaintGirons: B387
BSAK: B40
BSAM: B362, B379
BSAMF: B379

BSAO: B363
BSAP: B364
BSAS: B383
BSASarthe: B356
BSASD: B385
BSAT: B386
BSATarbes: B354
BSATG: B259
BSAV: B141, B381
BSaverne: B422
BSAVerviers: B442
BSAVienne: B359
BSAW: B55
BSAWL: B55
BSBAP: B390
BSBE: B389
BSBorda: B391
BSBS: B185
BSC: B183
BSCC: B142
BSCr: B186
BSEAA: B141
BSEAbb: B395
BSEAude: B401
BSEAv: B397
BSEBour: B393
BSEDV: B400
BSEE: B143
BSEHA: B398
BSELot: B399
BSemEAAValladolid: B141
BSESS: B403
BSete: B403
BSF: B404-B406
BSFAC: B404
BSFE: B405
BSFN: B406
BSG: B238
BSGAO: B407
BSGR: B238
BSGRE: B408
BSGW: B55
BSH: B352
BSHAB: B412
BSHABr: B413
BSHAcRoum: B344
BSHAGeneve: B415
BSHAL: B416
BSHAM: B418
BSHAMaur: B417
BSHAN: B419
BSHAOr: B420
BSHAP: B421
BSHAPar: B409
BSHAR: B352
BSHAV: B423

BSHB: I154
BSHBulg: I154
BSHCorbeil: B414
BSHCorreze: B436
BSHDS: B426
BSHGien: B411
BSHMaroc: B424
BSHProv: B410
BSHY: B439
BSI: B189
BSiena: B180
BSL: B428
BSl: B451
BSLP: B428
BSM: B149
BSMar: B182
BSN: B431
BSNAF: B361
BSNAin: B430
BSNAP: B432
BSNEP: B432
BSNR: B239
BSOAS: B349
BSocAChamp: B367
BSocArchAl: B365
BSocArchEureetLoir: B370
BSocArcVarna: I161
BSocBulg: I154
BSocEtSciAude: B401
BSocHistBulg: I154
BSocLittHistBrie: B429
BSOS: B349
BSOSt: B349
BSPA: B181
BSPABA: B181
BSPF: B435
BSPiac: B187
BSPiem: B181
BSPN: B188
BSR: P36
BSRAA: B365
BSRAAL: B365
BSRP: P36
BSRPapers: P36
BSRRG: B238
BSS: B438
BSSHC: B437
BSSHN: B437
BSSHS: B438
BSSNN: B402
BSt: B11, B67
BStAc: B240
BStM: B149
BSTPP: B441
BSz: B235
BT: B100

BTAM: B443
BTarn-et-Garone: B259
BTextilAnc: B321
Btfg: R117
BTh: B443
BTN: B101
BTonnerre: B378
BTorino: B181
BTournai: B441
BTours: B386
BTTK: B45
Bu: B448
BucksRecords: R36
BuCo: B159
BUComp: B145
BudapestReg: B234
Bude: C165
BudR: B234
BudReg: B234
BuJb: B448
BulArchMaroc: B260
BulASE: B261
BulCom: B159
BulComMonIst: B237
BulCorrespHellenique: B284
Bull: Bulletin, Bullettino. <u>See
    also Boll, B (followed by the
    next capitalized letter) and BM
    (followed by the next capital-
    ized letter)</u>.
Bull: B166
BullAcBelgique: B243
BullAcCrac: B245
BullAIEMA: B304
BullAIEtSEEur: B265
BullAmerOrient: B251
BullAmSchPrehistResearch: B252
BullAmSocPap: B253
BullAnaldHistRom: B255
BullAntB: B1
BullAntBesch: B1
BullAntFr: B361
BullArch: B160, B258
BullArchAlg: B257
Bullarchcom: B159
BullarchComite: B258
BullarchcommunalediRoma: B258
BullArchComTravHist: B257
BullArchComTravHisteScient: B257
BullArcheol: B258
BullArchHist: B258
BullArchMaroc: B260
BullArchNap: B147
BullarchSens: B383
BullAriegeois: B387
BullAssBude: B264

BullBA: B336
BullBAHongr: B336
BullBdCelticStudies: B270
BullBelg: B243
BullBeziers: B380
BullBoardofCelticStud: B270
BullBorda: B391
BullBrie: B429
BullBude: B264
BullCaire: B314
BullCentroArchitettura: B155
BullCercArchHesbayeCondroz: B274
BullClevelandMuseum: B276
BullClL: B243
BullClLetBA: B243
BullCom: B159
BullComArch: B159
BullComm: B159
BullCommAntSic: B158
BullCommArchCom: B159
BullCommArchNarbonne.: B279
BullComRoma: B159
BullComun: B159
BullComunale: B159
BullCorrHell: B284
BullCorrHellenique: B284
Bulld'Alexandrie: B365
BullDalm: V58
Bulldel'acroydeBelgClLet: B243
BulldelaSecHistdel'AcRoum: B352
BulldelaSocArchd'Alexandrie: B365
BulldellaCommArchCommdiRoma: B159
BulldellaCommarchmunic: B159
BulldI: B166
BulldInst: B166
BulldiPaletnItal: B179
BulldIstGerm: M193
Bulldpaletn: B179
BullDR: B167
BullDrome: R128
BullEcc: B323
BullEp: B290, B289
Bullep: B290, B289
BullEpigdelaGaul: B289
BullEpigr: B290, B289
Bullepigr: B290, B289
BulletdellInstArch: B166
BullEtOrient: B291
BullFoggArtMus: B294
BullGBude: B264
BullGers: B376
BullGov: B159
BullHispanique: B300
BullHistMetalGroup: J109
BullIDR: B167
BullIFAO: B314

BullIFAOC: B314
BullImp: B177
BullImpero: B177
BullInst: B166
BullInstArchBulg: I153
BullInstArchBulgare: I153
BullInstArchLiegeois: B309
BullInstArchSofia: I153
BullInstBulg: I153
BullInstClassStudies: B311
BullInstClSt: B311
BullInstd'Egypte: B312
BullInstEg: B312
BullInstEgypt: B312
BullInstFranc: B314
BullInstFrancArchOrient: B314
BullIstDirRom: B167
BullJPES: B318
BullJRylLibr: B319
BullKNOB: B340
BullLot: B399
BullLyons: B357
BullMem: Bulletin et Memoires.
  See also Bull....
BullMemBordeaux: B366
BullMetrMus: B326
BullMetrMusArt: B326
BullMetropolMuseum: B326
BullMFA: B333
BullMMA: B326
BullMNatVarsovie: B338
BullMon: B327
BullMonumental: B327
BullMus: B177
BullMusAnthrPrehistMonaco: B328
BullMusBeyrouth: B331
BullMuseesRouyaux: B329
BullMuseumBoston: B333
BullMusFA: B333
BullMusFarEasternAntiqu: B342
BullMusFineArtsBoston: B329
BullMusFrance: M305-M306
BullMusHistMulhouse: B335
BullMusImp: B177
BullMusLyon: B337
BullMusNatVarna: I161
BullMusroyartethist: B329
BullMusRoyBruxelles: B329
BullNap: B147
Bullnapol: B147
BullOran: B407
Bullpal: B179
BullPalentnItal: B179
BullPerigord: B421
BullPristina: G49
BullROM: B344

BullRoum: B352
BullRylandsLibr: B319
BullSarajevo: G52
BullSete: B403
BullSFN: B406
BullSoc: See also BS.
BullSocAlex: B365
BullSocAnt: B361
BullSocAntFrance: B361
BullSocAnthrParis: B360
BullSocArchChampenoise: B367
BullSocArchCopte: B368
BullSocArchdAlexandrie: B365
BullSocArchduMididelaFrance: B379
BullSocArcheolAlex: B365
BullSocArchHistChatillonnais: B374
BullSocArchScilettrdeBeziers: B380
BullSocBulg: I153
BullSocConsMonHistAlsace: B392
BullSocNatAntiquFrance: B361
BullSocNivernaise: B431
BullSocNormandeEtPrehist: B432
BullSocPolymathMorbihan: B433
BullSocPrehistAriege: B434
BullSocPrehistFrance: B435
BullSocRoyBelgAnthrPrehist: B390
BullSocSemur: B438
BullSousse: B384
BullSPF: B435
BullStrasb: B293
BullTrimInstArchLuxembourg: B310
BullVexin: B262
BullVienne: B359
BulMonIst: B237
BurgenlHeimatbl: B446
BurgHbl: B446
BurlM: B447
Burs: B448
Bursian: B448
BursianJahresb: B448
BursJahr: B448
BursJahresb: B448
BursJb: B448
BursJber: B448
BUS: B293
BUSC: B145
BUSS: B241
BUST: B241
ButlletiAssCat: B448
BUZFF: Z13
BV: B460, B23, B110
BVAB: B1
BVallad: B141
BVar: B248
BVBl: B23
BVC: B54

BVendome: B381
BVichy: B423
BVitoria: B139
BWANT: B42
BWaremme: B307
BWHA: B444
BWKPr: W31
BWPr: W31
BYale: B445
BYaleU: B445
ByJ: B458
BYonne: B439
BySl: B451
ByZ: B461
Byz: B452
ByzantinZtschr: B461
ByzantZeitschr: B461
ByzBul: B453
Byzbulg: B453
ByzF: B454
ByzForsch: B454
ByzJ: B458
ByzJb: B458
ByzMet: B455
ByzNeer: B457
ByzNeerl: B457
ByzneugrJahrb: B458
ByzS: B451
ByzSl: B451
ByzSlav: B451
ByzundNeugrJahb: B458
ByzZ: B461
ByzZeit: B461
ByzZeitschr: B461
ByzZeitschrift: B461
ByzZs: B461
BZ: B20, B105, B461
BZAW: Z22
BZG: B20
BzN: B37
BzNf: B37
BZNW: Z52

C

C: Cahiers, Casopis, Catalogue,
  Chronique, Classical, Collection,
  Communicazioni, Communications,
  Compte-rendu, Corpus, Cuadernos.
C: C220, D21, D23
C: See also Cah, Cahiers.
C&M: C138
C&S: C275
C&W: T94
C&WTrans: T94
CA: C6, S126, C106, C159, C252,
  C260, B24, P197
CAAAH: C5
CAAH: C5
CAB: C172, C106
CAD: A621
Caesaraug: C3
CAF: C167, S68
CAG: C173
CAH: C45
Cah: See also Cahiers, C (followed
  by the next capitalized letter).
CAHA: C5
CahA: C6
CahAlsaciens: C5
CahANord-Est: C8
CahArch: C6
CahArchetHistAlsace: C5
CahArchHistBerry: C7
CahArt: C11
CahASubaqu: C10
CAHB: C7
CahBrux: C13
CahByr: C14
CahByrsa: C14
CAHC: C261
CahCivMed: C16
CahCM: C16
CahDelFrIran: C17

CahHist: C23
CahHistArch: C24
CahHistM: C25
CahHistMond: C25
Cahiers: See also Cah, C (followed
  by the next capitalized letter).
CahiersAlsaciens: C5
CahiersArch: C6
CahiersArcheol: C6
CahiersArchetHistAlsace: C5
Cahiersd'histmond: C25
CahiersLigPrehistArch: C30
CahiersLigures: C25
CahiersNum: C34
CahiersTechniques: C40
CahLig: C30
CahLor: C31
CahMariemont: C32
CahMed: C33
CahN: C34
CahNum: C34
CahOr: C35
CahRhodBord: C37
CahSar: C39
CahStMichel: C38
CahTech: C40
CahTun: C41
CahTunisie: C41
CAIBL: C185
CAIL: C185
CairoDeutInstAgyptAltMitt: M191
CAJ: A609, J98, C102
Calculi: C44
CalifStClAnt: C131
CalNob: C43
CAMB: C123
CambsASP: P195
CampagneSocMagnaGrecia: A666
CAMT: C227

CAN: C257
CanadJour: C52
CAncH: C45
CANE: C8
CANES: C203
CAntiqFPL: C157
Capit: C54
CAR: C9
Car: C56-C57
CArch: C6
CArchAls: C5
CarmAntSoc: T93
CarmLatEpigr: C58
CarnJb: C60
CarnuntumJb: C60
CArt: C192
Cas: Časopis.
CASA: C254
CASAE: A304
CASJ: J98
CasMoravMuz: C63
CasMusSlovSpol: C64
CasNarodMuz: C65
CasopisBrno: C63
CasopisBrünn: C63
CasopisOlmütz: C68
CasopisOpava: C66
CasopisPraha: C65
CasSlezskeMuz: C66
CAStMicheldeCuxa: C38
CASubaqu: C10
Cat, Catal: Catalogue, Catalogus.
CatalBM[place]: B211
CatalBrux: C87
Catalcodhag: C87-C93
Catalgen: C74
CatalGraecGerm: C90
CatalGraecParis: C88
CatalGraecVatic: C89
CatalGrGerm: C90
CatalGrParis: C88
CatalGrVatic: C89
CatalLatBrux: C87
CatalLatParis: C91
CatalLatRom: C92
CatalLatVatic: C93
Catcodastrgr: C86
Catgen: C75
CatLitPap: B222
CB: C132, A676, C165, C13, C274, S128
CBa: C12
CBerry: C7
CBHByz: C204
CBM[place]: B211
CBMW: C282

CBQ: C95
CC: C205
CCAB: C248
CCAG: C86
CCatt: C127
CCC: C128
CCCA: C206
CCDS: C207
CCer: C15
CCG: C205
CCH: C109
CCh: C205
CChL: C205
CChr: C205
CChrL: C205
CCL: C205
CCM: C16
CCO: C72
CCS: C124, C46
CCSG: C205
CCSL: C205
CCTC: C47
CdA: C254
CDAFI: C17
CdByrsa: C14
CdE: C118
CdEg: C118
CdeT: C41
CE: C118, C58, C96
CEA: C18
CEEN: C264
CEFR: C162
CEG: C262
CEg: C118
CEM: C263
CeM: C130
CEN: B275
CeN: C140
CENB: B275
CentAsiaJ: C102
CEpigr: C58
Cerc, Cercet: Cercetări.
CercetArhBuc: C106
CercetIst: C107-C108
CercetIstIasi: C108
CercIst: C107-C108
CERP: C126
CES: B224
CeSDIR: A650
CeskCasHist: C109
CESSA: C74
CF: C133, R160
CFC: C265
CFHB: C209
CFilos: C266
CFS: C19

CGA: C105
CGC: B211
CGC[place]: B211
CGF: C168, F58
CGFPap: C169
CGFPR: C169
CGL: C210
CG1: C210
CGLC: C48
CG1L: C210
CG1Lat: C210
CGP: C103
CGRAR: C20
CGS: C272
CGT: C49
CH: Code of Hammurabi, Corpus Hippo-
  craticum, Code Hittite.
CH: C23
CHA: C24
ChArchLiege: C117
CHE: C267
ChHist: C121
CHist: C121, C247
CHistArch: C24
CHJ: C50
CHJZ: C268
CHK: L13
ChK: C116
CHL: C111, C21
ChLA: C111
CHM: C25
ChNI: C114
CHP: C269
CHR: C97
ChrAM: K21
Chrd'Eg: C118
ChrEg: C118
ChroE: C118
Chron: Chronique.
Chron: C120
Chrond'Eg: C118
ChrondEgypte: C118
ChronEg: C118
Chronika: A470
ChroniqueArchLiege: C117
ChronLind: L58
ChronMP: C120
Chronology: C120
ChronOr: C119
ChSB: K20
ChT: C110
ChtM: C22
CHum: C188
ChW: C112
CI: Codex Iustinianus.
CIA: C212, C195

CIAG: C172
CIAtt: C212
CIC: Corpus Iuris Canonici
CIC: Corpus Iuris Civilis.
CIC-CI: -Codex Iustinianus.
CIC-Dig: -Digesta
CIC-Inst: -Institutiones.
CIC-Nov: -Novellae.
CICO: Corpus Iuris Canonici Ori-
  entalis.
CIE: C213
CIEtr: C213
CIG: C214
CIGr: C214
CIH: C215
CII: C218, C217, C219
CIIC: C216
CIIns: C216
CIJ: C219
CIJud: C219
CIL: C220
CILL: C26
CIMA: C27
CIMGL: C27
CIMRM: C221
CIN: A51
CinArtB: C123
CIRB: K41
CIRM: C221
CIS: C222
CISA: C196
CISem: C222
CISoc: C28
CIst: C107-C108
CIstaMilano: C195
CItRom: A650
CIust: Codex Iustinianus.
Civcatt: C127
CivCattol: C127
CJ: C135, C134, C136-C137
CJ: Codex Iustinianus.
CJC: Corpus Iuris Civilis.
CJI: C219
CJL: C52
CL: C31
Cl: Classical.
CLA: C152, C111
Class: Classical.
ClassJ: C135, C134, C136-C137
ClassJourn: C135, C134, C136-C137
ClassPhil: C142
ClassQuart: C143
ClassRev: C144
ClassStud: C148
ClassW: C148
Clavis: C149-C150

ClB: C132
ClBull: C132
CLD: C29
CLE: C58
CLEp: C58
CletMed: C138
ClJ: C135, C134, C136-C137
ClJourn: C135, C134, C136-C137
ClMed: C138
ClMediaev: C138
ClMus: C139
ClO: C141
CLPA: C30
ClPh: C142
ClPhil: C142
ClQ: C143
ClQu: C143
ClQuart: C143
ClR: C144
ClRev: C144
ClRh: C129
ClRhod: C129
CLS: C181-C182
ClW: C148
CM: C138, C151, C32
CM[name of province]: C70
CMA: C80-C81
CMAG: C80
CMAL: C81
CMed: C33
CMedH: C51
CMG: C223
CMGr: C197
CMH: C51
CML: C224
CMMB: C63
CMMS: C225
CMP: C120
CMP[name of province]: C70
CMRDM: C226
CMS: C225
CMSS: C64
CMT: C227
CMu: C139
CN: C34, C140
CNA: C257-C258
CNI: C83, C114
CNJ: C53
CNM: C65
CNST: T92
CNV: C147
CO: C141, C35
CoBApx: S126
CoddLatAnt: C152
CodGreg: Codex Gregorianus.
CodHermog: Codex Hermogenianus.

CodIust: Codex Iustinianus.
CodJust: Codex Iustinianus.
CodMan: C153
CodTheod: Codex Theodosianus.
Coh: D21, D23
Coll: Collection.
CollAlex: C159
CollAmisHist: C160
CollByz: C161
ColldeTrav: C164
CollEFR: C165
Com: Comité, Comitato.
Com: C171
ComAttFrag: C167
ComErm: S117
ComGraecFrag: C168
ComGrFrag: C168
ComM: C176
Comm: Commentaria, Communications,
    etc.; Commission, Commissione,
    etc.
CommBiblHistMedHungar: C177
CommHistArtMed: C177
ComminAristGraeca: C172
CommunicReiCretRomFaut: C179
CommVieuxParis: P211
CompLit: C180
CompRendAcadInsc: C185
Comptesrend: C185
Comptesrendus: C185
ComptesrendAcInscr: C185
ComptesRendusAcInscr: C185
ComptesRendusParis: C185
ComRomFrag: C170
CongrAFr: S68
CongresPrehistFrance: C190
CongrNacArq: C257
ConnArts: C192
ContributiIstStAnt: C196
COr: C119
COrdPtol: C228
CornishArch: C201
Corp: Corpus. _See also C (follow-
    ed by the next capitalized let-
    ter)._
CorpGl: C210
Corpglosslat: C210
CorpGrChristlInschr: C211
Corpinscrattic: C212
CorpInscrEt: C213
CorpInscrGraec: C214
CorpInscrLat: C220
CorpInscrSem: C222
CorpInscrSemit: C222
CorpjurCan: Corpus iuris Canonici.
CorpMedGraec: C223

CorpMedLat: C224
CorpPapRain: C33
CorpPoesEpGraecLud: C246
CorppoesepGraeclud: C246
CorpPoetLat: C235
CorpScEcclLat: C237
CorpScriptEcclLat: C237
Corpusinscriptgrace: C214
CorrBlatt: K42
CorseHist: C247
Corsi: C248
CorsiRav: C248
CorsiRavenna: C248
COWA: C1-C2
CP: C142
CPar: C238, C240
CPC: C229
CPCA: U16
CPCP: U17
CPEGL: C246
CPF: C190
CPG: C149, C234
CPH: C142, C230, C283
CPHerm: C230
CPhil: C142
CPJ: C231
CPJud: C231
CPL: C150, C232, C235
CPP: C208
CPUG: C270
CPR: C233
CQ: C143
CQu: C143
CR: Compte-rendu
CR: C144, C185, C129, 057
CrA: C252
CRAc: C185
CRAcadInsc: C185
CRAcadInscr: C185
CRAccInscr: C185
CRAcInscr: C185
CRAcInscrB-L: C185
CRAI: C185
CRAIBL: C185
CRAP: 057
CRAPE: M115
CrArch: C254
CrArte: C252
Crarte: C252
CRAS: D86
Crd'A: C252
CRDAC: A650
CRdel'Acaddesinscr: C185
CREAM: C71
CREBM: B212
CrestChron: K53

CRF: C170
CRH: B281
CRh: C129
CRhod: C129
CRIPEL: C36
CritAr: C252
CRL: C145
CrNA: C258
CronArch: C254
CronAStorArt: C254
CronErc: C255
CronErcol: C255
CronPomp: C256
CrowtherFPL: C259
CRPetersb: 057
CRPetersbourg: 057
CRR: C155, R338
CRRA: C187
CRRAI: C187
CRRBM: B213
CRS: C188
CrSt: C251
CS: C253, C249, C281, C2
CSAV: S26
CSAVvBrne: S26
CSCA: C131
CSCH: C109
CSCO: C236
CSCOScriptcopt: C236
CSCOScriptSyr: C236
CSCOSS: C236
CSCP: C200
CSCT: C166
CSDIR: A650
CSEL: C237
CSG: C205
CSGP: C189
CSHB: C239
CSHByz: C239
CSIR: C241
CSL: C205
CSM: C66
CSPM: C74
CSPS: C67
CSSH: C183
CStor: C253
CT: Codex Theodosianus.
CT: B215, C110, C41
CTC: C94
CTCBM: B226
CTD: C158
CTER: C271
CTH: C85
CTh: Codex Theodosianus.
CTheod: Codex Theodosianus.
Cuad: Cuadernos. See also C (fol-

lowed by the next capitalized
letter).
CuadArqBar: C261
CuadernosHistPrim: C269
CuadernosMadrid: C269
CuadernosPrehGranada: C270
CuadFil: C266
CuadFilCl: C265
CuadFilolClas: C265
CuadRom: C271
CUCDBulletin: B285
CUE: C242
CUF: C165
CULR: C98
CumbandWestAAST: T94
CurrentAnthr: C280
CV: C147, C175
CV[name of country]: C243
CVA: C243-C244
CVH: C245
CVind: C175
CVMSO: C68
CW: C148, T94
CWAT: T94
CZN: C69

D

D: Dictionary, Dictionnaire, etc.;
  Denkschriften.
D: A335, B99, D92, F65, I80, S288
D&GTrans: T95
DA: D27, D41, D75
Da: D1
DAA: D6, D14
DAB: D43, D33
DABF: D33
DAC: D42
DACIA: D1
DACL: D44
DAC1: D44
Dacor: D2
DAdW: J20, A12, M230, S91
DAEM: D27
DAES: P198
DAFA: M117
DAFI: C17
DAG: D37
DAGM: D27
DAGR: D41
DAI: De Administrando Imperio
  (Constantine Porphyrogenitas).
DAI: D80, I130, J21, M7, M190-M193
DAI-Athens: M192
DAJ: D20
DAN: D86
DanskeVidSelsk: H93
DArch: D38
DarSag: D41
DARSAGL: D41
DarSag1: D41
DarSaglio: D41
DAU: A137
DAW: I130, J21, M7, M190-M193
DAWW: D19
DB: D46, D4
DBS: D46

DBW: D18
DC: Dio Cassius
DCA: D48
DCB: D49
DC-F: G55
DCG: D47
DChAE: D9
DChAH: D9
DCS: D82
DD: M257
DdA: D38
DDC: D50
DDG: D92
DE: D78, E159
DEAR: D78
DebreceniME: D5
DebreMuzEvk: D5
DEG: D52
DegrI: I78
DEI: D79
DEL: D53-D54
DELG: D52
DELL: D53
Delos: E164
Delphi: F50
Delt: A470
Deltchr: D9
Deltion: A470
DeltionChrist: D9
DemSupplCom: S276
Denkm: D16, D13-D17
Denkmäler: D13, D13-D17
DenkmalBadenWürttemberg: D18
DenkmPflBadWürt: D18
DenkschriftenWien: D19
DenkschriftenWienAk: D19
DerbyshireArchJ: D20
Dergi: D65
DeriMuzEvk: D5

DessILS: I80
DeutschArchäolInsJahrb: J21
DeutschArchäolInstMittRöm: M193
DeutscheAkadWissenBerlinSchr: S45
DeutscheLitztg: D29
DF: D97
DFA: D93
DG: D92, D59, T95, D95
DGE: D36, D40
DGG: D92
DH: Dionysius of Halicarnassus.
DHA: D39
DHGE: D56
DI: S17
Di: Digest (of Roman law).
DialA: D38
DialArch: D38
DialdiArch: D38
DicdelaBibleSuppl: D46
Dict: D41
DictAnt: D41
DictBibl: D46
Dictetym: D51, D53
Dictgeog: D55
DictSp: D60
DID: D66
Didot: B99
DIEE: D10
DIEH: D10
Dig: Digest (of Roman law).
DInschr: S17
DIR: D83
DIRAT: D81
DiscExcavScot: D73
DISO: D57
Diss: Dissertation, Dissertationes,
   etc.
Diss: D76
DissAbstr: D75
DissArch: R56
DissinaugBat: D74
DissPan: D76
DissPann: D76
DissPontAcc: A668
DistBraga: D77
Ditt: S288
DittenbOGI: O45
DittenbSyll: S288
DizEp: D78
DizEpigr: D78
DJ: Didius Julianus.
DJb: D96
DJbN: N124
DJbNum: N124
DJD: D72
DK: F65, Z88

DKD: D28
DKuDenkmPfl: D28
DL: Diogenes Laertius.
DL: D29
DLiteraturZ: D29
DLL: D58
DLZ: D29
DLz: D29
DM: D4
DMBl: D30
DM/DB: D4
DME: D5
DMG: D82
DM/PNB: P158
DNG: D59
DO: D11
DOC: C71
Doc: Documents, Documenti, etc.
DocantdellAfrtal: D80
DocRom: D83
Docs: D82
DOGWV: W39
DOLG: D87-D88
Dolg: D87-D88
DolgCluj: D87
DolgKolozsvar: D87
DolgKvar: D87
DolgozatokKolozsvar: D87
DolgozatokSzeged: D88
DolgSzeged: D88
DOMH: D12
DOP: D98
DOPap: D98
DOPapers: D98
DOS: D99
DossAParis: H88
DossArch: H88
DossArcheologie: H88
DOT: D100
DOW: C71
Doxa: D91
DoxGr: D92
DoxGraec: D92
DPAA: A668
DPK: D26
DPOA: E81
DR: D31, D90
DRCharl: D84
DresdnerKunstbl: D94
DrP: R325
DS: Diodorus Siculus.
DS: D41, D60, D101
DSAM: D60
DSp: D60
DSz: D101
Dt: Deutsches.

DTA: D8
DTC: D61, D65
DTCFD: D65
DTCFDergisi: D65
DTFDAnk: D65
DThC: D61
DuC: G55
DUJ: D102
DumbartonOP: D98
DumbPap: D98
DuraEuroposFinRep: E159
DuraEuroposPrelRep: E160
DuSz: D101
DuSzK: D101
DVI: De viris illustribus.
DVLG: D32
DWA: D19
DZGW: H116

E

E: Encyclopaedia, Encyclopédie,
   etc.; Epetēris; Etudes, Estudios,
   etc.
E: E50, E64, L93
E&G: E22
E&J: D81
EA: A471, P131, E25, E47
EAA: E32, E104
EaChQu: E3
EAD: E164
EADelos: E164
EAE: E158
EAF: E114
EAH: E96
EANimes: B288
EAO: E122
EAST: E102
EAux: E5
EAZ: E115
EAZeits: E115
EB: E34, E105, E123, R143
EBibl: E105
EBS: E56
EC: E124, E129, E107, E35
ECBranco: E106
EcHistR: E9
EchO: E6
EchOr: E6
ECl: E107
EClas: E107
ECo: E128
EconHistRev: E9
EconHR: E9
EcStor: E7
ED: E63, E164
EDelph: F50
EDR: E63
EE: E64, E108, E54
EEA: E68

EEAth: E83, E86
EEBS: E56
EEcl: E108
EEE: E55
EEF: E72, M113, M121, R84
EEKM: E58
EEKS: E57
EEpigr: E64
EES: G73, M113, M121, R84
EEst: E54
EEStM: E59
EETh: E85
EEThess: E85
EF: E97, E131
EFs: E109
EG: E88, E70, E76
EGA: E1
EGF: E67
EGH: E101
EGIM: E166
EGK: E76
EGP: E2
EgR: E15
EgriME: E13
EgriMuzE: E13
EgriMuzEv: E13
EgyptUrk: A94
EH: Ergänzungsheft.
EH: E132, E162
EHBS: E56
EHCM: E58
EHG1: E46
EHHD: E61
EHPhR: E134
EHPR: E134
EHR: E45, E79, E91
EHSM: E59
EI: E36, E37, E95
EIAH: E96

EIHD: E61
Einz: Einzelschriften.
Einzelaufn: P131
EIP: E161
EJ: D81, E10, E17, E38, E80, E95
EJER: E71
EKEEK: E60
EkklAl: E24
EL: E65, E135, E167
ELE: E26
ELFS: E152
ELH: E39
EllJb: E28
EllwangerJb: E28
EM: Etymologicum Magnum.
EM: E29, D53
Em: E29
EMAAA: E62
EMC: C147
EME: E13
EMF: E44
EmiliaPrRom: E30
EN: E136
EncBiblia: E33
EncBrit: E34
Enchoria: E31
Enciclarteant: E32
EncIs: E36
EncIt: E37
EncPhotTEL: E40
EnglishHistRev: E45
EntretiensHardt: E49
EO: E6
EOL: J8
EOMIA: E4
EOr: E6
EP: Etymologicum Parvum.
EP: E138-E140
EPap: E138
Epet: Epēteris.
Epet: E56
Epetk: E58
EpEtr: E69
EpGr: E76, E70
EpGraecFrag: E67
EpGrFr: E67
EpGrFrag: E67
EPh: E139
Eph: A471
EPhAHA: E141
EphArch: A471
EpHBSp: E56
EphDac: E63
EphDR: E63
Ephem: A471
Ephemepigr: E64

EphEp: E64
EphEpgr: E64
EphEpigr: E64
EPhK: E14
EphL: E65
EPhM: E143
EPhS: H47
EpicGraecFrag: E67
EpicGrFrag: E67
Epig: E79
EpigAnek: E78
EpigrAst: E72
EpigrGr: E76
EpigrStud: E82
EpigrVostok: E74
EpigStud: E82
Epist: E84-E87
EpistGr: E88
EpistGraec: E88
EpistologGraec: E88
EPK: E14
EpMesArch: E62
EpMyc: I28
EPRO: E144
EPRODER: E144
ER: E145
Er: E90
ERA: E72
EranJb: E91
EranosJb: E91
EranosJhb: E91
ErdelyiMuzeum: E93-E94
ErdM: E94, E93
ErdMuz: E94, E93
ErdMuzEvk: E94
ERE: E41
Erg: Erganzungsheft.
ErgH: Erganzungsheft.
Ergon: E96
ErIs: E95
ErIsr: E95
ERL: E73
ERVC: E117
ES: E120, E82, E100, E103
ESA: E155
ESAR: E11
ESB: E16
ESeg: E111
ESFM: E110
ESM: C154
Esp: R40
ESPAHA: E112
EssexArchHist: E102
EssexArchSocTrans: E102
EstAAlava: E104
EstB: E105

EstBib: E105
EstCl: E107
EstClas: E107
EstdeArqAlavesa: E104
EstudExtremenos: R137
ET: E151, E165
Et: Etudes. <u>See also E (followed
  by the next capitalized letter)</u>.
ETAC: E121
ETAM: E150
EtBalk: E123
EtBalkan: E123
EtByz: R143
EtChypr: E125
EtCl: E127, E126
EtClass: E127, E126
Etclass: E127, E126
EtCret: E129
EtdePap: E138
Etepigretphilol: E130
EtGe: Etymologicum Magnum Genuinum.
EtGu: Etymologicum Gudianum.
EtHist: E133
EThL: E66
Ethn: E113
EthnArchZ: E115
EthnArchZeitschr: E115
EthnogArchForsch: E113
EthnogrAZ: E115
EthnolAnz: E116
EThR: E149
ETL: E66
EtM: Etymologicum Magnum.
EtMag: Etymologicum Magnum.
EtNum: E136
EtO: E137
EtP: E138
EtPal: S224
EtPap: E138
EtPelop: E139
EtPezenas: E140
EtRel: E149
EtThas: E146
EtThH: E147
EtThHS: E148
EtTr: E151
EtTrav: E151
Etudesclass: E127, E126
EtudesCret: E129
EtW: L14
EtymMagn: Etymologicum Magnum.
EUA: E42
EUI: E43
EV: E74
EvkDebrecen: D5
EvkEger: E13

EvkMiskolc: H54
EvkNyiregyhaza: N132
EvkönyveDebrecen: D5
EvkönyveNyiregyhaza: N132
EvkönyveSzeged: M272
EvkSzeged: M272
EVP: E118
EvT: E157
EvTh: E157
ExcArqenEspana: E158
ExcArqEsp: E158
ExplDelos: E164
ExpTim: E165
EzhegodnikGIM: E166

F

F: Folia; Fontes, Fonti.
F&B: F38
F&F: F40
FA: F5, F21, F4
FAC: F57
FakDerg: D65
FAP: F27-F28
FastCap: F6
FastConsImp: F7
Fasti: F5
FastiA: F5
FastiArch: F5
FAttCom: F57
FB: F38
FberBadWürt: F74
FBSchwaben: F77
FBSM: F38
FC: F7
FCap: F6
FCG: F58
FCGM: F58
FCIR: F7
FD: F50
FdD: F50
FDE: F51
FdeDelphes: F50
FDelphes: F50
FdTh: F53
FdX: F54
FE: F39
FelRev: F12
Festschrift [personal name]: See
    the special section in the in-
    troduction about Festschriften.
FF: F40
FG: F68
FGH: F60
FGrH: F60
FgrH: F60

FGrHist: F60
FH: E75, F8, F75
FHA: F29
FHDR: F30
FHG: F61
FI: F14
FIB: F14
FiE: F39
FIFAO: F52
FiL: F43
FilIst: F14
FilKözl: F15
FImp: F7
FinsktMus: F18
FIR: F31-F32
FIRA: F31-F32
FITA: F70
FIul: F48
FK: F15, F20, F41
FKS: F72
FL: F25, F49, F55
FleckJahrb: N27
FleckJSuppl: N27
FLing: F22
FLMV: M329
FlorMitt: M204
FM: M329 (=motif)
FMD: F78
FMRD: F78
FMRL: F79
FMS: F73
FMZ: F67
FOA: F35
FÖ: F76
FOE: F76
FOEG: F44
FöldrKözl: F20
FoggArtMusAcqu: A29
FOL: F22

FolA: F21
FolArch: F21
Folarch: F21
FoldrKoz: F20
FoliaArch: F21
FoliaOrient: F23
Folk: F24
FolOr: F23
FondHardt: E49
FoniurRomant: F31-F32
Font: F31-F32
FontAPos: F27
Fontes: F31-F33
FontesAH: F26
FontesArch: F26
FontesArchHung: F26
FontesArchPosnan: F27
FontesArchPrag: F28
Fonti: F34
FontIurRom: F31-F32
Fonttopveturbpert: F33
FOR: C62
ForFor: F40
ForschFortschr: F40
ForschinEphesos: F39
ForschKA: F42
ForschLauriacum: F43
ForschuFortschr: F40
ForschVolksLand: F46
FPEL: F63
FPG: F62
FPL: C259, F63
FPR: F64
FR: F9, F12, G129
Frag: See also F (followed by the
  next capitalized letter).
FragComGraec: F58
FragGrHist: F60
FragHistGraec: F61
FragPoetEpic: F63
FragPoetRom: F64
FrankfMünzztg: F67
FranLA: S167
FrK: F20
FRLANT: F45
FrMz: F67
FrühMitAltSt: F73
FrühmitaltSt: F73
FrühmittelalterlStud: F73
FS: M328 (=shape), F77, F71, F66
FSHA: M122
FStI: F34
FTVURP: F33
FuB: F38
FuBerHessen: F75
FuBerÖ: F76

FuBerSchwab: F77
FuF: F40
FundberausSchwaben: F77
FundberBaden-Württemberg: F74
FundberHessen: F75
FundberÖsterreich: F76
FundberSchwaben: F77
FunGrRF: G77
FUR: F36, P135
FurtReich: G129
FurtwR: G129
FVL: F46
FVLK: F46
FVS: F65
FZPhTh: F69

G

G: Giornale; Geschichte; Glasnik;
  Godishnik;
G: G136, G135
G&L: G9
G&R: G83
GA: G10, G75
GABH: G58
GacNum: G1
GAG: G134
GAL: G28
Gal: G2
GalliaPrehist: G3
GalliaPrhist: G3
GALS: G28
GandR: G83
GAR: G83
GaR: G83
GArb: G10
Gaz: Gazette.
GazArch: G5
Gazarch: G5
GazBA: G6
GazdBA: G6
GB: G82, G70
GBA: G6
GBK: G17
GBKO: G17
GBL: G29
GCBM: B211
GCFI: G4
GCNAC: G85
GCS: G105
GDA: G86
GdA: G27
GDI: S17
GE: G81
GEL: G87
GelAnz: G12
GelAnzdKbayerAkdWiss: G12

Geog: Géographie, Geography, Geo-
  graphical, etc.
GeogGraecMin: G19
GeogGrMin: G19
GeogLatMin: G22
GeogrAnz: G18
GeographJ: G21
GeogrJourn: G21
GeogrZ: G23
Geol: Géologie, Geology, Geologi-
  cal, etc.
GEPB: G81
Ger: G26
GerefTTS: G25
Ges: Gesellschaft.
Gesch: Geschiedenis, Geschichte,
  Geschichtliche, etc.
GettyMus: J1
GEW: G106
GF: G107
GFF: G42
GFI: G41
GG: G108, G20
GGA: G66
GGAnz: G66
GGFR: G89
GGL: G31, G30
GGM: G19
GGMM: G19
GGP: G90
GGR: G32
GGrL: G31, G30
GH: G76
GHA: A85
GHÅ: A85
GHI: S74, S75
GIBM: B217
GIC: I47
GIF: G43

GIMB: B217
GiornItFilNap: G43
GiornStorLunig: G58
GJ: G21, G14
GJb: G68
GKV: G33
GL: G79, G54, G9, G111, G16
Gl: G56
GlasgowArchJ: G48
GlasnikLjubljana: G50
GlasnikPriština: G49
GlasnikSAN: G51
GlasnikSANU: G51
Glasnik-Sarajevo: G52
GlasnikSarajevoArh: G52
GlasSAN: G51
GlasSANU: G51
GlHrvM: G52
GLK: G79
GLL: G46
GlL: G54
GLM: G22
GLMBosn: G52
GlMSar: G52
GlMSlov: G50
GLO: G74
GlosArchSocTrans: T91
GlossLat: G54
GLP: S72, G92
GLS: G133
GM: G69, G44
GMDS: G50
GMK: G63
GMKM: G49
GMPN: G40
GMSar: G52
GMus: G71
GN: Gl, Nl, Gll, E20
Gn: G57
GNS: G7, S49
God: Godishnik.
GodDuhak: G59
GodišnikPlovdiv: G60, G62
Godišnik-Sofia: G61
GodišnjakPomorMuzKotoru: G63
GodMuzPlov: G60, G62
GodMuzPlovdiv: G60, G62
GodMuzSofia: G61
GodNarM: G61
GodPlovdiv: G60, G62
GodSof: G64
GöttAbh: A10
GöttAnz: G66
GöttGAnz: G66
GöttgelAnz: G66
GöttGelAnzeigen: G66

GöttgelehrteAnz: G66
GöttMisz: G69
GöttNach: Nl
GöttNachr: J10
GOKD: G8
GORILA: R47
Gorila: R47
GotArk: G72
GottAbh: A10
GottAnz: G66
GottGAnz: G66
GottgelAnz: G66
GottGelAnzeigen: G66
GottgelehrteAnz: G66
GottMisz: G69
GottNach: J10
GottNachr: Nl
GP: G98, G40
GPN: G122
GPNBM: G62
GPVJ: J63
GR: F20
GR&BS: G102
GramLat: G79
GrammGraec: G78
GrammLat: G79
GrammRomFrag: G77
GrandR: G83
GrazBeitr: G82
GRBM: G100
GRBr: G99
GRBS: G102
GRBSA: G101
GRBStud: G100
GRByzS: G102
GrCBM: B211
GrDI: S17
Greg: G104
GrEtWb: G106
GrEW: G106
GRF: G77
GrG: G32
GrGFR: G89
GrGr: G108, G78
GrHistInscr: S74, S75
GrInsBrM: B217
GRJ: G103
GrKrieg: G110
GRL: G34
GrL: G79
GrLat: G79
GrLyrPoet: G92
GRM: G73
GrMünz: G112
GrMyth: G113
GrPapBrM: B221

GrPl: G123
GrRF: G77
GrRomanPapyri: G124
GrRomByzSt: G102
GRT: H95
GSAN: G51
GSANU: G51
GSCE: S286
GSJb: G132
GSP: G45
GTT: G25
GV: G130-G131
GVI: G130
GVK: G131
GW: G36
GWU: G35
Gymn: G136, G135
GZ: G65
GZM: G52
GZMA: G52
GZMBH: G52
GZME: G52
GZMS: G52
GZMSarajevo: G52

H

H: Histoire, History, Historical,
   etc.; Handbuch; Handelingen.
H: H58, H60
H&T: H111
H&W: C174
HA: H50, H77, H1
HA: Scriptores Historiae Augustae.
Ha: H55
HAAN: H86
HAB: H66
HAC: H89
HadArch: H1
HadashotArch: H1
HadtörtKözl: H3
HAE: H78, H9
HAEp: H78
HAEpigr: H78
HaG: H24
HallWPr: H5
HambBeitrA: H6
HambBeitrN: H7
HambKuSamml: J28
Handb: Handbuch.
HandbAlt: H11
HandbderOr: H18
HanddArch: H12
HandelOudheidMechelen: H21
HanG: H8
HAnt: H77
HarburgerJahrb: H25
HarvardThR: H31
HarvSt: H30
HarvStClPhil: H30
HarvStud: H30
HarvStudClassPhil: H30
HarvTheolRev: H31
HarvThRev: H31
HarvThRev: H29
HarzZ: H33

HASB: H36
HAT: H10
HAW: H11
HaWpr: H5
HB: H11
Hb: Handbuch.
HBA: H6
HBArch: H12
HbAT: H10
HbAW: H11
HbKG: H16
HbKlAlt: H1
HBN: H7
HbNT: H17
HBo: H69
HbOr: H18
HBr: D17
HBS: P242
HCC: R334
HChI: H13
HchI: H13
HCT: H91
HdA: H11-H12
HdArch: H12
HdAW: H11
HDB: D45
Hdb: H11
HdbArchäol: H12
HdbitDial: H15
HdO: H18
HE: G84, H67, H92, E41
HebrUCA: H35
HeidAbh: A18
HeidAkAbh: A18
HeidAkSb: S92
HeidSitz: S92
HeJb: H38
Hell: H46
HellOxy: Hellenica Oxyrhynchia.

Helm: H49
HelvA: H50
HelvArch: H50
HelvetArch: H50
HelvetiaArch: H50
HERE: E41
Herm: H58, H57
HERM-BR: D17
HertfordshireArch: H59
Hesp: H60
HessJbLandesgesch: H63
HFM: H93
Hft: Heft.
HG: G136
HGAudenarde: A235
HGBruges: H19
HGD: H14
HGGand: H22
HGM: H94
HGRT: H95
HH: H74, H119
HhGl: H75
HHM: H120
HibJ: H72
HID: H15
HispAnt: H77
HispAntEpigr: H78
HispSacra: H79
Hist: Histoire, Historisch, Hist-
    orical, etc.
Hist: H80-H81, H84
HistCas: H90
HistEsp: H92
HistJ: H97
HistJbGraz: H98
HistJUBirmingham: H100
HistNum: H106
HistoriaZAltGesch: H80
HistriaA: H87
HistriaArch: H87
HistRomRel: H109
HistRomReliquiae: H109
HistSt: H110
HistTid(C): H113
HistTidskr: H113, H112, H114
HistToday: H115
HistZ: H118
HistZbor: H117
HistZeit: H118
HistZeitschr: H118
HistZeitschrift: H118
HJ: H97
HJAS: H26
HJB: H97
HJGraz: H98
HJL: H63

HJLinz: H99
HK: H3
HKAT: G67
HKL: H68
HKT: H69
HKZM: H23
HL: H39, H102
HLB: H27
HLB&P: H103
H1K: H42
HLKMalines: H21
HM: H121, H104
HME: H4
HMemAcRIBL: M97
HMI: H2
HN: H106, H105
HNT: H17
HO: Hellenica Oxyrhynchia.
HO: H18
HOLKMalines: H21
HOME: H54
HommePrehist: H122
HOr: H18
HPG: H107
HPN: H107
HR: H108
HRF: M102
HRR: H109
HRRel: H109
HS: H79, A359
HSClPh: H30
HSCP: H30
HSEH: S107
HSM: H28
HSPh: H30
HSS: H29
HStClPh: H30
HT: I120, H115, H62
HTC: H113, H112, H114
HThK: H53
HThR: H31
HTR: H70
HTr: H70
HTS: H112-H114, H32
HUCA: H35
HuH: H64
HumG: G136
HumLov: H128
Hunter: C76
HV: H116
HVS: H116
HW: H71, C174
HWPr: H5
HZ: H118, H117

I

I: Izvestiia; Institut, Istituto,
   etc.; Inscriptiones, Inschriften,
   etc.; International, Internazion-
   ale, etc.
IA: I53, I111, I142
IAA: I150
IAAK: I33
IAE: I94
IAI: I153
IAK: I156, I33
IAM: I61, I128
IAMY: I128
IAN: I152
IANA: I167
IANE: I93
IAP: I115
IBAI: I153
IBC: I42
IBK: I30
IBM: B217
IBoT: I129
IBR: I41
IBulg: I54
IC: I47
ICC: I95
ICERV: I48
ICK: I49
ICos: I46
ICr: I47
ICret: I47
ICreticae: I47
ICS: I45, I5
ICUR: I44
ICVR: I44
ID: I51, I143
IDB: I99
IDelos: I51
IdgForsch: I19
IdgGr: I20

IdgJb: I21
IDidyma: I32
IDR: I50
IEE: H96
IEG: I2
IEJ: I126
IEK: I34
IEW: I18
IExJ: I126
IF: I19, I130, I92
IFAnz: A398
IFAO: M125
IFil: I31
IFZ: I137
IFZArm: I137
IG: I52, I29
IGA: I53
IGAIMK: I155
IGB: I54, I35
IGBR: I54
IGBulg: I54
IGCH: I105
IGCh: R44
IGCS: I96
IGD: I7
IGdial: I55
IGForsch: I19
IgForsch: I19
IGH: S74
IGI: I70
IGLB: I14
IGLMP: I116
IGLR: I60
IGLS: I62-I63
IGLSYR: I62
IGLSyr: I62
IGR: I56
IGrB: I54
IgrForsch: I19

IGROM: I56
IGRom: I56
IGRR: I56
IGRRP: I56
IGS: I57-I58
IGSept: I57
IGSI: I58, I70
IGUR: I59
IGUrbesRomae: I59
IH: I23
IHA: I24
IHC: I65
IHCS: I65
IHEV: I66
IHH: I67
IHV: I66
II: I68
IIA: I9
IICAbstracts: A604
IIID: I69
IIJ: I17
IIt: I68
IIug: I77
IJ: I21, I113, R45
IJb: I21
IJG: R45
IJNA: I97
IKMK: I141
IKMKözl: I141
IKourion: I71
IL: I25
ILA: I72-I73, I85
ILAf: I72
ILAfr: I72
ILAl: I73
ILAlg: I73
ILC: I74
ILChV: I74
ILCV: I74
IldeGaule: I82
ILER: I75
ILG: I76
ILGN: I76
ILGNarb: I76
ILindos: I40
ILing: I11
ILIug: I77
IllLondonNews: I6
ILLP: I118
ILLR: I78
ILLRP: I78
IllVat: I8
ILM: I79
ILMar: I79
ILMaroc: I79
ILN: I6

ILS: I80
ILSard: I119
ILT: I83
ILTG: I82
ILTun: I83
IM: I131, I26
Imag: I9-I10
ImagIGA: I10
ImagInscrAttic: I9
IMagn: I36
IMagnesia: I36
IMaroc: I79
IMDAI: I131
IMErgH: I131
IMGA: I102
IMP: I116
Imp: Imperial, etc.
IMS: I84
IMU: I144
IN: I145
InDel: I51
IndForsch: I19
IndiceHistEsp: I16
IndogermF: I19
IndoGermForsch: I19
IndogForsch: I19
InF: I31
Inf&Trab: I27
InfA: I22
InfArqu: I22
InFil: I31
InfMemExcArq: I26
InformesyMem: I26
IngaunaetIntemelia: R283, R301
INJ: I127
Inscr: Inscriptiones, Inscriptions
    etc.
InscPontEuxini: I86
InscrAsMin: R44
InscrBritChrist: I42
InscrBulg: I54
InscrChrist: I43
InscrChristUR: I44
InscrCos: I46
InscrCret: I47
InscrdeDelos: I51
InscrDelos: I51
InscrDidyma: I32
InscrGr: I52
InscrGraec: I52
InscrGraecadresRompert: I56
InscrGreacAntiq: I53
InscrGrAntiq: I53
InscrGreclatlaSyrie: I62-I63
InscrGrLatSyrie: I62-I63
InscriptCret: I47

InscrItal: I68
InscrIug: I77
Inscrjurid: R45
InscrKourion: I71
InscrLatAfr: I72
InscrLatAlg: I73
InscrLatChristVet: I74
Inscrlatd'Afrique: I72
Inscrlatgaule: I76
Inscrlatiug: I77
Inscrlatlibreipublicae: I78
InscrLatLibRP: I78
InscrLatSel: I80
InscrLatTroisGaules: I82
InscrLindos: I40
InscrMaroc: I79
InscrMusAlex: I117
InscrOl: I37
InscrOlymp: I37
InscrOrell: I81
InscrorseptPonEux: I86
InscrPerg: I38
InscrPhilae: I64
InscrPrien: I39
InscrPyliae: I87
InscrRomAlg: I89
InscrRomGal: I90
InscrRomTripol: I91
InscrSardegna: I119
InscrTunisie: I83
Inst: Institut, Institute.
InsvPriene: I39
IntJNA: I97
IntJournal: J10
Inv: I101
InvArch[name of country]: I104
INVENTARIA: I104
InvLuc: I107
InvMos: I102
InvMosI-III: I102
InvMosAfrique: I102
InvMosaïques: I102
InvtArch[name of country]: I104
InvWaddington: I103
IOlympia: I37
IOSPE: I86
IosPE: I86
IP: I87, I133
IparME: I108
IPE: I86
IPEK: I109
Ipek: I109
IPergamon: I38
Iphilae: I64
IPQ: I1
IPriene: I39

IPS: I15
IRA: I89
IRAIK: I164
IRAIMK: I155
IRAN: I152
IrAn: I111
IranAnt: I111
IranicaAnt: I111
IrAnt: I111
IRAO: I156
IRF: A64
IRG: I90
IRN: I88
IRT: I91
Irtört: I114
IRTr: I91
ISA: S272
ISard: G91
ISardegna: I119
ISE: I121
Isl: I125, I124
ISPh: I98
IsraelExplJournal: I126
IsraelExplorJournal: I126
IsrEJ: I126
IstambAMüzYil: I128
IstanbForsch: I130
IstanbulArkMuzYilligi: I128
IstanbulerMitt: I131
IstArkMuzYill: I128
IstCas: I138
IstFilZhurANArmian: I137
IstForsch: I130
IstGl: I139
IstMitt: I131
IstRom: I132
IstSSSR: I136
IstZap: I134
IstZhurn: I135
IsvestijaDruzestvo: I153, I154,
   I161
It: Itinerarium Antonini Augusti.
It: I114
ItDial: I143
ItinAnt: Itinerarium Antonini Au-
   gusti.
ItR: I147
ItRom: I147
ITUAK: I166
IURA: I148
IVAD: I161
IVGO: I168
IvM: I36
IvO: I37
IvOl: I37
IvP: I38

J

J: Journal, Jahrbuch, Jahresbericht,
  Jaarsboek.
JA: J93, J13, J21
JAA: J96
JaabAkAmst: J2
JAAC: J87
JaarberExOrienteLux: J8
JaarberichteEOL: J8
JaarsTerpenGroningen: J7
JAC: J14
JadZbor: J9
JadZborn: J9
JAeAC: J87
JAfrHist: J88
JAfricanHist: J88
Jahrb: Jahrbuch. See also Jb and
  J (followed by the next capital-
  ized letter).
Jahrb: J21, N27
JahrbAltkde: J13
JahrbAnz: A421
JahrbBodendenMeck: B118
JahrbDAI: J21
JahrbdArchInst: J21
JahrbdInst: J21
JahrbdÖsterraechInst: J74
JahrbdStaatlKunstsammlungenBad-
  Württ: J52
JahrbfAltert: J13
JahrbfclPhil: N27
JahrbfclPhilSuppl: N27
JahrbfPhiluPädogSuppl: N27
JahrbHistMusBern: J17
JahrbHistVerDilling: J30
JahrbHistVerLiechten: J31
JahrbKunsthSamml: J36
JahrbNumismGeldgesch: J45
JahrbNumuGeldgesch: J45
JahrbOberösterrMusealver: J46

JahrbOsterreichByzantGesell: J47
JahrbPreussKunstsamml: J48, J16
JahrbRGZM: J49
JahrbSchweizGesellUrgesch: J50
JahrbSchweizGesUrgesch: J50
Jahrbuch: J21
JahrbuchfdclPhilSuppl: N27
JahrbuchRGZM: J49
JahrbZentralKomm: W25
Jahres: See also Jahresber, Jahr-
  esh.
Jahresb: B448
Jahresber: See also Jb, Jahres.
Jahresber: B448
JahresberBayerBodendenkmal: J61
JahresberGesProVindonissa: J63
JahresberGPV: J63
JahresberHistMusBern: J62
JahresberHistVerDillingen: J30
JahresberHistVerOberpfalz: J67
JahresberHistVerStraubing: J69
JahresberichtProVindon: J63
JahresberichtZürich: J78
JahresberOberösterrMusealver: J46
JahresberSchweizGesUrgesch: J50
JahresberSchweizLandesmusZürich:
  J78
JahresberTrier: T112
JahresbFortschrAltertswiss: B448
JahresbNaturhistGesNürnberg: J73
JahresbPVB: J75
JahresbSchweizUrgesch: J50
Jahresh: J74
JahreshBeiblatt: J74
JahreshdesÖsterrArchInst: J74
JahreshÖsterrArchInst: J74
JahresschrHalle: J72
JAI: J21, J74, J90
JAK: J13

JAME: N132
Jameson: C163
JAN: J116
JAnthrInst: J90
JAntIre: J132
JARCE: J89
JArchNum: J116
JArchSc: J91
JAS: J92
JAs: J93
JASAH: J133
JAScien: J91
JAsiat: J93
JAuC: J14
JAUK: J12
JAW: B448
JAWG: J10
JAWL: J3
JAWM: J11
JAZU: R3
JB: B448
Jb: Jahrbuch, Jaarboek. See also
   Jahrb and J (followed by the
   next capitalized letter).
JBAA: J96
JbAC: J14
JbAChr: J14
JbAltKde: J13
JbArchI: J21
JBArchInst: J21
JBAW: J15
JbAWG: J10
JBB: J61
JbB: J61
Jbb: Jahrbücher. See also Jahrb
   and J (followed by the next cap-
   italized letter).
JbBerlin: J20
JbBerlMus: J16
JBBernHistMus: J17
JbBernHistMus: J17
JbbfclPh: N27
JbBHM: J17
JbBM: J16
JbCoburgLandesst: J19
JbDAI: J21
JberEOL: J8
JberHistGesGraub: J64
JberInstVgFrankf: J70
JBerlM: J16
JbGfnf: T112
JbGött: J10
JbGOst: J26
JbGPV: J63
JbHVFL: J31
JbInst: J21

JbKlF: A160
JbKMusSchonKunstAntwerp: A288
JbKSWien: J36
JbKunsthistSammlWien: J36
JbKuSammlBadWürt: J52
JbKW: J37
JBL: J18, J95
JbLKNÖ: J38
JbLKNOE: J38
JbLN: J38
JbLW: J40
JBM: J17
JbMainz: J11
JBMe: B118
JBMeck: B118
JbMunchen: J15
JbMusLinz: J46
JbNG: J45
JbNum: J45
JbÖBG: J47
JbÖByz: J47
JbOÖMV: J46
JbPhPäd: N21
JbPrKs: J48
JBR: J94
JbRGZ: J49
JbRGZM: J49
JBritArchAss: J96
JbSchweizGesUrFrühgesch: J50
JbSchwGesUrgesch: J50
JbSGU: J50
JbSGUF: J50
JbSL: J54
JbSLM: J78
JbStiftPreussKulBes: J55
JbStKunstsammlDresden: J53
JbVerGeschWein: J57
JbVGSW: J57
JbVLkNÖ: J38
JbVorarlberg: J58
JbWels: J43
JbZMusMainz: J49
JbzMusMainz: J49
JCC: W25
JChesterArchSoc: J98
JCL: J19
JClS: J100
JCPh: N27
JCS: J101, J100
JCunSt: J101
JDAI: J21
JdAI: J21
JDAIAA: A421
JDArchInst: J21
JDI: J21
JdI: J21

JdIErg: J21
JDM: D5
JdS: J130
JE: J84
JEA: J104
JEArch: J104
JEgArch: J104
JEgyptArchaeol: J104
JEH: J102
JEHV: J22
JEOL: J8
JESHO: J103
JFA: J105
JfA: J13
JFieldA: J105
JFieldArch: J105
JFL: J23
JfLW: J40
JfNG: J45
JfNum: J45
JG: S44
Jg: Jaargang.
JGKAE: J27
JGKM: J24
JGlassStud: J107
JGlSt: J107
JGMOD: J25
JGOL: J4
JGS: J107
JhAC: J14
JHAG: J64
JHAW: J29
JhbInst: J21
JHellSt: J108
JHI: J111
JHistId: J111
JHistStud: J110
JHK: J28
JHM: J113
JHMS: J109
JHMT: J65
JhOAI: J74
JhOestArchI: J74
JHPh: J114
JhrbAC: J14
JHS: J108
JHSt: J108
JHVD: J30
JHVF: J34
JHVG: J32
JHVGR: J66
JHVL: J31
JHVM: J33
JHVS: J69
JHVSe: J68
JIAN: J116

JIC: J142–J143
JIES: J114
JIN: J116
JIntArNum: J116
JIntNum: J116
JJE: J82
JJP: J119
JJR: J118
JJS: J118
JJurP: J119
JJurPap: J119
JKAF: A160
JKBW: J52
JKD: J53
JKF: A160
JKGV: J35
JKH: J71
JK1F: A160
JK1Ph: N27
JKPh: N27
JKS: J36
JKSW: J36
JL: J120
JLNOE: J38
JLW: J40
JManch: J121
JMHR: J42
JMM: J41
JMP: J5, Z83
JMS: J122
JMV: J72
JMW: J43
JNedGen: J5
JNES: J123
JNFI: J44
JNG: J45
JNGG: J45
JNSL: J124
JO: J74
JOAI: J74
JOAIBeibl: J74
JOAIW: J74
JOB: J47
JOBG: J47
JOByz: J47
JÖ: J74
JOEAI: J74
JÖB: J47
JÖBG: J47
JÖEAI: J74
JOEB: J47
JÖByz: J47
JOEByz: J47
JOOEM: J46
JOstArchInst: J74
JOU: J6

JourHellStud: J108
Journal: <u>See also Journ, J (followed</u>
  <u>by the next capitalized letter)</u>.
JournalInternatd'ArchNumism: J116
Journalinternd'archeolnumism: J116
JournalNearEastStud: J123
JournalofEgArch: J104
JournalRomStud: J129
JournalSocAntiquIreland: J132
Journ: Journal. <u>See also Journal,</u>
  <u>J (followed by the next capital-</u>
  <u>ized letter)</u>.
JournAs: J93
JournAsiatSoc: J92
JournBibLit: J95
JournClassSocPhil: J99
JournEgArch: J104
JournHellSt: J108
JournintArchnum: J116
JournIntern: J116
JournofEgArch: J104
JournofEgyptArchaeol: J104
JournofJurPap: J119
JournofPapyr: J119
JournofPhil: J125
JournofRomStud: J129
JournoftheAntInst: J90
JournPhil: J125
JournRomSt: J129
JournRoyGeogSoc: J106
JournSav: J130
JournWaltersGallery: J139
JournWarburgInst: J140
JP: J125
JPalOrS: J117
JPEK: I109
JPh: J125-J126
JPhilos: J126
JPK: J48
JPKS: J48
JPM: J81
JPME: J81
JPOS: J117
JPrKS: J48, J16
JQR: J85
JR: J127
JRAI: J90
JRAS: J92
JRelig: J127
JRGM: J49
JRGS: J106
JRGZ: J49
JRGZM: J49
JRGZMainz: J49
JRH: J128
JRIBA: J112

JRomStud: J129
JRS: J129
JRSA: J134, J132
JRSAI: J132
JRSt: J129
JS: J130
JSAH: J133
JSav: J130
JSchrSbg: J76
JSchrVgHalle: J72
JSEA: M128
JSemSt: J131
JSExc: M128
JSGU: J50
JSJ: J136
JSMCA: J76
JSocArchH: J133
JSoG: J51
JSOR: J135
JSOT: J137
JSPK: J55
JSS: J131
JSSt: J131
JStGall: J77
JThS: J138
JThSt: J138
JTS: J138
JUAG: O48
JUD: J56
JUMP: M312
JurPap: J144
JuznFil: J145
JVA: B193
JVEG: J8
JVGW: J57
JVH: J80
JVL: J58
JVSTL: J72
JVT: J7
JWAG: J139
JWalt: J139
JWaltersArtGal: J139
JWarb: J140
JWCI: J140
JWG: J59
JWI: J140
JZK: W25

K

K: Közleményei; Korrespondenzblatt; Kratkie Soobshcheniia.
K: C167, K31
KA: K73
KAH: K11
KAI: K4
KairMitt: M191
KAJ: K12
KantStud: K5
KAR: K13
Kart: K6
Karth: K6
KAV: K14
KazakAkHabarlary: I151
KB: K10, K54, K71
KBH: K82
KBN: K41
KBN(CIRB): K41
KBO: K15
KBo: K15
KBS: K7
KC: See also KrSoob, KratSoob.
KC: K53, K45, K46, K70
KCh: K53
KChron: K53
KCOAM: K50
KCsA: K40
KdO: K68
Ke: K18
KEH: K77
KEK: K58
KerDo: K19
KF: K25
KG: A687
Kg: Königliche.
KGL: G79
KHAT: K76
KHC: K76
KHKM: K78

KHM: K67
KHTs: K38
KIAM: K64
KIB: K71
KiB: K71
KirchPA: P217
KJ: J34
KJb: K74
KJPOV: K65
KJVFG: K34
KK: K80, K53
KKhr: K53
KKI: K57
Kl: K31
KlassPhilStud: K23
KlF: K25
KlMünz: K26
KlP: K28
KlPauly: K28
KlPW: K28
KlRE: K28
KlSchr: Kleine Schriften.
KlT: K29
KM: M191
KMT: K52
KNNÖ: K62
KNOB: B340
KölnerJahrbVorFrühgesch: K34
KölnJbVFrühGesch: K34
KölnJbVorFrühGesch: K34
Közl: K44, M19
KözlCluj: K44
Közlemenyek-Cluj: K44
KözlKvar: K44
KolnerJahrbVor-uFruhgesch: K33
KolnJbVFruhGesch: K33
KolnJbVorFruhGesch: K33
KomaromMegMuzKöz: K37
KomaromMK: K37

KorrBlattVerSiebenLandeskunde: S85
KorrblDtGesAnthrEthUrgesch: K42
KorrblGesamtver: Bll4
KorrblWestdnZeitschr: K43
Közl: M19, K44
KözlCluj: K44
Közlemenyek-Cluj: K44
KözlKvar: K44
KP: K28
KPG: K75
KPN: K27
KR: P174
KraSoob: K45
KraSoobInstA; K45-K46
KratSoob: See also KC, KrSoob.
KratSoobInstArkANSSSR: K45
KratSoobInstArkANUSSR: K46
KratSoobInstEtnogr: K47
KratSoobInstMaterKult: K45
KratSoobInstNarodAz: K48
KratSoobOGAM: K50
KrCh: K53
KretChron: K53
Kretchron: K53
KritChron: K53
KritJahrFortschrromPhilogie: K59
KrSoIIMK: K45
KrSoob: See also KratSoob, KS.
KrSoobInstSlav: K49
KrSoobKiev: K46
KrSoobMoscou: K45
KrVJSchr: K60
KS: Kratkie Soobshcheniia. See
   also KrSoob.
KS: K45, K81
KSAMP: K50
KSIA: K45-K46
KASIANSSSR: K45
KSIAANUSSR: K46
KSIAK: K46
KsiaKiev: K46
KSIAM: K45
KSIIMK: K45
KSIMK: K45
KSKiev: K46
KSMoscova: K45
KSOdessa: K50
KSOGAM: K50
KSp: K81
KSz: K17
KT: K32, K29, K38
KTEMA: K61
KTU: K9
KUB: K16
KuGeschAnz: K72
KunglVitHistAntikAkadÅrsbok: A9

Kunstchr: K70
KunstOr: K68
KuOr: K68
KuWeltBerlMus: K69
KV: U25
KVGR: K60
KVHA: A9
KVMW: K39
KVSL: S85
KwartalnikHist: K79
KwartHistKulMat: K78
KwartHistKulMater: K78
KwHist: K79
KwKl: K80
KX: K53
KyprSpud: K81
KZ: Z72

L

L: Lettere, Lettres, etc.; Lexicon,
  Lexikon.
L: L8
L&G: L18
L&L: L66
L&S: L67
LA: S167, L21, L38
La: L7
LAAA: A224
LAalst: L3
LAC: A376
LÄ: L38
LÄS: L26
LAF: L68
LandKunVierJBl: L5
LANG: L6
Lang: L6
L'AntCl: A376
LAntClas: A376
LAnthr: A339
LAnthrop: A339
LapSept: L8
LAR: A200
LAS: L26
LaSicilartedarch: S83
LaurAqu: L21
LAW: L39
LB: B12
LBalk: B12
LBer: L62
LBW: V75
LChrI: L40
LCL: L80
LCM: L77
LCS: R55
LD: D13
LdM: L44
LDPK: L10
LdR: L78

LE: Z95
LEC: E127
LegSacr: L23
LegXII: The Twelve Tables.
LeipzhistAbhandl: L27
LeipzStud: L28
LenzN: L30
LetMatSrp: L34
Lett: Lettere, Lettres.
LEW: L14
Lex: Lexicon, Lexikon.
LexAW: L39
Lexis: R50
LexMyth: A688
LextotLatin: T79
LexVindob: L46
LF: L71, L49, L56
LFE: L41
LfgrE: L41
LFLW: V75
Lg: L6
LgDiss: L6
LGM: L42
LGRM: A688
LGRR: L11
LGS: L23
LgSuppl: L6
LGVI: L70
LH: L15, L92
LHerle: L4
LHommepreh: H122
LHS: L15
LHSz: L15
LI: L33
LIA: L65
Lib: L52-L53
LibAnt: L51
LibColon: Libri Coloniarum.
LibicaAnthropol: L52

LibicaArcheol: L53
LibyaAnt: L51
LiddSc: G87
LIHH: I67
LIMC: L43
LIn: L64
LincolnshireHistArch: L57
LincRc: R69
LincsAASocRep: R85
LindTempChron: L58
Ling: L61
LingBalk: B12
LingBibl: L63
LinzAF: L68
LisFil: L71
ListyFil: L71
Lit: L74
LitA: L76
LitArts: L76
LitblfgermuromPhil: L73
Litt: L74
LivAnn: A224
LiverpAn: A224
LiverpoolAAA: A224
LiverpoolAnnals: A224
LJ: L55
LL: M257
LLoon: D58
LM: L85
LMA: L44, M279
LMGL: L69
LMH: M260
LMS: L12
LMTS: L12
LN: L50
LOC: L75
Loeb: L80
LoebClassLibr: L80
LOS: L84
LP: S72, L48, P146
LPP: P83
LPPR: L24
LpzÄgStud: L26
LR: L78
LRBC: L13
LRE: H101, L16
LS: G87, L8, L17, L79
LSAG: L79
LSAM: L82
LSCG: L83
LSJ: G87
LSKPh: L28
LSLSuppl: G87
LSt: L28
LThK: L45
LThPh: L22

LTK: L45
LTL: T79
LTU: L89
LUÅ: A86
LüB: L86
LünebergerB: L86
LünebergerBl: L86
LünebergerMusbl: L87
LuJ: L55
LW: V75, L91
LXX: Septuagint Version of the
  Bible.
LydWb: L91
LZ: L72
LZB: L72

M

M: Materialy, Materiale, etc.; Med-
ede(e)lingen, Meddelelser, etc.;
Mélanges; Memoires, Memorie, Mem-
orias, etc.; Miscellanea; Mitteil-
lungen; Monatsbericht; Monumenta,
Monumenti; Magyar.
M: M226, R333
M&H: M80
MA: M246, M249-M251, M279, M40,
M51, M112
MA: Monumentum Ancyranum.
MAAL: M246
MAAN: M106
MAAR: M110
MAARome: M110
MAB: M95
MAb: M42
MAByz: M253
MAcA: M100
MAcBelg: M95
MAcBes: P212
MAcDijon: M99
MAcM: M98
MAcPat: A657
MACr: M247
MAcS: M104
MAcSavoie: M101
MAD: M50
MadriderMitt: M7
MadrMitt: M7
MÄS: M281
MAev: M81
MAF: M138
MAG: M184, M183
MagGr: M10
MAGW: M184
MAGWien: M184
MagyTud: M17-M21
MAGZ: M185

MAH: M87
MAHCUM: M240
MAI: M191-M193, M97, M21
MainfränkJbGeschKunst: M23
MAInstUngAk: M21
MainzerZeitschr: M24
MAIS: M180
MAIT: M102
MAK: M47
Maked: M25
MAKW: M182
MAL: M107, M246
MALinc: M246, M107
MAM: M178
MAMA: M255
MAmAcadRome: M110
MAN: M30
Man: M28
MANE: M241
ManEG: M31
MAntFr: M138
ManthropGesWien: M184
MAOG: M183
MAP: M49
MAPM: M74
MAPS: M111
MAR: M49, M254
MarbJb: M34
MarbJbKw: M34
MarbWP: M35
MarbWPr: M35
MarmPar: Marmor Parium.
MAS: M281
MASCAJourn: M1
MASCANews; M2
MASP: M48, M103
MAST: M109
MAT: M102, M109
Mat: Materialy, Materiale, Materi-

aux, etc.
MatA: M43
MatArch: M43
MatArchKrakow: M43
MatArh: M51
MatArhKiev: M48
MatArhSevPrincornom: M48
MatArkhSO: M45
MàtArkhSP: M48
MaterialyArch: M43
MatEtnGruz: M55
MatHistPrimetNatHomme: M56
MatiIss: M58
MatIss: M58
MatIstMuz: M59
MatIstBucuresti: M59
MatKiev: M54
MatMinsk: M44
MatMosKvaLeningrad: M58
MatPetrograd: M49
MatpoArkh: M45
MatRiga: M57
MatsiCercArh: M51
MatStar: M61
MatSzczecin: M64
MatTbilissi: M46
Matt-Syd: R333
MatWarszawa: M61
MatZachodnioPomorskie: M64
MAV: M105
MAW: M69
MB: Monatsberichte.
MB: M300, M282, M5, M168, M153
MBal: M36
MBerl: M234
MBerlGesAnthrop: M187
MBK: M188
MBlVFrühGesch: M198
MBNG: M186
MBP: M282
MBPR: M282
MBS: M114
MBV: M283
MBVF: M289
MC: M236
MCA: M51
MCACote-d'Or: M116
MCArh: M51
MCAT: M302
MCC: M189
McClean: C79
MCHACourtrai: H20
MChius: E119
MCl: M236
MCM: M169
MCom: M170

MCr: M303-M304
MCRAPE: M115
MCSA: M155
MCSN: M52
MCV: M88
McW: S71
MD: M53
MDAC: M119
MDAF: M120
MDAFA: M117
MDAI: M190, M130
MDAIA: M192
MDAIAthAbt: M192
MDAI(B): B9
MDAIBagAbt: B9
MDAI(I): I131
MDAI(K): M191
MDAI(M): M7
MDAIMadAbt: M7
MDAI(R): M193
MDAIRomAbt: M193
MDAI(T): A446
MDAPV: M54
MDAW: M230
MdF: M305-M306
MDI: M190
MdI: M190, M123
MDIAA: M191
MDIäAK: M191
MDIAK: M191
MDIK: M191
MDOG: M194
MDOrG: M194
MDP: M130
MDPV: M206
Med: Medede(e)lingen, Meddelanden,
    Meddelelser.
MedAkWet: M69
MeddelelserNCG: M71
MeddelelsGlyptKøb: M71
MeddelLinköping: M72
MeddelLund: M68
MeddelLundUHistMus: M68
Meded: M70
Mededeelingen: M69
MededelNedenInstRom: M70
MededRom: M70
MededRome: M70
MedelhavsMusB: B324
MedelhBull: B324
MedHum: M80
MedKonNederlAkadWet: M69
MedNC: M71
MedNederlHistInstRom: M70
MedNIRome: M70
MedRen: M78

MedRenSt: M78
MedSpin: M77
MedSt: M78
MEE: M83
MEFR: M87
MEFRA: M87
MEFR(MA-TM): M87
MeH: M80
MeinFCG: M87
Mel: Mélanges. See the special
    section about Festschriften in
    the introduction.
Mélanges: M87
Mélanges[followed by personal
    name]: See the special section
    about Festschriften in the in-
    troduction.
MelangesArcheolHist: M87
MelangesBeyrouth: M91
Melangesd'arch: M87
MelangesEcoleFrancRome: M87
MelArcheoletHist: M87
MelArchhist: M87
MelBeyrouth: M91
Meldarch: M87
Meld'Archetd'Hist: M87
Meldel'ecfrdeRom: M87
MelEcFranc: M87
MelGr: M89
MelRom: M87
MelRome: M87
MelStJ: M91
MelStJoseph: M91
MelUnivBeyr: M91
MelUnivSJoseph: M91
MelUSJ: M91
Mem: Mémoires, Memorie, Memoria,
    etc. See also M (followed by
    the next capitalized letter).
MemAAR: M110
MemAccadLincei: M107
MemAccadNapoli: M106
MemAccBologna: M108
MemAccdItalia: M107
MemAccIt: M107
MemAccLinc: M107
MemAccLincd'Italia: M107
MemAccNap: M106
MemAccNapoli: M106
MemAccPont: A668
MemAccTor: M108
MemAcInscr: M97, M118
MemAL: M107
MemAmAc: M110
MemAmAcadRome: M110
MemAmAcRome: M110

MemAmerAcad: M110
MemAmerAcadRome: M110
MemAngers: M100
MemAnt: M112
MemAntiq: M112
MemAube: M135
MemBologna: M108
MemCACO: M116
MemChalonS: M146
MemClL: M95, M126
Memcour: M95
Memdel'AcaddInscr: M118
MemdelaSocdeLingdeParis: M149
MemDepCoted'Or: M116
MemDijon: M99
MemExc: M128
MemFERT: M127
MemIFAO: M125
MemInst: M125
MemInstCaire: M125
MemInstCorArch: M123
MemInstFranc: M125
MemInstFrancaisarchor: M125
MemInstNatFr: M97
MemJuntaExc: M128
MemLinc: M107
MemLincei: M107
MemMA: M131
MemMAA: M131
MemMAProv: M131
MemMidi: M142
MemMiss: M129
MemMissCaire: M129
MemMusAProvinc: M131
MemMusArq: M131
MemMusArquProvinciales: M131
MemNap: M106
MemNapoli: M106
MemorieAccNapoli: M106
MemorieLincei: M107
MemPont: A668
MemPontAcc: A668
MemRAH: M96
MemRendAccZelAcireale: M133
MemSLing: M149
MemSocAF: M138
MemSocAnt: M138
MemSocAntPicardie: M139
MemSocEduenne: M144
MemSocLing: M149
MemSocnatantFrance: M138
MemSocNatAntiquFrance: M138
MemSocPrehistFranc: M150
MemStorForogiuliesi: M152
MemStorFriuli: M152
MemStPetersbourg: M103

MemToulouse: M102
MemTouraine: M143
MEpitömüveszet: M11
MEPR: V41
METEE: P243
MetMusBull: B316
MetMusStud: M158
MEtr: M256
MetrMusJ: M157
MetrMusStud: M158
MetrMusStudies: M158
MetrolScript: M156
MF: M6
MFA: A298, B333
MFAB: B333
MFME: M272
MFO: M91
MG: M257, M10, M93
MGAA: M257
MGAEU: M187
MGAuctant: M257
MGD: M257
MGDD: M257
MGeneve: M309
MGEpist: M257
MGEpp: M257
MGH: M257
MGHAA: M257
MGHBriefe: M257
MGHCapit: M257
MGHConc: M257
MGHConst: M257
MGHDD: M257
MGHDipl: M257
MGHDiplKar: M257
MGHDiplKarGerm: M257
MGHDiplRegImp: M257
MGHDtChron: M257
MGHDtMa: M257
MGHEp: M257
MGHEpp: M257
MGHEpSel: M257
MGHFontIur: M257
MGHFontIurNS: M257
MGHForm: M257
MGHGestPontRom: M257
MGHLibelli: M257
MGHLibriConfr: M257
MGHLL: M257
MGHLLNat: M257
MGHNecr: M257
MGHPoetae: M257
MGHQuellGeistGesch: M257
MGHScriptRerGerm: M257
MGHScriptRerGermNS: M257
MGHScriptRerLangob: M257

MGHScriptRerMerov: M257
MGHSS: M257
MGHStaatsschr: M257
MGI: M307-M308
MGJ: M231
MGL: M326
MGLex: M326, M257
MGLibLit: M257
MGLL: M257
MGPL: M257
MGpoetlat: M257
MGR: M173, M269
MGrecs: M259
MGScr: M257
MGScript: M257
MGScriptrerGerm: M257
MGScriptrerLang: M257
MGScrrermerov: M257
MGSL: M197
MGSLK: M197
MGSS: M257
MGStGall: M215
MGV: M327
MGWJ: M231
MH: M310, M80
MHAR: M134
MHB: B334
MHistVerPfalz: M200
MHJ: M82
MHKK: M67
MHSM: M271
MHVP: M200
MHVS: M199
MhVSt: M201
MI: M190, M123
MIA: M192, M58
MIAMoskva: M58
MIB: M237, M108
MIBT: M323
MIE: M124
MIFAC: M125
MIFAO: M125
MigPG: P89
MigPL: P90
MIGRA: M172
MIL: M126
MIO: M202
MIÖG: M209
MIOEG: M209
MIOGesch: M209
MIOF: M202
MIR: M193
Misc: Miscellanea.
MiscBarc: M168
MiscCom: M170
MiscFranc: M171

MiscGraec: M172
MiscStLCristAnt: M176
MiscStorValdelsa: M175
MiskME: H54
MiskolciHOME: H54
MiskolciME: H54
MitropOlteniei: M181
Mitt: Mitteilungen. See also M
  (followed by the next capitalized
  letter).
Mitt: M190
MittAlterKomWestfalen: M182
MittAltKommWestfalen: M182
MittAntGesell: M185
MittAnthrGes: M184
MittAnthrGesWien: M184
MittAntiquGesZürich: M185
MittArchInst: M21
Mittbayernumismges: M186
MittBosnien: W36
MittDAI: M190
MittDArchinst: M193
MittDeutschPalV: M194
MittdNumismatGesinWien: M210
MittDtOrientGes: M194
MittdVorderasGes: M221
MittGesSalzburgerLandeskde: M197
MitthdarchInstzuAthen: M192
MitthdeutarchInstzuAthen: M192
MitthdesarchInstinAthen: M192
MitthdKKCentralKomm: M189
MittHeddernheim: M214
MittHistVerPfalz: M200
MittIÖG: M209
MittKairo: M191
MittNassAK: N11
MittNumGes: M210
MittÖstArbeitsg: M208
MittÖstArbeitsgemUruFrühgesch: M208
MittOrGes: M194
MittPhilWien: M220
MittPrähisKommWien: M213
MittprähKom: M213
MittZentral-Komm: M189
MittZentrKom: M189
MittZK: M189
MittZurich: M185
MJ: M312
MJb: M284
MJBK: M284
MJSEA: M128
MJSExc: M128
MK: M12
MkB: M278
MKE: M324
MKErt: M324

MKhr: M160
MKIF: M204
MKS: M203
MKszle: M12
MKultistFlorenz: M204
MKZ: M189
ML: A688, M246, S75, R345, M227
MLatJb: M223
MLauriacum: M205
MLH: M266
MLI: M267
MLJ: M227
MLN: M228
MLS: M167
MLST: M224
MLW: M225
MM: M7, A55, M13, M285
MMA: M164, M242
MMABull: B332
MMAF: M129
MMAFC: M129
MMAGAuk: M290
MMAGListe: M290
MMAI: M268, M130
MMAJ: M157
MMAP: M131
MMB: M269, M291
MMC: M189, M262
MME: M163
MMezöMKözl: M19
MMFC: M129
MMM: T26
MMR: M165
MMS: M158
MMusLauricum: M205
MMuzeum: M13
MMVLaur: M205
MN: M314, M174
Mn: M226
MNANS: M314
MNAW: M69
MNC: M261
MNCG: M71
MNDPV: M206
Mnem: M226
Mnemos: M226
MNeuchatel: M313
MNGW: M233
MNIR: M70
MNM: N22
MNy: M14-M15
MNyor: M15
MO: M235
MÖGMM: M210
MÖIG: M209
MÖNG: M210

MOENG: M210
MOeNG: M210
MONumGes: M210
MOG: M207
MOGMM: M210
MOIG: M209
Mon: Monumenti, Monuments.
Mon: M265, M245
MonA: M249-M250
MonAL: M246
MonAnc: Monumentum Ancyranum.
MonAnnBull: M245
MonAnndInst: M245
MonAnt: M246
MonAntined: M248
MonAntLinc: M246
MonAntLincei: M246
MonantLincei: M246
MonArch: M249-M250
MonArteAnt: M252
MonAsMinAnt: M255
MonatsbBerl: M234, M230
Mondell'Inst: M265, M245
Mondoclass: M236
MondI: M265, M245
MondInst: M265, M245
MondL: M246
MonedAnnalidInst: M245
MonetMemPiot: M268
MonEtr: M256
MONG: M210
MonGermHist: M24
MonGermHistAuctAnt: M257
MonGermHistScr: M257
MonGr: M259
Monin: M264-M265
MonInst: M265, M245
MonLinc: M246
MonLincei: M246
MonmouthshireAnt: M238
MonnGr: M239
MonPiot: M268
MonPitt: M270
MonStud: M229
MonumAncyr: Monumentum Ancyranum.
Monumentet: M244
MonumentsineddelInstarch: M265
MonumentsPiot: M268
MONumGes: M210
MOr: M235
Mor: Morale, Morali.
MoraFerencMusEv: M272
MosAntIt: M274
Mostra: M275
MostraetrMil: M275
Mous: M276-M277

MP: M328, M86, M316, M322
MPA: M234
MPASI: M270
MPER: M210
MPERNS: M210
MPG: P89
MPh: M296
MPhL: M315
MPiot: M268
MPK: M213
MPL: P90
MPont: M316
MPrHistKomWien: M213
MR: M162
MRP: M317
MRR: M9, D22
MRS: M78
MRT: M16
MS: M79, M156
MSAcAube: M135
MSACharente: M141
MSAF: M138
MSAHteSaone: M137
MSALH: M132
MSAM: M142
MSAMarne: M136
MSAMF: M142
MScRel: M90
MSE: M144
MSED: M145
MSF: M152
MSG: M319, P87
MsGeschJud: M231
MSGr: P87
MSHAL: M147
MSHChalon: M146
MsHöhSch: M232
MsJ: M312
MSL: M149, P88, M62
MSLC: M176
MSLStD: M148
MSNACreuse: M51
MSocAntFr: M138
MSR: M90
MSS: M286
MssgrecsParis: M33
MST: M224
MSVal: M175
MT: M325, M84, M318
MTA: M19
MTAIIOsztKözl: M19-M20
MTAIOSztKözl: M19-M20
MTAK: M19-M20
MTAKII: M19-M20
MTAOKII: M19-M20
MTANyelvesIrodOK: M20

MTANyelvirodOK: M20
MTATarstörtOK: M19
MTATarsTörtTudOK: M19
MThM: M73
MThZ: M287
MTS: M263
MTud: M17
MUB: M71
MüJbb: M284
MünchAkAb: A11
MünchAkSb: S90
MünchBeitr: M282
MünchBeitrzPap: M282
MünchJahrb: M284
MuenchJahrbBildK: M284
MünchJb: M284
MünchnerJahrb: M284
MünchStSprWiss: M286
MüncJahrbbildKunst: M284
MünJbBildK: M284
MüTZ: M287
Müved: M280
MüvesErtes: M321
MüvtörtErt: M321
MuJb: M284
MuJbb: M284
MuM: M290
MUMCAH: M240
MunchAkAb: A11
MunchAkSb: S90
MunchBeitr: M282
MunchBeitrzPap: M282
MunchJahrb: M284
MunchJahrbBildK: M284
MunchJb: M284
MunchnerJahrb: M284
MunchStSprWiss: M286
MuncJahrbbildKunst: M284
MuncJbBildK: M284
MundM: M290
MuNDPV: M206
MunJbBildK: M284
Mus: Museum, Museo.
Mus: M293
MusÅrbokTrondheim: A5
MusÅrsberetTrondheim: A5
MusAfr: M298
MusAlt: M299
MusArbokTrondheim: M293
MusArsberetTrondheim: M293
MusB: M300
MusBelg: M300
MusBelge: M300
MusChius: E119
MusClasAnt: M301
MusCrit: M303-M304

MuseoChius: E119
MusetCollAlgTun: M302
MusetCollAlTun: M302
MuseumUnesco: M295
MusFr: M305-M306
MusGallIt: M307-M308
MusGr: M319
MusHelv: M310
MusIt: M311
MUSJ: M91
MusJ: M312
MusN: M314
MusNot: M314
MusNotAmNumSoc: M314
MüTZ: M287
Muved: M280
MüvesErtes: M321
MüvtortErt: M321
MuZ: M26
MuzEvkSzeged: M272
MuzHa'aretzBull: B334
MuzPamkul: M322
MuzPamKult: M322
MV: M329
MVAAG: M221
MVAeG: M221
MVAG: M221
MVEOL: M75
MVFC: M216
MVG: M221
MVGBH: M217
MVGN: M218
MVHB: M219
MV1AC: M76
MVN: M63
MVPhW: M220
MW: M86, M177, S71
Mw: M85
MWP: M35
MWPr: M35
MycSem: M167
MythGr: M330
MythGraec: M330
MythLex: A688
Mythogr: S64
MythVat: S64
MZ: M24, M26-M27
MZK: M189
MzZts: M24

N

N: Nachrichten; Neue, New; Nouveau, Nouvelles, Nuovo; Norsk; Numis-matic.
N: T83
N&C: N57
N&D: N78
NA: N10, N25
NAA: N9, N79
NAC: N1
Nachr: Nachrichten.
NachrblDtVorzeit: N5
NachrGesWissGött: N1
NachrGiessen: N2
NachrGött: N1
NachrGöttingen: N1
NachrNiedersachsUrgesch: N3
NAG: N1
NAH: N81
NAHisp: N81
NAJN: N71
NAK: N16
NAKg: N1
NAM: N87
NAMC: N82
NAMSL: N87
NAnt: N126
NapNobil: N8
NAR: N75
NarodAziiAfriki: N9
NassAnn: N10
Nat: National, etc.
NatA: N12
NationalmusArbejdsmark: N12
NAV: N24
NAVen: A557
NAWG: N1
NB: N6, N77, N84
NBACr: N127
NBArchChrist: N127

NBC: B4
NBK: N53
NBull: N127
NBullArchChrist: N127
NC: N106, C96, N15, N57
NCE: C96
NCGPhilhistKL: N1
NCGS: F56
NChr: N106
NCirc: N107
NClio: N88
NCr: N106
ND: N128, N94
NDI: N129
NdS: N83
NDSA: N83
Ndsc: N83
NdtV: N2
NDV: N55
NE: N108
Neap: N14
NED: N41
NederlandsHistInsRomeMed: M70
NedThT: N18
NedTT: N18
NEH: N89
NEphemSemEpigr: N26
NeprErt: N22
NEst: N13
NET: A198
NetD: N78
NeueHeidelbJahrb: H38
NeueJ: N27
NeueJahrb: N27
NeueJahrbKlAlt: N27
NeueJahrbKlasAltertum: N27
NeueJahrbPhil: N27
NeuJbfKlAlt: N27
NewPalSoc: N42

NewsletterASOR: N50
NewsletterUg: N51
NF: Neue Folge.
NfDV: N2
NG: N40
NGA: N1
NGBG: N34
NGFG: N35
NGG: N1
NGGW: N1
NGH: N3
NGML: N95
NGu: N40
NGW: N1
NGWG: N1
NH: N60, N62, N98
NHisp: N98
NHJ: H38, N65
NHVSGall: N36
NHVStGall: N36
NiceHist: N52
NieuwsbullKNOB: B340
NJ: Novellae.
NJ: N27
NJA: N27
NJAB: N27
NJADB: N27
NJahrb: N27
NJahrbbklAlt: N27
NJahrbfPhiluPad: N27
NJb: N27
NJbAnt: N27
NJbb: N27
NJbbKlassAlt: N27
NJDTh: N28
NJfWiss: N27
NJhb: N27
NJhbAlt: N27
NJKA: N27
NJKlA: N27
NJL: N76
NJPP: N27
NJW: N27
NJWJ: N27
NK: N110
NKJ: N17
NKNOB: B340
NKöZ: N110
NL: N112
NLB: N113
NLb: N113
NListy: N111
NLOB: N114
NMagHanau: N29
NMS: N85
NN: N115

NNÅ: N66
NNA: N66
NNb: N115
NNM: N116
NNMANS: N116
NNSU: N4
NNUM: N67
Nom: N58
NomChron: N59
NomKhron: N59
NorArchRev: N75
NorfolkArch: N70
NorthStaffordJFieldStud: N72
NorTTS: N68
NoSc: N83
Not: N83
NotAHisp: N81
NotArch: N82
NotArqHisp: N82
NotDign: Notitia Dignitatum.
Notdsc: N83
NoticiarioArqHisp: N81
NoticiarioArquHispanico: N81
NotizArch: N82
NotizieScavi: N83
NotSc: N83
NotScav: N83
NotScavi: N83
Nouv: Nouvelle.
NouvAnnalesdel'Instarch: N86
NouvArch: N87
NouvArchMiss: N87
NouvClio: N88
NouvMemdel'Academie: M95
NouvRevTheol: N92
NovDI: N129
NovPPbibl: N93
NovT: N96
NPB: N93
NPh: N20
NPhilUnt: N30
NPhM: N39
NPhU: N30
NPS: N42, N61
NPSS: N61
NR: N117
nr: nieuwe reeks.
NRevhistdeDroitfretetr: R176
NRFC: N90
NRH: N91, R176
NRHD: R176
NRivStor: N130
NRS: N130
NRT: N92
NRTh: N92
NS: New Series, Nuova Sèrie, etc.

NS: N83, N122, N120, N118-N119
NSA: N83
NSANS: N122
NSB: N5
NSb: N118
NSc: N83
NScavAnt: N83
NS(Czech): N118
NSf: N120
NSFC: T89
NSJFS: N72
NSJL: N54
NS(USSR): N119
NSW: N37
NT: New Testament.
NT: N96, N46
NTA: N43
NTAb: N43
NTD: N46
NTF: N69
NTJ: N31
NTS: N44-N45, N76
NTSt: N44-N45
NTT: N56
NuD: N129
NumAntCl: N105
NumChr: N106
NumChron: N106
NumCirc: N107
NumEpigr: N108
NumHisp: N98
NumiEpig: N108
NumiSfrag: N120
NumismaticaRom: N101
NumismatZtschr: N124
NumJ: N109
NumK: N110
NumKözl: N110
NumLB: N113
NumListPraha: N111
NumListy: N111
NumLit: N112
NumNachrBl: N115
NumRev: N117
NumSbor: N119
NumSfrag: N120
NumSt: N122
NumStockholm: N121
NumVij: N123
NumZ: N124
NumZeit: N124
NumZeitr: N124
NumZeitrWien: N124
NumZft: N124
NumZtschr: N124
NuovaAnt: N126

NuovaBulldiArchcristiana: N127
NuovaRivstor: N130
NuovBull: N127
NuovDidask: N127
NV: N130
NVVI: N19
NVVIČ: N19
NWAnt: N32
NyE: N131
NyiregyhaziJAME: N132
NyiregyhaziME: N132
NyirME: N132
NyJME: N132
NyME: N132
NYRB: N47
NYReview: N47
NZ: N124
NZKG: N38
NZNJ: N48

O

Ö: This letter is filed as if spelled oe in German words.

O: Ostraca. Usually followed by name of place where kept or the editor's name. See special section on papyri in the introduction.

O: Opuscula.

O: I13, I15

O&P: I100

OA: 020-022, 029

OABud: 030

OAIKairo: U26

OAr: 036

OArqPort: A591

OAth: 022

OB: 038

OBA: O1

OBGV: 061

OBodl: G93

ObzorPrehist: 06

OC: 031, 039

OCA: 039

OCD: 062

OChP: 040

OChr: 031

OCP: 040

OCT: S59

ODCC: 063

ÖAIKairo: U26

OECT: 064

OED: N41

ÖJ: J74

OEJH: J74

ÖJh: J74

Öjh: J74

OeJh: J74

Qejh: J74

ÖJhBeibl: J74

OeJhh: J74

OesterrArchäolInstJahresh: J74

ÖstJahresh: J74

ÖstJahreshefte: J74

ÖstJahrh: J74

ÖstJh: J74

OEZKD: O7

ÖZV: O8

OF: O17, O47

OG: 053

OGI: 045

OGIS: 045

OGRL: O2

OH: O4

OHR: 033

OIAS: A622

OIC: C178

OIP: P244

OIS: S160

OJ: J74, O12

OJh: J74

Ojh: J74

OJhBeibl: J74

OJhh: J74

OJN: J74

OKS: 054

OKT: 018

OLA: 042

OlAusgr: A691

OlBer: B48

OLD: 065

OlErg: O16

OlForsch: O17

OLP: 043

OltR: O14

Olympia: O16

OLZ: 041

OM: 052

OMich: G94

OML: 059
OMLeiden: 059
OMML: 059
OMRegTarsEvk: 048
OMRL: 059
OMRO: 059
OMROL: 059
OMROLeiden: 059
OMSzepMuzEvk: 049
OMT: 066
ON: 015
OOEH: 03
OÖHBL: 03
OOslo: 056
OP: 05-06
OpA: 020-021
OpArch: 020-021
OpAth: 022
OPhW: 024
OpR: 025
OpRom: 025
OpusArch: 020-021
OpusAth: 022
OpuscArch: 020-021
OpuscArchaeol: 020-021
OpuscAthen: 022
OpusPh: 024
OR: 025, 014
Or: 035, 028, 046
OrAnt: 029
OrArch: 036
OrBd: 035
OrBibl: 038
OrChr: 031
OrChrist: 031
OrChrP: 040
OrChrPer: 040
ORF: 026-027
ORFr(Malc): 027
ORFr(Meyer): 026
OrGraecInscrSel: 045
OrGrInscrSel: 045
OrGrIS: 045
OrientalisticheLz: 041
OrientLovan: 042-043
OrientLovanPeriod: 043
OrientSuecana: 044
OrInstSt: S160
ORL: 02
OrLov: 042-043
ORm: 059
OrNS: 035
ORom: 025
OrphF: 047
OrphFrag: 047
OrRund: K17

OrS: 044
OrSuec: 044
OrSyr: 034
ORTE: 048
ORund: K17
OS: 034, 054
OsjeckiZb: 051
OsjeckiZbor: 051
OsjZbor: 051
OsnabrückMitt: 052
OsterrJahresh: J74
OstJahresh: J74
OstJahrh: J74
OstJh: J74
Ostr: Ostraca. Usually followed
   by location or editor's name.
   See special section on Papyri
   in the introduction.
Ostr: G114
OStras: G109
OStrasb: G109
OstrBrWilb: 055
OstrBodl: G93
OstrMich: G94
OstrStrassb: G109
OstrWilbour: 055
OT: Old Testament.
OtcetPetrograd: 057
OTheb: T33
OTKT: 018
OTS: 060
Oud: Oudheidkunde
OudheidkMededelingen: 059
OudhMeded: 059
OudMed: 059
OWilb: 055
OWilbBrookl: 055
OWilck: G114
OxfClassDict: 062
OxfLatDic: 065
Oxford: S59
OZ: 051
OZb: 051
OZV: 08

P

P: Papers; Philosohpy, Philosophi-
cal, etc.; Philology, Philologi-
cal, etc.; Praktika; Problems,
Problemy, etc.; Proceedings; Pro-
cès-Verbaux; Publications, Pubbli-
cazioni, etc.
P: Papyrus/-i. Usually followed by
location or the editor's name;
see the special section on papyri
in the introduction.
P: N6, P80
P&IdeF(M): P81
P&P: P85
PA: P217, P26, P92, P181, P233
PAA: P168
PAAH: P169
PAAR: P37
PAberd: C77
PAberdeen: C77
PAbinn: A23
PAC: M257
PACA: P187
PACPhA: P188
PACT: P1
PAE: P169, P184
PAES: P245
PAH: P154
Pal: P181
Palaeo: P15
PalEF: P20
PalEFA: P20
PalEQ: P21
PalestExplQuarterly: P21
PalExplFundAnnual: P20
PalExplQu: P21
PalJahrb: P18
PalJb: P18
PalSb: P22
PalSborn: P22

PalSoc: P14
PAM: P26
PamA: P26
PamArch: P26
PamatkyArch: P26
PamatkyArcheol: P26
PAmh: A152
PamSlow: P29
PamTurkm: P28
Pan: P30
PannSzle: P31
PAnt: A357
PAntin: A367
PaP: P85
Pap: Papyrus/-i. Usually followed
by location or the editor's
name. See the special section
on papyri in the introduction.
See also P (followed by the
next capitalized letter).
Pap: Papers.
PAPA: P189
PapAmSchAth: P35
PapASA: P35
PapBrux: P41
PapCastr: P42
PapColon: W33
PapER: M210
PapersASA: P35
PapersASAthens: P35
PapersBritSchoolRome: P36
PapersBrSchRome: P36
PapersBsRome: P36
PapGM: P47
PAPhilos: P190
PAPhS: P190
PapLugdBat: P58
PapOx: O68
PapPrimer: P65

PAPS: P190
PapyrLugdoBat: P58
PAR: P182
Par: P80
Para; P80
ParadGraecRel: P78
Paravia: C238, C240
PArch: P233
PardPass: P83
PArg: P91
ParodEpicGrRel: P76
ParoladPassato: P83
ParPas: P83
PASA: P35
PASAth: P35
PASAthens: P35
PASb: P99
PatGraec: P89
PAthen: P69
PatLat: P90
PatrGr: P89
PatrLat: P90
PatrolGr: P89
PatrolLat: P90
PatrOr: P87
PaulWiss: R20
PB: P94
PBA: P194
PBad: V23
PBaden: V23
PBâle: P62
PBas: P62
PBasel: P62
PBerlLeihg: B64
PBerlMöller: G115
PBerlZill: V52
PBerlZilliacus: V52
PBF: P166
PBN: P40
PBour: P40
PBouriant: P40
PBS: P249
PBSR: P36
PC: I120
PCA: P197
PCair: C42
PCaireGoodspeed: G95
PCaireMaspero: P54
PCairePreisigke: G127
PCairGoodsp: G95
PCairIsid: A486
PCairIsidor: A486
PCairMasp: P54
PCairoZeno: Z75
PCairPreis: G127
PCairZen: Z75

PCAS: P195
PCIA: P39
PCM: P54
PCorn: G97
PCornell: G97
PColZen: Z76
PCPhS: P196
PCPS: P196
PCZ: Z75
PD: P152
PDAA: P136
PDANHS: P199
PDAR: P137
PdeV: P179
PDNHAS: P199
PdO: P84
PdP: P83
PDVHL: P17
PecsiME: J81
PEdfou: T15
PEdfu: T15
PEdg: S73
PEdgar: S73
PEFA: P20
PEFAnn: P20
PEFQ: P21
PEFQS: P21
PEFQSt: P21
PEleph: E27
Pelop: P97
PEnt: E48
Penteux: E48
PEQ: P21
PER: M212, P140
PErl: P73
PetGeogrMitt: P104
PF: P101, P118
PfälzerH: P106
PFamTeb: F3
PFamTebt: F3
PFay: F11
PfH: P106
PFlor: P53
PFouad: P43
PFrankf: G116
PFreib: M195
PG: P87
PGen: P44
PGiess: G119
PGiss: G119
PGissUniv: M211
PGL: P86
PGM: P47
PGoodspCair: G95
PGot: P51
PGoth: P51

PGP: P226
PGR: P78
PGrad: G120
PGraecMag: P47
PGrenf: A111
PGrenfell: A111
PGur: G99
PGurob: G96
PH: P228
Ph: P107
Ph&PhenR: P122
Ph&Rh: P125
PhA: P108
PHal: D64
PHalle: D64
PHamb: G117
PHarr: R67
PHarris: R67
PHaun: P45
PHeid: V24
PHib: H73
PHibeh: H73
Phil: Philosophical, etc.; Philolo-
    gical, etc.
Phil: P107
PhilAnt: P117
PhilClass: P109
PhilMus: P111
Philol: P107
PhilolSuppl: P107
PhilosQ: P123
PhilPatr: P121
PhilRev: P124
PhilStud: P112
PhilUnters: P113
PhilWoch: P114
PhilWochenschr: P114
PhJ: P119
PhLA: P120
PhM: A555
PHolm: P46
PhQ: P123
PhR: P124, P126
PhRdschau: P126
PhRev: P124
PhS: P112
PhStudiën: P112
PhU: P113
PhW: P114
PIand: P56
PID: P164
PIDO: P185
PIF: P81
PILux: P246
PIR: P218
PJ: P18

PJb: P18
Pjb: P18
PJena: J83
PK: P27
PKaran: P57
PKarGoodsp: P57
PKF: P252
PKFil: P252
PKG: P216
PKGL: G111
PkleinForm: G118
PKlForm: G118
PKOM: A575
PKroll: P240
PKU: U20
PKV: P227
PL: P90, P13, P95
PLAC: M257
PLAV: P34
PLBat: P58
PLeid: P48
PLesbFrg: P146
PLF: P146
PLG: P144
PLille: P50
PLilleII: P59
PLips: G128
PLitLond: B222
PLM: P143
PLond: B221
PLond1912-29: J89
PLondLit: B222
PLondon: B221
PLP: P221
PLRE: P222
PLund: A684
PLundUnivBibl: A684
PM: P11, T75, P104, P155, P171,
    P229
PMAA: P177
PMAAR: P37
PMac: P171
PMag: P47
PMagd: P59
PMB: B345
PME: P219
PMelGr: P145
PMerton: D25
PMeyer: G126
PMG: P145
PMGM: P133
PMH: P157
PMich: M159
PMichael: P60
PMichaelides: P60
PMichTeb: P71

PMichZen: Z77
PMil: P61
PMilanRUniv: P74
PMilVogl: P74
PMilVogliano: P74
PMLA: P2
PMonac: B459
PN: P12, P158, P183
PNB: P158
PNervia: P183
PNess: E160
PO: O68, P87, P238
POC: P214
Poetlyrgr: P144
PoetMelGr: P145
PoetRomVet: P148
Pol: P150
PoM: P11
POsl: P63
POslo: P63
POxf: S112
POxford: S112
POxfordWegener: S112
POxy: O68
PP: P83, P6, P139, P220
PPar: N80
PParis: N80
PPE: Periplus Ponti Euxini.
PPetr: F19
PPF: P147
PPhil: P64
PPhilad: P64
PPrinc: P66
PPrincet: P66
PPrincRoll: P67
PProcHampshireFieldClub: P38
PPS: P204, P170
PPtol: R201
PPUD: P176
PQ: P123
PR: P124
PraceA: P160-P161
PraceiMaterialy: P163
PrähistBl: P165
PrähistZeitschr: P167
PraehistZft: P167
PrähZ: P167
PraehZ: P167
PrähZs: P167
PrahistBl: P165
PRain: M212
PrakAkAth: P168
Prakt: P168-P169
PraktAkad: P168
PraktAkAth: P168
PraktArchEt: P169

Praktika: P168-P169
PraktikaArchEt: P169
PraktikaAthen: P168-P169
PrdeV: P179
PRE: R20
Préhist: Préhistoire, Préhistor-
    ique, etc.
PRein: P52
PReinach: P52
PRendelHarris: R67
PreussJb: P175
PRev: R201
PRevLaws: R201
PRevenueLaws: R201
PrFil: P162
PRIA: P201
PRIMI: P74
PriscLatMonEpigr: P180
PrJb: P175
PrMac: P171
Probl: Problemy, Problemes.
ProblMuz: P186
ProbVostok: N9
Proc: Proceedings. See also P
    (followed by the next capital-
    ized letter).
ProcAfrClAss: P187
ProcAmerPhilSoc: P190
ProcBrAc: P194
ProcBritAc: P194
ProcBritAcad: P194
ProcCambr: P195
ProcCambridgeAntiquSoc: P195
ProcCambridgeAntSoc: P195
ProcCambridgePhilSoc: P196
ProcCambrPhilSoc: P196
ProcCambrPhSoc:P196
ProcDevonArchExplSoc: P198
ProcDevonArchSoc: P198
ProcDorsetNaturHistArchSoc: P199
ProcDorsetNHandAS: P199
ProcDorsetSoc: P199
ProceedAntiquarScotland: P207
ProceedingsSBA: P208
ProceedoftheBritAcad: P194
ProceedrphilosSocofGlasgow: P203
ProceedsScotl: P207
ProcNewc: P206
ProcofPrehSoc: P204
ProcPhilAs: P189
ProcPhilSoc: P190
ProcPrehistSoc: P204
ProcPrHistSoc: P204
ProcPrSoc: P204
ProcPS: P204
ProcRGS: P200

ProcRNS: P202
ProcRoyalIrishAcad: P201
ProcRoyIrishAcad: P201
ProcSocAntiquLondon: P205
ProcSocAntiquScotland: P207
ProcSocAntiqScotland: P207
ProcSomersetArchNaturHistSoc: S113
ProcSuffolkInstArch: P209
Progr: Programmschrift.
PropKg: P216
PrOrChr: P214
ProsImpRom: P218
ProsMilEq: P219
ProsopAtt: P217
ProsopImpRom: P218
ProsopPtol: P220
ProsopRom: P215
ProspArch: P224
ProspezioniArch: P224
ProsPtol: P220
PRossGeorg: P68
Prov: Province, Provincie, etc.
ProvHist: P228
ProvLucca: P231
PrS: S15
PRU: P19
PRUM: P74
PRVR: P148
PRyl: C78
PrZ: P167
PrzArch: P233
PrzegArch: P233
PrzegladArch: P233
PrzegladHist: P234
PrzHum: P234-P235
PrzKl: P237
PrzOr: P238
PS: P14, P22, P88
PSA: P205
PSAAthen: P69
PSAL: P205
PSAM: P249
PSAN: P206
PSAS: P207
PSAScot: P207
PSb: P22
PSBA: P208
PSBH: P208
PSC: P102
PSemArag: C3
PSHAL: P250
PSI: P55
PSL: P205
PSM: P7
PSN: P206
PSorb: P70

PSRL: P153
PStras: G121
PStrasb: G121
PStrassb: G121
PSuffolkIArch: P209
PsVTGr: P239
PSyr: P88
PSz: P31
PT: P172
PTaur: P49
PTeb: T10
PTebt: T10
PThead: P72
PThR: P178
PTK: P142, P173
PTor: P49
PUAES: P247
Pub: Publications. See also P
    (followed by the next capital-
    ized letter).
PubHistInstLuxembourg: P246
PublServAntiquMaroc: P249
PubLux: P248
PUnivGiss: M212
PUnivMilan: P74
PV: P227, P159, P179
PVars: P75
PVarsov: P75
PVAveyron: P213
PVB: J75
PVBesançon: P212
PVindBoswinkel: E18
PVindobBosw: E18
PVindobSijp: E19
PVindobSijpesteijn: E19
PVS: P210
PW: P114, R20
PWarr: W3
PWarren: W3
PWRE: R20
PWürzb: M222
PYale: Y5
PYaleInv: Y5
Pyr: P251
PZ: P167
PZenCol: Z76
PZilliac: V52

Q

Q: Quaderni, Quarterly; Quellen.
Q&F: Q30
QAL: Q1
QAP: Q28
QAR: Q2
QC: Q3
QCLBS: Q21
QCLCS: Q22
QCLL: Q23
QCLM: Q24
QCLOS: Q25
QCLRS: Q26
QDAJ: Q27
QDAP: Q28
QDAPal: Q28
QFC: Q4
QFIAB: Q30
QGMath: Q32
QGMed: Q33
QGN: Q33
QIFL: Q7
QILCL: Q8
QISA: Q9
QJS: Q29
QM: Q11
QMAB: Q12
QS: Q14
QSAE: Q15
QSGMath: Q32
QSGMed: Q33
QSGNM: Q33
QSt: P21, Q31
QTicNumAntClas: N103
QTLCG: Q16
QTTA: Q17
QU: Q18
Quad: Quaderni.
QuadALibia: Q1
QuadArchLibia: Q1

QuadAReggio: Q2
QuaderniArcheolLibia: Q1
QuadIstFilGr: Q5-Q6
QuadIstTop: Q10
QuadStor: Q14
QuadTopAnt: Q10
QuadUrbin: Q19
QuAntPal: Q28
QuarterlyAntiquPalestine: Q28
QuarterlyStat: P21
QUC: Q19
QUCC: Q19
QuellStudGeschNat: Q32
QuSt: P21, Q32

R

R: Rassegna; Reallexikon; Recher-
   ches; Recueil; Rendiconti; Reper-
   toire; Report; Revue, Review, Re-
   vista, etc.; Rivista; Richerche;
   Rocznik; Royal, Reale.
R&C: S212
RA: R99, R111, R20
RAA: R73, R108-R109, R111
Raa: R73
RAAM: R108
RAAN: R68
RABM: R105
RABo: R70
RABol: R70
RAC: R22, R268, R100, R110, R269
RACAntNat: R100
RAcC: R249
RACF: R100
RACh: R22
RACome: R269
RAComo: R269
RACr: R268
RACrist: R268
RadJAZ: R4
RadJAZU: R4
RadNoviSad: R3
RadoviJAZU: R3
RadoviZabreb: R5
RadoviZadar: R6
RadVoivodMuz: R3
RadVojvMuz: R3
RadVojvodjMuz: R3
RAE: R101
RARG: R21
RAEst: R101
RAf: R94
RAfr: R94
RAgen: R96
RAHA: R102

RAI: R69, C187
RAIB: R70
RAL: R69
RALinc: R69
RAM: R185
RAN: R103
RANap: R68
RANarb: R103
RAntChrist: R22
RAnthr: R97-R98
RAO: R38
RAr: R99
RArch: R99
RArchBiblMus: R105
RArchHistArtLouvain: R102
RArt: R108, R204
RArtAncMod: R108
RArtChr: R110
RArts: R107
RArtsAs: R109
RAS: Q13
RAss: R111
Rass: Rassegna. See also R (fol-
   lowed by the next capitalized
   letter).
Rassd'A: R9
RassdellArteAnteMod: R9
RassegnaItal: R11
Rassegnanum: R14
RassegnaStSalern: R16
RassIGI: R282
RassLazio: R12
RassMon: R14
RassStorSalern: R16
RAssyr: R111
RASyr: R104
RAu: R112
RAuv: R112
RavBl: R17

RAvr: R113
RazpraveSAZU: R19
RB: R119, R118, R24, R121
RBA: R115
RBAH: R115
RBAHA: R115
RBArch: R115
RBasPoitou: R114
RBelgArch: R115
RBelgNum: R116
RBen: R118
RBi: R119
RBibIt: R271
RBibl: R119
Rbibl; R119
RBK: R25
RbK: R25
RBN: R116
RBNum: R116
RBo:R120
RBP: R117
RBPH: R117
RBPh: R117
RBPHH: R117
RBPhH: R117
RBPhil: R117
RBS: R59
RByz: R24
RC: R125, R349
RCAccLinc: R69
RCActa: A80
RCAJ: J97
RCAS: J97
RCC: R124
RCCM: R273
RCEA: R74
RCGO: R30
RCHM: I106
RChr: R355
RCl: R122
RCommingens: R123
RCr: R125
RCRF: A80, C179
RCRFActa: A80
RCulMedioev: R273
RD: R176, R56
RdA: R267
RDAC: R83
RDCiv: R274
RDDA: R56
RdE: R129
RdEg: R129
RdeG: R165
RdeGuimaraes: R165
RDGE: R322
RDI: R276

RdLinc: R69
RdNap: R68
RdPontAcc: A668
RdQ: R227
RE: R20
REA: R140, R130, R141
RealEnc: R20
ReallexderVergesch: R28
ReallexfurAntundChrist: R22
ReallexVorg: R28
RealVorg: R28
REAnc: R140
REAr: R141
REArm: R141
REAug: R142
ReAug: R29
REB: R143, R192
REByz: R143
REC: R136
Rec: R41
Recarchoreint: R38
RecArtMus: R35
RecAug: R29
RecBuckinghamshire: R36
RecConst: R49
RecConstantine: R49
RecdeTrav: R53
RechdePap: R31
RechScRelig: R33
RechSR: R33
RecPhL: R32
RecSciRel: R33
RecSocJBodin: R52
RecSR: R33
RecTh: R34
RecTrav: R53
Recueil: R42
RecueildeTravaux: R53
REE: R137, R277
REG: R144
REg: R129
RegA: R130
RegDolgEötvös: R56
RegeszetiTan: R58
RegFuz: R57
RegTan: R58
REgypt: R129
REH: R145
REHom: R146
REI: R148, R278
REIA: R27
ReiCretRomFautActa: A80
REIE: R147
REIslam: R148
REIt: R149
REJ: R150

REJuivHJud: R150
REL: R151
Rel: R63
RELat: R151
RELig: R301
RELO: R195
RelStud: R64
RelVeruVorarb: R63
Rend: Rendiconti.
RendAccadLincei: R69
RendAccArchNap: R68
RendAccIt: R69
RendAccLinc: R69
RendAccNap: R68
RendAccNaples: R68
RendAccNapoli: R68
RendBologna: R70
Rendic: Rendiconti.
RendicAccBologna: R70
RendicAccd'Italia: R69
RendicAccLincei: R69
RendicAccPont: A668
RendicIstLomb: R71
RendicontiAccadLincei: R69
RendicontiAccadNapoli: R68
RendicontiLincei: R69
RendicontiPontAccArch: A668
RendIstLomb: R71
RendLinc: R69
RendLincei: R69
RendNap: R68, R72
RendNapoli: R68, R72
RendPARA: A668
RendPont: A668
RendPontAc: A668
RendPontAcc: A668
RendPontAccadArch: A668
RendPontifAccad: A668
RendRIstLombSceLett: R71
RendrIstLombSciLettedArti: R71
RenQ: R65
REp: R132
RepCypr: A295, R83
RepEgExplSoc: R84
REPh: R131
REpigr: R132
RepKunstW: R76
RepKunstw: R76
RepMalta: R88
ReportCouncilBritArch: R82
RepPAS: R78
Reprel: R79
RepTransDevonshire: R87
RepUFS: R78
Repvases: R81
REPW: R20

RerItalSS[NS]: R89
RernatscrGraecmin: R90
RernatscrGrmin: R90
RERoum: R152
RES: R75, R135, R153-R154
RESE: R155
RESEE: R155
RESl: R154
RET: R134
RETAnc: R140
RETArm: R141
RETGr: R144
Rev: Revue, Review, Revista. _See_
  also R (followed by the next
  capitalized letter).
RevA: R99
RevAC: R110
RevAfr: R94
RevAfriquefranc: R95
RevAnthr: R97-R98
RevArch: R99
Revarch: R99
RevArchBiblMus: R105
RevArcheol: R79
RevArchEstetCentreEst: R101
RevArchNarbonn: R103
RevArh: R106
RevArhiv: R106
RevArtAnc: R108
RevArtAncetMod: R108
RevArts: R107
RevB: R117
RevBelgArch: R115
RevBelgedArchetdHistdelart: R115
RevBelgedeNum: R116
RevBelgedePhiletd'Hist: R117
RevBelgePhilHist: R117
RevBelgNum: R116
RevBelgPhil: R117
RevBen: R118
RevBibl: R119
Revbibl: R119
RevClasica: R122
RevCoursConf: R124
Revcr: R125
RevCrit: R125
Revd'Anthropol: R97
Revd'Assyr: R111
RevdeEstExtremenos: R137
Revd'Egypt: R129
Revdel'Orchret: R214
RevdePhil: R217
RevdesEtAnc: R140
RevdhistetdeLittRelig: R180
Revdrcan: R127
RevDrome: R128

RevduNord: R211
RevEA: R140
RevEE: R137
RevEG: R144
RevEgyptol: R129
RevEHom: R146
RevEIE: R147
RevEL: R151
RevEp: R132
RevEpigr: R132
Revepigr: R132
Revespdercan: R133
RevET: R134
RevEtAnc: R140
Revetanc: R140
RevEtArmen: R141
RevEtByz: R143
RevEtGr: R144
Revetgr: R144
RevEtGrec: R144
RevEtHist: R145
RevEthn: R138
Revetind: R147
RevEtJ: R150
RevEtLat: R151
Revetlat: R151
RevEtn: R139
RevEtSEEUr: R155
RevGer: R163
RevGuim: R165
RevGuimaraes: R165
RevH: R168
RevHDr: R175
RevHE: R177
RevHist: R167-R168
Revhistdr: R176
RevHistRel: R183
Revhistrel: R183
RevHPhilos: R149, R182
RevHRelig: R183
RevIEI: R11
RevInstEstIsl: R190
RevIOAL: R195
RevIst: R197
RevistaABM: R105
RevistaArchivos: R105
RevLouvre: R204
RevMuz: R209-R210
RevMuzMMon: R210
RevMuzMMuz: R210
RevNum: R212
Revnum: R212
RevNumism: R212
RevOChr: R214
RevOrChr: R214
RevOrLat: R215

RevPH: R222
RevPhil: R217, R219
Revphil: R217
RevPhilol: R217
RevPhilos: R218
Revpreh: R223
RevPrehist: R6, R223
RevQuestionshist: R225
RevRel: R183
RevSciRel: R236
RevScPhilTheol: R235
RevScRel: R236
RevSR: R236
RevThPhilos: R244
Revue: <u>See also Rev and R (follow-
    ed by the next capitalized let-
    ter)</u>.
RevueAnthr: R97-R98
RevueArch: R99, R104
Revuearch: R99, R104
RevueArchCentre: R100
RevueArcheol: R99
RevueArchEstetCentreEst: R101
RevueAssyriol: R111
RevueBelgeArchetHistArt: R115
RevueNum: R212
RevVivarais: R251
REW: R345
RF: R80, R57, R160, R281
RfAC: R22
RFC: R280
RFE: R159
RFIC: R280
RFIC1: R280
RFil: R281
RFilC1: R280
Rfilcl: R280
RFilIstC1: R280
RFLL: R156
RG: R41, R165, R257
RGA: R41, R26
RGBR: R40
RGE: R161
RGe: R163
RGevaudan: R164
RGF: R309
RGG: R61
RGK: R310
RGKB1: R310
RGKomm: B52
RGKorrB1: R310
RGKorrBlatt: R310
RGL: R162
RGMG: R42
RGP: R350
RGSA: R10

RGuimar: R165
RGVV: R63
RGZM: J49
RH: R168
RHA: R189
RHArd: R171
RHAs: R189
RHAuv: R166
RHavre: R39
RHB: I133
RHBord: R172
RHC: R174
RHCM: R173
RHD: R175-R176
RHDFE: R176
RHDroitFrE: R176
RHE: R177
RHEF: R179
RheinischMuseumPhilol: R254
RheinMus: R254
RheinMusBonn: R253
RheinMuseum: R254
RheinVb: R255
RheinViertJbl: R255
RheinVjsbll: R255
RheinZ: R256
RHES: R178
Rhet: R257
RhetGr: R257
RhetGraec: R257
RhetLatMin: R258
RhG: R257
RhGr: R257
RHist: R168
RHistBulg: I133
RHistCivMaghreb: R173
RHistDroit: R176
RHistRel: R183
RHitt: R189
RHittAs: R189
RhLatmin: R258
RHLR: R180
RHM: R254, R311
RhM: R254
RHMM: R181
RhMus: R254
RhN: R252
RhodeIsland: B347
RHPhilos: R234
RHPhilRel: R182
RHPhR: R182
RHPR: R182
RHR: R183
RHRel: R183
RHS: R184
RHSE: R186

RHSEE: R186
RHSpir: R185
RHT: R187
RHV: R188
RhV: R255
RI: R197
RIA: R285
RIAF: R216
RIASA: R285
RIB: R335, R70
RIBAJournal: J112
RIBWürttemb: R312
RIC: R333
RicMed: R260
RicR: R261
RicRel: R261
RicStBrindisi: R262
RIDA: R191
RIEB: R192
RIFD: R284
RIG: R43
RIGI: R282
RIHM: R193
RIJG: R45
RIL: R71, R46
RILA: R1
Rila: R1
RILC: R11
RILdiScienzeeLettere: R71
RIN: R286
RINA: R285
RINASA: R285
RIngIntem: R283, R301
RIntDroitsAnt: R191
RINum: R286
RIO: R194
RIOAL: R195
RIOno: R194
RIPh: R196
RIR: R98
RIS: R89
RISA: R351
RIScG: R287
RISG: R287
RIslamique: R148
RIst: R197
RIstRom: R198
RIT: R313
RItNum: R286
RIU: R314
Riv: Rivista. See also R (follow-
    ed by the next capitalized let-
    ter).
Riv: R280
RivAC: R268
RivAc: R268

RivAntr: R266
RivArchchrist: R268
RivArchClassica: A430
RivArchComo: R269
Rivarchcr: R268
RivArchCrist: R268
RivArchCristiana: R268
RivArcheolComo: R269
RivArte: R270
RivCalabreseStorGeogr: R292
Rivd or Rivdi: See also Riv (follow-
   ed by the next capitalized let-
   ter).
RivdArchCrist: R268
RivdiAntr: R266
RivdiCulturaClasseMed: R273
RivdiDirCiv: R274
RivdiFil: R280
RivdiFiloledIstrclassica: R280
RivDirComm: R275
RivEst: R279
RivFC: R280
RivFil: R280
RivFilCl: R280
RivFilIstrCl: R280
RivFilol: R280
RivFilos: R281
RivIA: R285
RivIGI: R282
RivIndGrecItal: R282
RivIndogrecoit: R282
RivIng: R283, R301
RivIngIntem: R283, R301
RivInguana: R283, R301
RivIst: R285
RivIstArch: R285
RivIstArcheStArte: R285
RivItalNum: R286
Rivitalperlescgiur: R287
RivItNum: R286
RivNum: R286
RivScienzePreist: R288
RivScPr: R288
RivSO: R302
RivSo: R302
RivStAnt: R290, R289
RivStCl: R299
RivStFen: R300
RivStLig: R301
RivStOr: R302
RivStor: R295
RivStorant: R290, R289
RivStordellAntichita: R290
RivStorIt: R295
RivStorTicinese: R295
RivStudiOrient: R302

RivStuLig: R301
RIW: R312
RJE: R199
RJKG: R315
RK: R62
RKR: R62
RKW: R76
RL: R28, R69, R202, R232
RLA: R23
R1A: R23
RLAC: R22
RLAF: R200
RLAM: R176
RLAss: R23
RLC: R11
RLexAssyr: R23
RLexVorgesch: R28
RLibourne: R169
RLing: R232
RLiÜ: R316
RliO: R316
RLiR: R203
RLM: R258
RLÜ: R316
RLouvre: R204
RLU: R317
RLV: R28
RLVG: R28
RM: M193, R254
RMaine: R170
RMAL: R207
RManche: R126
RMBord: R208
RMD: R318
RMeta: R205
RMfPh: R254
RMIsr: R13
RML: A688
RMM: R206, R209-R210
RMon: R14
RMP: R254
RMPH: R304
RMTHD: R48
RN: R212, R14
RNeosc: R220
RNord: R211
RNP: R220
RNSGM: R90
RNum: R212, R14
RO: R213, R308
RO(RÜ): R320
ROB: B51
ROC: R214
RocenkaProstejov: R304
ROChr: R214
RocOr: R308

RoczBiałostocki: R305
RoczHist: R306
RoczMuzNarodWarszawie: R307
RoczMuzWarsz: R307
RÖ: R320
ROE: R320
RömGermF: R309
RömGermKorrbl: R310
RömInschrWürttemb: R312
RömMitt: M193
RömMitteilungen: M193
RömMitth: M193
RömQ: R322
RömQSchr: R322
RömQuart: R322
RömQuartalSchrift: R322
RömQuartschr: R322
RömQuSchr: R322
RömStaatsr: R325
RömStrafr: R326
ROL: R215
RomBarb: R348
RomCont: R342
RomForsch: R346
RomGermF: R309
RomGermKorrbl: R310
RomInschrWurttemb: R312
RomMitt: M193
RomMitteilungen: M193
RomMitth: M193
RomQ: R322
RomQSchr: R322
RomQuart: R322
RomQuartalSchrift: R322
RomQuSchr: R322
RomR: R344
RomStaatsr: R325
RomStrafr: R326
ROnom: R194
RozCeskAkad: R354
RozprPraze: R354
RP: R321, R77, R37, R217
RPAA: A668
RPAN: R224
RPARA: A668
RPCC: R336
RPF: R221
RPGR: R77
RPH: R222, R217, R50
RPh: R217
RPhil: R217, R219
RPhilos: R217, R219
RPhL: R218
RPhLHA: R217
RPLHA: R217
RPorto: R157

RPR: R321
RPrehist: R223
RprR: R321
RQ: R322, R227
RQA: R322
RQH: R225
RQS: R322, R226
RQu: R322
RQuestHist: R225
RQum: R227
RR: R79, R228, R321, R339, R344
RRA: R69
RRAL: R69
RRAM: R340
RRC: R338, C155
RRCH: R337
RRG: R324, R323
RRGR: R79
RRH: R230
RRHA: R231
RRouergue: R229
RRoumaineHist: R230
RRoumaineHistArt: R231
RRoumHist: R230
RS: R330-R331, R80, R237, R240,
    M179
RS1909: R331
RSA: R289-R290
RSAA: Z62, R291
RSAAA: R291
RSAC: R49
RSAChar: R51
RSAL: R86
RSav: R233
RSB: R298
RSBN: R298
RSBodin: R52
RSC: R299, R293
RScF: R15
RSCI: R293
RScPhilT: R235
RScPr: R288
RScR: R33, R236
RScRel: R33, R236
RScRelig: R33, R236
RSDI: R294
RSF: R272, R300
RSGR: R80
RSH: S50
RSHum: R234
RSI: R295
RSL: R301
RSLig: R301
RSLR: R296
RSN: R239
RSNormandie: R238

RSO: R302
RSOr: R302
RSP: R288, R303
RSPh: R235
RSPhTh: R235
RSPomp: R303
RSPT: R235
RSPTh: R235
RSR: R33, R325
RSRS: R236
RSS: R16, S50
RST: R297
RSt: R80
RStBizNeoll: R298
RStFen: R300
RStLig: R301
RStO: R302
RStorAnt: R289
RStPomp: R303
RStudFen: R300
RStudLiguri: R301
RSV: Revised Standard Version of
    the Bible.
RT: R53, R246, R352-R353
RTAM: R34
RTarn: R241
RTD: R353
RTE: O48
RTh: R242, R245
RThA: R34
RThAM: R34
RThL: R243
RThom: R245
RThPh: R244
RTrav: R53
RTS: R66
RUB: R247
RUC: R248
RUComp: R249
RUKR: R62
RUL: R156
RUM: R249
RUP: R157
RusChr: R355
RUT: R158
RV: R28
RVA: R54
RVAP: R54
RvEtByz: R143
RVF: R250
RVivarais: R251
RVM: R3
RVV: R63
Rz: R327
RZPR: R327
RZZP: R256

S

S: Sammlung; Sbornik; Scriptorum,
  Scriptores, etc.; Sitzungsbericht;
  Skrifter; Soobshcheniia; Studi,
  Studies, etc.; Sylloge.
S&C: S66
SA: S126, S150, S156
SAA: S129, B365
SaalbgJb: S3
SaalbJb: S3
SaalburgJahrb: S3
SAB: S90-S91
SABeaune: M140
SAC: S282
Saec: S7
SächsGWAbh: S94
SächsGWB: B55
SAF: B361
SAH: S92
SAI: S165
Sait: S10
SAK: S272
SAL: R86
SAl: S9
SAM: S90
Sammelb: S15
SammelblHistVerIngolstadt: S14
SAN: S1, G51, S135
SAn: S101
San: S1
SANE: S122
SANH: S113
SANU: G51, S135
SAO: S155
SAOC: S160
SAPO: B355
SAr: S126
SArB: B387
SAriegeoise: B387
SavZeitschr: Z61

SavZtschr: Z61
SAW: S93
SAWW: S93
SB: Sitzungsberichte. _See also_
  Sitz and Sb.
SB: S15, S123, G108
Sb: Sitzungsberichte, Sbornik.
  See also Sitz and Sbor.
SBA: S90-S91
SbAkadWien: S93
SBAKBerlin: S91
SBAW: S90
SBB: S90
SbB: S90-S91
SBBA: S90-S91
SbBAW: S90
SBBayerAk: S90
SbBayern: S90
SbBayr: S90
SBBerl: S91
SbBerl: S91
SBBerlin: S91
SbBerlin: S91
SbBrno: S34, S26-S27
SBF: S167
SBFLA: S167
SbgJ: S3
SBGU: S15
SBGUBh: S15
SBH: S92
SBHeid: S92
SbHeid: S92
SBHeidelb: S92
SbHeidelb: S92
SBHeilelbAk: S92
SBHeidelberg: S92
SbHeidelberg: S92
SbKomPhil: S29
SBLeipz: S94

SBLpz: S94
SBM: S264
SbM: S90
SBMünch: S90
SBMünchen: S90
SbMünchen: S90
SBN: R298
SbNM: S31
SbNMPraha: S31
SbNU: S32
SBo: S86
SBÖAK: S93
SbÖAW: S93
SBÖsterr: S93
Sbor: Sbornik.
SborBrno: S34, S26-S27
SborNarodMuzPraze: S31
SbornikBratislava: S29
SbornikBrno: S34, S26-S27
SbornikCeskSpolArch: S27
SbornikCSSA: S27
SbornikFilFakUnivBrnoE: S34
SbornikPraha: S31
SbornikSofia: S32
SbornikTurcianSvMartin: Z16
SborPraciFilosFakBrno: S34
SBOsterr: S93
SBP: S91
SbPAW: S91
SbPH: H83
SBPreussAk: S91
SBS: S263
SbV: S35
SBVG: S39
SBWA: S93
SBWien: S93
SbWien: S93
SBWienerAk: S93
SByz: R298
SC: S124, S153, S177
Sc: Scienze, Science, etc.
ScaenRomFrag: S36
SCCluj: S170
SCE: S286
ScE: S51
SCG: S299
SchArch: P160
SchildSteier: S41
SchL: J78
SchlesVorzeit: S43
SChM: S119
Schol: Scholia.
SchrBerlin: S45
SchriftenzUr-uFrühgeschdSchweiz:
  S47
SchSt: S41

SchweizerMünzbl: S49
SchwMbll: S49
SchwNR: R239
SchwNumR: R239
SchwZfGesch: S50
SCI: S59
SCIA: S171-S172
SciAm: S53
SCIV: S173
SCIVA: S173
SCL: S174
SClas: S177
SCMB: S67
SCN: S175
SCNum: S175
SCO: S178
ScotAForum: S54
ScotHistR: S55
SCP: S179
SCPitesti: S182
Script: S57
ScriptHier: S60
ScriptMetr: M156
SCS: S176
SCSA: S27
SCSC: S176
SCSCluj: S176
ScSCluj: S176
SCSibiu: S181
SD: S186, S185
SDAHS: S187
SDAW: S91
SDB: D46
SDHI: S184
SDSD: S186
SE: Sextus Empiricus.
SE: S188, S51, S127, S283
SEC: S106
SECN: B394
Sef: S69
SEG: S277
SEH: S107
SEHHW: S107
SEHRE: S108
SEJG: S5
SelPap: S72
SEM: B396
Sem: Semestriel.
Sem: S77
SemKond: A273
SemKondakov: A273
SEP: S280
SEPRE: S199
Ser: Series, Série, etc.
SERP: S199
SET: S271

SETU: S271
SEV: A311
SF: S28, S34, S269
SFECAG: F13
SFMA: S191
SFSS: S13
SG: S38, S193
SGAIMK: P185
SGDI: S17
SGE: S117
SGHI: S75
SGK: S46
SGLG: S18, S195
SGM: S38
SGMII: S118
SH: S196, S4, S137
SHA: Scriptores Historiae Augustae.
SHA: S92
SHAS: B422
SHASenlis: C186
SHAW: S92
SHb: S6
SHist: S197-S198
SHMH: B425
SHP: S146
SI: S201
SIB: S200
SicA: S82
SicArch: S82
SicGym: S84
SicGymn: S84
SichArch: S82
SiciliaArch: S82
Siciliaartedearch: S83
SICV: S287
SIFC: S201
SIG: S288
SILTA: S202
SIMA: S215
SIO: S289
SIRIS: S290
Sitz: Sitzungsberichte. See also
    SB, Sb and S (followed by the
    next capitalized letter).
SitzAkadWisBerlin: S93
SitzAkadWisWien: S93
SitzBayAkadWis: S90
SitzBayAkWiss: S90
SitzBer: S93
SitzberBayerAkadWissPhilHistKl:
    S90
SitzberBerlAkad: S93
SitzberHeidAkad: S92
SitzberkbAkWiss: S90
SitzbHeidelbAkad: S92
SitzgbBerlin: S91

SitzgMünchen: S90
SitzgWien: S93
SitzLeipzig: S94
SitzpreussAkdWissphil-histKl: S91
SitzPreussAkWill: S91
SitzungsberichteBerlin: S91
SitzungsberichteWien: S93
SitzungsbHeidelbAkad: S92
SitzWien: S93
SIV: S125
SIVP: S125
SJ: S3
SJLA: S203
SJT: S56
SJTh: S56
SK: A273
SKond: A273
SKR: A364
Skr: Skrifter. See also S (fol-
    lowed by the next capitalized
    letter).
SkrifterTrondheim: S96
SkrLund: S100
SkrUppsala: S95
SkSvInsiAthen: S98
SL: S152, S205, S273
SlA: S104, S101
SlAnt: S101
SlArch: S104
SlavAnt: S101
SlaviaAnt: S101
SlavRev: S103
SLG: S278
SLGPage: S278
Sl0cc: S102
SlovA: S104
SlovArch: S104
SlovenskaArch: S104
SlovNum: S105
SlovNumiz: S105
SLS: A299
SLSAnnRpt: A299
SM: See also StM...
SM: C176, M38, S49, S61, S62,
    S213-S214
SMA: S147
SMAN: S208
SMB: S49
SMBFB: F38
SMC: C84
SMEA: S216
SMIA: S273
SMID: S219
SMIM: S209-S210
SMJP: S211
SMK: S114

SMMIM: S210
SMMuz: S210
SMon: S218
SMS: S301
SMSA: S8
SMSR: S212
SMSS: Z16
SMTM: S207
SMYA: S274
SN: S76
SNG[by country, place or collection name]: S291
SNR: R239
SNRA: S33
SNRK: S154
SNVA: S97
SO: S292, S222
SOAI: S115
SOAr: S268
SOAW: S93
Soc: Society, Société, etc.
SocGeoAOran: B407
SOAI: S115
SOAW: S93
SoesterZ: S110
SoestZ: S110
SOF: S269
Soforsch: S269
SOliv: S221
SomersetArchNatHist: S113
SomogyiMK: S114
SonderschrOAI: S115
SoobANGruzSSR: S116
SoobErm: S117
SoobErmit: S117
SoobGErmitazh: S117
SoobGMuzIzobIskPushkin: S118
SoobGruz: S116
SoobKhersonMuz: S119
SoobPus: S118
SoobsGosudErmitLeningrad: S117
SoproniSz: S117
SOsl: S292
SOslo: S292
SovA: S126
SovArch: S126
SovArh: S126
SovArkh: S126
SovEtn: S127
SovetskajaArch: S126
SP: S72, S229, S234
Sp: S130, S135
SPA: S91
SPASR: S275
SPAW: S91
SpBAN: S133

Spe: S130
SPFB: S34
SPFBA: S34
SPFBE: S34
SPFFBU: S34
SPFFBUA: S34
SPFFBUE: S34
SPh: S229
SpHist: S132
SPhNC: S229
SPhP: S293
SPhS: S230
SPicen: S233
SpinksnumCirc: N107
Spl: Supplement.
SpomenikSAN: S135
SpomSAN: S135
SpomSANU: S135
SPP: S296, S223
SPrAW: S91
SprawA: S138
SprawozdArchKrakow: S138
SprawozWarszawa: S139
Spud: S140
SQS: S16
SR: S240-S241, S237, A364, S239
SRF: S36
SRG: M257
SRH: S63
SRIL: S238
SRMG: P77
SRS: S65
SS: M257, S244, H41
SSAC: S249
SSard: S244
SSAW: S94
SSB: B440
SSCA: S148
SSIR: S99
SSL: S131, S242
SSP: S245
SSR: S240
SSRH: S63
SSz: S121
SSzK: S121
ST: S251-S252, S254
St: See also Stud (followed by the next capitalized letter).
St: R325
StA: S163-S164
Sta: S145
StAC: S161
StädelJb: S144
StAltägKul: S157
StANT: S158
Star: S145

StavangMusÅrbok: S127
StBiFranc: S167
StBiz: R298
StBoT: S168
StByz: R298
StC: S169
StCercIstVeche: S173
StCIstor: S171-S172
StCl: S177
StClas: S177
StClOr: S178
StCNum: S175
StCom: S180-S182
StComPitesti: S182
StComSibiu: S181
StCons: S183
StDhj: S184
StDoc: S184
StE: S188
SteDocdiStorediDiritto: S186
SteM: S212
SteMat: S212
StEtr: S188
StFilCl: S201
StGen: S192
StGenuensi: S193
STh: S254
StHell: S196
StiftHamburgKuSamml: E98
StIt: S201
StItal: S201
StItFil: S201
StJ: S142
STK: S2
STL: S255
StM: See also SM (followed by the
    next capitalized letter).
StM: S208, S213-S214
StMagreb: S206
StMatAn: S208
StMatPloiesti: S211
StMatSR: S212
StMatTgMures: M38
StMatTirguMures: M38
StMisc: S217
StMiscRom: S217
StMSR: S212
StN: S220
StOliv: S221
StOR: S222
StOr: S222
StoriaeLett: S152
StPapyr: S244
StPB: S228
StPhil: S232
StPhilon: S231

StPohl: S234
StR: R325
Str: R326
Strarohrvprosvj: S146
StRom: S240-S241, S239-S241
StRomagnoli: S239
StrR: R326
StSalent: S243
StSard: S244
StSem: S246
StSl: S247
StSt: S249
StStA: S249
StT: S252
StuCo: S180
Stud: See also St.
StudActaOrient: S155
StudAlb: S156
StudAmst: S159
StudArch: S163-S164
StudBal: S166
StudBibl: S167
StudByz: R298
StudCercIstorVeche: S173
StudCercIstVeche: S173
StudCercNum: S175
StudChrist: S161
StudClas: S177
StudClasseOr: S178
StudComPest: S180
StudComunBrukenthal: S181
StudComunPitesti: S182
StudDocHistetIuris: S184
StudDocHistIur: S184
StudetDoc: S184
StudetDocariuraorantpert: S185
StudetDocHistetIuris: S184
StudEtr: S188
StudFilol: S190
StudGen: S192
StudGeschKultAlt: S194
StudHist: S197-S198
StudiaCluj: S257
StudiClasseOrient: S178
Studiitaldifilcl: S201
StudiMatdiStoriadellaRelig: S212
StudiMaterialidiArcheNum: S208
StudiMatStReligioni: S212
Studistor: S249
StudistorAntclass: S249
StudIstoriaArtei: S171-S172
StudIt: S201
StudItal: S201
StudItFilCl: S201
StudjineZvestiAUSAV: S261
StudMag: S206

StudMagr: S206
StudMatIstMedie: S209
StudMatMuzIstMil: S210
StudMatMuzTirguMures: S207
StudMatStorRel: S212
StudMed: S214
StudMisc: S214
StudMon: S218
StudOrient: S222
StudPal: S223
StudPap: S244
StudPat: S226
StudPatr: S227
StudPic: S233
StudPicena: S233
StudPont: S235
StudRevIst: R197
StudRom: S239-S241
StudRomagn: S239
StudSal: S243
StudSard: S244
StudStobi: S162
StudStor: S248-S249
StudTeol: S251
StudTest: S252
StudTrent: S256
StudUrb: S258
StudUrbSerA: S258
StudUrbSerB: S258
StudVem: S259
StudVenez: S259
StudZvesti: S261
StudZvestiAUSAV: S261
StundTzGeistesgeschdesMA: S253
StUrbin: S258
StuSl: S247
StVF: S149
STYill: S21
StzProblGesch: S236
SUBB: S257
SUBsHag: S265
Subshag: S265
SUC: S265
SudhArch: S267
Süost-Forsch: S269
Sum: S270
SuomenAikakauskirija: S274
SuomenMus: F18
Suost-Forsch: S269
Supp: Supplement, Supplementum, etc.
SuppCom: S276
SuppEpigr: S277
SupplCom: S276
SupplEG: S277
SupplEpigrgr: S277
SupplLyrGraec: S278

SurreyAC: S279
SurreyArchColl: S279
SussexAC: S282
SussexArchColl: S282
SV: S85, S141
SVEA: S284
SvenskaFornmTidskr: S285
SVF: S149
SVGB: S48
SvS: S41
SvTK: S2
SWC: S19
SWI: S260
SWP: S281
Sy: S300
Syd: C155
Syll: Sylloge.
Syll: S288
Sylloge: S288
SymbOsl: S292
SymbOslo:S292
SympPreh: S296
SynaxariumCP: S297
SynaxEcclCP: S297
SynCP: S297
SynOr: S298
SyOs: S292
SyOsl: S292
Syr: S300
SZ: Z61
Sz: S302
SzA: S126
Sza: S126
SZAUSAV: S261
Szaz: S302
SzegediME: M272
SzegediMFME: M272
SzekszardiME: S304
Szeph: S305
SZG: S50
SzMK: B336
SzovArch: S126
SzVMK: S303

T

T: Texts, Textes; Theological, The-
  ologisches, etc.; Tidskrift,
  Tijdschrift; Trabalhos; Transac-
  tions; Travaux; Trudy; Tome, Tom-
  os, etc.
T: B100
T&C: T11
T&MByz: T108
T&R: T110
TA: T18
TabDefix: D8
TabDefixAud: D7
TabIg: Tabulae Iguvinae.
TabPeut: Tabula Peutingeriana.
TAD: T129
TAE: T81
TAik: T18
TAM: T69
TanBpMultjabol: T6
TAPA: T87
TAPHA: T87
TAPhA: T87
TAPhilosSoc: T88
TAPHO: T87
TAPhS: T88
TAPS: T88
Tarb: T8
TAVO: T128
TB: T75
TBGAS: T91
TBM: T6
TBVG: T61
TC: T71, T2
TCam: T71
TCamir: T71
TCL: T25
TCS: T29
TCs: T71
TCSup: T71

TCWA: T94
TD: S272
TDA: T73
TDNS: T96
TDNT: T50
TDoAx: T73
TE: T117
Techn&Cult: T11
TED: T130
TeherF: T12
TeherForsch: T12
TelAvivJInstA: T14
Teub: B100
Teubner: B100
TextMJ: T28
TF: T64
TFByzNgPhil: T22
TfK: T63
TFMSA: T97
TG: T65
TGF: T83-T84
TGL: T54
TGrF: T83-T84
TH: T66
Th&G: T36
TH&Ph: T40
THBl: T67
ThBl: T35
ThebOstr: T33
ThEE: T57
TheolLiteraturzeit: T39
TheolRu: T44
TheolSzle: T47
TheolWB: T49
Thes: T56
ThesLiL: T56
ThesLinLat: T56
ThesLL: T56
THeth: T23

ThG: T54
ThGL: T54
ThGl: T36
ThJb: T37
ThJbb: T37
ThLB: T38
ThLbl: T38
ThLGr: T54
ThLL: T56
ThLZ: T39
ThLz: T39
ThPQ: T41, Q20
ThQ: T42
ThR: T43-T44
ThRdsch: T44
ThRev: T43
ThRundschau: T44
ThRv: T43
ThS: T45-T46
ThStKr: T46
ThW: T50
ThWAT: T49
ThWB: T50
ThWNT: T50
ThZ: T51
TIB: T3
Tijd: R175
Tijdschr: R175
TimesLSuppl: T1
TIR: T4
TitAsMin: T69
TitCalymn: T70
TitCam: T71
TKB: T7
TLE: T20
TLL: T56
TLS: T1
TLZ: T39
TM: T108: T32
TMEFA: T109
TMMM: T26
TO: T33
TOAMGE: T124
TONGE: T125
TörtRegErt: T77
TörtSzle: T78
TotLatLexikon: T79
TP: Tabula Peutingeriana.
TP: T80
Tp: Trudy.
TPAPA: T87
TPAPHA: T87
TPh: T64
TPhS: T100
TPQ: T41
TPS: T100

TR: T43, R175
Tr: Transactions, Travaux. See
    also Trans, T (followed by the
    next capitalized letter).
Tr: T82
Trab: Trabalhos.
TrabAntrEtnSocPortug: T81
TrabAntrPorto: T80
TrabPreh: T80
TragGraecFrag: T83-T84
Traité: T86
Trans: Transactions. See also T
    (followed by the next capital-
    ized letter).
TransAASocDurhamNorthumb: T97
TransAct: T87
TransactAmPhilAss: T87
TransAm: T87
TransAmerPhilAss: T87
TransAmPhilAss: T87
TransAmPhilologAss: T87
TransandProcAmphilAss: T87
TransAPA: T87
TransAPhA: T87
TransB'hamArchSoc: T90
TransB'hamWarwksArchSoc: T90
TransBirminghamArchSoc: T90
TransBristGloucesArchSoc: T91
TransBristolandGlosAS: T91
TransCumbandWestmA&ASoc: T94
TransCumberlandArchSoc: T94
TransD&GNH&ASoc: T95
TransDumfriesGallNatHistAntSoc:
    T95
TransDumfriesandGallowayNHandAS:
    T95
TransEssexArchSoc: E102
TransLancsandCheshAntiqSoc: T98
TransLichfield&SStaffsA&HS: T104
TransLichSSTaffsArchHistSoc: T104
TransLincei: T106
TransLondonM'sexArchSoc: T99
TransPhilAs: T87
TransProcAmerPhilAss: T87
TransProcBirminghamArchSoc: T90
TransRSocLit: T103
TransSBA: T102
TransShropshireAS: T101
TransSocBiblArch: T102
TransSStaffArchHistSoc: T104
TransWorcArcSoc: T105
TrAPhAss: T87
TravMem: T108
TrBristol: T91
TrCumb: T94
TRF: T85

TRG: R175
TrGF: T85
TrGraecFrag: T83-T84
Tribus: T111
TriererZeitschr: T114
TriererZGeschKunst: T114
TriererZtschr: T114
TrierZ: T114
trim: trimestriel.
TrM: T108
TrMem: T108
TromsøMusÅrsberetning: T115
TrPr: T80
TRu: T44
TrudErm: T117
TrudIstMuz: T118
TrudTbil: T121
TrudTomsk: T127
TrudyAlma-Ata: T122
TrudyBaku: T120
TrudyErmit: T117
TrudyGErmitazh: T117
TrudyGosudMuzMoskva: T118
TrudyĪUTAKE: T123
TrudyTbilissi: T121
TrZ: T114
TrZtschr: T114
TS: R175, T30, T45
TSBA: T102
TSPAE: T81
TSt: T30
TSz: T78
TT: T48, T131
TTAE: T131
TTAED: T131
TThZ: T112
TTK: T132, B45
TTKR: K8
TTKRap: K8
TTKY: T132
TTKYayinlarindan: T132
TU: T28
TUAS: T17
Tusc: T133
TürkAD: T129
TürkArkDerg: T129
TürkArkDergisi: T129, T131
TürkEtDerg: T130
TürkTAED: T131
TürkTarDerg: T131
TuU: T28
TV: T21
TvG: T65
TW: T74
TWAS: T135
TWNT: T50
TZ: T114, T51

U

U: This letter is filed as if spelled ue in German words.
U: Uchenye Zapiski; University, Université, etc.
U&O: U12
UALG: U23
UAVA: U24
UCPCA: U16
UCPCP: U17
UCPPh: U17
UE: U29
UF: U7
UFAS: U30
UGA: U33
UgaritF: U7
UgFo: U7
UgHb: U8
UgMan: U9
UgTb: U10
UH: U21
UIZ: U11
UJA: U13
UK: U22
UkrIstZhurnal: U11
UkrIstZur: U11
UKV: U25
ULIAARpt: A297
UlsterJArch: U13
UlsterJournalArch: U13
UM: U9
UMB: U18
UMBS: P249
UMME: M163
Univ: University, Université, etc.
UnivIllStLangLit: S204
UnivLiverpoolAnnArchAnthr: A224
UnivOldsaksamlÅrbokOslo: A7
UnivOldsaksamlSkrifterOslo: U15
UPMB: U18

UpplandsFornmTidskr: U27
UppsÅrsskr: U28
UPZ: U35
Urk: U34-U35
Urkunden: U34
UrSchw: U31
US: U31
UT: U10
UUÅ: U28
UZ: Uchen ye Zapiski.
UZLG: U2
UZLGPI: U2
UZMK: U3
UZML: U3
UZPenz: U1
UZPerm: U4
UZTart: T72

V

V: Verhandelingen, Verhandlungen;
  Veröffentlichungen; Vestnik, Vjes-
  nik, Vijesti, etc.; Voprosy; Vor-
  träge.
VAB: V69
VAHD: V58
VAHDal: V58
VAMZ: V59
VAN: V32
VANSSSR: V32
VAR: V70
VariaBio-Arch: V2
VARS: V70
VarSpom: V3
VarstSpom: V3
VAS: V71
Vasenlisten: V4
VAWAmst: V20
VBGAEU: V17
VBoT: V30
VBW: V73
VC: V53, V9
VCH: V49
VChr: V53
VD: V10
VDI: V33
VDIst: V33
VDP: V21
VDPh: V21
VDrIst: V33
Ver: Verein.
VerderTürkGesch-Komm: T132
VErev: I167
Verh: Verhandelingen, Verhandlung-
  en. See also V (followed by the
  next capitalized letter).
VerhandlHistVerNiederbayern: V18
VerhandlHistVerOberpfalz: V19
VerhBerlGesAnthrEthnUrgesch: V17

Veröff: Veröffentlichungen. See
  also V (followed by the next
  capitalized letter).
VeröffIOBerl: V25
VeröffMün: V26
VeröffMusPotsdam: V28
VerslagAssen: V29
VesciAkBSSR: V31
VesDrevIstor: V33
Vest: Vestnik. See also Vjes-
  and V (followed by the next cap-
  italized letter).
VestAkNauk: V32
VestDrIst: V33
VestGosMuzGruz: V34
VestLU: L35
VestMoscovU: V39
VestMU: V39
VeszpME: V44
VeszpremiMuzK: V44
VeszpremMegyeiMuzKözlem: V44
VeszpremMk: V44
VetChr: V45
VetChrist: V45
VeteraChr: V45
VF: V77
VFM: V63
VFS: F65
VfSW: V51
VGH: V4
VGN: J79
VH: V59
VHAD: V59
VHVN: V18
VHVO: V19
VI: V66
VictCoHist: V49
VID: V78
VIE: V6

VigChr: V53
VigChrist: V53
VIMinsk: V65
VIMoscou: V66
VIO: V25
VIst: V66
VIVI: V67
VivPens: R119
VIZ: V60
VizVrem: V57
VJa: V64
VJaz: V64
VjesAMuzZagreb: V59
VjesDal: V58
Vjesnik-Split: V58
VjesnikZagreb: V58
VjestnikHAD: V59
VKF: V68
VKhark: V35
VKU: V36
VL: V55
VLFH: V15
VLU: V37
VLVH: V27
VLvov: V38
VMAE: M29
VMG: V34
VMK: V44
VMKH: V54
VMMK: V44
VMU: V39
VMUFG: V28
VMUFilol: V39
VMUist: V39
VNAW: V20
VoennoIstZhurnal: V60
VOKKUAN: V40
VONA: I167
Vop: Voprosy.
VopFilol: V62
VopFilos: V63
VopIst: V66
VopJaz: V64
VoprIst: V66
VorgeschichtlJb: V72
VorgeschJahrb: V72
Vorsokr: F65
VortWarb: V73
VP: V12
VR: V74
VS: F65, V5, V50, V61, V71
VSSuppl: V50
VSW: V51
VSWG: V51
VSz: D101
VT: V46, V7

VTM: V7
VTS: V46
VuG: V11
VV: V57
VVAP: M74
VVDPh: V21
VVIAc: V22
VVMB: V42
VVS: V43

W

W: Wiadomości; Wiener; Wissenschaft-
  liche; Wörterbuch.
W: I2
W&D: W55
W&S: W47
WA: W17
WAAFLN: W33
Wad: I103
Waddington: I103
WaG: W6
WAGB: W31
Wallraf: W2
WAM: W30
WArch: W17
Warch: W53
WB: W20, W21, W48
Wb: Wörterbuch.
Wb: W48
WBll: W21
WbM: W49
WbMyth: W49
WbMythol: W49
WBS: W22
WByzSt: W22
WD: A128
WdF: W5
WDI: V33
WdO: W8
WdZ: W9
WE: W51
Weber: D24
WeltGesch: W6
WeltIsl: W7
WeOr:W8
WestdtZeitschr: W9
WestdZeit: W9
WestdZeitGeschuKunst: W9
WestfälForsch: W11
WF: W11

WfKlPh: W46
WFON: W15
WG: W6
WGBl: W16, W23
WGbl: W16, W23
WH: L14
WHB: W24
Wiad: W17
WiadA: W17
WiadArch: W17
WiadNum: W18
WiadNumArch: W19
WiadomArch: W17
WiadomosciArch: W17
Wien: <u>See also W (followed by the
  next capitalized letter)</u>.
WienAkDis: D19
WienAkSb: S93
WienAnz: A399
WienBlätterFreundedAntike: B20
WeinerDenkschr: D19
WienerJahrbdLit: J39
WienerPrähistZeitschr: W25
WienerSt: W27
WienerVorlBl: W28
WienGbl: W23
WienJahresh: J74
WienPrähZ: W26
WienSitzb: S93
WienSt: W27
WienStud: W27
WienZKundeMorg: W29
WienZtsMorg: W29
WiltANatHistMag: W30
WiltsArchNaturHistMag: W30
WiltsMag: W30
WinckProgr: W31
WinterthurJb: W32
WissJZGreifswald: W40

WissLiteraturanz: W35
WissMittBosnuHerzeg: W36
WissZHalle: W44
WissZJena: W41
WissZRostock: W45
WJ: W57, W32
WJA: W57
WJh: J74
WJKG: W25
WJKg: W25
WK: W34
WKlPh: W46
WKP: W46
WkP: W46
WKPh: W46
WkPh: W46
WM: W36
WMANT: W37
WMBH: W36
WMK: R330
WMM: R319
WMR: R330
WN: W18
WNA: W19
WNZ: N124
WO: W8
Wo: W46
WochKlassPhilol: W46
WochklPhil: W46
WochKlPhilol: W46
Wört: W48
WorcesterMuseumNews: N49
WorldA: W53
Wort: W48
WP: R330, V16, W1
Wp: R330
WPZ: W26
WRJ: W3
WrzbJhrbb: W57
WS: W27, S23
Ws: S23
WSL: U19
WSM: C156
WSt: W27
WStudien: W27
WüJbb: W57
WürttFranken: W56
WürzbJ: W57
WürzbJahrbfdAlt: W57
WürzJbAltWiss: W57
WürzJbb: W57
WuJbb(WüJbb): W57
WUNT: W38
WUS: W50
WuS: W47
WV: W28

WVDO: W39
WVDOG: W39
WZ: Wissenschaftliche Zeitschrift.
WZ: W12
WZBerlin: W42
WZGreifswald: W40
WZHalle: W44
WZHW: W44
WZJena: W41
WZKM: W29
WZLeipzig: W43
WZM: W29
WZMorg: W29
WZRostock: W45

X-Y-Z

XP: C115

Y: Yearbook; Yayinlari.
YAJ: Y8
YaleAssociatesBul: B445
YaleClassStudies: Y1-Y2
YaleClSt: Y1-Y2
YaleUnivB: B445
YBC: B4
YC1S: Y1-Y2
YC1St: Y1-Y2
YCS: Y1-Y2
YearsW: Y9
Yediot: B318
YLG: Y6
YNER: Y3
YorkshireArchJ: Y8
YorkshireArchJournal: Y8
YOS: Y4
YOSR: Y4
YUTAKE: T123
YW: Y7
YWCS: Y7

Z: Zapiski; Zbornik; Zeitschrift.
ZA: Z86, Z25
ZAe: Z20
ZÄAK: Z20
ZAEK: Z20
ZÄS: Z19
ZAeS: Z19
ZÄSA: Z19
ZAESA: Z19
ZAesth: Z20
ZAG: Z18
ZAK: Z62
ZANO: Z2

ZAnt: Z85
ZapiskiOdessa: Z5-Z6
ZapOdessArkObshch: Z5
ZArch: Z23
ZAS: Z19
ZASA: Z19
ZAss: Z25
ZAssyr: Z25
ZATW: Z22
ZAVA: Z25
ZAW: Z22
ZBayLandGesch: Z26
ZBB: Z78
ZbBibl: Z78
ZBildK: Z27
ZBK: Z27
ZBL: Z26
Zbor: Zbornik.
ZborArheolMuz: Z7
ZborNarodMuzBeogradu: Z12
ZbornikBeograd: Z12, Z8
ZbornikLjubljana: Z9
ZbornikRadBeograd: Z14
ZbornikRadNarMuzBeograd: Z12
ZborSlovMuz: Z15
ZborSlovNarodMuz: Z15
ZborZadar: Z10
ZBreisgauGeschVer: S40
ZC: Z91
ZCas: Z81
ZChrK: Z28
ZCP: Z47
ZcPh: Z47
ZD: Z92
ZDA: Z29
ZdeutschPalVer: Z32
ZdFinnAltersGes: S274
ZDMG: Z30
ZDMGSuppl: Z30

ZdPalv: Z32
ZDPV: Z32
ZDVGMS: Z34
ZDVK: Z35-Z36
ZE: Z37
Zeit: See also Zft, Zt, Ztschr and
    Z (followed by the next capital-
    ized letter).
ZeitfArchit: Z38
ZeitfEthn: Z37
ZeitfNum: Z53
ZeitföstGymn: Z31
ZeitfVerglSprachf: Z72
ZeitöstGymn: Z31
ZeitschrArch: Z23
ZeitschrArchMittelalter: Z24
ZeitschrdSavingyStiftung: Z61
ZeitschrEthn: Z37
Zeitschrfdalterth: Z21
ZeitschrfPapuEpigr: Z55
ZeitschrfVergleichSprach: Z72
ZeitschrHalleWittenberg: W44
Zeitschrift: Z19
ZeitschrMährLandesmus: C63
ZeitschrNumBerlin: Z53
ZeitschrÖsterrGymn: Z31
ZeitschrSavingyStift: Z61
ZeitschrSavStiftgRomAbt: Z61
ZeitschrSchweizArchKungtgesch: Z62
ZeitsfAssyr: Z25
Zeph: Z79
Zetem: Z80
ZEthnol: Z37
ZfA: Z23, Z19
ZfAE: Z19
ZfAss: Z25
ZfBK: Z27
ZfCeltPh: Z47
ZfCPh: Z47
ZfdA: Z29
ZfdAW: Z21
ZfdPh: Z33
ZfE: Z37
ZfEthn: Z37
ZfEthVerh: Z37
ZFF: Z9
ZFFB: Z8
ZfG: Z42
ZfK: Z50
ZfKg: Z50
ZfN: Z53
ZfNum: Z53
ZfOrtsnamenforsch: Z51
ZfPapEp: Z55
ZfRechtsgesch: Z58
ZfRG: Z61

Zft: Zeitschrift. See also Zeit,
    Ztschr and Z (followed by the
    next capitalized letter).
ZftEthn: Z37
ZftfEthn: Z37
ZftNum: Z53
ZftON: Z51
ZftRechtsg: Z58
ZftVglSpr: Z72
ZfurdieöstGym: Z31
ZG: Z42
ZGdA: Z38
ZGeschOberrhein: Z39
ZGeschSaar: Z40
ZGeshcvMülheim: Z41
ZGLE: Z95
ZGLEN: Z95
ZGO: Z39
ZGS: Z40
ZGSHG: Z43
ZGW: Z42
ZHVS: Z44
ZHVSt: Z44
ZivaAnt: Z85
ZJKF: Z90
ZK: Z50, Z46
ZKG: Z48
ZKircheng: Z48
ZKT: Z45
ZKTh: Z45
ZKuGesch: Z50
ZKunst: Z50
ZKunstg: Z50
ZKunstW: Z35-Z36
ZKWL: Z49
ZLUMS: Z11
ZMG: Z30
ZMNP: Z82
ZMP: Z83
ZN: Z53, Z51, Z94
ZNF: Z51
ZNM: Z12
ZNORAO: Z4
ZNTW: Z52
ZntW: Z52
ZNum: Z53
ZNW: Z52
ZNWBeih: Z52
ZO: Z53
ZOAO: Z5
ZÖG: Z31
ZöstG: Z31
ZöstGym: Z31
ZofN: Z86
ZoG: Z31
ZON: Z51

ZONF: Z51
ZOOID: Z6
ZOrtsnam: Z51
ZostG: Z31
ZostGym: Z31
ZPalV: Z32
ZPE: Z55
ZPFZ: Z13
ZPhF: Z56
ZPhKr: Z57
ZPR: R327
ZpravyCSSA: Z89
ZpravyJKF: Z90
ZpravyPraha: Z89
ZPTh: E156
ZR: Z58, Z14
ZRAO: Z2
ZRelGg: Z59
ZRG: Z61, Z59
ZRg: Z58
ZRGG: Z59
ZRGR: Z61
ZRP: Z60
ZRPh: Z60
ZRVI: Z14
ZS: Z64
ZSAKg: Z62
ZSav: Z61
ZSavStiftg: Z61
ZSchlesHolstGesch: Z43
ZSchwAKg: Z62
ZSchwAlt: Z62
ZSchwArch: Z62
ZSchweizKg: Z62
ZSchweizArchKunstgesch: Z62
ZSchwG: Z62
ZsddeutschenmorgendGes: Z30
ZSem: Z64
ZsfRelGeistGesch: Z59
ZSK: Z63
ZSkopje: Z7
ZSNM: Z15
ZSR: Z61
ZSRGRA: Z61
ZSS: Z61
ZSSR: Z61
ZSSRA: Z61
ZSSRG: Z61
ZSSRomAbt: Z61
ZSSt: Z61
ZSTh: N33
ZT: Z93
ZThK: Z65
ZTK: Z65
ZtN: Z53
Ztschr: See also Zeit, Zeitschr,

Z (followed by the next capi-
talized letter).
ZtschrEthn: Z37
ZtschrKunstgesch: Z50
ZtschrNum: Z53
ZtschrON: Z51
ZtschrSavStift: Z61
ZVerglSprF: Z72
ZVergSprach: Z74
ZVerHessischeGesch: Z67
ZvglSpr: Z72
ZVHG: Z66
ZVHGL: Z67
ZVI: Z14
ZVL: Z70
ZVLGA: Z68
ZVR: Z71
ZVRW: Z71
ZVS: Z72, Z69
ZVSpr: Z72
ZVV: Z69
ZWG: S267
ZWL: Z74
ZWT: Z73
ZWTh: Z73

CYRILLIC

A: Archeion; Archaiologikon.
ΑΑΑ: A469
ΑΒΜ: A476
ΑΒΜΕ: A476
ΑΔ: A470
ΑΕ: A471
ΑΕΜ: A473
'Ανάλεκτα: A469
ΑρχαιολΔελτ: A470
ΑρχΒυζΜνμμυΕλλ: A476
ΑρχΕφημ: A471
ΑρχΠοντ: A474
Δ: Deltion.
Δελτ: Deltion.
Δελτ: A470
ΔελτΕτΕλλ: D10
ΔελτΧριστΑρχΕτ: D9
ΔΕΝΑ: J1116
ΔΙΕΕ: D10
ΔΧΑΕ: D9
E: Epetēris; Ephēmeris; Epis-
 tēmonikē Epetēris.
ΕΑ: A471
ΕΕ: E54
ΕΕΒΣ: E56
ΕΕΕ: E55
ΕΕΘΣΑ: E87
ΕΕΚΣ: E57
ΕΕΦΣΠΑ: E86
ΕλλΦιλολΣυλλ: H47
Επ: Epetēris.
ΕπΕτΒυζΣπ: E56
ΕπΕτΚρητΣπ: E57
ΕπιστΕπΦιλΣχΑ: E86
ΕπΜεσΑρχ: E86
Εφημ: Ephēmeris.
Εφημ: A471
Εφημαρχαιολ: A471
ΕΦΣ: H47

ΗΧ: E53
ΘΗΕ: T57
Θησ: T53
ΙΕΕ: H96
ΚρΧρον: K53
ΚρητΧρον: K53
ΚυπρΣπουδ: K81
ΚΧ: K53
Λαογρ: L7
Μακ: M25
ΜΒ: M153
ΜΕΕ: M83
ΜκΒ: M278
ΜουσΣμυρν: M278
ΝεοςΕλλ: N21
Π: Praktika.
ΠΑΑ: P168
ΠΑΑΕ: P169
ΠΑΕ: P169
Παρν: P82
Πολεμ: P150
ΠρακτΑρχΕτ: P169
Σ: Scholia.
ΧΡ: C115
Χρονικά: A470

GREEK

АДСВ: A347
АИУ: A582
АМА: A348
АО: A585
Бългезик: B242
B: Voprosy; Vestnik, Viestnik, etc.
ВВ: V57
Ви: V65-V66
ВизВрем: V57
ВизОбоз: R121
ВЛГУ: V37
ВОКК: V40
ВопросыИст: V65-V66
ВЯ: V64
Г: Godishnik etc.
ГАИМК: P185
ГНБМ: G62
ГНМПл: G60
ГПНЬМ: G62
ДРАН: D86
Ж: Zhurnal
ЖМНП: Z82
З: Zapiski
ЗКВ: Z3
ЗОАО: Z5
ЗООИД: Z6
ЗРАО: Z2
И: Izvestiia; Instituta; Istoriko.
ИАД: I153
ИАИ: I153
ИАК: I156
ИАН: I152
ИАНО: I149
ИБАД: I153
ИБАИ: I153
ИГАИМК: I155
ИЖ: I135
ИТОИАЭ: I165
ИФЖ: I137
КС: Kratikie Soobshcheniia
КС: K45

КСИА: K45-K46
КСИИМК: K45
КСИНА: K48
КСОАМ: K50
M: Materialy.
МАГК: M46
МАК: M47
МАР: M49
МИА: M58
МКА: M60
МСб: S32
НС: N119
НумСб: N118
ПАС: P99
ПС: P22
ПЭС: P98
C: Soobshcheniia; Sovetskaia;
     Sbornik.
СА: S127
СбМАЭ: S30
СВ: S128
СГАИМК: P185
СовАрх: S126
СоветАрхеол: S126
СовЭтн: S127
СЭ: S127
СЯ: S78
T: Trudy.
ТГИМ: T118
ТГЭ: T117
ТОВЭ: T126
Тр: Trudy.
ТрИЯ: T119
ТрЮТАКЭ: T123
ТХЭ: T116
У: Ucheniye.
УЗМГПИ: U3
УЗЛГУ: U4
УЗСГПИ: U5
ЭВ: E74
ЮТАКЭ: T123

PART II

BIBLIOGRAPHIC DESCRIPTIONS

A

Å is filed as if spelled Aa.

ABS INTERNATIONAL GUIDE to CLASSI-
    CAL STUDIES   see   I96.

ABS QUARTERLY CHECKLIST of ...
    STUDIES   see   Q21-Q26.

A1
AGR; Akten der Gesellschaft für
    Griechische und Hellenistische
    Rechtsgeschichte. Cologne
    1975-

AIESEE BULLETIN   see   B265.

ASCA NEWSLETTER   see   M2.

A2
AUMLA; journal of the Australasian
    Universities Language and Liter-
    ature Association.   Victoria &
    Christchurch 1953-   . Earlier
    name of the association: Austra-
    lasian Universities Modern Lan-
    guage Association. (AUMLA).

A3
AACHENER KUNSTBLÄTTER. Aachen
    1906?-   .
    --. Sonderschrift. 1928?-   .

Ålin, P.   see   E44.

A4
AARBØGER for NORDISK OLDKYNDIGHED
    og HISTORIE. Copenhagen 1866-   .

ÅRBOK see also ÅRSBOK.

ÅRBOK. BERGENS MUSEUM   see   A6.

A5
ÅRBOK. Kongl. NORSKE VIDENSKABERS
    SELSKAB MUSEET. Trondheim
    1894-   . 1894-50 title: Årsber-
    etning.

ÅRBOK. SAMLING av NORDISKE OLDSAKER
    (Univ. Oslo)   see   A7.

ÅRBOK. STAVANGER MUSEUM   see   S147.

A6
ÅRBOK. UNIVERSITETETS i BERGEN.
    Bergen 1883-   . 1883-91 title:
    Bergens Museums. Aarsberetning.
    1892-1946/7 title: Bergens
    Museums Årbok.

A7
ÅRBOK UNIVERSITETETS OLDSAKSAMLING.
    Oslo 1927-   . Title varies
    slightly.

A8
ÅRSBERÄTTELSE. Kungl. HUMANISTISKA
    VETENSKAPSSAMFUNDET i LUND =
    Bulletin de la Société Royale des
    Lettres de Lund. Lund 1918/9-56.

ÅRSBERETNING. Kongl. NORSKE VIDENS-
    KABERS SELSKAB MUSEET   see   A5.

AARSBERETNING. STAVANGER MUSEUM
    see   S147.

ÅRSBERETNING. TROMSØ MUSEUM   see
    T115.

ÅRSBOK   see also ÅRBOK.

A9
ÅRSBOK. Kungl. VITTERHETS-, HISTO-
RIE- og ANTIKVITETSAKADEMIEN.
Stockholm 1926-   .

ÅRSHEFTE. STAVANGER MUSEUM   see
S147.

ÅRSSKRIFT. GÖTEBORGS UNIVERSITET
see A85.

ÅRSSKRIFT. LUNDS UNIVERSITET   see
A86.

ÅRSSKRIFT. UPPSALA UNIVERSITET
see U28.

A10
ABHANDLUNGEN der AKADEMIE der
WISSENSCHAFTEN zu GÖTTINGEN.
Göttingen 1838/41-1892. Issued
under the Academy's earlier
name: K. Gesellschaft der Wissenschaften zu Göttingen. (AGG).
--. Philologisch-historische
Klasse. 1896-   . Variant
name of the class: Historisch-
philologische Klasse.

ABHANDLUNGEN. AKADEMIE der WISSEN-
SCHAFTEN, HEIDELBERG. PHILOSO-
PHISCH-HISTORISCHE KLASSE see
A18.

ABHANDLUNGEN. AKADEMIE der WISSEN-
SCHAFTEN und der LITERATUR in
MAINZ. GEISTES- und SOCIALWIS-
SENSCHAFTLICHE KLASSE see A15.

ABHANDLUNGEN. AKADEMIE der WISSEN-
SCHAFTEN, MÜNCHEN see A11.

A11
ABHANDLUNGEN der (K.) BAYERISCHEN
AKADEMIE der WISSENSCHAFTEN.
Academy's name changes slightly.
(ABAW, AbhMünch).
--. Historische Klasse 1833-
1904/9.
--. Philosophisch-historische
Klasse. 1835-   . 1835-1908
name: Philosophisch-philolo-
gische Classe. 1909-28 issued
by the Philosophisch-philolo-

gische Klasse and the Historische
Klasse.

ABHANDLUNGEN und BERICHTE des
HEIMATSMUSEUMS GOTHA see G71.

ABHANDLUNGEN. BERLIN see A12.

A12
ABHANDLUNGEN der DEUTSCHEN AKADE-
MIE der WISSENSCHAFTEN zu BER-
LIN. Berlin 1804-1907. Issued
under the Academy's earlier
name: (K.) Preussische Akademie
der Wissenschaften. (AbhBerlin,
APAW, ADAW).
--. Philosophisch-historische
Klasse. 1908-49.
--. Klasse für Sprachen, Liter-
atur und Kunst. 1950-   .
--. Klasse für Gesellschafts-
wissenschaften. 1950-53.
--. Klasse für Philosophie,
Geschichte, Staats-, Rechts-,
und Wirtschaftswissenschaften.
1955-   . Names of the classes
change slightly.

A13
ABHANDLUNGEN des DEUTSCHEN ARCH-
ÄOLOGISCHEN INSTITUTS, KAIRO.
(ADIK).
--. Ägyptologische Reihe.
Glückstadt etc. 1958-   .
--. Islamische Reihe. Cairo
1959-   .
--. Koptische Reihe. Wiesbaden
1962-   .

A14
ABHANDLUNGEN der DEUTSCHEN ORIENT-
GESELLSCHAFT. Berlin 1956-   .

A15
ABHANDLUNGEN der GEISTES- und
SOCIALWISSENSCHAFTLICHEN KLASSE.
AKADEMIE der WISSENSCHAFTEN und
der LITERATUR in MAINZ. Mainz
1950-   . (AbhMainz).

A16
ABHANDLUNGEN zur GESCHICHTE der
MATHEMATISCHEN WISSENSCHAFTEN
mit EINSCHLUSS ihrer ANWENDUNGEN.
Leipzig 1877-1913.

A17
ABHANDLUNGEN zur GESCHICHTE der
  NATURWISSENSCHAFTEN und der MEDI-
  ZIN. Erlangen 1922-25.

ABHANDLUNGEN. GESELLSCHAFT zu
  WISSENSCHAFTEN zu GÖTTINGEN
  see A10.

ABHANDLUNGEN. GÖTTINGEN see A10.

A18
ABHANDLUNGEN der HEIDELBERGER
  AKADEMIE der WISSENSCHAFTEN.
  PHILOSOPHISCH-HISTORISCHE KLASSE.
  Heidelberg 1913-35 1950-   .
  (AHAW, AbhHeidelberg).

ABHANDLUNGEN. HISTORISCHE KLASSE.
  AKADEMIE der WISSENSCHAFTEN,
  MÜNCHEN see A11.

ABHANDLUNGEN. HISTORISCH-PHILOLO-
  GISCHE KLASSE. AKADEMIE der
  WISSENSCHAFTEN zu GÖTTINGEN
  see A10.

ABHANDLUNGEN des HISTORISCHEN VER-
  EINS des KANTONS BERN see A508.

ABHANDLUNGEN. KLASSE für GESELL-
  SCHAFTSWISSENSCHAFTEN. AKADEMIE
  der WISSENSCHAFTEN zu BERLIN
  see A12.

ABHANDLUNGEN. KLASSE für PHILOSO-
  PHIE, GESCHICHTE, STAATS-,
  RECHTS-, und WIRTSCHAFTSWISSEN-
  SCHAFTEN. AKADEMIE der WISSEN-
  SCHAFTEN zu BERLIN see A12.

ABHANDLUNGEN. KLASSE für SPRACHEN
  LITERATUR und KUNST. AKADEMIE
  der WISSENSCHAFTEN zu BERLIN
  see A12.

ABHANDLUNGEN. KÖNIGLICHE ... see
  ABHANDLUNGEN ... (the word
  königliche is disregarded in
  filing, but may have been regarded in forming an abbreviation).

A19
ABHANDLUNGEN für die KUNDE des MOR-
  GENLANDES. Leipzig 1859-   .

ABHANDLUNGEN. LEIPZIG see A21.

ABHANDLUNGEN. MAINZ see A15.

ABHANDLUNGEN. MÜNCHEN see A11.

A20
ABHANDLUNGEN der NATURHISTORISCHEN
  GESELLSCHAFT zu NÜRNBERG. Nürn-
  berg 1858-   .

ABHANDLUNGEN. PHILOLOGISCH-HISTOR-
  ISCHE KLASSE. AKADEMIE der WIS-
  SENSCHAFTEN zu GÖTTINGEN see
  A10.

A21
ABHANDLUNGEN der PHILOLOGISCH-HIS-
  TORISCHE KLASSE der SÄCHSISCHEN
  AKADEMIE der WISSENSCHAFTEN.
  Leipzig 1850-   . 1856-1918
  name of the Academy: K. Sächs-
  ische Gesellschaft der Wissen-
  schaft. (ASAW, AbhLeipzig).

ABHANDLUNGEN. PHILOSOPHISCH-HIS-
  TORISCHE KLASSE. AKADEMIE der
  WISSENSCHAFTEN zu BERLIN see
  A12.

ABHANDLUNGEN. PHILOSOPHISCH-HIS-
  TORISCHE KLASSE. AKADEMIE der
  WISSENSCHAFTEN, HEIDELBERG
  see A18.

ABHANDLUNGEN. PHILOSOPHISCH-HIS-
  TORISCHE KLASSE. AKADEMIE der
  WISSENSCHAFTEN, MÜNCHEN see
  A11.

ABHANDLUNGEN. PHILOSOPHISCH-PHILO-
  LOGISCHE CLASSE. BAYERISCHE AKA-
  DEMIE der WISSENSCHAFTEN see
  A11.

ABHANDLUNGEN der PREUSSISCHEN AKA-
  DEMIE der WISSENSCHAFTEN zu
  BERLIN see A12.

ABHANDLUNGEN der SÄCHSISCHEN AKA-
  DEMIE der WISSENSCHAFTEN. PHI-
  LOLOGISCH-HISTORISCHE KLASSE
  see A21.

ABHANDLUNGEN der SÄCHSISCHEN GE-
  SELLSCHAFTEN. PHILOLOGISCH-HIS-
  TORISCHE KLASSE see A21.

A22
ABHANDLUNGEN zur THEOLOGIE des
ALTEN und NEUEN TESTAMENTS.
Zurich 1941?-   .

ABHANDLUNGEN der TSCHECHOSLOWAK-
ISCHEN AKADEMIE der WISSENSCHAF-
TEN see R354.

A23
ABINNAEUS ARCHIVE: papers of a
Roman officer in the reign of
Constantius II / H. I. Bell et
al. Oxford 1962. (PAbinn).

A24
ABRUZZO (Istituto di Studi Abruz-
zesi). Rome 1963-   .

ABS INTERNATIONAL GUIDE to CLASSI-
CAL STUDIES see I96.

A25
ACADEMIA (R. Academia de Bellas
Artes de San Fernando). Madrid
1951-   .

ACADEMY see A26.

A26
ACADEMY and LITERATURE. London
1869-1916. 1869-02, 1905-10
and 1914 title: Academy.

A27
ACCADEMIE e BIBLIOTECHE d'ITALIA;
annali della Direzione Generale
delle Accademie e Biblioteche.
Rome 1927-   .

A28
ACME; annali della Facoltà di
Filosofia e Lettere dell'Univer-
sità degli Studi di Milano.
Milan 1948-   .

A29
ACQUISITIONS. FOGG ART MUSEUM.
Cambridge, Mass. 1959/62-   .

A30
ACROPOLE; revue du monde hellén-
ique. Monaco & Paris 1925-36.

ACTA and ACTES are here interfiled.

A31
ACTA ACADEMIAE ABOENSIS: HUMANI-
ORA. Åbo 1920-   .

A32
ACTES de l'ACADÉMIE nationale des
SCIENCES, BELLES-LETTRES et ARTS
de BORDEAUX. Bordeaux 1838-   .
1848-59 title: Recueil des Actes.
Issued under the earlier names
of the academy: Académie royale
and Impériale.

A33
ACTA ACADEMIAE VELEHRADENSIS.
Velehrad 1905-   .

ACTA ANTIQUA see A35.

A34
ACTA ANTIQUA ACADEMIAE SCIENTIARUM
HUNGARICAE. Budapest 1951-   .
(ActaAntHung, AAntHung, AcAn).

A35
ACTA ANTIQUA et ARCHAEOLOGICA.
Szeged 1958-   . Title of vols.
1-2: Acta Universitatis Szegediensis: Sectio Antiqua. Sub-title
of vols. 3-4: Acta Antiqua.

A36
ACTA APOSTOLORUM APOCRYPHA / R.A.
Lipsius & M. Bonnet. Leipzig
1891-1903. Reprint Hildesheim
1972.

A37
ACTA APOSTOLOCAE SEDIS; commen-
tarium officiale. Rome 1909-

A38
ACTA ARCHAEOLOGICA. Copenhagen
1930-   . (ActaA, ActaArch).

ACTA ARCHAEOLOGICA (Ljubljana
1950-   .) see A571.

A39
ACTA ARCHAEOLOGICA ACADEMIAE SCIEN-
TIARUM HUNGARICAE. Budapest
1951-   . (AArchHung, ActaArch-
Hung).

A40
ACTA ad ARCHAEOLOGIAM et ARTIUM

HISTORIAM PERTINENTIA. Oslo
1962-   .
--. Series Altera. Rome 1981- .

A41
ACTA ARCHAEOLOGICA CARPATHICA.
Krakow 1958-   .

A42
ACTA APOSTOLICAE SEDIS: commen-
drid 1943-   .

A43
ACTA ARCHAEOLOGICA LODZIENSIA.
Lodz 1951-   . 1951-61 title:
Acta Archaeologica Universitatis
Lodziensis.

ACTA ARCHAEOLOGICA MUSEI NATIONALIS
HUNGARICI see A438.

ACTA ARCHAEOLOGICA UNIVERSITATIS
LODZIENSIS see A43.

ACTES de l'ATHOS see A45, A75,
A77, A89, A91.

A44
ACTA BALTICO-SLAVICA. Bialystok,
Poland 1964-   .

A45
ACTES de CHILANDER / L. Petit &
B. Korablev. Amsterdam 1975.
(Actes de l'Athos; 5). Originally
published as a supplement to
Vizantiiski Vremennik.

A46
ACTA CLASSICA (Universitatis Scientiarum Debreceniensis). Debrecen
1965-   . (ACD).

A47
ACTA CLASSICA; verhandelinge von
die Klassieke Vereniging van
Suid-Afrika = Proceedings of the
Classical Association of South
Africa. Capetown 1958-   .

A48
ACTA et COMMENTATIONES UNIVERSITA-
TIS TARTUENSIS (DORPATENSIS) B:
Humaniora. Tartu 1921-   .

A49
ACTA CONCILIORUM OECUMENICORUM /
E. Schwartz & J. Straub. Berlin
etc. 1925-   . (ACO).

A50
ACTES du ... CONGRESSO INTERNAZIO-
NALE di ARCHEOLOGIA CLASSICA.
place varies 1905-   .

A51
ACTES du ... CONGRÈS INTERNATIONAL
de NUMISMATIQUE. place varies
1891-

A52
ACTES du ... CONGRÈS INTERNATIONAL
des ORIENTALISTES. place varies
1873-   .

A53
ACTES du CONGRÈS NATIONAL des
SOCIÉTÉS SAVANTES. Section de
Philologie et d'Histoire jusqu'à
1610. Paris 95- 1970-   .
Formerly issued with the Bulletin
Philologique et Historique.

A54
ACTES de DIONYSIOU / N. Oikonomides. Paris 1968. (Archives de
l'Athos; 4).

A55
ACTA et DIPLOMATA GRAECA MEDII
AEVI / F. Miklosich & J. Müller.
Vienna 1860-90. Reprint Aalen
1968.

ACTA et DISSERTATIONES ARCHAEOLO-
GICAE see A570.

A56
ACTES d'ESPHIGMÉNOU / J. Lefort.
Paris 1973. (Archives de l'Athos;
6).

A57
ACTA ETHNOGRAPHICA (Magyar Tudományos Akademia). Budapest
1950-   .

A58
ACTA FRATRUM ARVALIUM edidit quae
post annum MDCCCLXXIV reperta
sunt / A. Pasoli. Bologna 1950.

(Univ. Bologna. Facoltà di Lettere e Filosofia. Studi e Ricerche; 7).

A59
ACTES GRECS de S. MARIA di MESSINA
/ A. Guillou. Palermo 1963.
(Istituto Siciliano di Studi
Bizantini e Neoellenici. Testi e
Monumenti. Testi; 8).

A60
ACTA HISTORICA (Magyar Tudományos
Akademia). Budapest 1951- .

A61
ACTA HISTORICA (Societatis Acade-
mica Dacoromana). Rome 1959- .

A62
ACTA HISTORIAE ARTIUM (Magyar Tudományos Akademia). Budapest
1953- .

A63
ACTA HISTORICA NEERLANDICA. Leiden
1966- .

ACTA INSTITUTI ACADEMIAE JUGOSLA-
VICAE SCIENTIARUM et ARTIUM in
ZADAR see R3.

ACTA INSTITUTI ATHENIENSIS Regni
SUECIAE see S98, O22.

A64
ACTA INSTITUTI ROMANI FINLANDIAE.
Helsinki 1963- .

ACTA INSTITUTI ROMANI regni SUECIAE
see S99, O20, O25.

A65
ACTA IRANICA; encyclopédie per-
manente des études iraniennes.
Leiden
--. 1. Sér.: Commemoration Cyrus.
1974.
--. 2. Sér.: Hommages et Opera
Minora. 1975- .
--. 3. Sér.: Textes et Mémoires.
1975- .
--. 4. Sér.: Répertoires.
1979- .

A66
ACTES de KUTLUMUS / P. Lemerle.
Paris 1945-46. (Archives de
l'Athos; 2).

A67
ACTA LINGUISTICA (Magyar Tudományos Akadémia). Budapest 1951- .

A68
ACTA LITTERARIA (Magyar Tudományos
Akadémia). Budapest 1957- .

ACTA LITTERARUM ac SCIENTIARUM
UNIVERSITATIS SZEGEDIENSIS see
A88.

A69
ACTA MARTYRUM et SANCTORUM / P.
Bedjan. Leipzig & Paris 1890-
97.

A70
ACTA y MEMORIAS de la SOCIEDAD ES-
PAÑOLA de ANTROPOLOGÍA, ETNOGRA-
FÍA y PREHISTORIA, MADRID.
Madrid 1921- .

A71
ACTA MUSEI NAPOCENSIS. Cluj
1964- . (ActaMN, AMN).

ACTA MUSEI NATIONALIS PRAGAE see
S31.

ACTA MUSEI SILESIAE see C66.

A72
ACTA NUMISMÁTICA. Barcelona
1971- .

A73
ACTA ORIENTALIA (Magyar Tudományos
Akadémia). Budapest 1950- .

A74
ACTA ORIENTALIA (Societatis Orientales: Danica, Finlandica, Norvegica, Suecica). Copenhagen
& Lund 1922/3- .

A75
ACTES du PANTOCRATOR / L. Petit.
Amsterdam 1964. (Actes de l'A-
thos; 2). Originally published
in 1903 as supplement to Vizantiiski Vremennik.

A76
ACTA PHILOLOGICA (Societas Acade-
mica Dacoromana). Rome 1958-   .

A77
ACTES de PHILOTHÉE / W. Regel et
al. Amsterdam 1975. (Actes de
l'Athos; 6). Originally published
in 1913 as a supplement to Vizantiiski Vremennik.

A78
ACTA PRAEHISTORICA et ARCHAEOLO-
GICA. Berlin 1970-   . (APA).

A79
ACTES du PROTATON / D. Papachryssanthou. Paris 1975. (Archives
de l'Athos; 7).

A80
ACTA. REI CRETARIAE ROMANAE FAUTO-
RUM. Bonn etc. 1960-   .
--. Supplementum. 1974-   .

A81
ACTA SANCTORUM / J. Bollandus et
al. Antwerp 1643-   . New ed.
Paris 1863-   . (AASS, ActSS).

A82
ACTA SANCTAE SEDIS. Rome 1865-
1908.

A83
ACTA SEMINARII NEOTESTAMENTICI
UPSALIENSIS. Uppsala 1936-65.

ACTA SOCIETATIS HISTORIAE OULOUEN-
SIS see S197.

A84
ACTES de la SOCIÉTÉ JURASSIENNE
d'ÉMULATION. Dellmont 1849-   .
1849-56 title: Coup d'Oeil sur
les Travaux de la Société Jurassienne d'Émulation. 1876-77
tilte: Émulation jurassienne.

A85
ACTA UNIVERSITATIS GOTHOBURGENSIS
= Göteborgs Universitets Årsskrift. Gothenburg 1895-   .
1895-1954 Swedish title: Göteborgs Högskolas Årsskrift.

A86
ACTA UNIVERSITATIS LUNDENSIS =
Lunds Universitets Årsskrift.
Lund 1864-1904.
--. Afdelning 1. Teologi, juri-
dik och humanistiska ämnen.
1905-   .

A87
ACTA UNIVERSITATIS PALACKIANAE
OLOMUCENSIS HISTORICA. Prague
1960-   .

ACTA UNIVERSITATIS STOCKHOLMIENSIS
see S148.

A88
ACTA UNIVERSITATIS SZEGEDIENSIS.
Cluj & Szeged. Title varies:
Acta litterarum ac scientiarum.
--. Sectio Geographico-historica.
1932-   .
--. Section Philologica.
1924-   . Suspended 1941-47.

ACTA UNIVERSITATIS SZEGEDIENSIS.
ACTA ANTIQUA see A35.

ACTA UNIVERSITATIS SZEGEDIENSIS.
SECTIO ANTIQUA see A35.

A89
ACTES de XENOPHON / L.Petit. Amsterdam 1964. (Actes de l'Athos;
1). Originally published in 1903
as a supplement to Vizantiiski
Vremennik.

A90
ACTES de XÉROPOTAMOU /J. Bompaire.
Paris 1964. (Archives de l'Athos;
3).

A91
ACTES de ZOGRAPHOU / W. Regel et
al. Amsterdam 1969. (Actes de
l'Athos; 4). Originally published in 1907 as a supplement
to Vizantiiski Vremennik.

A92
ACTIVITATEA MUZEELOR. Cluj
1955-   .

Adrados, F. Rodriguez see D40.

A93
AEGYPTIACA HELVETICA. Geneva
 1974-   .

A94
ÄGYPTISCHE URKUNDEN aus den STAAT-
 LICHEN MUSEEN zu BERLIN. GRIECH-
 ISCHE URKUNDEN. Berlin 1895-   .
 Title varies slightly. (BGU).

A95
ÄGYPTOLOGISCHE ABHANDLUNGEN. Wiesbaden 1960-   .

A96
ÄGYPTOLOGISCHE FORSCHUNGEN. Glückstadt 1936-   .

A97
AEGYPTUS; rivista italiana di egit-
 tologia e di papirologia. Milan
 1920-   .

A98
AERIAL ARCHAEOLOGY. 1977-   .

A99
AEVUM; rassegna di scienze, storiche, linguistiche e filologiche. Milan 1927-   .

A100
AFRICA (Institut National d'Archéologie et d'Art). Tunis
 1966-   .

AFRICA (Naples 1882-85) see A101.

A101
AFRICA ITALIANA. Naples 1882-1937.
 Title varies: 1882-85: Africa;
 1886-1912 as the society's Bollettino.

A102
AFRICA ITALIANA; rivista di storia
 e d'arte. Bergamo 1927-41.

Äg is filed as if spelled Aeg.

A103
AIDS and RESEARCH TOOLS in ANCIENT
 NEAR EASTERN STUDIES. Malibu,
 CA. 1977-   . (ARTANES).

AIESEE BULLETIN see B265.

Aistleitner, J. see W50.

AKADÉMIAI ÉRTESITÜ see M17.

A104
AKKADICA. Brussels 1977-   .

A105
AKKADISCHES HANDWÖRTERBUCH / W.
 von Soden. Wiesbaden 1965-   .
 (AHW).

A106
AKROTERION; quarterly for the
 classics in South Africa. Stel-
 lenbosch.1969?-   .

AKTEN der GESELLSCHAFT für GRIECH-
 ISCHE und HELLENISTISCHE RECHTS-
 GESCHICHTE see A1.

A107
ALALAKH TABLETS / D. J. Wiseman.
 London 1953. (Occasional Publi-
 cations of the British Institute
 of Archaeology at Ankara; 2).
 (AT).

al-ANDALUS see A205.

A108
ALBA REGIA; annales Musei Stephani
 Regis. Székesfehérvár 1960?-   .

A109
ALBANIA; revue d'archéologie, d'art
 et des sciences appliquées et
 dans les Balkans. Milan etc.
 1925-39.

A110
ALBUM of DATED LATIN INSCRIPTIONS /
 J. S. & A. E. Gordon. Berkeley
 1958-65.

ALESIA see P181.

Alexander, M. A. see C227.

A111
ALEXANDRIAN EROTIC FRAGMENTS and
 OTHER GREEK PAPYRI, chiefly
 ptolemaic / B. P. Grenfell.
 Oxford 1896. Second vol. appeared
 in 1897 as New Classical Frag-
 ments and Other Greek and Latin
 Papyri. (PGrenf).

A112
ALFA (Univ. Marilia. Departamento
de Letras). Marilia, Brazil
?- .

Alföldy, G. see F8, R313.

Ålin, P. see E44.

A113
ALKMAARS JAARBOEKJE. Alkmaar ?- .

A114
ALLGÄUER GESCHICHTSFREUND. Kempten
1888-1903 1909-39?

ALLGEMEINER PHILOLOGISCHER ANZEIGER
see E14.

A115
ALLGEMEINE ZEITSCHRIFT für GE-
SCHICHTE. Berlin 1844-46.

ALMANACH. AKADEMIE der WISSENSCHAF-
TEN, WIEN see A117.

A116
ALMANACH de BRIOUDE e son ARRONDIS-
SEMENT. Brioude 1920-   .

A117
ALMANACH. ÖSTERREICHISCHE AKADEMIE
der WISSENSCHAFT. Vienna
1851-   . 1851-1917 title:
Kaiserliche Akademie der Wissenschaften in Wien.

ALMANACH. WIEN see A117.

A118
ALON (Israel Numismatic Society).
Tel Aviv ?-   .

A119
ALT-THÜRINGEN. Weimar 1953/4-   .

A120
ALTAMURA; bolletino dell'Archivio
Biblioteca-Museu Civico. Bari
etc. 1954-60.

A121
ALTBAYERISCHE MONATSSCHRIFT. Munich 1899-1925.

A122
ALTE und MODERNE KUNST. Vienna

1956-   .

A123
ALTE ORIENT. Leipzig 1899-   .
(AO).

A124
ALTER ORIENT und ALTES TESTAMENT.
Neukirchen-Vluyn 1969-   .
(AOAT).
--. Sonderreihe. 1971-   .
(AOATS).

A125
ALTEN SPRACHEN. Frankfurt a.M.
1936-41.

A126
ALTERTÜMER von PERGAMON. Berlin,
Leipzig 1885-   . (AvP).

A127
ALTERTUM. Berlin 1955-   .

A128
ALTINDISCHE GRAMMATIK / J. Wackernagel & A. Debrunner. Göttingen
1896-   . (Göttinger Sammlung
indogermanischer Grammatiken
und Wörterbücher).

A129
ALTORIENTALISCHE DENKMÄLER im VOR-
DERASIATISCHEN MUSEUM zu BERLIN /
G. R. Meyer. Leipzig 1965.

A130
ALTORIENTALISCHE FORSCHUNGEN. Ber-
lin 1974-   . Subseries of
Schriften zur Geschichte und
Kultur des Alten Orients.

A131
ALTORIENTALISCHE TEXTE zum ALTEN
TESTAMENT / H. Gressmann. 2.
Aufl. Berlin 1926.

A132
ALTORIENTALISCHE TEXTE und BILDER
zum ALTEN TESTAMENT / H. Gressmann. 2. Aufl. Berlin 1926-27.
1st edition 1909.

A133
ALTORIENTALISCHE TEXTE und UNTER-
SUCHUNGEN / B. Meissner. Lei-
den 1916-20.

A134
ALTRÖMISCHE IUS / M. Kaser. Göttingen 1949.

A135
ALTSCHLESIEN. Breslau 1922-   .

A136
ALTSCHLESISCHE BLÄTTER. Breslau 1926-   .

A137
ALTSPRACHLICHE UNTERRICHT. Stuttgart 1951-   .

A138
ALUTA (Muzeul Judetean). Sfântul Gheorghe 1969-   .

Aly, W. see M195.

A139
ALZEYER GESCHICHTSBLÄTTER. Alzey 1964-   .

AMARNA TAFELN see E25.

A140
AMBIX (Society for the Study of Alchemy and Early Chemistry). London 1937-   . Suspended 1938-46.

A141
AMERICAN ANTHROPOLOGIST. Washington D.C. 1888-   .

AMERICAN BIBLIOGRAPHIC SERVICE INTERNATIONAL GUIDE to CLASSICAL STUDIES see I96.

A142
AMERICAN CLASSICAL REVIEW. New York 1971-73.

A143
AMERICAN HISTORICAL REVIEW. New York 1895-   . (AHR).

A144
AMERICAN JOURNAL of ANCIENT HISTORY. Cambridge, Mass. 1976-   .

A145
AMERICAN JOURNAL of ARCHAEOLOGY. Baltimore etc. 1885-   . Title

of vols. 1-11: American Journal of Archaeology and of the History of the Fine Arts. (AJA).

A146
AMERICAN JOURNAL of NUMISMATICS. New York etc. 1866-1924. Early title: American Journal of Numismatics and Bulletin of the American Numismatic and Archaeological Society.

A147
AMERICAN JOURNAL of PHILOLOGY. Baltimore 1880-   . (AJPh, AJP, AJPhil).

A148
AMERICAN JOURNAL of SEMITIC LANGUAGES and LITERATURES. Chicago etc. 1885-1941. 1884-95 title: Hebraica. (AJSL).

A149
AMERICAN NUMISMATIC SOCIETY. CENTENIAL PUBLICATION / H. Inghalt. New York 1958.

AMERICAN NUMISMATIC SOCIETY. MUSEUM NOTES see M314.

AMERICAN NUMISMATIC SOCIETY. NUMISMATIC NOTES and MONOGRAPHS see N116.

AMERICAN NUMISMATIC SOCIETY. NUMISMATIC STUDIES see N122.

A150
AMERICAN ORIENTAL SERIES. New Haven 1925-   . (AOS).

A151
AMERICAN STUDIES on PAPYROLOGY. New Haven 1966-   .

A152
AMHERST PAPYRI / B. P. Grenfell & A. S. Hunt. London 1900-01. (PAmh).

A153
AMISTAD; boletín del Museo Municipal. Barcelona ?-   .

A154
AMPURIAS; revista de arqueología,
prehistoria y etnología. Barcelona 1939-   .

A155
AMSTERDAM CLASSICS in LINGUISTICS.
Amsterdam 1800-1925.

A156
AMSTERDAMER BEITRÄGE zur ÄLTEREN
GERMANISTIK. Amsterdam 1972-   .

AMTLICHE BERICHTE aus den Königlichen KUNSTSAMMLUNGEN see B65.

A157
AMTSBLATT der STADT WIEN. Vienna
1954-   .

Amundsen, L. see G94, O56, P63.

A158
ANADOLU = Anatolia; revue annuelle
d'archéologie. Ankara 1956-   .
1956-64 title: Anatolia = Ana-
dalu.

A159
ANADOLU; revue des études d'arché-
ologie et d'histoire en Turque.
Ser. 1: Préhistoire, Antiquité,
Byzance. Paris 1951-   .

A160
ANADOLU ARASTIRMALARI; Jahrbuch
für kleinasiatische Forschung.
Ankara & Istanbul 1950/1-   .
1950-53 published as the Jahrbuch für kleinasiatische Forschungen.

A161
ANAIS de HISTÓRIA. Assiz
1968/9-   .

A162
ANAIS do INSTITUTO do VINHO do
PÔRTO. Oporto 1940-   .

A163
ANAIS do MUNICIPIO de FARO. Faro
?-   .

ANAL-: entries beginning with this
spelling are here interfiled.
See also ANN- and ANU-.

ANALEKTA see A469.

A164
ANALECTA AUGUSTINIANA. Rome
1905-   .

A165
ANALECTA BIBLICA. Rome 1952-   .

A166
ANALECTA BOLLANDIANA. Brussels
1882-   . (AB).

A167
ANALES del CENTRO de CULTURA VAL-
ENCIANA. Valencia 1928-36
1940-   .

A168
ANALELE DOBROGEI = Dobrudscha
Annalen. Dobruja etc. 1920-28.

A169
ANALES de FILOLOGÍA CLÁSICA.
Buenos Aires 1939-   . Early
volumes have title: Anales
del'Instituto de Literaturas
Clásicos.

A170
ANALECTA FRANCISCANA. Quarracchi
1885-   .

A171
ANALES de HISTORIA ANTIGUA y MEDIE-
VAL. Buenos Aires 1948-   .

A172
ANALI HISTORIJSKOG INSTITUTA (Jugo-
slovenska Akademija Znanosti i
Umjetnosti). Dubrovnik 1952-   .

A173
ANALECTA HYMNICA MEDII AEVI. Leipzig 1886-1922. Reprint New York
1961.

A174
ANALES del INSTITUTO de ESTUDIOS
GERUNDENSES. Gerona 1946-   .

ANALES del'INSTITUTO de LITERATURAS
CLÁSICOS see A169.

A175
ANALECTA LOVANIENSIA BIBLICA et

ORIENTALIA. Gembloux etc.
1934-   .

A176
ANALECTA MALACITANA (Facultad de
Filosofía y Letras. Univ. de
Malaga). Malaga 1978-   .

A177
ANALECTA ORDINIS SANCTI BASILII
MAGNI. Rome
--. I. Opera 1949?-   .
--. II. Analecta 1950?-   .
--. III. Documenta 1952?-   .

A178
ANALECTA ORIENTALIA. Rome 1931- .
Suspended 1942-44. (AnOr, Anal-
Or).

A179
ANALECTA ROMANA INSTITUTI DANICI.
Copenhagen 1960-   .
--. Supplementum. 1960-   .

A180
ANALELE ROMÂNO-SOVIETICE. Bucha-
rest 1946-49.
--. Seria Istorie-filosofie.
1949-51.
--. Seria Istorie. 1952-   .

A181
ANALECTA SACRA TARRACONENSIA; revista de ciencias histórico-
eclesiásticas. Barcelona
1925-   . Suspended 1937-39.

A182
ANALELE UNIVERSITĂŢII BUCUREŞTI:
Ştiinţe Sociale. Istorie. Bucharest 13- 1964-   . Continues
in part the Analele Universităţii Bucureşti. Ştiinţe Social
and continues its numbering.
(AUB).

A183
ANALELE UNIVERSITĂŢII din CRAIOVA:
Seria Istorie, Geografie, Filo-
logie. Craiova 1972-   .

A184
ANALES de la UNIVERSIDAD de MUR-
CIA. Murcia 1945-   . In
1954/5 split into 13 sections

including Derecho and Filosofia
y Letras.

A185
ANALELE UNIVERSITĂŢII din TIMIŞO-
ARA: Seria Ştiinţe filologice.
Timisoara, Roumania 1963-   .

ANATOLIA see A158.

A186
ANATOLIAN STUDIES. London 1951- .
(AS, AnatSt).

A187
ANTOLICA. Leiden & Istanbul
1967-   .

A188
ANATOLISCHE PERSONENNAMENSIPPEN /
L. Zgusta. Prague 1964. (Dis-
sertationes Orientales; 2).

A189
ANCIENT CHRISTIAN WRITERS; the
works of the Fathers in translation. New York 1946-   .

A190
ANCIENT CULTURE and SOCIETY. London 197?-   .

A191
ANCIENT EGYPT and the EAST. London
1914-35. 1914-32 title: Ancient
Egypt.

A192
ANCIENT EGYPTIAN MATERIALS and
INDUSTRIES / A. Lucas. Rev. J. R.
Harris. 4. ed. London 1962. 1st
edition 1926.

A193
ANCIENT EGYPTIAN ONOMASTICA / A.
H. Gardiner. London 1947.

A194
ANCIENT GAZA / W. M. F. Petrie.
London 1931-52. (Publications of
the Egyptian Research Account;
53, 56, 64).

A195
ANCIENT INDIA. New Delhi 1946-   .

A196
ANCIENT NEAR EAST; supplementary
texts and pictures relating to
the Old Testament / J. B. Pritchard. Princeton 1969.
--. Vol. II: a new anthology of
texts and pictures. 1975.

A197
ANCIENT NEAR EAST in PICTURES RELA-
TING to the OLD TESTAMENT / J. B.
Pritchard. Princeton 1954.
(ANEP).

A198
ANCIENT NEAR EASTERN TEXTS RELATING
to the OLD TESTAMENT / J. B.
Pritchard. 3. ed. Princeton 1969.
1st edition 1950. (ANET).

A199
ANCIENT PEOPLES and PLACES. New
York & London 1956-   .

A200
ANCIENT RECORDS of ASSYRIA and
BABYLONIA / D. D. Luckenbill.
Chicago 1926-27. Reprint New
York 1968.

A201
ANCIENT RECORDS of EGYPT / J. H.
Breasted. Chicago 1906-07.
(ARE).

A202
ANCIENT ROMAN STATUTES / A. C.
Johnson. Austin 1961. (Corpus
of Roman Law; 2).

A203
ANCIENT SOCIETY. Louvain 1970-   .

A204
ANCIENT WORLD. Chicago 1978-   .

A205
al-ANDALUS: revista de las Escuelas
de Estudios Araba de Madrid y
Granda. Madrid 1933-   .

Andersen, C. see L39.

Andrews, E. A. see L17.

A206
ANDREWS UNIVERSITY SEMINARY STUD-
IES. Berrien Springs, Mich.
1965-   .

A207
ANECDOTA ATHENIENSIA et alia / A.
Delatte. Paris 1927-39.

A208
ANECDOTA GRAECA / I. Bekker. Berlin 1814-21. Reprint Graz 1965.

A209
ANEDOCTA GRAECA / J. F. Boissonade.
Paris 1833. Reprint Hildesheim
1962.

A210
ANECDOTA GRAECA e codd. manuscrip-
tis bibliothecarum oxoniensium /
J. A. Cramer. Oxford 1835-37.

A211
ANECDOTA GRAECA; e codd. mss. bibl.
reg. parisin./ L. Bachmann.
Leipzig 1828. Reprint Hildesheim
1965.

A212
ANECDOTA GRAECA e codd. manuscrip-
tis bibliothecae regiae parisi-
enses / J. A. Cramer. Oxford
1839-41. Reprint Hildesheim 1967.

A213
ANECDOTA MEDICA GRAECA / F. Z.
Ermerins. Leiden 1840. Reprint
Amsterdam 1963.

A214
ANECDOTA VARIA GRAECA et LATINA /
R. Schoell & W. F. A. Studemund.
Berlin 1886.

A215
ANGELOS; Archiv für neutestament-
liche Zeitgeschichte und Kultur-
kunde. Leipzig 1925-32.

A216
ANIMA. Vierteljahresschrift für
praktische Seelsorge. Olten
1946-   .

A217
ANKARA ARKEOLOJI MÜZESINDE BULUNAN
BOĞAZKÖY TABLETLERI. Istanbul
1948.

ANKARA ÜNIVERSITESI DIL ve TARIH-
COĞRAFYA FAKÜLTESI DERGISI see
D65.

ANN-: entries beginning with this
spelling are here interfiled.
See also ANAL- and ANU-. For
Slavic titles beginning Annuaire
see also GODISHNIK.

A218
ANNALES de l'ACADÉMIE de MÂCON.
Macon 1851-   .

A219
ANNALES ACADEMIAE SCIENTIARUM FEN-
NICAE. Series B. = Suomalainen
Tiedeakatemian Toimituksia. Sar-
ja B. Helsinki 1909-   .

A220
ANNUARIO. ACCADEMIA ETRUSCA di
CORTONA. Cortona etc. 1934?-   .

A221
ANNUARIO della ACCADEMIA delle
SCIENZE di TORINO. Turin
1877/8-   . Academy's name
changes slightly.

A222
ANNUAL. AMERICAN SCHOOLS of ORIEN-
TAL RESEARCH. New Haven
1919/20-   . Also issued under
Association's earlier name:
American Schools of Oriental
Research in Jerusalem. (AASOR).

A223
ANNALES ARCHÉOLOGIQUES. Paris
1844-81. Suspended 1873-80.

A224
ANNALS of ARCHAEOLOGY and ANTHRO-
POLOGY. Liverpool 1908-48.
(LAAA, AAA, LivAnn).

A225
ANNALES ARCHÉOLOGIQUES ARABES
SYRIENNES. Damascus 1956-   .
1951-65 title: Annales Archéologiques de Syrie. (AAAS, AAS).

ANNUAL of the ARCHAEOLOGICAL MU-
SEUMS of ISTANBUL see I128.

ANNALES ARCHÉOLOGIQUES de SYRIE
see A225.

ANNUAIRE des ARCHIVES MÉDIÉVALES
see E62.

ANNUAL. ART & ARCHAEOLOGY DIVI-
SION. ROYAL ONTARIO MUSEUM see
A300.

ANNUAIRE d'ART PRÉHISTORIQUE et
ETHNOGRAPHIQUE see I109.

A226
ANNUAIRE de l'ASSOCIATION pour
l'ENCOURAGEMENT des ÉTUDES
GRECQUES en FRANCE. Paris 1867-
87.

ANNUAL of the AYASOFYA MUSEUM see
A696.

ANNALES des BASSES-ALPES see
A267.

ANNUAIRE de la BIBLIOTHÈQUE NA-
TIONALE et du MUSÉE à PLOVDIV
see G62.

A227
ANNALES de BOURGOGNE. Dijon etc.
1929-   .

A228
ANNALES de BRETAGNE et des PAYS
de l'OUEST. Rennes 1886-   .
Title varies slightly.

A229
ANNUAL. BRITISH SCHOOL at ATHENS.
London 1894/5-   . (BSA, ABSA).

A230
ANNALES du CENTRE d'ÉTUDE des RE-
LIGIONS (Univ. Brussels). Brus-
sels 1962-   .

A231
ANNALES du CENTRE UNIVERSITAIRE
MÉDITERRANÉEN. Nice 1946/7-   .

A232
ANNALES du CERCLE ARCHÉOLOGIQUE du

CANTON de SOIGNIES. Soignies
1894-   .

A233
ANNALES du CERCLE ARCHÉOLOGIQUE
d'ENGHIEN. Enghien 1880-   .

A234
ANNALES du CERCLE ARCHÉOLOGIQUE
et FOLKLORIQUE de la LOUVIÈRE
et du CENTRE. Mariemont ?-   .

A235
ANNALES du CERCLE ARCHÉOLOGIQUE et
HISTORIQUE d'AUDENAERDE = Handelingen van den Oudheid en Geschiedkundigen Kring van Oudenaarde. Audenarde 1906-   .
Suspended during World War II?.

A236
ANNALES du CERCLE ARCHÉOLOGIQUE de
MONS. Mons 1856/7-   .

ANNALES du CERCLE ARCHÉOLOGIQUE du
PAYS de WAES see A292.

ANNALES. CERCLE ARCHÉOLOGIQUE de la
VILLE et de l'ANCIEN PAYS de TER-
MONDE see G8.

ANNALES du CERCLE HISTORIQUE et
ARCHÉOLOGIQUE de RENAIX see
A266.

A237
ANNALES du CERCLE HUTOIS des SCI-
ENCES et BEAUX-ARTS, HUY. Huy
1875-   . Suspended during
World War II?.

A238
ANNUAIRE des CINQ DÉPARTEMENTS de
la NORMANDIE. Caen etc. 1835- .
1835-59 title: Annuaire des Cinq
Départements de l'Ancienne Normandie.

A239
ANNUAIRE du COLLÈGE de FRANCE.
Paris 1901-   .

A240
ANNUAL. DEPARTMENT of ANTIQUITIES
of JORDON. Amman 1951-   .
(ADAJ).

A241
ANNUAIRE de l'ÉCOLE PRATIQUE des
HAUTES ÉTUDES. IVe SECTION:
Sciences Philologiques et His-
toriques. Paris 1869-   .
Title varies slightly.

A242
ANNUAIRE de l'ÉCOLE PRATIQUE des
HAUTES ÉTUDES. Ve SECTION: Sci-
ences Religieuses. Paris &
Melun 1889/92-   .

A243
ANNALES: ÉCONOMIES, SOCIÉTÉS, CIVI-
LISATIONS. Paris 1946-   .
(AnnalesESC).

A244
ANNUAL EGYPTOLOGICAL BIBLIOGRAPHY
= Bibliographie Égyptologique
Annuelle. Leiden 1947-   .

A245
ANNÉE ÉPIGRAPHIQUE; revue des
publications épigraphiques relatives à l'antiquité romaine.
Paris 1888-   . (AE).

ANNALES de l'EST see E121.

A246
ANNALES de l'EST NANCY. Nancy
etc. 1887-   .

A247
ANNALES d'ÉTHIOPIE. Paris & Addis
Ababa 1955-   .

ANNALI FACOLTÀ di ECONOMIA e COM-
MERCIO in VERONA (Univ. Padua)
see A328.

ANNALES de la FACULTÉ des LETTRES
d'AIX. SERIE CLASSIQUE see
E127.

A248
ANNALI della FACOLTÀ di LETTERE,
FILOSOFIA e MAGISTERO. UNIV. di
CAGLIARI. Cagliari 1926-   .
(AFLC).

A249
ANNALI della FACOLTÀ di LETTERE e
FILOSOFIA. UNIV. di BARI. Bari
1954-   .

A250
ANNALI della FACOLTÀ di LETTERE e
  FILOSOFIA. UNIV. di LECCE.
  Lecce ?-   .

A251
ANNALI della FACOLTÀ di LETTERE e
  FILOSOFIA. UNIV. di MACERATA.
  Macerata 1968-   .

A252
ANNALI della FACOLTÀ di LETTERE e
  FILOSOFIA. UNIV. di NAPOLI.
  Naples 1951-   .

A253
ANNALI della FACOLTÀ di LETTERE e
  FILOSOFIA. UNIV. di PADOVA.
  Florence 1976-   .

A254
ANNALI della FACOLTÀ di LETTERE e
  FILOSOFIA. UNIV. degli STUDI di
  PERUGIA. Perugia 1963/4-   .

A255
ANNALES de la FACULTÉ des LETTRES
  et des SCIENCES HUMAINES. UNIV.
  AIX-MARSEILLES. Gap etc.
  1907-   . Faculty's name varies
  slightly.

A256
ANNALES de la FACULTÉ des LETTRES
  et SCIENCES HUMAINES. UNIV.
  DAKAR. Dakar 1971-   .

A257
ANNALES de la FACULTÉ des LETTRES
  et SCIENCES HUMAINES. UNIV. de
  NICE. Nice 1967-   .

A258
ANNALES publiées par la FACULTÉ
  des LETTRES et SCIENCES HUMAINES.
  UNIV. de TOULOUSE. Toulouse
  1951-   .

A259
ANNALI della FACOLTÀ di MAGISTERO.
  UNIV. di BARI. Bari 1959-   .

A260
ANNALI della FACOLTÀ di MAGISTERO.
  UNIV. di LECCE. Bari 1970/1-   .

A261
ANNALI della FACOLTÀ di MAGISTERO
  UNIV. di PALERMO. Palermo
  1950-   .

ANNUAIRE. FACULTÉ de PHILOSOPHIE
  de l'UNIVERSITÉ de SKOPJE see
  G65.

A262
ANNALES. FÉDÉRATION ARCHÉOLOGIQUE
  et HISTORIQUE de BELGIQUE.
  place varies 1885-   .

A263
ANNALES. FRANCUSKI INSTITUT, ZA-
  GREB = Institut Français de
  Zagreb. Zagreb 1937-47
  1953/4?-   .

A264
ANNALES FRIBOURGEOISES. Friburg
  1913-   .

A265
ANNALES de GÉOGRAPHIE. Paris
  1891-   .

A266
ANNALEN van de GESCHIED- en OUD-
  HEIDKUNDIGE KRING van RONSE =
  Annales du Cercle Historique et
  Archéologique de Renaix. Ronse
  ?-   .

A267
ANNALES de HAUTE-PROVENCE. Digne
  1880-   . Title until 1958:
  Annales des Basses-Alpes. Suspended 1921-24.

A268
ANNUARIUM HISTORIAE CONCILIORUM
  = Internationale Zeitschrift für
  Konziliengeschichtsforschung.
  Munich etc. 1969-   .

ANNALES d'HISTOIRE du DROIT see
  C283.

A269
ANNALEN des HISTORISCHEN VEREINS
  für den NIEDERRHEIN. Cologne
  1855-   .
  --. Beiheft. 1896-?.

ANNALES de l'INSTITUT ARCHÉOLO-
GIQUE (Rome) see A271.

ANNALI dell'INSTITUTO ARCHEOLOGICA
(Rome) see A271.

A270
ANNALES de l'INSTITUT ARCHÉOLO-
GIQUE du LUXEMBOURG. Arlon
1847/9-   . 1847-55 title: Annales de la Société pour la Conservation des Monuments Historiques et des Oeuvres d'Art dans
la Province de Luxembourg.

ANNALES de l'INSTITUT ARCHÉOLO-
GIQUE du LUXEMBOURG. SUPPLEMENT
see B310.

A271
ANNALI dell'INSTITUTO di CORRIS-
PONDENZA ARCHEOLOGICA = Annales
de l'Institut de Correspondance
Archéologique. Rome & Berlin
1829-85. 1843, 1845-53 title:
Annales de l'Institut Archéolo-
gique = Annali dell'Instituto
Archeologica. 1854-56 published
in the Institute's Monumenti,
Annali e Bullettini.

A272
ANNALES de l'INSTITUT d'ÉTUDES
ORIENTALES (Univ. d'Alger).
Algiers 1934/5-   .

ANNALES INSTITUT FRANÇAIS de ZA-
GREB see A263.

A273
ANNALY INSTITUTA IMENI N.P. KONDA-
KOVA = Annales de l'Institut Kondakov. Belgrad 1927-40. 1927-36
title: Seminarium Kondakovianum.

ANNALES de l'INSTITUT KONDAKOV
see A273.

A274
ANNUAIRE de l'INSTITUT de PHILOLO-
GIE et d'HISTOIRE ORIENTALES et
SLAVES (Univ. Brussels). Brus-
sels etc. 1932/3-   . 1932-35
issued by the Institut de Philo-
logie et d'Histoire Orientales.
(AIPhO, AIPHOS).

A275
ANNALES de l'INSTITUT de PHILOSO-
PHIE (Univ. Libre de Bruxelles).
Brussels 1969-   .

A276
ANNALES INSTITUTORUM quae provehen-
dis humanioribus disciplinis
artibusque colendis a variis in
urbe erecta sunt nationibus.
Rome 1928-   .

A277
ANNALES ISLAMOLOGIQUES. Cairo
1954-   . 1954-57 title: Mélanges Islamologiques.

ANNALI dell'ISTITUTO di CORRIS-
PONDENZA ARCHEOLOGICA see A271.

A278
ANNUARIO dell'ISTITUTO GIAPPONESE
di CULTURA. Rome 1963/4-   .

A279
ANNALI dell'ISTITUTO ITALIANO di
NUMISMATICA. Rome 1954-   .
(AIIN),

A280
ANNALI dell'ISTITUTO ITALIANO per
gli STUDI STORICI. Naples
1967/8-   .

A281
ANNALI dell'ISTITUTO ORIENTALE.
(Univ. Napoli). Naples 1929-38
1940-58. Institute's name varies
slightly.
--. Sezione di Archeologia e
Storia Antica. Seminario di
Studi Mondo Classico. 1960?-   .
--. Sezione Filologico-Letter-
aria. 1960?-   .
--. Sezione di Linguistica.
1959-   .
--.--. Quaderni. 1960-   .

ANNALI. ISTITUTO SUPERIORE ORIEN-
TALE, NAPLES see A281.

ANNALI dell'ISTITUTO UNIVERSITARIO
ORIENTALE di NAPOLI see A281.

ANNUAIRE du JÁSZMÚZEUM de JÁSZ-
BERÉNY see J82.

A282
ANNALES. LABORATOIRE de RECHERCHE
des MUSÉES de FRANCE. Paris
1970-   .

A283
ANNALI LATERANENSI (Pontificio
Museo Missionario Etnologico).
Rome 1937-   .

A284
ANNUAL of LEEDS UNIVERSITY. ORIEN-
TAL SOCIETY. Leiden 1958/9-   .

A285
ANNALI del LICEO CLASSICO G. GARI-
BALDI di PALERMO. Palermo ?-   .

A286
ANNALES LITTÉRAIRES de l'UNIVERSITÉ
de BESANÇON. Paris etc. 1946-53.
1946-47 title: Annales littéraires de Franche-Comité.
--. Sér. Archéologie. 1954-   .

ANNALES. MAṢLAḤAT al-ĀTHĀR see
A304.

ANNUAIRE. al-MATḤAF al-YŪNĀNĪ al-
RŪMĀNĪ, ALEXANDRIA see A289.

A287
ANNALES du MIDI; revue de la FRANCE
MÉRIDIONALE. Toulouse 1889-   .
(AMidi).

ANNALES MUSEI AGRIENSIS see E13.

ANNUAIRE des MUSÉES d'ANTIQUITÉS
d'ISTANBUL see I128.

ANNUAIRE du MUSÉE national ARCHÉ--
OLOGIQUE de PLOVDIV see G60.

A288
ANNUAIRE des MUSÉES royaux des
BEAUX-ARTS de BELGIQUE = Jaar-
boek der Koninklijke Museums
voor Schoone Kunsten van België.
Antwerp 1938-   .

ANNUAIRE du MUSÉE BULGARE de SOFIA
see G61.

ANNALES MUSEI DEBRECENIENSIS de
FRIDERICO DÉRI nominati see D5.

ANNUAIRE du MUSÉE d'EGER see E13.

ANNALES du MUSÉE FERENC MÓRA see
M272.

A289
ANNUAIRE du MUSÉE GRECO-ROMAIN
d'ALEXANDRIE. Alexandria
1932/3-   . 1932/3 title: Annuario del Museo Greco-Romano.

ANNUAIRE des MUSÉES d'ISTANBUL
see I128.

ANNALES MUSEI MISKOLCIENSIS de
HERMAN OTTÓ nominati see H54.

ANNALES MUSEI nationalis SLOVACI
see Z16.

ANNUAIRE du MUSÉE national de SOFIA
see G61.

ANNALES MUSEI SZEKSZÁRDIENSIS de
BÉRI BALOGH ÁDAM nominati see
S304.

ANNUAIRE du MUSÉE national de
VARSOVIE see R307.

A290
ANNALES de NANTES et du PAYS
NANTAIS. Nantes ?-   .

A291
ANNALES de NORMANDIE. Caen 1951-   .

ANNUAL. ONTARIO MUSEUM see A300.

ANNUAL. ORIENTAL SOCIETY. LEEDS
UNIVERSITY see A284.

A292
ANNALEN van den OUDHEIDKUNDIGE
KRING van het LAND van WAAS =
Annales du Cercle Archéologique
du Pays de Waes. St. Niklaas
1862-   .

ANNUAL. PALESTINE EXPLORATION FUND
see P20.

A293
ANNALES des PAYS NIVERNAIS. Nevers
?-   .

A294
ANNÉE PHILOLOGIQUE; bibliothèque
critique et analytique de l'antiquité greco-latine. Paris
1924/6-   . (APh).

ANNUAL REPORT and BULLETIN. INSTI-
TUTE of ARCHAEOLOGY (Univ. London) see A297.

A295
ANNUAL REPORT of the DIRECTOR of
the DEPARTMENT of ANTIQUITIES of
CYPRUS. Nicosia 1949-   .
Supplements and at times replaces
the Report of the Department of
Antiquities of Cyprus. (ARDC).

A296
ANNUAL REPORT. FOGG ART MUSEUM
(Harvard Univ.). Cambridge,
Mass. 1898-   .

A297
ANNUAL REPORT. INSTITUTE of ARCH-
AEOLOGY. (Univ. London). London
1937-56. 1955/6 title: Annual
report and bulletin.

A298
ANNUAL REPORT of the MUSEUM of.
FINE ARTS, BOSTON. Boston etc.
1876-   .

ANNUAL REPORTS and PROCEEDINGS.
BARROW NATURALISTS' FIELD CLUB
see B15.

A299
ANNUAL REPORT of the SOCIETY for
LIBYAN STUDIES. London
1969/70-   .

ANNUAL REPORT and TRANSACTIONS of
the NORTH STAFFORDSHIRE FIELD
CLUB see T89.

A300
ANNUAL. ROYAL ONTARIO MUSEUM. ART
& ARCHAEOLOGY DIVISION. Toronto
1959-   .

ANNUAIRE SCIENTIFIQUE de la FACULTÉ
de PHILOSOPHIE de l'UNIVERSITÉ
d'ATHÈNES see E86.

A301
ANNUARIO della SCUOLA ARCHEOLOGICA
di ATENE e delle MISSIONI ITALI-
ANI in ORIENTE. Bergamo 1914-
Variant title: Annuario della
Scuola Archeologica Italiana.
(ASAtene, ASAA).

ANNUARIO della SCUOLA ARCHEOLOGICA
ITALIANA see A301.

A302
ANNALI della SCUOLA NORMALE SU-
PERIORE di PISA. CLASSE di LET-
TERE e FILOSOFIA. Pisa etc.
1873-   . Subtitle until 1929:
Filosofia e Filologia. 1922-27
name of the school: R. Scuola
Normale Superiore Universitaria
di Pisa.

ANNALES. SECTIO CLASSICA (UNIV.
BUDAPEST) see A327.

ANNALES. SECTIO HISTORICA (UNIV.
BUDAPEST) see A327.

ANNALES. SECTIO LINGUISTICA.
(UNIV. BUDAPEST) see A327.

ANNALES. SECTIO PHILOLOGICA.
(UNIV. BUDAPEST) see A327.

A303
ANNALI del SEMINARIO GIURIDICO
UNIV. di PALERMO. Palermo
1912-   .

A304
ANNALES du SERVICE des ANTIQUITÉS
de l'ÉGYPT. Cairo 1900-   .
(ASAE).
--. Supplement. 1946-   .

ANNALES du SERVICE ARCHÉOLOGIQUES
de l'IRAN see A628.

ANNALI. SEZIONE di ARCHEOLOGIA e
STORIA ANTICA see A281.

ANNALI. SEZIONE FILOLOGICO-LETTER-
ARIA. ISTITUTO ORIENTALE di NA-
POLI see A281.

ANNALI. SEZIONE LINGUISTICA. ISTI-
TUTO ORIENTALE di NAPOLI see
A281.

A305
ANNUAIRE de la SOCIÉTÉ des AMIS de
  la BIBLIOTHÈQUE de SELESTAT.
  Selestat 1952?-   .

A306
ANNESCI. SOCIÉTÉ des AMIS du VIEIL
  ANNECY. Annecy 1953-   .

ANNÁLES SOCIÉTÉ ARCHÉOLOGIQUE de
  l'ARRONDISSEMENT de NIVELLES
  see A309.

A307
ANNALES de la SOCIÉTÉ royale
  d'ARCHÉOLOGIE de BRUXELLES.
  Brussels 1887-   . Society's
  name varies slightly.

A308
ANNUAIRE de la SOCIÉTÉ royale
  d'ARCHÉOLOGIE de BRUXELLES.
  Brussels 1890-   .

A309
ANNALES de la SOCIÉTÉ d'ARCHÉOLOGIE
  d'HISTOIRE et de FOLKLORE de NI-
  VELLES et du BRABANT WALLON.
  Nivelles etc. 1890-   . Also
  published under the earlier
  names of the society: Société
  Archéologique de l'Arondisse-
  ment de Nivelles and Société
  Archéologique et folklorique de
  Nivelles et du Brabant Wallon.

A310
ANNALES de la SOCIÉTÉ ARCHÉOLOGIQUE
  de NAMUR. Namur 1849-   .

ANNUAIRE de la SOCIÉTÉ ARCHÉOLO-
  GIQUE de la PROVINCE de CONSTAN-
  TINE see R49.

ANNALES de la SOCIÉTÉ pour la CON-
  SERVATION des MONUMENTS HISTO-
  RIQUES et des OEUVRES d'ART dans
  la PROVINCE de LUXEMBOURG see
  A270.

ANNALES de la SOCIÉTÉ d'ÉMULATION
  pour l'HISTOIRE et des ANTIQUI-
  TÉS de la FLANDRE see H19.

A311
ANNUAIRE. SOCIÉTÉ d'ÉMULATION de

la VENDÉE.   La Roche-sur-Yon
  1855-   .

ANNUAIRE de la SOCIÉTÉ des ÉTUDES
  BYZANTINES see E56.

ANNALES de la SOCIÉTÉ pour l'ÉTUDE
  de l'HISTOIRE et des ANTIQUITÉS
  de la FLANDRE OCCIDENTALE see
  H19.

A312
ANNUAIRE de la SOCIÉTÉ FRANÇAISE
  de NUMISMATIQUE.   Paris
  1866-   . Society's name 1866-
  88: Société Française de Numismatique et d'Archéologie.

A313
ANNALES de la SOCIÉTÉ d'HISTOIRE
  et d'ARCHÉOLOGIE de l'ARRONDIS-
  SEMENT de SAINT-MALO. Mortain
  1900-   . Society's name until
  1950: Société Historique et
  Archéologique de l'Arrondissement de Saint-Malo.

A314
ANNUAIRE de la SOCIÉTÉ d'HISTOIRE
  et d'ARCHÉOLOGIE de DAMBACH-la-
  VILLE, BARR, OBERNAI. Barr
  1967-   .

ANNALES de la SOCIÉTÉ d'HISTOIRE
  et d'ARCHÉOLOGIE de GAND see
  H22.

A315
ANNUAIRE. SOCIÉTÉ d'HISTOIRE et
  d'ARCHÉOLOGIE de la LORRAINE =
  Jahrbuch der Gesellschaft für
  Lothringische Geschichte und
  Altertumskunde. Matz 1888/9-   .

A316
ANNUAIRE de la SOCIÉTÉ HISTORIQUE
  et LITTERAIRE de COLMAR. Colmar
  1950?-   .

A317
ANNUAIRE de la SOCIÉTÉ d'HISTOIRE
  des RÉGIONS de THANN-GUEBWILLER.
  Mulhouse & Colmar 1948/50?-   .

A318
ANNUAIRE de la SOCIÉTÉ d'HISTOIRE

SÜNDGOVIENNE = Jahrbuch des
Sundgauvereins. Mulhouse
1952?-   .

A319
ANNUAIRE de la SOCIÉTÉ d'HISTOIRE
du VAL et de la VILLE de MUNSTER.
Munster 1927-   . Some volumes
also have title: Jahrbuch des
Geschichtsvereins für Stadt und
Tal Münster. Suspended 1939-57.

ANNALES. SOCIÉTÉ IMPERIALE ...
see ANNALES. SOCIÉTÉ ... (the
word imperiale is disregarded
in filing, but may have been
regarded in forming an abbreviation).

A320
ANNALES de la SOCIÉTÉ des LETTRES,
SCIENCES et ARTS des ALPES-MARI-
TIMES. Nice 1865-   .

ANNALES. SOCIÉTÉ NATIONALE ... see
ANNALES. SOCIÉTÉ ... (the word
nationale is disregarded in
filing, but may have been regarded in forming an abbreviation).

ANNALES. SOCIÉTÉ ROYALE ... see
ANNALES. SOCIÉTÉ ... (the word
royale is disregarded in filing
but may have been regarded in
forming an abbreviation).

A321
ANNALES de la SOCIÉTÉ SCIENTIFIQUE
et LITTÉRAIRE de CANNES et de
l'ARRONDISSEMENT de GRASSE.
Cannes etc. 1868-78/9 1928-   .
Earlier title: Mémoires de la
Société des Sciences Naturelles
(et Historiques) des Lettres et
des Beaux-arts de Cannes et de
l'Arondissement de Grasse.

A322
ANNALES de la SOCIÉTÉ des SCIENCES
NATURELLES et d'ARCHÉOLOGIE de
TOULON et du VAR. Toulon
1947?-   . Society's name var-
ies slightly.

ANNUAIRE. SOCIÉTÉ SUISSE de PHILO-
SOPHIE see S232.

ANNUAIRE de la SOCIÉTÉ SUISSE de
PRÉHISTOIRE et d'ARCHÉOLOGIE
see J50.

ANNUARIO della SOCIETÀ SVIZZERA di
PREISTORIA e d'ARCHEOLOGIA see
J50.

A323
ANNALI di STORIA del DIRITTO.
Milan 1957-   .

ANNUAL. SVENSKA TEOLOGISKA INSTITU-
TET see A324.

A324
ANNUAL of the SWEDISH THEOLOGICAL
INSTITUTE in JERUSALEM. Leiden
1962-   .

ANNÉE THÉOLOGIQUE see A325.

A325
ANNÉE THÉOLOGIQUE AUGUSTINIENNE.
Paris 1940-54. 1940-51 title:
Année Théologique.

A326
ANNALI TRIESTINI (Univ. Triesti).
Triesti 1929-   .
--. Sez. Ia.: Giurisprudenza,
economica, lettere. 1947-   .

ANNALES. UNIVERSITÉ d'AIX-MAR-
SEILLES. FACULTÉ des LETTRES et
des SCIENCES HUMAINES see A255.

ANNALI. UNIVERSITÀ di BARI. FACOLTÀ
di LETTERE e FILOSOFIA see
A249.

ANNALI. UNIVERISTÀ di BARI. FACOLTÀ
di MAGISTERO see A259.

A327
ANNALES UNIVERSITATIS scientiarum
BUDAPESTINENSES de ROLANDO EÖT-
VÖS nominatae. Budapest.
--. Sectio Classica. 1972-   .
--. Sectio Historica. 1957-   .
--. Sectio Linguistica. 1970-   .
--. Sectio Philologica. 1957-   .

ANNALI. UNIVERSITÀ di CAGLIARI.
FACOLTÀ di LETTERE, FILOSOFIA
e MAGISTERO see A248.

ANNALI. UNIVERSITÀ di LECCE. FACOL-
TÀ di LETTERE e FILOSOFIA   see
A250.

ANNALI. UNIVERSITÀ di LECCE. FACOL-
TÀ di MAGISTERO   see A260.

ANNALI. UNIVERSITÀ di MACERATA. FA-
COLTÀ di LETTERE e FILOSOFIA
see A251.

ANNALI. UNIVERSITÀ di NAPOLI. FA-
COLTÀ di LETTERE e FILOSOFIA
see A252.

ANNALES. UNIVERSITÉ de NICE. FACUL-
TÉ des LETTRES et SCIENCES
HUMAINES   see A257.

A328
ANNALI. UNIVERSITÀ di PADOVA. FA-
COLTÀ di ECONOMIA e COMMERCIO
in VERONA. Verona 1965-   .

ANNALI. UNIVERSITÀ di PADOVA. FA-
COLTÀ di LETTERE e FILOSOFIA
see A253.

ANNALI UNIVERSITÀ di PALERMO. FA-
COLTÀ di MAGISTERO see A261.

ANNALI. UNIVERSITÀ di PALERMO.
SEMINARIO GIURIDICO   see A303.

A329
ANNALES de l'UNIVERSITÉ de PARIS.
Paris 1926-41 1947-   .

ANNALI. UNIVERSITÀ degli studi di
PERUGIA. FACOLTÀ di LETTERE e
FILOSOFIA see A254.

ANNUAIRE. UNIVERSITÉ de SKOPJE.
FACULTÉ de PHILOSOPHIE   see G65.

ANNUAIRE de l'UNIVERSITÉ de SOFIA
see G64.

ANNALES. UNIVERSITÉ de TOULOUSE.
FACULTÉ des LETTRES et SCIENCES
HUMAINES see A258.

ANNALES de l'UNIVERSITÉ de TOU-
LOUSE-LE MIRAIL see P25.

A330
ANNALES VALAISANNES. Lausaunne
etc. 1916-   . Publication
suspended during World War II?

ANNALEN. VEREIN für NASSAUISCHE
ALTERTUMSKUNDE und GESCHICHTS-
FORSCHUNG see N10.

A331
ANNUAL. WORCESTER ART MUSEUM.
Worcester, Mass. 1935/6-   .

A332
ANTE-NICENE CHRISTIAN LIBRARY;
translations of the Fathers down
to 325 A.D. Edinburgh 1867-72.
Available in several printings.

A333
ANTEMURALE (Institutum Historicum
Polonicum Romae). Rome 1954-   .

A334
ANTHOLOGIA GRAECA / H. Beckby.
Munich 1965. 1st edition 1957-58.

A335
ANTHOLOGIA LYRICA GRAECA / E.
Diehl. 3. ed. Leipzig 1949-52.
(Bibliotheca Scriptorum Graecorum
et Romanorum Teubneriana). 1st
edition 1925.

A336
ANTHROPOLOGIA HUNGARICA. Budapest
1956-   . 1956-61 title: Crania
Hungarica.

A337
ANTHROPOLÓGIAI KÖZLEMÉNYEK. Budapest 1957-   .

A338
ANTHROPOLOGICAL QUARTERLY. Washington D.C. 1928-   . 1928-52
title: Primitive man.

A339
ANTHROPOLOGIE. Paris 1890-   .
(L'Anthr).

A340
ANTHROPOLOGIE. Hamburg 1952-   .

A341
ANTHROPOLOGIE; časopis věnovaný
  fysické anthropologii. Prague
  1923-   .

A342
ANTHROPOLOGIE (Marovske Muzeum).
  Brno 1962-   .

A343
ANTHROPOS; revue internationale
  d'ethnologie et de linguistique.
  Friburg 1906-   .

A344
ANTICHITÀ. Rome 1947-50.

A345
ANTICHITÀ ALTOADRIATICHE. Udine
  1972-   .

A346
ANTICHITÀ PISANE. Pisa 1974-   .

A347
ANTICHNAĬA DREVNOST'I SREDNIE VEKA.
  Sverdlovsk 19??-   . Part of the
  Uchenve Zapiski of the Ural'ski
  Gosudarstvennyi Universitet.

A348
ANTICHNYI MIR i ARKHEOLOGIIA.
  Saratov 1972-   .

A349
ANTICHTHON; journal of the Australian Society for Classical Studies. Sydney 1967-   .

A350
ANTIEK. Lochem 1966-   .

A351
ANTIK TANALMÁNYOK = Studia Antiqua.
  Budapest 1954-   . (AntTan, AT).

A352
ANTIKE. Berlin & Leipzig 1925-44.

A353
ANTIKE und ABENDLAND. Hamburg
  1945-   . (AuA).

A354
ANTIKE und CHRISTENTUM / F. J. Dölger & T. Klauser. Münster 1929-

50. None published 1931, 1933,
  1935, 1937-39, 1941-49.

A355
ANTIKE DENKMÄLER (Kaiserliches
  Deutsches Archäologisches Insti-
  tut). Berlin 1886/90-1927/31?.
  (AD).

A356
ANTIKEN GEMMEN / A. Furtwängler.
  Leipzig 1900. Reprint Amsterdam
  1964-65. (AG).

A357
ANTIKE GEMMEN in DEUTSCHEN SAMMLUN-
  GEN. Munich 1968-   . (AGDS,
  AGD).

A358
ANTIKEN GEMMEN des KUNSTHISTORIS-
  CHEN MUSEUMS in WIEN. Munich
  1973-   .

A359
ANTIKE INSCHRIFTEN aus JUGOSLAVIEN
  / V. Hoffiller & B. Saria. Za-
  greb 1938. Only vol. 1 appeared.
  (AIJ).

A360
ANTIKE KUNST. Basel etc. 1958-   .
  (AK, AntK).

A361
ANTIKE MÜNZEN und GESCHNITTENE
  STEINE. Berlin 1969?-   .

A362
ANTIKEN MÜNZEN NORD-GRIECHENLANDS /
  F. Imhoof-Blumer. Berlin 1898-
  1935.

A363
ANTIKE PLASTIK. Berlin 1962-   .

A364
ANTIKEN SARKOPHAGRELIEFS / C. Robert
  & C. Rodenwaldt et al. Berlin
  1980-   .

A365
ANTIKE WELT. Zurich 1970-   .
  (AW).

A366
ANTIKVARISK TIDSKRIFT för SVERIGE.
Stockholm 1864-1924. Title of
vols. 1-17: Antiqvarisk tidskrift
för Sverige.

A367
ANTINOOPOLIS PAPYRI / C. H. Roberts
et al. London 1950-67. (Egypt
Exploration Society. Graeco-
Roman Memoirs; 28, 37, 47).
(PAnt).

A368
ANTIOCH REVIEW. Yellow Springs,
Ohio 1941-   .

ANTIQ-: entries beginning with
this spelling are here interfiled.

A369
ANTIQUA; Special-Zeitschrift für
prähistorische Archäologie und
einschlägige Gebiete. Zurich
1883-91.

A370
ANTIQUA; Veröffentlichungen der
Schweizerischen Gesellschaft für
Ur- und Frühgeschichte. Basel
1973-   .

A371
ANTIQUARY; a magazine devoted to
the study of the past. London
1880-1915.

A372
ANTIQUITAS. Salerno 1946-47.

A373
ANTIQUITY. Gloucester 1927-   .

A374
ANTIQUITÉS AFRICAINES. Paris
1967-   . (AntAfr).

A375
ANTIQUITIES of ATHENS / J. Stuart
& N. Revett. London 1762-1830.
Reprint New York 1980-   .

A376
ANTIQUITÉ CLASSIQUE. Brussels
1932-   . (AC, AntCl).

ANTIQUARIAN COMMUNICATIONS (Cambridge Antiquarian Society) see
P195.

A377
ANTIQUITAS HUNGARICA. Budapest
1947-   .

A378
ANTIQUARIES JOURNAL (Society of
Antiquaries of London). London
1921-   . (AntJ, AJ).

A379
ANTIQUITÉS NATIONALES. Saint Ger-
main en Laye 1969?-   .

ANTIQUITÉS NATIONALES et INTERNA-
TIONALES see A477.

A380
ANTIQUITÄTEN RUNDSCHAU. Eisenach
1902-32.

A381
ANTIQUITY and SURVIVAL. The Hague
1955/6-   .

ANTIQVARISK TIDSKRIFT för SVERIGE
see A366.

ANTIQUITÉ VIVANTE see Z85.

A382
ANTONIANUM; periodicum philosophi-
co-theologicum trimestre. Rome
1926-   .

ANU-: entries beginning with this
spelling are here interfiled.
See also ANAL- and ANN-.

A383
ANUARUL COMISIUNII MONUMENTELOR IS-
TORICE. SECTIA PENTRU TRANSILVA-
NIA. Cluj 1926/8-   .

A384
ANUARIO del CUERPO FACULTATIVO de
ARCHIVEROS, BIBLIOTECARIOS y
ARQUEÓLOGOS. Madrid 1881-82
1934-35. Title varies slightly.

A385
ANUARIO de ESTUDIOS MEDIEVALES.
Barcelona 1964-   .

A386
ANUARIO de FILOLOGIA. Barcelona
  1975-   .

A387
ANUARIO de HISTORIA. Mexico City
  1961-   .

A388
ANUARIO de HISTORIA del DERECHO
  ESPAÑOL. Madrid 1924-   .
  (AHDE).

A389
ANUARI. INSTITUT d'ESTUDÍS CATALANS.
  SECCIÓ HISTÓRICO-ARQUEOLÓGICA.
  Barcelona 1907-31. Vols. 1-4
  issued without name of section.

A390
ANUARUL INSTITUTULUI de ISTORIE şi
  ARHEOLOGIE. Cluj 1959-   .

A391
ANUARUL INSTITUTULUI de ISTORIE şi
  ARHEOLOGIE. Iaşi 1964-   .

A392
ANUARUL INSTITUTULUI de STUDII CLA-
  SICE. Cluj 1928/32-44/8. (AISC).

A393
ANUARIO de PREHISTORIA MADRILEÑA.
  Madrid 1930-33/5?

A394
ANUARUL UNIVERSITĂTII din BUCUREŞTI.
  Bucharest 1930/1-   .

ANZEIGER see A421.

ANZEIGER der AKADEMIE der WISSEN-
  SCHAFTEN in KRAKAU. PHILOLOGISCHE
  und HISTORISCH-PHILOSOPHISCHE
  CLASSE see B246.

ANZEIGER. AKADEMIE der WISSENSCHAF-
  TEN, MÜNCHEN see G12.

ANZEIGER der AKADEMIE der WISSEN-
  SCHAFTEN in WIEN. PHILOSOPHISCH-
  HISTORISCHE KLASSE see A399.

A395
ANZEIGER für die ALTERTUMSWISSEN-
  SCHAFT. Innsbruck etc. 1948-   .
  (AnzAlt, AnzAW).

ANZEIGER der BAYERISCHEN AKADEMIE
  der WISSENSCHAFTEN see G12.

A396
ANZEIGER für DEUTSCHES ALTERTUM und
  DEUTSCHE LITTERATUR. Berlin
  1876-   .

ANZEIGER für ELSÄSSISCHE ALTERTUMS-
  KUNDE see C5.

A397
ANZEIGER des GERMANISCHEN NATIONAL-
  MUSEUMS. Nuremberg 1884/6-   .

A398
ANZEIGER für INDOGERMANISCHE
  SPRACH- und ALTERTUMSKUNDE.
  Strasbourg 1891-1930? Supplement
  to Indogermanische Forschungen.

ANZEIGER. MÜNCHEN see G12.

A399
ANZEIGER der ÖSTERREICHISCHEN AKA-
  DEMIE der WISSENSCHAFTEN. PHILO-
  SOPHISCH-HISTORISCHE KLASSE.
  Vienna 1864-   . Name of Aca-
  demy also appears as Akademie
  der Wissenschaften in Wien (other
  minor changes). (ANZWien, AAWW).

ANZEIGER. PHILOSOPHISCH-HISTORISCHE
  KLASSE. ÖSTERREICHISCHE AKADEMIE
  der WISSENSCHAFTEN see A399.

A400
ANZEIGER für SCHWEIZERISCHE ALTER-
  TUMSKUNDE = Indicateur d'Anti-
  quités Suisses. Zurich 1868-
  1938. 1868 title: Berichte der
  Antiquarischen Gesellschaft in
  Zurich. Continued as Zeitschrift
  für schweizerische Archäologie
  und Kunstgeschichte; supersedes
  Anzeiger für schweizerische
  Geschichte und Altertumskunde.

A401
ANZEIGER für SCHWEIZERISCHE GE-
  SCHICHTE und ALTERTUMSKUNDE = Indicateur d'Histoire et d'Antiquités Suisses. Zurich 1855-69. Superseded by Anzeiger für schweizerische Altertumskunde.

ANZEIGER. WIEN   see   A399.

A402
APERION; a journal for ancient
  philosophy and science. Clayton,
  Victora 1966-   .

A403
APOLLO; a journal of the arts.
  London 1925-   .

A404
APPENZELLISCHE JAHRBÜCHER.   Trogen
  1854-56/7 1860-84 1886-   .

A405
APULUM; acta Musei Apulensis. Alba
  Iulia 1939-   .

A406
AQUILEIA NOSTRA; bollettino dell'As-
  sociazione Nazionale per Aquileia.
  Milan & Aquileia 1930-   .

Arango-Ruiz, V. see I58.

ARBEITEN des ARCHÄOLOGISCHEN INSTI-
  TUTS der k. Ung. Horothy Miklós
  UNIVERSITÄT see D88.

A407
ARBEITEN zur LITERATUR und GE-
  SCHICHTE des HELLENISTISCHEN JU-
  DENTUMS. Leiden 1968-   .

ARBEITEN der TOMSKER STAATSUNIVER-
  SITÄT see T127.

A408
ARBEITS- und FORSCHUNGSBERICHTE
  zur SÄCHSISCHEN BODENKMALPFLEGE.
  Leipzig etc. 1956-   .

A409
ARBEITSBLÄTTER für RESTAURATOREN.
  Mainz 1968-   .

ÅRBOK is filed as if spelled AARBOK.

A410
ARBOR; revista general del Consejo
  Superior de Investigaciones
  Científicas. Madrid 1944-   .

A411
ARCADIA; Zeitschrift für verglei-

chende Literaturwissenschaft.
  Berlin 1966-   .

A412
ARCHÄOGRAPHIE. Berlin 1969-   .
  Subtitle through 1975: Archäologie und elektronische Datenver-
  arbeitung.

ARCHAEOL-, ARCHÄOL- and ARCHEOL-:
  entries beginning with this
  spelling are here interfiled.
  See also ARCHAIOL-, ARKHEOL-
  ARHEOL- and ARQUEOL-.

A413
ARCHAEOLOGY. Cambridge, Mass.
  1948-   .

A414
ARCHEOLOGIA. Rome 1962-   .

A415
ARCHEOLOGIA. Paris 1964-   . Subtitle until 1976: Trésor des
  áges.

A416
ARCHEOLOGIA. Torun 1968-   . Subseries of the Nauki Humanisty
  Cznospoleczne of the University
  of Torun.

A417
ARCHAEOLOGIA; or miscellaneous
  tracts relating to antiquity.
  London 1770-   .

A418
ARCHEOLOGIA; rocznik Instytutu His-
  torii Kultury Materialnej Polska
  Akademii nauk. Warsaw 1947-   .
  Earlier issued by the Pánstwowe
  Muzeum Archeologiczne and the
  Towarzystwo Archeologiczne.

A419
ARCHÉOLOGIE (Centre National de
  Recherches Archéologiques en
  Belgique). Wezembeek ?-   .

ARCHÉOLOGIE (Kiev 1947-   ) see
  A579.

ARCHÉOLOGIE (Paris 1954-   ) see
  A286.

A420
ARCHAEOLOGIA AELIANA. Newcastle-
upon-Tyne 1822-   .

A421
ARCHÄOLOGISCHER ANZEIGER. Berlin
1849-67 1889-   . 1849-67 published as a supplement to Archäologische Zeitung; 1889-1975 as a
supplement to the Jahrbuch des
Deutschen Archäologischen Instituts. (ArchAnz).

A422
ARCHAEOLOGIE AUSTRIACA. Vienna
1948-   .

A423
ARCHÉOLOGIE en BAS-LIMOUSIN. Tulle
1965-   .

A 424
ARCHAEOLOGIA BELGICA. Brussels
1950-   .

A425
ARCHÄOLOGISCHE BIBLIOGRAPHIE. Berlin etc. 1913-   . 1913-72 issued as a supplement to the Jahrbuch des Deutschen Archäologischen Instituts. 1913-31 title:
Bibliographie zum Jahrbuch des
Deutschen Archäologischen Instituts. Continues bibliographies
published earlier in the Jahrbuch.

A426
ARCHAEOLOGICAL BIBLIOGRAPHY for
GREAT BRITAIN and IRELAND. Lon-
don 1940-   . 1940-47 title:
Archaeological Bulletin for the
British Isles. 1948-49 title:
Archaeological Bulletin for Great
Britain and Ireland.

A427
ARCHÉOLOGIE en BRETAGNE. Brest
1974?-   .

ARCHAEOLOGICAL BULLETIN for the
BRITISH ISLES see A426.

A428
ARCHAEOLOGIA CAMBRENSES. London
1846-   .

A429
ARCHAEOLOGIA CANTIANA (Kent Archaeological Society). London
1858-   .

A430
ARCHEOLOGIA CLASSICA. Rome
1949-   . (ArchClass, ArchCl,
AC).

A431
ARCHAEOLOGY of CRETE / J. D. S.
Pendlebury. London 1939. (Me-
theun's Handbooks of Archaeology). Several reprints in the
1960'S.

A432
ARCHÄOLOGISCH-EPIGRAPHISCHE MIT-
THEILUNGEN aus OESTERREICH-UN-
GARN. Vienna 1877-97. (AEM).

A433
ARCHAEOLOGIAI ÉRTESITÖ. Budapest
1868-   . (ArchErt, AErt, AE).

ARCHEOLOGIJA un ETNOGRAFIJA see
A567.

A434
ARCHÄOLOGISCHE FORSCHUNGEN. Berlin
1975-   .

A435
ARCHÄOLOGISCHE FÜHRER der SCHWEIZ.
Basel 197?-   .

A436
ARCHAEOLOGIA GEOGRAPHICA; Beiträge
zur vergleichenden geographisch-
kartographischen Methode in der
Urgeschichtsforschung. Hamburg
1950-   .

A437
ARCHAEOLOGICA HOMERICA. Göttingen
1967-   .

A438
ARCHAEOLOGIA HUNGARICA; a Magyar
Nemzeti Múzeum régészeti osztályának kiadványai = Acta archaeologica Musei Nationalis Hungarici. Budapest 1926-   . Suspended 1944-49?

ARCHAEOLOGIA HUNGARICA (1939-45)
   see F21.

A439
ARCHÄOLOGISCHE INFORMATIONEN.
   Cologne 1972-   .

A440
ARCHÄOLOGISCHES INTELLIGENZBLATT
   zur ALLGEMEINEN LITERATUR ZEI-
   TUNG. Halle 1833-37.

ARCHAEOLOGIA IUGOSLAVICA see
   A442.

A441
ARCHAEOLOGICAL JOURNAL. London
   1844-   . (ArchJ, AJ).

A442
ARCHAEOLOGIA JUGOSLAVICA. Belgrad
   1954-   . (ArchIug).

A443
ARCHÄOLOGISCHES KORRESPONDENZBLATT.
   Mainz 1971-   .

A444
ARCHAEOLOGIAI KÖZLEMÉNYEK. Budapest 1859-99.

A445
ARCHÉOLOGIE MÉDIÉVALE. Caen
   1971-   .

A446
ARCHÄOLOGISCHE MITTEILUNGEN aus
   IRAN. Berlin 1929-   . Sus-
   pended 1939-67. (AMI, AMIran).
   --. Ergänzungsband. 1938-   .
   Suspended 1939-77.

A447
ARCHÄOLOGISCHE NACHRICHTEN aus
   BADEN. Freiburg i.B. ?-   .

A448
ARCHAEOLOGICAL NEWS. Tallahassee
   1972-   .

A449
ARCHAEOLOGICAL NEWS LETTER. London
   1948-   .

A450
ARCHAEOLOGICAL NEWSLETTER. (Ameri-
can Schools of Oriental Research).
Ann Arbor, Mich. 1939-   .

ARCHAEOLOGICAL NEWSLETTER (Jerusalem) see H2.

A451
ARCHAEOLOGIA OXONIENSIS. Oxford
   1892-95.

A452
ARCHAEOLOGIA POLONA. Warsaw etc.
   1958-   .

A453
ARCHEOLOGIA POLSKI. Wroclaw etc.
   1957-   .

ARCHEÓLOGO PORTUGUÊS see A591.

A454
ARCHAEOLOGICAL REPORT (Egypt Exploration Fund). London 1890/1-
   1912/3.

A455
ARCHAEOLOGICAL REPORTS. London
   1954-   . Prior to 1954 included
   in the Journal of Hellenic Studies; since 1954 issued as a supplement to that journal.

A456
ARCHAEOLOGICAL REVIEW. Bristol,
   Eng. 1966-   .

A457
ARCHEOLOGIKÉ ROZHLEDY = Nouvelles
   Archéologiques. Prague 1949-   .
   (AR).

A458
ARCHÄOLOGIE des SCHWEIZ = Archéologie Suisse = Archeologia Svizzera. Basel 1978-   .

A459
ARCHAEOLOGIA SCOTIA. Edinburgh
   1792-1890.

A460
ARCHAEOLOGICA SLOVACA. Bratislava
   --. Fontes. 1957-   .
   --. Monographiae. 1957-   .

ARCHÉOLOGIE SOVIETIQUE see S126.

A461
ARCHEOLOGICKÉ STUDIJNI MATERIÁLY.
  Prague 1964-   .

ARCHÉOLOGIE SUISSE see A458.

ARCHAEOLOGICAL SURVEY of EGYPT see
  M113.

ARCHEOLOGIA SVIZZERA see A458.

A462
ARCHÄOLOGISCHE VERÖFFENTLICHUNGEN
  (Deutsches Archäologisches Institut. Abteilung Kairo). Berlin
  1970-   .

A463
ARCHAEOLOGIA VIVA. Paris 1968-69.
  Published in English, French,
  and German editions.

A464
ARCHÄOLOGISCHE ZEITUNG. Berlin
  1843-85. (AZ, ArchZeit).
  --. Beilage. 1844-48.

ARCHÄOLOGISCHE ZEITUNG. SUPPLEMENT
  see A421.

A465
ARCHAEOMETRY. Oxford 1958-   .

A466
ARCHAIC GREEK GEMS / J. Boardman.
  London & Evanston, Ill. 1968.

A467
ARCHAIOGNŌSIA. Athens 1980-   .

ARCHAIOL-: see also ARCHAEOL-,
  ARKHEOL-, ARHEOL- and ARQUEOL-.

A468
ARCHAIOLOGIA. Athens 1981-   .

A469
ARCHAIOLOGIKA ANALEKTA ex ATHĒNŌN
  = Athens Annals of Archaeology.
  Athens 1968-   . (AAA).

A470
ARCHAIOLOGIKON DELTION. Athens
  1915-33/5 1960-   . In two sections: Chronika and Meletai.
  (ArchDelt, Deltion, AD).

A471
ARCHAIOLOGIKĒ EPHĒMERIS. Athens
  1837-60 1862-74 1883-   .
  1837-60 1883-1909 title: Ephēmeris Archaiologikē. (AE, Ephem).

A472
ARCHEION EKKLĒSIASTIKĒS HISTORIAS.
  Istanbul 1911-   .

A473
ARCHEION EUBOÏKŌN MELETŌN. Athens
  1935-   .

A474
ARCHEION PONTOU. Athens 1928-   .

A475
ARCHEION THESSALIKŌN MELETŌN. Volos
  Volos 1972-   .

A476
ARCHEION tōn VYZANTINŌN MNĒMEIŌN
  tēs HELLADOS. Athens 1935-   .
  (ABME).

A477
ARCHÉOCIVILISATION. Paris 1960-63
  1966-   . 1960-63 title: Antiquités nationales et internationales.

A478
ARCHEOGRAFO TRIESTINO; raccolta di
  memoire, notize e documenti per
  sevire alla storia di Trieste,
  del Friuli e dell'Istria.
  Trieste 1829-37 1869-   .

ARCHEOL-: see ARCHAEOL- (entries
  beginning with these spellings
  are interfiled). See also ARCH-
  AIOL-, ARKHEOL-, ARHEOL-, and
  ARQUEOL-.

ARCHIEF voor NEDERLANDSCHE KERKGE-
  SCHIEDENIS see N16.

A479
ARCHITECTURA; Zeitschrift für Geschichte der Architektur. Munich
  1971-   .

A480
ARCHITETTURA e ARTI DECORATIVE; rivista d'arte e di storia. Milan
  1921-

ARCHIV, ARCHIVE, ARCHIVIO, ARCH-
IVO and ARCHIVUM are here interfiled. See also ARQUIVO.

A481
ARCHIVUM; revista de la Facultad de
    Filosofia y Letras. Univ. de
    Oviedo. Oviedo 1951-   .

A482
ARCHIV für ÄGYPTISCHE ARCHÄOLOGIE.
    Vienna 1938-   . Vol. 1 only
    published?

A483
ARCHIVIO per l'ALTO ADIGE. Alto
    Adige 1906-   . Variant title:
    Archivo per l'Alto Adige.

A484
ARCHIV für ANTHROPOLOGIE, VÖLKERFOR-
    SCHUNG und KOLONIALEN KULTURWAN-
    DEL. Brunswick 1866-1943. 1866-
    1936 title: Archiv für Anthropo-
    logie. 1937-38 title: Archiv für
    Anthropologie und Volkerforschung.

A485
ARCHIVIO per l'ANTROPOLOGIA e
    l'ETNOLOGIA. Florence 1871-   .

ARCHIVES de l'ATHOS see A54, A56,
    A66, A79, A90.

A486
ARCHIVE of AURELIUS ISIDORUS in the
    EGYPTIAN MUSEUM, CAIRO and the
    UNIVERSITY of MICHIGAN / A. E. R.
    Boak & H. C. Youtie. Ann Arbor,
    Mich. 1960. (PCairIsid).

A487
ARCHIV für BEGRIFFSGESCHICHTE.
    Bonn 1955-   .

A488
ARCHIVIO della CULTURA ITALIANA.
    Rome 1932-   . 1932-33 title:
    Archivio di Storia della Filoso-
    fia. 1934-38 title: Archivio di
    Storia della Filosofia Italiana.

A489
ARCHIVIO. DEPUTAZIONE ROMANA di STO-
    RIA PATRIA. Rome 1877-   . Soci-
    ety's name until 1934: Società
    Romana di Storia Patria.

A490
ARCHIVO ESPAÑOL de ARQUEOLOGÍA.
    Madrid 14- 1940-   . Supersedes in
    in part Archivo Espanol de Arte
    y Arqueología (1925-37) and con-
    tinues its numbering. (AEArq,
    AEA, ArchEspArq).

ARCHIVO ESPAÑOL de ARQUEOLOGÍA
    SUPPLEMENT see H78.

A491
ARCHIVO ESPAÑOL de ARTE. Madrid
    14- 1940-   . Supersedes in
    part Archivo Espanol de Arte y
    Arqueología (1925-37) and contin-
    ues its numbering. (AEA, AEArte).

A492
ARCHIVO ESPAÑOL de ARTE y ARQUEOLO-
    GÍA. Madrid 1925-37.

A493
ARCHIVUM EURASIAE MEDII AEVI.
    Lissi 1975-   .

A494
ARCHIVUM EUROPAE CENTRO-ORIENTALIS.
    Budapest 1935-   .

A495
ARCHIVUM FRANCISCANUM HISTORICUM.
    Quaracchi & Rome 1908-   .

A496
ARCHIV für FRANKFURTS GESCHICHTE und
    KUNST. Frankfurt a.M. 1839-58.
    1860-84 1888-1920 1925-   .

A497
ARCHIVUM FRATRUM PRAEDICATORUM
    Rome 1931-   .

ARCHIV für GESCHICHTE und ALTERTHUM-
    SKUNDE von OBERFRANKEN see A498.

ARCHIV für GESCHICHTE der MATHEMA-
    TIK, der NATURWISSENSCHAFTEN und
    der MEDIZIN see Q33.

ARCHIV für GESCHICHTE der MEDIZIN
    see S267.

ARCHIV für GESCHICHTE der NATURWIS-
    SENSCHAFTEN und der MEDIZIN see
    Q33.

A498
ARCHIV für GESCHICHTE von OBER-
  FRANKEN. Bayreuth 1838-
  Earlier title: Archiv für Ge-
  schichte und Alterthumskunde von
  Oberfranken.

A499
ARCHIV für GESCHICHTE der PHILOSO-
  PHIE. Stuttgart & Berlin 1888-   .
  Title varies: 1895-1924: Archiv
  für Philosophie. 1925-30: Archiv
  für Geschichte der Philosophie
  und Soziologie. Suspended 1933-
  39.

A500
ARCHIVIO GIURIDICO. Bologna
  1868-   .

A501
ARCHIVIO GLOTTOLOGICO ITALIANO.
  Rome etc. 1873-   . Suspended
  1943-49. (AGI).

A502
ARCHIV für HESSISCHE GESCHICHTE und
  ALTERTUMSKUNDE. Darmstadt 1835-
  84 1894-   .
  --. Ergänzungsband. 1901-   .

A503
ARCHIVO HISPALENSE; revista histo-
  rica, litteraria y artística.
  Seville 1886-88.

A504
ARCHIVES d'HISTOIRE DOCTRINALE et
  LITTÉRAIRE du MOYEN ÂGE. Paris
  1926/7-   . (AHDLMA, AHMA).

A505
ARCHIVES d'HISTOIRE du DROIT ORIEN-
  TAL. Brussels 1937-47 1952-53.
  In 1952 and 1953 this journal
  combined with Revue Internationale
  des Droits de l'Antiquité and
  continued under its own title,
  with the title Revue Internationale etc. as a subtitle. Since
  1954 publication has been under
  the title Revue Internationale
  etc. (AHDO, AHDO-RIDA).

A506
ARCHIVE for HISTORY of EXACT SCIEN-
  CES. Berlin 1960-   .

A507
ARCHIVUM HISTORIAE PONTIFICIAE.
  Rome 1963-   .

A508
ARCHIV des HISTORISCHEN VEREINS des
  KANTONS BERN. Bern 1848-   .
  1848-54 title: Abhandlungen des
  Historischen Vereins des Kantons
  Bern.

ARCHIVO IBEROAMERICANO de HISTORIA
  de la MEDICINA y ANTROPOLOGÍA
  MÉDICA see A616.

A509
ARCHIVES de l'INSTITUT de PALÉON-
  TOLOGIE HUMAINE. Paris 1927-   .

ARCHIVES INTERNATIONALES d'ETHNO-
  GRAPHIE see I94.

A510
ARCHIVIO INTERNAZIONALE di ETNO-
  GRAFIA e PREISTORIA. Turin
  1958-   .

A511
ARCHIVES INTERNATIONALES d'HISTOIRE
  des SCIENCES. Paris 1947-   .

ARCHIV für KEILSCHRIFTFORSCHUNG
  see A523.

A512
ARCHIV für KULTURGESCHICHTE. Berlin 1903-   . Suspended 1945-49.

ARCHIV für KUNDE ÖSTERREICHISCHER
  GESCHICHTSQUELLEN see A520.

A513
ARCHIV für LATEINISCHE LEXICOGRA-
  PHIE und GRAMMATIK. Leipzig
  1884-1908. (ALL, ALLG).

ARCHIVUM LATINITATIS MEDII AEVI
  see B273.

A514
ARCHIVOS LEONESES. Leon 1947?-

A515
ARCHIVUM LINGUISTICUM. Glasgow
  1949-   .

A516
ARCHIV für LITERATUR- und KIRCHEN-
GESCHICHTE des MITTELALTERS.
Freiburg i.B. 1885-1900. Title
of vol. 7: Literatur und Kirchen-
geschichte des Mittelalters.

A517
ARCHIV für LITURGIEWISSENSCHAFT.
Regensburg 1950-   .

A518
ARCHIVES des MISSIONS SCIENTIFIQUES
et LITTÉRAIRES. Paris 1850-57
1864-72 1873-90.

A519
ARCHIV für MUSIKWISSENSCHAFT.
Leipzig etc. 1918-   . Suspended
1927-52.

A520
ARCHIV für ÖSTERREICHISCHE GE-
SCHICHTE. Vienna 1848-   .
1848-65 title: Archiv für Kunde
Österreichischer Geschichtsquel-
len.

A521
ARCHIV ORIENTÁLNÍ. Prague 1929- .
1943-44 title: Archivum Orientale
Pragense. (ArOr).

A522
ARCHIVES de l'ORIENT CHRÉTIEN.
Paris 1932-   . Vol. 2 published
in 1932; vol. 1 in 1948.

A523
ARCHIV für ORIENTFORSCHUNG. Berlin
etc. 1923-   . Title of vols.
1-2: Archiv für Keilschriftforschung. (AfO, AOF).
--. Beiheft. 1936?-   .

A524
ARCHIVES de l'ORIENT LATIN. Paris
1881-   . Reprint New York 1978.

ARCHIVUM ORIENTALE PRAGENSE see
A521.

A525
ARCHIV für PAPYRUSFORSCHUNG und
VERWANDTE GEBIETE. Leipzig &
Berlin 1900-   . (APF).

ARCHIVUM PHILOLOGICUM see E14.

ARCHIV für PHILOLOGIE und PÄDAGO-
GIK see N27.

A526
ARCHIVES de PHILOSOPHIE. Paris
1923-   .
--. Supplément Bibliographie.
1929-   .

ARCHIV für PHILOSOPHIE see A499.

A527
ARCHIVO de PREHISTORIA LEVANTINA.
Valencia 1928-   .

A528
ARCHIV für RELIGIONSWISSENSCHAFT.
Leipzig etc. 1898-   . (ARW).

A529
ARCHIVUM ROMANICUM; nuova rivista
di filologia romanza. Florence
& Geneva 1917-41.

A530
ARCHIVES ROYALES de MARI / A. Par-
rot & G. Dossin. Paris 1950- .
Transcriptions and Transactions
of Archives Royales de Mari:
Textes.

A531
ARCHIVES ROYALES de MARI : textes /
G. Dossin et al. Paris 1941- .
(Musée du Louvre. Département des
Antiquités Orientales. Textes
Cunéiformes; 22-31).

A532
ARCHIVES de SAINT JEAN-PRODROME sur
le MONT MÉNÉCÉE. Paris 1955.
(Bibliothèque Byzantine. Documents; 3).

ARCHIVIO. SOCIETÀ ROMANA di STORIA
PATRIA see A489.

A533
ARCHIVES de SOCIOLOGIE des RELI-
GIONS. Paris 1956-   .

A534
ARCHIVIO di STATO di VENEZIA / A.
da Mosto. Rome 1937-   .

A535
ARCHIVIO STORICO di BELLUNO, FELTRE
e CADORE. Feltre 1929-   .

A536
ARCHIVIO STORICO della CALABRIA.
Mileto-Catanzaro 1912/3-18?

A537
ARCHIVIO STORICO per la CALABRIA e
la LUCANIA. Rome 1931-

ARCHIVIO STORICI per la CITTÀ e
COMUNI del CIRCONDARIO (e della
DIOCESI) di LODI see A540.

A538
ARCHIVIO STORICO per la DALMAZIA.
Rome 1926-   .

ARCHIVIO di STORIA della FILOSOFIA
(ITALIANA) see A488.

A539
ARCHIVIO STORICO ITALIANO. Florence
1842-51 1855-63 1865-   .

A540
ARCHIVIO STORICO LODIGIANO (Biblioteca Comunale Laudense). Lodi
1881-   . 1881-1900 title: Archivio Storico per la Città e Comuni
del Circondario (e della Diocesi)
di Lodi.

A541
ARCHIVIO STORICO LOMBARDO. Milan
1874-   .

A542
ARCHIVIO STORICO MESSINESE. Messina 1900-27/34 1939/48-   . Replaced 1936-38 by Bollettino Storico Messinese.

A543
ARCHIVIO STORICO PRATESE. Prato
1916-   . Suspended 1918 1922-23.

A544
ARCHIVIO STORICO per la PROVINCIA
di SALERNO. Naples 1921-27 1933-
35?

A545
ARCHIVIO STORICO per la PROVINCIE
NAPOLETANE. Naples 1876-   .

A546
ARCHIVIO STORICO per la PROVINCIE
PARMENSI. Parma 1892-   . Vols.
1-8 have added title page: Atti
e Memoire della R. Deputazione
di Storia Patria per le Provincie
Parmensi, ser. 4.

A547
ARCHIVIO STORICO PUGLIESE. Bari
1948-   .

A548
ARCHIVIO STORICO SARDO. Cagliari
1905-   . Suspended 1943-53?

ARCHIVIO STORICO per la SICILIA
see A549.

A549
ARCHIVIO STORICO SICILIANO. Palermo 1873-1934 1946-   . Suspended
1935-45 and replaced by Archivio
Storico per la Sicilia.

A550
ARCHIVIO STORICO per la SICILIA OR-
IENTALE. Catana 1904-   . Sus-
pended 1936-47 and replaced by
Bollettino Storico Catanese.

A551
ARCHIVIO STORICO SIRACUSANO. Syra-
cuse 1955-   .

A552
ARCHIVIO STORICO di TERRA di LAVORO.
Caserta 1956-   .

A553
ARCHIVIO STORICO TICINESE. Belin-
zona, Switz. 1960-   .

A554
ARCHIVES SUISSES d'ANTHROPOLOGIE
GÉNÉRALE. Geneva 1914-   . Sus-
pended 1923-27 and 1942-47.

A555
ARCHIV für SYSTEMATISCHE PHILOSO-
PHIE und SOCIOLOGIE. Berlin etc.
1868-   . 1868-94 title: Philosophische Monatshefte. 1895-1924
title: Archiv für Systematische
Philosophie.

A556
ARCHIV für URKUNDENFORSCHUNG.
Leipzig 1907-44.

A557
ARCHIVIO VENETO. Venice 1871- .
1891-1921 title: Nuovo Archivio
Veneto. 1922-26 title: Archivio
Veneto-tridentino.

ARCHIV des VEREINS für GESCHICHTE
und ALTERTÜMER des HERZOGTÜMER
see S142.

A558
ARCHIV des VEREINS für SIEBENBÜR-
GISCHE LANDESKUNDE. Sibiu 1843-
51 1853-1936.

A559
ARCHIV und WISSENSCHAFT. SCHRIFTEN-
REIHE der ARCHIVALISCHEN ZEIT-
SCHRIFT. Munich 1957- .

A560
ARCTOS; acta philologica Fennica.
Helsinki 1930-31 1954- .

A561
ARDENNE et FAMENNE; art-archéolo-
gie-histoire-folklore. Remicourt
1958- .

ARENA see S143.

A562
ARETHUSA. Buffalo, N.Y. 1968- .

A563
ARÉTHUSE; revue trimestrielle d'art
et d'archéologie. Paris 1923-31.

A564
ARGIVE HERAEUM / C. Walstein et al.
Boston 1902-05.

A565
ARGO; informativno glasilo za arhe-
ologijo, zgodovino umetnosti in
muzeologijo. Ljubljana 1962- .

A566
ARGOVIA; Jahresschrift der Histo-
rischen Gesellschaft des Kantons
Aargau. Aarau 1860- .

ARHEOL-: entries beginning with
this spelling are here interfiled. See also ARKHEOL- (for
other Slavic titles), ARCHAEOL-,
ARCHAIOL- and ARQUEOL-.

A567
ARHEOLOGIJA un ETNOGRAFIJA. Riga
1957- . 1957 title: Archeologija un Etnografia.

A568
ARHEOLOGIA MOLDOVEI. Bucharest
1961- . (ArhMold).

A569
ARHEOLOŠKI PREGLED. Belgrad
1959- .

A570
ARHEOLOŠKI RADOVI i RASPRAVE =
Acta et Dissertationes Archaeolo-
gicae. Zagreb 1959- .

A571
ARHEOLOŠKI VESTNIK = Acta Archaeo-
logica. Ljubljana 1950- .
(AV).

A572
ARHIVELE OLTENIEI. Craiova 1920?-
48?

A573
ARIEL; a review of arts and sciences in Israel. Jerusalem
1962- .

A574
ARION; a journal of humanities and
the Classics. Boston etc. 1962-
70 1974- .

A575
ARKEOLOJ MÜZELERI YAYINLARI (Istanbul Arkeoloji Müzeleri). Istanbul 1916- . Title varies:
vols. 1-5: Publikationen; 6-7:
Publications. 8-15: Istanbul
(Asariatika) Müzeleri Neşriyati.

A576
ARKHEOGRAFICHESKIĬ EZHOGODNIK.
Moscow 1957- .

ARKHEOL-: See also ARHEOL- (for

other Slavic titles), ARCHAEOL-,
ARCHAIOL- and ARQUEOr.

A577
ARKHEOLOGIIA (Bŭlgarska Akademiĭa
na Nautike. Arkheologicheski
Institut i Muzei). Sofia
1959-   .

A578
ARKHEOLOGIIA. Kiev 1971-   . Supersedes an earlier publication
with the same title.

A579
ARKHEOLOGIIA = Archéologie. Kiev
1947-   ?

A580
ARKHEOLOGIIA i ÉTNOGRAFIIA BASHKI-
RII. Ufa 1962-   .

A581
ARKHEOLOGICHESKIE ISSLEDOVANIIA
v GRUZII. Tiflis ?-   .

A582
ARKHEOLOGICHESKIE ISSLEDOVANIIA na
UKRAINE. Kiev 1965/6-   .

A583
ARKHEOLOGIIA i ISTORIIA BOSPORA.
Simferopol 1952-   .

A584
ARKHEOLOGICHESKIE IZVIESTIIA i ZA-
METKI (Moskovskoe Arkheologich-
eskoe Obshchestvo). Moscow
1873-1899/1900?

A585
ARKHEOLOGICHESKIE OTKRYTIIA (Akademiia Nauk SSSR. Institut Arkheologii). Moscow 1965-   .

A586
ARKHEOLOGICHNI PAMIATKY URSR.
Kiev 1949-   .

A587
ARKHEOLOGICHESKIE RASKOPI v ARMENII.
Erivan 1950-   .

A588
ARKHEOLOGICHESKII SBORNIK. Leningrad 1959-   .

A589
ARKHITEKTURA. Moscow 1945-   .

ARMÉE ROMAINE et les PROVINCES
see C20.

Arndt, P. see D15, G125, P131.

Arndt, W. F. see G88.

Arnim, H. von see S149.

ARQUEOL-: See also ARCHAEOL-,
ARKHEOL-, ARHEOL- and ARCHAIOL-.

A590
ARQUEOLOGIA e HISTORIA. Lisbon.
Lisbon 1922-32 1945-   .

A591
ARQUEÓLOGO PORTUGUÊS. Lisbon 1895-
1930/1 1951-   . 1895-1931 title: Archeólogo Português.

A592
ARQUIVO de BEJA. Beja 1944?-   .

A593
ARRABONA (Györi Múzeum Évkönyve).
Györ etc. 1959-   .

ÅRS is filed as if spelled AARS.

A594
ARS ASIATICA. Brussels 1914-35.

A595
ARS HISPANIAE. Madrid 1947-   .

A596
ARS HUNGARICA. Budapest 1932-   .

A597
ARS ISLAMICA. Ann Arbor, Mich.
1934-51.

A598
ARS ORIENTALIS. Baltimore 1954-   .

ÅRSBERETNING is filed as if spelled
AARSBERETNING.

ÅRSBOK is filed as if spelled AARS-
BOK.

ÅRSSKRIFT is filed as if spelled
AARSSKRIFT.

A599
ARSE (Centro Arqueológico Sagun-
tino). Sagunto ?-   .

ART, ARTA, ARTE and ARTI are here
    interfiled.

A600
ARTE. Rome, Milan 1968-   . Re-
    vival of Arte; rivista di storia
    dell'arte medioevale e moderna
    (1898-1963).

A601
ARTE ANTICA e MODERNA. Bologna
    1958-   .

A602
ART and ARCHAEOLOGY. Washington,
    D.C. etc. 1914-34.

A603
ARTA și ARHEOLOGIA REVISTĂ. Iasi
    1927-38?

A604
ART and ARCHAEOLOGY TECHNICAL AB-
    STRACTS. New York etc. 1955- .
    1955-65 title: I.I.C. Abstracts;
    abstracts of the technical liter-
    ature on archaeology and the fine
    arts.

A605
ART BULLETIN. New York etc. 1913-
    1913-   . 1913-18 title: Bulle-
    tin of the College Art Associa-
    tion of America. Other minor
    changes. (ArtB).

A606
ARTE ETRUSCA / G. Q. Giglioni.
    Milan 1935.

A607
ARTI FIGURATIVE; rivista d'arte
    antica e moderna. Rome 1945-   .

A608
ART JOURNAL. London 1839-1912.
    1839-48 title: Art Union. Also
    published in an American edition
    in New York 1875-87.

A609
ART JOURNAL. New York etc. 1941-

Title of vols. 1-19: College
Art Journal.

A610
ARTE LOMBARDA. Milan 1955-   .
    --. Monografie. 1966-   .

A611
ART QUARTERLY. Detroit 1938-   .

ART REVIEW see K38.

A612
ART STUDIES; medieval, renaissance
    and modern. Princeton 1923-31.

ART UNION see A608.

A613
ARTE VENETA. Venice 1947-   .

A614
ARTIBUS ASIAE. Hellerau-Dresden
    1925-   .
    --. Supplementum. 1937-   .

A615
ARTIUM SCRIPTORES / L. Radermacher.
    Vienna 1951. (Österreichische
    Akademie der Wissenschaften.
    Philosophisch-historische Klasse.
    Sitzungsberichte; 227, 3).

ASCA NEWSLETTER see M2.

A616
ASCLEPIO. Madrid 1949-   . 1949-
    53 title: Archivos Iberoamerican-
    os de Historia de la Medicina.
    1954-63 title: Archivo Iberoamer-
    icano de Historia de la Medicina
    y Antropología Médica.

A617
ASCULUM. Pisa 1975-   .

A618
ASIATISCHE STUDIEN = Études Asia-
    tiques. Bern 1947-   .

A619
ASPECTS of GREEK and ROMAN LIFE.
    London 1967?-   .

A620
ASSUR. Malibu, CA. 1974-   .

(Monographic Journals of the
Near East).

A621
ASSYRIAN DICTIONARY (Oriental In-
stitute). Chicago 1956-   .
(CAD).

A622
ASSYRIOLOGICAL STUDIES (Oriental
Institute). Chicago 1931-   .
(OIAS).

A623
ASSYRIOLOGISCHE BIBLIOTHEK. Leipzig 1881-1927 1933-   .

A624
ASSYRIOLOGISCHE STUDIEN / B. Meissner. Berlin 1903-13. (Mitteilungen der Vorderasiatischen Gesellschaft; VIII, 3; IX, 3; X, 4;
XII, 3; XV, 5; XVIII, 2).

A625
ASSYRISCHE RECHTSURKUNDEN / J.
Kohler & A. Ungnad. Leipzig 1913.

A626
ATENE e ROMA. Messina & Florence
1898-   . Suspended 1941-50?
(A&R).

A627
ATENEO VENETO; rivista di scienze,
lettere ed arti. Venice 1812- .
Variant title: Ateneo di Venezia.
Suspended 1946-48.

A628
ĀTHAR-é ĪRĀN; annales du Service
Archéologique de l'Iran. Paris
1936-49. Suspended 1939-48.

A629
ATHĒNA; syngramma periodikon tēs en
Athēnais Epistēmonikēs Hetaireias.
Athens 1889-   . Suspended 1933
1936 1942-47.

A630
ATHENAEUM; a journal of literature,
science, the fine arts, music
and the drama. London 1828-
1921.

A631
ATHENAEUM; studi periodici di let-
tère e storia dell'antichità.
Pavia 1913-   .

.A632
ATHĒNAION. Athens 1872-81.

A633
ATHENIAN AGORA; results of excava-
tions conducted by the American
School of Classical Studies at
Athens. Princeton 1953-   .

A634
ATHENIAN FINANCIAL DOCUMENTS in the
5th century/ B. D. Meritt. Ann
Arbor, Mich. 1932. (University
of Michigan Humanistic Series;
27).

A635
ATHENIAN TRIBUTE LISTS / B. D. Meritt, H. T. Wade Gery & M. F.
McGregor. Cambridge, Mass. 1939-
53. (ATL).

ATHENISCHE MITTEILUNGEN   see   M192.

ATHENS ANNALS of ARCHAEOLOGY   see
A469.

A636
ATIQOT.(Dept. of Antiquities, Is-
rael). Jerusalem
--. English series. 1955-   .
--. Hebrew series. 1955-   .
Vols. 1-3 appeared in English and
Hebrew editions, identical in
content. Beginning with vol. 4
the contents are different.

A637
ATLANTIS; archéologie scientifique
et traditionnelle. Vincennes
?-   .

A638
ATLAS ARCHÉOLOGIQUE de l'ALGÉRIE /
S. Gsell. Algers & Paris 1911.
Reprint Osnabrück 1973.

A639
ATLAS ARCHÉOLOGIQUE de la TUNISIE /
E. Babelon, R. Cagnat, S. Rein-
ach et al. Paris 1892-1932.

ATTI: See also ATTI e MEMORIE.

ATTI. ACCADEMIA degli AGIATI in
ROVERETO see A645.

ATTi della reale ACCADEMIA di ARCH-
EOLOGIA, LETTERE e BELLE ARTI di
NAPOLI see R68.

A640
ATTI dell'ACCADEMIA COSENTINA.
Cosenza 1838-   . Suspended 1894-
1928. Title varies slightly.

ATTI della reale ACCADEMIA d'ITALIA
see A642, M107, N83, R69, T106.

A641
ATTI della ACCADEMIA LIGURE di SCI-
ENZE e LETTERE di GENOVA. Genoa
etc. 1890-   . 1890-1921 title:
Atti della Società Ligustica di
Scienze Naturali e Geografiche;
1922-35 title: Atti della Società
Ligustica di Scienze e Lettere;
1936-40 title: Atti della Società
di Scienze e Lettere di Genova.

A642
ATTI della ACCADEMIA nazionale dei
LINCEI. Rome 1870-76/7. Contin-
ues in part Atti dell'Accademia
Pontificia dei Nuovi Lincei.
Superseded by the Academy's Tran-
uniti and Memorie. A number of
subsequent publications of the
Academy also bear the series ti-
tle Atti. Academy's name 1939-43:
Accademia d'Italia.

ATTI della ACCADEMIA nazionale dei
LINCEI see also M107, N83,
R69, T106.

ATTI. ACCADEMIA NAZIONALE ... see
ATTI. ACCADEMIA ... (the word
nazionale is disregarded in filing, but may have been regarded
in forming an abbreviation).

A643
ATTI. R. ACCADEMIA PELORITANA, MES-
SINA. Messina 1878-1935?
--. Classe di Scienze, Storiche
e Filologiche. 1938-   .
--. Classe di Lettere, Filosofia
e Belle Arte. 1937-   .

A644
ATTI dell'ACCADEMIA PONTANIANA.
Naples 1832-1933 1947/8-   .
Supersedes the Atti published
under the Academy's earlier name:
Societa Pontaniana, Naples (1810-
20). 1934-44 united with the Atti
della Accademia di Scienze Morali
e Politiche to form Atti della
Accademia Pontaniana di Scienze
Morali e Politiche.

ATTI della ACCADEMIA PONTANIANA di
SCIENZE MORALI e POLITICHE see
A644, A648.

A645
ATTI. ACCADEMIA ROVERETANA degli
AGIATI. Rovereto 1826-   .
Published under the earlier names
of the Academy: Accademia di Scienze, Lettere ed Arti degli Agiati in Rovereto and Accademia
degli Agiati di Rovereto.

A646
ATTI dell'ACCADEMIA di SCIENZE, LET-
TERE e ARTI di FALERMO. Palermo
1755-80 1845-89 1891-   . 1755-
80 title: Saggi di Dissertazioni
dell'Accademia Palermitana del
Buon Gusto. Other minor changes
in title.

A647
ATTI dell'ACCADEMIA di SCIENZE, LET-
TERE e ARTE di UDINE. Udine 1842-
52/3 1867-   . Title of vols. 1-
3: Relazione Interno degli Atti.
Also published under earlier
names of the Academy: Accademia
di Udine.

A648
ATTI. ACCADEMIA nazionale di SCI-
ENZE MORALI e POLITICHE, NAPOLI.
Naples 1864-   . 1934-44 united
with Atti dell'Accademia Pontani-
ana to form Atti della Accademia
Pontaniana di Scienza Morali e
Politiche. Academy's name changes
slightly.

A649
ATTI della ACCADEMIA delle SCIENZE
di TORINO. Turin 1865-1926. Aca-

demy's name varies slightly.
--. Classe di Scienze Morali,
Storiche e Filologiche.
1927/8-   .

ATTI dell.'ACCADEMIA di UDINE   see
A647.

A650
ATTI. CENTRO RICERCHE DOCUMENTAZI-
ONE sull'ANTICHITÀ CLASSICA. Milan 1967/8-   . (Biblioteca
Storica Universitaria). 1967-
76 issued by the Centro Studi
e Documentazione sull'Italia Romana.
--. Monografie e Supplemento.
1972-   .

ATTI. CENTRO STUDI e DOCUMENTAZIONE
sull'ITALIA ROMANA see A650.

A651
ATTI dei CIVICI MUSEI di STORIA ed
ARTE di TRIESTE. Trieste ?-   .

ATTI. CLASSE di LETTERE, FILOSOFIA
e BELLE ARTI. ACCADEMIA PELORITA-
NA, MESSINA   see A643.

ATTI. CLASSE di SCIENZE, MORALI,
STORICHE e FILOLOGICHE. ACCADEMIA
delle SCIENZE di TORINO see
A649.

ATTI. CLASSE di SCIENZE, STORICHE
e FILOLOGICHE. ACCADEMIA PELORI-
TANA, MESSIANA see A643.

A652
ATTI della COMMISSIONE CONSERVATRICE
dei MONUMENTI e BELLE ARTI della
PROVINCIA di TERRA di LAVORO.
Caserta 1870-96.

A653
ATTI del ... CONGRESSO NAZIONALE di
STUDI ROMANI. Rome etc. 1928- .

ATTI. CORSI d'ARTE RAVENNATE e BI-
ZANTINA see C248.

ATTI. COSENTINA see A640.

A654
ATTI. DEPUTAZIONE di STORIA PATRIA

per la LIGURIA. Genoa 1858-   .
Title of vols. 1-64: Società Ligure di Storia Patria.

ATTI. FIRENZE see A659.

ATTI. GENOVA see A641.

A655
ATTI dell'ISTITUTO VENETO di SCI-
ENZE, LETTERE ed ARTI. Venice
1840-   .
--. Pt. 2 Sez. 2: Classe di Sci-
enze Morali. 1934-   .

ATTI. LIGURE see A641.

ATTI. LIGUSTICA see A641.

A656
ATTI e MEMORIE. ACCADEMIA di AGRI-
COLTURA, SCIENZE e LETTERE, VER-
ONA. Verona 1807-   . 1807-99
title: Memorie. Academy's name
changes slightly.

ATTI e MEMORIE dell'ACCADEMIA FIO-
RENTINA di SCIENZE MORALI "La
COLOMBARIA" see A659.

A657
ATTI e MEMORIE dell'ACCADEMIA PA-
TAVINA di SCIENZE, LETTERE ed
ARTI. Padua 1884/5-   . Since
vol. 51 issued in 3 parts; Atti,
Memorie della Classe di Scienze
Fisico-Mathematica and Memorie
della Classe di Scienze Morali.

A658
ATTI e MEMORIE. ACCADEMIA di SCI-
ENZE, LETTERE ed ARTI in MODENA.
Modena 1833/58-   . 1833-82
title: Memorie.

A659
ATTI e MEMORIE. ACCADEMIA TOSCANA
di SCIENZE e LETTERE "La COLOM-
BARIA. Florence 1856/90-   .
Title until 1936: Atti della Società Colombaria di Firenze. 1943-
50 title: Atti e Memorie dell'Accademia Fiorentina di Scienze Morali "La Colombaria".

A660
ATTI e MEMORIE. ACCADEMIA VERGILI-
ANA di SCIENZE, LETTERE ed ARTE
di MANTOVA. Mantua 1868-   .
Earlier title: Atti e Memorie
della R. Accademia Virgiliana di
Mantova.

ATTI e MEMORIE. COLOMBARIA see A659.

A661
ATTI e MEMORIE. DEPUTAZIONE di
STORIA PATRIA per le ANTICHE PRO-
VINCIE MODENENSI. Modena 1892- .
Suspended 1938-47 and replaced by
the Studi e Documenti. Deputaz-
ione di Storia Patria per l'Emi-
lia e la Romagna. Sezione di Mo-
dena. Supersedes in part the
Atti e Memorie. Deputazioni di
Storia Patria per le Provincie
Modenesi e Parmensi.

A662
ATTI e MEMORIE. DÉPUTAZIONE di STO-
RIA PATRIA per la PROVINCIE delle
MARCHE. Ancona 1895-   . Sus-
pended 1934-36.

ATTI e MEMORIE della R. DEPUTAZIONE
di STORIA PATRIA per le PROVINCIE
PARMENSI see A546.

A663
ATTI e MEMORIE. DEPUTAZIONE di STO-
RIA PATRIA per le PROVINCIE di
ROMAGNA. Bologna 1862-70 1875-76
1883-1945.

ATTI e MEMORIE. FIRENZE see A659.

A664
ATTI e MEMORIE dell'ISTITUTO ITAL-
IANO di NUMISMATICA. Rome 1912-
34.

ATTI e MEMORIE. MANTUA see A660.

ATTI e MEMORIE. MODENA see A658.

ATTI e MEMORIE. PADOVA see A657.

A665
ATTI e MEMORIE della SOCIETÀ IS-
TRIANA di ARCHEOLOGIA e STORIA
PATRIA. Venice etc. 1885-   .

A666
ATTI e MEMORIE della SOCIETÀ MAGNA
GRECIA. Rome 1925-32 1954-   .
Variant title: Campagne della
Società Magna Grecia. (AHiMGr,
ASMG).

ATTI e MEMORIE della SOCIETÀ MAGNA
GRECIA. SUPPLEMENTO see A537.

A667
ATTI e MEMORIE della SOCIETÀ TIBUR-
TINA di STORIA e d'ARTE, TIVOLI.
Tivoli 1921-   . Suspended 1944-
50.

ATTI e MEMORIE. VERONA see A656.

ATTI. MESSINA see A643.

ATTI. NAPOLI see A644, A648, A671.

ATTI. PALERMO see A646.

ATTI. PONTIFICIA ACCADEMIA dei NUO-
VI LINVEI see A669.

A668
ATTI della PONTIFICIA ACCADEMIA RO-
MANA di ARCHEOLOGIA. Rome
--. Ser. 1-2: Dissertazione. 1821-
64 1881-1921.
--. Ser. 3. Memorie (Serie in 4°)
1923/4-   . (MemPontAcc).
--. --. Memorie. (Serie in 8°).
1975-   .
--. --. Rendiconti. 1921-   .
(RendPontAcc, RPAA).

A669
ATTI. PONTIFICIA ACCADEMIA delle
SCIENZE. Rome 1847-1934/5. Aca-
demy's earlier name: Accademia
Pontificia dei Nuovi Lincei.

ATTI. REALE ACCADEMIA ... see ATTI.
ACCADEMIA ... (the word reale is
disregarded in filing, but may
have been regarded in forming an
abbreviation).

ATTI e RENDICONTI. ACCADEMIA di SCI-
ENZE, LETTERE ed ARTI degli ZEL-
ANTI see M133.

ATTI e RENDICONTI. ACIREALE   see
M133.

ATTI della SOCIETÀ di ARCHEOLOGIA
e BELLE ARTE per la PROVINCIA
di TORINO see A670.

ATTI della SOCIETÀ COLOMBARIA di
FIRENZE see A659.

ATTI della SOCIETÀ LIGURE di STORIA
PARTIA see A654.

ATTI della SOCIETÀ LIGUSTICA di
SCIENZE e LETTERE see A641.

ATTI della SOCIETÀ LIGUSTICA di
SCIENZE NATURALI e GEOGRAFICHE
see A641.

A670
ATTI della SOCIETÀ PIEMONTESE di
ARCHEOLOGIA e BELLE ARTE. Turin
1875-   . 1875-1906 title: Atti
della Società di Archeologia e
Belle Arte per la Provincia di
Torino.

A671
ARTI. SOCIETÀ PONTANIANA, NAPOLI.
Naples 1810-20. Continued by
Atti dell'Accademia Pontaniana
(1832-   ).

ATTI. SOCIETÀ ROMANA di ANTROPOLO-
GIA see R266.

ATTI della SOCIETÀ di SCIENZE e
LETTERE di GENOVA see A641.

ATTI. TORINO see A649.

ATTI. UDINE see A647.

ATTI. VENEZIA see A655.

ATTI. VERONA see A656.

A672
ATTIC BLACK FIGURED LEKYTHOI / C.
H. E. Haspels. Paris 1936. (Travaux et Mémoires. École Française
d'Athènes; 4). (ABL).

A673
ATTIC BLACK FIGURED VASE-PAINTERS /

J. D. Beazley. Oxford 1956. Reprint New York 1978. (ABV).

A674
ATTIC RED FIGURED VASES in AMERICAN
MUSEUMS / J. D. Beazley. Cambridge, Mass. 1918. Reprint Rome
1967.

A675
ATTIC RED-FIGURE VASE PAINTERS /
J. D. Beazley. 2. ed. Oxford
1963. 1st edition 1942. (ARV).

A676
ATTIC VASE PAINTINGS in the MUSEUM
of FINE ARTS, BOSTON / L. D.
Caskey & J. D. Beazley. London
1931-64. (CB).

A677
AUCTARIUM BIBLIOTHECAE HAGIOGRA-
PHICAE GRAECAE / F. Halken.
Brussels 1969. (Subsidia Hagio-
graphica; 47).

Audollent, A. M. H. see D7.

A678
AUFSTIEG und NIEDERGANG der RÖM-
ISCHEN WELT / H. Temporini. Berlin & New York 1972-   . Dedi-
cated to J. Vogt. (ANRW).

A679
AUGUSTINIAN STUDIES. Villanova
1970-   .

A680
AUGUSTINIANA. Louvain 1951-   .

A681
AUGUSTINIANUM (Collegium Internationale Augustinianum). Rome
1961-   .

A682
AUGUSTINUS (Padres Agustinos Reco-
letos). Madrid 1956-   .

AUMLA see A2.

A683
AUREUS; Zeitschrift für Numismatik
und Geldwesen. Munich 1959-   .

A684
AUS der PAPYRUSSAMMLUNG der UNI-
  VERSITÄTSBIBLIOTHEK in LUND.
  Lund 1935-52. (Humanistiska Vet-
  enskapssamfundet i Lund. Årsber-
  ättelse). (PLund).

A685
AUSA; publicación trimestral del
  patronato de estudios ausonenses.
  Vich ?-   .

A686
AUSERLESENE GRIECHISCHE VASENBILDER
  / E. Gerhard. Berlin 1840-58.

A687
AUSFÜHRLICHE GRAMMATIK der GRIECH--
  ISCHEN SPRACHE / R. Kühner, F.
  Blass & B. Gerth. 3. ed. Hann-
  over 1890-1904. 1st edition 1834-
  35. (KG).

A688
AUSFÜHRLICHES LEXIKON der GRIECH-
  ISCHEN und RÖMISCHEN MYTHOLOGIE /
  W. H. Roscher. Leipzig 1884-
  1937. Reprint Hildesheim 1965-78.
  (ML).

A689
AUSGRABUNGEN in BERLIN. Berlin
  1970-   .

A690
AUSGRABUNGEN und FUNDE; Nachrichtenblatt für Vor- und Frühgeschichte. Berlin 1956-   .

A691
AUSGRABUNGEN zu OLYMPIA / E. Curtius et al. Berlin 1876-81.

A692
AUSONIA; rivista della Società
  Italiana di Archeologia e Storia
  dell'Arte. Rome 1906-21. Suspended 1916-18.

Austin, C. see C169.

AUSTRALASIAN UNIVERSITIES (MODERN
  LANGUAGE / LANGUAGE and LITERA-
  TURE) ASSOCIATION. JOURNAL see
  A2.

A693
AUSTRALIAN BIBLICAL REVIEW. Mel-
  bourne 1951-   .

A694
AUSTRALIAN JOURNAL of BIBLICAL
  ARCHAEOLOGY. Sydney 1968-   .

AUSTRIA ROMANA see P182.

A695
AUVERGNE LITTÉRAIRE, ARTISTIQUE
  et HISTORIQUE. Clermont-Ferrand
  1924-   .

A696
AYASOFYA MÜZESI YILLIGI = Annual
  of the Ayasofya Museum. Istanbul
  1957/8-   . Published as part
  of the Museum's Yayinlari.

Azara, A. see N94, N129.

AZÄRBAJGAN SSR ELMLÄR AKADEMYAN-
  YNYN CHÄBÄRLÄRI see I150.

B

B1
BABESCH; bulletin antieke beschaving. Leiden 1926- . 1926-69
title: Bulletin van de Vereeninging tot Bevordering der Kennis
van de Antieke Beschaving. 1970-
75 title: Bulletin Antieke Beschaving. (BABESCH, BABesch,
BVAB)

Babelon, E. see D22, T86, I103,
R41, A639.

B2
BABYLONIACA; études de philologie
assyro-babylonienne. Paris
1907-37.

B3
BABYLONIAN EXPEDITION of the UNI-
VERSITY of PENNSYLVANIA. Phila-
delphia 1893-1911.

B4
BABYLONIAN INSCRIPTIONS in the
COLLECTION of James B. Nies,
YALE UNIV. New Haven 1917-   .
Editor 1917-25: A. T. Clay.

B5
BABYLONISCHE BRIEFE aus der ZEIT
der HAMMURAPI-DYNASTIE / A. Ungnad. Leipzig 1914. (Vorderasiatische Bibliothek; 6).

Bachmann, L. see A211.

B6
BADENER NEUJAHRSBLÄTTER. Baden
1925-   .

B7
BADISCHE FUNDBERICHTE. Freiburg
i.B. 1925-   .
--. Sonderheft. 1962-   .

B8
BADISCHE HEIMAT; mein Heimatland.
Freiburg i.B. etc. 1914-42
1950-   . 1914-42 title: Mein
Heimatland. Absorbed Oberrhein-
isches Heimat (formerly Badische
Heimat) in 1950.

Baehrens, E. see F63-F64, P143.

B9
BAGHDADER MITTEILUNGEN (Deutsches
Archäologisches Institut. Abtei-
lung Baghdad). Berlin 1960-   .
(BaM, MDAI(I)).
--. Beiheft. 1968-   .

Bailey, A. see D54.

B10
BALCANIA. Bucharest 1938-45?.

B11
BALKAN STUDIES. Thessalonike
1960-   .

B12
BALKANSKO EZIKOZNANIE = Linguistique Balkanique. Sofia 1959-   .

B13
BALTISCHE STUDIEN. Stettin
1832-   .

B14
BANATICA (Muzeul Judeţean). Reşiţa, Romania ?-   .

Barkóczi, L. see R314.

Barnett, R. D. see C83.

B15
BARROW NATURALISTS' FIELD CLUB and
   LITERARY and SCIENTIFIC ASSOCIA-
   TION [Annual Reports and Pro-
   ceedings]. Barrow-in-Furness
   1876/7-1910/2 1928/9-   .

Barton, G. A. see R351.

B16
BASELBIETER HEIMATBLÄTTER. Basel
   ?-   .

B17
BASELBIETER HEIMATBUCH. Liestal
   1941-   .

B18
BASLER BEITRÄGE zur GESCHICHTSWIS-
   SENSCHAFT. Basel 1938-   .

BASLER JAHRBUCH see B19.

B19
BASLER STADTBUCH. Basel etc.
   1879-   . 1879-1959 title: Basler Jahrbuch.

B20
BASLER ZEITSCHRIFT für GESCHICHTE
   und ALTERTUMSKUNDE. Basel
   1902-   .

B21
BASTAN CHENASSI va HONAR-EIRAN =
   Revue d'Archéologie et d'Art
   Iraniens. Teheran 1970?-   .

Bataille, A. see P43.

Battisti, C. see D79.

Baudrillart, A. see D56.

Bauer, W. see G88.

Baumbach, L. see M327.

Baumeister, A. see D16.

B22
BAYERISCHE BLÄTTER für das GYMNASI-
   ALSCHULWESEN. Bamburg & Munich
   1864-1935. 1864-74 and 1881-91
   title: Blätter für das bayerische Gymnasialschulwesen. 1875-
   80 title: Blätter für das bayerische Gymnasial- und Realschulwesen. 1892-1916 title: Blätter
   für das Gymnasial-Schulwesen.

B23
BAYERISCHE VORGESCHICHTSBLÄTTER.
   Munich 1921-   . 1921-42 title:
   Bayerische Vorgeschichtsfreund.
   (BVBl).

BAYERISCHE VORGESCHICHTSFREUND
   see B23.

B24
BEAUX ARTS; chronique des arts et
   de la curiosité. Paris 1883-
   1940. 1883-1922 title: Chronique
   des arts et de la curiosité.

Beazley, J. D. see A673-A675.
   P80, A674, A676, B110, D33,
   E118.

Bechtel, F. see S17, G122.

Beckby, H. see A334.

B25
BEDFORDSHIRE ARCHAEOLOGICAL JOUR-
   NAL. Luton 1962-   .

Bedjan, P. see A69.

Bees, N. A. see C211.

BEIBLATT ... BEIHEFT ... look under
   the name of the journal.

BEIHEFTE zum ALTEN ORIENT see
   M273.

B26
BEITRÄGE zur ÄGYPTISCHEN BAUFOR-
   SCHUNG und ALTERTUMSKUNDE. Ber-
   lin etc. 1926-   .

B27
BEITRÄGE zur ALLGEMEINEN und VER-
GLEICHENDEN ARCHÄOLOGIE. Munich
1979- . (BAVA).

B28
BEITRÄGE zur ANTHROPOLOGIE und UR-
GESCHICHTE BAYERNS. Munich
1876/7-1915.

B29
BEITRÄGE zur ARCHÄOLOGIE. Würzburg 1970- .

B30
BEITRÄGE zur ASSYRIOLOGIE und SE-
MITISCHEN SPRACHWISSENSCHAFT.
Leipzig 1890-1927. Variant title:
Beiträge zur Assyriologie und
Vergleichenden Semitischen
Sprachwissenschaft. (BAS).

B31
BEITRÄGE zum ASSYRISCHEN WÖRTER-
BUCH / B. Meissner. Chicago
1931-32. (Assyriological Studies.
Oriental Institute of the Univ.
of Chicago).

BEITRÄGE zur BIBLISCHEN LANDES-
und ALTERTUMSKUNDE see Z33.

B32
BEITRÄGE zur DEUTSCHEN VOLKS- und
ALTERTUMSKUNDE. Hamburg 1954- .

B33
BEITRÄGE zur FÖRDERUNG CHRISTLICHER
THEOLOGIE. Gütersloh 1897- .

B34
BEITRÄGE zur GESCHICHTE DORTMUNDS
und der GRAFSCHAFT MARK. Dortmund 1875- .

BEITRÄGE zur GESCHICHTE des
NIEDERRHEINS see D96.

B35
BEITRÄGE zur HISTORISCHEN THEOLO-
GIE. Tübingen 1929- . Sus-
pended 1937-49.

B36
BEITRÄGE zur KUNDE der INDOGERMAN-
ISCHEN SPRACHEN. Göttingen
1877-1906. (BB).

B37
BEITRÄGE zur NAMENFORSCHUNG. Heidelberg 1949/50- . (BN).

B38
BEITRÄGE zur OBERPFALZFORSCHUNG.
Kallmünz 1965- .

B39
BEITRÄGE zur RHEINISCHEN KUNSTGE-
SCHICHTE und DENKMALPFLEGE. Düsseldorf 1970- . (Kunstdenkmäler des Rheinlandes. Beiheft;
16, etc.).

B40
BEITRÄGE zur SARRLÄNDISCHEN ARCH-
ÄOLOGIE und KUNSTGESCHICHTE.
Saarbrücken ?- .

B41
BEITRÄGE zur SAARLÄNDISCHEN ARCH-
LICHEN ARCHÄOLOGIE des MITTELMEER
-KULTURRAUMES. Berlin 1965- .
Vol. 2 was published in 1962.

BEITRÄGE zur VATERLÄNDISCHEN GE-
SCHICHTE see S39.

B42
BEITRÄGE zur WISSENSCHAFT vom
ALTEN und NEUEN TESTAMENT.
Stuttgart 1908- .

B43
BÉKÉS MEGYEI MÚZEUMOK KÖZLEMÉNYEI.
Szeged 1971- .

Bekker, I. see A208.

B44
BELFAGOR; rassegna di varia umanità. Florence etc. 1946- .

BELGISCH TIJDSCHRIFT voor OUDHEID -
KUNDE en KUNSTGESCHIEDENIS see
R115.

BELGISCH TIJDSCHRIFT voor PHILOLO-
GIE en GESCHIEDENIS see R117.

Bell, H. I. see A23, B221, D25,
J86.

B45
BELLETEN (Türk Tarih Kurumu). Ankara 1937- .

Bellinger, A. R. see C71.

Bennett, E. L. see K32, M325, N23.

Benson, J. L. see G33.

B46
BERCEO; boletín del Instituto de
  Estudios Riojanos. Logroño
  1946-   .

Berg, P. see C207.

BERGENS MUSEUMS ÅRBOK see A6.

BERGENS MUSEUMS AARSBERETING see
  A6.

BERGENS MUSEUMS SKRIFTER see U14.

Bergk, T. see P144.

B47
BERGOMUM (Civica Biblioteca; Aten-
  eo di Scienze, Lettere ed Arti).
  Bergamo 1907-   . 1907-26 title:
  Bollettino. Civica biblioteca.

BERICHT, BERICHTE and BERICHTEN
are here interfiled.

BERICHTE. AKADEMIE der WISSENSCHAF-
  TEN zu LEIPZIG (1846-48) see
  B55.

BERICHTE. AKADEMIE der WISSENSCHAF-
  TEN zu LEIPZIG (1849-61) see
  S94

BERICHTE der ANTIQUARISCHEN GESELL-
  SCHAFT in ZURICH see A400.

B48
BERICHTE über die AUSGRABUNGEN in
  OLYMPIA. Berlin 4- 1940/1-   .
  Vols. 1-3 published in the Jahrbuch des Deutschen Archäologischen Instituts; 52, 53, 56
  (1937-38, 1941).

BERICHTE der CHRISTLICH-ARCHÄOLO-
  GISCHEN GESELLSCHAFT zu ATHEN
  see D9, B458.

B49
BERICHTE zur DEUTSCHEN LANDESKUNDE.

Leipzig etc. 1941-   . Suspended
  1944-48.
--. Sonderheft. 1942.

BERICHTE über die FORTSCHRITTE der
  RÖMISCH-GERMANISCHEN FORSCHUNGEN
  see B52.

BERICHT der KONSERVATORS der GE-
  SCHICHTLICHEN DENKMÄLER im
  SAARGEBIET see B53.

BERICHTE. LEIPZIG (1846-48) see
  B55.

BERICHTE. LEIPZIG (1849-61) see
  S94.

B50
BERICHTE und MITTHEILUNGEN des AL-
  TERTUMSVEREINS in WIEN. Vienna
  1854-1919.

BERICHT des OBERÖSTERREICHISCHEN
  MUSEALVEREINS see J46.

B51
BERICHTEN van de RIJKSDIENST voor
  het OUDHEIDKUNDIG BODEMONDERZOEK
  = Proceedings of the State Service for Archaeological Investi-
  gations in the Netherlands. Am-
  ersfoort 1950-   . (BerROB,
  ROB).

B52
BERICHTE der RÖMISCH-GERMANISCHE
  KOMMISSION des DEUTSCHEN ARCHÄ-
  OLOGISCHEN INSTITUTS, Frankfurt
  a.M. Berlin 1904-   . 1904-
  06/7 title: Berichte über die
  Fortschritte der römisch-ger-
  manischen Forschungen. Insti-
  tute's name varies slightly.
  (BRGK, BerRGK).

BERICHTE der SÄCHSISCHEN AKADEMIE
  der WISSENSCHAFTEN see S94.

BERICHTE. SÄCHSISCHE GESELLSCHAFT
  zu LEIPZIG (1846-48) see B55.

BERICHTE der SÄCHISCHEN GESELL-
  SCHAFT der WISSENSCHAFTEN (1849-
  61) see S94.

B53
BERICHT der STAATLICHEN DENKMAL-
PFLEGE im SAARLAND. Saarbrucken
?-   . Title before 1953 (vols.
1-5): Bericht der Konservators
der Geschichtlichen Denkmäler
im Saargebiet.

BERICHT der TOMSKER STAATS-UNIVER-
SITÄT see T127.

B54
BERICHT des VEREINS CARNUNTUM in
WIEN. Vienna 1887?-1933.

BERICHTE über die VERHANDLUNGEN
der SÄCHSISCHEN AKADEMIE der
WISSENSCHAFTEN see S94.

B55
BERICHTE über die VERHANDLUNGEN der
SÄCHSISCHEN GESELLSCHAFT der
WISSENSCHAFT zu LEIPZIG. Leipzig
1846-48. Continued in Classes.

BERICHTE über der VERHANDLUNGEN der
SÄCHSISCHEN GESELLSCHAFT der
WISSENSCHAFTEN. PHILOLOGISCH-
HISTORISCHE KLASSE see S94.

B56
BERICHTIGUNGSLISTE der GRIECHISCHEN
PAPYRUSURKUNDEN aus ÄGYPTEN / F.
Preisigke. Berlin 1913-   .

BERKS, BUCKS and OXON ARCHAEOLOGI-
CAL JOURNAL see B57.

B57
BERKSHIRE ARCHAEOLOGICAL JOURNAL.
Reading etc. 1889-   . 1889-95
title: Quarterly Journal. Berkshire Ashmolean Society. 1895-
1930 title: The Berks, Bucks and
Oxon Archaeological Journal.

BERKSHIRE, BUCKINGHAMSHIRE and
OXFORDSHIRE ARCHAEOLOGICAL JOUR-
NAL see B57.

BERLINER ... (Berliner Jahrbuch ...,
Berliner Zeitschrift ...) see
also JARHBUCH ...., ZEITSCHRIFT...

B58
BERLINER BEITRÄGE zur VOR- und
FRÜHGESCHICHTE. Berlin 1957-   .

B59
BERLINER BLÄTTER für MÜNZ-, SIEGEL-
und WAPPENKUNDE. Berlin 1863-
71/3.

B60
BERLINER BLÄTTER für VOR- und FRÜH-
GESCHICHTE. Berlin 1952-   .

B61
BERLINER BYZANTINISCHE ARBEITEN.
Berlin 1956-   .

B62
BERLINER JAHRBUCH für VOR- und
FRÜHGESCHICHTE. Berlin 1961- .
(BJV).

B63
BERLINER KLASSIKER TEXTE. Berlin
1904-   . Suspended 1924-38.
(BKT).

B64
BERLINER LEIHGABE GRIECHISCHER
PAPYRI / T. Kalen et al. Up-
psala 1932-77. (Uppsala Uni-
versitets Årsskrift 1932.
Filosofi, Spräkvetenskap och
Historiska Vetenskaper; 1).
Vol. 2 appeared as Studia Graeca
Upsaliensia, 12. (PBerlLeihg).

BERLINER MÜNZBLÄTTER see D30.

B65
BERLINER MUSEEN; Berichte aus den
preussischen Kunstsammlungen.
Berlin 1907-73. 1907-18 title:
Amtliche Berichte aus den Königlichen Kunstsammlungen. Suspended
1944-50. (BerlMus).

B66
BERLINER NUMISMATISCHE ZEITSCHRIFT.
Berlin 1949-   .

BERLINER PHILOLOGISCHE WOCHEN-
SCHRIFT see P114.

B67
BERLINER STUDIEN für KLASSISCHE
PHILOLOGIE und ARCHÄOLOGIE.
Berlin 1883-98.

B68
BERYTUS; archaeological studies.
  Beirut & Copenhagen 1934-   .

BEZZENBERGERS BEITRÄGE zur KUNDE
  der INDOGERMANISCHEN SPRACHEN
  see B36.

B69
BIBBIA e ORIENTE. Milan etc.
  1959-   .

B70
BIBLE et TERRE SAINTE. Paris
  1957-   .

B71
BIBLE e VIE CHRÉTIENNE. Paris
  1953-   .

B72
BIBLICA (Pontificium Institutum
  Biblicum). Rome 1920-   .
  The Elenchus Bibliographicus
  Biblicus was included for the
  years 1950-67, after which
  it assumed separate publication.

B73
BIBLICA et ORIENTALIA (Pontificum
  Institutum Biblicum). Rome
  1928-   . Earlier title: Sacra
  Scriptura Antiquitatibus Orien-
  talibus Illustrata.

B74
BIBLICAL ARCHAEOLOGIST. New Haven
  1938-   . (BA).

B75
BIBLICAL WORLD. Chicago 1893-
  1920.

B76
BIBLIOGRAPHICAL BULLETIN of the
  GREEK LANGUAGE = Deltion Vivlio-
  graphias tēs Hellēnikēs Glossēs.
  Athens 1973-   . (BGL).

B77
BIBLIOGRAPHIE ANALYTIQUE de l'AF-
  RIQUE ANTIQUE. Paris 1961/2-   .

BIBLIOGRAPHIE ÉGYPTOLOGIQUE AN-
  NUELLE see A244.

BIBLIOGRAPHIE zum JAHRBUCH des
  DEUTSCHEN ARCHÄOLOGISCHEN
  INSTITUTS see A425.

BIBLIOTHECA, BIBLIOTHEK and BIBLI-
  OTHÈQUE are here interfiled.

B78
BIBLIOTHECA AEGYPTIACA. Brussels
  1931-   .

B79
BIBLIOTHEK der ALTEN WELT. Zurich
  --. Alte Orient Reihe. 1950-   .
  --. Antike und Christentum
  Reihe. 1949-   .
  --. Griechische Reihe. 1947-   .
  --. Römische Reihe. 1949-   .

B80
BIBLIOTHÈQUE ARCHÉOLOGIQUE et HIS-
  TORIQUE (Institut Français
  d'Archéologie de Beyrouth).
  Paris 1921-   . (BAH).

BIBLIOTHÈQUE des CAHIERS de l'IN-
  STITUT de LINGUISTIQUE de LOU-
  VAIN see C26.

B81
BIBLIOTHECA CLASSICA ORIENTALIS.
  Berlin 1956-69. (BCO).

B82
BIBLIOTHÈQUE de l'ÉCOLE des CHAR-
  TES. Paris 1839/0-   .

B83
BIBLIOTHÈQUE des ÉCOLES FRANÇAISES
  d'ATHÈNES et de ROME. Rome
  1877-   . (BEFAR).

B84
BIBLIOTHÈQUE de l'ÉCOLE des HAUTES
  ÉTUDES SCIENCES, PHILOLOGIQUES
  et HISTORIQUES. Paris 1869-   .

B85
BIBLIOTHÈQUE d'ÉTUDES de l'INSTITUT
  FRANÇAIS d'ARCHÉOLOGIE ORIENTALE.
  Cairo 1908-   .

B86
BIBLIOTHÈQUE de la FACULTÉ de
  PHILOSOPHIE et LETTRES de l'UNI-
  VERSITÉ DE LIÈGE. Liège 1897-   .

B87
BIBLIOTHECA GEOGRAPHORUM ARABICO-
RUM / M. J. de Goeje. 2. ed.
Leiden 1906. 1st edition 1870-
94.

BIBLIOTHECA GRAECA MEDII AEVI
see M153.

B88
BIBLIOTHECA HAGIOGRAPHICA GRAECA /
F. Halkin. 3. ed. Brussels 1969.
(Subsidia Hagiographica; 47).
(BHG).

B89
BIBLIOTHECA HAGIOGRAPHICA LATINA.
Brussels 1898-1901. (Subsidia
Hagiographica; 6). Reprint
Brussels 1949. (BHL).

B90
BIBLIOTHECA HAGIOGRAPHICA ORIENTA-
LIS / P. Peeters. Brussels
1910. (Subsidia Hagiographica;
10). Reprint Profondeville 1954.
(BHO).

B91
BIBLIOTHÈQUE HISTORIQUE VAUDOISE.
Lausanne 1940-   .

B92
BIBLIOTHECA HUMANITATIS HISTORICA.
Budapest 1936-   .

B93
BIBLIOTHÈQUE d'HUMANISME et RE-
NAISSANCE; travaux et documents.
Paris & Geneva 1941-   .

B94
BIBLIOTHEK der KIRCHENVÄTER. 2.
Aufl. Munich 1911-38. 1st edition
1869-88. (BKV).

B95
BIBLIOTHEK der KLASSISCHEN ALTER-
TUMSWISSENSCHAFT. Heidelberg
1911-   .

B96
BIBLIOTHECA MESOPOTAMICA. Malibu,
CA. 1975-   . (BM).

BIBLIOTHÈQUE NATIONAL. Catalogue
des Monnaies de l'Empire Romain
see C82.

B97
BIBLIOTHECA ORIENTALIS. Leiden
1943-   . (BiOr, BO).

BIBLIOTHECA PHILOLOGICA CLASSICA
see B448.

B98
BIBLIOTHECA PRAEHISTORICA HISPANIA.
Madrid 1958-   .

B99
BIBLIOTHECA SCRIPTORUM GRAECORUM
editore A. FIRMIN-DIDOT. Paris
1858-90?

B100
BIBLIOTHECA SCRIPTORUM GRAECORUM
et ROMANORUM TEUBNERIANA. Leipzig 1849-   .
--. Scriptores Graeci.
--. Scriptores Romani.
Since the end of World War II
appears in two distinct publish-
ers' series; one located in
Leipzig and the other in Stuttgart.

B101
BIBLIOTHECA THEOLOGICA NORVEGICA.
Oslo 1967-   .

BIBLIOTHÈQUE de l'UNIVERSITÉ de
LIÈGE. FACULTÉ de PHILOSOPHIE
et LETTRES see B86.

B102
BIBLIOTHEK und WISSENSCHAFT.
Wiesbaden 1964-   .

B103
BIBLISCHER KOMMENTAR: Altes Testament / M. Noth et al. Neukirchen-Vluyn 1976-   .

B104
BIBLISCHES REALLEXIKON / K. Galling. Tübingen 1937. (Handbuch
zum Alten Testament, I. Reihe).

B105
BIBLISCHE ZEITSCHRIFT. Paderborn
1903-39 1957-   . (BZ).

Bickel, E. see K23.

B106
BICKEL'S COIN and MEDAL NEWS =
  Munt en Medaljenuus. Johannes-
  berg 1965?-75?

Bieber, M. see H95.

Bigorra, S. Mariné see I66.

B107
BIJDRAGEN tot de GESCHIEDENIS IN-
  ZONDERHEID van het oud HERTOGDOM
  BRABANT. Antwerp 1902-   .
  Title varies slightly.

B108
BIJDRAGEN voor de GESCHIEDENIS der
  NEDERLANDEN. The Hague 1946-69.

B109
BIJDRAGEN en MEDEDELINGEN BETREF-
  FENDE de GESCHIEDENIS der NEDER-
  LANDEN. The Hague 85- 1970-   .
  Formed by the merger of Bijdragen
  voor de Geschiedenis der Nederlanden and Bijdragen en Mededelingen van het Historisch Genootschap, and continues the
  numbering of the latter.

B110
BILDER GRIECHISCHEN VASEN / J. D.
  Beazley & P. Jacobthal. Berlin
  1930-39. English edition Mainz
  1974-   .

B111
BILLEDTAVLER til KATALOGET over
  ANTIKE KUNSTVAERKER (Ny Carlsberg
  Glyptotek). Copenhagen 1907-   .
  --. Supplement. 1915.

BIOGRAPHISCHES JAHRBUCH für ALTER-
  TUMSKUNDE see B448.

B112
BIOGRAPHOI: vitarum scriptores
  graeci minores / A. Westerman.
  Brunswick 1845. Reprint Amsterdam 1964.

B113
BIULETYN NUMÍZMATYCZNY. Warsaw
  1965-   .

Bivona, L. see I118.

BLÄTTER für das BAYERISCHE GYMNASI-
  AL- und REALSCHULWESEN see B22.

B114
BLÄTTER für DEUTSCHE LANDESGE-
  SCHICHTE. Berlin 1852-   .
  1852-1935 title: C/Korrespondenz-
  blatt. Gesamtverein der Deutschen
  Geschichts- und Altertumsverein.
  Suspended 1943-50.

B115
BLÄTTER für DEUTSCHE PHILOSOPHIE.
  Berlin 1927-44.

BLÄTTER für das GYMNASIALSCHULWE-
  SEN see B22.

B116
BLÄTTER für HEIMATKUNDE (Histor-
  ischer Verein für Steiermark).
  Graz 1923-   .

B117
BLÄTTER für MÜNZFREUNDE und MÜNZ-
  FORSCHUNG. Leipzig etc. 1865-   .
  Until 1874 issued as a supple-
  ment to Numismatischer Verkehr.

Blanchet, A. see C62.

Blass, F. see A687, G80.

Blegen, C. W. see P12.

Blinkenberg, C. S. see I40, L58.

Bliss, F. J. see E161.

Boak, A. E. R. see A486, P71.

Boardman, J. see A466, G89, O18.

Bode, G. H. see S64.

B118
BODENDENKMALPFLEGE in MECKLENBURG;
  Jahrbuch. Schwerin 1953-   .
  Cover title: Jahrbuch für Boden-
  denkmalpflege in Mecklenburg.

B119
BODLEIAN LIBRARY RECORD. Oxford
  1938-   .

Boeckh, A.   see   C214.

B120
BOGHAZKÖI-STUDIEN / O. Weber.
  Leipzig 1917-   .

BOGHAZKOY-TAFELN im ARCHÄOLOGISCHEN
  MUSEUM im ISTANBUL see I129.

B121
BOGHAZKÖI-TEXTE in UMSCHRIFT / E.
  Forrer. Leipzig 1922-26. (Wissenschaftliche Veröffentlichung
  der Deutschen Orientgesellschaft;
  41-42).

Boisacq, É.   see   D51.

Boissonade, J. F.   see   A209.

B122
BOKA; zbornik radova iz nauke, kul-
  ture i umjetnosti. Ercegnovi
  1969-   .

BOLETÍN:
  See also BULLETIN, BOLLETTINO,
  BULETINUL and BUTLLETÍ.

BOLETÍN de la real ACADEMIA de
  BUENAS LETRAS de BARCELONA see
  B449.

B123
BOLETÍN de la real ACADEMIA de
  CIENCIAS BELLAS LETRAS y NOBLES
  ARTES de CÓRDOBA. Córdoba
  1922-   .

B124
BOLETÍN de la real ACADEMIA ESPAÑ-
  OLA. Madrid 1914-   . Suspended
  1936-45.

B125
BOLETÍN de la real ACADEMIA GALLE-
  GA. La Caruña 1906-   .

B126
BOLETÍN de la real ACADEMIA de la
  HISTORIA. Madrid 1877-   .
  (BRAH).

B127
BOLETÍN ARQUEOLÓGICO. Tarragona.
  1901-08 1914-20 1921-36 1943-   .

B128
BOLETÍN ARQUEOLÓGICO del SUDESTE
  ESPAÑOL. Cartagena 1945-   .
  (BASE).

B129
BOLETÍN. ASOCIACIÓN ESPAÑOLA de
  ORIENTALISTAS. Madrid 1965-   .
  (BAEO).

B130
BOLETÍN de la BIBLIOTECA MENÉNDEZ
  y PELAYO. Santander 1919-   .
  Suspended 1934-44.

B131
BOLETÍN de la BIBLIOTECA-MUSEO-
  BALAGUER. Villanueva y Geltru
  1884-   .

BOLETÍN de la COMISIÓN PROVINCIAL
  de MONUMENTOS HISTÓRICOS y ARTÍS-
  TICOS de BURGOS see B138.

B132
BOLETÍN de la COMISIÓN PROVINCIAL
  de MONUMENTOS HISTÓRICOS y ARTÍS-
  TICOS de LUGO. Lugo 1941-   .

B133
BOLETÍN de la COMISIÓN PROVINCIAL
  de MONUMENTOS HISTÓRICOS y ARTÍS-
  TICOS de ORENSE. Orense 1898-   .

B134
BOLETÍN de FILOLOGÍA (Univ. de
  Montevideo). Montevideo 1936/7-
  51/2?

B135
BOLETÍN del INSTITUTO de ESTUDIOS
  ASTURIANOS. Oviedo 1947-   .
  (BIEA).

B136
BOLETÍN del INSTITUTO de ESTUDIOS
  GIENNENSES. Jaen 1953-   .

B137
BOLETÍN del INSTITUTO de ESTUDIOS
  HELÉNICOS (Univ. de Barcelona).
  Barcelona ?-   .

B138
BOLETÍN de la INSTITUCIÓN FERNÁN-
  GONZALES. Burgos 1922?-   .

1922?-45 title: Boletín de la
Comisión Provincial de Monumentos
Históricos y Artísticos de Bur-
gos.

B139
BOLETÍN de la INSTITUCIÓN SANCHO
el SABIO. Vitoria 1957-   .

B140
BOLETÍN del MUSEI ARQUEOLÓGICO
PROVINCIAL de ORENSE. Orense
1943-   .

BOLETÍN REAL ... see BOLETÍN ...
(the word real is disregarded in
filing, but may have been regarded in forming an abbreviation).

B141
BOLETÍN del SEMINARIO de ESTUDIOS
de ARTE y ARQUEOLOGÍA (Univ. Valladolid). Valladolid 1932-   .
1932-53 title: Boletín de trabajos. (BSEAA, BSAA).

B142
BOLETÍN de la SOCIEDAD CASTELLON-
ENSE de CULTURA. Castellón
1920-36.

B143
BOLETÍN de la SOCIEDAD ESPANOLA
de EXCURSIONES; arte, arqueología, historia. Madrid 1893-   .
Suspended 1936-39.

B144
BOLETÍN de la real SOCIEDAD VASCON-
GADA de AMIGOS del PAÍS. San
Sebastian 1945-   .

BOLETÍN de TRABAJOS del SEMINARIO
de ESTUDIOS de ARTE y ARQUEOLO-
GIA see B141.

BOLETÍN. UNIVERSIDAD de BARCELONA.
INSTITUTO de ESTUDIOS HELÉNICOS
see B137.

B145
BOLETÍN de la UNIVERSIDAD de SAN-
TIAGO de COMPOSTELA. Santiago
de Compostela 1929-   .

BOLETÍN. UNIVERSIDAD de VALLADOLID.
SEMINARIO de ESTUDIOS de ARTE y
ARQUEOLOGÍA see B141.

Bollandus, J. see A81.

BOLLETTINO and BULLETTINO are here
interfiled. See also BULLETIN,
BULETINUL, BOLETIN and BUTLETTI.

BULLETTINO degli ANNALI dell'INSTI-
TUTO di CORRESPONDENZA ARCHEOLO-
GICO see B166.

B146
BOLLETTINO di ARCHEOLOGIA CRISTI-
ANA. Rome etc. 1863-94. Super-
seded by Nuovo Bullettino di
Archeologia Cristiana. (BAC).

B147
BULLETTINO ARCHEOLOGICO NAPOLETANO.
Naples 1842-48 1852-60.

BULLETTINO di ARCHEOLOGIA e STORIA
(DALMATA/PATRIA) see V58

B148
BOLLETTINO d'ARTE del Ministero
della Pubblica Istruzione. Rome
1907-   . Suspended 1938-47
and replaced by Le Arte (1938-
43. (BdA, BA, BArte).

BOLLETTINO. ASSOCIAZIONE ARCHEO-
LOGICA ROMANA see R341.

B149
BOLLETTINO dell'ASSOCIAZIONE INTER-
NAZIONALE degli STUDI MEDITERRA-
NEI. Rome 1930-36. (BStM).

B150
BOLLETTINO della BADIA GRECA di
GROTTAFERRATA. Grottaferrata
1947-   .

B151
BOLLETTINO della CAPITOLE. Rome
1935-36. Published during the
suspension of Capitolium.

B152
BOLLETTINO del CENTRO CAMUNO di
STUDI PREISTORICI. Brescia
1964/5-   .

B153
BOLLETTINO. CENTRO INTERNAZIONALE
di STUDI d'ARCHITETTURA ANDREA
PALLADIO. Vicenza 1959-   .

BOLLETTINO del CENTRO INTERNAZION-
ALE per lo STUDIO dei PAPIRI
ERCOLANESI see C255.

B154
BOLLETTINO. CENTRO di STUDI FILO-
LOGICI e LINGUISTICI SICILIANI.
Palermo 1953-   .

B155
BOLLETTINO del CENTRO di STUDI per
la STORIA dell'ARCHITETTURA.
Rome 4- 1945-   . Centro's
name varies slightly.

B156
BOLLETTINO del CIRCOLO NUMISMATICO
NAPOLITANO. Naples 1916-   .

BOLLETTINO. CIVICA BIBLIOTECA.
BERGAMO see B47.

B157
BOLLETTINO dei CLASSICI (Comitato
per la Preparazione dell'Edizione
Nazionale dei Classici Greci e
Latini). Rome 1940-42 1945-   .
Title until 1969?: Bollettino
del Comitato per la Preparazione
... (BPEC).

BOLLETTINO del COMITATO per la PRE-
PARAZIONE della EDIZIONE NAZI-
ONALE dei CLASSICI GRECI e LA-
TINI see B157.

B158
BULLETTINO della COMMISSIONE di
ANTICHITÀ e BELLE ARTE in SICI-
LIA. Palermo 1864-75.

B159
BULLETTINO della COMMISSIONE ARCHE-
OLOGICA COMUNALE di ROMA. Rome
1872-   . (BullCom, BullComm,
BCAR, BCom).

BULLETTINO della COMMISSIONE ARCHE-
OLOGICA COMUNALE di ROMA. SUP-
PLEMENT see B177.

B160
BULLETTINO della DEPUTAZIONE ABRUZ-
ZESI di STORIA PATRIA. Aquila
1889-   . Also issued under
the variant names of the Society:
Società di Storia Patria Anton
Ludovico Antinori negli Abruzzi
& Deputazione di Storia Patria
per gli Abruzzi.

BULLETTINO. DEPUTAZIONE di STORIA
PATRIA per gli ABRUZZI see
B160.

BOLLETTINO della DEPUTAZIONE di
STORIA PATRIA per la LIGURIA.
SEZIONE INGAUNA e INTEMELIA.
see R301.

B161
BOLLETTINO della DEPUTAZIONE di
STORIA PATRIA per l'UMBRIA.
Perugia 1895-   .

B162
BOLLETTINO ECONOMICO della CAMERA
di COMMERCIO, INDUSTRIA, ARTIGI-
ANATO e AGRICOLTURA. Ravenna
1946-   .

B163
BOLLETTINO di FILOLOGIA CLASSICA.
Turin 1894-1942.

BULLETTINO dell'ISTITUTO ARCHEO-
LOGICO GERMANICO. SEZIONE ROMA-
NA see M193.

B164
BOLLETTINO dell'ISTITUTO nazionale
di ARCHEOLOGIA e STORIA dell'ARTE.
Rome 1922-   . Institute's name
varies slightly.

B165
BOLLETTINO dell'ISTITUTO CENTRALE
del RESTAURO. Rome 1950-   .

B166
BULLETTINO dell'INSTITUTO di COR-
RESPONDENZA ARCHEOLOGICA = Bul-
letin de l'Institut de Correspon-
dance Archéologique. Rome &
Berlin 1829-85. 1829 title:
Bullettino degli Annali dell'In-
stituto di Correspondenza Arche-

ologico. 1854-55 published in
the Institute's Monumenti, Annali e Bullettini. (BullInst,
BdI).

B167
BULLETTINO dell'ISTITUTO di DIRIT-
TO ROMANO "Vittorio Scialoja"
(Univ. Rome). Rome 1888-   .
(BIDR).

BOLLETTINO dell'ISTITUTO nazionale
del DRAMMA ANTICO see D69.

B168
BOLLETTINO dell'ISTITUTO di FILOLO-
GIA GRECA (Univ. Padova). Rome
1974-   .

BOLLETTINO dell'ISTITUTO NAZIONALE
see BOLLETTINO dell'ISTITUTO ...
(the word nazionale is disregarded in filing, but may have been
regarded in forming an abbreviation).

B169
BOLLETTINO dell'ISTITUTO di STORIA
e di ARTE del LAZIO MERIDIONALE.
Rome ?-   .

B170
BOLLETTINO dell'ISTITUTO STORICO
ARTISTICO ORVIETANO. Orvieto
1945-   .

B171
BULLETTINO dell'ISTITUTO STORICO
ITALIANO per il MEDIO EVO e
ARCHIVIO MURATORINO. Rome
1886-   . 1886-1921 title: Bul-
lettino dell'Istituto Storico
Italiano. 1923-33 title: Bul-
lettino dell'Istituto Storico
Italiano e Archivio Muratoriano.

BOLLETTINO dell'ISTITUTO per la
STORIA della SOCIETÀ e dello
STATO VENEZIANO see S259.

B172
BOLLETTINO ITALIANO di NUMISMATICA
e di ARTE della MEDAGLIA. Milan
1903-18. 1903-06 title: Bollettino di Numismatica e di Arte
della Medaglia.

B173
BOLLETTINO del MUSEO CIVICO di
PADOVA. Padua 1898-1914 1925- .

B174
BULLETTINO dei MUSEI CIVICI VENE-
ZIANI. Venice 1956-   .

B175
BOLLETTINO dei MUSEI COMUNALI di
ROMA. Rome 1954-   . (BollMC).

B176
BOLLETTINO. MUSEI FERRARESI. Ferrara ?-   .

B177
BULLETTINO del MUSEO dell'IMPERO
ROMANA. Rome 1930-42. Supplement to the Bullettino della Commissione Archeologica Comunale
di Roma. (BMusImp, BMIR).

BOLLETTINO di NUMISMATICA e di
ARTE della MEDAGLIA see B172.

B178
BOLLETTINO NUMISMATICO di LUIGI
SIMONETTI. Florence 1964-   .

B179
BULLETTINO di PALETNOLOGIA ITALI-
ANA. Rome etc. 1875-   .
1941/2-53 title: Preistoria; bol-
lettino di paletnologia italiana.
(BPI, BullPaletnItal).

B180
BULLETTINO SENESE di STORIA PATRIA.
Siena 1894-   .

BOLLETTINO della SEZIONE di CUNEO
R. DEPUTAZIONE SUBALPINA di
STORIA PATRIA see B183.

BOLLETTINO. SOCIETÀ AFRICANA
d'ITALIA see A101.

B181
BOLLETTINO della SOCIETÀ PIEMONTESE
di ARCHEOLOGIA e di BELLE ARTI.
Turin 1917-35 1947-   .

BOLLETTINO della SOCIETÀ STORICO-
ARCHEOLOGICA INGAUNA e INTEMELIA
see R301.

B182
BOLLETTINO della SOCIETÀ STORICA
MAREMMANA. Grosseto ?-   .

BOLLETTINO. SOCIETÀ di STORIA PAT-
RIA ANTON LUDOVICO ANTINORI
negli ABRUZZI see B160.

B183
BOLLETTINO della SOCIETÀ per gli
STUDI STORICI ARCHEOLOGICI ed
ARTISTICI nella PROVINCIA di
CUNEO. Cuneo 1929-44 1949-   .
Title varies: 1929-34: Communica-
zioni; 1935: Communicazioni della
R. Deputazione Subalpina di Stor-
ia Patria. Sezione di Cuneo;
1936-44: Bollettino della Sezione
di Cuneo della Deputazione di
Storia Patria.

B184
BOLLETTINO di STORIA dell'ARTE.
Salerno 1951-   .

B185
BOLLETTINO STORICO-BIBLIOGRAFICO
SUBALPINO. Turin 1896-   .

BOLLETTINO STORICO CATANESE see
A550.

B186
BOLLETTINO STORICO CREMONESE.
Cremona 1931-   .

BOLLETTINO STORICO MESSINESE see
A542.

B187
BOLLETTINO STORICO PIACENTINO.
Piacenza 1906-   .

B188
BOLLETTINO STORICO per la PROVINCIA
di NOVARA. Novara 1907-   .

B189
BOLLETTINO STORICO della SVIZZERA
ITALIANA. Bellinzona 1879-   .
Suspended 1913-14 1916-20.

Bompaire, J. see A90.

Bond, E. A. see P14.

B190
BONNER BIBLISCHE BEITRÄGE. Bonn
1950-   .

B191
BONNER GESCHICHTSBLÄTTER. Bonn
1937-   .

B192
BONNER HEFTE zur VORGESCHICHTE.
Bonn 1971-   .

BONNER HISTORIA-AUGUSTA-COLLOQUIUM
see H89.

B193
BONNER JARHBÜCHER des RHEINISCHEN
LANDESMUSEUMS in BONN und des
VEREINS von ALTERTUMSFREUNDEN im
RHEINLANDE. Bonn 1842-   .
1842-94 title: Jahrbücher des
Vereins von Alterthumsfreunden
im Rheinlande. Other minor title
changes. Suspended 1943-47.
(BJ, BJb, BJbb, BonnJahrb).

Bonnet, H. see R21.

Bonnet, M. see A36.

B194
BOOKLIST (Society for Old Testament
Studies). n.p. 1946-   .

B195
BOREAS; münstersche Beiträge zur
Archäologie. Münster 1978-   .

B196
BOREAS; Uppsala studies in ancient
Mediterranean and Near Eastern
civilizations. Uppsala 1970-   .
(Acta Universitatis Upsaliensis).

Bosanquet, R. C. see U20.

Bosch y Gimpera, P. see F29.

Boswinkel, E. see E18.

Botterweck, G. J. see T49.

Bowra, C. M. see G92.

B197
BRABANTS HEEM; tweemaandelijks

tidsschrift voor Brabantse Heem-
en Oudheidkunde. Eindhoven
1949-   .

B198
BRACARA AUGUSTA; revista cultural
da Câmara Municipal de Braga.
Braga 1935-   . 1935-49 title:
Braga.

Bradeen, D. W. see S189.

B199
BRADFORD ANTIQUARY. Bradford
1888-   .

BRAGA see B198.

Brandt, P. see C246, P76.

B200
BRAUNSCHWEIGISCHE HEIMAT. Brunswick ?-   .

B201
BRAUNSCHWEIGISCHES JAHRBUCH.
Brunswick 1902-   . 1902-38
title: Jahrbuch des Geschichtsvereins für das Herzogtum Braunschweig.

Bréal, M. J. A. see D54.

Breasted, J. H. see A201.

Breccia, E. see I117.

B202
BREMER ARCHÄOLOGISCHE BLÄTTER.
Bremen 1960-   .

B203
BREMISCHES JAHRBUCH. Bremen
1864-   .

B204
BRESLAUER PHILOLOGISCHE ABHANDLUN-
GEN. Breslau 1887-1914.

B205
BRETTENER JAHRBUCH für KULTUR und
GESCHICHTE. Bretten 1959-   .

BRÈVES COMMUNICATIONS de l'INSTITUT
de la CULTURE MATERIELLE de l'AC-
ADÉMIE des SCIENCES de l'URSS
see K45.

Brice, W. C. see I85.

Briggs, C. A. see H34.

B206
BRITANNIA; a journal of Romano-
British and kindred studies.
London 1970-   .

B207
BRITISH ARCHAEOLOGICAL ABSTRACTS.
London 1968-   .

B208
BRITISH ARCHAEOLOGICAL REPORTS.
Oxford 1974-   . (BAR).

B209
BRITISH MUSEUM. CATALOGS. BRONZES.
Catalogue of the Bronzes, Greek,
Roman and Etruscan in the Department of Greek and Roman Antiquities / H. B. Walters. London
1899.

B210
BRITISH MUSEUM. CATALOGS. COINS.
BYZANTINE. Catalogue of the Im-
perial Byzantine Coins / W.
Wroth. London 1908.

B211
BRITISH MUSEUM. CATALOGS. COINS.
GREEK.[arranged by place].
Catalogue of the Greek Coins.
London 1873-1927. (BMC, BMC
(place), BMCGC).

B212
BRITISH MUSEUM. CATALOGS. COINS.
ROMAN. EMPIRE. Coins of the Roman Empire / H. Mattingly. London 1923-   . (CREBM,BMCRE).

B213
BRITISH MUSEUM. CATALOGS. COINS.
ROMAN. REPUBLIC. Coins of the
Roman Republic / H. A. Grueber.
London 1910. (CRRBM).

B214
BRITISH MUSEUM. CATALOGS. GEMS.
Catalogue of the Engraved Gems
and Cameos, Greek, Etruscan and
Roman / H. B. Walters. London
1926. (BMCG).

B215
BRITISH MUSEUM. CATALOGS. INSCRIP-
TIONS. CUNEIFORM. Cuneiform Texts
from Babylonian Tablets. London
1896-   .

B216
BRITISH MUSEUM. CATALOGS. INSCRIP-
TIONS. CUNEIFORM. Hittite Texts
in the Cuneiform Character from
Tablets in the British Museum /
H. C. Rawlinson. London 1920.

B217
BRITISH MUSEUM. CATALOGS. INSCRIP-
TIONS. GREEK. Collection of An-
cient Greek Inscriptions / C. T.
Newton. Oxford 1874-1916.
(GIBM, IBM, BMI).

BRITISH MUSEUM. CATALOGS. IVORIES
see C83.

B218
BRITISH MUSEUM. CATALOGS. JEWEL-
LERY. Catalogue of the Jewellery
Greek, Etruscan and Roman, in the
Departments of Antiquities / F.
H. Marshall. London 1911.
(BMCJ).

B219
BRITISH MUSEUM. CATALOGS. LAMPS.
Catalogue of the Greek and
Roman Lamps in the British Mu-
seum / H. B. Walters. New ed.
London 1975-   .

B220
BRITISH MUSEUM. CATALOGS. MARBLES.
Description of the Collection of
Ancient Marbles in the British
Museum / T. Combe et al. London
1812-61.

B221
BRITISH MUSEUM. CATALOGS. PAPYRI.
Greek Papyri in the British
Museum / F. G. Kenyon, H. I.
Bell et al. London 1893-   .
(PLond).

B222
BRITISH MUSEUM. CATALOGS. PAPYRI.
Catalogue of the Literary Papyri
/ H. J. M. Milne. London 1927.
(PLondLit).

B223
BRITISH MUSEUM. CATALOGS. RINGS.
Catalogue of the Finger Rings,
Greek, Etruscan and Roman, in the
Departments of Antiquities / F.
H. Marshall. London 1907.
(BMCR).

B224
BRITISH MUSEUM. CATALOGS. SCARABS.
Catalogue of Egyptian Scarabs
etc. / H. R. Hall. London
1913-   . Vol. 1 only published?

B225
BRITISH MUSEUM. CATALOGS. SCULP-
TURE. Catalogue of Sculpture in
the Department of Greek and Roman
Antiquities / A. H. Smith. Lon-
don 1892-1904. Vol. 1 appeared
in 2nd edition (1928) by F. N.
Pryce.

B226
BRITISH MUSEUM. CATALOGS. TERRA-
COTTAS. Catalogue of the Terra-
cottas in the Department of
Greek and Roman Antiquities / R.
A. Higgins. New ed. London
1954-   . 1st edition 1903 by
H. B. Walters.

B227
BRITISH MUSEUM. CATALOGS. VASES.
Catalogue of the Greek and Etrus-
can Vases. London 1893-   .

B228
BRITISH MUSEUM QUARTERLY. London
1926-   . Suspended 1941-50.
(BMQ).

B229
BRITISH NUMISMATIC JOURNAL and
PROCEEDINGS of the BRITISH NUMIS-
MATIC SOCIETY. London 1903-   .

Brockelmann, C. see G28.

Brommer, F. see V4.

B230
BROOKLYN MUSEUM BULLETIN. Brooklyn 1939-60.

Broughton, T. R. S. see M9.

Brown, F. see H34.

Bruce, J. C. see L8.

Bruckmann, F. see D15, D17,
    G125.

Bruckner, A. see C111.

B231
BRUGGER NEUJAHRSBLÄTTER (Kultur-
    gesellschaft des Bezirks Brugg).
    Brugg 1890-   .

Brugmann, K. see G108.

Brugsch, H. K. see D55, T55.

Brunn, H. see D15, G125, R263.

Bruns, C. G. see F32.

B232
BRUTIUM. Reggio di Calabria
    1957-   .

Bruyère, B. see T15.

Buchberger, M. see L46

Buckler, W. H. see G91.

B233
BUCKNELL REVIEW. Lewisburg, Pa.
    1941-   . 1941-54 title: Buck-
    nell University Studies. Sus-
    pended 1941-49.

BUCKNELL UNIVERSITY STUDIES see
    B233.

B234
BUDAPEST RÉGISÉGEI (Budapesti Tör-
    téneti Múzeum). Budapest 1889- .
    (BpR).

BUDAPESTI RUNDSCHAU see B235.

B235
BUDAPESTI SZEMLE. Budapest 1857-
    69 1873-1919?.

Buecheler, F. see C58.

B236
BÜNDNER MONATSBLATT; Zeitschrift

für Bundnerische Geschichte,
    Heimat- und Volkskunde. Chur
    1850-57 1881 1914-   . Title
    until 1951: Bündnerisches Monats-
    blatt.

BULETINUL, BULETIN and BULETINI
are here interfiled. See also
BULLETIN, BOLLETTINO and BOLETIN.

B237
BULETINUL COMISIUNII MONUMENTELOR
    ISTORICE a ROMÂNIEI. Bucharest
    1908-42? Continued by Revista
    Muzeelor?

BULETINUL MONUMENTELOR ISTORICE
    see B237.

BULETINI i MUZEUMIT të KOSOVË ME-
    TOHIS see G49.

BULETINUL. SECJTIUNEA ISTORICĂ.
    ACADEMIA ROMÂNĂ see B352.

BULETIN per SHKENCAT SHOQERORE
    see B241.

B238
BULETINUL SOCIETATII GEOGRAFICE
    din republica socialista RO-
    MANIA. Bucharest 1876-? 1971- .

B239
BULETINUL SOCIETATII NUMISMATICE
    ROMÂNE. Bucharest 1904-   .
    (BSNR).

BULETINUL SOCIETATII regale RO-
    MÂNE de GEOGRAFIE see B238.

B240
BULETINUL ŞTIINŢIFICE. ACADEMIA
    ROMÂNĂ. SECTIA de ŞTIINŢE ISTO-
    RICE, FILOZOFICE şi ECONOMICE.
    Bucharest ?-   . Continues the
    Bulletin de la Section Histo-
    rique, Académie Roumaine?

B241
BULETIN i UNIVERSITETIT SHTETËROR
    të TIRANES. SERIA SHKENCAT
    SHOQËRORE. Tiranë 1951-63
    1951-57 title: Buletin per Shken-
    cat Shoqërore.

B242
BULGARSKI EZIK. Sofia 1951-   .

BULLETIN see also BULLETIN INFOR-
MATION, BOLLETTINO, BULETINUL,
BOLETIN, GLASNIK, IZVESTIĬA,
VESTNIK.

B243
BULLETINS. ACADÉMIE royale de
BELGIQUE. Brussels 1832-98.
--. Classe des Lettres, des
Sciences Morales et Politiques.
1899-   . Suspended 1915-18.
--. Classe des Beaux Arts.
1915-   .
(BAB).

B244
BULLETIN de l'ACADÉMIE DELPHINALE.
Grenoble 1836-   .

B245
BULLETIN de l'ACADÉMIE d'HIPPONE.
Bona, Algeria 1865-   .

BULLETIN. ACADÉMIE IMPERIALE ...
see BULLETIN. ACADÉMIE ... (the
word imperiale is disregarded in
filing, but may have been regarded in forming an abbreviation).

BULLETIN. ACADÉMIE NATIONALE ...
see BULLETIN. ACADÉMIE ... (the
word nationale is disregarded in
filing, but may have been regarded in forming an abbreviation).

BULLETIN de l'ACADÉMIE de NÎMES
see B351.

B246
BULLETIN international de l'ACAD-
ÉMIE POLONAISE des SCIENCES et
des LETTRES. Krakow 1889-1945?
1889-1901 title: Anzeiger der
Akademie der Wissenschaften in
Krakau. Philologische und Historisch-philosophische Classe.
1903-17 title also in French:
Bulletin international de l'Académie des Sciences de Cracovie.
Classe de Philologie, Classe
d'histoire et de philosophie.

BULLETIN.ACADÉMIE ROUMAINE. SEC-
TION HISTORIQUE see B352.

BULLETIN. ACADÉMIE ROYALE ... see
BULLETIN. ACADÉMIE ... (the word
royale is disregarded in filing,
but may have been regarded in
forming an abbreviation).

BULLETIN. ACADÉMIE des SCIENCES,
BELLES-LETTRES et ARTS de BE-
SANÇON see P212.

BULLETIN. ACADÉMIE des SCIENCES
de BULGARE. INSTITUT d'HISTOIRE
see I157.

BULLETIN international de l'ACA-
DÉMIE des SCIENCES de CRACOVIE.
CLASSE de PHILOLOGIE, CLASSE
d'HISTOIRE et de PHILOSOPHIE
see B245.

BULLETIN of the ACADEMY of SCIENCES
of the GEORGIAN SSR see S116.

BULLETIN. ACADÉMIE royale des
SCIENCES, des LETTRES et des
BEAUX ARTS de BELGIQUE see
B243.

BULLETIN de l'ACADÉMIE des
SCIENCES (de l'URSS/ de Russie)
see I152.

BULLETIN de l'ACADÉMIE SERBE des
SCIENCES. CLASSE des SCIENCES
SOCIALES see Z17.

B247
BULLETIN de l'ACADÉMIE et de la
SOCIÉTÉ LORRAINES des SCIENCES.
Nancy 1961-   . 1961-62 title:
Bulletin de la Société Lorraine
des Sciences. Variant title:
Bulletin Trimestriel.

B248
BULLETIN de l'ACADÉMIE du VAR.
Toulon 1833-65 1868-99 1901-
Academy's name varies: Société
des Sciences, Arts et Belles-
Lettres, au Departement du Var;
Société des Sciences, Belles-
Lettres, et Arts du Var; Société
Académique du Var.

B249
BULLETIN international de l'ACA-
DÉMIE YOUGOSLAVE des SCIENCES et
des BEAUX-ARTS et BELLES-LETTRES.
Zagreb 1932-   . Suspended
1956-63?

BULLETIN de l'ALLIANCE NUMISMATIQUE
de BELGIQUE see B250.

B250
BULLETIN mensuel de l'ALLIANCE NUM-
ISMATIQUE EUROPÉENNE. Antwerp
1950-   . Vol. 1 published under
the name of Alliance Numismatique
de Belgique.

BULLETIN of the AMERICAN INSTITUTE
for IRANIAN ART and ARCHAEOLOGY
see B317.

BULLETIN of the AMERICAN INSTITUTE
for PERSIAN ART and ARCHAEOLOGY
see B317.

BULLETIN of the AMERICAN NUMISMATIC
and ARCHAEOLOGICAL SOCIETY see
A146.

B251
BULLETIN of the AMERICAN SCHOOLS of
ORIENTAL RESEARCH. Baltimore
etc. 1919-   . (BASOR, BASO).

B252
BULLETIN of the AMERICAN SCHOOL of
PREHISTORIC RESEARCH. Cambridge,
Mass. 1926-   .

B253
BULLETIN. AMERICAN SOCIETY of
PAPYROLOGISTS. New Haven etc.
1963/4-   . (BASP).

BULLETIN. AMIS de MONTLUÇON see
B346.

B254
BULLETIN des AMIS d'ORANGE.
Orange ?-   .

BULLETIN des AMIS SUISSES de la
CERAMIQUE see M203.

B255
BULLETIN ANALYTIQUE d'HISTOIRE
ROMAINE. Strasbourg 1962-   .

B256
BULLETIN d'ANCIENNE LITTÉRATURE et
d'ARCHÉOLOGIE CHRÉTIENNES. Paris
1911-14.

BULLETIN ANNUEL ... see BULLETIN
... (the word annuel is disregarded in filing, but may have
been regarded in forming an
abbreviation).

BULLETIN ANTIEKE BESCHAVING see
B1.

BULLETIN trimestriel des ANTIQUITÉS
AFRICAINES see R95.

B257
BULLETIN d'ARCHÉOLOGIE ALGÉRIENNE.
Paris 1962/5-   . (BAA).

B258
BULLETIN ARCHÉOLOGIQUE du COMITÉ
des TRAVAUX HISTORIQUES et
SCIENTIFIQUES. Paris 1883-   .
1883-85 title: Bulletin du Comité
des Travaux Historiques et Scientifique: Archéologie. (BAC).

B259
BULLETIN ARCHÉOLOGIQUE, HISTORIQUE,
et ARTISTIQUE de la SOCIÉTÉ ARCH-
ÉOLOGIQUE de TARN-et-GARONNE.
Montauban 1869-   . Title
varies slightly.

BULLETIN d'ARCHÉOLOGIE et d'HIS-
TOIRE DALMATE see V58.

BULLETIN ARCHÉOLOGIQUE et HISTO-
RIQUE de la SOCIÉTÉ ARCHÉOLOGIQUE
de TARN-et-GARONNE see B259.

B260
BULLETIN d'ARCHÉOLOGIE MAROCAINE.
Casablanca 1956-   . (BAM).

BULLETIN ARCHÉOLOGIQUE POLONAIS
see W17.

BULLETIN ARCHÉOLOGIQUE de la SOCIÉ-
TÉ ARCHÉOLOGIQUE de TARN-et-GAR-
ONNE see B259.

BULLETIN d'ARCHÉOLOGIE et de STA-
TISTIQUE de la DRÔME see R128.

B261
BULLETIN d'ARCHÉOLOGIE SUD-EST
   EUROPÉENNE. Bucharest 1969-   .

B262
BULLETIN ARCHÉOLOGIQUE du VEXIN
   FRANÇAIS. Guiry-en-Vexin ?-   .

BULLETIN. ART MUSEUM. RHODE ISLAND
   SCHOOL of DESIGN see B347.

BULLETIN. ASSOCIATION des AMIS (des
   ÉGLISES et) d'ART COPTES see
   B368.

B263
BULLETIN semestriel de l'ASSOCIA-
   TION des CLASSIQUES de l'UNIVER-
   SITÉ de LIÈGE. Heusy-Verviers
   1953-   .

BULLETIN of the ASSOCIATES in
   FINE ARTS at YALE UNIVERSITY
   see B445.

B264
BULLETIN de l'ASSOCIATION GUILLAUME
   BUDÉ. Paris 1923-   . 1941-50
   replaced by Lettres d'humanité.
   --. Supplement critique. 1929-38.
   (BAGB).

BULLETIN. ASSOCIATION INTERNATION-
   ALE des ÉTUDES BYZANTINES see
   B305.

BULLETIN. ASSOCIATION INTERNATION-
   ALE pour l'ÉTUDE de la MOSAÏQUE
   ANTIQUE see B304.

BULLETIN. ASSOCIATION INTERNATION-
   ALE d'ÉTUDES PATRISTIQUES see
   B306.

B265
BULLETIN de l'ASSOCIATION INTERNA-
   TIONALE d'ÉTUDES du SUD-EST
   EUROPÉEN. Bucharest 1963-   .
   Half title: AIESEE Bulletin.

B266
BULLETIN de l'ASSOCIATION INTERNA-
   TIONALE pour l'HISTOIRE du VERRE.
   Liège 1962-   . Vols. 1-4 issued
   under the association's earlier
   name: Journées Internationales
   du Verre.

BULLETIN de l'ASSOCIATION du MUSÉE
   de SLOVÉNIE see G50.

B267
BULLETIN de l'ASSOCIATION des NA-
   TURALISTES de la VALLÉE du LOING
   et du MASSIF de FONTAINEBLEAU.
   Paris 1913-   . Suspended
   1939-47?

B268
BULLETIN de l'ASSOCIATION PRO AVEN-
   TICO. Lausanne 1887-   .

BULLETIN de l'AUVERGNE see B302.

BULLETIN. BELGIQUE see B243.

B269
BULLETIN des BIBLIOTHÈQUES de
   FRANCE. Paris 1956-   . (BBF).

BULLETIN BIMESTRIEL ... see BUL-
   LETIN ... (the word bimestriel
   is disregarded in filing, but
   may have been regarded in forming an abbreviation).

B270
BULLETIN of the BOARD of CELTIC
   STUDIES. Cardiff 1921/3-   .

B271
BULLETIN. BRITISH SCHOOL of ARCHAE-
   OLOGY in JERUSALEM. London
   1922-25.

BULLETIN. BRUXELLES see B243.

B272
BULLETIN of the BYZANTINE INSTITUTE
   (of America). Paris & Boston
   1946-50. (BByzt).

B273
BULLETIN du CANGE; archivum latinitatis medii aevi. Paris & Brussels 1924-   . (ALMA).

BULLETIN. CENTRE INTERNATIONAL
   d'ÉTUDE de TEXTILES ANCIENS
   see B321.

B274
BULLETIN du CERCLE ARCHÉOLOGIQUE
   HESBAYE-CONDROZ. Amay ?-   .

B275
BULLETIN du CERCLE d'ÉTUDES NUMIS-
   MATIQUES. Brussels 1964-   .

BULLETIN. CLASSE des BEAUX ARTS.
   ACADÉMIE Royale de BELGIQUE
   see B243.

BULLETIN. CLASSE des HUMANITÉS.
   ACADÉMIE des SCIENCES de l'URSS
   see I152.

BULLETIN de la CLASSE des LETTRES,
   des SCIENCES, MORALES et POLI-
   TIQUES. ACADÉMIE Royale de
   BELGIQUE see B243.

B276
BULLETIN of the CLEVELAND MUSEUM
   of ART. Cleveland 1914-   .

BULLETIN of the COLLEGE ART ASSO-
   CIATION see A605.

B277
BULLETIN du COMITÉ ARCHÉOLOGIQUE
   de LEZOUX. Lezoux ?-   .

BULLETIN du COMITÉ des TRAVAUX
   HISTORIQUES et SCIENTIFIQUE:
   ARCHÉOLOGIE see B258.

BULLETIN de la COMMISSION des
   ANTIQUITÉS DÉPARTEMENTALES du
   PAS-de-CALAIS see B280.

B278
BULLETIN de la COMMISSION des
   ANTIQUITÉS de SEINE-MARITIME.
   Rouen ?-   .

BULLETIN de la COMMISSION (impériale) ARCHÉOLOGIQUE (RUSSIA)
   see I156.

B279
BULLETIN de la COMMISSION ARCHÉOLO-
   GIQUE de NARBONNE. Narbonne
   1876-77 1890-   . Until 1890
   under an earlier name: Commission
   Archéologique et Litteraires de
   l'Arrondissement de Narbonne.

B280
BULLETIN de la COMMISSION DÉPARTEM-
   ENTALE des MONUMENTS HISTORIQUES
   du PAS-de-CALAIS. Arras etc.
   1848-1930. Also under the earlier
   name of the Commission: Commission des Antiquités Départementales du Pas-de-Calais.

B281
BULLETIN de la COMMISSION royale
   d'HISTOIRE = Handelingen van de
   koninklijke Commissie voor Geschiedenis. Brussels 1834/7-   .
   1834-1902 title: Compte-rendu
   des Séances de la Commission
   Royale d'Histoire. Suspended
   1914-19.

B282
BULLETIN de la COMMISSION HISTO-
   RIQUE et ARCHÉOLOGIQUE de la
   MAYENNE. Mayenne 1878/9-   .
   1878-87 title: Procès-verbaux
   et Documents.

B283
BULLETIN de la COMMISSION royale
   des MONUMENTS et des SITES.
   Brussels 1950-   . Supersedes
   in part Bulletin des Commission
   Royales d'Art et d'Archéologie.

B284
BULLETIN de CORRESPONDANCE HELLE-
   NIQUE. Paris 1877-   . 1877-
   1928 vols. also have Greek
   title: Deltion Hellēnikēs Allelographias. (BCH).
   --. Supplement. Paris 1973-   .

B285
BULLETIN. COUNCIL of UNIVERSITY
   CLASSICAL DEPARTMENTS. London
   etc. 1972-   .

B286
BULLETIN CRITIQUE du LIVRE FRAN-
   ÇAIS. Paris 1945-   . (BCLF).

B287
BULLETIN de la DIANA (Société Historique et Archéologique du For-
   ez). Montbrison 1880-   .

BULLETIN DOCUMENTAIRE de la
   SOCIÉTÉ ACADÉMIQUE des HAUTES-
   PYRÉNÉES see B354.

B288
BULLETIN annuel. ÉCOLE ANTIQUE de
  NÎMES. Nimes ?-   .

B289
BULLETIN ÉPIGRAPHIQUE. Vienne,
  France 1881-86. 1881-83 title:
  Bulletin Épigraphique de la
  Gaule.

B290
BULLETIN ÉPIGRAPHIQUE. Paris
  1888-   . Published as part of
  the Revue des Études Grecques.
  Since 1938 compiled by J. & L.
  Robert. (Bullepigr).

BULLETIN ÉPIGRAPHIQUE de la GAULE
  see B289.

B291
BULLETIN d'ÉTUDES ORIENTALES (Institut Français de Damas). Damascus 1931-   . (BEO).

B292
BULLETIN des ÉTUDES PORTUGAISES.
  Coimbra 1931-   .

B293
BULLETIN de la FACULTÉ des LETTRES
  de STRASBOURG. Strasbourg
  1922-   .

B294
BULLETIN of the FOGG ART MUSEUM.
  Cambridge, Mass. 1931-   .

BULLETIN GENERAL de la SOCIÉTÉ ACA-
  DÉMIQUE des HAUTES-PYRÉNÉES see
  B354.

BULLETIN trimestriel de GÉOGRAPHIE
  et d'ARCHÉOLOGIE see B407.

B295
BULLETIN du GROUPEMENT ARCHÉOLO-
  GIQUE du MÂCONNAIS. Mâcon ?-   .

B296
BULLETIN du GROUPE ARCHÉOLOGIQUE
  du NOGENTAIS. Nogent sur
  Seine 1962-   .

B297
BULLETIN du GROUPEMENT ARCHÉOLO-

GIQUE de SEINE-et-MARN. Melun
  ?-   .

B298
BULLETIN des GROUPES de RECHERCHES
  ARCHÉOLOGIQUES du DÉPARTEMENT
  de la LOIRE. Saint-Étienne
  ?-   .

B299
BULLETIN du GROUPE de RECHERCHES
  et d'ÉTUDES de la CÉRAMIQUES.
  Beauvais ?-   .

B300
BULLETIN HISPANIQUE. Bordeaux
  etc. 1899-   .

B301
BULLETIN of the HISTORY of MEDI-
  CINE. Baltimore 1933-   . 1933-
  38 title: Bulletin of the Insti-
  tute of the History of Medicine,
  Johns Hopkins Univ.

BULLETIN of the HISTORICAL METAL-
  LURGY GROUP see J109.

B302
BULLETIN HISTORIQUE et SCIENTI-
  FIQUE de l'AUVERGNE. Clermont-
  Ferrand 1881-   . 1925-31 title:
  Bulletin de l'Auvergne.

B303
BULLETIN HISTORIQUE, SCIENTIFIQUE,
  LITTÉRAIRE, ARTISTIQUE et AGRI-
  COLE. SOCIÉTÉ ACADÉMIQUE du PUY
  et de la HAUTE-LOIRE. Le Puy
  1911-   . Also published by
  the Society under its earlier
  names: Société Scientifique et
  Agricole de la Haute Loire; Société d'Agriculture, Sciences,
  Arts et Commerce de du Puy et
  de la Haute Loire.

BULLETIN HISTORIQUE, SCIENTIFIQUE
  LITTERAIRE, ARTISTIQUE et AG-
  RICOLE. SOCIÉTÉ d'AGRICULTURE,
  SCIENCES, ARTS et COMMERCE de
  du PUY de la HAUTE LOIRE/SOCIÉTÉ
  SCIENTIFIQUE et AGRICOLE de la
  HAUTE LOIRE   see B303.

BULLETIN HISTORIQUE trimestriel.
SOCIÉTÉ des ANTIQUAIRES de la
MORINIE see B362.

BULLETIN INFORMATION ... see also
BULLETIN ...

B304
BULLETIN d'INFORMATION. ASSOCIATION
INTERNATIONALE pour l'ÉTUDE de la
MOSAÏQUE ANTIQUE. Paris 1968- .
(BullAIEMA).

B305
BULLETIN d'INFORMATION et de COOR-
DINATION de l'ASSOCIATION INTER-
NATIONALE des ÉTUDES BYZANTINES.
Athens & Paris 1964-   .

B306
BULLETIN d'INFORMATION et LIAISON
de l'ASSOCIATION INTERNATIONALE
d'ÉTUDES PATRISTIQUES. Amsterdam 1968-   .

B307
BULLETIN d'INFORMATION de la SOCI-
ÉTÉ d'ARCHÉOLOGIE et d'HISTOIRE
de WAREMME et ENVIRONS. Waremme ?-   .

BULLETIN de l'INSTITUT ARCHÉOLO-
GIQUE (Sofia 1910-   .) see
I153.

B308
BULLETIN of the INSTITUTE of ARCH-
AEOLOGY (Univ. London). London
1958-   .

BULLETIN de l'INSTITUT ARCHÉOLO-
GIQUE BULGARE see I153.

BULLETIN. INSTITUT d'ARCHÉOLOGIE
et d'HISTOIRE de l'ART. OFFICE
INTERNATIONALE see B343.

B309
BULLETIN de l'INSTITUT ARCHÉOLO-
GIQUE LIÉGEOIS. Liège 1852-   .

B310
BULLETIN trimestriel de l'INSTITUT
ARCHÉOLOGIQUE du LUXEMBOURG.
Arlon 1925-   . Supplement to
the Institute's Annales.

BULLETIN de l'INSTITUT ARCHÉOLO-
GIQUE RUSSE à CONSTANTINOPOLE
see I164.

B311
BULLETIN of the INSTITUTE of CLAS-
SICAL STUDIES (Univ. London).
London 1954-   . Title of vols.
1-2: Supplementary Papers. (BICS).
--. Supplement. 1955-   .

BULLETIN de l'INSTITUT de CORRES-
PONDANCE ARCHÉOLOGIQUE see
B166.

B312
BULLETIN de l'INSTITUT d'ÉGYPTE.
Alexandria & Cairo 1859-   .
Issues until 1918 under insti-
tute's earlier name: Institut
Égyptien. (BIE).

B313
BULLETIN et mémoires. INSTITUT des
FOUILLES de PRÉHISTOIRE et
d'ARCHÉOLOGIE des ALPES-MARI-
TIMES. Nice ?-   .

B314
BULLETIN de l'INSTITUT FRANÇAIS
d'ARCHÉOLOGIE ORIENTALE. Cairo
1901-   . (BIFAO, BIAO).

BULLETIN de l'INSTITUT d'HISTOIRE
ACADÉMIE des SCIENCES de BULGARE
see I157.

B315
BULLETIN de l'INSTITUT HISTORIQUE
BELGE de ROME. Rome 1919-   .
(BIBR).

BULLETIN of the INSTITUTE of the
HISTORY of MEDICINE (Johns Hopkins Univ.) see B301.

B316
BULLETIN de l'INSTITUT royal du
PATRIMOINE ARTISTIQUE. Brussels
1958-   .

BULLETIN INTERNATIONAL ... see
BULLETIN ... (the word international is disregarded in filing,
but may have been regarded in
forming an abbreviation).

BULLETIN. INTERNATIONAL ASSOCIA-
TION for SOUTH EASTERN EUROPEAN
STUDIES. see B265.

BULLETIN. INTERNATIONAL MEDITERRAN-
EAN RESEARCH ASSOCIATION see
B149.

B317
BULLETIN of the IRANIAN INSTITUTE
of AMERICA. New York 1931-   .
Also under the Institute's earlier names: American Institute for
Persian Art and Archaeology; American Institute for Iranian Art
and Archaeology.

B318
BULLETIN of the ISRAEL EXPLORATION
SOCIETY. Jerusalem 1933-   .
1933-50 title: Bulletin of the
Jewish Palestine Exploration
Society.

BULLETIN of the JEWISH PALESTINE
EXPLORATION SOCIETY see B318.

B319
BULLETIN of the JOHN RYLANDS LIBRA-
RY. Manchester, Eng. 1903-   .
Title of vol. 1: Quarterly Bul-
letin. (BJRL).

BULLETIN. JOURNÉES INTERNATIONALES
du VERRE see B266.

BULLETIN des KONINKLIJKE ... see
BULLETIN... (the word koninklijke
is disregarded in filing, but
may have been regarded in forming
an abbreviation).

B320
BULLETIN du LABORATOIRE du MUSÉE du
LOUVRE. Paris 1956-   .

B321
BULLETIN de LIAISON du CENTRE
INTERNATIONAL d'ÉTUDE des TEX-
TILES ANCIENS. Lyons 1955-   .

B322
BULLETIN LINGUISTIQUE. Bucharest,
Paris etc. 1933-   .

B323
BULLETIN de LITTÉRATURE ECCLÉSIA-
STIQUE. Toulouse 1877-   .
Title before 1898: Bulletin Thé-
ologique, Scientifique et Lit-
téraire.

BULLETIN LOCAL de la SOCIÉTÉ ACA-
DÉMIQUE des HAUTES-PYRÉNÉES
see B354.

BULLETIN MAURITSHUIS see B348.

B324
BULLETIN. MEDELHAUSMUSEET = Bulletin. Museum of Mediterranean
and Near Eastern Antiquities.
Stockholm 1961-   .

B325
BULLETIN of MEDITTERANEAN ARCHAE-
OLOGY. Highland Heights, Ky.
1975/6-   ?. Only vol. 1 published?

BULLETIN et MÉMOIRS ... see BUL-
LETIN ... (the word mémoirs is
disregarded in filing, but may
have been regarded in forming
an abbreviation).

BULLETIN MENSUEL ... see BULLETIN
... (the word mensuel is disregarded in filing, but may have
been regarded in forming an
abbreviation).

B326
BULLETIN of the METROPOLITAN MUSEUM
of ART. New York 1905-   .
(BMMA, BMM).

B327
BULLETIN MONUMENTAL. SOCIÉTÉ FRAN-
ÇAISE d'ARCHÉOLOGIE. Paris
1834-   . (BM).

B328
BULLETIN du MUSÉE d'ANTHROPOLOGIE
PREHISTORIQUE. Monaco 1954-   .
Title of vol. 1: Publications.

BULLETIN des MUSÉES royaux des ARTS
DÉCORATIFS et INDUSTRIELS see
B329.

B329
BULLETIN des MUSÉES royaux d'ART
et d'HISTOIRE. Brussels 1901-14
1929-   . 1901-11 title: Bulletin des Musées Royaux des Arts
Décoratifs et Industriels. 1912-
14 title: Bulletin des Musées
Royaux du Cinquantenaire.

B330
BULLETIN des MUSÉES royaux des
BEAUX-ARTS de BELIGIQUE = Bulle-
tin der Koninklijke Musea voor
Schöne Kunsten van België.
Brussels 1952-   .

B331
BULLETIN du MUSÉE de BEYROUTH.
Beirut & Paris 1937-   . (BMB,
BMBeyrouth, BMBeyr, BMusBeyr).

BULLETIN du MUSÉE de BOSNIE-HERZÉG-
OVINE à SARAJEVO see G52.

B332
BULLETIN MUSEUM BOYMANS van BEUN-
INGEN. Rotterdam 1937-   .
Suspended 1937-50.

BULLETIN du MUSÉE national de BUR-
GAS see I158.

BULLETIN des MUSÉES royaux du CIN-
QUANTENAIRE see B329.

BULLETIN du MUSÉE d'ÉTAT de CHER-
SONÈSE TAURIQUE see K20.

BULLETIN of the MUSEUM of FAR
EASTERN ANTIQUITIES see B342.

B333
BULLETIN of the MUSEUM of FINE
ARTS. Boston 1903-   . 1903-27
title: Museum of Fine Arts Bulletin. (BMFA, BMusB).

BULLETIN des MUSÉES de FRANCE
see M305-M306.

BULLETIN du MUSÉUM de GÉORGIE
see V34.

B334
BULLETIN. MUSEUM HAARETZ. Tel Aviv
1959-   .

B335
BULLETIN du MUSÉE HISTORIQUE de
MULHOUSE. Mulhouse 1876-   .

BULLETIN du MUSÉE HISTORIQUE RÉ-
GIONAL de VELIKO TĂRNOVA see
I163.

B336
BULLETIN du MUSÉE national HONGROIS
des BEAUX-ARTS = Magyar Nemzeti
Múzeum, Szépmüvésti Múzeum Köz-
leményei. Budapest 1947-   .
Title varies slightly.

BULLETIN du MUSÉE national KOLAROV-
GRAD see I160.

BULLETIN du MUSÉE de KOSOVO et
METOHIE see G49.

BULLETIN des MUSÉES LYONNAIS see
B337.

BULLETIN. MUSEUM of MEDITERRANEAN
and NEAR EASTERN ANTIQUITIES
see B324.

BULLETIN du MUSÉE MILITAIRE à
BELGRADE see V42.

B337
BULLETIN des MUSÉES et MONUMENTS
LYONNAIS. Lyons 1952-   .
1952-59 title: Bulletin des
Musées Lyonnais.

BULLETIN du MUSÉE de la RÉPUBLIQUE
SOCIALISTE de BOSNIE-HERZÉGOVINE
à SARAJEVO see G52.

BULLETIN des MUSÉES ROYAUX ...
see BULLETIN des MUSÉS ... (the
word royaux is disregarded in
filing, but may have been regarded in forming an abbreviation).

BULLETIN du MUSÉE national de RUSE
see I159.

BULLETIN der koninklijke MUSEA voor
SCHÖNE KUNSTEN van BELGIË see
B330.

BULLETIN du MUSÉE national de SU-
MEN see I160.

BULLETIN du MUSÉE national de VAR-
NA see I161.

B338
BULLETIN du MUSÉE national de VAR-
SOVIE. Warsaw 1960-   .

B339
BULLETIN des MUSÉES de la VILLE
d'ANGERS. Angers 1928-   .
1928-61 title: Cahiers de Pincé
et des Musées de la Ville d'Angers.

B340
BULLETIN. Koninklijke NEDERLANDSE
OUDHEIDKUNDIGE BOND. Amsterdam
& Leiden 1899-   . 1921-46
title: Oudheidkundig Jaarboek.
1948-   includes its Nieuws-
bulletin, a separately paged section of the Bulletin. (BKNOB).

BULLETIN of the NORTHAMPTONSHIRE
FEDERATION of ARCHAEOLOGICAL
SOCIETIES see N73.

B341
BULLETIN de NUMISMATIQUE. Brussels & Paris 1891-1906.

B342
BULLETIN. ÖSTASIATISKA MUSEET.
Stockholm 1929-   . Museum's
English name: Museum of Far
Eastern Antiquities. Its earlier
name: Östasiatiska Samlingarna.

BULLETIN. ÖSTASIATISKA SAMLINGARNA
STOCKHOLM see B342.

B343
BULLETIN de l'OFFICE INTERNATIONALE
des INSTITUTS d'ARCHÉOLOGIE et
d'HISTOIRE de l'ART. Paris
1934-37. Variant title: Bulletin
Periodique.

B344
BULLETIN of the royal ONTARIO MU-
SEUM. ART and ARCHAEOLOGY DIVI-
SION. Toronto 1923-58. Suspend-
ed 1932-45 and part of 1955-56.

BULLETIN. PACIFIC SCHOOL of RELI-
GION see P3.

BULLETIN. PALESTINE ARCHAEOLOGICAL
MUSEUM see B345.

B345
BULLETIN. PALESTINE MUSEUM (Jeru-
salem). Liverpool 1924-27.
Museum's variant name: Palestine
Archaeological Museum.

BULLETIN PÉRIODIQUE de l'OFFICE
INTERNATIONALE des INSTITUTS
d'ARCHÉOLOGIE et d'HISTOIRE de
l'ART see B343.

BULLETIN de PHILOSOPHIE MÉDIÉVALE
see B427.

BULLETIN des PROCÈS-VERBAUX de la
SOCIÉTÉ d'ÉMULATION HISTORIQUE
et LITTÉRAIRE d'ABBEVILLE see
B395.

B346
BULLETIN RÉGIONAL. AMIS de MONTLU-
ÇON. Montluçon 1912-   .

BULLETIN REVUE. SOCIÉTÉ d'ÉMULA-
TION et des BEAUX-ARTS du BOUR-
BONNAIS see B393.

B347
BULLETIN of the RHODE ISLAND
SCHOOL of DESIGN - MUSEUM NOTES.
Providence 1913-   . Title
varies slightly.

B348
BULLETIN van het RIJKS-MUSEUM =
Bulletin Mauritshuis. Amsterdam
1953-   .

B349
BULLETIN of the SCHOOL of ORIENTAL
and AFRICAN STUDIES. UNIVERSITY
of LONDON. London 1917-   .
Title through 1938: Bulletin of
the School of Oriental Studies.
(BSOAS, BSOS).

B350
BULLETIN der SCHWEIZERISCHEN GE-
SELLSCHAFT für ANTHROPOLOGIE und
ETHNOLOGIE = Bulletin de la Soci-
été Suisse d'Anthropologie et
d'Ethnologie. Bern 1914-   .

BULLETIN SCIENTIFIQUE de l'ACADÉ-
MIE des SCIENCES (de l'URSS/de
Russie) see I152.

BULLETIN SCIENTIFIQUE de la SOCI-
ÉTÉ de BORDA see B391.

B351
BULLETIN des SÉANCES de L'ACADÉMIE
de NÎMES. Nîmes 1842-   .
1842-78 title: Procès-verbaux
(other slight changes).

B352
BULLETIN de la SECTION HISTORIQUE.
ACADÉMIE ROUMAINE. Bucharest
1912/3-1935? (BHAcRoum).

BULLETIN SEMESTRIEL ... see BULLE-
TIN ... (the word semestriel is
disregarded in filing, but may
have been regarded in forming
an abbreviation).

B353
BULLETIN de la SOCIÉTÉ ACADÉMIQUE
d'AGRICULTURE des SCIENCES, ARTS
et BELLES-LETTRES du DÉPARTEMENT
de l'AUBE. Troyes ?-   .

BULLETIN de la SOCIÉTÉ ACADÉMIQUE
DÉPARTEMENT de l'AUBE see B353.

B354
BULLETIN de la SOCIÉTÉ ACADÉMIQUE
des HAUTES-PYRÉNÉES. Tarbes
1853-   . Title varies: Bulletin
General, Bulletin Local, Bulletin
Documentaire.

BULLETIN. SOCIÉTÉ ACADÉMIQUE du
PUY et de la HAUTE LOIRE see
B303.

BULLETIN. SOCIÉTÉ ACADÉMIQUE du
VAR see B248.

B355
BULLETIN. SOCIÉTÉ AGRICOLE, SCI-
ENTIFIQUE et LITTÉRAIRE des
PYRÉNÉES ORIENTALES. Perpignon
1833-   . Name of Society
1833-39: Société Philomathique
de Perpignon.

BULLETIN de la SOCIÉTÉ d'AGRICUL-
TURE, LETTRES, SCIENCES et ARTS
du DÉPARTEMENT de HAUTE-SAÔNE
see M137.

B356
BULLETIN de la SOCIÉTÉ d'AGRICUL-
TURE, SCIENCES et ARTS de la
SARTHE. Le Mans 1883-   .
Society's name varies slightly.

B357
BULLETIN de la SOCIÉTÉ des AMIS du
MUSÉE d'ARRAS. Arras ?-   .

B358
BULLETIN de la SOCIÉTÉ des AMIS
du MUSÉE de DIJON. Dijon
1952/4-   .

B359
BULLETIN de la SOCIÉTÉ des AMIS de
VIENNE. Vienne, France 1905-   .

BULLETIN de la SOCIÉTÉ d'ANTHROPO-
LOGIE de BRUXELLES see B390.

B360
BULLETIN et mémoires de SOCIÉTÉ
d'ANTHROPOLOGIE de PARIS. Paris
1859-   . Earlier title: Bulletin.

B361
BULLETIN de la SOCIÉTÉ nationale
des ANTIQUAIRES de FRANCE. Paris
1857-   . Society's name changes
slightly. (BSAF, BAF, BSNAF,
BAntFr).

B362
BULLETIN de la SOCIÉTÉ des ANTI-
QUAIRES de la MORINIE. Saint
Omer 1852/6-   . 1852-1932
title: Bulletin Historique Tri-
mestriel.

B363
BULLETIN de la SOCIÉTÉ des ANTI-
QUAIRES de l'OUEST. Poitiers
1834-   . (BSAO).

B364
BULLETINS de la SOCIÉTÉ des ANTI-
QUAIRES de PICARDIE. Amiens
1841-   . cover title of some

numbers: Bulletin Trimestriel.
(BSAP).

BULLETIN. SOCIÉTÉ d'ARCHÉOLOGIE ...
and BULLETIN. SOCIÉTÉ ARCHEOLO-
GIQUE ... are here interfiled.

B365
BULLETIN de la SOCIÉTÉ d'ARCHÉOLO-
GIE d'ALEXANDRIE. Alexandria
etc. 1898-   . Society's name
changes slightly. (BSAA, BSAA1).

BULLETIN de la SOCIÉTÉ ARCHÉOLO-
GIQUE de BÉZIERS see B380.

B366
BULLETIN et Mémoires de la SOCIÉTÉ
ARCHÉOLOGIQUE de BORDEAUX. Bordeaux 1874-   . 1874-1912 were
issued without titles; frequently
refered to as Actes in the tables
of contents. Individual fasc. for
1911-23 were variously called Mémoires, Procès verbaux, Procès
verbaux des Séances, Procès verbaux et Notes Succintes. 1917-
title: Bulletin et Mémoires.

BULLETIN de la SOCIÉTÉ ARCHÉOLO-
GIQUE BULGARE see I153.

B367
BULLETIN de la SOCIÉTÉ d'ARCHÉOLO-
GIQUE CHAMPENOISE. Reims 1907- .
Suspended 1915-20.

B368
BULLETIN de la SOCIÉTÉ d'ARCHÉOLO-
GIE COPTE. Cairo 1935-
Society's name changes; 1935:
Association des Amis des Eglises
et d'Art Coptes; 1936-37: Asso-
ciation des Amis de l'Art Copte.

B369
BULLETIN et Mémoires de la SOCIÉTÉ
ARCHÉOLGOIQUE du DÉPARTEMENT
d'ILLE-et-VILAINE. Rennes 1861-
Title of vol. 1: Mémoires.

B370
BULLETIN. SOCIÉTÉ ARCHÉOLOGIQUE
d'EURE-et-LOIR. Chartres ?-   .

B371
BULLETIN de la SOCIÉTÉ ARCHÉOLO-

GIQUE du FINISTÈRE. Quimper
1873-   .

BULLETIN de la SOCIÉTÉ ARCHÉOLO-
GIQUE du GERS see B376.

B372
BULLETIN et Mémoires de la SOCIÉTÉ
ARCHÉOLOGIQUE et HISTORIQUE de
l'ARRONDISSEMENT de FOUGERES.
Fougeres 1957-   .

B373
BULLETIN de la SOCIÉTÉ ARCHÉOLO-
GIQUE et HISTORIQUE de BEAUVIS.
Beauvais ?-   .

B374
BULLETIN de la SOCIÉTÉ ARCHÉOLO-
GIQUE et HISTORIQUE du CHÂTIL-
LONNAIS. Châtillon-sur-Seine
1881-99.

B375
BULLETIN de la SOCIÉTÉ ARCHÉOLO-
GIQUE et HISTORIQUE du LIMOUSIN.
Limoges 1846-   .

B376
BULLETIN de la SOCIÉTÉ ARCHÉOLO-
GIQUE, HISTORIQUE, LITTÉRAIRE et
SCIENTIFIQUE du GERS. Auch
1900-   . Also issued under the
Society's earlier names: Société
Archéologique du Gers and Société
d'Histoire et d'Archéologie du
Gers.

B377
BULLETIN de la SOCIÉTÉ ARCHÉOLO-
GIQUE et HISTORIQUE de l'ORLÉAN-
NAIS. Orleans 1848/51-
Society's name through 1873: So-
ciété Archéologique de l'Orléan-
nais.

B378
BULLETIN annuel de la SOCIÉTÉ
d'ARCHÉOLOGIE et d'HISTOIRE du
TONNERROIS. Tonnerre, France
1938-   . Title varies slightly.
Suspended 1939-50.

BULLETIN. SOCIÉTÉ d'ARCHÉOLOGIE et
d'HISTOIRE de WAREMME et ENVIRONS
see B307.

B379
BULLETIN de la SOCIÉTÉ ARCHÉOLO-
GIQUE du MIDI de la FRANCE. Tou-
louse 1869-   .

BULLETIN de la SOCIÉTÉ ARCHÉOLO-
GIQUE de MORBIHAN   see   B433.

BULLETIN de la SOCIÉTÉ ARCHÉOLO-
GIQUE de l'ORLÉANNAIS   see   B377.

B380
BULLETIN de la SOCIÉTÉ ARCHÉOLO-
GIQUE, SCIENTIFIQUE et LITTÉRAIRE
de BÉZIERS. Béziers 1836-   .
Society's name until 1860: Soci-
été Archéologique de Béziers.

B381
BULLETIN de la SOCIÉTÉ ARCHÉOLO-
GIQUE, SCIENTIFIQUE et LITTÉRAIRE
du VENDÔMOIS. Vendôme 1862-   .
Society's name until 1966: Soci-
été Archéologique du Vendômois.

B382
BULLETIN de la SOCIÉTÉ ARCHÉOLO-
GIQUE et SCIENTIFIQUE de NOYON.
Noyon ?-   .

B383
BULLETIN de la SOCIÉTÉ ARCHÉOLO-
GIQUE de SENS. Sens 1846-   .

B384
BULLETIN de la SOCIÉTÉ ARCHÉOLO-
GIQUE de SOUSSE. Sousse 1903-   .
Suspended 1914-29.

BULLETIN de la SOCIÉTÉ ARCHÉOLO-
GIQUE à STALIN   see   I161.

B385
BULLETIN de la SOCIÉTÉ d'ARCHÉOLO-
GIE et de STATISTIQUE de la
DRÔME. Valence 1866-   . Soci-
ety's name until 1910: Société
Départementale d'Archéologie et
de Statistique de la Drôme.

B386
BULLETIN trimestriel de la SOCIÉTÉ
ARCHÉOLOGIQUE de TOURAINE. Tours
1868/70-   . Title of vols. 1-
11: Bulletin.

BULLETIN de la SOCIÉTÉ ARCHÉOLO-
GIQUE à VARNA   see   I161.

BULLETIN de la SOCIÉTÉ ARCHÉOLO-
GIQUE du VENDÔMOIS   see   B381.

B387
BULLETIN annuel. SOCIÉTÉ ARIÈGE-
OISE des SCIENCES, LETTRES et
ARTS. Saint Girons 1882-   .
Earlier title: Bulletin.

B388
BULLETIN de la SOCIÉTÉ d'ART et
d'HISTOIRE du DIOCÈSE de LIÈGE.
Liège 1881-   . Suspended 1914-
22.

B389
BULLETIN de la SOCIÉTÉ BELFORTAINE
d'ÉMULATION. Belfort 1872-   .

B390
BULLETIN de la SOCIÉTÉ royale
BELGE d'ANTHROPOLOGIE et de PRÉ-
HISTOIRE. Brussels 1882-   .
Variant title: Bulletin et Mé-
moires. Society's name until
1932: Société d'Anthropologie de
Bruxelles.

B391
BULLETIN de la SOCIÉTÉ de BORDA.
Dax 1876-   . Earlier titles:
Bulletin Scientifique and Bulle-
tin Trimestriel.

BULLETIN de la SOCIÉTÉ BOURBONNAISE
des ÉTUDES LOCALES   see   N84.

B392
BULLETIN de la SOCIÉTÉ pour la CON-
SERVATION des MONUMENTS HISTO-
RIQUES d'ALSACE = Mitteilungen
der Gesellschaft für Erhaltung
der Feschichtlichen Denkmäler im
Elsass. Strasbourg 1856/7-1926.

BULLETIN de la SOCIÉTÉ DÉPARTEMEN-
TALE d'ARCHEOLOGIE et de STATIS-
TIQUE de la DRÔME   see   B385.

B393
BULLETIN de la SOCIÉTÉ d'ÉMULATION
du BOURBONNAIS. Moulins 1892-   .
1892-1902 title: Bulletin Revue.

Société d'Émulation et des Beaux-Arts du Bourbon. Suspended 1914-18.

B394
BULLETINS et mémoires. SOCIÉTÉ d'ÉMULATION des CÔTES-du-NORD. Saint Brieuc 1861-   .

B395
BULLETIN de la SOCIÉTÉ d'ÉMULATION HISTORIQUE et LITTÉRAIRE d'ABBE-VILLE. Abbeville 1877/80-   . Title varies: Bulletin des Procès-verbaux, Bulletin trimestriel.

B396
BULLETIN et mémoires. SOCIÉTÉ d'ÉMULATION de MONTBÉLIARD. Montbéliard ?-   .

B397
BULLETIN de la SOCIÉTÉ d'ÉTUDES d'AVALLON. Avallon 1859-   .

BULLETIN de la SOCIÉTÉ d'ÉTUDES des HAUTES-ALPES see A398.

B398
BULLETIN de la SOCIÉTÉ d'ÉTUDES HISTORIQUES, SCIENTIFIQUES et LITTÉRAIRES des HAUTES-ALPES. Gap 1882-   . Society's name until 1917: Société d'Études des Hautes-Alpes.

B399
BULLETIN de la SOCIÉTÉ des ÉTUDES LITTÉRAIRES, SCIENTIFIQUES et ARTISTIQUES du LOT. Cahors 1873-   . Variant title: Bulletin Trimestriel. Vols. 4- (1878-) also include the society's Procès-verbaux des Séances.

B400
BULLETIN de la SOCIÉTÉ d'ÉTUDES SCIENTIFIQUES et ARCHÉOLOGIQUES de DRAGUIGNAN. Draguignan 1855-   . Vols. 31- (1916/7-) include the society's Mémoires.

B401
BULLETIN de la SOCIÉTÉ d'ÉTUDES SCIENTIFIQUES de l'AUDE. Carcassonne 1890-   .

B402
BULLETIN de la SOCIÉTÉ d'ÉTUDE des SCIENCES NATURELLES de NÎMES. Nîmes 1873-   .

B403
BULLETIN de la SOCIÉTÉ d'ÉTUDES SCIENTIFIQUES de SÈTE et de la RÉGION. Sète ?-   .

B404
BULLETIN de la SOCIÉTÉ FRANÇAISE d'ARCHÉOLOGIE CLASSIQUE. Paris 1967-   . Published as a separately paged section of Revue Archéologique.

B405
BULLETIN de la SOCIÉTÉ FRANÇAISE d'ÉGYPTOLOGIE. Paris 1949-   . Variant title: Bulletin Trimestriel.

B406
BULLETIN de la SOCIÉTÉ FRANÇAISE de NUMISMATIQUE. Paris 1946-   . (BSFN).

B407
BULLETIN trimestriel de la SOCIÉTÉ de GÉOGRAPHIE et d'ARCHÉOLOGIE de la PROVINCE d'ORAN. Oran 1878/81-   . Variant titles: Bulletin Trimestriel de Géographie et d'Archéologie and Bulletin.

B408
BULLETIN de la SOCIÉTÉ GÉOGRAPHIE de l'ÉGYPTE. Cairo 1876-1912 1917-   . Name of Society 1876-81: Société Khédiviale de Géographie. 1917-22 name: Société Sultanieh.

B409
BULLETIN de la SOCIÉTÉ HISTORIQUE et ARCHÉOLOGIQUE "Les AMIS des ANTIQUITÉS de PARTHENAY". Parthenay ?-   .

B410
BULLETIN de la SOCIÉTÉ d'HISTOIRE et d'ARCHÉOLOGIE de l'ARRONDIS-SEMENT de PROVINS. Provins 1892-   .

B411
BULLETIN de la SOCIÉTÉ HISTORIQUE
    ARCHÉOLOGIQUE et ARTISTIQUE du
    GIENNOIS. Gien ?-   .

B412
BULLETIN de la SOCIÉTÉ d'HISTOIRE
    et d'ARCHÉOLOGIE de BEAUCAIRE.
    Beaucaire ?-   .

B413
BULLETIN de la SOCIÉTÉ d'HISTOIRE
    et d'ARCHÉOLOGIE de BRETAGNE.
    Rennes 1920-   . Suspended
    1939-42.

B414
BULLETIN de la SOCIÉTÉ HISTORIQUE
    et ARCHÉOLOGIQUE de CORBEIL,
    d'ÉTAMPES et du HUREPOIX. Paris
    1895-   .

B415
BULLETIN de la SOCIÉTÉ d'HISTOIRE
    et d'ARCHÉOLOGIE de GENÈVE.
    Geneva 1892/7-   .

BULLETIN de la SOCIÉTÉ d'HISTOIRE
    et d'ARCHÉOLOGIE du GERS   see
    B376.

B416
BULLETIN de la SOCIÉTÉ HISTORIQUE
    et ARCHÉOLOGIQUE de LANGRES.
    Langres 1872-   .

B417
BULLETIN de la SOCIÉTÉ d'HISTOIRE
    et d'ARCHÉOLOGIE de la MAURIENNE.
    Savoie ?-   .

B418
BULLETIN de la SOCIÉTÉS d'HISTOIRE
    et d'ARCHÉOLOGIE de la MEUSE.
    Bar-le-Duc 1964-   .

B419
BULLETIN de la SOCIÉTÉ HISTORIQUE
    et ARCHÉOLOGIQUE de NOGENT-sur-
    MARNE et du CANTON de NOGENT.
    Nogent-sur-Marne 1950-   .

B420
BULLETIN de la SOCIÉTÉ HISTORIQUE
    et ARCHÉOLOGIQUE de l'ORNE.
    Alençon 1882-   .

B421
BULLETIN de la SOCIÉTÉ HISTORIQUE
    et ARCHÉOLOGIQUE du PÉRIGORD.
    Perigueux 1874-   .

B422
BULLETIN. SOCIÉTÉ d'HISTOIRE et
    d'ARCHÉOLOGIE de SAVERNE et de
    ses ENVIRONS. Saverne 1938-   .
    Variant title: Bulletin Trimes-
    triels.

B423
BULLETIN de la SOCIÉTÉ d'HISTOIRE
    et d'ARCHÉOLOGIE de VICHY et des
    ENVIRONS. Vichy 1938-   .

BULLETIN de la SOCIÉTÉ HISTORIQUE
    BULGARE   see   I154.

BULLETIN de la SOCIÉTÉ HISTORIQUE
    et ETHNOLOGIQUE de la GRÈCE   see
    D10.

B424
BULLETIN de la SOCIÉTÉ d'HISTOIRE
    du MAROC. Rabat 1968-   .

B425
BULLETIN. SOCIÉTÉ d'HISTOIRE et du
    MUSÉE d'HUNINGUE et du CANTON de
    HUNINGUE. Huningue ?-   .

B426
BULLETIN de la SOCIÉTÉ HISTORIQUE
    et SCIENTIFIQUE des DEUX-SÈVRES.
    Niort 1912-   .

BULLETIN. SOCIÉTÉ IMPÉRIALE ...
    see BULLETIN. SOCIÉTÉ ... (the
    word impériale is disregarded
    in filing, but may have been
    regarded in forming an abbrevia-
    tion).

B427
BULLETIN de la SOCIÉTÉ INTERNATION-
    ALE pour l'ÉTUDE de la PHILOSO-
    PHIE MÉDIÉVALE. Louvain
    1959-   . Variant title: Bul-
    letin de Philosophie Médiévale.

BULLETIN de la SOCIÉTÉ KHÉDIVIALE
    de GÉOGRAPHIE   see   B408.

BULLETIN de la SOCIÉTÉ royale des
    LETTRES de LUND   see   A8.

B428
BULLETIN de la SOCIÉTÉ de LINGUIS-
TIQUE de PARIS.   Paris 1869-   .
(BSL).

B429
BULLETIN de la SOCIÉTÉ LITTÉRAIRES
et HISTORIQUES de la BRIE.   Meaux
1893-   .

BULLETIN de la SOCIÉTÉ LORRAINES
des SCIENCES   see   B247.

BULLETIN. SOCIÉTÉ NATIONALE ...
see BULLETIN. SOCIÉTÉ ... (the
word nationale is disregarded
in filing, but may have been
regarded in forming an abbreviation).

B430
BULLETIN de la SOCIÉTÉ des NATURA-
LISTES et des ARCHÉOLOGIQUES de
l'AIN.   Bourg 1896/7-   .

B431
BULLETIN de la SOCIÉTÉ NIVERNAISE
des LETTRES, SCIENCES et ARTS.
Nivers 1851/4-55 1867-80 1883-   .
Society's name varies slightly.

B432
BULLETIN de la SOCIÉTÉ NORMANDE
d'ARCHÉOLOGIE PRÉHISTORIQUE et
HISTORIQUE.   Louviers etc.
1893-   . Former title: Bulletin
de la Société Normande d'Études
Prehistoriques.

BULLETIN de la SOCIÉTÉ NORMANDE
d'ÉTUDES PRÉHISTORIQUES   see
B432.

BULLETIN. SOCIÉTÉ PHILOMATHIQUE de
PERPIGNON   see   B355.

B433
BULLETIN mensuel de la SOCIÉTÉ
POLYMATHIQUE du MORBIHAN.   Vannes
1857-   . 1857-59 title: Société
Archéologique du Morbihan.

B434
BULLETIN de la SOCIÉTÉ PRÉHISTO-
RIQUE de l'ARIÈGE.   Tarascon-sur-
Ariège 1946-   .

B435
BULLETIN de la SOCIÉTÉ PRÉHISTO-
RIQUE FRANÇAISE.   Paris 1904-63.
Name varies slightly.

BULLETIN, SOCIÉTÉ ROYALE ... see
BULLETIN. SOCIÉTÉ ... (the word
royale is disregarded in filing,
but may have been regarded in
forming an abbreviation).

BULLETIN trimestriel. SOCIÉTÉ des
SCIENCES et ARTS de BAYONNE   see
B440.

BULLETIN. SOCIÉTÉ des SCIENCES,
ARTS et BELLES-LETTRES du TARN
see   R241.

BULLETIN. SOCIÉTÉ des SCIENCES,
BELLES-LETTRES et ARTS du DÉ-
PARTEMENT du VAR   see   B248.

B436
BULLETIN de la SOCIÉTÉ SCIENTI-
FIQUE, HISTORIQUE et ARCHÉOLO-
GIQUE de la CORRÈZE.   Brive
1878-   .

B437
BULLETIN de la SOCIÉTÉ des SCIENCES
HISTORIQUES et NATURELLES de la
CORSE.   Bastia 1881-   .

B438
BULLETIN de la SOCIÉTÉ des SCIENCES
HISTORIQUES et NATURELLES de
SEMUR-en-AUXOIS.   Semur-en-Auxois
1864-   . Suspended 1900 & 1923-
27.

B439
BULLETIN de la SOCIÉTÉ des SCIENCES
HISTORIQUES et NATURELLES de
l'YONNE.   Auxerre 1847-   .

B440
BULLETIN. SOCIÉTÉ des SCIENCES,
LETTRES et ARTS de BAYONNE.
Bayonne 1873-   . Title varies
slightly.

BULLETIN de la SOCIÉTÉ SUISSE d'AN-
THROPOLOGIE et d'ETHNOLOGIE
see   B350.

BULLETIN de la SOCIÉTÉ SULTANIEH
de GÉOGRAPHIE see B408.

B441
BULLETIN de la SOCIÉTÉ TOURNAI-
SIENNE de PALÉONTOLOGIE et de
PRÉHISTOIRE. Tournai ?-   .

B442
BULLETIN de la SOCIÉTÉ VERVIÉTOISE
d'ARCHÉOLOGIE et d'HISTOIRE.
Verviers 1898-   .

B443
BULLETIN de THÉOLOGIE ANCIENNE et
MÉDIÉVALE. Louvain 1929-   .

BULLETIN THÉOLOGIQUE, SCIENTIFIQUE
et LITTÉRAIRE see B323.

BULLETIN of the TOMSK STATE UNI-
VERSITY see T127.

BULLETIN TRIMESTRIEL... see BULLE-
TIN ... (the word trimestriel
is disregarded in filing, but
may have been regarded in forming
an abbreviation).

BULLETIN. UNIVERSITY MUSEUM (Univ.
Pennsylvania). see U18.

BULLETIN. UNIVERSITÉ de STRASBOURG.
FACULTÉ des LETTRES see B293.

BULLETIN van de VEREENINGING tot
BEVORDERING der KENNIS van de
ANTIEKE BESCHAVING see B1.

B444
BULLETIN van de WERKGROEP HISTORIE
en ARCHEOLOGIE onder auspiciën
van het Koninklijk ZEEUWS
GENOOTSCHAP der WETENSCHAPPEN.
Middelburg ?-   .

B445
BULLETIN. YALE UNIVERSITY ART
GALLERY. New Haven 1926-   .
1926-57 title: Bulletin of the
Associates ·in Fine Arts at Yale
University. 1961-64 title: Yale
Art Gallery Bulletin.

BULLETTINO see BOLLETTINO (the
words are interfiled). See also
BOLETIN, BULLETIN and BULETINUL.

BÜNDNER MONATSBLATT see B236.

Buonamici, G. see E69.

B446
BURGENLÄNDISCHE HEIMATBLÄTTER.
Eisenstadt 1932-   .

B447
BURLINGTON MAGAZINE. London
1903-   . 1903-47 title: Burlington Magazine for Connois-
seurs.

Burnet, J. see E2.

B448
BURSIANS JAHRESBERICHT über die
FORTSCHRITTE der KLASSISCHEN
ALTERTUMSWISSENSCHAFT. Berlin &
Leipzig 1873-1944/5. Title varies
slightly. (JAW).
--. Beilage: Biographisches
Jahrbuch für Altertumskunde.
1878-1943.
--. Beiblatt: Bibliotheca philo-
logica classica. 1874-1938.

Bury, J. B. see H117.

B449
BUTLLETI de l'ACADEMIA de BONAS
LLETRAS de BARCELONA. Barcelona
1901-   . 1901-30 title: Bole-
tín. Real Academia de Buenas
Letras de Barcelona.

B450
BUTLLETI. ASSOCIACIÓ CATALANA
d'ANTROPOLOGIA, ETNOLOGIA i
PREHISTORIA. Barcelona 1923-26.

BYZANT-: entries beginning·with
this spelling are here interfiled.

BYZANTINA see V79.

B451
BYZANTINOSLAVICA. Prague 1929-   .
Suspended 1939-46.

B452
BYZANTION. Brussels etc. 1924-   .

B453
BYZANTINO-BULGARICA. Sofia 1962- .

BYZANTINA CHRONIKA see V57.

B454
BYZANTINISCHE FORSCHUNGEN. Amsterdam 1966- .

B455
BYZANTINA kai METABYZANTINA. Malibu, CA. 1978- . (BKM).

B456
BYZANTINE and MODERN GREEK STUDIES.
   Oxford 1975- .

B457
BYZANTINA NEERLANDICA. Leiden
   --. Series A: Textus. 1969- .
   --. Series B: Studia. 1970- .

BYZANTINA kai NEOELLĒNIKA CHRONIKA
   see B458.

B458
BYZANTINISCH-NEUGRIECHISCHE JAHR-
   BÜCHER. Berlin & Athens 1920-
   1945/9? 1926-35 also had Greek
   title: Vyzantina kai Neoellēnika
   Chronika. Vols. 10-11 and 13-14
   included the Berichte der Christ-
   lich-archäologischen Gesellschaft
   zu Athen. (Deltion tēs Christianikēs Archaiologikēs Hetaireia).
   (BNJ).

BYZANTINISCH-NEUGRIECHISCHE JAHR-
   BÜCHER. BEIHEFTE see T22.

B459
BYZANTINISCHE PAPYRI in der K.
   HOF- und STAATSBIBLIOTHEK zu
   MÜNCHEN / A. Heisenberg & L.
   Wenger. Leipzig & Berlin 1914.
   (Veröffentlichungen aus der
   Papyrussammlung der K. Hof- und
   Staatsbibliothek zu München; I).
   (PMonac).

B460
BYZANTINA VINDOBONENSIA. Vienna
   1966- .

B461
BYZANTINISCHE ZEITSCHRIFT. Munich
   1892- . (BZ, ByzZ).

C

C1
COWA BIBLIOGRAPHY; current publi-
cations in old world archaeology.
Cambridge, Mass. 1957-   .

C2
COWA SURVEY: current work in old
world archaeology. Cambridge,
Mass. 1957-   .

Cabrol, F. see D44.

Cadell, H. see P70.

C3
CAESARAUGUSTA (Seminario de Arqueología y Numismática Aragonesas).
Saragossa 1951-   . 1951-53
title: Publicaciones.
--. Anejo. 1966-   . Issued
as part of the series Monografí-
as Arqueológicas.

C4
CAESARODUNUM. Tours etc. 1969-   .

Cagnat, R. see A639, I56, I72.

C5
CAHIERS ALSACIENS d'ARCHÉOLOGIE
d'ART et d'HISTOIRE. Strasburg
1909-   . Former titles: Anzeiger für elsässische Altertumskunde, Cahiers d'archéologie et
d'histoire d'Alsace.

C6
CAHIERS ARCHÉOLOGIQUES; fin de
l'antiquité et moyen-age. Paris
1945-   . (CArch, CahA).

CAHIERS d'ARCHÉOLOGIE et d'HISTOIRE
d'ALSACE see C5.

C7
CAHIERS d'ARCHÉOLOGIE et d'HIS-
TOIRE du BERRY. Bourges
1965-   .

C8
CAHIERS d'ARCHÉOLOGIE du NORDEST.
Laon 1958-   .

C9
CAHIERS d'ARCHÉOLOGIE RÉGIONALE.
Roanne ?-   .

C10
CAHIERS d'ARCHÉOLOGIE SUBAQUA-
TIQUE. Fréjus 1972-   .

C11
CAHIERS d'ART. Paris 1926-   .
Suspended 1941-43.

C12
CAHIERS du BAZADAIS. Bazas ?-   .

C13
CAHIERS BRUXELLOIS. Brussels
1956-   .

C14
CAHIERS de BYRSA (Tunis. Musée
Lavigerie). Paris 1951-   .

C15
CAHIERS de la CÉRAMIQUE, du VERRE
et des ARTS du FEU. Sèvres
1955-   . Earlier title:

Cahiers de la Ceramique et des Arts du Feu.

C16
CAHIERS de CIVILISATION MÉDIÉVALE X^e-XIIe SIÈCLES. Poitiers 1958-   .
--. Supplément. 1960?-   .

C17
CAHIERS de la DÉLÉGATION ARCHÉOLO-GIQUE FRANÇAISE en IRAN. Paris 1971-   .

C18
CAHIERS des ÉTUDES ANCIENNES. Montreal 1972-   .

C19
CAHIERS FERDINAND de SAUSSURE. Geneva 1941-   .

C20
CAHIERS du GROUPE de RECHERCHES sur l'ARMÉE ROMAINE et les PROVINCES. Paris 1977-   .

C21
CAHIERS de la HAUTE-LOIRE. Le Puy 1965-   .

C22
CAHIERS HAUT-MARNAIS. Chaumont 1946-   .

C23
CAHIERS d'HISTOIRE.   Grenoble etc. 1956-   .

C24
CAHIERS d'HISTOIRE et d'ARCHÉOLO-GIE. Nîmes 1931-   .

C25
CAHIERS d'HISTOIRE MONDIALE = Journal of World History = Cuadernos de Histoira Munidal. Paris 1953-   . (CHM).

CAHIERS. INSTITUT for GRAESK og LATINSK MIDDELALDERFILOLOGI see C27.

C26
CAHIERS de l'INSTITUT de LINGUIS-TIQUE (Univ. Louvain). Louvain 1972-   .
--. Bibliothèque. 1976-   .

C27
CAHIERS de l'INSTITUT du MOYEN-ÂGE GREC et LATIN (Univ. Copenhagen). Copenhagen 1969-   .

C28
CAHIERS INTERNATIONAUX de SOCIO-LOGIE. Paris 1946-   .

C29
CAHIERS LÉOPOLD DELISLE. (Société Parisienne d'Histoire et d'Archéologie Normandes). Paris 1947-   .

C30
CAHIERS LIGURES de PRÉHISTOIRE et d'ARCHÉOLOGIE. Montpellier 1952-   . 1952 title: Cahiers de Préhistoire et d'Archéologie.

C31
CAHIERS LORRAINS. Metz 1922-   . 1922 title: Cahier Lorrain.

C32
CAHIERS de MARIEMONT. Morlanwelz 1970-   .

C33
CAHIERS MÉDULIENS. Lesparre ?-   .

C34
CAHIERS NUMISMATIQUES. Paris 1964-   .

C35
CAHIERS de l'ORONTE. Beirut 1965-   .

CAHIERS de PINCÉ et des MUSÉES de la VILLE d'ANGERS see B339.

CAHIERS de PRÉHISTOIRE et d'ARCHÉOLOGIE see C30.

C36
CAHIERS de RECHERCHES de l'INSTITUT de PAPYROLOGIE et d'ÉGYPTOLOGIE de LILLE. Lille 1973-   .

C37
CAHIERS RHODANIENS. Lyon 1953-   . 1953 title: Cahiers Valentinois.

CAHIERS de RUSSIE et CHRÉTIENTÉ
see R355.

C38
CAHIERS de SAINT-MICHEL de CUXA.
Prades-Codalet 1970-   .

C39
CAHIERS SARREGUEMINOIS. Sarregue-
mines 1964?-   .

C40
CAHIERS TECHNIQUES de l'ART.
Strasburg 1947-   .

C41
CAHIERS de TUNISIE. Tunis
1953-   . (CT).

CAHIERS VALENTINOIS see C37.

C42
CAIRO PAPYRI / B. P. Grenfell & A.
S. Hunt. Oxford 1903. (Catalogue
Général des Antiquités Égypti-
ennes du Musée du Caire; 10.).
(PCair).

C43
CALABRIA NOBILISSMA; periodico di
arte, storia e letteratura Calabrese. Consenza 1947-   .

C44
CALCULI (Dept. of Classics. Dart-
mouth). Hanover, N.H. 1967-79.

Calderini, A. see P61.

CALIFORNIA PUBLICATIONS In CLAS-
SICAL ARCHAEOLOGY see U16.

CALIFORNIA PUBLICATIONS in CLAS-
SICAL PHILOLOGY see U17.

CALIFORNIA STUDIES in CLASSICAL
ANTIQUITY see C131.

Cambitoglou, A. see R54.

C45
CAMBRIDGE ANCIENT HISTORY. Cambridge 1923-39. Revised edition
of vol. 1-2 (1961-71) in 71
fasc; these reissued with some
changes in 1970-77 in 5 vols.
(CAH).

CAMBRIDGE ANTIQUARIAN COMMUNICA-
TIONS see P195.

C46
CAMBRIDGE CLASSICAL STUDIES.
Cambridge 1936-   .

C47
CAMBRIDGE CLASSICAL TEXTS and COM-
MENTARIES. Cambridge 1965-   .

C48
CAMBRIDGE GREEK and LATIN CLASSICS.
Cambridge 1970?-   .

C49
CAMBRIDGE GREEK TESTAMENT for
SCHOOLS and COLLEGES. Cambridge
1881-1933. Appeared in several
printings.

C50
CAMBRIDGE HISTORICAL JOURNAL. London etc. 1923-57.

C51
CAMBRIDGE MEDIEVAL HISTORY. Cambridge 1911-36. 2nd edition of
vol. 4 (Byzantium) published
1966-67. (CMH).

CAMPAGNE de la SOCIETÀ MAGNA GRECIA
see A666.

C52
CANADIAN JOURNAL of LINGUISTICS =
Revue Canadienne de Linguis-
tique. Toronto 1954-   .
1954-61 title: Journal of the
Canadian Linguistic Association.

C53
CANADIAN NUMISMATIC JOURNAL.
Ottawa 1956?-   .

Cantineau, J. see I101.

C54
CAPITOLIUM. Rome 1925-   . Suspended 1935-36 during which
time it was replaced by Bollettino della Capitole..

C55
CAPYS; annuario degli Amici di Capua. Capua ?-   .

Caquot, A. see T27.

Carratelli, G. Pugliese see I120.

Carratelli, I. Pugliese see T71.

Carcopino, J. see M40.

Carducci, G. see R89.

Carettoni, G. see P135.

C56
CARINTHIA; Zeitschrift für Vater-
  lanskunde, Belehrung und Unter-
  haltung. Klagenfurt 1811-90.
  Superseded by Carinthia I and
  Carinthia II.

C57
CARINTHIA I; Mitteilungen des Ge-
  schichtsvereines für Kärnten.
  Klagenfurt 81- 1891-   .

C58
CARMINA LATINA EPIGRAPHICA / F.
  Buecheler & E. Lommatzsch.
  Leipzig 1895-1926. (Bibliotheca
  Scriptorum Graecorum et Roman-
  orum Teubneriana). (CE, CLE).

C59
CARNIOLA; Zeitschrift für Heimatkunde. Laibach 1908-18.

C60
CARNUNTUM JAHRBUCH. Vienna
  1955-   .

C61
CARPICA (Muzeul de Istorie din
  Bacău). Bacău ?-   .

C62
CARTE ARCHÉOLOGIQUE de la GAULE
  ROMAINE / A. Blanchet et al.
  Paris 1931-   . (Forma Orbis
  Romani).

Cary, M. see 062.

Caskey, L. D. see A676.

C63
ČASOPIS. MORAVSKÉHO MUSEA v BRNĚ
  = Acta Musei Moraviae. Brno

1901-   . 1901-19 and 1941-43
  title: Zeitschrift des Mährischen Landesmuseums. Name of
  museum varies slightly.

C64
ČASOPIS MUSEÁLNEJ SLOVENSKEJ SPO-
  LOČNOSTI. V. Turčiansky Sv. Mar-
  tin 1898-   .

ČASOPIS MUZEJNÍHO SPOLKU OLOMUCK-
  ÉHO see C68.

C65
ČASOPIS NÁRODNIHO MUZEA. Prague
  1827-1935. Continued in parts.
  --. [Pt. 2]: Historické Muzeum.
  ?-   . Variously called Oddíl
  Duchovědný and Oddíl věd
  společeských.

C66
ČASOPIS SLEZSKÉHO MUZEA = Acta
  Musei Silesiae. Opava 1951-
  54/5.
  --. Ser. B. Vedy Historicke =
  Historia. 1951-   .

C67
ČASOPIS SPOLEČNOSTI PŘÁTEL STARO-
  ŽITNOSTI ČESKÝCH v PRAZE.
  Prague 1893-   . Title varies
  slightly.

C68
ČASOPIS VLASTENECKÉHO SPOLKU MU-
  SEJNIHO OLOMOUCI. Olomouc
  1884-   . Title of vols. 1-2
  Časopis Muzejního Spolku Olomu-
  ckého; other slight variations.

C69
ČASOPIS za ZGODOVINO IN NARODOPIS-
  JE. Maribor 1904-40? Suspended
  1916.

Casson, L. see E160.

C70
CATÁLOGO MONUMENTAL de la PROVEN-
  CIA de [name of province].
  place and date varies.

CATALOGUE of the BRONZES, GREEK,
  ROMAN and ETRUSCAN in the DEPART-
  MENT of GREEK and ROMAN ANTIQUI-
  TIES, BRITISH MUSEUM see B209.

C71
CATALOGUE of BYZANTINE COINS in the
DUMBARTON OAKS COLLECTION and in
the WHITTEMORE COLLECTION / A. R.
Bellinger & P. Grierson. Wash-
ington, D.C. 1966-   .

C72
CATALOGUE of COINS of the ROMAN
EMPIRE in the ASHMOLEAN MUSEUM.
Oxford 1975-   .

C73
CATALOGUE des CYLINDRES, CACHETS
et PIERRES GRAVÉES de STYLE
ORIENT du MUSÉE du LOUVRE / L.
Delaporte. Paris 1920.

CATALOGUE of EGYPTIAN SCARABS, etc.
in the BRITISH MUSEUM see B224.

C74
CATALOGUE of EGYPTIAN SCARABS,
SCARABOIDS, SEALS and AMULETS
in the PALESTINE ARCHEOLOGICAL
MUSEUM / A. Rowe. Cairo 1936.

CATALOGUE of the ENGRAVED GEMS and
CAMEOS, GREEK, ETRUSCAN and RO-
MAN in the BRITISH MUSEUM. see
B214.

CATALOGUE of the FINGER RINGS,
GREEK, ETRUSCAN and ROMAN in the
Department of Antiquities,
BRITISH MUSEUM see B223.

C75
CATALOGUE GÉNÉRAL des ANTIQUITÉS
ÉGYPTIENNES du MUSÉE du CAIRE.
Cairo 1901-   .

CATALOGUE of the GREEK COINS in
the BRITISH MUSEUM see B211.

C76
CATALOGUE of GREEK COINS in the
HUNTERIAN COLLECTION / G. Mac-
Donald. Glasgow 1899-1905.

CATALOGUE of the GREEK and ETRUSCAN
VASES in the BRITISH MUSEUM see
B227.

C77
CATALOGUE of GREEK and LATIN PA-

PYRI and OSTRACA in the posses-
sion of the UNIVERSITY of ABER-
DEEN / E. G. Turner. Aberdeen
1939. (Aberdeen University
Studies; 116). (PAberd).

C78
CATALOGUE of the GREEK PAPYRI in
the JOHN RYLANDS LIBRARY, MAN-
CHESTER / A. S. Hunt et al.
Manchester 1911-52. (PRyl).

CATALOGUE of the GREEK and ROMAN
LAMPS in the BRITISH MUSEUM
see B219.

CATALOGUE of the IMPERIAL BYZANTINE
COINS in the BRITISH MUSEUM
see B210.

CATALOGUE of the JEWELLERY, GREEK,
ETRUSCAN and ROMAN, in the DE-
PARTMENTS of ANTIQUITIES, BRI-
TISH MUSEUM see B218.

CATALOGUE of the LITERARY PAPYRI
in the BRITISH MUSEUM see B222.

C79
CATALOGUE of the McCLEAN COLLEC-
TION of GREEK COINS, Fitzwilliam
Museum, Cambridge / S. W. Grose.
Cambridge 1923-39.

C80
CATALOGUE des MANUSCRITS ALCHI-
MIQUES GRECS / J. Bidet et al.
Brussels 1924-   .

C81
CATALOGUE des MANUSCRITS ALCHI-
MIQUES LATINS / J. Bidet. Brus-
sels 1939-51?

C82
CATALOGUE des MONNAIES de l'EMPIRE
ROMAIN, BIBLIOTHÈQUE NATIONALE
/ J. B. A. Giard. Paris
1976-   .

C83
CATALOGUE of the NIMRUD IVORIES:
with other examples of ancient
Near Eastern ivories in the
British Museum / R. D. Barnett.
2. ed. London 1975. 1st edition
1957.

CATALOGUE of SCULPTURE in the DE-
PARTMENT of GREEK and RCMAN ANTI-
QUITIES, BRITISH MUSEUM see
B225.

C84
CATALOGUE of the SPARTA MUSEUM /
M. N. Tod & A. J. B. Wace.
Oxford 1906.

C85
CATALOGUE des TEXTES HITTITES / E.
Laroche. Paris 1971. (Études
et Commentaires; 75).

C86
CATALOGUS CODICUM ASTROLOGORUM
GRAECORUM. Brussels 1898-1953?
(CCAG).

C87
CATALOGUS CODICUM HAGIOGRAPHICORUM
BIBLIOTHECAE REGIAE BRUXELLENSIS.
Brussels 1886-89. (Subsidia
Hagiographica; 1).

C88
CATALOGUS CODICUM HAGIOGRAPHICORUM
GRAECORUM BIBLIOTHECAE NATIONALIS
PARISIENSIS. Brussels 1896-   .

C89
CATALOGUS CODICUM HAGIOGRAPHICORUM
GRAECORUM BIBLIOTHECAE VATICANAE.
Brussels 1899.

C90
CATALOGUS CODICUM HAGIOGRAPHICORUM
GRAECORUM GERMANIAE, BELGII,
ANGLIAE. Brussels 1913. (Sub-
sidia Hagiographica; 13).

C91
CATALOGUS CODICUM HAGIOGRAPHICORUM
LATINORUM ANTIQUIORUM SAECULO
XVI qui asservantur in BIBLIO-
THECA NATIONALI PARISIENSI.
Brussels 1889-93. (Subsidia
Hagiographica; 2).

C92
CATALOGUS CODICUM HAGIOGRAPHICORUM
LATINORUM BIBLIOTHECARUM ROMAN-
ORUM PRAETER quam VATICANAE.
Brussels 1909.

C93
CATALOGUS CODICUM HAGIOGRAPHICORUM
LATINORUM BIBLIOTHECAE VATICANAE.
Brussels 1910. (Subsidia Hagio-
graphica; 11).

C94
CATALOGUS TRANSLATIONUM et COMMEN-
TARIORUM: medieval and renaissance Latin translations and
commentaries; annotated lists
and guides / P. O. Kristeller.
Washington D.C. 1960-   .

C95
CATHOLIC BIBLICAL QUARTERLY. Washington D.C. 1939-   . (CBQ).

C96
CATHOLIC ENCYCLOPEDIA. New York
1907-14. Revised edition (1967-
79) has title: New Catholic
Encyclopedia.

C97
CATHOLIC HISTORICAL REVIEW. Washington D.C. 1915-   .

C98
CATHOLIC UNIVERSITY of AMERICA
LAW REVIEW. Washington D.C.
1950-   .

Catling, H. W. see C282.

CAUCASIAN and NEAR EASTERN STUDIES
see K7.

Cauer, P. see D36.

Cavenaile, R. see C232.

C99
CELTIBERIA; revista del Centro
de Estudios Sorianos. Soria
1951-   .

C100
CELTICUM. Rennes 1961-   .

C101
CENTAURUS; international magazine
of the history of science and
medicine. Copenhagen 1950-   .

C102
CENTRAL ASIATIC JOURNAL. The
  Hague 1955- .

C103
CENTRAL GAULISH POTTERS / J. A.
  Stanfield & G. Simpson. New
  York & London 1958. (CGP).

CENTRALBLATT see ZENTRALBLATT.

C104
CENTUMCELLAE (Associazione Archeologica "Centumcellae"). Civi-
  tavecchia ?- .

C105
CÉRAMIQUE GÉOMÉTRIQUE de l'ARGOLIDE
  / P. Courbin. Paris 1966. (Bibliothèque des Écoles Françaises
  d'Athènes et de Rome; 208).

C106
CERCETĂRI ARHEOLOGICE în BUCUREŞTI.
  Bucharest 1963- .

CERCETĂRI FILOZOFICE see R160.

C107
CERCETĂRI ISTORICE. Bucharest
  1979- .

C108
CERCETĂRI ISTORICE = Des Recherches
  Historiques. Iaşi 1970- .

C109
ČESKOSLOVENSKY ČASOPIS HISTORICKY.
  Prague 1953- .

Chabot, J. B. see R46, S298.

Chadwick, J. see D82, K32, M325,
  M327.

C110
CHAMBER TOMBS at MYCENAE / A. J.
  B. Wace. Oxford 1932. (Archae-
  ologia; 82).

Chantraine, P. see D52, G76.

C111
CHARTAE LATINAE ANTIQUIORES; fac-
  simile edition of Latin charters
  prior to the ninth century / A.

Bruckner & R. Marichal. Olten
  1954- . (ChLA).

Chatelain, L. see I79.

CHECKLIST of STUDIES see Q21-Q26.

Cheetham, S. see D48.

C112
CHERCHEURS de la WALLONIE. Yvoz-
  Ramet ?- .

CHERSONESSKIĬ SBORNIK see K20.

C113
CHIRON (Kommission für Alte Geschichte und Epigraphik des
  Deutschen Archäologischen Instituts). Munich 1971- .

Christ, W. von see G31.

C114
CHRISTIAN NEWS FROM ISRAEL. Jerusalem 1949- .

C115
CHRISTIANISMOS. Rome 1978- .

C116
CHRISTLICHE KUNSTBLÄTTER. Linz
  1860- .

CHRONICA ALIAQUE VARIA DOCUMENTA
  ad HISTORIAM FRATRUM MINORUM
  SPECTANTIA see A170.

CHRONIKA see A470.

CHRONIKA ARKHEOLOGII ta MISTETSVA
  see K21.

C117
CHRONIQUE ARCHÉOLOGIQUE du PAYS
  de LIÈGE. Liège 1906- .

CHRONIQUE des ARTS et de la CURI-
  OSITÉ see B24.

C118
CHRONIQUE d'ÉGYPTE. Brussels
  1925- . (CE, ChrE, CdE).

C119
CHRONIQUES d'ORIENT / S. Reinach.
  Paris 1883-95.

C120
CHRONOLOGY of MYCENAEAN POTTERY /
A. Furumark. Stockholm 1941.
Reprinted in 1972 as Skrifter
utgivna av Svenska Institutet;
Athen, 4°; 22). (CMP).

C121
CHURCH HISTORY. New York etc.
1932-   .

C122
CICERONIANA. Rome 1959-64 1973-   .

C123
CINCINNATI ART MUSEUM BULLETIN.
Cincinnati 1930-41 1950-   .
Replaced 1942-May 1950 by its
Newsletter (1942-45) and its
News (1946-50).

C124
CINCINNATI CLASSICAL STUDIES. Leiden etc. 1967-73 1977-   . 1967-
73 title: University of Cincinnati Classical Studies.

C125
CISALPINA: atti del Convegno sull'
attività archeologica nell'Italia
settentrionale. Milan 1959-   .

C126
CITIES of the EASTERN ROMAN PRO-
VINCES / A. H. M. Jones. Oxford
1937-   .

C127
CIVILTÀ CATTOLICA. Rome 1850-   .

C128
CIVILTÀ CLASSICA e CRISTIANA.
Genoa 1980-   .

C129
CLARA RHODOS. Rhodes 1928-41.
(ClRh).

CLASS-: entries beginning with this
spelling are here interfiled.

C130
CLASSICA; boletin de pedagogia e
cultura. Lisbon 1977-   .

C131
CLASSICAL ANTIQUITY. Berkeley, CA.

1968-   . 1968-81 title: California Studies in Classical
Antiquity.

C132
CLASSICAL BULLETIN. Chicago
1925-   . (CB).

C133
CLASSICAL FOLIA; studies in the
Christian perpetuation of the
classics. New York 1946-   .
1946-59 title: Folia.
--. Supplement. Huntington,
N.Y. 1953-   .

C134
CLASSICAL JOURNAL. London 1810-29.

C135
CLASSICAL JOURNAL. Chicago
1905-   . (CL, ClJ).

C136
CLASSICAL JOURNAL (Virgil Society:
Malta Branch). Valetta 1947-   ..

C137
CLASSICAL JOURNAL and SCHOLARS RE-
VIEW. Boston 1830-31.

C138
CLASSICA et MEDIEVALIA. Copenhagen 1938-   . (C&M, ClMed).

C139
CLASSICAL MUSEUM. London 1844-50.

C140
CLASSICI e NEO-LATINI. Aosla & Modena 1905- ? No more published?

CLASSICAL NEWS and VIEWS see C147

C141
CLASSICAL OUTLOOK. New York
1923-   . 1923-36 title: Latin
Notes.

C142
CLASSICAL PHILOLOGY. Chicago
1906-   . (CPh, CP, ClPh).

C143
CLASSICAL QUARTERLY. London & Oxford 1907-   . (CQ).

C144
CLASSICAL REVIEW. London & Oxford
   1887-   . (CR, ClRev, ClR).

C145
CLASSICAL ROMAN LAW / F. Schulz.
   Oxford 1951.

C146
CLASSICAL STUDIES (Dept. of Classics Univ. Kyoto). Kyoto
   1980?-   .

C147
CLASSICAL VIEWS = Echos du Monde
   Classique. Toronto 1956-   .
   1956-81 English title: Classical
   News and Views.

CLASSICAL WEEKLY see C148.

C148
CLASSICAL WORLD. New York 1907- .
   1907-57 title: Classical Weekly.
   (CW).

C149
CLAVIS PATRUM GRAECORUM. Turnhout
   1974-   . (Corpus Christianorum).

C150
CLAVIS PATRUM LATINORUM / E. Dekkers
   & A. Gaar. 2. ed. Steenbrugis
   1961. (Sacris erudis; 3). 1st
   edition 1951.

Clermont-Ganneau, C. S. see E122.

Clinton, H. F. see F9.

C151
CLIO MEDICA; a series of primers
   on the history of medicine.
   New York 1930-   .

C152
CODICES LATINI ANTIQUIORES. Oxford
   1972-   . 1st edition 1934-66;
   supplement 1971. (CLA).

C153
CODICES MANUSCRIPTI. Vienna
   1975-   .

Cohen, H. see D21, D23.

C154
COINAGE of the EASTERN SELEUCID
   MINTS from SELEUCUS I to ANTI-
   OCHUS III / E. T. Newell. New
   York 1938. (Numismatic Studies,
   1).

C155
COINAGE of the ROMAN REPUBLIC /
   E. A. Sydenham. London 1952.
   Reprint New York 1976.

C156
COINAGE of the WESTERN SELEUCID
   MINTS from SELEUCUS I to ANTI-
   OCHUS III / E. T. Newell. New
   York 1941. (Numismatic Studies;
   4).

C157
COINS and ANTIQUITIES LTD. FIXED
   PRICE LIST. London 1970-78?

COINS of the ROMAN EMPIRE in the
   BRITISH MUSEUM see B212.

COINS of the ROMAN REPUBLIC in the
   BRITISH MUSEUM see B213.

Coldstream, J. N. see G24, G90.

C158
COLLANA di TESTI e DOCUMENTI per lo
   STUDIO dell'ANTICHITÀ. Milan
   1959-   .

Collart, P. see P40, P52.

C159
COLLECTANEA ALEXANDRINA; reliquiae
   minores poetarum graecorum aeta-
   tis Ptolemaicae 323-146 A. C.,
   epicorum, elegiacorum, lyricorum,
   ethicorum / J. U. Powell. Oxford 1925. Reprint Oxford 1970.

COLLECTED PAPERS of the ZAGREB LAW
   SCHOOL see Z13.

C160
COLLECTION des "AMIS de l'HISTOIRE".
   Luxemburg 1958?-   .

COLLECTION of ANCIENT GREEK INSCRIP-
   TIONS in the BRITISH MUSEUM see
   B217.

COLLECTION BUDÉ see C165.

C161
COLLECTION BYZANTINES (Association
   Guillaume Budé). Paris 1926?- .

C162
COLLECTION de l'ÉCOLE FRANÇAISE de
   ROME. Rome 1964- . 1964-71
   title: Mélanges d'Archéologie
   et d'Histoire. Supplement.

C163
COLLECTION R. JAMESON. Paris 1913-
   32.

COLLECTIONS of the SURREY ARCHAEO-
   LOGICAL SOCIETY see S279.

C164
COLLECTION de TRAVAUX de l'ACADÉMIE
   INTERNATIONALE d'HISTOIRE des
   SCIENCES. Paris & Leiden
   1948- .

C165
COLLECTION des UNIVERSITÉS de
   FRANCE (Association Guillaume
   Budé). Paris 1920- . (CUF).

COLLEGE ART JOURNAL see A609.

Collingwood, R. G. see R335.

Collitz, H. see S17.

Collomp, P. seee G121.

C166
COLUMBIA STUDIES in the CLASSICAL
   TRADITION. Leiden 1976- .

Combe, T. see B220.

C167
COMICORUM ATTICORUM FRAGMENTA / T.
   Kock. Leipzig 1880-88. (CAF).

C168
COMICORUM GRAECORUM FRAGMENTA / G.
   Kaibel. Berlin 1899. (Poetarum
   Graecorum Fragmenta; VI, 1).
   (CGF).

C169
COMICORUM GRAECORUM FRAGMENTA in

PAPYRI REPERTA / C. Austin. Berlin 1973.

C170
COMICORUM ROMANORUM FRAGMENTA prae-
   ter Plautum et Terentium / O.
   Ribbeck. 3. ed. Leipzig 1897.
   (Bibliotheca Scriptorum Grae-
   corum et Romanorum Teubneriana).
   Published as vol. 2 of his Scae-
   nicae Romanorum Poesis Fragmenta.
   (CRF).

C171
COMMENTARI; rivista di critica e
   storia dell'arte. Florence &
   Rome etc. 1950- .

C172
COMMENTARI dell'ATENEO di BRESCIA.
   Brescia 1808- . 1808-11 title:
   Commentarj della Accademia di
   Scienze, Lettere, Agricultura ed
   Arti del Dipartimento del Mella.

C173
COMMENTARIA in ARISTOTELEM GRAECA.
   Berlin 1882-1909. (CAG).

COMMENTARJ see C172.

C174
COMMENTARY on HERODOTUS / W. W.
   How & V. Wells. Oxford 1912.
   Reprinted with corrections 1928
   and 1975.

C175
COMMENTATIONES VINDOBONENSES.
   Vienna 1935- .

C176
COMMUNICATION MONOGRAPHS. Falls
   Church etc..1934- . 1934-75
   title: Speech Monographs.

COMMUNICAÇÕES, COMMUNICATIONES,
   COMMUNICATIONS and COMMUNICAZIONI
   are here interfiled.

COMMUNICATIONES ex BIBLIOTHECA HIS-
   TORIAE MEDICAE HUNGARICA see
   C177.

COMMUNICAZIONI della R. DEPUTAZIONE
   SUBALPINA di STORIA PATRIA. SE-
   ZIONE CUNEO see B183.

C177
COMMUNICATIONES de HISTORIA ARTIS
  MEDICINAE. Budapest 1955-   .
  Earlier title: Communicationes
  ex Bibliotheca Historiae Medicae
  Hungarica = Országos Orvostörté-
  neti Könyvtar Közleményei.

COMMUNICATIONS du MUSÉE NATIONAL de
  l'ÉRMITAGE see S117.

C178
COMMUNICATIONS. ORIENTAL INSTITUTE
  (Univ. Chicago). Chicago
  1922-   . (OIC).

C179
COMMUNICATIONES. REI CRETARIAE
  ROMANAE FAUTORUM. Haverford, Pa.
  1958-   .

COMMUNICAÇÕES dos SERVICOS GEOLO-
  GICOS do PORTUGAL see C189.

COMMUNICAZIONI della SOCIETÀ per
  gli STUDI STORICI, ARCHEOLOGICI
  ed ARTISTICI nella PROVINCIA di
  CUNEO see B183.

C180
COMPARATIVE LITERATURE. Eugene,
  Oregon 1949-   .

C181
COMPARATIVE LITERATURE STUDIES.
  College Park, Md. 1964-   .
  Continues journal by same title
  published in Cardiff 1940-46.

C182
COMPARATIVE LITERATURE STUDIES =
  Cahiers de Littératures Comparées.
  Cardiff 1940-46.

C183
COMPARATIVE STUDIES in SOCIETY and
  HISTORY. The Hague 1958-   .
  --. Supplement. 1961-   .

C184
COMPOSTELLANUM. Santiago de Compostela 1956-   .

C185
COMPTES-RENDUS des séances de l'ACA-
  DÉMIE des INSCRIPTIONS et BELLES-

LETTRES. Paris 1857-   .
  (CRAI, CRAIBL).

COMPTE-RENDU. ACADÉMIE des SCIEN-
  CES, ARTS et BELLES-LETTRES
  de DIJON see M99.

COMPTES RENDUS de l'ACADÉMIE des
  SCIENCES de (l'URSS/RUSSIE)
  see D86.

COMPTE-RENDU de la COMMISSION impériale ARCHÉOLOGIQUE (Leningrad) see O57.

COMPTE-RENDU des séances de la COM-
  MISSION royale d'HISTOIRE see
  B281.

COMPTE RENDU de la session. CON-
  GRÈS PRÉHISTORIQUE de FRANCE
  see C190.

COMPTES RENDU M.A.P. see S139.

C186
COMPTES-RENDUS et MÉMOIRES. SOCIÉTÉ
  d'HISTOIRE et d'ARCHÉOLOGIE de
  SENLIS. Senlis 1862-   .

C187
COMPTE RENDU de la ... RENCONTRE
  ASSYRIOLOGIQUE INTERNATIONALE.
  place varies 1950-   .

COMPTE-RENDU. SOCIÉTÉ nationale
  HAVRAISE d'ÉTUDES DIVERSES
  see R50.

C188
COMPUTERS and the HUMANITIES.
  Flushing 1966-   .

C189
COMUNICAÇÕES dos SERVICOS GEOLÓGI-
  COS do Portugal. Lisbon 1885-   .
  Variant title: Communicações.
  Also issued under the earlier
  names of the service: Direcção
  dos Trabalhos Geologicos.

Conder, C. R. see S280-S281.

CONGRÈS, CONGRESO and CONGRESSO
  are here interfiled.

CONGRÈS ARCHÉOLOGIQUE de FRANCE
see S68.

CONGRÈS INTERNATIONAL d'ARCHÉOLO-
GIE CLASSIQUE see A50.

CONGRÈS INTERNATIONAL de NUMISMA-
TIQUE see A51.

CONGRÈS INTERNATIONAL des ORIENTAL-
ISTES see A52.

CONGRESSO NACIONAL de ARQUEOLOGÍA
see C257.

CONGRESSO NAZIONALE di STUDI ROMANI
see A653.

C190
CONGRÈS PRÉHISTORIQUE de FRANCE.
Compte rendu. Paris 1905-   .

C191
CONIMBRIGA; revista do Instituto
de Arqueologia (Univ. Coimbra).
Coimbra 1959-   .

C192
CONNAISSANCE des ARTS. Paris
1952-   . 1952 title: Connaisseur.

CONNAISSEUR see C192.

C193
CONNOISSEUR. London 1901-   .

Contenau, G. see T2.

C194
CONTREBIS (Lancaster Archaeological Society). Lancaster
1973?-   .

C195
CONTRIBUTI dell'ISTITUTO di ARCHE-
OLOGIA (Univ. Milan). Milan
1967-   .

C196
CONTRIBUTI dell'ISTITUTO di STORIA
ANTICA. Milan 1972-   . (Sci-
enze Storiche). (Pubblicazione
della Università Cattolica del
Sacro Cuore).

C197
CONVEGNO di STUDI sulla MAGNA
GRAECA. Naples 1961-   .

C198
CONVIVIUM: filosofía, psicología,
humanidades. Barcelona 1956-   .

C199
CONVIVIUM; rivista di lettere,
filosofia e storia. Turin
1929-   .

Conway, R. S. see P164.

C200
CORNELL STUDIES in CLASSICAL
PHILOLOGY. Ithaca 1887-   .

Cornford, F. M. see P142.

C201
CORNISH ARCHAEOLOGY. Camborne
1962-   .

C202
CORNUCOPIAE (Ancient Coin Society
of Canada). Toronto 1972-   .

C203
CORPUS of ANCIENT NEAR EASTERN
SEALS in North American Collec-
tions. New York & Washington,
D.C. 1948-   . (Bollingen
series; 14).

C204
CORPUS BRUXELLENSE HISTORIAE BYZAN-
TINAE. Brussels 1935-   .
--. Forma Imperii. 1939-   .
--. Subsidia. 1954-   .

C205
CORPUS CHRISTIANORUM. Turnhout.
(CC).
--. Series Graeca. 1977-   .
--. Series Latina. 1953-   .

C206
CORPUS CULTUS CYBELAE ATTIDISQUE /
M. J. Vermaseren. Leiden
1977-   . (Études Préliminaires
aux Religions Orientales dans
l'Empire Romain; 50). (CCCA).

C207
CORPUS CULTUS DEAE SYRIAE / P.
  Berg. Leiden 1972-   . (Études
  Préliminaires aux Religions Ori-
  entales dans l'Empire Romain;
  28). (CCDS).

C208
CORPUS of DATED PALESTINIAN POTTERY
  / J. G. Duncan. London 1930.
  (British School of Archaeology
  in Egypt. Publications of the
  Egyptian Research Account; 49).

C209
CORPUS FONTIUM HISTORIAE BYZANTINAE.
  Berlin 1967-   . Some vols.
  also in the series: Dumbarton
  Oaks Texts.

C210
CORPUS GLOSSARIORUM LATINORUM a G.
  Loewe incohatum ed. G. GÖTZ.
  Leipzig 1888-1923. Reprint Am-
  sterdam 1965. (CGL).

C211
CORPUS der GRIECHISCH-CHRISTLICHEN
  INSCHRIFTEN von HELLAS / N. A.
  Bees. Athens 1940. Vol. 1 only
  published.

C212
CORPUS INSCRIPTIONUM ATTICARUM.
  Berlin 1873-97. Reissued in
  1903 as Inscriptiones Graecae,
  1-3. (CIA).

C213
CORPUS INSCRIPTIONUM ETRUSCARUM.
  Leipzig 1893-   . (CIE).

C214
CORPUS INSCRIPTIONUM GRAECARUM / A.
  Boeckh. Berlin 1828-77. Reprint
  Hildesheim 1977. (CIG).

C215
CORPUS INSCRIPTIONUM HETTICARUM /
  L. Messerschmidt. Berlin 1900-
  06. (Mitteilungen der Vorderasia-
  tischen Gesellschaft; V, 4-5;
  VII, 3; XI, 5). (CIH).

C216
CORPUS INSCRIPTIONUM INSULARUM

CELTICARUM / R. A. S. Macalister.
  Dublin 1945-   .

C217
CORPUS INSCRIPTIONUM IRANICARUM.
  London 1955-   .
  --. Supplementary Series.
  1972-   .

C218
CORPUS INSCRIPTIONUM ITALICARUM
  ANTIQUIORIS AEVI / A. Fabretti.
  Turin 1867. Supplements appeared
  1872-80.

C219
CORPUS INSCRIPTIONUM IUDAICARUM /
  J. B. Frey. Rome 1936. Only
  vol. 1 published. 1975 reprint
  had title: Corpus of Jewish
  Inscriptions. (CIJ).

C220
CORPUS INSCRIPTIONUM LATINARUM.
  Berlin 1863-   . (CIL).

CORPUS INSCRIPTIONUM LATINARUM
  SUPPLEMENT see E64.

C221
CORPUS INSCRIPTIONUM et MONUMENTOR-
  UM RELIGIONIS MITHRIACAE / M. J.
  Vermaseren. The Hague 1956-   .
  (CIMRM).

CORPUS INSCRIPTIONUM REGNI BOSPOR-
  ANI see K41.

C222
CORPUS INSCRIPTIONUM SEMITICARUM.
  Paris 1881-   . (CIS).

CORPUS of JEWISH INSCRIPTIONS see
  C229.

C223
CORPUS MEDICORUM GRAECORUM. Leip-
  zig & Berlin 1908-   . (CMG).
  --. Supplementum. 1934-   .
  --. Supplementum Orientale.
  1963-   .

C224
CORPUS MEDICORUM LATINORUM. Berlin
  & Leipzig 1915-   . (CML).

C225
CORPUS der MINOISCHEN und MYKEN-
ISCHEN SIEGEL. Berlin 1964-   .
(CMMS).

C226
CORPUS MONUMENTORUM RELIGIONIS DEI
MENSIS. Leiden 1971-78. (Études
Préliminaires aux Religions
Orientales dans l'Empire Romaine
19).

C227
CORPUS des MOSAÏQUES de TUNISIE /
M. A. Alexander & M. Ennaifer.
Tunis 1973-   .

C228
CORPUS des ORDONNANCES des PTOLE-
MÉES / M. T. Lenger. Brussels
1980. (Mémoire de la Classe des
Lettres. Académie Royale de
Belgique. Collection in 8°; II
64, 2). Reprint with corrections
of 1964 edition. (COrdPtol).

C229
CORPUS PAPYRORUM CHRISTIANARUM
(Macquarie University). North
Ryde, N.S.W. In progess.

C230
CORPUS PAPYRORUM HERMOPOLITANORUM /
C. Wessely. Leipzig 1905-   .
((Studien zur Palaeographie
und Papyruskunde; 5). (CPHerm).

C231
CORPUS PAPYRORUM JUDAICORUM / V.
A. Tcherikover & A. Fuks. Cam-
bridge, Mass. 1957-64. (CPJud).

C232
CORPUS PAPYRORUM LATINORUM / R.
Cavenaile. Wiesbaden 1956-58.
(CPLat).

C233
CORPUS PAPYRORUM RAINERI / C. Wes-
sely et al. Vienna 1895-   .
(CPR).

C234
CORPUS PAROEMIOGRAPHORUM GRAECORUM
/ E. L. Leutsch & F. G. Schneide-
win. Göttingen 1839-51. Reprint
Hildesheim 1958-65.

CORPUS POESIS EPICAE GRAECAE
LUDIBUNDAE see C246.

C235
CORPUS POETARUM LATINORUM / J. P.
Postgate. 2. ed. London 1905-
20.

C236
CORPUS SCRIPTORUM CHRISTIANORUM
ORIENTALIUM. Louvain etc.
1903-   . Issued in 4 sections:
1) Scriptores Aethiopici; 2)
Scriptores Arabici; 3) Scriptores
Coptici; 4) Scriptores Syri.
(CSCO).

C237
CORPUS SCRIPTORUM ECCLESIASTICORUM
LATINORUM. Vienna 1866-   .
(CSEL).

C238
CORPUS SCRIPTORUM GRAECORUM PARA-
VIANUM. Turin 1975-   .

C239
CORPUS SCRIPTORUM HISTORIAE BYZAN-
TINAE / B. G. Niebuhr. Bonn
1828-97. (CSHB).

C240
CORPUS SCRIPTORUM LATINORUM PARA-
VIANUM. Rome & Turin 1916-   .

C241
CORPUS SIGNORUM IMPERII ROMANI =
Corpus der Skulpturen der Röm-
ischen Welt = Corpus of the
Sculpture of the Roman World =
Corpus des Sculptures du Monde
Romain. (CSIR).
--. Deutschland. Bonn 1973-   .
--. Great Britain. London
1975-   .
--. Österreich. Vienna 1967-   .
--. Pologne. Warsaw 1972-   .

C242
CORPUS delle URNE ETRUSCHE di ETÀ
ELLENISTICA. Florence 1975-   .

C243
CORPUS VASORUM ANTIQUORUM [arranged
by country]. place varies
1923-   . (CVA).

C244
CORPUS VASORUM ARRETINORUM; a catalogue of the signatures, shapes,
and chronology of Italian sigillata / A. Oxe. Bonn 1968. (Antiquitas, Reihe 3; 1-4).

C245
CORPUS VASORUM HISPANORUM. Madrid
1944-   .

C246
CORPUSCULUM POESIS EPICAE GRAECAE
LUDIBUNDAE / P. Brandt & C. Wachs-
muth. Leipzig 1885-88. (Biblio-
theca Scriptorum Graecorum et
Romanorum Teubneriana).

CORRESPONDENZBLATT see KORRESPON-
DENZBLATT.

C247
CORSE HISTORIQUE, ARCHÉOLOGIQUE,
LITTÉRAIRE, SCIENTIFIQUE.
Ajaccio 1961-   . Earlier ti-
tles: Revue d'Études Corses and
Revue d'Études Historiques,
Littéraires et Scientifiques
Corses.

CORSI d'ARTE RAVENNATE e BIZANTINA
see C248.

C248
CORSO di CULTURA dull'ARTE RAVEN-
NATE e BIZANTINA. Ravenna
1955-   . Variant titles: Corsi
di Cultura sull'Arte Ravennate e
Bizantina, Corsi d'Arte Ravennate e Bizantina.

Corswant, W. see D43.

Cougny, E. see E77.

COUNCIL for OLD WORLD ARCHAEOLOGY
see C1-C2.

COUP d'OEIL sur les TRAVAUX de la
SOCIÉTÉ JURASSIENNE d'ÉMULATION
see A84.

Courbin, P. see C105.

COWA BIBLIOGRAPHY see C1.

COWA SURVEY see C2.

Cramer, J. A. see A212, A210.

CRANIA HUNGARICA see A336.

Crawford, D. S. see P60.

Crawford, M. H. see R338, R337.

C249
CRETAN SEALS / V. E. G. Kenna.
Oxford 1960.

CRETICA CHRONICA see K53.

C250
CRISIA; culegere de materiale şi
studii. Oradia, Romania ?-   .

C251
CRISTIANESIMO nella STORIA. Bologna 1980-   .

C252
CRITICA d'ARTE. Florence 1935-50
1954-   . Suspended 1943-49.

C253
CRITICA STORICA. Florence 1962- .

C254
CRONACHE di ARCHEOLOGIA e di STORIA
dell'ARTE. Catania 1962-   .

C255
CRONACHE ERCOLANESI. Naples
1971-   .

C256
CRONACHE POMPEIANE. Naples
1975-   .

C257
CRONICA. CONGRESO NACIONAL de
ARQUEOLOGIA. place varies
1949-   .

C258
CRONICA NUMISMATICĂ si ARHEOLOGICĂ.
Bucharest 1920-39?

Cross, F. L. see 063.

C259
CROWTHER (D. J.) LTD. [Fixed Price
List]. London 1966-69.

C260
CUADERNOS de ARAGÓN. Saragossa
   1966-   . (Publicación. Institución Fernando el Católico;
   403).

C261
CUADERNOS de ARQUEOLOGÍA e HISTORIA
   de la CIUDAD. Barcelona
   1960-   .

C262
CUADERNOS de ESTUDIOS GALLEGOS.
   Santiago de Compostela 1944-   .

C263
CUADERNOS de ESTUDIOS MANCHEGOS.
   Ciudad Real 1947-   .

C264
CUADERNOS de ETNOLOGÍA y ETNOGRA-
   FÍA de NAVARRA. Pamplona
   1969-   .

C265
CUADERNOS de FILOLOGÍA CLÁSICA.
   Madrid 1971-   .

C266
CUADERNOS de FILOSOFÍA. Buenos
   Aires 1948-   .

CUADERNOS de HISTORIA see V66.

C267
CUADERNOS de HISTORIA de ESPAÑA.
   Buenos Aires 1944-   .

C268
CUADERNOS de HISTORIA "JERONIMO
   ZURITA". Saragossa 1951-   .
   (Publicación Institución
   Fernando el Católico).

CUADERNOS de HISTORIA MUNDIAL see
   C25.

C269
CUADERNOS de HISTORIA PRIMITIVA.
   Madrid 1946-   .

C270
CUADERNOS de PREHISTORIA de la
   UNIVERSIDAD de GRANDA. Granada
   1976-   .

C271
CUADERNOS de TRABAJOS de la ESCUELA
   ESPAÑOLA de HISTORIA y ARQUEOLO-
   GIA en ROMA. Rome etc. 1912-24
   1952-   . Name of the school
   varies slightly.

C272
CULTS of the GREEK STATES / L. R.
   Farnell. Oxford 1896-1909. Reprint Chicago 1971 and New Ro-
   chelle 1977.

C273
CULTURA; rivista di filosofia, letteratura e storia. Rome 1963- .

C274
CULTURA BIBLICA. Segovia 1944-   .

C275
CULTURA e SCUOLA. Rome 1961-   .

C276
CULTURES. (UNESCO). Paris 1973-   .
   Also issued in a French edition.

C277
CUMANIA; Acta Museorum ex Comitatu
   Bács-Kiskun. Kecskemet 1972-   .

C278
CUMIDAVA; culegere di studii și
   cercetări a Muzeului Judetean
   Brasov, Romania ?-   .

Cumont, F. see T26, F51.

CUNEIFORM TEXTS from BABYLONIAN
   TABLETS in the BRITISH MUSEUM
   see B215.

C279
CUNOBELIN; yearbook of the British
   Association of Numismatic Societies. Birmingham 1954-   . Subtitle formerly used as title.

C280
CURRENT ANTHROPOLOGY. Chicago
   1960-   .

Curtius, E. see A691.

C281
CYLINDER SEALS; a documentary essay

on the art and religion of the
ancient Near East / H. Frankfort.
London 1939. Reprint London 1965.

C282
CYPRIOTE BRONZEWORK in the MYCE-
    NAEAN WORLD / H. W. Catling.
    Oxford 1964. (Oxford Monographs
    on Classical Archaeology; 9).

C283
CZSAOPISMO PRAWNO-HISTORYCZNE = An-
    nales d'Histoire du Droit.   Posnan
    etc. 1948-   .

D

Đ1
DACIA. Bucharest 1924-48. 1957-   .

Dack, E. Van't see P220.

D2
DACOROMANIA; Cluj 1920/1-   .

d'Amelio, M. see N129.

da Mosto, A. see A534.

D3
DANUBIUS (Muzeul de Istorie).
  Galati 1967?-   .

Daremberg, C. V. see D41.

Dareste, R. see R45.

Daris, S. see P61.

David, M. see P65.

Davies, A. Morpurgo see M326.

Dawkins, R, M. see U20.

DAWNA KULTURA see Z88.

D4
[DAYBOOKS for KNOSSOS] / D. Macken-
  zie. Manuscript in Ashmolean
  Museum, Oxford.

D5
DEBRECENI DÉRI MŰZEUM ÉVKÖNYVE =
  Annales Musei Debreceniensis de
  Friderico Déri nominati. Deb-
  recen 1933-   . (DME).

Debrunner, A. see G80, A128.

D6
DEDICATIONS from the ATHENIAN
  AKROPOLIS / A. E. Raubitschek.
  Cambridge, Mass. 1949.

D7
DEFIXIONUM TABELLAE quotquot inno-
  tuerunt / A. M. H. Audollent.
  Paris 1904.

D8
DEFIXIONUM TABELLAE ATTICAE / R.
  Wuensch. Berlin 1897. Published
  as an appendix to vol. 3, 3 of
  the Corpus Inscriptionum Atticarum.

de Goeje, M. J. see B87.

Degrassi, A see I78, F6-F7.

Deimel, A. see S273.

Dekkers, E. see C150.

Delaporte, L. see C73.

Delatte, A. see A207.

Del Chiaro, M. A. see E117.

Delehaye, H. see S297.

DELTION see A470.

D9
DELTION tēs CHRISTIANIKĒS ARCHAI-

OLOGIKĒS HETAIREIAS. Athens
1892-1911 1924-27 1959-   .
Ser. 3 (1932-38) originally published as Abt. 4 of Byzantinisch-
neugriechische Jahrbücher 10-11,
13-14.

DELTION HELLENIKĒS ALLELOGRAPHIAS
see B284.

D10
DELTION tēs HISTORIKĒS kai ETHNOLO-
GIKĒS HETAIREIAS tēs HELLADOS =
Bulletin de la Société Histor-
ique et Ethnologique de la Grèce.
Athens 1883-   . Suspended 1904-
09, 1929-55.

DELTION VIVLIOGRAPHIAS tēs HELLĒ-
NIKĒS GLOSSĒS see B76.

Demiańczuk, J. see S276.

D11
DEMOTIC OSTRACA from the COLLEC-
TIONS at OXFORD, PARIS, BERLIN
and CAIRO / G. Mattha. Cairo
1945. (Publications de la Société Fouad I de Papyrologie.
Textes et Documents; 6).

D12
DEMOTIC OSTRACA from MEDINET HABU /
M. Lichtheim. Chicago 1957. (Univ. of Chicago. Oriental Institute Publications; 80).

D13
DENKMÄLER aus ÄGYPTEN und AETHIO-
PIEN / R. Lepsius. Berlin 1849-
56. (LD).

D14
DENKMÄLER ANTIKER ARCHITEKTUR.
Berlin 1932-   .

D15
DENKMÄLER GRIECHISCHER und RÖM-
ISCHER SKULPTUR / H. Brunn, F.
Bruckmann & P. Arndt. Munich
1888-1935? (BrBr).

D16
DENKMÄLER des KLASSISCHEN ALTER-
TUMS zur ERLÄUTERUNG des LEBENS
der GRIECHEN und RÖMER in RELI-

GION, KUNST und SITTE / A. Baumeister. Munich & Leipzig 1885-
88.

D17
DENKMÄLER der MALEREI des ALTER-
TUMS / P. Hermann & F. Bruck-
mann. Munich 1904-?

DENKMALPFLEGE see D28.

D18
DENKMALPFLEGE in BADEN-WÜRTTEMBERG.
Stuttgart 1972-   .

DENKMALPFLEGE und HEIMATSCHUTZ
see D28.

DENKSCHRIFTEN. AKADEMIE der WIS-
SENSCHAFTEN in WIEN. PHILOSO-
PHISCH-HISTORISCHE KLASSE see
D19.

D19
DENKSCHRIFTEN der ÖSTERREICHISCHEN
AKADEMIE der WISSENSCHAFTEN.
PHILOSOPHISCH-HISTORISCHE
KLASSE. Vienna 1850-   .

DENKSCHRIFTEN. PHILOSOPHISCH-HIS-
TORISCHE KLASSE. ÖSTERREICHISCHE
AKADEMIE der WISSENSCHAFTEN see
D19.

DENKSCHRIFTEN. WIEN see D19.

Denniston, J. D. see G98.

D20
DERBYSHIRE ARCHAEOLOGICAL JOURNAL.
London etc. 1879-   . 1879-1960
title: Journal. Derbyshire Arch-
aeological and Natural History
Society.

DERGISI. DIL ve TARIH-COĞRAFYA FA-
KÜLTESI see D65.

DÉRI MÚZEUM ÉVKÖNYVE see D5.

de Rossi, G. B. see I44, R331.

Deroy, L. see I28.

DES RECHERCHES HISTORIQUES see
C108.

Desborough, V. R. d'A. see G86,
L12, P226.

DESCRIPTION of the COLLECTION of
ANCIENT MARBLES in the BRITISH
MUSEUM see B220.

D21
DESCRIPTION GÉNÉRALE des MONNAIES
de la RÉPUBLIQUE ROMAINE COMMU-
NÉMENT APPELÉES MÉDAILLES CONSU-
LAIRES / H. Cohen. Paris 1857.

D22
DESCRIPTION HISTORIQUE et CHRONO-
LOGIQUE des MONNAIES de la RÉPUB-
LIQUE ROMAINE VULGAIREMENT APPE-
LÉES MONNAIES CONSULAIRES / E.
C. F. Babelon. Paris etc. 1885-
86. Reprint Bologna 1963.

D23
DESCRIPTION HISTORIQUE des MONNAIES
FRAPÉES sous l'EMPIRE ROMAIN COM-
MUNEMENT APPELÉES MEDAILLES IM-
PÉRIALES / H. Cohen. 2. éd. Paris
1880-92. 1st edition 1859-68.
Reprint edition Graz 1955.

D24
DESCRIPTIVE CATALOGUE of the COL-
LECTION of GREEK COINS FORMED by
Sir Hermann WEBER / L. Forrer.
London 1922-29. Reprint New York
1975.

D25
DESCRIPTIVE CATALOGUE of the GREEK
PAPYRI in the COLLECTION of Wil-
fred MERTON / H. I. Bell et al.
London 1948-67. Volume 3 appeared
as Supplement 18 to the Bulletin
of the Institute of Classical
Studies. (PMert).

Dessau, H. see I80.

D26
DESTRUCTION of the PALACE at KNOS-
SOS / M. R. Popham. Gothenburg
1970. (Studies in Mediterranean
Archaeology; 12).

D27
DEUTSCHES ARCHIV für ERFORSCHUNG
des MITTELALTERS. Weimar etc.

1937-   . 1937-44 title: Deutsches Archiv für Geschichte des
Mittelalters. Suspended 1944-50.

DEUTSCHES ARCHIV für GESCHICHTE
des MITTELALTERS see D27.

DEUTSCHES JAHRBUCH für NUMISMATIK
see N124

D28
DEUTSCHE KUNST und DENKMALPFLEGE.
Munich etc. 1899-1943 1948
1952-   . Title varies: 1899-
1922 & 1930-33: Denkmalpflege;
1923-29: Denkmalpflege und
Heimatschutz; 1934-43: Deutsche
Kunst und Denkmalpflege; 1948:
Kunstpflege.

D29
DEUTSCHE LITERATURZEITUNG für
KRITIK der INTERNATIONALEN
WISSENSCHAFT. Berlin 1880-   .
Title varies slightly. Suspended
1945-47. (DLZ).

D30
DEUTSCHE MÜNZBLÄTTER. Berlin etc.
1880-1943. 1880-1933 title:
Berliner Münzblätter.

D31
DEUTSCHE REVUE. Berlin 1877-1922.

D32
DEUTSCHE VIERTELJAHRSSCHRIFT für
LITERATURWISSENSCHAFT und
GEISTESGESCHICHTE. Stuttgart
etc. 1923-   . Suspended 1945-
48.

DEUTSCHE ZEITSCHRIFT für Ge-
SCHICHTSWISSENSCHAFT see H116.

D33
DEVELOPMENT of ATTIC BLACK-FIGURE
/ J. D. Beazley. Berkeley 1951.
(Sather Classical Lectures; 24).

Devijver, H. see P219.

D34
DIADORA (Arheoloski Muzej). Zadar
1959-   .

D35
DIALECTICA; international review
of philosophy of knowledge.
Neuchâtel 1947-   .

D36
DIALECTORUM GRAECARUM EXEMPLA EPI-
GRAPHICA POTIORA / E. Schwyzer.
Leipzig 1923. Reprint Hildesheim
1960. Based on P. Cauer's Dialec-
tus Inscriptionum Graecarum.
(DGE).

D37
DIALECTS of ANCIENT GAUL / J. Whatmough. 2. ed. Cambridge, Mass.
1970. 1st edition 1950.

DIALECTUS INSCRIPTIONUM GRAECARUM
see D36.

D38
DIALOGHI di ARCHEOLOGIA.   Rome &
Milan 1967-77? 1979-   .

D39
DIALOGUES d'HISTOIRE ANCIENNE.
Paris 1974-   . Part of the
Annales litteraires de l'Univer-
sité de Besançon.

DIANA see B287.

D40
DICCIONARIO GRIEGO-ESPAÑOL / F.
Rodriguez Adrados & E. Gangutia
et al. Madrid 1980-   .

DICHTUNG und VOLKSTUM   see E153.

DICTIONARY and DICTIONNAIRE are
here interfiled. See also DIZI-
ONARIO, DICCIONARIO.

D41
DICTIONNAIRE des ANTIQUITÉS GREC-
QUES et ROMAINES / C. V. Daremberg & E. Saglio. Paris 1877-
1919. Appeared in several printings. Reprint Graz 1962. (DA, DS,
DAGR).

D42
DICTIONARY of the APOSTOLIC CHURCH
/ J. Hastings. Edinburgh 1915-
18.

D43
DICTIONNAIRE d'ARCHÉOLOGIE BIBLI-
QUE / W. Corswant & E. Urech.
Neuchâtel 1956.

D44
DICTIONNAIRE d'ARCHÉOLOGIE CHRÉTI-
ENNE et de LITURGIE / F. Cabrol
& H. Leclercq. Paris 1907-53.
(DACL).

D45
DICTIONARY of the BIBLE / J. Hastings. New York etc. 1898-
1904. Appeared in several printings.

D46
DICTIONNAIRE de la BIBLE / F. G.
Vigouroux. Paris 1895-1912.
(DB).
--. Supplement. 1928-   .
(DBS).

D47
DICTIONARY of CHRIST and the GOS-
PELS / J. Hastings. New York
1906-08. Reprint Grand Rapids,
Mich. 1973.

D48
DICTIONARY of CHRISTIAN ANTIQUI-
TIES / W. Smith & S. Cheetham.
London 1876-80. Appeared in many
printings and editions.

D49
DICTIONARY of CHRISTIAN BIOGRAPHY
LITERATURE, SECTS and DOCTRINES
/ W. Smith & H. Wace. London
1877-87. Version in 1 vol. by   .
Wace & W. C. Piercy appeared
in 1911 under similiar title.

D50
DICTIONNAIRE de DROIT CANONIQUE /
R. Naz. Paris 1935-65.

D51
DICTIONNAIRE ÉTYMOLOGIQUE de la
LANGUE GRECQUE / E. Boisacq. 4.
éd. Heidelberg 1950. 1st edition
1916.

D52
DICTIONNAIRE ÉTYMOLOGIQUE de la

LANGUE GRECQUE / P. Chantraine.
Paris 1968-   .

D53
DICTIONNAIRE ÉTYMOLOGIQUE de la
LANGUE LATINE / A. Ernout & M.
Meillet. 4. éd. Paris 1967. 1st
edition 1932.

D54
DICTIONNAIRE ÉTYMOLOGIQUE LATIN /
M. J. A. Bréal & A. Bailey. Paris 1885. Appeared in numerous
editions and printings.

D55
DICTIONNAIRE GÉOGRAPHIQUE de l'AN-
CIENNE ÉGYPTE / H. K. Brugsch.
Leipzig 1879-80. Reprint Hilde-
sheim & New York 1974.

D56
DICTIONNAIRE d'HISTOIRE et de GÉO-
GRAPHIE ECCLÉSIASTIQUE / A. Baud-
rillart et al. Paris 1912-   .
(DHGE).

D57
DICTIONNAIRE des INSCRIPTIONS SÉ-
MITIQUES de l'OUEST / C. F. Jean
& J. Hoftijzer. Nouv. éd.
Leiden 1965. 1st edition 1954.

D58
DICTIONNAIRE de la LANGUE LOUVITE /
E. Laroche. Paris 1959. (Bibliothèque Archéologique et Historique de l'Institut Français
d'Archéologie d'Istanbul; 6).

D59
DICTIONNAIRE des NOMS GÉOGRAPHIQUES
contenus dans les textes hiéro-
glyphiques / T. Gauthier. Cairo
1925-31. Reprint Osnabrück 1975.

D60
DICTIONNAIRE de SPIRITUALITÉ AS-
CÉTIQUE et MYSTIQUE, DOCTRINE et
HISTOIRE / M. Viller et al. Pa-
ris 1932-   .

D61
DICTIONNAIRE de THÉOLOGIE CATHO-
LIQUE / A. Vacant et al. Paris
1903-50. (DTC).

D62
DIDASKALIKON (Athénée de Liège.
Centre de Recherche et de Docu-
mentation pour l'Enseignement du
Grec). Liege 1960-   .

D63
DIDASKALOS (Joint Association of
Classical Teachers). London
1963-76.

Didot, A. F.   see   B99.

Diego Santos, F.   see   E72.

Diehl, E.   see   A335, I74, P148.

Diels, H.   see   F65, D92, P147.

DIETHNES EPHEMERIS tēs NOMISMA-
TIKES ARCHAIOLOGIAS   see   J116.

Dietrich, M.   see   K9.

D64
DIKAIOMATA; Auszüge aus alexand-
rinischen Gesetzen und Verord-
nungen in einem Papyrus des
Philologischen Seminars der
Universität Halle. Berlin 1913.
(PHal).

D65
DIL ve TARIH-COĞRAFYA FAKÜLTESI
DERGISI = Revue de la Faculté
de Langues, d'Histoire et de
Géographie. Ankara 1942-   .

D66
DIN ISTORIA DOBROGEI / D. M. Pippidi et al. Bucharest 1900-   .

Dindorf, L. A.   see   H94.

D67
DIOGÈNE (Conseil International de
la Philosophie et des Sciences
Humaines). Paris 1952-   .

D68
DIOGENES (International Council
for Philosophy and Humanistic
Studies). New York 1952-   .
Also in French edition.

D69
DIONISO (Istituto Nazionale del
    Dramma Antico). Syracuse 1929- .
    1929-30 title: Bolletino dell'Is-
    tituto Nazionale del Dramma An-
    tico.

D70
DIONYSIUS (Dept. of Classics Dal-
    house Univ.). Halifax 1977-   .

D71
DIOTIMA; epithēorēsis philosophi-
    kēs ereunēs. Athens 1973-   .

Diringer, D. see I115.

D72
DISCOVERIES in the JUDAEAN DESERT.
    Oxford 1955-   .

D73
DISCOVERY and EXCAVATIONS, SCOT-
    LAND. Dundee 1955-   .

DISSERTATION, DISSERTATIONES, DIS-
    SERTATIONS and DISSERTAZIONE
    are here interfiled.

DISSERTATION ABSTRACTS see D75.

DISSERTATIONES ARCHAEOLOGICAE see
    R56.

D74
DISSERATIONES INAUGURALES BATAVAE
    ad RES ANTIQUAS PERTINENTES.
    Leiden 1940-   . Suspended
    1941-44.

D75
DISSERTATIONS INTERNATIONAL. Ann
    Arbor 1938- . 1938-51 title:
    Microform abstracts. 1952-69
    title: Dissertation abstracts.

D76
DISSERTATIONES PANNONICAE. Buda-
    pest.
    --. Ser. I. 1940-46 196?-   .
    --. Ser. II. 1933-44.
    Series I and II issued by the
    Institute of Numismatics and
    Archaeology, Pázmány Univ. Series
    I being issued in reprint. New
    editions are being issued by the

National Museum of Hungary.
    (DissPan).

DISSERTAZIONE della PONTIFICIA AC-
    CADEMIA ROMANA di ARCHEOLOGIA
    see A668.

D77
DISTRITO de BRAGA. Braga ?-   .

Dittenberger, W. see I37, S288,
    O45.

D78
DIZIONARIO EPIGRAFICO di ANTICHITÀ
    ROMANE / E. de Ruggero. Rome
    1886-   .

D79
DIZIONARIO ETIMOLOGICO ITALIANO /
    C. Battisti. Florence 1975.
    1st edition 1950?

DOBRUDSCHA ANNALEN see A168.

DOCUMENT, DOCUMENTE, DOCUMENTI and
    DOCUMENTS are here interfiled.

D80
DOCUMENTI ANTICHI dell'AFRICA
    ITALIANA. Bergamo 1932-36.

DOCUMENT ARCHEOLOGIA see H88.

D81
DOCUMENTS ILLUSTRATING the REIGNS
    of AUGUSTUS and TIBERIUS / V.
    Ehrenberg & A. H. M. Jones. 2.
    ed. Oxford 1976. 1st edition
    1949.

D82
DOCUMENTS in MYCENAEAN GREEK / J.
    Chadwick. 2. ed. Cambridge 1973.
    1st edition 1956 by J. Chadwick
    & M. Ventris. (Docs).

D83
DOCUMENTE PRIVIND ISTORIA ROMÂNIEI
    / M. Roller. Bucharest
    --. A. Moldova. 1951-   .
    --. B. Tara Românească. 1951- .
    --. C. Transilvania. 1951-   .

DOCUMENTS du PROCHE-ORIENT ANCIEN
    see E81.

D84
DOCUMENTS et RAPPORTS de la SOCI-
ÉTÉ PALÉONTOLOGIQUE et ARCH-
ÉOLOGIQUE de l'ARRONDISSEMENT
JUDICIAIRE de CHARLEROI. Char-
leroi 1864-   . Name of society
varies slightly.

D85
DŌDŌNĒ (Philosophikē Scholē. Panepistēmion Ioanninōn). Ioannina
1972-   .

Dölger, F. J. see A354.

D86
DOKLADY. AKADEMIĨA NAUK SSSR =
Comptes Rendus de l'Académie des
Sciences de l'URSS. Leningrad
1922-63. 1922-25 title: Doklady
Rossiĩskoĩ Akademii Nauk = Comp-
tes Rendus de l'Académie des
Sciences de Russie.

DOKLADY ROSSIĨSKOĨ AKADEMII NAUK
see D86.

DR. A. PETERMANNS MITTEILUNGEN aus
JULIUS PERTHES' GEOGRAPHISCHER
ANSTALT see P104.

D87
DOLGOZATOK az ERDÉLYI NEMZETI MŪZE-
UM ÉREM-ES RÉGISÉGTĂRABÓL = Travaux de la Section Numismatique
et Archéologique du Musée National de Transylvanie à Kolozsvár.
Cluj 1910-19.

D88
DOLGOZATOK a MAGYAR KIRALYI HORTHY
MIKLÓS TUDOMÁNY-EGYETEM RÉGISÉG-
TUDOMÁNYI INTÉZETÉBŌL = Arbeiten
des Archäologischen Institut der
k. ung. Miklós Universität.
Szeged 1925-43. Also issued under
the earlier name of the university: Franz Josef University. Some
early volumes also had the French
title: Travaux de l'Institut
Archéologique de l'Université
Francois-Joseph.

DOLGOZATOK a SZEGEDI TUDOMÁNY-EGYE-
TEM RÉGISÉGTUDOMÁNYI INTEZETÉBŌL
see D88.

D89
DONAURAUM. Vienna 1956-   .

Donner, H. see K4.

D'Ors, A. see E71.

DOSSIERS de l'ARCHÉOLOGIE see
H88.

Dossin, G. see A530-A531.

D90
DOWNSIDE REVIEW. Bath etc. 1880- .

D91
DOXA; rassegna critica di antichità
classica. Rome 1948-51.

D92
DOXOGRAPHI GRAECI / H. Diels. Berlin & Leipzig 1879. Reprint Berlin 1958.

DR. A. PETERMANNS MITTEILUNGEN aus
JUSTUS PERTHES' GEOGRAPHISCHER
ANSTALT see P104.

D93
DRAMMATIC FESTIVALS of ATHENS / A.
W. Pickard-Cambridge. 2. ed.
Oxford 1968. 1st edition 1953.

DRESDENER GALERIE BLÄTTER see D94.

D94
DRESDENER KUNSTBLÄTTER; Monatsschrift der Staatlichen Kunstsammlungen Dresden. Dresden
1957-   . 1957-59 title: Dresdener Galerie Blätter.

Driver, S. R. see H34.

DROIT PUBLIC ROMAIN see R325.

Dü filed as if it were spelled Due.

DuCange, C. see G55.

Ducati, P. see S151.

Duchesne, L. see L48.

D95
DÜRENER GESCHICHTSBLÄTTER. Düren
1955-   .

D96
DÜSSELDORFER JAHRBUCH; Beiträge zur
  Geschichte des Niederrheins.
  Düsseldorf 1886-   . 1886-1912
  title: Beiträge des Niederrheins.

D97
DUISBERGER FORSCHUNGEN; Schriften-
  reihe für Geschichte und Heimatkunde Duisburges. Duisburg-Ruh-
  rort 1957-   .

D98
DUMBARTON OAKS PAPERS. Cambridge,
  Mass. 1941-   . (DOP).

D99
DUMBARTON OAKS STUDIES. Washington
  D.C. 1950-   .

D100
DUMBARTON OAKS TEXTS. Washington
  D.C. 1967-   .

D101
DUNÁNTÚLI SZEMLE. Szombathely
  1933-   . Vols. 1-6 as Vasi
  Szemle.

Duncan, J. G. see C208.

D102
DURHAM UNIVERSITY JOURNAL. Durham
  1876-   .

D103
DURIUS; boletín castellano de estudios clásicos. Valladolid 1973
  1973-   .

E

E1
EARLY GREEK ARMOUR and WEAPONS from the END of the BRONZE AGE to 600 B.C. / A. Snodgrass. Edinburgh 1964.

E2
EARLY GREEK PHILOSOPHY / J. Burnet. 4. ed. New York & London 1930. 1st edition 1895.

E3
EASTERN CHURCHES QUARTERLY. Ramsgate 1936-64.

Ebeling, E. see I33, K12-K13, R23.

Ebert, M. see R28.

E4
ECCLESIAE OCCIDENTALIS MONUMENTA IURIS ANTIQUISSIMA / C. H. Turner & E. Schwartz. Oxford 1899-1939.

E5
ÉCHO d'AUXERRE. Auxerre ?-   .

ÉCHOS du MONDE CLASSIQUE see C147.

E6
ÉCHOS d'ORIENT. Paris 1897-1942. (EO).

E7
ECONOMIA e STORIA. Rome 1954-   .
--. Biblioteca. Milan 1959-   .

E8
ECONOMIC HISTORY REVIEW. Utrecht etc. 1927-   .

E9
ECONOMIC HISTORY of ROME / T. Frank. London & Baltimore 1927. Reprint New York 1973.

E10
ECONOMIC JOURNAL (Royal Economic Society). London etc. 1891-   .

E11
ECONOMIC SURVEY of ANCIENT ROME / T. Frank. Baltimore 1933-40. Reprint New York 1973. (ESAR).

E12
EDDA; nordisk tidsskrift for literaturforskning. Oslo 1914-   .

Edgar, C. C. see M159, S72-S73, Z75, Z77.

Edmonds, J. M. see F57, L93.

EESTI VABARIIGI TARTU ÜLIKOOLI TOIMETUSED, TARTU see A48.

Eger, O. see G119.

E13
EGRI MÚZEUM ÉVKÖNYVE = Annales Musei Agriensis. Eger 1963-   .

E14
EGYETEMES PHILOLOGIAI KÖZLÖNY. Budapest 1877-1948. Suspended

June 1944–May 1946. At head of
title: Archivum Philologicum.
(EPhK).

EGYPT EXPLORATION FUND see EGYPT
EXPLORATION SOCIETY.

EGYPT EXPLORATION SOCIETY. ARCHAE-
OLOGICAL SURVEY of EGYPT see
M113.

EGYPT EXPLORATION SOCIETY. GRAECO-
ROMAN MEMOIRS see G73.

EGYPT EXPLORATION SOCIETY. MEMOIRS
see M121.

EGYPT EXPLORATION SOCIETY. REPORT
see R84.

EGYPTIAN EXPEDITION PUBLICATIONS
see P243.

E15
EGYPTIAN RELIGION. New York 1933–
36.

EGYPTIAN RESEARCH ACCOUNT see
P241.

Ehrenberg, V. see D81.

E16.
EIGEN SCHOON en de BRABANDER.
Brussels 1911–   .

E17
EINBECKER JAHRBUCH. Einbeck ?-   .

E18
EINIGE WIENER PAPYRI / E. Boswinkel. Leiden 1942. (Papyrologica Lugduno-Batava; 2). (PVindobBosw).

E19
EINIGE WIENER PAPYRI / P. J. Sijpesteijn. Leiden 1963. (Papyrologica Lugduno-Batava; 11).
(PVindobSijp).

E20
EINLEITUNG in die ALTERTUMSWISSEN-
SCHAFT / E. Norden & A. Gercke.
4. Aufl. Leipzig & Berlin
1932-   . 1st edition 1910-12.

EINZELSCHRIFT [journal name] ...
look under the name of the
journal.

E21
EIRENE; studia graeca et latina.
Prague 1960-   .

E22
EISZEITALTER und GEGENWART; Jahrbuch der deutschen Quartärver-
einigung. Oehringen 1951-   .

Eitrem, S. see P63.

E23
EKKHART; Jahrbuch für das Badner
Land. Freiburg i.B. ?-   .

E24
EKKLESIATIKE ALETHEIA. Istanbul
1881-1923.

E25
EL-AMARNA TAFELN / J. A. Knudtzon.
Leipzig 1908-15. (Vorderasia-
tische Bibliothek; 2).

E26
ELEMENTI di LINGUA ETRUSCA / M.
Pallottino. Florence 1936.

ELENCHUS BIBLIOGRAPHICUS BIBLICUS
see B72.

E27
ELEPHANTINE PAPYRI / O. Rubensohn.
Berlin 1907. (Ägyptische Urkun-
den aus den K. Museen in Berlin:
Griechischen Urkunden: Sonder-
heft). (PEleph).

E28
ELLWANGER JAHRBUCH; ein Volksbuch
für Heimatpflege in Virngau und
Ries. Ellwangen ?-   .

E29
EMERITA; boletín de lingüística y
filología clásica. Madrid
1933-   .

E30
EMILIA PREROMANA. Bologna 1948-   .

ÉMULATION JURASSIENNE see A84.

E31
ENCHORIA; Zeitschrift für Demo-
tistik und Koptologie. Wiesbaden 1971-   .

ENCICLOPEDIA, ENCICLOPÉDIE, ENCY-
CLOPAEDIA and ENCYCLOPEDIA are
here interfiled.

E32
ENCICLOPEDIA dell'ARTE ANTICA,
CLASSICA e ORIENTALE. Rome
1958-   .

E33
ENCICLOPEDIA de la BIBLIA. 2. ed.
Barcelona 1969. 1st edition 1963-
65?.

E34
ENCYCLOPAEDIA BRITANNICA. Chicago
etc. 1974. The most famous scho-
larly editions are the 11th
(1910-11) and 14th (1929). 1st
edition 1771.

E35
ENCICLOPEDIA CATTOLICA. Vatican
City 1948-54.

E36
ENCYCLOPAEDIA of ISLAM. New ed.
Leiden 1954-   . 1st edition
1913. (EI).

E37
ENCICLOPEDIA ITALIANA di SCIENZE,
LETTERE ed ARTI. Rome 1929-37.
--. Appendice. 1938-   .

E38
ENCYCLOPAEDIA JUDAICA. Berlin
1928-34.

E39
ENCICLOPEDIA LINGUÍSTICA HISPÁNICA.
Madrid 1960-   .

E40
ENCYCLOPÉDIE PHOTOGRAPHIQUE de
l'ART. Paris 1935-38. Published
by Éditions TEL.

E41
ENCYCLOPAEDIA of RELIGION and
ETHICS / J. Hastings. Edinburgh
etc. 1908-26. (ERE).

E42
ENCICLOPEDIA UNIVERSALE dell'ARTE.
Venice 1958-67. (EUA). -

E43
ENCICLOPEDIA UNIVERSAL ILUSTRADE.
Madrid 1935-   .

E44
ENDE der MYKENISCHEN FUNDSTÄTTEN
auf dem GRIECHISCHEN FESTLAND /
P. Ålin. Lund 1962. (Studies
in Mediterranean Archaeology; 1).

Engelmann, H. see I34.

E45
ENGLISH HISTORICAL REVIEW. London
1886-   . (EHR).

E46
ENGLISH-HITTITE GLOSSARY / H. A.
Hoffner. Paris 1967. (Revue
Hittite et Asianique; 25).

E47
ENKOMI-ALASIA / C. F. A. Schaeffer.
Paris 1952. (Publications de la
Mission Archéologique Française
et de la Mission du Gouvernement
de Chypre à Enkomi; 1).

Ennaifer, M. see C227.

E48
ENTEUXEIS; requêtes et plaintes
adressées au roi d'Égypte au
IIIᵉ siècle avant J.C. / O.
Guéraud. Cairo 1931. (Publica-
tions de la Société Royale
Égyptienne de Papyrologie.
Textes et Documents; 1).
(PEnteux).

E49
ENTRETIENS sur l'ANTIQUITÉ CLAS-
SIQUE (Fondation Hardt pour
l'Étude de l'Antiquité Classique). Vandoeuvres-Genève
1952-   .

E50
EOS; commentarii Societatis Philo-
logae Polonorum = Czasopismo
filologiczne. Lemberg 1894-   .
--. Supplementa. 1925-   .

E51
EOS; syngramma periodikon philologias epistēmōn, viomēchanias kai
politeiographias. Athens 1836-
37?

E52
EOS; Zeitschrift für Philologie
und Gymnasialwesen. Würzburg
1864-66.

E53
EPEIRŌTIKA CHRONIKA. Ioannina
1926-38?

E54
EPEIRŌTIKĒ HESTIA. Ioannina
1952-   .   .

EPETĒRIS tou ARCHEIOU tēs HISTORIAS
tou HELLĒNIKOU DIKAIOU see E61.

E55
EPETĒRIS EPISTEMONIKŌN EREUNŌN
(Panepistēmion Athēnōn). Athens
1967/8-   .

E56
EPETĒRIS HETAIREIAS BYZANTINŌN
SPOUDŌN = Annuaire de la Soci-
été des Études Byzantines.
Athens 1924-   . (EEBS).

E57
EPETĒRIS tēs HETAIREIAS KRĒTIKŌN
SPOUDŌN. Athens 1938-41?

E58
EPETĒRIS HETAIREIAS KYKLADIKŌN
MELETŌN. Athens 1961-   .

E59
EPETĒRIS. HETAIREIA STEREOELLA-
DIKŌN MELETŌN. Athens 1968-

E60
EPETĒRIS. KENTRON EPISTĒMONIKŌN
EREUNŌN KYPROU. Leukosia
1968-   .

E61
EPETĒRIS tou KENTROU EREUNĒS tēs
HISTORIAS tou HELLĒNIKOU
DIKAIOU. Athens 1948-   .
1948-62 title: Epetēris tou
Archeiou tēs Historias tou Hel-
lēnikou Dikaiou.

E62
EPETĒRIS tou MESSAIŌNIKOU ARCHEIOU.
Athens 1939-   . Some issues
have French title: Annuaire des
Archives Médiévales.

EPHEMERIS and EPHEMERIDES are
here interfiled.

EPHEMERIS ARCHAIOLOGIKĒ see A471.

E63
EPHEMERIS DACOROMANA: annuario
della Scuola Romena di Roma.
Rome 1923-   .

E64
EPHEMERIS EPIGRAPHICA; corpus
inscriptionum latinarum supplementum. Rome 1872-1913.
(EE, EphEpigr, EphEp).

E65
EPHEMERIDES LITURGICAE. Rome etc.
1887-   . 1937-47 issued in
two parts: Pars Prior; Analecta
historico-ascetica; Pars Altera;
Ius et praxis liturgica.

E66
EPHEMERIDES THEOLOGICAE LOVANIEN-
SIS: commentarii de re theologiae et cannonica. Louvain
1924-   .

E67
EPICORUM GRAECORUM FRAGMENTA / G.
Kinkel. Leipzig 1877. (Biblio-
theca Scriptorum Graecorum et
Romanorum Teubneriana). Vol. 1
only published.

E68
EPIGRAFIA EBRAICA ANTICA, 1935-
1950 / S. Moscati. Chicago &
Rome 1951. (Biblica et Orientalia; 15).

E69
EPIGRAFIA ETRUSCA / G. Buonamici.
Florence 1932.

E70
EPIGRAFIA GRECA / M. Guarducci.
Rome 1967.

E71
EPIGRAFÍA JURIDICA de la ESPAÑA
ROMANA / A. D'Ors. Madrid
1953. (Istituto Nacional de
Estudios Juridicos. Publicaci-
ones. Ser. 5: Textes Juridicos
Antiquos).

E72
EPIGRAFÍA ROMANA de ASTURIAS / F.
Diego Santos. Oviedo 1959.

E73
EPIGRAFÍA ROMANA de LÉRIDA / F.
Lora Peinado. Lérida 1973.

E74
EPIGRAFIKA VOSTOKA. Moscow etc.
1947-   .

E75
EPIGRAMMATA; Greek inscriptions in
verse from the beginnings to the
Persian war / P. Friedländer &
H. B. Hoffleit. Berkeley 1948.

E76
EPIGRAMMATA GRAECA ex LAPIDIBUS
CONLECTA / G. Kaibel. Berlin
1878-   .

E77
EPIGRAMMATUM ANTHOLOGIA PALATINA
cum planudeis. Vol. III: Appendix
/ E. Cougny. Paris 1890. (Bibliotheca Scriptorum Graecorum
editore A. Firmin-Didot).

E78
EPIGRAPHAI ANEKDOTOI ANAKALYPHTHEI-
SAI kai EKDOTHEISAI hypo tou
ARCHAIOLOGIKOU SYLLOGOU. Athens
1852-70.

E79
EPIGRAPHICA. Milan 1939-   .

E80
EPIGRAPHICAL JOURNEY in ASIA MINOR
/ J. R. S. Sterrett. Boston
1888. (American School of Classical Studies at Athens. Papers,
1883/4; 2).

E81
ÉPIGRAPHIE: documents du Proche-
Orient ancien. Brussels 1976- .

E82
EPIGRAPHISCHE STUDIEN. Cologne
1967-   . Vols. 1-4 issued as
Beihefte der Bonner Jahrbücher;
bd. 11, 21, 22, 25.

E83
EPISTEME; rivista critica di storia delle scienze mediche e
biologiche. Milan 1964-   .

EPISTĒMONIKĒ EPETĒRIS. ARISTOTE-
LION PANEPISTĒMION. PHILOSO-
PHIKĒ SCHOLĒ see E85.

E84
EPISTĒMONIKĒ EPETĒRIS. ETHNIKON
kai KAPODISTRIAKON PANEPISTĒMION.
Athens 1902/3-21/2. Also issued
under the earlier name of the
institution: Ethnikon Panepistēmion. Continued by the Epistēmonikē Epeteris of the individual
schools.

EPISTĒMONIKĒ EPETĒRIS. ETHNIKON
kai KAPODISTRIAKON PANEPISTĒMION.
PHILOSOPHIKĒ SCHOLE see E86.

EPISTĒMONIKĒ EPETĒRIS. ETHNIKON
kai KAPODISTRIAKON PANEPISTĒMION.
THEOLOGIKĒ SCHOLE see E87.

EPISTĒMONIKĒ EPETĒRIS. ETHNIKON
PANEPISTĒMION, ATHĒNAI see E84.

E85
EPISTĒMONIKĒ EPETĒRIS tēs PHILOSO-
PHIKĒS SCHOLĒS tou ARISTOTELEIOU
PANEPISTĒMIOU. Thessalonika
1927-   .

E86
EPISTĒMONIKĒ EPETĒRIS tēs PHILOSO-
PHIKĒS SCHOLĒS tou PANEPISTĒMIOU
ATHĒNŌN = Annuaire Scientifique
de la Faculté de Philosophie de
l'Université d'Athènes. Athens
1935-   .

E87
EPISTĒMONIKĒ EPETĒRIS tēs THEOLOGI-
KĒS SCHOLĒS tou PANEPISTĒMIOU
ATHĒNŌN. Athens 1924-   .

E88
EPISTOLOGRAPHI GRAECI / R. Hercher.
  Paris 1873. (Scriptorum Graecorum
  Bibliotheca editore A. Firmin-
  Didot). Reprint Amsterdam 1963.

E89
EPITHEORĒSIS ARCHAIAS PHILOLOGIAS
  kai HISTORIAS = Revue de Philologie et d'Histoire Ancienne =
  Zeitschrift für alte Philologie
  und Geschichte. Athens 1960-   .

E90
ERANOS; acta philologica Suecana.
  Uppsala 1896-   .

E91
ERANOS JAHRBUCH. Zurich 1933-   .
  --. Papers from the Eranos Year-
  books. New York 1954-   .

E92
ERASMUS; speculum scientiarum =
  international bulletin of contem-
  porary scholarship. Brussels
  etc. 1947-   . Subtitle also
  in French.

E93
ERDÉLYI MÚZEUM. Cluj 1874-   .
  1936 title: Múzeum; a Múzeum-Eg-
  yesület közlönye.

E94
ERDÉLYI MÚZEUM-EGYLET ÉVKÖNYVEI.
  Cluj 1859-78.

E95
ERETZ ISRAEL; archaeological, his-
  torical and geographical studies.
  Jerusalem 1951-   .

E96
ERGON tēs ARCHAIOLOGIKĒS HETAIRE-
  IAS. Athens 1954-   .

E97
ERLANGER FORSCHUNGEN. Erlangen
  --. Reihe A: Geisteswissenschaft.
  1954-   .

Erman, A. see W48.

Ermerins, F. Z. see A213.

Ernout, A. see D53.

E98
ERWERBUNGEN (Stiftung zur Förderung der Hamburgischen Kunstsammlungen). Hamburg 1956-   .

E99
ESHKOLOT = Scholia; commentationes
  de antiquitate classica. Jerusalem 1954-   .

E100
ESPAÑA SAGRADA / E. Flórez. Madrid 1747-1849. Reprint Nendeln
  1966.

Espérandieu, É. see I76, R40.

E101
ESSAYS in GREEK HISTORY / H. T.
  Wade-Gery. Oxford 1958.

E102
ESSEX ARCHAEOLOGY and HISTORY.
  Colchester 1852-   . 1852-1973
  title: Transactions of the
  Essex Archaeological Society.
  (TransEssexArchSoc).

E103
ESSLINGER STUDIEN. Esslingen
  ?-   .

Estienne, H. see T54.

E104
ESTUDIOS de ARQUEOLOGÍA ALAVESA.
  Vitoria 1966-   .

E105
ESTUDIOS BÍBLICOS. Madrid 1929-
  36 1941-   .

E106
ESTUDIOS de CASTELO BRANCO. Castelo Branco 1961-   .

E107
ESTUDIOS CLÁSICOS. Madrid 1950-   .

E108
ESTUDIOS ECLESIÁSTICOS. Madrid
  1922-   . Suspended July 1936-
  March 1942.

ESTUDIOS EXTREMEÑOS   see   R137.

E109
ESTUDIOS FILOSÓFICOS.   Valladolid
   etc. 1951/2-   .

E110
ESTUDIOS, NOTAS y TRABELHOS de SER-
   VICO de FOMENTO MINEIRO.   Lisbon
   1945-   .

E111
ESTUDIOS SEGOVIANOS.   Segovia
   1949-   .

E112
ESTUDIOS del SEMINARIO de PREHIS-
   TORIA ARQUEOLOGÍA et HISTORIA
   ANTIGUA de la FACULTAD de FILO-
   SOFÍA y LETRAS de ZARAGOZA.
   Saragosa ?-   .

E113
ETHNOGRAPHIA.   Budapest 1890-   .

ETHNOGRAPHIE SOVIETIQUE   see   S127.

E114
ETHNOGRAPHISCH-ARCHÄOLOGISCHE FOR-
   SCHUNGEN.   Berlin 1953-59.

E115
ETHNOGRAPHISCH-ARCHÄOLOGISCHE
   ZEITSCHRIFT.   Berlin 1960-   .
   (EAZ).

E116
ETHNOLOGISCHER ANZEIGER.   Stuttgart 1926-35/40.

Etienne, H.   see   T54.

E117
ETRUSCAN RED-FIGURED VASE PAINTING
   at CAERE / M. A. Del Chiaro.
   Berkeley 1974.

E118
ETRUSCAN VASE-PAINTING / J. D.
   Beazley.   Oxford 1947.   (Ox-
   ford Monographs on Classical
   Archaeology).

E119
ETRUSCO MUSEO CHIUSINO / F. Inghirami.   Fiesole 1832-33.

E120
ETRUSKISCHE SPIEGEL / E. Gerhard.
   Berlin 1834-97. Reprint New
   York & Berlin 1974.

E121
ÉTUDES d'ARCHÉOLOGIE CLASSIQUE.
   Nancy 1955-   . Subseries of
   Annales de l'Est.

E122
ÉTUDES d'ARCHÉOLOGIE ORIENTALE /
   C. S. Clermont-Ganneau.   Paris
   1880-97. (Bibliothèque de l'École Pratique des Hautes Études;
   44, 113).

ÉTUDES ASIATIQUES   see   A618.

E123
ÉTUDES BALKANIQUES.   Sofia 1964-   .

ÉTUDES BYZANTINES   see   R143.

E124
ÉTUDES CELTIQUES.   Paris 1936-   .

E125
ÉTUDES CHYPRIOTES.   Paris 1963-   .

E126.
ÉTUDES CLASSIQUES.   Namur 1932-   .
   (LEC, EtCl).

E127
ÉTUDES CLASSIQUES.   Paris & Marseilles 1963?-   . (Annales
   de la Faculté des Lettres d'Aix;
   39 etc.).

ÉTUDES de CONSERVATION   see   S183.

E128
ÉTUDES CORSES.   Ajaccio 1973-   .

E129
ÉTUDES CRÉTOISES.   Paris 1928-   .

E130
ÉTUDES ÉPIGRAPHIQUES et PHILOLO-
   GIQUES / L. Robert.   Paris 1938.
   (Bibliothèque de l'École des
   Hautes Études, Sciences, Histor-
   iques et Philologiques; 272).

E131
ÉTUDES FORÉZIENNES. Saint-Étienne
  1968-   .

E132
ÉTUDES HAGUENOVIENNES. Hagenau
  1948 1950/5-   . 1950/5 title:
  Études Haguenauiennes. Suspended
  1971-78.

E133
ÉTUDES HISTORIQUES (Bǔlgarska Akademiĩa na Naukite). Sofia
  1960-   .

E134
ÉTUDES d'HISTOIRE et de PHILOSOPHIE
  RELIGIEUSES. Strasbourg etc.
  1922-   .

E135
ÉTUDES de LETTRES. Lausanne
  1934-   .

ÉTUDES de MÉTAPHYSIQUE et de MO-
  RALE see R206.

E136
ÉTUDES NUMISMATIQUES. Brussels
  1960-   .

E137
ÉTUDES ORIENTALES (Institut Fran-
  çaise d'Archéologie de Stamboul).
  Paris 1935-   .

ÉTUDES PALMYRÉNIENNES see S224.

E138
ÉTUDES de PAPYROLOGIE. Cairo
  1932-   .

E139
ÉTUDES PÉLOPONNÉSIENNES. Paris
  1960-   .

E140
ÉTUDES sur PÉZENAS et sa RÉGION.
  Pézenas ?-   .

E141
ÉTUDES de PHILOLOGIE, d'ARCHÉOLOGIE
  et d'HISTOIRE ANCIENNES. Rome
  & Brussels 1934-   .

E142
ÉTUDES PHILOSOPHIQUES. Marseilles
  etc. 1926-   .

E143
ÉTUDES de PHILOSOPHIE MÉDIÉVALE.
  Paris 1922-   .

E144
ÉTUDES PRÉLIMINAIRES aux RELIGIONS
  ORIENTALES dans l'EMPIRE ROMAIN.
  Leiden 1961-   . (EPRO).

ÉTUDES et RECHERCHES d'HISTOIRE
  ANCIENNE see S173.

ÉTUDES et RECHERCHES LINGUISTIQUES
  see S174.

ÉTUDES RHODANIENNES see R162.

E145
ÉTUDES ROUSSILLONNAISES; revue
  d'histoire et d'archéologie.
  Perpignan 1951-   .

E146
ÉTUDES THASIENNES. Paris 1944-   .

E147
ÉTUDES de THÉOLOGIE HISTORIQUE.
  Paris 1910-   .

E148
ÉTUDES de THÉOLOGIE et d'HISTOIRE
  de la SPIRITUALITÉ. Paris
  1943-   .

E149
ÉTUDES THÉOLOGIQUES et RELIGIEUSES.
  Montpellier 1926-   .

E150
ÉTUDES et TRAVAUX d'ARCHÉOLOGIE
  MAROCAINE. Rabat 1965-   .

E151
ÉTUDES et TRAVAUX du CENTRE d'ARCH-
  ÉOLOGIE MÉDITERRANÉENNE de l'A-
  CADÉMIE POLONNAISE des SCIENCES
  = Studia i Prace du Zakɫadu Arch-
  eologii Śródziemnomorskiej. Pol-
  ska Akademia Nauk. Warsaw.
  1959-   .

ÉTUDES et TRAVAUX. INSTITUT des
ÉTUDES RHODANIENNES (Univ. Lyons)
see R162.

Eula, E.   see   N94.

E152
EUNOMIA. Ephemeridis Listy Filologické supplementum. Prague
1957-   .

E153
EUPHORION; Zeitschrift für Littera-
turgeschichte. Heidelberg
1894-   . 1934-44 title: Dichtung und Volkstum. None published
1940.

E154
EUPHROSYNE. Lisbon 1957-61
1967-   .

E155
EURASIA SEPTENTRIONALIS ANTIQUA.
Helsinki 1927-38. (ESA).

E156
EVANGELISCHE FREIHEIT. Frankfurt
a.M. 1879-1920. 1879-1900 title:
Zeitschrift für praktische Theologie. 1901-06 title: Monatsschrift für die kirchlichen
Praxis.

E157
EVANGELISCHE THEOLOGIE. Munich
1934-   .

Evans, A. J.   see   P11, P173,
S61, N77.

ÉVKÖNYVE, DEBRECENI DÉRI MÚZEUM
see D5.

ÉVKÖNYVE, EGRI MÚZEUM see E13.

ÉVKÖNYVE. HERMAN OTTÓ MÚZEUM see
H54.

ÉVKÖNYVE, IPARMÜVESZETI MÚZEUM
see I108.

ÉVKÖNYVE. JANUS PANNONIUS MÚZEUM
see J81.

ÉVKÖNYVE, JÁSZBERÉNYI JÁSZMÚZEUM
see J82.

ÉVKÖNYVE. MÓRA FERENC MÚZEUM see
M272.

ÉVKÖNYVE, NYIREGYHÁZI JÓSA ANDRÁS
MÚZEUM see N132.

ÉVKÖNYVE, ORSZÁGOS MAGYAR RÉGÉSZETI
TÁRSULAT see O48.

ÉVKÖNYVE, ORSZÁGOS MAGYAR SZÉP-
MÜVÉSZETI MÚZEUM see O49.

ÉVKÖNYVE, SZEKSZÁRDI BÉRI BALOGH
ÁDAM MÚZEUM see S304.

EX ORIENTE LUX see J8.

E158
EXCAVACIONES ARQUEOLOGICAS en
ESPANA. Madrid 1962-   .
(EAE).

E159
EXCAVATIONS at DURA EUROPOS. London & New Haven 1943-   . Pre-
liminary reports began in 1929.

E160
EXCAVATIONS at NESSANA. Princeton.
--. Vol. 2. Literary Papyri / L.
Casson & E. L. Hettich. 1950.
--. Vol. 3. Non-literary Papyri
/ C. J. Kraemer. 1958. (PNess).

E161
EXCAVATIONS in PALESTINE during the
years 1898-1900 / F. J. Bliss &
R. A. S. Macalister. London
1902.

E162
EXEGETISCHES HANDBUCH zum ALTEN
TESTAMENT / J. Nickel. Münster
i.W. 1911-   .

E163
EXPEDITION. Philadelphia 1958-   .

E164
EXPLORATIONS ARCHÉOLOGIQUES de
DÉLOS. Paris 1909-   . (EAD,
EADélos).

E165
EXPOSITORY TIMES. Edinburgh
1889-   .

E166
EZHEGODNIK GOSUDARSTVENNOGO ISTOR-
  ICHESKOGO MUZEĬA. Moscow 1958- .
  Supersedes an earlier title
  (1883-1925) with the same title.

E167
EZIK i LITERATURA. Sofia 1946-   .

F

Fabretti, A. see C218.

F1
FABULA; Zeitschrift für Erzählfor-
schung. Berlin 1957-   . Subtitle also in English and French.

F2
FAENZA (Museo Internazionale delle
Ceramiche). Faenza 1913-   .

Falkenstein, A. see N40.

F3
FAMILY ARCHIVE from TEBTUNIS / B.
A. von Groningen. Leiden 1950.
(Papyriologica Lugduno-Batava;
6). (PFamTebt).

Farnell, L. R. see C272.

F4
FASTI AEDELICII von der Einrich-
tung der plebejischen Ädilität
bis zum Tode Caesars / J. Seidel.
Breslau 1908.

F5
FASTI ARCHAEOLOGICI; annual bul-
letin of classical archaeology.
Florence 1946-   . (FA).

F6
FASTI CAPITOLINI / A. Degrassi.
Turin 1954. (Corpus Scriptorum
Latinorum Paravianum).

F7
FASTI CONSOLARI dell'IMPERO ROMANO

/ A. Degrassi. Rome 1952.
(Sussidi Eruditi; 3).

F8
FASTI HISPANIENSES / G. Alföldy.
Wiesbaden 1969.

F9
FASTI ROMANI; the civil and literary chronology of Rome and Constantinople, from the death of
Justin II / H. F. Clinton. Oxford 1845-50. Reprint New York
1965.

F10
FAVENTIA (Dept. de Filología Clás-
sica de la Univ. de Barcelona).
Barcelona 197?-   .

F11
FAYUM TOWNS and their PAPYRI / B.
P. Grenfell et al. London 1900.
(Egypt Exploration Fund. Graeco-
Roman Memoirs; 3). (PFay).

F12
FELIX RAVENNA. Faenza 1911-   .

FESTSCHRIFT: See special section
about Festschriften in the
introduction.

Fick, A see G122.

F13
FIGLINA (Société Française d'Étude
de la Céramique Antique en Gaule).
Lyon 1976-   .

F14
FILE de ISTORIE (Muzeul de Istoria).
  Bistrita 1971-   .

F15
FILOLÓGIAI KÖZLÖNY. Budapest
  1955-   .

F16
FILOSOFIA. Turin 1950-   .

F17
FILOSOFIA. Lisbon 1954-   .

FINSKA FORNMINNESFÖRENINGENS TID-
  SKRIFT see S274.

F18
FINSKT MUSEUM. Helsinki 1894-   .
  1903-09 issued as vols. 10-16 of
  Suomen Museo.

Fiorelli, G. see P154.

Fitz, J. see R317.

FIXED PRICE LIST [coin dealer]
  see C157, C259.

FLECKEISENS JAHRBUCH für KLASS-
  ISCHE PHILOLOGIE see N27.

F19
FLINDERS PETRIE PAPYRI / J. P. Ma-
  haffy & J. G. Smyly. Dublin
  1891-1905. (Royal Irish Academy.
  Cunningham Memoirs; 8-9, 11).
  (PPetr).

Flórez, E. see E100.

FÖLDRAJZI KÖZLEMÉNYEK see F20.

FOGG ART MUSEUM. ACQUISITIONS
  see A29.

F20
FÖLDRAJZI KÖZLEMÉNYEK = Geographische Mitteilungen = Geographical
  Review. Budapest 1873-   . Suspended 1949-52.

FOLIA see C133.

F21
FOLIA ARCHAEOLOGICA; a Magyar
  Nemzeti Múzeum - Törteneti Mú-
  zeum évkönyve. Budapest
  1939-   . At head of title
  1939-45: Archaeologia hungarica.
  Suspended 1946-53. (FA, Fol-
  Arch).

F22
FOLIA LINGUISTICA; acta Societatis
  Linguisticae Europaeae. The
  Hague 1967-   .

F23
FOLIA ORIENTALIA. Krakow 1959-   .

F24
FOLK; Dansk etnografisk tidsskrift.
  Copenhagen 1959-   .

F25
FOLK-LORE; quarterly review of
  myth, tradition, institution
  & custom. London 1890-   .

FONDATION HARDT pour l'ÉTUDE
  de l'ANTIQUITÉ CLASSIQUE see
  E49.

F26
FONTES ARCHAEOLOGICI HUNGARIAE.
  Budapest 1973-   .

F27
FONTES ARCHAEOLOGICI POSNANIENSES;
  annales Musei Archeologici Posnanienses. Posen 1950-   .
  1950-52 title: Fontes Praehistorici.

F28
FONTES ARCHAEOLOGICI PRAGENSES.
  Prague 1958-   .

F29
FONTES HISPANIAE ANTIQUAE / A.
  Schullen & P. Bosch y Gimpera.
  Barcelona 1922-59?

F30
FONTES HISTORIAE DACOROMANAE.
  Bucharest 19??-   .

F31
FONTES IURIS ROMANI ANTEJUSTINIANI

/ S. Riccobono et al. 2. ed.
Florence 1968-   . 1st edition
1908. (FIRA).

F32
FONTES IURIS ROMANI ANTIQUI / C. G.
  Bruns. Tubingen 1860. Appeared
  in numerous editions.

FONTES PRAEHISTORICI see F27.

F33
FONTES ad TOPOGRAPHIAM VETERIS UR-
  BIS ROMAE PERTINENTES / G. Lugli.
  Rome 1952-   .

F34
FONTI per la STORIA d'ITALIA.
  Rome 1887-   .

Forcellini, E. see T79.

F35
FORMAE ORBIS ANTIQUI / H. Kiepert.
  Berlin 1894-1913. (FOA).

FORMA ORBIS ROMANI see C62.

F36
FORMA URBIS ROMAE / R. A. Lanciani. Mediolani 1901?

FORMA URBIS ROMAE (1960) see P135.

F37
FORNVÄNNEN; tidskrift för Svensk
  antikvarisk = journal of Swedish
  antiquarian research. Stockholm
  1906-   .

Forrer, E. see B121.

Forrer, L. see D24.

F38
FORSCHUNGEN und BERICHTE (Staatliche Museen). East Berlin
  1957-   .

F39
FORSCHUNGEN in EPHESOS. Vienna
  1906-   . (FiE).

F40
FORSCHUNGEN und FORTSCHRITTE; Korrespondenzblatt der deutschen

Wissenschaft und Technik. Berlin 1925-   . Suspended 1945-
47. (FuF).

F41
FORSCHUNGEN auf KRETA 1942 / F.
  Matz. Berlin 1951.

F42
FORSCHUNGEN zur KUNSTGESCHICHTE
  und CHRISTLICHEN ARCHÄOLOGIE.
  Wiesbaden etc. 1952-   .

F43
FORSCHUNGEN in LAURIACUM. Linz
  1950-   . (FiL).

F44
FORSCHUNGEN zur OSTEUROPÄISCHEN
  GESCHICHTE. Wiesbaden 1954-   .

F45
FORSCHUNGEN zur RELIGION und LITER-
  ATUR des ALTEN und NEUEN TESTA-
  MENTS. Göttingen 1903-   .
  (FRLANT).

F46
FORSCHUNGEN zur VOLKS- und LAN-
  DESKUNDE. Sibiu 1959-   .

F47
FORUM; revue du Groupe d'Archéologie Antique du TCF. Paris
  ?-   .

F48
FORUM IULII (Museo Archeologico
  Nazionale di Cividale del Fri-
  uli). Cividale 1977-   .

F49
FORUM der LETTEREN. Leiden
  1960-   .

Foucart, P. see V75.

F50
FOUILLES de DELPHES. Paris
  1902-   . (FD, FdD).

F51
FOUILLES de DOURA-EUROPOS / F.
  Cumont. Paris 1932. (Bibliothèque Archéologique et Historique; 9).

F52
FOUILLES de l'INSTITUT FRANÇAIS
d'ARCHÉOLOGIE ORIENTALE. Cairo
1921/3-   .

FOUILLES et RECHERCHES (Académie
Bulgare des Sciences) see R18.

F53
FOUILLES de THORIKOS = Opgravingen
van Thorikos. Gent 1977-   .

F54
FOUILLES de XANTHOS. Paris
1958-   .

F55
FOUNDATIONS of LANGUAGE; international journal of language
and philosophy. Dordrecht &
Boston 1965-76.

F56
FRA NY CARLSBERG GLYPTOTEKS SAM-
LINGEN. Copenhagen 1920-   .

Fränkel, M. see I38.

FRAGMENTA, FRAGMENTE, FRAGMENTS
and FRAMMENTI are here interfiled.

F57
FRAGMENTS of ATTIC COMEDY after
Meineke / J. M. Edmonds. Leiden
1957-61.

F58
FRAGMENTA COMICORUM GRAECORUM / A.
Meineke. Berlin 1839-57. Reprint
Berlin 1970. (FCG).

F59
FRAMMENTI della COMMEDIA GRECA e
del MIMO nella SICILIA e nella
MAGNA GRECIA / A. Olivieri.
Naples 1930-   . (Biblioteca
Filologica Loffredo).

F60
FRAGMENTE der GRIECHISCHEN
HISTORIKER / F. Jacoby. Berlin
1923-   . Reprint Leiden 1954-
60. (FGH, FGrH, FGrHist).

F61
FRAGMENTA HISTORICORUM GRAECORUM
/ K. Müller. Paris 1848-78.
Appeared in several printings.
(FHG).

F62
FRAGMENTA PHILOSOPHORUM GRAECORUM
/ F. W. A. Mullach. Paris
1860-81.

FRAGMENTA POETARUM EPICORUM
et LYRICORUM see F63.

F63
FRAGMENTA POETARUM LATINORUM EPI-
CORUM et LYRICORUM praeter En-
nium et Lucilium post A. Baehrens
/ W. Morel. Leipzig 1927. (Bib-
liotheca Scriptorum Graecorum
et Romanorum Teubneriana).
(FPL).

F64
FRAGMENTA POETARUM ROMANORUM / E.
Baehrens. Leipzig 1886. (Bibliotheca Scriptorum Graecorum
et Romanorum Teubneriana).

F65
FRAGMENTE der VORSOKRATIKER / H.
Diels. 6. Aufl. Dublin & Zur-
ich 1972-73. 1st edition 1903.
Later editions revised by W.
Kranz.

FRAMMENTI see FRAGMENTI
(the words are interfiled)

F66
FRANCISCAN STUDIES. St. Bona-
venture N.Y. 1924-   .

Frank, T. see E11, E9.

Frankfort, H. see C281.

F67
FRANKFURTER MÜNZZEITUNG. Frankfurt. 1901-21 1930-33.

Fraser, P. M. see S108.

Frazer, J. G. see G70.

F68
FREIBURGER GESCHICHTSBLÄTTER.
  Freiburg i Ue 1894-   .

F69
FREIBURGER ZEITSCHRIFT für PHILO-
  SOPHIE und THEOLOGIE. Freiburg
  1954-   .

Frey, J. B. see C229.

Friedländer, P. see E75.

Friedrich, J. see H67-H68, H71.

Friis Johansen, K. see V5.

Frisk, H. see G106, P51.

F70
FROM IMPERIUM to AUTORITAS / M.
  Grant. Cambridge 1946. Reprinted
  with corrections 1969.

F71
FRÜHGRIECHISCHE SAGENBILDER / K.
  Schefold. Munich 1964.

F72
FRÜHKRETISCHEN SIEGEL / F. Matz.
  Berlin 1928.

F73
FRÜHMITTELALTERLICHE STUDIEN:
  Jahrbuch des Instituts für
  Frühmittelalterforschung der
  Universität Münster. Berlin
  1967-   .

Fuks, A. see C231.

Funaioli, G. see G77.

F74
FUNDBERICHTE aus BADEN-WÜRTTEMBERG.
  Stuttgart 1974-   .

F75
FUNDBERICHTE aus HESSEN. Darmstadt 1961-   .

F76
FUNDBERICHTE aus ÖSTERREICH.
  Vienna 1930-   .

F77
FUNDBERICHTE aus SCHWABEN. Stuttgart 1893-1973?.

F78
FUNDMÜNZEN der RÖMISCHEN ZEIT in
  DEUTSCHLAND. Berlin 1960-   .
  (FMRD).

F79
FUNDMÜNZEN der RÖMISCHEN ZEIT in
  GROSSHERZOGTUM LUXEMBURG = Mon-
  naies Antiques Découvertes au
  Grand-Duché de Luxembourg. Ber-
  lin 1972-   . (FMRL).

Funk, R. W. see G80.

Furtwängler, A. see G129, M86,
  A356, M330.

Furumark, A. see C120, M328.

G

Gaar, A. see C150.

G1
GACETA NUMISMATICA. Barcelona ?- .

Gaertringen, F. Hiller von see
I39.

G2
GALLIA. Paris 1943- .
--. Supplement. 1946- .

G3
GALLIA PRÉHISTOIRE. Paris 1958- .
--. Supplement. 1963- .

Gallavotti, C. see I87.

Galling, K. see B104.

Gangutia, E. see D40.

Ganneau, C. S. Clermont- see E122.

Gardiner, A. H. see T33, A193.

Garstang, J. see G20.

G4
GAULE (Société d'Histoire, d'Arch-
éologie et de Tradition Gauloise).
Paris 1956- .

Gauthier, H. see D59, L78.

G5
GAZETTE ARCHÉOLOGIQUE; recueil de
monuments pour sevir à la connaissance et à l'histoire de

l'art dans l'antiquité et le
moyen-âge. Paris 1875-89.

G6
GAZETTE des BEAUX ARTS. Paris
1859- . (GBA).

G7
GAZETTE NUMISMATIQUE. Brussels
1896-1913.

GAZETTE NUMISMATIQUE SUISSE see
S49.

G8
GEDENKSCHRIFTEN. OUDHEIDKUNDIGE
KRING voor het LAND van DENDER-
MONDE = Annales. Cercle Archéologique de la Ville et de l'Ancien Pays de Termonde. Termonde
1863- .

G9
GEIST und LEBEN. Würzburg 1926- .
1926-44 title: Zeitschrift für
Aszese und Mystik. Suspended
1945-46.

G10
GEISTIGE ARBEIT; Zeitung aus der
wissenschaftlichen Welt. Berlin
1934-44.

Gelb, I. J. see H119-H120.

G11
GELDGESCHICHTLICHE NACHRICHTEN.
Frankfurt a.M. 1966- .

GELEHRTE ANZEIGER. AKADEMIE der
WISSENSCHAFTEN, MÜNCHEN see
G12.

G12
GELEHRTE ANZEIGER der BAYERISCHEN
AKADEMIE der WISSENSCHAFTEN.
Munich 1835-60.

G13
GELRE. (Vereeninging tot Beoefening
van Geldersche Geschiedenis, Oudheidkunde en Recht). Arnhem
--. Bijdragen en mededeelingen.
1898- .
--. Werken. 1900- .

G14
GEMEENTELIJK JAARBOEK. The Hague
1957- . Supersedes earlier
journal by same name which ended
in 1941.

G15
GENAVA; bulletin du Musée d'Art et
d'Histoire, Genève. Geneva
1923- . Supersedes the Museum's
Compte Rendu and Genève.

G16
GENERAL LINGUISTICS. Lexington,
Ky. and University Park, Pa.
1955- .

G17
GENTSE BIJDRAGEN tot de KUNSTGE-
SCHIEDENIS en de OUHEIDKUNDE.
Antwerp 1934- . Title varies
slightly.

GEOGRAPH-: entries beginning with
this spelling are here interfiled.

G18
GEOGRAPHISCHER ANZEIGER. Gotha
1900- .

G19
GEOGRAPHI GRAECI MINORES / K. Mül-
ler. Paris 1855-82. (Bibliotheca
Scriptorum Graecorum editore A.
Firmin-Didot). Reprint Hildesheim
1965.

G20
GEOGRAPHY of the HITTITE EMPIRE /

J. Garstang & O. R. Gurney. Lon-
don 1959. (British Institute of
Archaeology at Ankara. Occasional
Publications; 5).

G21
GEOGRAPHICAL JOURNAL. London
1893- .

G22
GEOGRAPHI LATINI MINORES / A. Ries-
se. Heilbronn 1878. Reprint
Hildesheim 1964.

GEOGRAPHISCHE MITTEILUNGEN see
F20.

GEOGRAPHICAL REVIEW see F20.

G23
GEOGRAPHISCHE ZEITSCHRIFT. Wiesbaden etc. 1895- . Suspended
1945-62.

G24
GEOMETRIC GREECE / J. N. Coldstream. London & New York 1977.

Gercke, A. see E20.

G25
GEREFORMEERD THEOLOGISCH TIJD-
SCHRIFT. Heusden etc. 1900- .

Gerhard, E. see E120, A686.

G26
GERMANIA; Anzeiger der Römisch-
germanischen Kommission des
Deutschen Archäologischen Instituts. Frankfurt a.M. etc.
1917- .

Gerth, B. see A687.

Gery, H. T. Wade- see A635.

G27
GESCHICHTE des ALTERTUMS / E. Meyer.
3. Aufl. Stuttgart & Berlin.
1884- . Some volumes available
in 2nd and 3rd editions.

G28
GESCHICHTE der ARABISCHEN LITERA-
TUR / C. Brockelmann. 2. Aufl.

Leiden 1909. 1st edition 1897.
--. Supplementband. 1937-42.

G29
GESCHICHTE des BYZANTINISCHEN LIT-
ERATUR / K. Krumbacher. 2. Aufl.
Munich 1897. (Handbuch der Klas-
sischen Altertumswissenschaft;
Bd. 9, Abt. 1). 1st edition
1891.

G30
GESCHICHTE der GRIECHISCHEN LITER-
ATUR / A. Lesky. Bern 1971. 1st
edition 1957-58. Also available
in English translation.

G31
GESCHICHTE der GRIECHISCHEN LITER-
ATUR / W. Schmid & O. Stählin.
6. Aufl. Munich 1961-   .
(Handbuch der Altertumswissenschaft; Abt. 7). Based on W.
von Christ's work by the same
title. 1st edition 1908?   (GGL).

G32
GESCHICHTE der GRIECHISCHEN RELIG-
ION / M. P. Nilsson. 3. Aufl.
Munich 1967-   . (Handbuch der
Altertumswissenschaft; Abt. 5,
T. 2). 1st edition 1941-50.

G33
GESCHICHTE der KORINTHISCHEN VAS-
EN / J. L. Benson. Basel 1953.
(Arbeiten aus dem Archäologischen
Seminar der Universität Basel).
(GKV).

GESCHICHTE LATEINISCHER EINGENNAMEN
see Z95.

G34
GESCHICHTE der RÖMISCHEN LITERATUR
/ M. von Schanz, C. Hosius & G.
Krüger. 4. Aufl. Munich 1922-   .
(Handbuch der Altertumswissen-
schaft; Bd. 8).

G35
GESCHICHTE in WISSENSCHAFT und
UNTERRICHT. Stuttgart 1950-   .

G36
GESCHICHTSBLÄTTER für WALDECK und
PYRMONT. Arolsen, Ger. 1901-   .

G37
GESCHICHTSFREUND (Historischer
Verein der Fünf Orte Luzern, Uri,
Schwyz, Unterwalden und Zug).
Einsiedeln, Switz. 1843-   .

GESCHIEDENIS en AARDRIJKSUNDE see
T65.

G38
GESNERUS (Schweizerische Gesellschaft für Geschichte der Medizin und der Naturwissenschaften). Aarau 1943-   .

G39
GESTA (International Center of
Medieval Art). New Haven, Conn.
etc. 1963-   .

GETTY MUSEUM JOURNAL see J1.

G40
GEUZENPENNING; munt- en penning-
kundig nieuws. Amsterdam
1951?-   .

Giannini, A. see P78.

Giard, J. B. see C82.

Giglioni, G. Q. see A606.

Gildersleeve, B. L. see S299.

Gimpera, P. Bosch y see F29.

Gingrich, F. W. see G88.

G41
GIORNALE CRITICO della FILOSOFIA
ITALIANA. Florence & Messina
1920-   .

G42
GIORNALE FILOLOGICO FERRARESE.
Ferrara 1978-   .

G43
GIORNALE ITALIANO di FILOLOGIA.
Naples 1948-   . (GIF).

G44
GIORNALE di METAFISICA. Genoa
1946-   .

G45
GIORNALE degli SCAVI di POMPEI.
Naples 1861-65 1868-79.

GIORNALE STORICO e LETTERARIO della
LIGURIA/LUNIGIANA see G46.

G46
GIORNALE STORICO delle LUNIGIANA e
del TERRITORIO LUCENSE. Genoa
1900-23 1925-? 1950- . Title
varies; 1900-08: Giornale storico
e letterario della Liguria; 1909-
23: Giornale storico della Lunigiana; 1925-   : Giornale storico e letterario delle Lunigiana.

G47
GLADIUS; études sur les armes anciennes, l'armement, l'art militaire et la vie culturelle en
Orient et en Occident. Granada
etc. 1961- . Title also in
Arabic.

G48
GLASGOW ARCHAEOLOGICAL JOURNAL.
Glasgow 1969-   .

G49
GLASNIK MUZEJA KOSOVA i METOHIJE
= Buletini i Muzeumit të Kosovë
Metohis = Bulletin du Musée de
Kosovo et Metohie. Priština
1956-   .

G50
GLASNIK MUZEJSKEGA DRUŠTVA za
SLOVENIJO = Bulletin de l'Asso-
ciation du Musée de Slovénie.
Ljubljana 1919-45.

G51
GLASNIK. SRPSKA AKADEMIJA NAUKA i
UMETNOSTI. Belgrad 1949-   .
Name of the academy varies
slightly.

G52
GLASNIK ZEMALJSKOG MUZEJA BOSNE i
HERCEGOVINE u SARAJEVU = Bulletin
du Musée de la République Socia-
liste de Bosnie-Herzégovine à
Sarajevo. Sarajevo 1889-1940
1945- . Earlier title: Glasnik
Zemaljskog Muzeja u Sarajevu.

Beginning with N.S. 13 (1954)
issued in two series: Arheologija
= Archéologie and Etnologija =
Ethnologie (in 1954-57 called
Istorija i etnografija).

G53
GLOSSA; a journal of linguistics.
Burnaby, B.C. 1967-   .

G54
GLOSSARIA LATINI / W. M. Lindsay
et al. Paris 1926-31. (Nouvelle
Collection de Textes et Documents pub. sous le Patronage
de l'Association Guillaume
Budé).

G55
GLOSSARIUM MEDIAE et INFIMAE LATIN-
ITATIS CONDITUM / C. D. DuCange.
Originally published in 1678.
Appeared in many printings and
editions.

G56
GLOTTA; Zeitschrift für griechische
und lateinische Sprache. Göttingen 1909- . Suspended
1944-47 1949-50.

G57
GNOMON; kritische Zeitschrift für
die gesamte klassische Altertumswissenschaft. Berlin & Munich
1925-   . Suspended 1944-48.

Godart, L. see R47.

GODIŠEN, GODISHNIK and GODIŠNJAK
are here interfiled.

G58
GODIŠNJAK. AKADEMIJA NAUKA i
UMJETNOSTI BOSNE i HERCEGOVINE.
Sarajevo 1956- . 1956-65 pub-
lished by the Naučno Društvo N R
Bosne i Hercegovine.

G59
GODISHNIK na DUKHOVNATA AKADEMIĬA
"SVETI KLIMENT OKHRIDSKI" =
Annuaire de l'Académie de Théolo-
gie "St. Clement d'Ochrida".
Sofia 1950/1-   .

GODISHNIK na MUZEITE v PLOVDIVSKI
OKR'G see G60.

G60
GODISHNIK na NARODNIIA ARKHEOLO-
GICHESKI MUZEĬ, PLOVDIV = Annuaire du Musée National Archéologique de Plovdiv. Plovdiv
1948-   . 1953-55 title: Godishnik na Muzeite v Plovdivski Okr'g.
Continues Godishnik na Plovdivskata Narodna Biblioteka i Muzeĭ
v Plovdiv.

G61
GODISHNIK na NARODNIIA ARKHEOLO-
GICHESKI MUZEĬ = Jahrbuch des
Bulgarischen Archäologischen
Nationalmuseums. Sofia 1909/19-
42? Vols. 1-6? (1909-32/4?) is-
sued under titles: Godishnik na
Narodniia Muzei = Annuaire du
Musée National de Sofia.

GODISHNIK na NARODNATA BIBLIOTEKA
i MUZEĬ v PLOVDIV see G62.

GODISHNIK na NARODNATA BIBLIOTEKA
v PLOVDIV see G62.

GODISHNIK na NARODNIIA MUZEĬ, SOFIA
see G61.

GODIŠNAJK NAUČNO DRUŠTVO N R BOSNE
i HERCEGOVINE see G58.

G62
GODISHNIK na PLOVDIVSKATA NARODNA
BIBLIOTEKA i MUZEĬ v PLOVDIV =
Annuaire de la Bibliothèque Nationale et du Musée de Plovdiv.
Plovdiv 1905-47. 1921-27 title:
Godishnik na Narodnata Biblioteka
v Plovdiv = Annuaire de la Bibliothèque Nationale de Plovdiv.
1928-30 title: Godishnik na Narodnata Biblioteka i Muzeĭ v Plovdiv = Annuaire de la Bibliothèque Nationale et du Musée à
Plovdiv. Continued by Godishnik
na Narodniia Arkheologicheski
Muzeĭ, Plovdiv.

G63
GODIŠNJAK. POMORSKI MUZEJ. Kotor
Yugo. 1952-   .

G64
GODISHNIK na SOFIĬSKIIA UNIVERSI-
TET = Annuaire de l'Université
de Sofia. Sofia 1904/5-06/8.
--. Istoriko-filologicheski Fakultet = Faculté Historico-philologique. 5-46 1908/9-49/50.
--. Filologicheski Fakultet.
47- 1950/2-
--. Filosofsko-istoricheski Fakultet. 47- 1950/2-   .

G65
GODIŠEN ZBORNIK. FILOZOFSKI FAKUL-
TET na UNIVERZITETOT SKOPJE =
Annuaire. Faculté de Philosophie
de l'Université de Skopje.
Skopje 1948-   . 1948-61 title:
Godišen Zbornik. Filozofski Fak-
ultet. Istorisko-filološki Oddel.

GODIŠEN ZBORNIK. ISTORISKO-FILOLO-
ŠKI ODDEL. FILOZOFSKI FAKULTET.
UNIVERSITET SKOPJE see G65.

Goeje, M. J. see B87.

Gössler, P. see R312.

GÖTEBORGS HÖGSKOLAS ÅRSSKRIFT see
A85.

GÖTEBORGS UNIVERSITETS ÅRSSKRIFT
see A85.

GÖTTINGISCHER ANZEIGEN von GELEHR-
TEN SACHEN see G66.

G66
GÖTTINGISCHE GELEHRTE ANZEIGEN.
Göttingen 1739-   . 1739-52 ti-
tle: Göttingische Zeitungen von
Gelehrten Sachen. 1753-1801 ti-
tle: Göttingisch Anzeigen von
Gelehrten Sachen. (GGA).

G67
GÖTTINGEN HANDKOMMENTAR zum ALTEN
TESTAMENT. Göttingen 1892-   .
Some volumes in revised editions.

G68
GÖTTINGER JAHRBUCH. Göttingen
1952-   .

G69
GÖTTINGER MISZELLEN; Beiträge zur
ägyptologischen Diskussion.
Göttingen 1972-   .

GÖTTINGISCHE ZEITUNGEN von GELEHR-
TEN SACHEN see G66.

Götz, G. see C210.

Götze, A. see V30.

G70
GOLDEN BOUGH; a study in magic and
religion / J. G. Frazer. 3. ed.
New York 1911-15. Appeared in a
number of printings and editions.

Gomme, A. W. see H91.

Goodspeed, E. J. see G95, P57.

Gordon, A. E. see A110.

Gordon, C. J. see U8-U10.

Gordon, J. S. see A110.

G71
GOTHAER MUSEUMSHEFTE. Gotha
1964-   . Includes the Abhandlungen and Berichte des Heimatsmuseums Gotha.

G72
GOTLÄNDSKT ARKIV. Visby 1929-   .

Gow, A. S. F. see G84.

GRABUNGEN (Österreichisches Archäologisches Institut in Wien)
see J74.

G73
GRAECO-ROMAN MEMOIRS (Egypt Exploration Society). London 1898-   .

G74
GRAECOLATINA e ORIENTALIA. Bratislava 1969-   .

G75
GRÄZISTISCHE ABHANDLUNGEN. Cologne
1965-   .

Graffin, R. see P87-P88.

G76
GRAMMAIRE HOMÉRIQUE / P. Chantraine. Paris 1948-53. (Collection Philologie Classique).

G77
GRAMMATICAE ROMANAE FRAGMENTA / G.
Funaioli. Leipzig 1907. (Biblio-
theca Scriptorum Graecorum et
Romanorum Teubneriana). Only one
volume published. (GRF).

G78
GRAMMATICI GRAECI / R. Schneider
et al. Leipzig 1867-1910. Reprint Hildesheim 1965.

G79
GRAMMATICI LATINI / H. Keil. Leipzig 1857-80. Reprint Hildesheim
1961. (GL, GLK).

G80
GRAMMATIK des NEUTESTAMENTLICHEN
GRIECHISCH / F. Blass, A. De-
brunner & F. Rehkopf. 14. Aufl.
Göttingen 1976. 1st edition
1896? Also in English transla-
tion by A. Debrunner & R. W.
Funk, Cambridge & Chicago 1961.

G81
GRANDE ENCICLOPÉDIA PORTUGUESA e
BRASILEIRA. Lisbon & Rio de
Janeiro 1935-58.

Grant, M. see F70.

Grapow, H. see W48.

G82
GRAZER BEITRÄGE. Zeitschrift für
die klassische Altertumswissenschaft. Amsterdam 1973-   .

G83
GREECE and ROME. Oxford 1931-   .
(G&R, GaR).

G84
GREEK ANTHOLOGY: Hellenistic epi-
grams / A. S. F. Gow & D. L.
Page. Cambridge 1965.

GREEK and BYZANTINE STUDIES see
G102.

G85
GREEK COINS in NORTH AMERICAN COL-
LECTIONS. New York 1969-   .

G86
GREEK DARK AGES / V. R. d'A. Desborough. London & New York 1972.

G87
GREEK-ENGLISH LEXIKON / H. G. Liddell, R. Scott & H. S. Jones.
rev. ed. Oxford 1940. (LSJ).
--. Supplement / E. A. Barber
et al. 1968.

G88
GREEK-ENGLISH LEXICON of the NEW
TESTAMENT and other early Christian literature; a translation
and adaptation of W. Bauer's
Griechisch-deutsches Wörterbuch /
W. F. Arndt & F. W. Gingrich.
2. ed. London & Chicago 1969.
1st edition 1957.

G89
GREEK GEMS and FINGER RINGS / J.
Boardman. New York & London
1970.

G90
GREEK GEOMETRIC POTTERY / J. N.
Coldstream. London 1968. (Me-
thuen's Handbooks of Archaeology). (GGP).

GREEK GRAMMAR of the NEW TESTAMENT
and OTHER EARLY CHRISTIAN LITER-
ATURE see G80.

GREEK HISTORICAL INSCRIPTIONS see
S74.

G91
GREEK and LATIN INSCRIPTIONS / W.
H. Buckler & D. M. Robinson.
Leiden 1932. (Archaeological Ex-
ploration of Sardis; 7, 1).

GREEK LITERARY PAPYRI see S72.

G92
GREEK LYRIC POETRY from ALCMAN to
SIMONIDES / C. M. Bowra. 2. ed.
Oxford 1967. 1st edition 1961.

GREEK NON-LITERARY PAPYRI see
S72.

G93
GREEK OSTRACA in the BODLEIAN LI-
BRARY at OXFORD and various
other collections / J. G. Tait
et al. London 1930-64. (Egypt
Exploration Society. Graeco-Ro-
man Memoirs; 21, 33, 43).
(OBodl).

G94
GREEK OSTRACA in the UNIVERSITY of
MICHIGAN COLLECTION / L. Amundsen. Ann Arbor 1935. (University
of Michigan Studies, Humanistic
series; 34). (OMich).

G95
GREEK PAPYRI from the CAIRO MUSEUM;
together with papyri of Roman
Egypt from American Collections
/E. J. Goodspeed. Chicago
1902. Published in the Univ. of
Chicago's Decennial Publications,
5. (PCairGoodsp).

G96
GREEK PAPYRI from GUROB / J. G.
Smyly. Dublin 1921. (Royal
Irish Academy Cunningham Memoirs;
12). (PGur).

G97
GREEK PAPYRI in the LIBRARY of
CORNELL UNIVERSITY / W. L. West-
ermann & C. J. Kraemer. New
York 1926. (PCorn).

G98
GREEK PARTICLES / J. D. Denniston.
2. ed. Oxford 1954. 1st edition
1934.

G99
GREEK and ROMAN BRONZES / W. Lamb.
New York 1929. (Illustrated Li-
brary of Archaeology). Reprint
Wilmington, Del. 1979.

G100
GREEK, ROMAN and BYZANTINE MONO-
GRAPHS. Durham, N.C. etc.
1959-   .

G101
GREEK, ROMAN and BYZANTINE SCHOLAR-
LY AIDS. Cambridge, Mass.
1961-   .

G102
GREEK, ROMAN and BYZANTINE STUDIES.
Durham, N.C. etc. 1958-   .
1958 title: Greek and Byzantine
Studies. (GRBS).

G103
GREEK and ROMAN JEWELLERY / R. A.
Higgins. 2. ed. Berkeley & New
York 1980. 1st edition 1961.

Grégoire, H. see R44.

G104
GREGORIANUM; commentarii de re
theologica et philosophica.
Rome 1920-   .

Grenfell, B. P. see A111, A152,
C42, F11, H73, O68, R201, T10.

Grenier, A. see M30.

Gressmann, H. see A131-A132.

G105
GRIECHISCHEN CHRISTLICHEN SCHRIFT-
STELLER der ERSTEN JAHRHUNDERTE.
Leipzig 1897-   . 1897-1941.ti-
tle: Griechischen christlichen
Schriftsteller der ersten drei
Jahrhunderte. (GCS).

GRIECHISCHE DIALEKT-INSCHRIFTEN
see S17.

G106
GRIECHISCHES ETYMOLOGISCHES WÖRTER-
BUCH / H. Frisk. Heidelberg
1954-72. (Indogermanische Biblio-
thek. II. Reihe: Wörterbücher)
(GEW).

G107
GRIECHISCHE FESTE / M. P. Nilsson.
Darmstadt 1906. Reprint Milan
1975.

G108
GRIECHISCHE GRAMMATIK auf der
GRUNDLAGE von Karl BRUGMANNS

GRIECHISCHER GRAMMATIK / E.
Schwyzer. Munich 1939-71.
(Handbuch der Altertumswissen-
schaft; Abt. 2, Tl. 1).

G109
GRIECHISCHE und GRIECHISCH-DEMO-
TISCHE OSTRAKA der UNIVERSITÄTS-
und LANDESBIBLIOTHEK zu STRASS-
BOURG im ELSASS / P. Viereck.
Berlin 1923. (OStras).

G110
GRIECHISCHE KRIEGSSCHRIFTSTELLER /
H. A. T. Köchly & W. Rüstow.
Leipzig 1853-55. Reprint Osna-
brück 1969.

G111
GRIECHISCHEN LANDSCHAFTEN / A.
Philippson & E. Kirsten. Frank-
furt a.M. 1950-59.

G112
GRIECHISCHE MÜNZEN / F. Imhoof-
Blumer. Munich 1890. (Abhand-
lungen. Bayerische Akademie der
Wissenschaften. Philosophisch-
philologische Klasse; 18, 3).

G113
GRIECHISCHE MYTHOLOGIE / L. Preller & C. Robert. 5. Aufl. Berlin 1964-67. 1st edition 1894-
1926.

G114
GRIECHISCHE OSTRAKA aus ÄGYPTEN
und NUBIEN / U. Wilcken. Leipzig etc. 1899. Reprint Amsterdam 1970 and New York 1979.
(OWilck, WO).

G115
GRIECHISCHE PAPYRI aus dem BERLIN-
ER MUSEUM / S. Möller. Gothen-
burg 1929. (PBerlMöller).

G116
GRIECHISCHE PAPYRI aus dem BESITZ
des RECHTSWISSENSCHAFTLICHEN
SEMINARS der UNIVERSITÄT FRANK-
FURT / H. Lewald. Heidelberg
1920. (Sitzungsberichte der
Heidelberger Akademie der Wis-
senschaften. Philosophisch-

historische Klasse; 1920, Abh.
14). (PFrankf).

G117
GRIECHISCHE PAPYRUSURKUNDEN der
HAMBURGER STAATS- und UNIVERSI-
TÄTSBIBLIOTHEK / P. M. Meyer. et
al. Hamburg etc. 1911-54. Ti-
tle of vol. 2: Griechische Pa-
pyri der Hamburger Staats- und
Universitätsbibliothek mit eini-
gen Stücken aus der Sammlung
Hugo Ibscher. (PHamb).

G118
GRIECHISCHEN PAPYRUSURKUNDEN KLEIN-
EREN FORMATS / C. Wessely. Leip-
zig 1904-08. (Studien zur Palaeo-
graphie und Papyruskunde; 3, 7).
(PK1Form).

G119
GRIECHISCHE PAPYRI im MUSEUM des
OBERHESSISCHEN GESCHICHTSVER-
EINS zu GIESSEN / O. Eger et al.
Leipzig 1910-22. (PGiss).

G120
GRIECHISCHE PAPYRI der SAMMLUNG
GRADENWITZ / G. Plaumann. Hei-
delberg 1914. (Sitzungsberichte
der Heidelberger Akademie der
Wissenschaft. Philosophisch-His-
torische Klasse; 1914, Abh. 15).
(PGrad).

G121
GRIECHISCHE PAPYRUS der kaiserli-
chen UNIVERSITÄTS- und LANDES-
BIBLIOTHEK zu STRASSBURG = Pa-
pyrus Grecs de la Bibliothèque
Nationale et Universitaire de
Strasbourg / F. Preisigke, P.
Collomp, J. Schwartz et al.
Strasbourg etc. 1912-   . Vol.
3 published as Publications de
la Faculté des Lettres de l'Un-
iversité de Strasbourg; Vol. 4
is insseries Publications de la
Bibliothèque Nationale et Uni-
versitaire de Strasbourg.
(PStras).

G122
GRIECHISCHEN PERSONENNAMEN nach
ihrer BILDUNG / A. Fick & F.

Bechtel. 2. Aufl. Göttingen
1894. 1st edition 1874.

G123
GRIECHISCHE PLASTIK / G. Lippold.
Munich 1950. (Handbuch der Alter-
tumswissenschaft; III, 1).

G124
GRIECHISCHE ROMAN-PAPYRI und VER-
WANDTE TEXTE / F. Zimmermann.
Heidelberg 1936.

G125
GRIECHISCHE und RÖMISCHE PORTRÄTS
/ H. Brunn, P. Arndt & F. Bruck-
mann. Munich 1891-1935? (ABr).

G126
GRIECHISCHE TEXTE aus ÄGYPTEN /
P. M. Meyer. Berlin 1916.
(PMeyer).

G127
GRIECHISCHE URKUNDEN des ÄGYPTIS-
CHEN MUEUMS zu KAIRO / F. Prei-
sigke. Strasbourg 1911. (Schrif-
ten der Wissenschaftlichen
Gesellschaft zu Strassburg; 8).
(PCairPreis).

G128
GRIECHISCHE URKUNDEN der PAPYRUS-
SAMMLUNG zu LEIPZIG / L. Mitteis.
Leipzig 1906. (PLips).

GRIECHISCHE URKUNDEN. STAATLICHE
MUSEEN zu BERLIN   see   A94.

G129
GRIECHISCHE VASENMALEREI / A. Furtwängler & K. Reichhold. Munich
1904-32.

G130
GRIECHISCHE VERS-INSCHRIFTEN / W.
Peek. Berlin 1955. Verzeichnis
published in 1957. (GV).

G131
GRIECHISCHE VERSKUNST / U. v. Wilamowitz-Moellendorff. Berlin
1921.

GRIECHISCHEN ZAUBERPAPYRI   see
P47.

G132
GRIEFSWALD-STRALSUNDER JAHRBUCH.
  Putbus, Ger. 1961-   .

G133
GRIEKSCHE en LATIJNSCHE SCHRIJVERS
  met AANTEEKENINGEN. Leiden
  1923?-   .

Grierson, P. see C71.

Groningen, B. A. van see P65, F3.

Grose, S. W. see C79.

Grueber, H. A. see B213.

Gruen, E. S. see L11, R336.

G134
GRUNDRISS der AKKADISCHEN GRAMMA-
  TIK / W. von Soden. Rome 1952.
  (Analecta Orientalia; 33).
  (GAG).

Gsell, S. see A638, H86, I73.

Guarducci, M. see I47, E70.

Guéraud, O. see E48.

Güterbock, H. G. see S86.

Guillou, A. see A59.

Gurney, O. R. see G20.

Gusmani, R. see L33, L91.

Guy, P. L. O. see M84.

G135
GYMNASIUM. Paderborn 1883-1906.

G136
GYMNASIUM; Zeitschrift für Kultur
  der Antike und Humanistische
  Bildung. Leipzig & Heidelberg
  1890-   . 1890-1936 title: Humanistische Gymnasium. Suspended
  1943-49.

H

HABALARY. KAZAK SSR GYLYM AKADEMI-
JASYNYN see I151.

H1
HADASHOT ARHKE'OLOGIYOT = Archaeological Newsletter. Jerusalem
1961-

H2
HADASHOT MUZEON ISRAEL. Tel Aviv
?- .

H3
HADTÖRTÉNELMI KÖZLEMÉNYEK. Budapest 1888-1943 1954- .

Hahn, W. see M237.

H4
HAJDÚSAGI MÚZEUM ÉVKÖNYVE. Hajdu-
böszormény 1973- .

Halkin, F. see A677, B88, M33.

Hall, H. R. see B224.

H5
HALLISCHES WINCKELMANNSPROGRAMME
Halle 1876-1931? Suspended
1912-27.

Halm, K. F. see R258.

H6
HAMBURGER BEITRÄGE zur ARCHÄOLOGIE.
Hamburg 1971- .

H7
HAMBURGER BEITRÄGE zur NUMISMATIK

Hamburg 1947- . Called n.s.
in continuation of Verein der
Münzenfreunde in Hamburg. Veröffentlichungen. (HBN).

Hammond, N. G. L. see O62.

H8
HANAUER GESCHICHTSBLÄTTER. Hanau
1860-90 1911- . 1860-90 title:
Veröffentlichungen des Hanauer
Geschichts-Vereins.

H9
HANDBUCH der ALTCHRISTLICHEN EPI-
GRAPHIK / C. M. Kaufmann. Frei-
burg i.B. 1917.

H10
HANDBUCH zum ALTEN TESTAMENT.
Tübingen 1934- .

H11
HANDBUCH der ALTERTUMSWISSENSCHAFT.
Neu. Aufl. Munich 1911- .
1st edition (1892-1930) had ti-
tle: Handbuch der klassischen
Altertumswissenschaft.

H12
HANDBUCH der ARCHÄOLOGIE. 3. Aufl.
Munich 1969- . 1st (1895-
1913) and 2nd (1939-54) editions
published as part of the Handbuch der Klassischen Altertumswissenschaft. (HdArch).

H13
HANDBUCH der CHALDISCHEN INSCHRIF-

TEN / F. W. König. Graz 1955-57.
(Archiv für Orientforschung; Beiheft 8). Reprint Osnabrück 1967.

H14
HANDBUCH der GRIECHISCHEN DIALEKTE
/ A. Thumb. 2. Aufl. Heidelberg
1932-59. (Indogermanische Bibliothek. I. Reihe. Grammatik). Re-
visions by E. Kieckers & A.
Scherer. 1st edition 1909.

H15
HANDBUCH der ITALISCHEN DIALEKTE /
E. Vetter. Heidelberg 1953-   .

H16
HANDBUCH der KIRCHENGESCHICHTE / H.
Jedin. Freiburg 1962-   . Also
in English translation.

HANDBUCH der KLASSISCHEN ALTERTUMS-
WISSENSCHAFT see H11.

H17
HANDBUCH zum NEUEN TESTAMENT / H.
Lietzmann. Tübingen 1907-   .

H18
HANDBUCH der ORIENTALISTIK. Leiden
1952-   . (HbOr).

HANDELINGEN van de Koninklijke COM-
MISSIE voor GESCHIEDENIS see
B281.

H19
HANDELINGEN van het GENOOTSCHAP
voor GESCHIEDENIS GESTICHT te
BRUGGE = Annales de la Société
d'Émulation de Bruges. Bruges
1839-   . Variant French titles:
Annales de la Société d'Émulation
pour l'Histoire et les Antiquités
de la Flandre Occidentale; Annales
de la Société pour l'Étude de
l'Histoire et des Antiquités de
la Flandre Occidentale.

H20
HANDELINGEN. Koninklijke GESCHEID-
en OUDHEIDKUNDIGE KRING van KOR-
TRIJK = Mémoires du Cercle Royal
Historique et Archéologique de
Courtrai. Kortrijk 1908-15
1921-   .

HANDELINGEN. KONINKLIJKE ... see
HANDELINGEN ... (the word koninklijke is disregarded in filing,
but may have been regarded in
forming an abbreviation).

H21
HANDELINGEN. Koninklijke KRING voor
OUDHEIDKUNDE LETTEREN en KUNST
van MECHELEN. Malines-Mechelen
1889-   .

H22
HANDELINGEN der MAATSCHAPPIJ voor
GESCHIED- en OUDHEIDKUNDE te
GENT = Annales de la Société
d'Histoire et d'Archéologie de
Gand. Gent 1894-1923 1944-   .

HANDELINGEN van den OUDHEID- en
GESCHIEDKUNDIGEN KRING van
OUDENAARDE see A235.

H23
HANDELINGEN. Koninklijke ZUIDNEL-
ERLANDSE MAATSCHAPPIJ voor TAAL-
en LETTERKUNDE en GESCHIEDENIS.
Brussels ?-   .

H24
HANNOVERSCHE GESCHICHTSBLÄTTER.
Hannover 1898-1929 1930-   .
Suspended 1940-51.

Hansen, P. A. see L70.

H25
HARBURGER JAHRBUCH. Hamburg-Har-
burg 19??-   .

Harris, J. R. see A192.

H26
HARVARD JOURNAL of ASIATIC STUDIES.
Cambridge, Mass. 1936-   .

H27
HARVARD LIBRARY BULLETIN. Cam
bridge, Mass. 1947-59 1968-   .

H28
HARVARD SEMITIC MONOGRAPHS. Cambridge, Mass. 1968-   .

H29
HARVARD SEMITIC SERIES. Cambridge,
Mass. 1912-   .

H30
HARVARD STUDIES in CLASSICAL PHIL-
OLOGY. Cambridge, Mass. 1890-   .
(HSCP, HSPh, HarvSt).

H31
HARVARD THEOLOGICAL REVIEW. Cam-
bridge, Mass. 1908-   . (HThR,
HTR, HarvTheolRev).

H32
HARVARD THEOLOGICAL STUDIES. Missoula, Mont. etc. 1916-   . Suspended 1933-50.

H33
HARZ-ZEITSCHRIFT. Harzburg 1948-   .

Haspels, C. H. E.   see   A672.

Hastings, J.   see   E41, D42, D45,
D47.

Haug, F.   see   R312.

HAUPTBLATT. (Österreichisches
Archäologisches Institut in Wien
see   J74.

Haussig, H. W.   see   W49.

Head, B. V.   see   H106.

HEBRAICA   see   A148.

H34
HEBREW and ENGLISH LEXICON of the
OLD TESTAMENT / F. Brown, S. R.
Driver & C. A. Briggs. Oxford
1907. Reprint with corrections
Oxford 1957. Numerous printings.

H35
HEBREW UNION COLLEGE ANNUAL. Cin-
cinnati, Ohio 1904 1924-   .
(HUCA).

H36
HEFTE des ARCHÄOLOGISCHEN SEMINARS
der UNIVERSITÄT BERN. Bern
1975-   . (HASB).

H37
HEGAU (Verein für Geschichte des
Hegaus). Singen-Hohentwiel, Ger.
1956-   .

H38
HEIDELBERGER JAHRBÜCHER. Heidelberg 1891-1920 1924-41 1950-54
1957-   . 1891-1954 title:
Neue Heidelberger Jahrbücher.

H39
HEILIGE LAND. Cologne 1857-1914
1920-38 1951-   .

HEIMATBLÄTTER für den REICHSGAU
TIROL und VORARLBERG   see   T67.

H40
HEIMATSCHUTZ; Zeitschrift der
Schweizer Vereinigung für Hei-
matschutz. Olten etc. 1906?-   .

H41
HEINRICH SCHLIEMANNS SAMMLUNG
TROJANISCHER ALTERTÜMER / H.
Schmidt. Berlin 1902.

Heisenberg, A.   see   B459

H42
HELIKON; rivista di tradizione e
cultura classica. Naples
1961-   .

H43
HELINIUM; revue consacrée a l'archéologie des Pays-Bas, de la Belgique et du Grand Duché de Luxembourg. Wetteren, Belgium 1961-
1961-   .

H44
HELIOS. Lubbock, Texas 1975?-   .

H45
HELLENICA / L. Robert. Limoges
1940-   .

H46
HELLENIKA; philogikon, historikon
kai laographikon periodikon syngramma. Thessalonike 1928-39
1952-   .

H47
HELLENIKOS PHILOLOGIKOS SYLLOGOS.
Istanbul 1863-1914.

H48
HELLENISM. Chicago 1968-   .

HELLENISTIC EPIGRAMS see G84.

H49
HELMANTICA; revista de humanidades
clásicas. Salamanca 1950-   .

H50
HELVETIA ARCHAEOLOGICA. Basel
1970-   .

H51
HEMECHT; Zeitschrift für luxem-
burger Geschichte. Luxemburg
1948-   .

Henrichs, A. see P47.

H52
HEPHAISTOS; kritische Zeitschrift
zur Theorie und Praxis der Archäologie und angrenzender Wissenschaft. Bad Bramstedt 1979-   .

Hercher, R. see E88.

H53
HERDERS THEOLOGISCHER KOMMENTAR
zum NEUEN TESTAMENT. Freiburg
1953-   .

H54
HERMAN OTTÓ MÚZEUM ÉVKÖNYVE =
Annales Musei Miskolciensis de
Herman Ottó nominati. Miskolc
1957-   .

Hermann, P. see D17.

H55
HERMATHENA; a series of papers by
members of Trinity College,
Dublin. Dublin 1873-   .

H56
HERMENEUS; maandblad voor de antieke cultuur. Zwolle, Netherlands
1928/9-   .

H57
HERMES; collana di testi antichi.
Naples 195?-   . No longer
published?

H58
HERMES; Zeitschrift für klassische
Philologie. Berlin & Wiesbaden

1866-   . Suspended 1945-51.
--. Einzelschriften. 1936-   .

H59
HERTFORDSHIRE ARCHAEOLOGY. St. Al-
bans, Eng. 1968-   .

H60
HESPERIA (American School of Classical Studies at Athens). Cambridge, Mass. 1932-   . (Hesp).

H61
HESPERIAM (Joint Association of
Classical Teachers). London
1978-   .

H62
HESPERIS-TAMUDA. Rabat, Morroco
1960-   .

H63
HESSISCHES JAHRBUCH für LANDESGE-
SCHICHTE. Marburg 1951-   .

H64
HETHITER und HETHITISCH / F. Sommer.
Stuttgart 1947.

H65
HETHITICA / G. Jucquois. Louvain
1972-   . (Travaux de la Faculté
de Philosophie et Lettres de
l'Univ. Catholique de Louvain; 7).

H66
HETHITISCH-AKKADISCHE BILINGUE des
HATTUŠILI I / F. Sommer. Munich
1938. (Abhandlungen. Bayerische
Akademie der Wissenschaften.
Philosophisch-historische Abtei-
lung; n.F. 16). Reprint Hilde-
sheim 1974.

H67
HETHITISCHES ELEMENTARBUCH / J.
Friedrich. 2. Aufl. Heidelberg
1960-   . (Indogermanische
Bibliothek I. Reihe. Grammatiken).
1st edition 1940-46.

H68
HETHITISCHES KEILSCHRIFT-LESEBUCH /
J. Friedrich. Heidelberg 1960.
(Indogermanische Bibliothek 2.
Reihe: Wörterbücher).

H69
HETHITISCHE KEILSCHRIFTTEXTE aus
  BOGHAZKÖI in UMSCHRIFT / B.
  Hrozný. Leipzig 1919. (Boghazköi
  Studien; 3).

H70
HETHITISCHEN TOTENRITUAL / H. Otten.
  Berlin 1958. (Deutsches Akademie
  der Wissenschaften. Institut für
  Orientforschung. Veröffentlichun-
  gen; 37).

H71
HETHITISCHES WÖRTERBUCH / J. Friedrich. 2. Aufl. Heidelberg 1975- .
  (Indogermanische Bibliothek. Reihe
  2: Wörterbücher). (HW).

Hettich, E. L. see E160.

Heurtley, W. A. see P171.

H72
HIBBERT JOURNAL; a quarterly
  review of religion, theology
  and philosophy. London & Boston
  1902- .

H73
HIBEH PAPYRI / B. P. Grenfell et al.
  London 1906-55. (Egypt Exploration
  Society. Graeco-Roman Memoirs; 7,
  32). (PHib).

Hicks, E. L. see I46.

H74
HIÉROGLYPHES HITTITES / E. Laroche.
  Paris 1960.

H75
HIEROGLYPHISCH-HETHITISCHES GLOS-
  SAR / P. Meriggi. 2. Aufl. Wies-
  baden 1962.

Higgins, R. A. see B226, G103,
  M164.

Hill, P. V. see L13.

Hiller von Gaertringen, F. see
  I39.

H76
HISPANIA. Madrid 1940- .

H77
HISPANIA ANTIQUA. Vitoria 1971- .

H78
HISPANIA ANTIQUA EPIGRAPHICA. Ma-
  drid 1950/2- . Supplement to
  Archivo Español de Arquelogia.
  (HAE).

H79
HISPANIA SACRA. Madrid 1948- .

HIST-: entries beginning with this
  spelling are here interfiled.

H80
HISTORIA; revue d'histoire ancienne
  = Zeitschrift für alte Geschichte.
  Wiesbaden 1950- . (Hist).

H81
HISTORIA; studi storici per
  l'antichità classica. Milan
  1927-35. Continues Studi storici
  per l'antichità classica.

HISTORIA (Turčiansky Sv. Martin)
  see Z16.

H82
HISTORICA. (Academia Republicii
  Socialiste Romania. Centrul de
  Istorie, Filologie şi Etnografie
  din Craiova). Bucharest
  1970- .

H83
HISTORICA (Palackeho Universita,
  Olomouc. Filosofická Fakulta).
  Prague 1960?- . Variant title:
  Sborník Prací Historických.

HISTORY (Berwickshire Naturalists' Club) see P192.

H84
HISTORY (Historical Association).
  London 1912- .

H85
HISTRIA; monografie archeologică.
  Bucharest 1954- .

H86
HISTOIRE ANCIENNE de l'AFRIQUE du

NORD / S. Gsell. 3. ed. Paris
1928. Reprint of 1st edition
(1913) Osnabrück 1972. (HAAN).
.

H87
HISTRIA ARCHAEOLOGICA.   Pula
1970-   .

H88
HISTOIRE et ARCHÉOLOGIE: DOSSIERS.
Dijon 1973-   . 1973 title: Docu-
ment Archeologia; 1974-80 title:
Dossiers de l'Archéologie.

H89
HISTORIA-AUGUSTA-COLLOQUIUM.   Bonn
1963-   . (Antiquitas. Reihe 4;
Beiträge zur Historia Augusta-
Forschungen; 2 etc.).

H90
HISTORICKÝ ČASOPIS.   Bratislava
1940-   . 1940-52 title: Historický Sborník.

H91
HISTORICAL COMMENTARY on THUCYDIDES
/ A. W. Gomme. Oxford 1956.

H92
HISTORIA de ESPAÑA / R. Menéndez
Pidal. Madrid 1935-   .

HISTORISK-FILOLOGISKE MEDDELELSER
see H93.

H93
HISTORISK-FILOSOFISKE MEDDELELSER
(Dansk Videnskabernes Selskab).
Copenhagen 1917-   . Title of
vols. 1-36: Historisk-Filologiske
Meddelelser.

H94
HISTORICI GRAECI MINORES / L. A.
Dindorf. Leipzig 1870-77. (Bibliotheca Scriptorum Graecorum
et Romanorum Teubneriana).

H95
HISTORY of the GREEK and ROMAN
THEATER / M. Bieber. 2. ed.
Princeton 1961. 1st edition 1939.

H96
HISTORIA tou HELLĒNIKOU ETHNOUS.
Athens 1970-   .

H97
HISTORISCHES JAHRBUCH. Münster
etc. 1880-   . Suspended 1942-
48. (HJ).

H98
HISTORISCHES JAHRBUCH der STADT
GRAZ. Graz 1968-   .

H99
HISTORISCHES JAHRBUCH der STADT
LINZ. Linz 1955-   .

H100
HISTORICAL JOURNAL. Birmingham,
Eng. 1947-   .

H101
HISTORY of the LATER ROMAN EMPIRE
/ J. B. Bury. New York & London
1923. Appeared in several editions.

H102
HISTORIOGRAPHIA LINGUISTICA. Amsterdam 1974-   .

H103
HISTOIRE LOCALE, BEAUCE et PERCHE.
Chartres 1960-   .

H104
HISTORIA MATHEMATICA. New York &
London 1974-   .

HISTOIRE et MÉMOIRES de l'ACADÉ-
MIE des INSCRIPTIONS et BELLES-
LETTRES see M97.

HISTOIRE et MÉMOIRES de l'ACADÉMIE
des SCIENCES, INSCRIPTIONS, et
BELLES-LETTRES de TOULOUSE see
M102.

HISTOIRE et MÉMOIRES de l'INSTI-
TUT r. de FRANCE. CLASSE d'HIS-
TOIRE et de LITTÉRATURE ANCIENNE
see M97.

HISTORICAL METALLURGY see J109.

H105
HISTORISCHES NEUJAHRSBLATT. Alt-
dorf, Switz. 1895-31 ?-   .

H106
HISTORIA NUMORUM / B. V. Head. London 1911. Reprint London 1963. (HN).

H107
HISTORISCHEN PERSONENNAMEN des GRIECHISCHEN bis zur KAISERZEIT / F. Bechtel. Halle 1917. Reprint Hildesheim 1964. (HPN).

H108
HISTORY of RELIGIONS. Chicago 1961-   .

HISTORICAL REVIEW see Z81.

H109
HISTORICORUM ROMANORUM RELIQUIAE / H. Peter. Leipzig 1870-1906. Vol. 1 revised in 1914.

HISTORISCHE RUNDSCHAU see T78.

HISTORICKÝ SBORNÍK (Bratislava 1940-52) see H90.

HISTORICKÝ SBORNÍK (Bratislava 1961-   .) see Z15.

H110
HISTORICKÉ ŠTÚDIE. Bratislava 1955-   . Vols. 1-2 issued as supplements to Historický Časopis.

H111
HISTORY and THEORY. The Hague 1960-   .

H112
HISTORISK TIDSKRIFT. Stockholm 1881-   .

H113
HISTORISK TIDSSKRIFT. Copenhagen 1840-   . 1847-56 title: Nyt Historisk Tidsskrift.

H114
HISTORISK TIDSSKRIFT (Norske Historiske Forening). Oslo 1871-   .

H115
HISTORY TODAY. London 1951-   .

H116
HISTORISCHE VIERTELJAHRSCHRIFT. Leipzig etc. 1889-1939. 1889-98 title: Deutsche Zeitschrift für Geschichtswissenschaft.

H117
HISTORIJSKI ZBORNIK. Zagreb 1948-   .

H118
HISTORISCHE ZEITSCHRIFT. Munich & Berlin 1859-   . Suspended 1944-Apr. 49. (HZ).
--. Sonderheft. 1962-   .

H119
HITTITE HIEROGLYPHS / I. J. Gelb. Chicago 1931-   . (Studies in Ancient Oriental Civilizations; 2, etc.).

H120
HITTITE HIEROGLYPHIC MONUMENTS / I. J. Gelb. Chicago 1939. (Oriental Institute Publications; 45).

HITTITE TEXTS in the CUNEIFORM CHARACTER from TABLETS in the BRITISH MUSEUM see B216.

HÖFER, J. see L45.

Hoffiller, V. see A359.

Hoffleit, H. B. see E75.

Hoffner, H. A. see E46.

Hofmann, J. B. see L14-L15.

Hoftijzer, J. see D57.

H121
HOMER and the MONUMENTS / H. L. Lorimer. London 1950.

H122
HOMME PRÉHISTORIQUE. Paris 1903-28. Suspended 1915-25.

H123
HOMO. Toulouse 1953-   .

H124
HOMO. Göttingen etc. 1949-   .

H125
HOMONOIA; **year**book of the Chair of
  Greek Philology, Univ. of Buda-
  pest. Budapest 1979-   .

Hoops, J. see R26.

H126
HORIZON. New York 1958-   .

Hosius, C. see G34.

How, W. W. see C174.

Hrozný, B. see H69, I49, I67,
  S137.

Hübner, E. see I42, I65, M267.

Hultsch, F. see M156.

H127
HUMANIDADES (Univ. Pontificia de
  Comillas). Santander 1949-   .

H128
HUMANISTICA LOVANIENSIA; journal of
  neo-Latin studies. Louvain
  1928-   .

HUMANISTISCHE GYMNASIUM see G136.

H129
HUMANITAS; revista do Instituto de
  Estudios Clássicos. Coimbra
  1947-   .

Hunt, A. S. see A152, C42, C78,
  O68, S72.

Hunter, W. see C76, R334.

HUNTER COIN CABINET see C76, R334.

Hussey, J. M. see L75.

I

IIC ABSTRACTS   see   A604.

IPEK   see   I109.

I1
IPQ; international philosophical
  quarterly. New York 1961-   .

IURA   see   I148.

I2
IAMBI et ELEGI GRAECI ante ALEXAN-
  DRUM CANTATI / M. L. West. Ox-
  ford 1971-72.

I3
IAPIGIA; organo della Deputazione
  di Storia Patria per la Puglia.
  Bari 1930-   . Title of vols.
  1-3: Japigia.

Ideler, J. L.   see   P133.

IIC ABSTRACTS   see   A604.

I4
ILERDA (Instituto de Estudios Ler-
  denses). Lérida 1943-   .

I5
ILLINOIS CLASSICAL STUDIES.   Urbana, Ill. 1976-   .

I6
ILLUSTRATED LONDON NEWS.   London
  1842-   .   (ILN).

I7
ILLUSTRATIONS of GREEK DRAMA / A.
D. Trendall & T. B. L. Webster.
  London 1971.

I8
ILLUSTRAZIONE VATICANA.   Vatican
  City 1930-38.

I9
IMAGINES INSCRIPTIONUM ATTICARUM /
  J. E. Kirchner. 2. Aufl. Berlin
  1948. 1st edition 1935.

I10
IMAGINES INSCRIPTIONUM GRAECARUM
  ANTIQUISSIMARUM / H. Röhl. 3.
  Aufl. Berlin 1907. 1st edition
  1883.

Imhoof-Blumer, F.   see   A362,
  G112, K26, M239.

I11
INCONTRI LINGUISTICI (Univ. Trieste).   Trieste 1974-   .

I12
INDEX; quaderni camerti di studi
  romanistici = international
  survey of Roman law.   Camerino
  ?-   .

I13
INDEX of FIGURE-TYPES on TERRA
  SIGILLATA / F. Oswald. Liver-
  pool 1936-37. Appeared as supple-
  ment to vol. 23 of Annals of
  Anthropology and Archaeology.
  Reprint London 1964.

I14
INDEX GÉNÉRAUX du LINEAIRE B / J.
P. Olivier. Rome 1973. (Incuna-
bula Graeca; 52).

I15
INDEX of POTTERS' STAMPS on TERRA
SIGILLATA / F. Oswald. East
Bridgeford, Eng. 1931. Reprint
London 1964.

INDICADOR PREHISTÓRICO see U33.

INDICATEUR d'ANTIQUITÉS SUISSES
see A400.

INDICATEUR PRÉHISTORIQUE see
U33.

I16
INDICE HISTÓRICO ESPAÑOL; biblio-
grafiá historica de España e
hispanoamérica. Barcelona
1953-   .

I17
INDO-IRANIAN JOURNAL. The Hague
1957-   .

I18
INDOGERMANISCHES ETYMOLOGISCHES
WÖRTERBUCH / J. Pokorny. Bern
1948-69. (IEW).

I19
INDOGERMANISCHE FORSCHUNGEN.
Strasbourg & Berlin 1891-   .
(IF, IndogForsch).

INDOGERMANISCHE FORSCHUNGEN. BEI-
BLATT see A398.

I20
INDOGERMANISCHE GRAMMATIK / J.
Kuryłowicz. Heidelberg 1968.

I21
INDOGERMANISCHES JAHRBUCH. Strasburg etc. 1913-   .

I22
INFORMACIÓN ARQUEOLOGICA. Barcelona 1970-   .

INFORMATION CULTURELLE ARTISTIQUE
see I24.

I23
INFORMATION HISTORIQUE. Paris
1938?-   .

I24
INFORMATION d'HISTOIRE de l'ART.
Paris 1955-   . Title of vols.
1-2: Information Culturelle
Artistique.

I25
INFORMATION LITTÉRAIRE. Paris
1949-   .

I26
INFORMES y MEMORIAS (Servicio Nacional de Excavaciones Arqueológicas). Madrid 1942-   .

I27
INFORMES y TRABAJOS del INSTITUTO
de CONSERVACIÓN y RESTAURACIÓN
de OBRAS de ARTE, ARQUEOLOGÍA
y ETNOLOGIA. Madrid 1964-   .

Inghirami, F. see E119, M256.

Ingholt, H. see A149.

I28
INITIATION à l'ÉPIGRAPHIE MYCÉNI-
ENNE / L. Deroy. Rome 1962.
(Incunabula Graeca; 2).

I29
INNERRHODER GESCHICHTSFREUND.
Appenzell, Switz. 1953-   .

I30
INNSBRUCKER BEITRÄGE zur KULTUR-
WISSENSCHAFT. Innsbruck
1953-   .

I31
INOZEMNA FILOLOGIÏA. Lvov 1964- .

INSCHRIFTEN see also INSCRIPCIONES
and ISCRIZIONI.

I32
INSCHRIFTEN / A. Rehm. Berlin
1958. (Didyma; 2).

I33
INSCHRIFTEN der ALTASSYRISCHEN
KÖNIGE / E. Ebeling et al. Leip-

zig 1926. (Altorientalische Bibliothek; 1).

INSCHRIFTEN. DIDYMA   see   I32.

I34
INSCHRIFTEN von ERYTHRAI und KLAZ-
OMENAI / H. Engelmann & R. Merk-
elbach.   Bonn 1972. (Inschriften
Griechischer Städte aus Klein-
asien; 1).

I35
INSCHRIFTEN GRIECHISCHER BILDHAUER
/ E. Loewy. Leipzig 1885. Re-
print Chicago 1976.

I36
INSCHRIFTEN von MAGNESIA am MAEAN-
DER / O. Kern. Berlin 1900.

I37
INSCHRIFTEN von OLYMPIA / W. Dittenberger & K. Purgold. Berlin 1896. (Olympia; 5).

I38
INSCHRIFTEN von PERGAMON / M. Fränkel. Berlin 1890-95. (Altertümer von Pergamon; 8, 1-2).

I39
INSCHRIFTEN von PRIENE / C. Freid-
rich & F. Hiller von Gaertringen.
Berlin 1906. Reprint 1968.

INSCHRIFTEN. TARRACO   see   R313.

INSCHRIFTEN. WÜRTTEMBERG   see
R312.

INSCRIPCIONES, INSCRIPTIILE,
INSCRIPTIONES, INSCRIPTIONS and
INSCRIPTIONUM are here inter-
filed. See also INSCHRIFTEN and
ISCRIZIONI.

I40
INSCRIPTIONS / C. S. Blinkenberg.
Berlin 1941. (Lindos; fouilles
de l'Acropole; 2).

INSCRIPTIONES ANTIQUAE SEPTENTRIO-
NALIS PONTI EUXINI   see   I86.

I41
INSCRIPTIONES BAVARIAE ROMANAE /
F. Vollmer. Munich 1915.

I42
INSCRIPTIONES BRITANNIAE CHRISTI-
ANAE / E. Hübner. Berlin 1876.

I43
INSCRIPTIONS CHRÉTIENNES de la
GAULE antérieures au VIIIe
siècle / E. F. LeBlant. Paris
1856-65.

I44
INSCRIPTIONES CHRISTIANAE URBIS
ROMAE: NOVA SERIES / G. B. de
Rossi. Rome 1922. Continues work
by the same title by de Rossi
published 1861-88, of which
only vol. 1 and vol. 2, part 1
appeared; supplement in 1915.
(ICVR, ICUR).

I45
INSCRIPTIONS CHYPRIOTES SYLLABIQUES
/ O. Masson. Paris 1961. (Études
Chypriotes; 1). (ICS).

I46
INSCRIPTIONS of COS / W. R. Paton
& E. L. Hicks. Oxford 1891.

I47
INSCRIPTIONES CRETICAE opera et
consilio Friderici Halbherr
collectae / M. Guarducci. Rome
1935-   . (IC, ICr, InscrCret).

I48
INSCRIPCIONES CRISTIANAS de la
ESPAÑA ROMANA y VISIGODA / J.
Vives. Barcelona 1942. (Monumenta Hispaniae Sacra. Ser.
patristica; 2). Also issued as
vol. 18 of the 2nd series of the
Bibliotheca Histórica de la Biblioteca Balmes. Reissued with
supplement in 1969.

I49
INSCRIPTIONES CUNEIFORMES du KUL-
TEPE / B. Hrozný. Prague 1952-
62. (Monografie Archivu Orientálního; 14).

150
INSCRIPȚIILE DACIEI ROMANE / I. I.
Russu. Bucharest 1975-   .

151
INSCRIPTIONS de DELOS. Paris
1926-   . Serves as vol. 11 of
the Inscriptiones Graecae.
(ID).

152
INSCRIPTIONES GRAECAE. Berlin
1873-   . Revised editions of
some volumes 1913-   . Volume
1 in 3rd edition 1981. (IG).

153
INSCRIPTIONES GRAECAE ANTIQUISSI-
MAE praeter Atticas in Attica
repertas / H. Röhl. Berlin
1882. (IGA).

154
INSCRIPTIONES GRAECAE in BULGARIA
repertae / G. I. Mikhaĭlov.
Sofia 1958-   . (Academia Litterarum Búlgarica. Institutum
Archaeologicum. Series Epigraphica; 5, etc.). (IGB).

155
INSCRIPTIONES GRAECAE ad INLUSTRAN-
DAS DIALECTOS SELECTAE / F. Solm-
sen. 4. Aufl. Stuttgart 1966.
(Bibliotheca Scriptorum Grae-
corum et Romanorum Teubneriana).

156
INSCRIPTIONES GRAECAE ad RES ROMAN-
AS PERTINENTES / R. Cagnat et al.
Paris 1901-27. Reprint editions
Rome 1964 and Chicago 1975.

157
INSCRIPTIONES GRAECAE SEPTENTRI-
ONALIS. Berlin 1897-1908.
(Inscriptiones Graecae; 9).
Part 1 also published in 1897 as
Corpus Inscriptionum Graecorum
Graeciae Septentrionalis, 3,
fasc. 1.

158
INSCRIPTIONES GRAECAE SICILIAE
et INFIMAE ad IUS PERTINENTES /
V. Arangio-Ruiz & A. Olívieri.

Milan 1925-   . (Fondazione
Guglielmo Castelli; 3).

INSCRIPTIONES GRAECAE SICILIAE
et ITALIAE see 170.

159
INSCRIPTIONES GRAECAE URBIS ROMAE /
L. Moretti. Rome 1968-   .
(Studi Pubblicati dall'Istituto
Italiano per la Storia Antica;
17).

160
INSCRIPȚIILE GRECEȘTI și LATINE din
SECOLELE IV-XII DESCOPERITE in
ROMÂNIA / E. Popescu. Bucharest
1976. (Inscripțiile Antice din
Dacia și Scythia Minor).

161
INSCRIPTIONS GRECQUES et LATINES
recueilles en ASIE MINEURE / P.
LeBas & W. H. Waddington. Paris
1870. Originally published as
vol. 3. of their Voyages archéologiques en Grèce et en Asie
Mineure. Reprint Hildesheim
1972.

162
INSCRIPTIONS GRECQUES et LATINES
de la SYRIE / L. Jalabert & R.
Mouterde. Paris 1929-   .
(Haut Commissariat de la Répub-
lique Française en Syrie et au
Liban. Service des Antiquités et
de Beaux-Arts. Bibliothèque
Archéologique et Historique; 12,
etc.). (IGLSyr, IGLS).

163
INSCRIPTIONS GRECQUES et LATINES
de la SYRIE / W. H. Waddington.
Paris 1870. Reprint Rome 1968.

164
INSCRIPTIONS GRECQUES de PHILAE /
A. Bernand. Paris 1969.

165
INSCRIPTIONES HISPANIAE CHRISTIANAE
/ E. Hübner. Berlin 1871.
--. Supplement. 1900.

I66
INSCRIPCIONES HISPANIAS en VERSO /
S. Mariné Bigorra. Barcelona
1952. (Publicaciones de la Es-
cuela de Filología de Barcelona.
Filología Clásica; 11).

I67
INSCRIPTIONS HITTITES HIÉROGLY-
PHIQUES / B. Hrozný. Prague
1933-37. (Monografie Archivu
Orientálního; 1).

I68
INSCRIPTIONES ITALIAE. Rome
1931-   . (II, InscrIt).

I69
INSCRIPTIONES ITALIAE INFERIORIS
DIALECTICAE / I. V. TSvetaev.
Moscow 1886.

I70
INSCRIPTIONES ITALIAE et SICILIAE
/ G. Kaibel & A. Lebégue. Berlin 1903. (Inscriptiones Graecae;
14). 1890 edition appeared out-
side of the series and with
title: Inscriptiones Graecae
Siciliae et Italiae. (IGSI).

I71
INSCRIPTIONS of KOURION / T. B.
Mitford. Philadelphia 1971.
(Memoirs of the American Philo-
sophical Society; 83).

I72
INSCRIPTIONS LATINES d'AFRIQUE
(Tripolitaine, Tunisie, Maroc)
/ R. Cagnat et al. Paris
1923. (ILAf).

I73
INSCRIPTIONS LATINES d'ALGÉRIE /
S. Gsell. Paris 1922-   .
(ILAlg).

I74
INSCRIPTIONES LATINAE CHRISTIANAE
VETERES / E. Diehl. Berlin
1924-31. Corrected edition appeared in 1961 with supplement
by J. Moreau and H. Marrou.
(ILCV).

I75
INSCRIPCIONES LATINAS de la ES-
PAÑA ROMANA / J. Vives. Barcelona 1971-72. (Publicaciones
de los Departamentos de Filología Latina. Univ. de Barcelona).

I76
INSCRIPTIONS LATINES de la GAULE
(Narbonnaise) / É. Éspérandieu.
Paris 1929. (ILGN).

I77
INSCRIPTIONES LATINAE quae in IUGO-
SLAVIA inter annos MCMXL et
MCMLX repertae et edita sunt /
A. & J. Šašel. Ljubljana 1963.
(Situla; 5).

I78
INSCRIPTIONES LATINAE LIBERAE REI
PUBLICAE / A. Degrassi. Flo-
rence 1957-63. (ILLRP).

I79
INSCRIPTIONS LATINES du MAROC /
L. Chatelain. Paris 1942-   .
(ILM).

I80
INSCRIPTIONES LATINAE SELECTAE /
H. Dessau. Berlin 1892-1916.
Appeared in several printings
and reprint editions. (ILS).

I81
INSCRIPTIONUM LATINARUM SELECTARUM
amplissima collectio ad illustra-
dam romanae antiquitatis disci-
plinam accomodata ... / J. K.
von Orelli. Turici 1826-56.

I82
INSCRIPTIONS LATINES des TROIS
GAULES / P. Wuilleumier. Paris
1963. (Gallia. Supplement; 17).
(ILT).

I83
INSCRIPTIONS LATINS de la TUNISIE
/ A. Merlin. Paris 1944. (ILT).

INSCRIPTIONS. LINDOS see I40.

I84
INSCRIPTIONS de la MÉSIE SUPÉR-
IEURE / F. Papazoglou et al.
Belgrad 1976-   .

I85
INSCRIPTIONS in the MINOAN LINEAR
SCRIPT of CLASS A / W. C. Brice.
Oxford 1961.

I86
INSCRIPTIONES antiquae ORAE SEPTEN-
TRIONALIS PONTI EUXINI / V. Laty-
schev. Leningrad 1885-1901. 2nd
edition of vol. 1 1916.
(IOSPE).

INSCRIPTIONS. PHILAE see I64.

I87
INSCRIPTIONES PYLIAE ad Mycenaeum
aetatem pertinentes / C. Gallavotti & A. Sacconi. Rome 1961.
(Incunabula Graeca; 1).

I88
INSCRIPTIONES REGNI NEOPOLITANI /
T. Mommsen. Leipzig 1852.
(IRN).

I89
INSCRIPTIONS ROMAINES d'ALGÉRIE /
L. Renier. Paris 1855-86.

I90
INSCRIPCIONES ROMANAS de GALICIA.
Santiago de Compostela 1949-   .

I91
INSCRIPTIONS of ROMAN TRIPOLITANA /
J. M. Reynolds & J. B. Ward Per-
kins. Rome 1950? (IRT).

INSCRIPTIONS. SARDIS see G91.

I92
INSULA FULCHERIA (Museo Civico).
Crema, Italy 1962-   .

I93
INTERCONNECTIONS in the ANCIENT
NEAR-EAST / W. Smith. New Haven
1965.

INTERNATIONAL, INTERNATIONALE, IN-
TERNATIONALER and INTERNATIONALES
are here interfiled.

I94
INTERNATIONAL ARCHIVES of ETHNO-
GRAPHY = Internationales Archiv
für Ethnographie = Archives-
Internationales d'Ethnographie.
Leiden 1888-1968.

INTERNATIONAL CONGRESS of CLAS-
SICAL ARCHAEOLOGY see A50.

INTERNATIONAL CONGRESS of ORIEN-
TALISTS see A52.

I95
INTERNATIONAL CRITICAL COMMENTARY
[to the Bible]. Edinburgh &
London 1895-   .

I96
INTERNATIONAL GUIDE to CLASSICAL
STUDIES. Darien, Conn. 1961-78.
Variant title: ABS (American
Bibliographic Service) Inter-
national Guide to Classical
Studies.

INTERNATIONAL INSTITUTE (for
CONSERVATION of MUSEUM OBJECTS/
of HISTORIC and ARTISTIC WORKS)
ABSTRACTS see A604.

I97
INTERNATIONAL JOURNAL of NAUTICAL
ARCHAEOLOGY and UNDERWATER EX-
PLORATION. London 1972-   .

INTERNATIONAL NUMISMATIC CONGRESS
see A51.

INTERNATIONALER ORIENTALISTEN-
KONGRESS see A52.

INTERNATIONAL PHILOSOPHICAL QUAR-
TERLY see I1.

INTERNATIONAL REPERTORY of the LIT-
ERATURE of ART see R1.

INTERNATIONAL REVIEW of MILITARY
HISTORY see R193.

I98
INTERNATIONAL STUDIES in PHILOSOPHY
= Studi Internazionale di Filosofia. Turin 1969-   . Until
1973 title only in Italian.

I99
INTERPRETER'S DICTIONARY of the
   BIBLE. Nashville, Tenn. 1962.
   --. Supplement. 1976.

I100
INTRODUCTION to the STUDY of TERRA
   SIGILLATA / F. Oswald & T. D.
   Price. London 1920. Reprint
   Farmborough 1966.

I101
INVENTAIRE des INSCRIPTIONS de
   PALMYRE / J. Cantineau. Beirut
   1930- .

I102
INVENTAIRE des MOSAÏQUES de la
   GAULE et de l'AFRIQUE / G. Lafaye
   et al. Paris 1909- .

I103
INVENTAIRE SOMMAIRE de la COLLEC-
   TION WADDINGTON / E. Babelon.
   Paris 1897.

I104
INVENTARIA ARCHAEOLOGICA [arranged
   by country]. place varies
   1953?- .

I105
INVENTORY of GREEK COIN HOARDS /
   M. Thompson et al. New York
   1973. (IGCH).

I106
INVENTORY of the HISTORICAL MONU-
   MENTS in [name of county]
   (Royal Commission on Historical
   Monuments). London 1910?- .
   (RCHM).

INVESTIGATEUR see R145.

I107
INVIGILATA LUCERNIS; rivista
   dell'Istituto di Latino. (Univ.
   Bari). Bari 1979- .

IPARMÜVÉSZETI EVKÖNYVE see I108.

I108
IPARMÜVÉSZETI MÜZEUM és a HOPP
   FERENC KELETÁZSSIAI MÜVÉSZETI
   MÜZEUM ÉVKÖNYVE. Budapest

1954- . 1954-59 title: Iparmüvészeti Evkönyve.

I109
IPEK: Jahrbuch für prähistorische
   & ethnographische Kunst. Leipzig & Berlin 1925- . Subtitles
   also in French, Spanish, English
   and Italian. (IPEK, JPEK).

IPQ; international philosophical
   quarterly see I1.

I110
IRAN. London 1963- .

I111
IRANICA ANTIQUA. Leiden 1961- .

I112
IRAQ. London 1934- . Suspended
   1941-45.

I113
IRISH JURIST. Dublin 1935- .

I114
IRODALOMTÖRTÉNET = Literaturge-
   schichte. Budapest 1912- .
   Suspended 1948.

ISCRIZIONE see also INSCRIPCIONES
and INSCHRIFTEN.

I115
INSCRIZIONI ANTICO-EBRAICHE PALES-
   TINESI / D. Diringer. Florence
   1934. (Pubblicazioni della R. Uni-
   versità degli Studi di Firenze.
   Facoltà di Lettere e Filosofia.
   III ser.; 2).

I116
ISCRIZIONI GRECHE LAPIDARIE del
   MUSEO di PALERMO / M. T. Manni
   Piraino. Palermo 1973. (Sikelia.
   Serie Storica; 6).

I117
ISCRIZIONI GRECHE e LATINE / E.
   Breccia. Cairo 1911. (Catalogue
   Général des Antiquités d'Egyp-
   tiennes du Musée d'Alexandrie;
   1).

I118
ISCRIZIONI LATINE LAPIDARIE del
MUSEO di PALERMO / L. Bivona.
Palermo 1970. (Sikelia. Serie
Storica; 5).

I119
ISCRIZIONI LATINE della SARDEGNA /
G. Sotgiu. Padua 1961-   .

I120
ISCRIZIONI PREELENICHE di HAGIA
TRIADA in CRETA e della GRECIA
PENINSULARE / G. Pugliese Carratelli.   Rome 1945.   (Monumenti Antichi XL (1945),
422-610).

I121
ISCRIZIONI STORICHE ELLENISTICHE /
L. Moretti. Florence 1967-   .
(Biblioteca di Studi Superiore;
53).

I122
ISIS; international review devoted
to the history of sciences and
its cultural influences. Brussels etc. 1913-   . Suspended
1914-19.

I123
ISKUSSTVO. Moscow 1933-   . Suspended 1942-46.

I124
ISLAM. Strasbourg & Berlin 1910- .

I125
ISLAMICA. Leipzig 1924-35.

I126
ISRAEL EXPLORATION JOURNAL. Jerusalem 1950/1-   . (IEJ).

I127
ISRAEL NUMISMATIC JOURNAL. Tel
Aviv 1963-   .

ISTANBUL ARKEOLOJI MÜZELERI YAY-
INLARINDAN see A575.

I128
ISTANBUL ARKEOLJI MÜZELERI YIL-
LIĞI = Annual of the Archaeolo-
gical Museums of Istanbul.

Istanbul 1934-   . 1934 alternate titles: Istanbul Müzeleri
Yilliği = Annuaire des Musées
d'Antiquités d'Istanbul. 1937
parallel title: Annuaire des
Musées d'Istanbul. 1949-52 alternate title: Report. Archaeological Museums of Istanbul.

I129
ISTANBUL ARKEOLOJI MÜZELERINDE
BULUNAN BOĞAZKÖY TABLETLERINDEN
SEÇME METINLER. Istanbul 1944-
54. Vol. 2 also has German
title: Boghazkoy-Tafeln im Archäologischen Museum in Istanbul.

ISTANBUL ASARIATIKA MÜZELERI
NESRIYATI see A575.

I130
ISTANBULER FORSCHUNGEN. Berlin
1932-   . (IstForsch).

I131
ISTANBULER MITTEILUNGEN (Deutsches
Archäologisches Institut).
Istanbul 1933-   . (IM).

ISTANBUL MÜZELERI NESRIYATI see
A575.

ISTANBUL MÜZELERI YILLIĞI see
I128.

I132
ISTORIA ROMÎNE. Bucharest 1960- .

I133
ISTORICHESKI PREGLED (Bŭlgarsko
Istorichesko Druzhestvo). Sofia
1945-   .

I134
ISTORICHESKIE ZAPISKI (Akademiîa
Nauk SSSR. Institut Istorii).
Moscow 1937-   .

I135
ISTORICHESKII ZHURNAL. Moscow
1931-45.

ISTORICHESKIĬ ZHURNAL (Ljubljana
1947-   ) see Z81.

I136
ISTORIIA SSSR. (Akademiia Nauk
SSSR. Institut Istorii). Moscow
1957- .

I137
ISTORIKO-FILOLOGICHESKIĬ ZHURNAL
Erevan, Armenia 1958?- .

I138
ISTORISKI ČASOPIS = Revue Historique. Belgrad 1948- . Suspended 1968-70.

I139
ISTORISKI GLASNIK. Belgrad
1948- .

I140
ISTROS; revue roumaine d'archéolo-
gie et d'histoire ancienne.
Bucharest 1934- .

I141
ISTVÁN KIRÁLY MÚZEUM KÖZLEMÉNYEI.
Székesfehérvár 1956- .

I142
ITALIA ANTICHISSIMA. Reggio
1929-38.

I143
ITALIA DIALETTALE; rivista di
dialettologia Italiana. Pisa
1924- .

ITALIA DIALETTALE. SUPPLEMENTO
see S242.

I144
ITALIA MEDIOEVALE e UMANISTICA.
Padua 1958- .

I145
ITALIA NOSTRA. Rome 1957- .

I146
ITALIEN; Monatsschrift für Kultur,
Kunst und Literatur. Heidelberg
1927-30.

I147
ITINERARIA ROMANA: römisiche
Reisewege an der Hand der Tabula
Peutingeriana / K. Miller.
Stuttgart 1916. Reprint Rome
1964.

IUGOSLAVSKIĬ ISTORISCHESKIĬ ZHUR-
NAL see J142.

I148
IURA; rivista internazionale di
diritto romano e antico. Naples
1950- .

IZVESTIIA and IZVIESTIIA are here
interfiled.

I149
IZVESTIIA ABKHAZSKOGO NAUCHNOGO
OBSHCHESTVA = Bulletin de la
Société Scientifique d'Abkhasie.
Suchum 1925-26.

I150
IZVESTIIA AKADEMII NAUK AZERBAĬD-
ZHANSKOI SSR = AZĂRBAJGAN SSR
ELMLĂR AKADEMIJASYNYN CHĂBĂRĂRI.
Baku 1936-57.
--. Seriia obshchestvennykh
nauk. 1958-65.
--. Seriia istorii, filosofii i
Prava. 1966- .
--. Seriia literatury, iazyka i
iskusstva. 1966- .

I151
IZVESTIIA. AKADEMIIA NAUK KAZAKH-
SKOI. Seriia arkheologicheskaia.
Alma-Ata 1948- .

I152
IZVESTIIA AKADEMII NAUK SSSR.
Leningrad & Moscow 1836- .
Until 1928 title primarily or
only in French: Bulletin (1836-
42: Bulletin scientifique). Academy's name changes slightly.
--. Otdelenie literatury i iazyka. 1941- .
--. Otdelenie obshchestvennykh
nauk. 1928-37. 1928-30 as Otdelenie Gymanitarnykh = Classe
des humanités.
--. Seriia istorii i filosofii =
Série historique et philologique
1944-52.

I153
IZVESTIIA na ARKHEOLOGICHESKIIA
INSTITUT = Bulletin de l'Insti-
tut Archéologique (Bŭlgarska
Akademiia na Naukite). Sofia

1910-   . 1910-20 title: Izvestiĩa na Bŭlgarskoto Arkheologichesko Druzhestvo = Bulletin de
la Société Archéologique Bulgare.
1921-50 title: Izvestiĩa na Bŭlgarskiĩa Arkheologicheski Institut = Bulletin de l'Institut
Archéologique Bulgare.

IZVĨESTIĨA ARKHEOLOGICHESKOĬ KOM-
MISSII see I156.

IZVESTIĨA. BŬLGARSKA AKADEMIĨA
na NAUTIKE. INSTITUT za ISTORIĨA
see I157.

IZVESTIĨA na BŬLGARSKOTO ARKHEOLO-
GICHESKO DRUZHESTVO see I153.

IZVESTIĨA na BŬLGARSKIĨA ARKHEOLO-
GICHESKI INSTITUT see I153.

I154
IZVESTIĨA na BŬLGARSKOTO ISTORI-
CHESKO DRUZHESTVO = Bulletin de
la Société Historique Bulgare.
Sofia 1905?-   .

I155
IZVESTIĨA GOSUDARSTVENNOĬ AKADEMII
ISTORII MATERIAL'NOI KUL'TURY.
Leningrad 1921-35. 1921-25 pub-
lished as Izvestiĩa Rossiĭskoĭ
Akademii Istorii Material'noi
Kul'tury. (IGAIMK).

IZVESTIĨA. GOSUDARSTVENNOE GEOGRA-
FICHESKOE OBSHCHESTVO see I168.

I156
IZVESTIĨA GOSUDARSTVENNOĬ ROSSIĬ-
SKOĬ ARKHEOLOGICHESKOĬ KOMMISSII
= Bulletin de la Commission
Archéologique. Leiningrad 1901-
1918. Earlier title: Izvĩestiĩa
(Imperatorskoĭ) Arkheologische-
skoĭ Kommissiĭ.

IZVESTIĨA. GOSUDARSTVENNOE RUSSKOE
GEOGRAFICHESKOE OBSHCHESTVO
see I168.

IZVĨESTIĨA IMPERATORSKOĬ AKADEMII
NAUK see I152.

IZVĨESTIĨA IMPERATORSKOIĬ ARKHEOLO-
GICHESKOĬ KOMMISSII see I156.

IZVESTIĨA na INSTITUTA za BŬLGAR-
SKA ISTORIĨA, i Bŭlgarska Akademiĩa na NAUTIKE see I157.

IZVESTIĨA za INSTITUTA za ISTORIĨA,
ARKHEOLOGIĨA i FILOSOFIĨA, i
BŬLGARSKA AKADEMIIA na NAUTIKE
see I157.

I157
IZVESTIĨA na INSTITUTA za ISTORIĨA
i BŬLGARSKA AKADEMIĨA na NAUTIKE
= Bulletin de l'Institut d'Histoire. Académie des Sciences de
Bulgare. Section d'Histoire et
de Pédagogie. Sofia 1951-   .
Also issued under the earlier
name of the Institute: Instituta
za Bulgarska Istoriĩa and Instituta za Istoriĩa, Arkheologiĩa i
Filosofiĩa.

I158
IZVESTIĨA na NARODNIĨA MUZEĬ BUR-
GAS = Bulletin du Musée National
de Burgas. Sofia 1950-   .

IZVESTIĨA na NARODNIĨA MUZEĬ, KO-
LAROVGRAD see I160.

I159
IZVESTIĨA na NARDONIĨA MUZEĬ, RUSE
= Mitteilungen des Volksmuseums,
Russe. Varna, Bulgaria 1964- .

I160
IZVESTIĨA na NARDONIĨA MUZEĬ, SHU-
MEN = Bulletin du Musée National
de Sumen. Shumen 1960-   .

I161
IZVESTIĨA na NARODNIĨA MUZEĬ VARNA
= Bulletin du Musée National de
Varna. Varna 1951-   . Until
1964? issued by the Arkheologichesko Druzhestvo. Earlier titles: Izvestiĩa na Varnenskoto
Arkheologichesko Druzhestvo =
Bulletin de la Société Archéologique à Varna; Izvestiĩa na Varnenskoto Arkheologichesko Druzhestvo v. gr. Stalin = Bulletin de
la Société Archéologique à Stalin.

I162
IZVESTIĬA NIZHNE-VOLZHSKOGO INSTI-
   TUTA KRAEVEDENIĬA IMENI M. GOR'-
   KOGO. Saratov 19?-   .

IZVESTIĬA OBSHCHESTVENNYE NAUKI
   see I167.

I163
IZVESTIĬA na OKRĂZHNIĬA ISTORI-
   CHESKI MUZEĬ = Bulletin du Musée Historique Régional de Veliko Tărnova. Veliko Tărnovo
   ?-   .

IZVESTIĬA ROSSIĬSKOĬ AKADEMII
   ISTORII MATERIAL'NOI KUL'TURY
   see I155.

IZVESTIĬA ROSSIĬKOĬ AKADEMIĬA
   NAUK see I152.

I164
IZVĬESTIĬA RUSSKAGO ARKHEOLOGICHES-
   KAGO INSTITUTA v KONSTANTINOPOLIE
   = Bulletin de l'Institut Archéo-
   logique Russe à Constantinople.
   Odessa & Sofia 1896-1912. (IRAIK).

IZVESTIĬA. RUSSKOE GEOGRAFICHESKOE
   OBSHCHESTVO see I168.

I165
IZVESTIĬA TAVRICHESKOGO OBSHCHESTVA
   ISTORII, ARKHEOLOGII I ETNOGRAFII
   Simferopol 1927-29?

I166
IZVĬESTIĬA TAVRICHESKOĬ UCHENOĬ
   ARKHIVNOI KOMMISSII. Simferopol
   1887-1926.

IZVESTIĬA na VARNENSKOTO ARKHEOLO-
   GICHESKO DRUZHESTVO see I161.

I167
IZVESTIĬA. VESTNIK OBSHCHESTVENNYKH
   NAUK (Akademiĭa Nauk Armĭanskoi
   SSR). Erevan ?-   . Title
   until 1965: Izvestiĭa. Obshchest-
   vennye nauki.

I168
IZVESTIĬA VSEOSOĬUZNOGO GEOGRAFI-
   CHESKOGO OBSHCHESTVA. Leningrad
   1865-   . Issued under the

Society's earlier names; 1865-
1924: Russkoe Geograficheskoe
Obshchestvo; 1925-29: Gosudarstvennoe Russkoe Geograficheskoe
Obshchestvo; 1930-39: Gosudarstvennoe Geografischeskoe Obshchestvo.

J

J1
J. PAUL GETTY MUSEUM JOURNAL. Malibu, Ca. 1974-   .

JAARBERICHT, JAARBOEK, JAARBOEKJE,
   JAARSVERLAG and JAAROVERZICHT
   are here interfiled. See also
   JAHRBUCH and JAHRESBERICHT.

J2
JAARBOEK van de AKADEMIE van
   WETENSCHAPPEN, AMSTERDAM. Am-
   sterdam 1853-   .

J3
JAAROVERZICHT ARCHEOLOGISCHE WERK-
   GEMEENSCHAP LIMBURG. Maastricht
   ?-   .

JAARBERICHT, "EX ORIENTE LUX" see
   J8.

J4
JAARBOEKJE voor GESCHIEDENIS en
   OUDHEIDKUNDE van LEIDEN en OM-
   STREKEN. Leiden 1904-   .

JAARBOEK voor MUNT-en PENNINGKUNDE
   see J5.

JAARBOEK der Koninklijke MUSEUMS
   voor SCHOONE KUNSTEN van BELGIË
   see A288.

J5
JAARBOEK van het Koninklijk NEDER-
   LANDSCH GENOOTSCHAP voor MUNT-en
   PENNINGKUNDE. Amsterdam 1914-   .

J6
JAARBOEKJE van "OUD-UTRECHT".
   Utrecht 1924-   .

J7
JAARSVERLAG van de VEREENIGING
   voor TERPENONDERZOEK over de
   VEREENIGINGSJAREN. Groningen
   1917-   .

J8
JAARBERICHT. VOORAZIATISCH - EGYP-
   TISCH GENOOTSCHAP "EX ORIENTE
   LUX". Leiden 1933-   . (JEOL).

Jacobthal, P. see B110.

Jacoby, F. see F60.

J9
JADRANSKI ZBORNIK; prilozi za povijest istre, rijeke i hrvatskog
   primorja. Fiume 1956-   .

JAHRBUCH see also JAHRESBERICHT
   and JAARBERICHT.

JAHRBUCH für ÄSTHETIK und ALLGE-
   MEINE KUNSTWISSENSCHAFT see
   Z20.

J10
JAHRBUCH der AKADEMIE der WISSEN-
   SCHAFTEN, GÖTTINGEN. Göttingen
   & Berlin 1894-1943/4. 1894-1933
   title: Nachrichten; geschaftliche
   Mitteilungen. 1933/4-38/9 title:
   Nachrichten; Jahresbericht.

J11
JAHRBUCH. AKADEMIE der WISSEN-
    SCHAFTEN und der LITERATUR,
    MAINZ. Mainz 1950-   .

JAHRBUCH. AKADEMIE der WISSEN-
    SCHAFTEN, MÜNCHEN see J15.

J12
JAHRBUCH der ALBERTUS UNIVERSITÄT
    zu KÖNIGSBERG. Freiburg i.B.
    1951-   .

J13
JAHRBUCH für ALTERTUMSKUNDE.
    Vienna 1907-13.

J14
JAHRBUCH für ANTIKE und CHRISTEN-
    TUM. Münster 1958-   . (JbAC,
    AbAChr).

J15
JAHRBUCH der BAYERISCHEN AKADEMIE
    der WISSENSCHAFTEN. Munich
    1912-   .

JAHRBUCH. BERLIN see J20.

J16
JAHRBUCH der BERLINER MUSEEN. Ber-
    lin 1959-   . Subtitle: Jahrbuch
    der Preussichen Kunstsammlungen
    N.F.

J17
JAHRBUCH des BERNISCHEN HISTOR-
    ISCHEN MUSEUMS. Bern 1921-   .

JAHRBUCH für BODENDENKMALPFLEGE
    in MECKLENBURG see B118.

J18
JAHRBUCH für BRANDENBURGISCHE
    LANDESGESCHICHTE. Berlin
    1950-   .

JAHRBUCH des BULGARISCHEN ARCHÄO-
    LOGISCHEN NATIONALMUSEUMS,
    SOFIA see G61.

JAHRBUCH der K. K. CENTRAL COMMIS-
    SION zur ERFORSCHUNG und ERHAL-
    TUNG der BAUDENKMALE see W25.

J19
JAHRBUCH. COBURGER LANDESSTIFTUNG.
    Coburg 1956-   .

JAHRBUCH des DÉRI MUSEUMS see D5.

J20
JAHRBUCH der DEUTSCHEN AKADEMIE der
    WISSENSCHAFTEN zu BERLIN. Ber-
    lin 1939-   . Suspended 1942-45.

J21
JAHRBUCH des DEUTSCHEN ARCHÄOLO-
    GISCHEN INSTITUTS. Berlin
    1886-   . Institute's name
    changes slightly. (JDAI, JdI).
    --. Ergänzungshefte. 1881-   .

JAHRBUCH des DEUTSCHEN ARCHÄOLO-
    GISCHEN INSTITUTS. BEIBLATT
    see A421.

JAHRBUCH des DEUTSCHEN ARCHÄOLO-
    GISCHEN INSTITUTS. BEILAGE
    see A425.

J22
JAHRBUCH des EMSLÄNDISCHEN HEIMAT-
    VEREINS. Meppen 1953-   .

JAHRBUCH des FERENC MÓRA MUSEUMS
    see M272.

J23
JAHRBUCH für FRÄNKISCHE LANDES-
    FORSCHUNG. Erlangen 1935-   .

JAHRBUCH für die GESCHICHTE des
    HERZOGTUMS OLDENBURG see O12.

J24
JAHRBUCH für GESCHICHTE und KUNST
    des MITTELRHEINS und seiner
    NACHBARGEBIETE. Neuwied am
    Rhein 1949-   . 1949-50/1 title:
    Jahrbuch für Geschichte und Kul-
    tur des Mittelrheins und Seiner
    Nachbargebiete.

J25
JAHRBUCH für die GESCHICHTE MIT-
    TEL- und OSTDEUTSCHLANDS.
    Tübingen 1952-   .

J26
JAHRBUCH für die GESCHICHTE OST-
  EUROPAS. Wiesbaden 1936-41
  1953-   .

JAHRBUCH des GESCHICHTSVEREINS
  für das HERZOGTUM BRAUNSCHWEIG
  see B201.

JAHRBUCH des GESCHICHTVEREINS für
  STADT und TAL MÜNSTER see A319.

J27
JAHRBUCH der GESELLSCHAFT für
  BILDENDE KUNST und VATERLÄNDISCHE
  ALTERTÜMER zu EMDEN. Emden
  1872-   .

JAHRBUCH der GESELLSCHAFT für
  LOTHRINGISCHE GESCHICHTE und
  ALTERTUMSKUNDE see A315.

JAHRBUCH für GESETZGEBUNG, VERWAL-
  TUNG und VOLKSWISSENSCHAFT im
  DEUTSCHEN REICH see S44.

JAHRBUCH. GÖTTINGEN see J10.

J28
JAHRBUCH der HAMBURGER KUNSTSAMM-
  LUNGEN. Hamburg 1948-   .

J29
JAHRBUCH. HEIDELBERGER AKADEMIE
  der WISSENSCHAFTEN. Heidelberg
  1963/4-   .

J30
JAHRBUCH des HISTORISCHEN VEREINS
  DILLINGEN. Dillingen 1888-   .
  1888-95 title: Jahresbericht.

J31
JAHRBUCH des HISTORISCHEN VEREINS
  für das FÜRSTENTUM LIECHTENSTEIN.
  Vaduz 1901-   .

J32
JAHRBUCH des HISTORISCHEN VEREINS
  des KANTONS GLARUS. Glarus
  1865-   .

J33
JAHRBUCH des HISTORISCHEN VEREINS
  für MITTELFRANKEN. Ansbach
  etc. 1830-   . 1830-57 title:
  Jahresbericht.

J34
JAHRBUCH des HISTORISCHEN VEREINS
  für WÜRTTEMBERGISCH FRANKEN.
  Hall ?-   .

JAHRBUCH des JÁSZMÚZEUMS see
  J82.

JAHRBÜCHER für KLASSISCHE PHILO-
  LOGIE und PÄDAGOGIK see N27.

JAHRBUCH für KLEINASIATISCHE FOR-
  SCHUNGEN see A160.

J35
JAHRBUCH des KÖLNISCHEN GESCHICHTS-
  VEREINS. Cologne 1912-   .

JAHRBUCH der (KÖNIGLICH) PREUS-
  SISCHEN KUNSTSAMMLUNGEN see
  J48.

JAHRBUCH für KUNSTGESCHICHTE see
  W25.

JAHRBUCH des KUNSTHISTORISCHEN
  INSTITUTES (des K.K. ZENTRAL-
  KOMMISSION für DENKMALPFLEGE)
  see W25.

J36
JAHRBUCH der KUNSTHISTORISCHEN
  SAMMLUNGEN. Vienna 1883-   .
  Title varies slightly. Suspended
  1945-52.

J37
JAHRBUCH für KUNSTWISSENSCHAFT.
  Leipzig 1923-30.

JAHRBUCH für LANDESKUNDE und HEI-
  MATSCHUTZ von NIEDERÖSTERREICH
  (und WIEN) see J38.

J38
JAHRBUCH für LANDESKUNDE von NIE-
  DERÖSTERREICH. Vienna 1902-   .
  Variant titles: Jahrbuch für
  Landeskunde und Heimatschutz
  von Niederösterreich (und Wien).

JAHRBUCH des LINDEN-MUSEUMS see
  T111.

J39
JAHRBÜCHER der LITERATUR. Vienna
  1818-49.

J40
JAHRBUCH für LITURGIEWISSENSCHAFT.
   Munich 1921-41.

J41
JAHRBUCH der MÄNNER vom MORGEN-
   STERN, HEIMATBUND an ELB- und
   WESERMÜNDUNG. Hannover 1898-   .
   1898-1910 title: Jahresbericht
   der Männer vom Moregenstern,
   Heimatbund in Hannover.

JAHRBUCH. MÜNCHEN see J15.

JAHRBÜCHER des MUSEUMS der BILDEN-
   DEN KÜNSTE in BUDAPEST see O49.

JAHRBUCH des MUSEUMS von EGER
   see E13.

J42
JAHRBUCH des MUSEUMS HOHENLEUBEN-
   REICHENFELS. Hohenleuben ?-   .

J43
JAHRBUCH des MUSEALVEREINS WELS.
   Wels 1954-   .

J44
JAHRBUCH des NORDFRIESICHEN INSTI-
   TUTS. Bredstedt ?-   .

J45
JAHRBUCH für NUMISMATIK und GELD-
   GESCHICHTE. Kallmünz 1949-   .
   (JNG).

J46
JAHRBUCH des OBERÖSTERREICHISCHEN
   MUSEALVEREINS. Linz 1835-   .
   1835-93/4 title: Bericht.
   1894/5-1922/3 title: Jahresbericht. 1939-40 title: Jahrbuch
   des Vereins für Landeskunde und
   Heimatpflege im Gau Oberdonau.

J47
JAHRBUCH der ÖSTERREICHISCHEN
   BYZANTINISTIK. Vienna 1951-   .
   1951-68 title: Jahrbuch der
   Österreichischen Byzantinischen
   Gesellschaft. (JÖBG, JÖB).

JAHRBUCH der ÖSTERREICHISCHEN
   BYZANTINISCHEN GESELLSCHAFT
   see J47.

JAHRBÜCHER für PHILOLOGIE und
   PÄDAGOGIK see N27.

JAHRBUCH für PRÄHISTORISCHE und
   ETHNOGRAPHISCHE KUNST see I109.

J48
JAHRBUCH der PREUSSISCHEN KUNST-
   SAMMLUNGEN. Berlin 1880-1943/4.
   Former title: Jahrbuch der König-
   lich Preussischen Kunstsammlun-
   gen. Continued by Jahrbuch der
   Berliner Museen.

JAHRBUCH der PREUSSISCHEN KUNST-
   SAMMLUNGEN N.F. see J16.

J49
JAHRBUCH des RÖMISCH-GERMANISCHEN
   ZENTRAL MUSEUMS MAINZ. Mainz
   1954-   . (RGZM, JRGZ, JbRGZM).

J50
JAHRBUCH der SCHWEIZERISCHEN GE-
   SELLSCHAFT für URGESCHICHTE =
   Annuaire de la Société Suisse de
   Préhistoire et d'Archéologie =
   Annuario della Societa Svizzera
   di Preistoria e d'Archeologia.
   Zurich 1909-   . 1909-37 title:
   Jahresbericht. (JSGU).

JAHRBUCH. SCHWEIZERISCHE PHILOSO-
   PHISCHE GESELLSCHAFT see S232.

J51
JAHRBUCH für SOLOTHURNISCHE GE-
   SCHICHTE. Solothurn 1928-   .

J52
JAHRBUCH der STAATLICHEN KUNSTSAMM-
   LUNGEN in BADEN-WÜRTTEMBERG.
   Munich 1964-   .

J53
JAHRBUCH der STAATLICHEN KUNSTSAMM-
   LUNGEN, DRESDEN. Dresden
   1959-   .

J54
JAHRBUCH der STADT LINZ. Linz ?-
   1954. Suspended 1938-48.

J55
JAHRBUCH. STIFTUNG PREUSSISCHER
KULTURBESITZ. Berlin etc.
1962- .

JAHRBUCH des SUNGAUVEREINS see
A318.

JAHRBUCH des UNGARISCHEN ARCHÄO-
LOGISCHEN GESELLSCHAFT see O48.

J56
JAHRBUCH der UNIVERSITÄT DÜSSEL-
DORF. Düsseldorf 1968/9?- .

JAHRBÜCHER des VEREINS von ALTER-
THUMSFREUNDEN im RHEINLANDE
see B193.

J57
JAHRBUCH des VEREINS für GESCHICHTE
der STADT WIEN. Vienna 1939- .

JAHRBUCH des VEREINS für LANDES-
KUNDE und HEIMATPFLEGE im GAU
OBERDONAU see J46.

J58
JAHRBUCH. VORARLBERGER LANDESMU-
SEUMS VEREINS. Bregenz 1928- .

J59
JAHRBUCH für WIRTSCHAFTSGESCHICHTE.
Berlin 1960- .

J60
JAHRBÜCHER für WISSENSCHAFTLICHE
KRITIK zu BERLIN. Berlin etc.
1827-46.

JAHRBUCH der K. K. ZENTRAL KOM-
MISSION für ERFORSCHUNG und ER-
HALTUNG der KUNST- und HISTO-
RISCHEN DENKMALE see W25.

JAHRESBERICHT, JAHRESHEFTE and
JAHRESSCHRIFT are here inter-
filed. See also JAHRBUCH and
JAABERICHT.

J61
JAHRESBERICHT der BAYERISCHEN
BODENDENKMALPFLEGE. Munich
1960- .

J62
JAHRESBERICHT des BERNISCHEN HIS-
TORISCHEN MUSEUMS in BERN. Bern
1894-1920.

JAHRESBERICHT über die FORTSCHRIT--
TE der KLASSISCHEN (ALTERTUMS-
WISSENSCHAFT/PHILOLOGIE) see
B448.

JAHRESBERICHT der GESELLSCHAFT
für NÜTZLICHE FORSCHUNGEN zu
TRIER see T112.

J63
JAHRESBERICHT. GESELLSCHAFT pro
VINDONISSA, BASEL. Brugg
1906/7- .

J64
JAHRESBERICHT. HISTORISCH-ANTI-
QUARISCHE GESELLSCHAFT von GRAU-
BÜNDEN. Chur 1871- . Sus-
pended during World War II?

J65
JAHRESBERICHT des HISTORISCHEN
MUSEUMS SCHLOSS THUN. Thun
1923?- . Title changes
slightly.

JAHRESBERICHT des HISTORISCHEN
VEREINS DILLINGEN see J30.

J66
JAHRESBERICHT des HISTORISCHEN
VEREINS für die GRAFSCHAFT
RAVENSBERG. Bielefeld 1877- .
Suspended 1940-46.

JAHRESBERICHT des HISTORISCHEN
VEREINS für MITTELFRANKEN
see J33.

J67
JAHRESBERICHT des HISTORISCHEN
VEREINS von OBERPFALZ und
REGENSBURG. Ratisbon ?- .

J68
JAHRESBERICHTE der HISTORISCHEN
VEREINIGUNG SEETAL. Seengen
?- .

J69
JAHRESBERICHT des HISTORISCHEN

VEREINS für STRAUBING und UMGE-
BUNG. Staubing 1898-   .

J70
JAHRESBERICHT des INSTITUTS für
VORGESCHICHTE der UNIVERSITÄT
FRANKFURT am MAIN. Munich
1973-   .

J71
JAHRESSCHRIFT des KREISMUSEUMS
HALDENSLEBEN. Haldensleben
?-   .

JAHRESBERICHT der MÄNNER vom MOR-
GENSTERN, HEIMATBUND in HAN-
NOVER see J41.

J72
JAHRESSCHRIFT für MITTELDEUTSCHE
VORGESCHICHTE. Halle 1902-   .
Variant title: Jahresschrift für
die Vorgeschichte der Sächsisch-
thüringischen Länder. Suspended
1912-24 1941-48.

J73
JAHRESBERICHT der NATURHISTORISCHEN
GESELLSCHAFT NÜRNBERG. Nürnberg
1882-1906.

JAHRESBERICHT des OBERÖSTERREICH-
ISCHEN MUSEALVEREINS see J46.

J74
JAHRESHEFTE des ÖSTERREICHISCHEN
ARCHÄOLOGISCHEN INSTITUTES in
WIEN. Vienna 1898-   . 1940-43
title: Wiener Jahreshefte. Vols.
for 1960- called Hauptblatt with
supplements called Beiblatt
and Grabungen. Suspended 1944-
45. (JOEAI, JOAI, WJh).

J75
JAHRESBERICHT. PHILOLOGISCHER VER-
EIN zu BERLIN. Berlin 1875-1924.
Issued as part of Sokrates.

J76
JAHRESSCHRIFT des SALZBURGER MUSE-
UMS CAROLINO-AUGUSTEUM. Salz-
burg ?-   .

J77
JAHRESBERICHTE ST. GALLEN. St.
Gall ?-   .

JAHRESBERICHT der SCHWEIZERISCHEN
GESELLSCHAFT für URGESCHICHTE
see J50.

J78
JAHRESBERICHT. SCHWEIZERISCHES
LANDESMUSEUM. Zurich 1892-   .
1902-32 alternate title: Rapport
annuel. Musée National Suisse à
Zurich.

J79
JAHRESBERICHT. VEREIN für GESCHICH-
TE der STADT NÜRNBERG. Nürnberg
1879-   .

J80
JAHRESBERICHT des VEREINS für
HEIMATGESCHICHTE. Ober-Ramstadt
?-   .

JAHRESSCHRIFT für die VORGESCHICH-
TE der SÄCHSISCH-THURINGISCHEN
LÄNDER see J72.

Jalabert, L. see I62.

Jameson, R. see C163.

Jan, K. van see M319.

J81
JANUS PANNONIUS MÚZEUM ÉVKÖNYVE.
Pécs 1956-   .

JAPIGIA see I3.

J82
JÁSZBERÉNYI JÁSZMÚSEUM ÉVKÖNYVE
= Yearbook of the Jászmúzeum =
Jahrbuch des Jászmúzeums = An-
nuaire du Jászmúzeum de Jászber-
ény. Budapest 1937-38/43?

Jean, C.-F. see D57

Jedin, H. see H16.

Jeffery, L. H. see L79.

J83
JENAER PAPYRUS-URKUNDEN / F.
Zucker & F. Schneider. Greiz
1926. (PJena).

Jenson, C. see K23.

J84
JEWISH ENCYCLOPEDIA. New York &
London 1901-06.

J85
JEWISH QUARTERLY REVIEW. London
1888-1908.
--. n.s. Philadelphia 1910-   .
(JQR).

J86
JEWS and CHRISTIANS in EGYPT; the
Jewish trouble in Alexandria and
the Athanasian controversy / H.
I. Bell. London 1924. (Greek
Papyri in the British Museum).
(PLondVI).

Johansen, K. Friis   see V5.

Johnson, A. C.   see A202, P66.

Johnson, S. E.   see P164.

Jones, A. H. M.   see P222, C126,
D81, L16.

Jones, H. S.   see G87.

Jones, T. B.   see S271.

Jouguet, P.   see P50, P72.

J87
JOURNAL of AESTHETICS and ART
CRITICISM. Philadelphia etc.
1941-   .

J88
JOURNAL of AFRICAN HISTORY. London 1960-   .

J89
JOURNAL of the AMERICAN RESEARCH
CENTER in EGYPT. Boston 1962- .
(JARCE).

JOURNAL of the AMERICAN SOCIETY of
ARCHITECTURAL HISTORIANS   see
J133.

JOURNAL of ANCIENT HISTORY   see
V33.

J90
JOURNAL of the Royal ANTHROPOLO-

GICAL INSTITUTE of GREAT BRI-
TAIN and IRELAND. London 1871-
1965. (JRAI).

J91
JOURNAL of ARCHAEOLOGICAL SCIENCE.
London 1974-   .

JOURNAL of the ARCHITECTURAL,
ARCHAEOLOGICAL and HISTORICAL
SOCIETY (for the COUNTY and CITY)
of CHESTER (and NORTH WALES)
see J98.

J92
JOURNAL of the Royal ASIATIC
SOCIETY of GREAT BRITAIN and
IRELAND. London 1834-   .
(JRAS).

J93
JOURNAL ASIATIQUE. Paris 1822-   .
1828-35 title: Nouveau Journal
Asiatique. (JA, JAs).

JOURNAL of the AUSTRALASIAN UNI-
VERSITIES LANGUAGE and LITERA-
TURE ASSOCIATION   see A2.

J94
JOURNAL of BIBLE and RELIGION.
Wolcott, N.Y. 1933-   . 1933-
36 title: Journal. National
Association of Bible Instructors.

J95
JOURNAL of BIBLICAL LITERATURE.
Middleton, Conn. 1881-   .
1881-88 title: Journal of Bibli-
cal Literature and Exegesis.
Suspended 1889. (JBL).

J96
JOURNAL of the BRITISH ARCHAEOLO-
GICAL ASSOCIATION. London
1845-   . (JBAA).

JOURNAL of the CANADIAN LINGUISTIC
ASSOCIATION   see C52.

J97
JOURNAL of the Royal CENTRAL ASIAN
SOCIETY. London 1914-69.

J98
JOURNAL of the CHESTER and NORTH

WALES ARCHITECTURAL, ARCHAEO-
LOGICAL and HISTORICAL SOCIETY.
Chester 1849-85 1887-   .
Society's name changes; 1849-85:
Architectural, Archaeological
and Historical Society for the
County and City of Chester;
1887-92: Chester Archaeological
and Historical Society; 1893-
1914: Architectural, Archaeological and Historical Society
for Chester and North Wales.

J99
JOURNAL of CLASSICAL and SACRED
    PHILOLOGY. Cambridge 1854-59.

J100
JOURNAL of CLASSICAL STUDIES (Clas-
    sical Society of Japan = Seijo
    Kotengaku Kenkyu). Kyoto
    1953-   . (JCS).

J101
JOURNAL of CUNEIFORM STUDIES. New
    Haven etc. 1974-   . (JCS).

JOURNAL. DERBYSHIRE ARCHAEOLOGICAL
    and NATURAL HISTORY SOCIETY see
    D20.

JOURNAL. DURHAM UNIVERSITY see
    D102.

J102
JOURNAL of ECCLESIASTICAL HISTORY.
    London 1950-   .

J103
JOURNAL of the ECONOMIC and SOCIAL
    HISTORY of the ORIENT. Leiden
    1957-   . (JESHO).

J104
JOURNAL of EGYPTIAN ARCHAEOLOGY.
    London 1914-   . (JEA).

J105
JOURNAL of FIELD ARCHAEOLOGY.
    Boston 1974-   .

J106
JOURNAL of the Royal GEOGRAPHICAL
    SOCIETY. London 1831-80.

J107
JOURNAL of GLASS STUDIES. Corning
    N.Y. 1959-   . (JGS).

J108
JOURNAL of HELLENIC STUDIES.
    London 1880-   . Archaeological
    Reports appeared as part of the
    publication until 1954 when it
    began to appear as a supplement.

JOURNAL of HELLENIC STUDIES.
    SUPPLEMENT see A455.

JOURNAL of the HISTORICAL and ARCH-
    AEOLOGICAL ASSOCIATION of IRE-
    LAND see J132.

J109
JOURNAL of the HISTORICAL METALLUR-
    GY SOCIETY. London 1963-   .
    1963-73 title: Bulletin. Histor-
    ical Metallury Group. Variant
    title: Historical Metallurgy.

J110
JOURNAL of HISTORICAL STUDIES.
    Washington D.C. 1975-   .

J111
JOURNAL of the HISTORY of IDEAS.
    Lancaster, Pa. etc. 1940-   .

J112
JOURNAL of the Royal INSTITUTE of
    BRITISH ARCHITECTS. London
    1893/4-   . (JRIBA).

J113
JOURNAL of the HISTORY of MEDICINE
    and ALLIED SCIENCES. New York
    1946-   .

J114
JOURNAL of the HISTORY of PHILOSO-
    PHY. Berkeley 1963-   .

J115
JOURNAL of INDO-EUROPEAN STUDIES.
    Hattiesburg, Miss. 1973-   .

JOURNAL. INSTITUT HISTORIQUE see
    R145.

J116
JOURNAL INTERNATIONAL d'ARCHÉOLO-

GIE NUMISMATIQUE = Diethnēs
Ephēmeris tēs Nomismatikēs Arch-
aiologias. Athens 1898-1927.
(JIAN).

J117
JOURNAL of the ISRAEL ORIENTAL
SOCIETY. Jerusalem 1920-49.
1920-49 title: Journal of the
Palestine Oriental Society. Sus-
pended 1941-45. (JPOS).

J118
JOURNAL of JEWISH STUDIES. Cambridge 1948-   . (JJS).

J119
JOURNAL of JURISTIC PAPYROLOGY =
Rocznik Papirologii Prawniczej.
Warsaw 1946-   . (JJP, JJur-
Pap).

JOURNAL of the KILKENNY and SOUTH-
EAST of IRELAND ARCHAEOLOGICAL
SOCIETY see J132.

J120
JOURNAL of LINGUISTICS. London
1965-   .

J121
JOURNAL of the MANCHESTER UNIVER-
SITY EGYPTIAN and ORIENTAL SOCI-
ETY. Manchester 1911-   . 1911
title: Journal of the Manchester
Oriental Society. 1912-35 title:
Journal of the Manchester Egyp-
tian and Oriental Society.

J122
JOURNAL of MITHRAIC STUDIES.
London 1976-80.

JOURNAL. NATIONAL ASSOCIATION of
BIBLE INSTRUCTORS see J94.

J123
JOURNAL of NEAR EASTERN STUDIES.
Chicago 1942-   . (JNES).

J124
JOURNAL of the NORTH-WEST SEMITIC
LANGUAGES. Leiden 1971-   .

JOURNAL of the PALESTINE ORIENTAL
SOCIETY see J117.

J125
JOURNAL of PHILOLOGY. London &
Cambridge 1868-1920. (JournPhil,
JPh, JP).

JOURNAL of PHILOSOPHICAL STUDIES
see P116.

J126
JOURNAL of PHILOSOPHY. New York
etc. 1904-   . 1904-20 title:
Journal of philosophy, psycholo-
gy and scientific methods.
(JPhilos).

JOURNAL of PHILOSOPHY, PSYCHOLOGY
and SCIENTIFIC METHODS see
J126.

J127
JOURNAL of RELIGION. Chicago
1921-   . (JR).

J128
JOURNAL of RELIGIOUS HISTORY.
Sydney 1960-   .

J129
JOURNAL of ROMAN STUDIES. London
1911-   . (JRS).

JOURNAL of the ROYAL ... see JOUR-
NAL of the ... (the word royal
is disregarded in filing, but
may have been regarded in forming an abbreviation).

J130
JOURNAL des SAVANTS. Paris 1797
1816-   . (JS, JSav, JournSav).

J131
JOURNAL of SEMITIC STUDIES. Manchester 1956-   . (JSS).

J132
JOURNAL of the Royal SOCIETY of
ANTIQUARIES of IRELAND. Dublin
1849-   . 1849-53 title: Journal
of the Historical and Archaeological Association of Ireland.
1854-55 title: Proceedings and
Transactions of the Kilkenny and
Southeast of Ireland Archaeological Society. 1856-67 title:
Journal of the Kilkenny and

Southeast of Ireland Archaeolo-
gical Society. 1868-69 title:
Journal of the Historical and
Archaeological Association of
Ireland. 1870-89 title: Journal
of the Royal Historical and
Archaeological Association of
Ireland. 1890-91 title: Pro-
ceedings and Papers of the Royal
Society of Antiquaries of Ire-
land.

J133
JOURNAL of the SOCIETY of ARCHITEC-
TURAL HISTORIANS. Troy N.Y. &
Louisville, Ky. 1941-   . 1941-
44 title: Journal of the American
Society of Architectural Histo-
rians. (JSAH).

J134
JOURNAL of the Royal SOCIETY of
ARTS. London 1852-   .

J135
JOURNAL of the SOCIETY of ORIENTAL
RESEARCH. Chicago 1917-32.

J136
JOURNAL for the STUDY of JUDAISM
in the PERSIAN, HELLENISTIC and
ROMAN PERIOD. Leiden 1970-   .

J137
JOURNAL for the STUDY of the OLD
TESTAMENT. Sheffield 1976-   .

J138
JOURNAL of THEOLOGICAL STUDIES.
Oxford & London 1899-   .
(JTS, JThS).

J139
JOURNAL of the WALTERS ART GALLERY.
Baltimore 1938-   . (JWaH).

J140
JOURNAL of the WARBURG and COUR-
TAULD INSTITUTES. London
1937/8-   . 1937-39 title:
Journal of the Warburg Institute.
(JWI).

JOURNAL of WORLD HISTORY   see   C25.

Jucquois, G.   see   H65.

J141
JUDAICA.   Zurich 1945-   .

J142
JUGOSLOVENSKI ISTORIJSKI ČASOPIS
= Yugoslav Historical Revue =
Revue Historique Yougoslave =
Iugoslavskiĭ Istorischeskiĭ
Zhurnal.   Belgrad 1962-   .

J143
JUGOSLOVENSKI ISTORISKI ČASOPIS.
Ljubljana etc. 1935-39.

J144
JURISTISCHE PAPYRI / P. M. Meyer.
Berlin 1920.   (JurPap).

J145
JUŽHNOSLOVENSKI FILOLOG.   Belgrad
1913-   . Suspended 1914-20
1940-48.

K

K1
KADMONIYOT = Qadmoniot; quarterly
for the antiquities of Eretz Israel and Biblical Lands. Jerusalem
1968-   .

K2
KADMOS. Zeitschrift für vor- und
frühgriechische Epigraphik. Berlin 1962-   .

Kaibel, G.   see C168, I70.

K3
KAIROS. Zeitschrift für Religionswissenschaft und Theologie. Salz-
burg 1959-   .

Kalbfleisch, C.   see P56.

Kalen, T.   see B64.

K4
KANAANÄISCHE und ARÄMAISCHE IN-
SCHRIFTEN / H. Donner et al. 3.
Aufl. Wiesbaden 1971-76. 1st ed-
ition 1962-64.

K5
KANT-STUDIEN. Hamburg & Berlin
1897-   . Suspended 1937-41 1945-
52.

Karo, G.   see S38.

K6
KARTHAGO; revue d'archéologie africaine. Paris 1950-   .

Kase, E. H.   see P67.

Kaser, M.   see A134, R321, R327.

KATHOLIEKE UTRECHT   see S169.

Kaufmann, C. M.   see H9.

K7
KAVKAZSKO-BLIZHNEVOSTOCHNYĬ SBORNIK
= Caucasian and Near Eastern
Studies. Tiflis 1960-   . 1960
title: Vostochnyĭ Sbornik.

KAZAK SSR GYLYM AKADEMIJASYNYN
HABALARY   see I151.

K8
KAZI RAPORLARI ve BUNLARA ILGILI
ARASTIRMALAR. Istanbul 1935-   .
(Türk Tarih Kurumu Yayinlari;
ser. 5).

Keil, H.   see G79.

K9
KEILALPHABETISCHEN TEXTE aus UGARIT
/ M. Dietrich, D. Loretz & J.
Sanmarten. Kevelaer & Neukir-
chen-Vluyn. 1976-   . (Alter
Orient und Altes Testament; 24).

K10
KEILSCHRIFTLICHE BIBLIOTHEK / E.
Schrader. Berlin 1889-1900. Re-
print Amsterdam 1970.

K11
KEILSCHRIFTTEXTE aus ASSUR: HISTOR-
ISCHEN INHALTS / L. Messerschmidt
et al. Leipzig 1911-12. (Wissenschaftliche Veröffentlichungen
der Deutschen Orientgesellschaft;
16, 37). Published as part of
Ausgrabungen der Deutschen Orientgesellschaft in Assur.

K12
KEILSCHRIFTTEXTE aus ASSUR: JURIS-
TISCHEN INHALTS / E. Ebeling.
Leipzig 1927. (Wissenschaftliche
Veröffentlichen der Deutschen
Orientgesellschaft; 50). Published
as part of Ausgrabungen der Deut-
schen Orientgesellschaft in Assur.

K13
KEILSCHRIFTTEXTE aus ASSUR: RELIGIÖ-
SEN INHALTS / E. Ebeling. Leip-
zig 1915-23. (Wissenschaftliche
Veröffentlichung der Deutschen
Orientgesellschaft; 28, 34). Pub-
as part of Ausgrabungen der
Deutschen Orientgesellschaft in
Assur.

K14
KEILSCHRIFTTEXTE aus ASSUR: VER-
SCHIEDEDEN INHALTS / O. Schroeder.
Leipzig 1920. (Wissenschaftliche
Veröffentlichung der Deutschen
Orientgesellschaft; 3-5). Pub-
lished as part of Ausgrabungen
der Deutschen Orientgesellschaft
in Assur.

K15
KEILSCHRIFTTEXTE aus BOGHAZKÖI.
Berlin & Leipzig 1921-   . (Wissenschaftliche Veröffentlichungen
der Deutschen Orientgesellschaft;
30, etc). (KBo).

K16
KEILSCHRIFTURKUNDEN aus BOGHAZKÖI.
Berlin 1921-   . (KUB).

K17
KELETI SZEMLE = Revue Orientale.
Budapest 1900-32.

Keller, O. see R90.

K18
KÊMI; revue de philologie et
d'archéologie égyptiennes et coptes. Paris 1928-   .

Kenna, V. E. G. see C249.

Kenyon, F. G. see B221.

Kern, O. see I36, O47.

K19
KERYGMA und DOGMA. Göttingen
1955-   .

K20
KHERSONESSKIÏ SBORNIK; materialy
po arkheologii Khersonesa Tavricheskogo = Bulletin du Musée
d'État de Chersonèse Taurique.
Sevastopol 1926-30.

K21
KHRONIKA ARKHEOLOGII ta MISTETSVA.
Kiev 1930-31?.

K22
KHUDOZHNIK (Soiuz Zhudozhnikov
RSFSR Orgkomitet). Moscow
1958-   .

KIADVÁNYAI, SZEGEDI VÁROSI MÚZEUM
see S303.

Kieckers, E. see H14.

Kiepert, H. see F35.

Killen, J. T. see K32.

Kinkel, G. see E67.

Kirchner, J. E. see P217, I9.

Kirk, G. S. see P174.

Kirschbaum, E. see L40.

Kirsten, E. see G111.

Kitchener, H. H. see S281.

Kittel, G. see T50.

K23
KLASSISCH-PHILOLOGISCHE STUDIEN /

C. Jenson & E. Bickel. Bonn &
Leipzig 1927-   .

Klauser, T. see R22, A354.

K24
KLEARCHOS (Associazione Amici del
Museo Nazionale di Reggio Cala‾
bria). Reggio Calabria 1959-   .

KLEINE TEXTE für THEOLOGISCHE und
PHILOLOGISCHE VORLESUNGEN und
ÜBUNGEN see K29.

K25
KLEINASIATISCHE FORSCHUNGEN. Weimar
1927-30.

K26
KLEINASIATISCHE MÜNZEN / F. Imhoof-
Blumer. Vienna 1901-02. Reprint
Hildesheim 1974.

K27
KLEINASIATISCHE PERSONENNAMEN / L.
Zgusta. Prague 1964. (Česko-
slovenkà Akademie věd. Monografie
Orientálního Ústava ČSAN).

K28
KLEINE PAULY; Lexikon der Antike.
Stuttgart 1962-75.

K29
KLEINE TEXTE für VORLESUNGEN und
ÜBUNGEN. Bonn & Berlin 1902-   .
1905-11 title: Kleine Texte für
Theologische und Philologische
Vorlesungen und Übungen.

K30
KLEIO; tijdschrift voor oude talen
en antieke kultuur. Kapellen &
Louvain 1971?-   .

Kling, H. see M211.

K31
KLIO; Beiträge zur alten Geschichte.
Leipzig & Wiesbaden 1901-44
1959-   .

Klotz, A. see S36.

K32
KNOSSOS TABLETS / J. Chadwick & J.

T. Killen. 4. ed. Cambridge 1971.
1st edition 1956 by E. L. Bennett, J. Chadwick & M. Ventris.

Knudtzon, J. A. see E25.

Kock, T. see C167.

Köchly, H. A. T. G110.

K33
KÖLN; Vierteljahrsschrift für
Freunde der Stadt. Cologne
1955-   .

K34
KÖLNER JAHRBUCH für VOR- und FRÜH-
GESCHICHTE. Berlin 1955-   .

Koenen, L. see P240.

König, F. W. see H13.

Körte, G. see R263.

Kohler, J. see A625.

K35
KOINONIA (Associazione di Studi
Tardoantichi). Naples ?-   .

K36
KOKALOS (Istituto di Storia Antica
dell'Univ. di Palermo). Palermo
1955-   .

K37
KOMÁROM MEGYEI MÚZEUMOK KÖZLEMÉN-
YEI. Tata 1968-   .

KONGELIGE NORSKE SELSKABS SKRIFTER
see S96.

K38
KONSTHISTORISK TIDSKRIFT = Art Review. Stockholm 1932-   .

K39
KONTAKBLAD van de HISTORISCHE VER-
ENIGING van het LAND van MAAS en
WAAL. Nimegue ?-   .

Korablev, B. see A45.

K40
KÖRÖSI CSOMA-ARCHIVUM. Budapest
1923-43.

K41
KORPUS BOSPORSKIKH NADPISEĬ = Corpus Inscriptionum Regni Bosporani / V. V. Struve. Moscow & Leningrad 1965. (CIRB).

K42
KORRESPONDENZBLATT der DEUTSCHEN GESELLSCHAFT für ANTHROPOLOGIE, ETHNOLOGIE und URGESCHICHTE. Brunswick 1870-1920. 1870-1905 title: Correspondenzblatt.

KORRESPONDENZBLATT des GESAMTVEREINS der DEUTSCHEN GESCHICHTS- und ALTERTUMSVEREINS see B114.

KORRESPONDENZBLATT des VEREINS für SIEBENBURGISCHE LANDESKUNDE see S85.

K43
KORRESPONDENZBLATT des WESTDEUTSCHEN ZEITSCHRIFT für GESCHICHTE und KUNST. Trier 1882-1907.

Körte, G. see R263.

KÖZLEMÉNYEI, BEKES MEGYEI MÚZEUMOK see B43.

K44
KÖZLEMÉNYEK az ERDÉLYI NEMZETI MÚZEUM EREM es RÉGISÉGTÁRÁBÁL = Mitteilungen der Numismatisch-Archäologischen Abteilung des Siebenbürgischen National-Museums in Kolozsvár = Publications de la Section Numismatique et Archéologique du Musée de Transsylvanie à Kolozsavár. Cluj 1940-44.

KÖZLEMÉNYEI, ISTVÁN KIRÁLY MÚZEUM see I141.

KÖZLEMÉNYEI, KOMÁROM MEGYEI MÚZEUMOK see K37.

KÖZLEMÉNYEI, MAGYAR TUDOMÁNYOS AKADÉMIA FILOZÓFIAI es TÖRTENETTUDOMÁNYI OSZTÁLYANAK see M19.

KÖZLEMÉNYEI, MAGYAR TUDOMÁNYOS AKADÉMIA NYLEV és IRODALOMTUDOMANYI OSZTÁLYÁNAK see M20.

KÖZLEMÉNYEI, MAGYAR TUDOMÁNYOS AKADÉMIA. RÉGÉSZETI INTÉZET see M21.

KÖZLEMÉNYEI, SOMOGYI MÚZEUMOK see S114.

KÖZLEMÉNYEI, SZÉPMÚVÉSZETI MÚZEUM see B336.

KÖZLEMÉNYEI, VESZPRÉM MEGYEI MÚZEUMOK see V44.

Kraemer, C. J. see G97, E160.

K45
KRATKIE SOOBSHCHENIĬA. AKADEMIĬA NAUK SSSR. INSTITUT ARKHEOLOGII. Moscow & Leningrad 1939- . 1939-69 title: Kratkie Soobshcheniĭa o Dokladakh i Polevykh Issledovaniĭakh. 1939-60 issued by the Institut under its earlier name: Institut Istorii Material'noĭ Kul'tury, (KSIIMK, KSIA, KS).

KRATKIE SOOBSHCHENIĬA o DOKLADAKH i POLEVYKH ISSLEDOVANIĬAKH see K45.

KRATKIE SOOBSHCHENIĬA INSTITUTA ARKHEOLOGII (Moscow 1939-   .) see K45.

K46
KRATKIE SOOBSHCHENIĬA INSTITUTA ARKHEOLOGII (Akademiĭa Nauk URSR). Kiev 1952-   .

K47
KRATKIE SOOBSHCHENIĬA. INSTITUTA ETNOGRAFII (Akademiĭa Nauk SSSR). Moscow 1946-   .

KRATKIE SOOBSHCHENIĬA INSTITUTA ISTORII MATERIAL'NOĬ KUL'TURY see K45.

K48
KRATKIE SOOBSHCHENIĬA. INSTITUTA NARODOV AZII. AKADEMIĬA NAUK SSSR. Moscow 1951-   .

K49
KRATKIE SOOBSHCHENIĬA INSTITUTA. SLAVIĬANOVEDENIĬA. Moscow 1951-   .

KRATKIE SOOBSHCHENIĬA ODESSKOGO
  ARKHEOLOGICHESKOGO MUZEIĂ see
  K50.

K50
KRATKIE SOOBSHCHENIIA o POLEVYKH
  ARKHEOLOGICHESKIKH ISSLEDOVANIIAKH
  ODESSKOGO GOSUDAROTVENNOGO ARKHE-
  OLOGICHESKOGO MUZEIA. Odessa
  1961-   .

K51
KRATYLOS; kritisches Berichts- und
  Rezensionsorgan für Indogermanische und allgemeine Sprachwissenschaft. Wiesbaden 1956-   .

K52
KRETE, MYKENE, TROY / F. Matz.
  Stuttgart 1956. English edition
  1962: The Art of Crete and Early
  Greece.

K53
KRĒTIKA CHRONIKA. Heraklion
  1947-   .

K54
KRETISCHE BRONZERELEIFS / E. Kunze.
  Stuttgart 1931.

K55
KRĒTOLOGIA. Heraklion 1975-   .

Kristeller, P. O. see C94.

K56
KRITERION (Univ. de Minas Gerais.
  Faculdade de Filosofia). Belo
  Horizonte 1947/8-   .

K57
KRITIKA BURZHUAZNYKH KONTSEPTSIĬ
  VSEOBSHCHEĬ ISTORII. Kazan
  1972-   .

K58
KRITISCH-EXEGETISCHER KOMMENTAR
  über das NEUE TESTAMENT. Göttingen 1832-52. English edition
  1873-95.

K59
KRITISCHER JAHRESBERICHT über die
  FORTSCHRITTE der ROMANISCHEN
  PHILOLOGIE. Munich & Leipzig
  1890-1912.

K60
KRITISCHE VIERTELJAHRESSCHRIFT für
  GESETZGEBUNG und RECHTSWISSEN-
  SCHAFT. Munich? 1859-1944.

Kronasser, H. see V15.

Krüger, G. see G34.

Krumbacher, K. see G29.

K61
KTĒMA; civilisations de l'Orient,
  de la Grèce et de Rome antiques.
  Strasbourg 1976-   .

Kühner, R. see A687.

KUHNS ZEITSCHRIFT für VERGLEICHENDE
  SPRACHFORSCHUNG see Z72.

K62
KULTUR und NATUR in NIEDERÖSTER-
  REICH. Vienna 1976-   . Title
  of vol. 1: Neue Forschungen in
  Carnuntum.

K63
KUL'TURA i ISKUSSTVO ANTICHNOGO
  MIRA. Leningrad 3- 1962-   .
  Continues in part Kul'tura i
  Iskusstvo Antichnogo Mira i
  Vostoka.

K64
KUL'TURA i ISKUSSTVO ANTICHNOGO
  MIRA i VOSTOKA. Leningrad
  1958. Continued by Kul'tura
  i Iskusstvo Antichnogo Mira and
  Kul'tura i Iskusstvo Narodov
  Vostoka.

K65
KULTUREEL JAARBOEK voor de PROVIN-
  CIE OOST-VLAANDEREN. Gand ?-   .

K66
KULTUREN (Kulturhistoriska Före-
  ning för södra Sverize). Lund
  1935-   .

KUNGL. VITTERHETS HISTORIE- och
  ANTIKVITETSAKADEMIENS ÅRSBOK
  see A9.

Kunkel, W. see R323.

K67
KUNST in HESSEN und am MITTELRHEIN.
  Darmstadt 1961/2-   .

K68
KUNST des ORIENTS. Wiesbaden
  1950-   .

K69
KUNST der WELT in den BERLINER
  MUSEEN. Berlin 1962-   .

K70
KUNSTCHRONIK. Munich & Nuremburg
  1948-   .

K71
KUNSTGESCHICHTE in BILDERN. Bd. 1:
  Das Altertum / F. Winter. Leip-
  zig & Berlin 1898-99.

K72
KUNSTGESCHICHTLICHES JAHRBUCH der
  enna ètc. 1904-   .

KUNSTGECHICHTLICHES JAHRBUCH der
  BIBLIOTHECA HERTZIANA see R315.

KUNSTGESCHICHTLICHES JAHRBUCH
  der K. K. ZENTRAL KOMMISSION
  für ERFORSCHUNG und ERHALTUNG
  der KUNST- und HISTORISCHEN
  DENKMALE see W25.

K73
KUNSTMUSEETS AARSKRIFT. Copenhagen
  1914-   .

KUNSTPFLEGE see D28.

Kunze, E. see K54.

K74
KURTRIERISCHES JAHRBUCH. Trier
  1961-   .

Kuryłowicz, J. see I20.

K75
KURZBERICHTE aus dem PAPYRUSSAMM-
  LUNGEN (Universitäts Bibliothek,
  Giessen). Giessen 1956-   .

K76
KURZER HAND-COMMENTAR zum ALTEN
  TESTAMENT / D. K. Marti. Frei-
  burg i.B. 1897-1906.

K77
KURZGEFASSTES EXEGETISCHES HANDBUCH
  zum ALTEN TESTAMENT. Leipzig
  1838-   .

K78
KWARTALNIK HISTORII KULTURY MATER-
  IALNEJ. Warsaw 1953-   .

K79
KWARTALNIK HISTORYCZNY. Warsaw
  1887-   .

K80
KWARTALNIK KLASYCZYNY. Lvov 1927-
  34. Merged with Eos.

K81
KYPRIAKAI SPOUDAI. Nicosia
  1937-   .

K82
KYPROS, the BIBLE and HOMER / M.
  H. Ohnefalsch-Richter. Berlin
  1893.

L

L1
LABEO; rassegna di diritto romano.
  Naples 1955-   .

Lafaye, G. see I102.

Lagercrantz, O. see P46.

Lamb, W. see G99.

L2
LAMPAS; tijdschrift voor Nederlandse
  classici. Zwolle 1968-   .

Lampe, G. W. H. see P86.

Lanciani, R. A. see F36.

L3
LAND van AALST. St.-Gilles 1949- .

L4
LAND van HERLE. Heerlen ?-   .

L5
LANDESKUNDLICHE VIERTELJAHRSBLÄTTER.
  Trier 1955?- .

Lane, E. see C226.

L6
LANGUAGE (Linguistics Society of
  America). Baltimore etc. 1925- .
  --. Dissertations. 1927-   .
  --. Monographs. 1925-   .

Lansberger, B. see M62.

L7
LAOGRAPHIA. Athens 1909-   .

L8
LAPIDARIUM SEPTENTRIONALE / J. C.
  Bruce. Newcastle upon Tyne 1875.

Lara Peinado, F. see E73.

L9
LARES (Società di Etnografia Italiana). Florence 1930-   . Suspended 1943-48. Supersedes publication of same name which appeared 1912-14 in Rome.

Laroche, E. see C85, D58, H74,
  N60.

L10
LAST DAYS of the PALACE at KNOSSOS
  / M. R. Popham. Lund 1964.
  (Studies in Mediterranean Archae-
  ology; 5).

L11
LAST GENERATION of the ROMAN RE-
  PUBLIC / E. S. Gruen. Berkeley
  1974.

L12
LAST MYCENAEANS and THEIR SUCCES-
  SORS / V. R. d'A. Desborough.
  Oxford 1964.

L13
LATE ROMAN BRONZE COINAGE / P. V.
  Hill et al. London 1960. The
  articles in the book previously

appeared in Numismatic Circular,
1956-59. (LRBC).

L14
LATEINISCHES ETYMOLOGISCHES WÖRTER-
BUCH / A. Walde & J. B. Hofmann.
4. Aufl. Heidelberg 1965. (Indo-
germanische Bibliothek. II. Reihe.
Wörterbucher). 1st edition 1906.

L15
LATEINISCHE GRAMMATIK / M. Leumann,
J. B. Hofmann & A. Szantyr. Neu
Aufl. Munich 1972-79. (Handbuch
der Altertumswissenschaft; II).
Vol. 1 is a reprint of the 5th
edition 1926-28.

L16
LATER ROMAN EMPIRE 284-602 / A. H.
M. Jones. Oxford 1964.

L17
LATIN DICTIONARY founded on ANDREWS'
edition of FREUND'S Latin Dictionary / C. T. Lewis & C. Short. Oxford 1879. Appeared in many printings.

LATIN NOTES see C141.

L18
LATINA et GRAECA. Zagreb 1974?-   .

L19
LATINITAS; commentarii linguae latinae excolendae. Vatican City
1953-   .

L20
LATOMUS; revue d'études latines.
Brussels 1937-   .

Latte, K. see R324, L42.

Latyshev, V. see I86.

Lauffer, S. see P217.

L21
LAUREAE AQUINCENSES. Budapest 1938.
(Dissertationes Pannonicae; ser.
2, 10-11?).

L22
LAVAL THÉOLOGIQUE et PHILOSOPHIQUE.
Quebec City 1945-   .

LeBas, P. see V75, I61.

Lebégue, A. see I70.

LeBlant, E. F. see I43.

Leclercq, H. see D44.

Leemans, C. see P48.

Lefort, J. see A56.

L23
LEGES GRAECORUM SACRAE e TITULIS
COLLECTAE / J. von Prott & L.
Ziehen. Leipzig 1896-1906.

L24
LEGES PUBLICAE POPULI ROMANI / G.
Rotondi. Milan 1912. Reprint
Hildesheim 1966.

L25
LEIEGOUW. Kortrijk 1959-   .

L26
LEIPZIGER ÄGYPTOLOGISCHE STUDIEN.
Hamburg etc. 1935-   .

L27
LEIPZIGER HISTORISCHE ABHANDLUNGEN.
Leipzig 1906-16.

L28
LEIPZIGER STUDIEN zur CLASSISCHEN
PHILOLOGIE. Leipzig 1878-1902.

Lemerle, P. see A66.

L29
LEMOUZI; histoire, archéologie,
lettres et traditions lemousines.
Limoges etc. 1893-   .

Lenger, M. T. see C228.

L30
LENZBURGER NEUJAHRSBLÄTTER. Lenz-
burg, Switz. 19?-   .

L31
LEODIUM (Société d'Art et d'His-
toire du Diocèse de Liège).
Liège 1902-   .

L32
LEONARDO; rassegna mensile della
cultura italiana. Rome 1925-29.

Lepsius, R. see D13.

Lesky, A. see G30.

Lesquier, J. see P59.

L33
LESSICO ITTITO / R. Gusmani. Na-
ples 1968. (Introduzione allo
Studio Comparativo delle Lingue
Anatoliche; 1). Also as vol. 5
of Collano di Studi Classici.

L34
LETOPIS MATICE SRPSKE. Novi Sad &
Budapest 1824-   . Earlier ti-
tles: Serbski Lietopis & Srbski
Letopis.

L35
LETOPIS. SLOVENSKA AKADEMIJA ZNA-
NOSTI in UMETNOSTI v LJUBLJANI.
Ljubljana 1938/42-   .

Letronne, J. A. see N80.

LETTRES d'HUMANITÉ see B264.

L36
LEUCA (Istituto di Archeologia e
Storia Antica. Univ. Lecce).
Lecce 1978-   . (Collana
dell'Istituto di Archeologia e
Storia Antica; 1).

Leumann, M. see L15.

Leutsch, E. L. see C234.

L37
LEVANT (British School of Archaeology in Jerusalem). London
1969-   .

Lewald, H. see G116.

Lewis, C. T. see L17.

Lewis, D. see S75.

LEXICA, LEXICON and LEXIKON are
here interfiled.

L38
LEXIKON der ÄGYPTOLOGIE. Wiesbaden
1973?-   .

L39
LEXIKON der ALTEN WELT / C. Andersen. Zurich & Stuttgart 1965.

L40
LEXIKON der CHRISTLICHEN IKONO-
GRAPHIE / E. Kirschbaum et al.
Rome 1968-76.

L41
LEXIKON des FRÜGRIECHISCHEN EPOS /
B. Snell. Göttingen 1955-   .
(LFgrE, LFE).

L42
LEXICA GRAECA MINORA / K. Latte.
Hildesheim 1965.

L43
LEXICON ICONOGRAPHICUM MYTHOLOGIAE
CLASSICAE. Zurich & Munich
1981-   . (LIMC).

L44
LEXIKON des MITTELALTERS. Munich
& Zurich 1977-   .

L45
LEXIKON für THEOLOGIE und KIRCHE /
M. Buchberger, J. Höfer & K.
Rahner. Neue Aufl. Freiburg i.B.
1957-67. (LThK).

L46
LEXICON VINDOBONENSE / A. Nauck.
Leiningrad 1867. Reprint Hilde-
sheim 1965.

L47
LEXIS; Studien zur Sprachphiloso-
phie, Sprachgeschichte und Be-
griffsforschung. Lahr i.B.
1948-   .

LIBER ANNUUS see S167.

L48
LIBER PONTIFICALIS / L. Duchesne.
2. éd. Paris 1955-57. (Bibliothèque des Écoles Françaises
d'Athènes et de Rome, 2. sér.;
3). 1st edition 1886-92.

LIBICA see L52-L53.

L49
LIBRARY of the FATHERS. Oxford
   1838-74.

L50
LIBRARY NOTES (Friends of Duke
   University Library). Durham,
   N.C. 1936-   .

L51
LIBYA ANTIQUA. Tripoli 1964-   .
   --. Supplement. 1966-   .

L52
LIBYCA; Anthropologie, Préhistoire,
   Ethnographie. Algiers 1953-   .

L53
LIBYCA; série archéologie-épigra-
   phique. Algiers 1953-61. Superseded by Bulletin d'Archéologie
   Algerienne.

Lichtheim, M. see D12.

Liddell, H. G. see G87.

Lietzmann, H. see H17.

L54
LIMBURG. Maaseik 1919-   .

L55
LIMES u JUGOSLAVIJI. Belgrad
   1960-   .

L56
LIMESFORSCHUNGEN. Berlin 1959-   .

L57
LINCOLNSHIRE HISTORY and ARCHAE-
   OLOGY. Lincoln 1966-   .

L58
LINDISCHE TEMPELCHRONIK / C. S.
   Blinkenberg. Bonn 1915. (Kleine
   Texte für Vorlesungen und Übun-
   gen; 131).

Lindsay, W. M. see G54.

LING-: entries beginning with this
   spelling are here interfiled.

L59
LINGUA; international review of
   general linguistics. Haarlem
   1948-   .

L60
LINGUISTICS. The Hague 1963-   .

L61
LINGUISTIQUE. Paris 1965-   .

LINGUISTIQUE BALKANIQUE see B12.

L62
LINGUISTISCHE BERICHTE. Wiesbaden
   1969-   .

L63
LINGUISTICA BIBLICA. Bonn-Röttgen
   1970-   .

L64
LINGUISTIC INQUIRY. Cambridge,
   Mass. 1970-   .

L65
LINGUE dell'ITALIA ANTICA OLTRE il
   LATINO / V. Pasani. 2. ed.
   Turin 1964. 1st edition 1953.

L66
LINGUA e LITERATURA. São Paulo
   1972-   .

L67
LINGUA e STILE. Bologna 1966-   .

LINGVISTICHESKIE OCHERKI i ISSLE-
   DOVANIIA see S174.

L68
LINZER ARCHÄOLOGISCHE FORSCHUNGEN.
   Linz 1962-   .
   --. Sonderheft. 1964-   .

L69
LIPPISCHE MITTEILUNGEN aus GE-
   SCHICHTE und LANDESKUNDE. Det-
   mold 1903-   . 1903-56 title:
   Mitteilungen aus der Lippischen
   Geschichte und Landeskunde. Sus-
   pended 1940-48.

Lippold, G. see G123.

Lipsius, R. A. see A36.

L70
LIST of GREEK VERSE INSCRIPTIONS
   down to 400 B.C. / P. A. Hansen.
   Copenhagen 1975. (Opuscula
   Graecolatina; 3).

L71
LISTY FILOLOGIKÉ. Prague 1874-   .
   1874-86 title: Listy filologické
   a paedagogické. (LF).

LISTY FILOLOGICKÉ. SUPPLEMENTUM
   see E152.

LISTY FILOLOGICKÉ a PAEDAGOGICKE
   see L71.

L72
LITERARISCHES ZENTRALBLATT für
   DEUTSCHLAND. Leipzig 1850-1944.
   Title varies slightly.

LITERARY PAPYRI see S72.

LITERATUR- und KIRCHENGESCHICHTE
   des MITTELALTERS see A516.

L73
LITERATURBLATT für GERMANISCHE und
   ROMANISCHE PHILOLOGIE. Heilbronn
   1880-1944.

LITERATURGESCHICHTE see I114.

L74
LITTERIS; an international critical
   review of the humanities. Lund
   1924-30.

L75
LITURGIARUM ORIENTALIUM COLLECTIO /
   E. Renaudot & J. M. Hussey. 2.
   ed. Frankfurt 1847. 1st edition
   1716. Reprint Farnborough 1970.

L76
LITURGICAL ARTS. New York etc.
   1931-   .

LIVERPOOL ANNALS of ARCHAEOLOGY
   and ANTHROPOLOGY see A224.

L77
LIVERPOOL CLASSICAL MONTHLY.
   Liverpool 1976-   .

Livingstone, E. A. see O63.

L78
LIVRE des ROIS d'ÉGYPTE / H. Gauthier. Cairo 1907-17. (Mémoires
   publiés par les Membres de l'Institut Français d'Archéologie
   Orientale du Caire; 17-21).

Lobel, E. see P146.

L79
LOCAL SCRIPTS of ARCHAIC GREECE /
   L. H. Jeffery. Oxford 1961.

L80
LOEB CLASSICAL LIBRARY. London
   & Cambridge, Mass. 1912-   .
   (LCL).

Loesch, G. see M330.

Loewe, G. see C210.

Loewy, E. see I35.

L81
LOGOS; rivista internazionale di
   filosofia. Naples etc. 1914-   .

L82
LOIS SACRÉES de l'ASIE MINEURE / F.
   Sokolowski. Paris 1955. (École
   Française d'Athènes. Travaux et
   Mémoires; 9).

L83
LOIS SACRÉES des CITÉS GRECQUES /
   F. Sokolowski. Paris 1969.
   (École Française d'Athènes. Travaux et Mémoires des Anciens Membres Étrangers de l'École et de
   divers Savants; 18).

Lommatzsch, E. see C58.

L84
LONDON ORIENTAL SERIES. London
   1953-   .

Loretz, D. see K9.

Lorimer, H. L. see H121.

Lowe, E. A. see C152.

Lucas, A. see A192.

Luckenbill, D. D. see A200.

L85
LUDUS MAGISTRALIS (Centre de La-
    tin F. Peters). Brussels
    1965?-   .

L86
LÜNEBURGER BLÄTTER. Lüneburger,
    Ger. 1950-   .

L87
LÜNEBURGER MUSEUMSBLÄTTER, Lüne-
    burg 1904-28?.

Lugli, G. see F33.

LUNDS UNIVERSITETS ÅRSSKRIFT see
    A86.

L88
LUSTRUM; internationale Forschungs-
    berichte aus dem Bereich des
    Klassischen Altertums. Göttingen
    1956-   .

L89
LUVISCHE TEXTE in UMSCHRIFT / H.
    Otten. Berlin 1953. (Akademie
    der Wissenschaften zu Berlin.
    Institut für Orientforschung,
    Veröffentlichungen; 17).

L90
LYCHNOS; Lärdomshistoriska Samfund-
    ets Årsbok = Annual of the Swed-
    ish History of Science Society.
    Uppsala etc. 1936-   .

L91
LYDISCHES WÖRTERBUCH / R. Gusmani.
    Heidelberg 1964.

L92
LYKISCH und HITTITISCH / H. Peder-
    sen. 2. Aufl. Copenhagen 1945.
    (Kongelinge Videnskabernes Sel-
    skab. Historiskfilologiske Med-
    delelser; 30,4).

L93
LYRA GRAECA; being remains of all
    Greek lyric poetry from Eumelus
    to Timotheus, excepting Pindar

/ J. M. Edmonds. New York & London 1922-27. (Loeb Classical Library).

M

M1
MASCA JOURNAL. (Museum Applied Science Center for Archaeology. Univ. Museum). Philadelphia 1978/9- .

M2
MASCA NEWSLETTER (Applied Science Center. University Museum. Univ. Pennsylvania). Philadelphia 1965-77. Earlier title: ASCA Newsletter.

M3
MÅNADSBLAD Kongl. VITTERHETS-, HISTORIE- och ANTIQUITETS- AKADEMIENS. Stockholm 1872-1905.

M4
MAASGOUW; orgaan voor Limburgsche geschiedenis taal- en letterkunde. Maastricht 1879- . Suspended 1916-17.

Macalister, R. A. S. see C216, E161.

McClean, J. R. see C79.

McCrum, M. see S71.

MacDonald, G. see C76.

McDonald, W. A. see M163.

McGregor, M. F. see A635, S189.

Mackenzie, D. see D4, P158.

MACNE see M65.

M5
MADRIDER BEITRÄGE (Deutsches Archäologisches Institut. Abteilung Madrid). Mainz 1973- .

M6
MADRIDER FORSCHUNGEN (Deutsches Archäologisches Institut. Abteilung Madrid). Berlin 1956- .

M7
MADRIDER MITTEILUNGEN (Deutsches Archäologisches Institut. Madrider Abteilung). Heidelberg 1960- . (MM, MDAI(M), MadrMitt).

M8
MAGHREB; les documents marocains. Paris 1932- .

Magie, D. see R340.

M9
MAGISTRATES of the ROMAN REPUBLIC / T. R. S. Broughton. New York 1951-52. (MRR).
--. Supplement. 1960.

M10
MAGNA GRAECIA. Cosenza 1966- .

M11
MAGYAR ÉPITÖMÜVÉSZET. Budapest 1952- .

M12
MAGYAR KÖNYVSZEMLE. Budapest 1876- . Variant title: Magyarországi könyvészet.

M13
MAGYAR MÚZEUM. Budapest 1945-   .

MAGYAR NEMZETI MÚZEUM NÉPRAJZI OS-
ZTÁLYÁNAK ÉRTESITŐJE see N22.

MAGYAR NEMZETI MÚZEUM NÉPRAJZI TÁ-
RÁNAT ÉRTESITŐJE see N22.

MAGYAR NEMZETI MÚZEUM, SZÉPMÚVÉS-
ZETI MÚZEUM KÖZLEMÉNYEI see
B336.

MAGYARORSZÁGI KÖNYVÉSZET see M12.

M14
MAGYAR NYELV. Budapest 1905-   .

M15
MAGYAR NYELVŐR. Budapest 1872- .

M16
MAGYARORSZÁG RÉGÉSZETI TOPOGRÁFIA-
JA. Budapest 1966-   .

M17
MAGYAR TUDOMÁNY. Budapest 1890- .
1890-1955 title: Akadémiai Érte-
sítő.

M18
MAGYAR TUDOMÁNYOS AKADÉMIA ALMAN-
ACHJA. Budapest 1973-   . Title
varies slightly.

M19
MAGYAR TUDOMÁNYOS AKADÉMIA FILOZÓ-
FIAI és TORTÉNETTUDOMÁNYI. OSZ-
TÁLYÁNAK KÖZLEMÉNYEI. Budapest
1951-   . 1951-65 title: Magyar
Tudományos Akadémia Társadalmi
Törtenti Tudományok Osztályának.
Közleményei.

M20
MAGYAR TUDOMÁNYOS AKADÉMIA NYELV
és IRODALOMTUDOMANYI OSZTÁLYÁNAK
KÖZLEMÉNYEI. Budapest 1951-   .

M21
MAGYAR TUDOMÁNYOS AKADÉMIA RÉGÉS-
ZETI INTÉZETÉNEK KÖZLEMÉNYEI =
Mitteilungen des Archäologischen
Instituts der Ungarischen Akade-
mie der Wissenschaften. Buda-
pest 1970-   .

MAGYAR TUDOMÁNYOS AKADÉMIA TÁRSA-
DALMI TÖRTÉNETI TUDMÁNYOK OSZTÁL-
YÁNAK KÖZLEMÉNYEI see M19.

Mahaffy. J. P. see F19.

Mai, A. see N93.

M22
MAIA; rivista di letterature classiche. Florence etc. 1948-   .

M23
MAINFRÄNKISCHES JAHRBUCH für GE-
SCHICHTE und KUNST. Würzburg
1949-   .

M24
MAINZER ZEITSCHRIFT. Mainz
1906-   . (MZ).

MAJALLAT TĀRĪKH wa-HADĀRAT al-MAG-
HRIB see R173.

M25
MAKEDONIKA. Thessalonike 1940-   .

Malcovati, E. see O27.

MALEREIEN der KATAKOMBEN ROMS see
R330.

M26
MALEREI und ZEICHNUNG der GRIECHEN
/ E. Pfuhl. Munich 1923. Reprint
Rome 1969. (MuZ).

M27
MALEREI und ZEICHNUNG der KLASSI-
SCHEN ANTIKE / A. Rumpf. Munich
1953. (Handbuch der Archäologie;
4). Also in the series: Handbuch der Altertumwissenschaft;
6, 4.

MALTA see R88.

MÅNADSBLAD see M3.

Mangenot, E. see D61.

Manni Piraino, M. T. see I116.

M28
MANNUS; Zeitschrift für Vorgeschichte. Würzburg & Leipzig
1904-42/4.

MANNUS. SUPPLEMENT see N2.

Manteuffel, G. see P75.

M29
MANUEL d'ARCHÉOLOGIE ÉGYPTIENNE /
J. Vandier. Paris 1952- .

M30
MANUEL d'ARCHÉOLOGIE GALLO-ROMAINE
/ A. Grenier. Paris 1931- .

M31
MANUALE di ETEO GEROGLIFICO / P.
Meriggi. Rome 1966- . (Incu-
nabula Graeca; 13, etc,).

M32
MANUSCRIPTA. St. Louis, Mo.
1957- . Supersedes and reprints
the contents of two trial issues
published in 1954.

M33
MANUSCRITS GRECS de PARIS inventaire hagiographique / F. Halkin.
Brussels 1968. (Subsidia Hagiographica; 44).

M34
MARBURGER JAHRBUCH für KUNSTWISSEN-
SCHAFT. Marburg 1924- .

M35
MARBURGER WINCKELMANN-PROGRAMM.
Marburg 1947-51?

M36
MARE BALTICUM. Hamburg 1965/6- .

M37
MAREMMA. Grosseto 1924-36.

Marichal, R. see C111.

Mariné Bigorra, S. see I66.

M38
MARISIA (Muzeul Judeţean Mures).
Tîrgu Mureş 1965- . 1965-72
title: Studii şi materiale.
Suspended 1973-74.

M39
MARMATIA (Muzeul Judeţean Maramur-
es). Baia-Mare 1969- .

M40
MAROC ANTIQUE / J. Carcopino. Paris 1943. Appeared in many printings and editions.

Marshall, F. H. see B218-B223.

M41
MARSYAS; studies in the history of
art. New York 1941- .

Marti, D. K. see K76.

Marucchi, O. see R331.

MASCA JOURNAL see M1.

MASCA NEWSLETTER see M2.

Maspero, J. see P54.

Masson, O. see I45.

M42
MASTERS ABSTRACTS. Ann Arbor,
Mich. 1962- .

MATERIALE, MATERIALEN, MATERIALI,
MATERIAL'NAÏA, MATERIALS, MATERI-
ALY and MATERIAUX are here inter-
filed.

M43
MATERIALY ARCHEOLOGICZNE. Krakow
1959- .

MATERIAUX pour l'ARCHÉOLOGIE du
CAUCASE see M47.

MATERIAUX pour l'ARCHÉOLOGIE de la
RUSSIE see M49.

MATERIALE ARHEOLOGICE PRIVIND IS-
TORIA VECHE a R.P.R. see M51.

M44
MATERIALY po ARKHEOLOGII BSSR.
Minsk 1957- .

M45
MATERIALY po ARKHEOLOGII i DREVNEI
ISTORII SEVERNOI OSETII. Dzaud-
zhikau 1961- .

M46
MATERIALY po ARKHEOLOGII GRUZII i
KAVKAZA. Tiflis 1955- .

M47
MATERIALY po ARKHEOLOGII KAVKAZA
= Materiaux pour l'Archéologie
du Caucase. Moscow 1888-1916.

M48
MATERIALY z ARKHEOLOGII PIVNICHNOHO
   PRYCHORNOMOR'IA. Odessa 1959- .
   Variant title: Materialy po Ark-
   heologii Severnogo Prychornomor-
   'ĩa. (MASP).

M49
MATERIALY po ARKHEOLOGII ROSSĨI =
   Materiaux pour l'Archéologie de
   la Russie. Leningrad 1866-1918.

MATERIALY po ARKHEOLOGII SEVERNOGO
PRYCHORNOMOR'IA see M48.

M50
MATERIALS for the ASSYRIAN DICTION-
   ARY. Chicago 1952-   .

M51
MATERIALE și CERCETĂRI ARHEOLOGICE.
   Bucharest 1953-   . 1953 title:
   Materiale arheologice privind
   istoria veche a R.P.R. (MCA).

M52
MATERIALI e CONTRIBUTI per la STOR-
   IA della NARRATIVA GRECO-LATINA.
   Perugia 1976-   .

M53
MATERIALI e DISCUSSIONI per l'ANAL-
   ISI dei TESTI CLASSICI. Pisa
   1978-   .

M54
MATERIALY i DOSLIDZHENNIĨA z ARK-
   HEOLOGI i PRYKARPATTĨA i VOLYNI.
   Liev 1957?-   .

M55
MATERIALY po ETNOGRAFII GRUZII.
   Tiflis 1938-   .

M56
MATERIAUX pour l'HISTOIRE PRIMITIVE
   et NATURELLE de l'HOMME. Paris
   & Toulouse 1864-88.

M57
MATERIALY i ISSLEDOVANIĨA po ARK-

HEOLOGII LATVIĨSKOĨ. Riga
1957-   .

M58
MATERIALY i ISSLEDOVANIĨA po ARK-
   HEOLOGII SSSR = Materiaux et
   Recherches d'Archéologie de
   l'URSS. Moscow & Leningrad
   1940-   .

M59
MATERIALE de ISTORIE și MUZEOGRA-
   FIE. Bucharest 1964-   .

M60
MATERIAL'NAĨA KULTURA AZERBAĨD-
   ZHANA. Baku ?-1955.

MATERIAUX et RECHERCHES d'ARCHÉO-
LOGIE de l'URSS see M58.

M61
MATERIALY STAROŻYTNE (Panstwowe
   Muzeum Archeologiczne). Warsaw
   1956-   .

M62
MATERIALS for the SUMERIAN LEXICON
   = Materialen zum Sumerischen
   Lexikon./ B. Lansberger. Rome
   1937-   .

M63
MATERIALI per il VOCABOLARIO NEO-
   SUMERICO. Rome 1974-   .

M64
MATERIALY ZACHODNO-POMORSKIE (Mu-
   zeum Pomorza Zachodniego).
   Szczecin 1955-   .

MATICA SRPSKA see Z11.

M65
MATSNE; vestnik otdeleniĩa obshchestv nauk A.N. Grua. Tbilissi
   ?-   .

Mattha, G. see D11.

Mattingly, H. see B212, R333.

Matz, F. see F41, F72, K52.

Mc is filed as if spelled Mac.

M66
MEANDER; miesiecznik Poświęcony
Kulturze Świata Starozytnego.
Warsaw 1946-   .

MÉDAILLES CONSULAIRES see D21.

MÉDAILLES IMPÉRIALES see D23.

MEDDELANDEN, MEDDELELSER, MEDEDEE-
LINGEN, MEDEDELINGEN and MEDEDE-
LINGENBLAD are here interfiled.

MEDEDELINGEN. ACADEMIE van BELGIË.
KLASSE der LETTEREN see M76.

M67
MEDEDELINGEN van de HISTORISCHE
KRING KESTEREN en OMSTREKEN.
Kesteren ?-   .

MEDEDELINGEN. KLASSE der LETTEREN.
Koninklijke VLAAMSE ACADEMIE
van BELGIË see M76.

MEDEDE(E)LINGEN. KONINKLIJKE ...
see MEDEDE(E)LINGEN ... (the
word koninklijke is disregarded
in filing, but may have been
regarded in forming an abbreviation).

M68
MEDDELANDEN från LUNDS UNIVERSITETS
HISTORISKA MUSEUM = Mémoires du
Musée Historique de l'Université
de Lund. Lund 1918/19-   . Un-
til 1957 published as part of
the Årsberättelse Humanistiska
Vetenskapssamfundets: Lund.

M69
MEDEDEELINGEN der Koninklijke
NEDERLANDSE AKADEMIE van WETEN-
SCHAPPEN. AFDEELING LETTERKUNDE.
Amsterdam 1855-   . 1855-1919
title: Verslagen en Mededeelin-
gen.

M70
MEDEDELINGEN van het NEDERLANDSCH
HISTORISCH INSTITUT te ROME.
The Hague 1921-29 1931-   .
Spelling varies slightly.
(Meded, MNIR).

M71
MEDDELELSER fra NY CARLSBERG GLYP-
TOTEK. Copenhagen 1944-   .

M72
MEDDELANDEN från ÖSTERGÖTLANDS
FORNMINNES- och MUSEIFÖRENING.
Linköping 1903?-   .

M73
MEDDELELSER fra THORVALDSENS MU-
SEUM. Copenhagen 1929-   .
Publication dates erratic.

M74
MEDEDELINGENBLAD. VERENIGING van
VRIEDEN van het ALLARD PIERSON
MUSEUM. Amsterdam ?-   .

M75
MEDEDEELINGEN en VERHANDELINGEN.
VOORAZIATISCH-EGYPTISCH GENOOTS-
CHAP "EX ORIENT LUX". Leiden
1934-   .

M76
MEDEDEELINGEN van de Koninklijke
VLAAMSE ACADEMIE van BELGIË.
KLASSE der LETTEREN. Antwerp
1939-   . 1939-41 title: Ver-
slagen en mededeelingen.

M77
MEDEDELINGEN van WEGE het SPINOZA-
HUIS. Leiden 1934-   . Title
varies slightly.

MEDELSHAVSMUSEET BULLETIN see
B324.

M78
MEDIAEVAL and RENAISSANCE STUDIES.
London 1943-   .

M79
MEDIAEVAL STUDIES (Pontifical In-
stitute of Mediaeval Studies,
Toronto). New York etc. 1939- .

M80
MEDIEVALIA et HUMANISTICA. Boul-
der, Colo. 1943-   .

M81
MEDIUM AEVUM. Oxford 1932-   .

M82
MEDIZIN-HISTORISCHES JOURNAL. Hildesheim 1966-   .

MEDLEMSBLAD. NORDISK NUMISMATISK
UNIONS see N67.

M83
MEGALE HELLENIKE ENKYKLOPAIDEIA.
Athens 1926-   .

M84
MEGIDDO TOMBS / P. L. O. Guy. Chicago 1938. (Univ. of Chicago Oriental Institute Publications; 33).

Meiggs, R. see S75.

Meillet, A. see D53.

MEIN HEIMATLAND see B8.

Meineke, A. see F58.

Meissner, B. see A133, A624, B30, R23.

M85
MEISTERWERKE GRIECHISCHER KUNST /
K. Schefold. Basel 1960.

M86
MEISTERWERKE der GRIECHISCHEN PLASTIK / A. Furtwängler. Leipzig
1893. English edition New York
1895.

MÉLANGES: see special section about
Festschriften in the introduction.

M87
MÉLANGES d'ARCHÉOLOGIE et d'HISTOIRE
(École Française de Rome). Paris
1881-1970. (MEFR, MelRome).
--. Antiquite. 83- 1971-   .
(MEFRA).
--. Moyen Age; Temps Modern.
83- 1973-   .

MÉLANGES d'ARCHÉOLOGIE et d'HISTOIRE. SUPPLÉMENT see C162.

M88
MÉLANGES de la CASA de VELÁZQUEZ.
Paris 1965-   .

MÉLANGES de l'ÉCOLE FRANÇAISE de
ROME see M87.

MÉLANGES de la FACULTÉ ORIENTALE,
UNIVERSITÉ SAINT JOSEPH, BEIRUT
see M91.

M89
MÉLANGES GRÉCO-ROMAINS; tiré du
Bulletin Historico-philologique
de l'Académie Imperiale des Sciences de St. Petersbourg. Leningrad 1849/55-94?

MÉLANGES de l'INSTITUT des SCIENCES HISTORIQUE à ZADAR see
Z10.

MÉLANGES ISLAMOLOGIQUES see A277.

MÉLANGES de PHILOSOPHIE et de
MATHÉMATIQUE see M109.

M90
MÉLANGES de SCIENCES RELIGIEUSES.
Lille 1944-   . (MSR).

MÉLANGES. UNIVERSITÉ de BEYROUTH.
FACULTÉ ORIENTALE see M91.

M91
MÉLANGES de l'UNIVERSITÉ SAINT-
JOSEPH. Beirut 1906-   . 1906-
21 title: Mélanges de la Faculté
Orientale, Université Saint
Joseph. (MUSJ).

M92
MELTO; recherches orientales.
Kaslik 1965-   .

M93
MEMMINGER GESCHICHTSBLÄTTER.
Memminger 1912-40 1951-   .

M94
MEMNON; Zeitschrift für die Kunst-
und Kultur-Geschichte des alten
Orients. Leipzig 1907-15.

MÉMOIRES, MEMOIRS, MEMORIA, MEMOR-
IAS, MEMORIE and MEMORIILE are
here interfiled.

M95
MEMOIRES de l'ACADÉMIE Royale de

BELGIQUE = Verhandelingen Konin-
klijke Académie van België.
Brussels 1777-1904. Title varies
slightly.
--. Classe des Lettres et des
Sciences Morales et Politique.
  --. Collection in 4°. 1906- .
  --. Collection in 8°. 1906- .
--. Classes des Beaux Arts.
  --. Collection in 4°. 1919- .
  --. Collection in 8°. 1920- .

MÉMOIRES. ACADÉMIE de DIJON see
M99.

M96
MEMORIAS de la Real ACADEMIA de la
HISTORIA. Madrid 1796-1910.

MÉMOIRES. ACADÉMIE IMPERIALE ...
see MÉMOIRES. ACADÉMIE ... (the
word imperiale is disregarded
in filing, but may have been
regarded in forming an abbreviation).

M97
MÉMOIRES de l'ACADÉMIE des INSCRIP-
TIONS et BELLES LETTRES. (Insti-
tut de France). Paris 1803- .
Appeared under earlier title
Histoire et Mémoires and under
earlier names of the institute:
Institut National, Institut Ro-
yal, and the Classe d'Histoire
et de Litterature Ancienne.
Other additional minor changes.
(MemAcInscr).

MÉMOIRES. ACADÉMIE des INSCRIPTIONS
et BELLES LETTRES see also M118.

M98
MÉMOIRES de l'ACADÉMIE de METZ.
Metz 1819- . 1819-27 title:
Seance Générale. Société des
Lettres, Sciences et Arts (et
d'Agriculture) de Metz. Name of
Academy varies slightly.

MÉMOIRES. ACADÉMIE NATIONALE ...
see MÉMOIRES. ACADÉMIE ... (the
word nationale is disregarded in
filing, but may have been regarded in forming an abbreviation).

MEMORIILE. ACADEMIA ROMÂNĂ. SECTI-
UNEA ISTORICĂ see M134.

MÉMOIRES. ACADÉMIE ROYALE ... see
MÉMOIRES. ACADÉMIE ... (the
word royale is disregarded in
filing, but may have been regarded in forming an abbreviation).

M99
MÉMOIRES de l'ACADÉMIE des SCI-
ENCES, ARTS et BELLES-LETTRES
de DIJON. Dijon 1769-74 1782- .
Title varies: Nouveaux Mémoires
Séance Publique, Compte Rendu.
Academy's name also varies.

M100
MÉMOIRES de l'ACADÉMIE des SCI-
ENCES, BELLES-LETTRES et ARTS
d'ANGERS. Angers 1831- .
Earlier name of the Academy:
Société (Nationale/Imperiale)
d'Agriculture, Sciences et Arts.

MÉMOIRES. ACADÉMIE des SCIENCES,
BELLES-LETTRES et ARTS de BE-
SANÇON see P212.

M101
MÉMOIRES de l'ACADÉMIE des SCI-
ENCES, BELLES-LETTRES et ARTS
de SAVOIE. Chambéry 1825-72
1875- . Name of Academy
varies; until 1847: Société
(royale) Académique de Savoie.

M102
MÉMOIRES de l'ACADÉMIE des SCI-
ENCES, INSCRIPTIONS et BELLES-
LETTRES de TOULOUSE. Toulouse
1782- . 1807-41 title: Histoire et Mémoires. Name of Academy varies slightly.

MÉMOIRES. ACADÉMIE Royale des SCI-
ENCES, des LETTRES et des BEAUX
ARTS de BELGIQUE see M95.

M103
MÉMOIRES de l'ACADÉMIE Impériale
des SCIENCES de ST-PETERSBOURG.
Leningrad 1830/2-1859.

M104
MÉMOIRES de l'ACADÉMIE de STANIS-
LAS. Nancy 1754-59 1802-   .
1754-59 title: Mémoires. Société
Royale des Sciences et Belles-
Lettres de Nancy.

M105
MÉMOIRES de l'ACADÉMIE des VAU-
CLUSE. Vaison etc. 1882-   .

M106
MEMORIE delle ACCADEMIA di ARCHE-
OLOGIA, LETTERE e BELLE ARTI di
NAPOLI. Naples 1911-42 1951-   .

MEMORIE. ACCADEMIA d'ITALIA   see
M107.

M107
MEMORIE. ACCADEMIA nazionale dei
LINCEI. Rome 1870-   . 1879-
1939 as Classe di scienze morali,
storiche e filologiche. Academy's
name 1939-43: Accademia d'Italia.
Published as part of the Academy's
continuing Atti series.

MEMORIE. ACCADEMIA. NAPOLI   see
M106.

MEMORIE. ACCADEMIA PATAVINA di
SCIENZE, LETTERE ed ARTI. CLASSE
di SCIENZE MORALI, LETTERE ed
ARTI   see A657.

M108
MEMORIE dell'ACCADEMIA delle SCI-
ENZE dell'ISTITUTO di BOLOGNA.
Bologna 1850-1907.
--. Classe di Scienze Morali.
1906-   . Published in two
sections: Sezione di Scienze Stor-
ico-Filologiche and Sezione di
Scienze Giuridiche.

MEMORIE delle R. ACCADEMIA di
SCIENZE, LETTERE ed ARTE in MO-
DENA   see A658.

MEMORIE. ACCADEMIA di SCIENZE
LETTERE ed ARTI degli ZELANTI
see M133.

MEMORIE. ACCADEMIA di SCIENZE,
LETTERE e BELLE ARTI ACIREALE
see M133.

M109
MEMORIE dell'ACCADEMIA delle SCI-
ENZE di TORINO. Turin 1759-
1935? 1759 title: Miscellanea
Philosophico-mathematica. 1760-
73 title: Mélanges de Philoso-
phie et de Mathématique.
--. Classe di Scienze Morali,
Storiche e Filologiche. 1936-   .

MEMORIE. ACIREALE   see M133.

M110
MEMOIRS of the AMERICAN ACADEMY
in ROME. Bergamo etc. 1917-   .
(MAAR, MemAmAc).

M111
MEMOIRS of the AMERICAN PHILOSO-
PHICAL SOCIETY. Philadelphia
1935-   .

M112
MEMORIA ANTIQUITATIS. Piatra-
Neamt, Romania 1969-   .
(MemAntiq).

MÉMOIRES ARCHÉOLOGIQUE de PERSE
see M130.

M113
MEMOIRS. ARCHAEOLOGICAL SURVEY of
EGYPT. (Egypt Exploration Society). London 1893-   . Vols.
1-4 issued without title.

MÉMOIRES. BELGIQUE   see M95.

M114
MÉMOIRES de la BIBLIOTHÈQUE de la
SORBONNE. Paris 1980-   .

MEMORIE. BOLOGNA   see M108.

MÉMOIRES. BRUXELLES   see M95.

M115
MÉMOIRES du CENTRE de RECHERCHES
ANTHROPOLOGIQUE, PRÉHISTORIQUE,
et ETHNOLOGIQUE. Algiers
1963-   .

MÉMOIRES du CERCLE ROYALE HISTO-
RIQUE et ARCHÉOLOGIQUE de COUR-
TRAI   see H20.

MÉMOIRES. CLASSE des BEAUX-ARTS.
   ACADÉMIE de BELGIQUE   see M95.

MÉMOIRES. CLASSE des LETTRES et des
   SCIENCES MORALES et POLITIQUES.
   ACADÉMIE de BELGIQUE   see M95.

MEMORIE. CLASSE di LETTERE, SCIENZE,
   MORALI e STORICHE. ISTITUTO LOM-
   BARDO di SCIENZE e LETTERE   see
   M126.

MEMORIE. CLASSE di SCIENZE MORALI.
   ACCADEMIA delle SCIENZE dell'ISTI-
   TUTO di BOLOGNA   see M108.

MEMORIE. CLASSE di SCIENZE MORALI,
   LETTERE ed ARTI. ACCADEMIA PATA-
   VINA di SCIENZE, LETTERE ed ARTI
   see A657.

MEMORIE. CLASSE di SCIENZE, MORALI,
   STORICHE e FILOLOGICHE. ACCADEMIA
   delle SCIENZE di TORINO   see
   M109.

MÉMOIRES du COMITÉ des ORIENTALISTES
   (Akademiîa Nauk USSR)   see Z3.

M116
MÉMOIRES de la COMMISSION des ANTI-
   QUITÉS du DÉPARTEMENT de la CÔTE
   d'OR.   Dijon 1832-35 1838-   .

M117
MÉMOIRES de la DÉLÉGATION ARCHÉO-
   LOGIQUE FRANÇAISE de AFGHANISTAN.
   Paris 1928-   .

MÉMOIRES de la DÉLÉGATION ARCHÉO-
   LOGIQUE en IRAN   see M130.

MÉMOIRES de la DÉLÉGATION en PERSE
   see M130.

M118
MÉMOIRES présentés par DIVERS
   SAVANTS à l'ACADÉMIE des INSCRIP-
   TIONS et BELLES-LETTRES de l'IN-
   STITUT de FRANCE.   Paris
   --. I. Série. Sujets d'Érudition.
   1844-   .
   --. II. Série. Antiquités de la
   France.   1843-83.

M119
MÉMOIRES et DOCUMENTS publiés par
   l'ACADÉMIE CHABLAISIENNE.   Tho-
   non-les-Bains 1886-   .

M120
MÉMOIRES et DOCUMENTS publiés par
   l'ACADÉMIE du FAUCIGNY.   Bonne-
   ville ?-   .

M121
MEMOIRS. EGYPT EXPLORATION SOCIETY.
   London 1885-   .

M122
MÉMOIRES. FÉDÉRATION des SOCIÉTÉS
   d'HISTOIRE et d'ARCHÉOLOGIE de
   l'AISNE.   Laon etc. 1953/4-   .

M123
MEMORIE dell'INSTITUTO di CORRIS-
   PONDENZA ARCHEOLOGICA.   Rome
   1832-65.

M124
MÉMOIRES de l'INSTITUT d'ÉGYPTE.
   Cairo 1862-1916 1918-   . Ear-
   lier name of the Institute:
   Institut Égyptien.

MÉMOIRES de l'INSTITUT (r.) de
   FRANCE. ACADÉMIE des INSCRIP-
   TIONS et BELLES-LETTRES   see
   M97.

M125
MÉMOIRES de l'INSTITUT FRANÇAIS
   d'ARCHÉOLOGIE ORIENTALE.   Cairo
   1902-   . (MIFAO).

MEMORIE. ISTITUTO di BOLOGNA   see
   M108.

M126
MEMORIE dell'ISTITUTO LOMBARDO di
   SCIENZE e LETTERE, SCIENZE, MOR-
   ALI e STORICHE.   Milan 1843-1962.
   --. Classe di Lettere, Scienze,
   Morali e Storiche.   1963-   .

M127
MEMORIE. ISTITUTO STORICO ARCHEOLO-
   GICO (F.E.R.T.) e della R. DEPU-
   TAZIONE di STORIA PATRIA per
   RODI.   Rhodes 1933-38.

M128
MEMORIAS de la JUNTA SUPERIOR de
  EXCAVACIONES y ANTIQUEDADES.
  Madrid 1915-33?

MEMORIE. LOMBARDO see M126.

M129
MÉMOIRES publiés par les MEMBRES
  de la MISSION ARCHÉOLOGIQUE
  FRANÇAISE au CAIRE. Cairo
  1889-1937?

MEMORIE. MILANO see M126.

MÉMOIRES de la MISSION ARCHÉOLO-
  GIQUE FRANÇAISE au CAIRE see
  M129.

M130
MÉMOIRES de la MISSION ARCHÉOLO-
  GIQUE en IRAN. Paris 1900-   .
  Also under earlier and variant
  names: Délégation en Perse, Délé-
  gation Archéologique en Iran,
  Mission Archéologique de Susiane,
  Mission Archéologique de Perse.
  (MDP).

MÉMOIRES de la MISSION ARCHÉOLO-
  GIQUE de SUSIANE see M130.

M131
MEMORIAS de los MUSEOS ARQUEOLÓGI-
  COS PROVINCIALES. Madrid 1940- .

MÉMOIRES du MUSÉE HISTORIQUE de
  l'UNIVERSITÉ de LUND see M68.

MEMORIE. NAPOLI see M106.

MEMORIE. PADOVA see A657.

MEMORIE. PONTIFICIA ACCADEMIA ROMANA
  di ARCHEOLOGIA see A668.

M132
MÉMOIRES et PUBLICATIONS de la SO-
  CIÉTÉ des SCIENCES, des ARTS et
  des LETTRES du HEIMAT. Mons
  1839-   .

MEMORIAS. REAL ACADEMIA ... see
  MEMORIAS. ACADEMIA ... (the word
  real is disregarded in filing,
  but may have been regarded in
  forming an abbreviation).

M133
MEMORIE e RENDICONTI. ACCADEMIA di
  SCIENZE, LETTERE e BELLE ARTI
  ACIREALE. CLASSE di LETTERE.
  Acireale 1889-   . Title varies:
  1889-96: Atti e Rendiconti (1893-
  96: Classe Lettere e Arte); 1896-
  1918: Rendiconti e Memorie. Classe di Lettere; 1919-33: Memorie.
  Classe di Lettere. Also issued
  under the Accademy's earlier
  name: Accademia di Scienze, Lettere ed Arti degli Zelanti.

M134
MEMORIILE SECTIUNII ISTORICE, ACA-
  DEMIA ROMANA = Mémoires de la
  Section Historique de l'Académie
  Roumaine. Bucharest 3. ser.
  1922/3-   . Series 1 & 2 were
  published as part of the Academy's
  Analele.

M135
MÉMOIRES de la SOCIÉTÉ ACADÉMIQUE
  d'AGRICULTURE des SCIENCES, ARTS
  et BELLES-LETTRES du DÉPARTEMENT
  de l'AUBE. Troyes 1822-   .
  Society's name 1818-29: Société
  d'Agriculture, des Sciences, Arts
  et Belles-Lettres du Département
  de l'Aube.

M136
MÉMOIRES de la SOCIÉTÉ d'AGRICUL-
  TURE, COMMERCE, SCIENCES et ARTS
  du DÉPARTEMENT de la MARNE.
  Châlon-sur-Marne 1855-   .

M137
MÉMOIRES de la SOCIÉTÉ d'AGRICUL-
  TURE, LETTRES, SCIENCES et ARTS
  du DÉPARTEMENT de HAUTE-SAÔNE.
  Vesoul 1806-12 1824 1869-   .
  1869-1900 title: Bulletin. Name
  of society varies slightly.

MÉMOIRES de la SOCIÉTÉ d'AGRICUL-
  TURE, des SCIENCES, ARTS et
  BELLES-LETTRES du DÉPARTEMENT
  de l'AUBE see M135.

M138
MÉMOIRES de la SOCIÉTÉ nationale
  des ANTIQUAIRES de FRANCE. Paris
  1817-   . Society's name varies

slightly. (MAF, MSAF, MAntFr, MémSocAF).

M139
MÉMOIRES de la SOCIÉTÉ des ANTI-
QUAIRES de la PICARDIE. Amiens
--. Series in 4°. 1845-   .
--. Series in 8°. 1839-1920
1925-   .

M140
MÉMOIRES de la SOCIÉTÉ d'ARCHÉOLO-
GIE de BEAUNE. Beaune 1874-   .

MÉMOIRES. SOCIÉTÉ ARCHÉOLOGIQUE de
BORDEAUX see B366.

MÉMOIRES de la SOCIÉTÉ ARCHÉOLO-
GIQUE du DÉPARTEMENT d'ILLE-et-
VILAINE see B369.

M141
MÉMOIRES de la SOCIÉTÉ ARCHÉOLO-
GIQUE et HISTORIQUE de la CHAREN-
TE. Angoulême 1845-52 1856-   .

M142
MÉMOIRES de la SOCIÉTÉ ARCHÉOLO-
GIQUE du MIDI de la FRANCE.
Toulouse 1832/3-   .

M143
MÉMOIRES de la SOCIÉTÉ ARCHÉOLO-
GIQUE de TOURAINE. Tours
--. Série in 4°. 1869-1914.
--. Série in 8°. 1842-1928.

M144
MÉMOIRES de la SOCIÉTÉ ÉDUENNE.
Autun 1844-45 1872-   .

M145
MÉMOIRES de la SOCIÉTÉ d'ÉMULATION
du DOUBS. Besançon 1841-   .
Society's name changes 1841-54:
Société Libre d'Émulation du
Doubs; 1855-84: Société d'Émula-
tion du Département du Doubs.

MÉMOIRES. SOCIÉTÉ d'ÉTUDES SCIENTI-
FIQUES et ARCHÉOLOGIQUES de DRA-
GUIGNAN see B400.

M146
MÉMOIRES de la SOCIÉTÉ d'HISTOIRE
et d'ARCHÉOLOGIE de CHÂLON-sur-
SAÔNE. Châlon-sur-Saône 1844-   .

M147
MÉMOIRES de la SOCIÉTÉ HISTORIQUE
et ARCHÉOLOGIQUE de LANGRES.
Langres 1847-   . Suspended
1937-56.

MÉMOIRES. SOCIÉTÉ HISTORIQUES et
ARCHÉOLOGIQUES de PARIS et d'ILE-
de-FRANCE see P81.

MÉMOIRES. SOCIÉTÉ IMPÉRIALE ...
see MÉMOIRES. SOCIÉTÉ ... (the
word impériale is disregarded
in filing, but may have been
regarded in forming an abbreviation).

M148
MÉMOIRES de la SOCIÉTÉ des LETTRES
des SCIENCES des ARTS de l'AGRI-
CULTURE et de l'INDUSTRIE de
SAINT-DIZIER. Saint Dizier
1880-   .

MÉMOIRES de la SOCIÉTÉ LIBRE d'ÉM-
ULATION du DOUBS see M145.

M149
MÉMOIRES de la SOCIÉTÉ de LINGUIS-
TIQUE de PARIS. Paris 1868-1935.
(MSL).

MÉMOIRES. SOCIÉTÉ NATIONALE ...
see MÉMOIRES. SOCIÉTÉ ... (the
word nationale is disregarded in
filing, but may have been regarded in forming an abbreviation).

M150
MÉMOIRES de la SOCIÉTÉ PRÉHISTO-
RIQUE FRANÇAISE. Paris 1911-19.

MÉMOIRES. SOCIÉTÉ ROYALE ... see
MÉMOIRES. SOCIÉTÉ ... (the word
royale is disregarded in filing,
but may have been regarded in
forming an abbreviation).

MÉMOIRES. SOCIÉTÉ Royale des SCI-
ENCES et BELLES-LETTRES de
NANCY see M104.

M151
MÉMOIRES de la SOCIÉTÉ des SCIENCES
NATURELLES et ARCHÉOLOGIQUES de
la CREUSE. Guéret 1838/47-   .

MÉMOIRES de la SOCIÉTÉ des SCIENCES NATURELLES (et HISTORIQUES) des LETTRES et des BEAUX-ARTS de CANNES de l'ARONDISSEMENT de GRASSE see A321.

MEMORIE STORICHE CIVIDALESI see M152.

M152
MEMORIE STORICHE FOROGIULIESI. Friuli etc. 1905-   . Title of vols. 1-2: Memorie Storiche Cividalesi.

MEMORIE. TORINO see M109.

MEMORIE. VERONA see A656.

Menédez Pidal, R. see H92.

Meriggi, P. see H75, M31.

Meritt, B. D. see A634-A635.

Merkelbach, R. see I34.

Merlin, A. see I83.

Merton, W. see D25.

M153
MESAIONIKE BIBLIOTHEKE = Bibliotheca Graeca Medii Aevi / K. N. Sathas. Venice 1872. Reprint 1972.

M154
MESOPOTAMIA. Turin 1966-   .

M155
MESOPOTAMIA; Copenhagen studies in Assyriology. Copenhagen 1972- .

MESSAGER de l'EXARCHAT du PATRIARCHE RUSSE en EUROPE OCCIDENTALE see V41.

MESSAGER des FIDÈLES see R118.

Messerschmidt, L. see C215, K11.

M156
METROLOGICORUM SCRIPTORUM RELIQUIAE / F. Hultsch. Leipzig 1864-66. (Bibliotheca Scriptorum Graecorum et Romanorum Teubneriana). Reprint Stuttgart 1971.

METROPOLITAN MUSEUM of ART. EGYPTIAN EXPEDITION PUBLICATIONS see P243.

M157
METROPOLITAN MUSEUM JOURNAL. New York 1968-   .

M158
METROPOLITAN MUSEUM STUDIES. New York 1928-36.

Meyer, E. see G27.

Meyer, G. R. see A129.

Meyer, H. see O26.

Meyer, P. M. see G117, G126, J144.

Meyer-Lübke, W. see R345.

Micali, G. see M264.

Michalowski, K. see T15.

Michel, C. see R43.

M159
[MICHIGAN PAPYRI] / C. C. Edgar et al. Ann Arbor, Toronto etc. 1931-   . Volumes to date have appeared in several series: Univ. of Michigan Studies, Humanistic Series; American Philological Association Monographs; American Studies in Papyrology; and Studia Amstelodamensia ad Epigraphicam. (PMich).

MICHIGAN PAPYRI. PAPYRI from TEBTUNIS see P71.

MICHIGAN PAPYRI. ZENON PAPYRI see Z77.

MICROFORM ABSTRACTS see D75.

Migne, J. P. see P89-P90.

Mikhaĭlov, G. I. see I54.

Miklosich, F. see A55.

M160
MIKRASIATIKA CHRONIKA. Athens
  1938-   . Suspended 1941-47.

Miller, C. W. E. see S299.

Miller, K. see I147.

Milne, H. J. M. see B222.

M161
MIND; a quarterly review of psychology and philosophy. London
  1876-   .

M162
MINNESOTA MESSENIA EXPEDITION / W.
  A. McDonald & G. R. Rapp. Min-
  neapolis 1972.

M163
MINNESOTA REVIEW. Minneapolis
  1960-   .

M164
MINOAN and MYCENAEAN ART / R. Higgins. 2. ed. New York & London
  1981. 1st edition 1967.

M165
MINOAN-MYCENAEAN RELIGION and its
  SURVIVAL in GREEK RELIGION / M.
  P. Nilsson. 2. ed. Lund 1950.
  (Skrifter utgivna av Kungl. Hu-
  manistiska Vetenskapssamfundet i
  Lund; 9). 1st edition 1927.
  (MMR).

M166
MINOS; revista di filología egea.
  Salamanca 1951-   .
  --. Supplement 1956-   .

M167
MINUTES of the MEETINGS. MYCENAEAN
  SEMINAR. (Institute of Classical
  Studies. Univ. London). London
  1958?-   . Published as part of
  the Bulletin of the Institute
  1966-   .

MISCELANEA and MISCELLANEA are
  here interfiled.

MISCELLANEA d'ARTE see R270.

M168
MISCELLANEA BARCINONENSIA. Barcelona 1962-   .

M169
MISCELLANEA CLASSICO-MEDIEVALE.
  (Univ. Lecce). Lecce ?-   .

M170
MISCELÁNEA COMILLAS. Comillas,
  Spain 1943-   .

M171
MISCELLANEA FRANCESCANA; rivista di
  scienze, lettere ed arti. Rome
  1886-   . Title varies slightly.

M172
MISCELLANEA GRAECA. Ghent 1975-   .

M173
MISCELLANEA GRECA e ROMANA. Rome
  1965. (Studi pubblicati dell'Istituto Italiana per la Storia
  Antica; 16, etc.).

M174
MISCELLANEA NUMISMATICA. Naples
  1920-22.

MISCELLANEA PHILOSOPHICO-MATHEMA-
  TICA see M109.

M175
MISCELLANEA STORICA della VALDELSA.
  Castelfiorentino 1893-   .

M176
MISCELLANEA di STUDI di LETTERATURA
  CRISTIANA ANTICA. Cantania
  1947-   .

M177
MISCELLANEA WILBOURIANA (Brooklyn
  Musuem). Brooklyn 1972-   .

M178
MISSION ARCHÉOLOGIQUE de MARI / A.
  Parrot. Paris 1956-   . (Bibliothèque Archéologique et Historique; 65).

M179
MISSION de RAS SHAMRA / C. F. A.
  Schaeffer. Paris 1936-   .
  (Bibliothèque Archéologique et
  Historique; 21, etc.).

M180
MISSIONE ARCHEOLOGICA ITALIANA in
   SIRIA. Rome 1964-   .

Mitford, T. B.   see I71.

M181
MITROPOLIA OLTENIEI. Craiova ?- .

MITTEILUNGEN, MITTEILUNGSBLATT and
   MITTHEILUNGEN are here interfiled.

M182
MITTEILUNGEN der ALTERTUMS KOMMIS-
   SION für WESTFALEN. Münster
   1899-1922.

M183
MITTEILUNGEN. ALTORIENTALISCHE GE-
   SELLSCHAFT. Leipzig 1925-   .
   (MAOG).

M184
MITTEILUNGEN der ANTHROPOLOGISCHEN
   GESELLSCHAFT in WIEN. Vienna
   1870-   . Also issued under the
   earlier name of the society:
   Österreichische Gesellschaft für
   Anthropologie, Ethnologie, und
   Prähistorie. Suspended 1943-46.
   (MAGW, MAG).

M185
MITTEILUNGEN der ANTIQUARISCHEN GE-
   SELLSCHAFT in ZURICH. Zurich
   1837/41-   .

MITTEILUNGEN des ARCHÄOLOGISCHEN
   INSTITUTS der UNGARISCHEN AKADE-
   MIE der WISSENSCHAFTEN see M21.

M186
MITTEILUNGEN der BAYERISCHEN NUMIS-
   MATISCHEN GESELLSCHAFT. Munich
   1882-1937.

M187
MITTEILUNGEN der BERLINER GESELL-
   SCHAFT für ANTHROPOLOGIE, ETHNO-
   LOGIE und URGESCHICHTE. Berlin
   1965-   .

M188
MITTEILUNGEN. BERNER KUNSTMUSEUM.
   Bern 1955-   .

M189
MITTEILUNGEN des BUNDESDENKMALAM-
   TES. Vienna 1856-1924. 1856-1902
   title: Mitteilungen der K. K.
   Central-Commission (zur/für) Erforschung und Erhaltung der
   Baudenkmale. 1902-10 title: Mitteilungen der K. K. Central-Commission (zur/für) Erforschung
   und Erhaltung der Kunst- und Historischen Denkmale. 1911-17 title: Mitteilungen für Denkmalpflege. 1919 title: Mitteilungen
   des Staatsdenkmalamtes.

MITTEILUNGEN der K. K. CENTRAL-COM-
   MISION (zur/für) ERFORSCHUNG und
   ERHALTUNG der (BAUDENKMALE /
   KUNST- und HISTORISCHEN DENK-
   MALE) see M189.

M190
MITTEILUNGEN des DEUTSCHEN ARCHÄ-
   OLOGISCHEN INSTITUTS. Munich &
   Berlin 1948-53. (MdI, MDAI).

MITTEILUNGEN des DEUTSCHEN ARCHÄ-
   OLOGISCHEN INSTITUTS. ABTEILUNG.
   BAGHDAD see B9.

M191
MITTEILUNGEN der DEUTSCHEN ARCHÄ-
   OLOGISCHEN INSTITUTS. ABTEILUNG
   KAIRO. Wiesbaden etc. 1930-   .
   Some vols. published under vari-
   ant name of the institute:
   Deutsches Institut für Ägyptische
   Altertumskunde in Kairo. (MDAI(K)).

M192
MITTEILUNGEN des DEUTSCHEN ARCHÄ-
   OLOGISCHEN INSTITUTS. ATHENISCHE
   ABTEILUNG. Berlin etc. 1876- .
   Name of Institute varies slight-
   ly. Vol. 59 for 1944 issued in
   1948 (AM, AthMitt, MDAI(A)).
   --. Beiheft. 1971-   .

MITTEILUNGEN des DEUTSCHEN ARCHÄ-
   OLOGISCHEN INSTITUTS. MADRIDER
   ABTEILUNG. see M7.

M193
MITTEILUNGEN des DEUTSCHEN ARCHÄ-
   OLOGISCHEN INSTITUTS. RÖMISCHE
   ABTEILUNG = Bulletino dell'Isti-

tuto Archeologico Germanico,
Sezione Romana. Mainz etc.
1886-   . (RM, RömMitt,MDAI(R)).
--. Ergänzungsheft. 1931-   .

MITTEILUNGEN, DEUTSCHES INSTITUT
    für ÄGYPTISCHE ALTERTUMSKUNDE in
    KAIRO see M191.

M194
MITTEILUNGEN der DEUTSCHEN ORIENT
    GESELLSCHAFT zu BERLIN. Berlin
    1898-   .

M195
MITTEILUNGEN aus der FREIBURGER
    PAPYRUSSAMMLUNG / W. Aly et al.
    Heidelberg 1914-27. (Sitzungsber-
    ichte der Heidelberger Akademie
    der Wissenschaften; 1914, 2 and
    1916, 10. Abhandlungen der Heidel-
    berger Akademie der Wissenschaf-
    ten; 1927, 7). (PFreib).

MITTEILUNGEN der GESELLSCHAFT für
    ERHALTUNG der GESCHICHTLICHEN
    DENKMÄLER im ELSASS see B392.

M196
MITTEILUNGEN der GESELLSCHAFT für
    KIELER STADTGESCHICHTE. Kiel
    1877-   .

M197
MITTEILUNGEN der GESELLSCHAFT für
    SALZBURGER LANDESKUNDE. Salz-
    burg 1860-   .

M198
MITTEILUNGSBLATT. GESELLSCHAFT für
    VOR- und FRÜHGESCHICHTE. Bonn
    1970-   .

M199
MITTEILUNGEN des HISTORISCHEN VER-
    EINS des KANTONS SCHWYZ. Ein-
    siedeln 1882-   .

M200
MITTEILUNGEN. HISTORISCHER VEREIN
    der PFALZ. Spires 1870-   .
    Suspended 1933-52.

M201
MITTEILUNGEN des HISTORISCHEN VER-
    EINS für STEIERMARK. Gratz 1850-
    1903.

MITTEILUNGEN. INSTITUT für ÖSTER-
    REICHISCHES GESCHICHTSFORSCHUNG
    see M209.

M202
MITTEILUNGEN des INSTITUTS für ORI-
    ENTFORSCHUNG (Deutsches Akademie
    der Wissenschaft). Berlin
    1953-   . (MIO).

MITTHEILUNGEN aud JUSTUS PERTHES'
    GEOGRAPHISCHER ANSTALT see
    P104.

M203
MITTEILUNGSBLATT der KERAMIKFREUNDE
    der SCHWIEZ = Bulletin des Amis
    Suisses de la Ceramique. Basel
    1956-   .

MITTEILUNGEN. KLUB der MÜNZ und
    MEDAILLENFREUNDE in WIEN see
    M210.

M204
MITTEILUNGEN. KUNSTHISTORISCHES IN-
    STITUT, FLORENCE. Augsburg etc.
    1908-   . Suspended 1914-15
    1918 March 1919-July 1929 1942-
    52.

MITTEILUNGEN aus der LIPPISCHEN
    GESCHICHTE und LANDESKUNDE see
    L69.

MITTEILUNGEN der MUSEALVEREINS für
    SLOWIEN see G50.

MITTEILUNGEN der MUSEEN der KOMI-
    TATS BÉKÉS see B43.

M205
MITTEILUNGEN des MUSEUMSVEREINS
    "LAURIACUM". Enns, Austria ?-   .

M206
MITTHEILUNGEN und NACHRICHTEN.
    DEUTSCHER PALÄSTINA-VEREIN.
    Leipzig 1895-1912.

MITTEILUNGEN der NUMISMATISCH-ARCH-
    ÄOLOGISCHEN ABTEILUNG des SIEBEN-
    BURGISCHEN NATIONAL-MUSEUMS in
    KOLOZSVÁR see K44.

MITTEILUNGEN der NUMISMATISCHEN GE-
SELLSCHAFT in WIEN   see   M210.

M207
MITTEILUNGEN des OBERHESSISCHEN
GESCHICHTSVEREINS.   Giessen
1889-   .

M208
MITTEILUNGEN der ÖSTERREICHISCHEN
ARBEITSGEMEINSCHAFT für UR- und
FRÜHGESCHICHTE. Vienna 1950-   .
1950-57 title: Mitteilungen der
Urgeschichtlichen Arbeitsgemein-
schaft in der Anthropologischen
Gesellschaft in Wien.

MITTEILUNGEN. ÖSTERREICHISCHE GE-
SELLSCHAFT für ANTHROPOLOGIE,
ETHNOLOGIE, und PRÄHISTORIE
see M184.

MITTEILUNGEN der ÖSTERREICHISCHEN
GESELLSCHAFT für MÜNZ- und MEDAIL-
LENKUNDE in WIEN see M210.

M209
MITTEILUNGEN. ÖSTERREICHISCHES IN-
STITUT für GESCHICHTSFORSCHUNG.
Vienna 1880-   . Variant name of
Institute: Institut für Öster-
reichisches Geschichtsforschung.
(MIÖG, MIOEG).

M210
MITTEILUNGEN der ÖSTERREICHISCHEN
NUMISMATISCHEN GESELLSCHAFT.
Vienna 1890-   . Society's name
varies; 1890-1904: Klub der Münz
und Medaillenfreunde in Wien;
1905-18: Österreichische Gesellschaft für Münz- und Medaillen-
kunde in Wien; 1919-40: Numismatische Gesellschaft in Wien.

M211
MITTEILUNGEN aus der PAPYRUSSAMM-
LUNG der GIESSENER UNIVERSITÄTS-
BIBLIOTHEK / H. Kling et al.
Giessen 1924-39. (Schriften der
Hessischen Hochschulen, Univer-
sität Giessen). Index published
1975. (PGissUniv).

M212
MITTEILUNGEN aus der PAPYRUS-SAMM-

LUNG der ÖSTERREICHISCHEN NATION-
ALBIBLIOTHEK (Papyrus Erzherzog
Rainer). Vienna etc. 1887?-97.
Title varies slightly. (MPER).
--. Neue Serie. 1932-   .
(MPER NS).

M213
MITTEILUNGEN. PRÄHISTORISCHE KOM-
MISSION. AKADEMIE der WISSEN-
SCHAFTEN, VIENNA. Vienna 1888- .
Vol. 1 published in 1903.

M214
MITTEILUNGEN über RÖMISCHE FUNDE
in HEDDERNHEIM.   Frankfurt a.M.
1894-1918.

MITTEILUNGEN aus der SAMMLUNG der
PAPYRUS ERZHERZOG RAINER see
M212.

MITTEILUNGEN des STAATSDENKMALAM-
TES see M189.

MITTEILUNGEN der URGESCHICHTLICHEN
ARBEITSGEMEINSCHAFT in der AN-
THROPOLOGISCHEN GESELLSCHAFT in
WIEN see M208.

M215
MITTEILUNGEN zur VATERLÄNDISCHE
GESCHICHTE. St. Gallen 1862-   .
Suspended 1920-27 1940-52.

M216
MITTEILUNGEN des VEREINS der FREUN-
DE CARNUNTUMS. Vienna 1948-   .

MITTEILUNGEN des VEREINS für GE-
SCHICHTE und ALTERTUMSKUNDE zu
BAD HOMBURG vor der HÖHE see
M217.

M217
MITTEILUNGEN des VEREINS für GE-
SCHICHTE und LANDESKUNDE zu BAD
HOMBURG vor der HÖHE. Homburg
v.d.H. 1877-   . 1877-1936
title: Mitteilungen des Vereins
für Geschichte und Altertumskunde zu Bad Homburg vor der Hohe.

MITTEILUNGEN des VEREINS für GE-
SCHICHTE und LANDESKUNDE von
OSNABRÜCK see O52.

M218
MITTEILUNGEN des VEREINS für GE-
   SCHICHTE der STADT NÜRNBERG.
   Nürnberg 1879-   .

M219
MITTEILUNGEN des VEREINS für HEI-
   MATKUNDE in LANDKREIS BIRKENFELD.
   Birkenfeld ?-   .

M220
MITTEILUNGEN des VEREINS KLASSIS-
   CHER PHILOLOGEN in WIEN. Vienna
   1924-33. (MVPhW).

MITTEILUNGEN des VEREINS für KUNST
   und ALTERTUM in ULM und OBER-
   SCHWABEN see U12.

MITTEILUNGEN. VEREIN für NASSAU-
   ISCHE ALTERTUMSKUNDE und GE-
   SCHICHTSFORSCHUNG see N11.

MITTEILUNGEN des VOLKSMUSEUMS
   (Russe) see I159.

M221
MITTEILUNGEN. VORDERASIATISCH-ÄGYP-
   TISCHEN GESELLSCHAFT. Berlin
   1896-1944. (MVÄG, MVAeG, MVG).

M222
MITTEILUNGEN aus der WÜRZBURGER
   PAPYRUSSAMMLUNG / U. Wilcken.
   Berlin 1934. (Abhandlungen der
   Preussischen Akademie der Wissen-
   schaften. Philosophisch-Histor-
   ische Klasse; 1933, 6) (PWürzb).

MITTEILUNGEN der K. K. ZENTRALKOM-
   MISSION für DENKMALPFLEGE see
   M189.

M223
MITTELLATEINISCHES JAHRBUCH.
   Cologne 1964-   .
   --. Beihefte. Ratingen 1968-   .

M224
MITTELLATEINISCHE STUDIEN und
   TEXTE. Leiden 1965-   .

M225
MITTELLATEINISCHES WÖRTERBUCH bis
   zum ausgehenden 13. JAHRHUNDERT.
   Munich 1959-   .

Mitteis, L. see G128.

MITTHEILUNGEN see MITTEILUNGEN
   (the words are interfiled).

M226
MNEMOSYNE; bibliotheca classica
   Batava. Leiden 1852-62 1873-   .
   --. Supplement. 1938-   .
   (Mnem).

Mócsy, A. see R314.

M227
MODERN LANGUAGE JOURNAL. Menasha,
   Wisc. 1916-   .

M228
MODERN LANGUAGE NOTES. Baltimore
   1886-   .

Möller, S. see G115.

Mommsen, T. see R325-R326, I88.

M229
MONASTIC STUDIES. Pine City, N.Y.
   1963-   .

MONATSBERICHTE, MONATSBLATT and
MONATSSCHRIFT are here interfiled.

MONATSBERICHTE. K. AKADEMIE der
   WISSENSCHAFTEN zu BERLIN see
   M234.

MONATSBERICHTE. BERLIN (1856-81)
   see M234.

MONATSBERICHTE. BERLIN (1959-   )
   see M230.

M230
MONATSBERICHTE der DEUTSCHEN AKA-
   DEMIE der WISSENSCHAFTEN zu
   BERLIN. Berlin 1959-   .

M231
MONATSSCHRIFT für GESCHICHTE und
   WISSENSCHAFT des JUDENTUMS.
   Breslau etc. 1851-   .

M232
MONATSSCHRIFT für HÖHERE SCHULEN.
   Berlin 1902-38.
   --. Beiheft. 1930-33.

MONATSSCHRIFT für die KIRCHLICHEN
PRAXIS see E156.

M233
MONATSBLATT der NUMISMATISCHEN
GESELLSCHAFT in WIEN. Vienna
1898?-1915?

M234
MONATSBERICHTE der PREUSSISCHEN
AKADEMIE der WISSENSCHAFTEN zu
BERLIN. Berlin 1856-81. Contin-
ued as the Academy's Sitzungber-
ichte.

MONDE ANTIQUE et l'ARCHÉOLOGIE
see A348.

MONDE d'ISLAM see W7.

M235
MONDE ORIENTAL. Uppsala 1906-
39/41.

M236
MONDO CLASSICO. Turin 1931-52.

M237
MONETA IMPERII BYZANTINI / W. Hahn.
Vienna 1973-   .

MONITORE PREISTORICO see U33.

M238
MONMOUTHSHIRE ANTIQUARY. Ponty-
pool 1961-   .

MONNAIES ANTIQUES DÉCOUVERTES au
GRAND-DUCHÉ de LUXEMBOURG see
F79.

M239
MONNAIES GRECQUES / F. Imhoof-
Blumer. Amsterdam 1883.

M240
MONOGRAPHIES en ARCHÉOLOGIE et HIS-
TOIRE CLASSIQUE = Monographs in
Classical Archaeology and His-
tory. Montreal 1980-   .

M241
MONOGRAPHS on the ANCIENT NEAR
EAST. Malibu, CA. 1974-   .
(MANE).

M242
MONOGRAPHS on MEDITERRANEAN ANTI-
QUITY. Leiden 1967?-   .

M243
MONTFORT; Zeitschrift für Ge-
schichte, Heimat- und Volkskunde
Voralsberg. Dornbirn 1946-   .

MONUMENTA, MONUMENTET, MONUMENTI
and MONUMENTS are here interfiled.

M244
MONUMENTET (Ministria e aresimet
dhe Kultures, Instituti i Monu-
menteve te Kultures). Tirana
1971-   .

M245
MONUMENTI ANNALI e BULLETTINI pubblicati dall'INSTITUTO di CORRES-
PONDENZA ARCHAEOLOGICA. Rome
1854-56. 1856 title: Monumenti
ed Annali. Includes the Institute's Annali for 1854-56 and
the Bullettino for 1854-55.

MONUMENTI ed ANNALI pubblicati
dall'INSTITUTO di CORRESPONDENZA
ARCHEOLOGICA see M245.

M246
MONUMENTI ANTICHI dell'ACCADEMIA
nazionale dei LINCEI. Milan
1890-   . Name of Academy
varies slightly. (MonAnt, MALinc,
MA, MonAL).

M247
MONUMENTI di ANTICHITÁ CRISTIANA.
Vatican City 1929-   .

M248
MONUMENTI ANTICHI INEDITI; ovvero
notizie sulle antichità e belle
arti di roma. Rome 1784-89
1805-   .

M249
MONUMENTA ARCHAEOLOGICA. Prague
1948-   .

M250
MONUMENTA ARCHAEOLOGICA. Novi
Sad 1974-   .

M251
MONUMENTA ARCHAEOLOGICA. Los
  Angeles 1976-   .

MONUMENTS ARCHÉOLOGIQUES   see P26.

M252
MONUMENTI d'ARTE ANTICA.   Turin
  1937-   .

M253
MONUMENTS de l'ART BYZANTIN.   Paris
  1899-1930.

M254
MONUMENTA ARTIS ROMANAE.   Cologne
  & Berlin 1959-   .

M255
MONUMENTA ASIAE MINORIS ANTIQUA.
  London 1928-   . (Publications.
  American Society for Archaeolo-
  gical Research in Asia Minor).
  (MAMA).

MONUMENTS of CULTURE: new discoveries see P27.

M256
MONUMENTI ETRUSCHI / F. Inghirami.
  Fiesole 1821-26.

M257
MONUMENTA GERMANIAE HISTORICA.
  (MGH).
  SCRIPTORES.
    --. Auctores antiquissimi.
  1877-1919.
    --. Scriptores rerum Merovingi-
  carum. 1885-1919. Editio Altera. 1937-42.
    --. Scriptores rerum Langobar-
  dicarum et Italicarum. 1878.
    --. Gesta pontificum Romanorum.
  1898.
    --. Scriptores (in Folio).
  1826.
    --. Scriptores rerum Germani-
  carum, Nova series. 1922-   .
    --. Scriptores rerum Germani-
  carum in usum scholarum separ-
  atim editi. 1841-   .
    --. Scriptores qui vernacula
  lingua usi sunt = Deutsche
  Chroniken. 1877-1923.
    --. Libelli de lite imperatorum

et pontificum. 1891-97.
    --. Staatsschriften des spä-
  teren Mittelalters. 1941-   .
  LEGES.
    --. Leges (in Folio). 1835-
  89.
    --. Leges nationum Germanicar-
  um. 1892.
    --. Capitularia regum Francor-
  um. 1883-   .
    --. Concilia. 1893-1924.
    --. Constitutiones et acta
  publica imperatorum et regum.
  1893-   .
    --. Formulae Merowingici et
  Karolini aevi. 1882-86.
    --. Fontes iuris Germanici an-
  tiqui, Nova series. 1933-   .
    --. Fontes iuris germanici an-
  tiqui in usum scholarum separ-
  atim editi. 1869-   .
  DIPLOMATA.
    --. Diplomata (in Folio).
  1872.
    --. Diplomata Karolinarum =
  Urkunden der Karolinger.
  1906-
    --. Regum Burgundiae e stirpe
  Rudolfina Diplomata et Acta =
  Urkunden der Burgundischen
  Rudolfinger. 1977-   .
    --. Diplomata regum Germaniae
  ex stirpe Karolinorum = Urkunden der deutschen Karolinger. 1932-   .
    --. Diplomata regum et impera-
  torum Germaniae = Urkunden der
  deutschen Könige und Kaiser.
  1879-   .
    --. Laienfürsten- und Dynaste-
  nurkunden der Kaiserzeit.
  1941-49.
  EPISTOLAE.
    --. Epistolae (in Quarto).
  1887-1939.
    --. Die Briefe der deutschen
  Kaiserzeit. 1949-   .
    --. Epistolae saeculi XIII e
  regestis pontificum Romanorum
  selectae. 1883-94.
    --. Epistolae selectae.
  1916-   .
  ANTIQUITATES.
    --. Poetae Latini medii aevi.
  1881-   .
    --. Necrologia Germaniae.

1886-1920.
--. Libri memoriales. 1970.
--. Libri memoriales et Necro-
logia, Nova series. 1979-   .
--. Quellen zur Geistesge-
schichte des Mittelalters.
1955-   .
--. Deutsches Mittelalter.
Kritische Studientexte。
1937-   .

M258
MONUMENTA GRAECA et ROMANA. Leiden
1977-   .

M259
MONUMENTS GRECS (Association des
Études Grecques). Paris 1882-
97.

M260
 MONUMENTS HISTORIQUES. Paris
1936-   . 1936-76 title: Monuments historiques de la France.
Suspended 1940-54.

MONUMENTS HISTORIQUES de la
FRANCE see M260.

M261
MONUMENTS ILLUSTRATING NEW COMEDY /
T. B. L. Webster. 2. ed. London
1969. (Bulletin. Institute of
Classical Studies. Supplement;
24). 1st edition 1962.

M262
MONUMENTS ILLUSTRATING OLD and MID-
DLE COMEDY / T. B. L. Webster.
3. ed. London 1978. (Bulletin.
Institute of Classical Studies.
Supplement; 39). 1st edition 1960.

M263
MONUMENTS ILLUSTRATING TRAGEDY and
SATYR PLAYS / T. B. L. Webster.
2. ed. London 1967. (Bulletin.
Institute of Classical Studies.
Supplement; 20). 1st edition
1962.

M264
MONUMENTI INEDITI a ILLUSTRAZIONE
della STORIA degli ANTICHI POPO-
LI ITALIANI / G. Micali. Florence 1844.

M265
MONUMENTI INEDITI, pubblicati
dall'INSTITUTO di CORRESPONDENZA
ARCHEOLOGICA = Monuments inédits
pubbliés par l'Institut de Correspondance Archéologique. Rome
1829-85. Supplement 1891. Published irregularly (12 vols.
only). (MonInst, Mon d I).

MONUMENTI. INSTITUTO di CORRESPON-
DENZA ARCHEOLOGICA see M245,
M265.

M266
MONUMENTA LINGUARUM HISPANICARUM /
J. Untermann. Wiesbaden
1975-   .

M267
MONUMENTA LINGUAE IBERICAE / E.
Hübner. Berlin 1893.

M268
MONUMENTS et MÉMOIRES publiés par
l'ACADÉMIE des INSCRIPTIONS et
BELLES-LETTRES (Fondation E.
Piot). Paris 1894-   .
(MonPiot, MMAI).

MONUMENTS et MÉMOIRES (FONDATION
E.) PIOT see M268.

M269
MONUMENTA MUSICAE BYZANTINAE.
Copenhagen 1935-   .
--. Lectionaria. Brussels
1939-   .
--. Subsidia. 1935-   .
--. Transcripta. 1936-   .

MONUMENTS PIOT see M268.

M270
MONUMENTI della PITTURA ANTICA
SCOPERTI in ITALIA. Rome
1936-   . (MonPitt).

M271
MONUMENTA SPECTANTIA HISTORIAM SLAV-
ORUM MERIDIONALUM. Zagreb
1868-   .

Moortgat, A. see V70.

M272
MÓRA FERENC MŮZEUM ÉVKÖNYVE = Jahr-
buch des Ferenc Móra Museums =
Annales du Musée Ferenc Móra.
Szeged 1956-   . (MFME).

Morel, W. see F63.

Moretti, L. see I59, I121.

M273
MORGENLAND; Darstellung aus Ge-
schichte und Kultur des Osten.
Leipzig 1924-39. 1924-27 title:
Beihefte zum Alten Orient.

Morpurgo-Davies, A. see M326.

M274
MOSAICI ANTICHI in ITALIA. Rome
1967-   .
--. Studi Monografici. 1971-   .

Moscati, S. see E68.

Moss, R. L. B. see T75.

Mosto, A. da see A534.

M275
MOSTRA dell'ARTE e della CIVILTÀ
ETRUSCA / M. Pallottino. Milan
1955-   .

M276
MOUSEION. (International Museum Office). Paris 1927-46. Suspended
1941-44.

M277
MOUSEION; rivista di scienze classiche. Naples 1923-28.

M278
MOUSEION kai VIVLIOTHEKE tēs EVAN-
GELIKES SCHOLES. Smyrna 1873/5-
84/5?

Mouterde, R. see I62.

M279
MOYEN ÂGE; revue d'histoire et de
philologie. Paris 1888-   .
(MA).

Mü is filed as if spelled Mue.
(Ignore the " in Hungarian words).

M280
MŮEMLÉKVÉDELEM. Budapest 1957- .

Müller, I. P. E. see H11.

Müller, J. see A55.

Müller, K. see F61, G19.

<u>MÜNCHNER and MÜNCHENER are here
interfiled.</u>

M281
MÜNCHNER ÄGYPTOLOGISCHE STUDIEN.
Berlin 1962-   .

M282
MÜNCHENER BEITRÄGE zur PAPYRUSFOR-
SCHUNG und ANTIKEN RECHTSGE-
SCHICHTE. Munich 1915-   .

M283
MÜNCHNER BEITRÄGE zur VOR- und
FRÜHGESHICHTE. Munich 1950-   .

M284
MÜNCHNER JAHRBUCH der BILDENDEN
KUNST. Munich 1906-39 1950-   .
(MJb, MüJb).

M285
MÜNCHENER MUSEUM für PHILOLOGIE des
MITTELALTERS und der RENAISSANCE.
Munich 1911/22-1928/31. Suspended
1924-27.

M286
MÜNCHENER STUDIEN zur SPRACHWIS-
SENSCHAFT. Munich 1952-   .
(MSS).
--. Beiheft. 1952-   .

M287
MÜNCHNER THEOLOGISCHE ZEITSCHRIFT.
Munich 1950-   .

M288
MÜNSTER. Munich 1947-   .

M289
MÜNSTERSCHE BEITRÄGE zur VOR- und
FRÜHGESCHICHTE. Hildesheim
1964-   .

M290
MÜNZEN und MEDAILLEN A. G. Basel

--. Auktion [Katalog]. 1942-   .
--. Liste. 1942-   .
--. Sonderliste. 195?-   .

M291
MÜNZEN und MEDAILLENSAMMLER. Frie-
burg i.B. 1961-   .

Mullach, F. W. A. see F62.

Muratore, L. A. see R89.

Murray, G. see O61.

Murray, J. A. H. see N41.

MUSE-: entries beginning with this
spelling are here interfiled.

M292
MUSE (Museum of Art and Archaeology
Univ. Missouri). Columbus
1967-   .

M293
MUSÉON; revue d'études orientales.
Louvain etc. 1882-   . Title
of vol. 1: Revue des Sciences et
des Lettres. Suspended 1916-20.

M294
MUSEU; revista de arte, arqueología, tradicões. Oporto 1942-   .

M295
MUSEUM (UNESCO). Paris 1948-   .

M296
MUSEUM; tijdschrift voor filologie
en geschiedenes. Leiden 1893-
1959. (MPh).

M297
MUSEUMSKUNDE. Berlin 1905-24
1929-   .

M298
MUSEUM AFRICUM. West African journal of classical and related
studies. Ibadan, Nigeria
1972-   .

M299
MUSEUM der ALTERTHUMSWISSENSCHAFT.
Berlin 1807-10?

M300
MUSÉE BELGE; revue de philologie
classique. Louvain 1897-1930/2.
(MB).

M301
MUSEUM of CLASSICAL ANTIQUITES; a
series of papers on ancient art.
London 1851-53.

M302
MUSÉES et COLLECTIONS ARCHÉOLO-
GIQUES de l'ALGÉRIE et de la
TUNISIE. Paris 1890-   .

M303
MUSEUM CRITICUM; or, Cambridge
Classical researches. Cambridge
1813-26.

M304
MUSEUM CRITICUM. (Istituto di Filologia Classica. Univ. Bologna).
Bologna 4- 1969-   . Supersedes
Quaderni dell'Istituto di Filologia Greca, Univ. Cagliari and
continues its numbering.

MUSEUM of FINE ARTS BULLETIN see
B333.

M305
MUSÉES de FRANCE. Paris 1906-14.
1906-07 title: Musées et Monuments de France. 1908-10 title:
Bulletin des Musées de France.

M306
MUSÉES de FRANCE. Paris 1929-50.
1929-47 title: Bulletin des Musées de France. Suspended 1939-
46.

M307
MUSEI e GALLERIE d'ITALIA. Rome
1901-10.

M308
MUSEI e GALLERIE d'ITALIA. Rome
1956-   .

M309
MUSÉES de GENÈVE. Geneva 1944-   .

MUSEUM HAARETZ. BULLETIN see
B334.

M310
MUSEUM HELVETICUM; revue suisse
  pour l'étude de l'antiquité classique. Basel 1944-   . (MH,
  MusHelv).

M311
MUSEO ITALIANO di ANTICHITÀ CLASSI-
  CA. Florence 1884-90.

M312
MUSEUM JOURNAL (Univ. Museum. Univ.
  Pennsylvania). Philadelphia
  1910-35. (MJ).

MUSÉES et MONUMENTS de la CULTURE
  see M322.

MUSÉES et MONUMENTS de FRANCE . see
  M306.

M313
MUSÉE NEUCHÂTELOIS; recueil d'his-
  toire nationale et d'archéologie
  Neuchâtel. Neuchâtel 1864-   .

M314
MUSEUM NOTES (American Numismatic
  Society). New York 1945-   .
  (ANSMusN, MN, MN(ANS)).

MUSEUM NOTES (Rhode Island School
  of Design. Art Museum) see
  B347.

M315
MUSEUM PHILOLOGUM LONDINIENSE.
  Amsterdam 1975-   .

M316
MUSEO de PONTEVEDRA. Ponteverdra
  1942-   .

MUSEI REGIONALIS DEVENSIS see
  S24.

M317
MUSÉE du RETHÉLOIS et du PORCIEN.
  Rethel 1931-   .

M318
MUSEUM TUSCULUM (Institut for
  Klassisk Filologi). Copenhagen
  1958?-   .

M319
MUSICI SCRIPTORES GRAECI / K. v.
  Jan. Leipzig 1895. Supplement
  1899. Reprint Hildesheim 1962.

M320
MŰVÉSZET. Budapest 1902-17.

M321
MŰVÉSZETTÖRTÉNETI ÉRTESITÖ. Budapest 1952-   .

M322
MUZEI i PAMETNITSI na KULTURATA =
  Musées et Monuments de la Cul-
  ture. Sofia 1961-   .

M323
MUZEJ ISTOČNE BOSNE u TUZLI.
  Tuzla ?-   .

MŰZEUM see E93.

M324
MŰZEUM és KÖNYVTÁRI ÉRTESITÖ. Budapest 1907-18. (MKE).

M325
MYCENAE TABLETS / E. L. Bennett,
  J. Chadwick et al. I published
  in Proceedings of the American
  Philosophical Society 97, 4
  (1953) pp.422-701; II as Transactions of the American Philosophical Society 48, 7 (1958);
  III as Transactions of the American Philosophical Society 52, 7
  (1962).

M326
MYCENAEAE GRAECITATIS LEXICON / A.
  Morpurgo-Davies. Rome 1963.
  (Incunabula Graeca; 3).

MYCENAEAN BIBLIOGRAPHY see N23.

M327
MYCENAEAN GREEK VOCABULARY / J.
  Chadwick & L. Baumbach. Glotta
  46 (1963) pp.157-271.

M328
MYCENAEAN POTTERY / A. Furumark.
  Stockholm 1941. Reprinted in
  1972 as Skrifter utgivna av
  Svenska Institutet i Athen, 4°;
  22). (MP).

MYCENAEAN SEMINAR   see   M167.

M329
MYKENISCHE VASEN / A. Furtwängler
  & G. Loesch. Berlin 1866.

Mylonas, G. E. see T7.

M330
MYTHOGRAPHI GRAECI / R. Wagner et
  al. Leipzig 1894-1902. (Bibliotheca Scriptorum Graecorum et
  Romanorum Teubneriana).

MYTHOGRAPHI VATICANI see S64.

N

NACHRICHTEN and NACHRICHTENBLATT
are here interfiled.

NACHRICHTEN. AKADEMIE. GÖTTINGEN
see N1.

N1
NACHRICHTEN. AKADEMIE der WISSEN-
SCHAFTEN zu GÖTTINGEN. Göttingen 1845-93. Issued under the
society's earlier name: K. Gesellschaft der Wissenschaften
zu Göttingen.
--. Philologisch-historische
Klasse. 1894-1933. 1941-   .
Variant name of the Class: His-
torisch-Philologische Klasse.
--. I: Altertumswissenschaft.
1934/6-40.

NACHRICHTEN; geschaftliche Mitteilungen. AKADEMIE der WISSEN-
SCHAFTEN, GÖTTINGEN see J10.

N2
NACHRICHTENBLATT für DEUTSCHE VOR-
ZEIT. Leipzig & Wiesbaden 1925-
43. 1925 title: Nachrichtenblatt
der Gesellschaft für Deutsche
Vorgeschichte. Supplement to
Mannus: 1926-28.

NACHRICHTENBLATT der GESELLSCHAFT
für DEUTSCHE VORGESCHICHTE see
N2.

NACHRICHTEN. K. GESELLSCHAFT der
WISSENSCHAFTEN zu GÖTTINGEN see
N1

N3
NACHRICHTEN der GIESSENER HOCH-
SCHULGESELLSCHAFT. Giessen
1918-   .

NACHRICHTEN. GÖTTINGEN see N1.

NACHRICHTEN. HISTORISCH-PHILOLO-
GISCHE KLASSE. AKADEMIE der
WISSENSCHAFTEN zu GÖTTINGEN
see N1.

NACHRICHTEN: JAHRESBERICHT. AKA-
DEMIE der WISSENSCHAFTEN, GÖT-
TINGEN see J10.

N4
NACHRICHTEN aus NIEDERSACHSENS UR-
GESCHICHTE. Hannover 1927-   .

NACHRICHTEN. PHILOLOGISCH-HISTOR-
ISCHE KLASSE. AKADEMIE der WIS-
SENSCHAFTEN zu GÖTTINGEN see
N1.

N5
NACHRICHTEN des SCHWEIZERISCHEN
BURGENVEREINS = Revue de l'Asso-
ciation Suisse pour Châteaux et
Ruines. Zurich ?-   .

NACHRICHTENBLATT des VEREINS für
GESCHICHTE der STADT WIEN see
W23.

N6
NAMENBUCH, enthaltend alle GRIECH-
ISCHEN, LATEINISCHEN, HEBRÄ-
ISCHEN, ARABISCHEN und SONSTIGEN

SEMITISCHEN und NICHTSEMITISCHEN MENSCHENNAMEN, soweit sie in GRIECHISCHEN URKUNDEN / F. Preisigke. Heidelberg 1922. Reprint Amsterdam 1967. (NB).

N7
NAMURCUM (Société Archéologique de Namur). Namur 1924-   .

N8
NAPOLI NOBILISSIMA; rivista di topografia ed arte napoletana. Naples 1892-1906 1920-23.

N9
NARODY AZZI i AFRIKI. Moscow 1959-   . 1959-61 title: Problemy vostokovedeniia.

Nash, E.   see P137.

N10
NASSAUISCHE ANNALEN (Verein für Nassauische Altertumskunde und Geschichtsforschung). Wiesbaden 1827-   . 1827-1912 title: the society's Annalen. (NassAnn).

N11
NASSAUISCHE HEIMATBLÄTTER. Wiesbaden 1897/8-   . 1897-1913 title: Mitteilungen. Verein für Nassauische Altertumskunde und Geschichtsforschung.

N12
NATIONALMUSEETS ARBEJDSMARK. Copenhagen 1928-   . Title varies slightly.

Nauck, A.   see T83, L46.

Naz, R.   see D50.

N13
NEA HESTIA. Athens 1927-   .

N14
NEAPOLIS; rivista di archeologia e scienze affini per l'Italia meridionale e la Sicilia. Naples 1913-15.

N15
NECROCORINTHIA / H. Payne. Oxford

1931. Reprint College Park, Md. 1971. (NC).

N16
NEDERLANDSCH ARCHIEF voor KERKGESCHIEDENIS. The Hague 1884-1884-99 title: Archief voor nederlandsche Kerkgeschiedenis.

N17
NEDERLANDS KUNSTHISTORISCH JAARBOEK = Netherlands Yearbook for History of Art. Bussum 1947-   .

N18
NEDERLANDS THEOLOGISCH TIJDSCHRIFT. The Hague etc. 1946-   .

N19
NEKOTORYE VOPROSY VSEOBSHCHEÏ ISTORIÏ. Chelyabinsk 1965-   .

N20
NEOPHILOLOGUS; a modern language quarterly. The Hague etc. 1916-   . Suspended in 1945.

N21
NEOS HELLENOMNEMON. Athens 1904-27. Suspended 1917-20.

N22
NÉPRAJZI ÉRTESITÖ. Budapest 1900-   . Title varies: Néprajzi Osztálályanak Értesitöje; Néprajzi Táránat Értesitöje; Néprajzi Múzeum Értesitöje; Néprajzi Tára Értesitöje. Sometimes these variant titles appear as subtitles after Magyar Nemzeti Múzeum. Suspended 1917-25 1944-53.

NÉPRAJZI MÚZEUM ÉRTESITÖJE see N22.

NÉPRAJZI OSZTÁLÁYANAK ÉRTESITÖJE see N22.

NÉPRAJZI TÁRA ÉRTESITÖJE see N22.

NERVIA see P183.

NEŞRIYATI, ISTANBUL (ASARIATIKA) MÜZELERI see A575.

N23
NESTOR. Madison, Wisc. & Bloom-
ington, Ind. 1957-   . 1957-
June 1958 title: Mycenaean bibliography. For many years the
work of E. L. Bennett.

NETHERLANDS YEARBOOK for HISTORY
of ART see N17.

N24
NEUES aus ALT-VILLACH (Museum Stadt
Villach). Villach 1964-   .

N25
NEUES ARCHIV der GESELLSCHAFT für
ÄLTERE DEUTSCHE GESCHICHTSKUNDE.
Hannover 1876-1935. (NA).

N26
NEUE EPHEMERIS für SEMITISCHE EPI-
GRAPHIK. Wiesbaden 1972-   .

NEUE FORSCHUNGEN in CARNUNTUM see
K62.

NEUE HEIDELBERGER JAHRBÜCHER see
H38.

N27
NEUE JAHRBÜCHER für ANTIKE und
DEUTSCHE BILDUNG. Leipzig 1826-
1943. Published as a continuous
series, but with variant titles
and individual volume numbering;
1826-30: Jahrbücher für Philologie und Pädagogik; 1831-97:
Neue Jahrbücher für Philologie
und Pädagogik; 1898-1924: Neue
Jahrbucher für das Klassische
Altertum, Geschichte und Deutsche
Literatur und für Pädagogik;
1925-36: Neue Jahrbücher für
Wissenschaft und Jugenbildung;
1937: Neue Jahrbücher für
Deutsche Wissenschaft. Edited
by A. Fleckeisen for many years,
especially 1855-97.
--. Supplementbände. 1831-1903.
1831-53 title: Archiv für Philologie und Pädagogik. 1855-1903
title: Jahrbücher für Klassische
Philologie und Pädagogik.

N28
NEUE JAHRBÜCHER für DEUTSCHE THEO-
LOGIE. Bonn 1892-95.

NEUE JAHRBÜCHER für DEUTSCHE WIS-
SENSCHAFT see N27.

NEUE JAHRBÜCHER für das KLASSISCHE
ALTERTUM, GESCHICHTE und DEUTSCHE
LITERATUR und für PÄDAGOGIK see
N27.

NEUE JAHRBÜCHER für PHILOLOGIE und
PÄDAGOGIK see N27.

NEUE JAHRBÜCHER für WISSENSCHAFT
und JUGENBILDUNG see N27.

NEUER LITERATURANZEIGER see W35.

N29
NEUES MAGAZIN für HANAUISCHE GE-
SCHICHTE. Hanau 1949/50-51/4

N30
NEUE PHILOLOGISCHE UNTERSUCHUNGEN.
Berlin 1926-37.

N31
NEUES TRIERISCHES JAHRBUCH. Trier
1961-   .

N32
NEUE WEGE zur ANTIKE. Leipzig &
Berlin
--. 1. Darstellungen. 1925-37?
--. 2. Interpretationen. 1932-
37?

N33
NEUE ZEITSCHRIFT für SYSTEMATISCHE
THEOLOGIE und RELIGIONSPHILOS-
OPHIE. Berlin 1923-55 1959-   .
1923-55 title: Zeitschrift für
Systematische Theologie. 1959-
62 title: Neue Zeitschrift für
Systematische Theologie. Sus-
pended 1944-49.

NEUJAHRSBLATT für BASELS JUNGEND
see N34.

N34
NEUJAHRSBLATT. GESELLSCHAFT zur
BEFÖRDERUNG des GUTEN und GE-
MEINNÜTZINGEN. Basel 1821-   .
1821-71 title: Neujahrsblatt für
Basels Jugend.

N35
NEUJAHRSBLÄTTER. GESELLSCHAFT für
    FRÄNKISCHE GESCHICHTE. Würzburg
    1906-   .

N36
NEUJAHRSBLATT. HISTORISCHER VEREIN
    des KANTONS ST. GALLEN. St.
    Gallen 1861-   .

N37
NEUJAHRSBLATT der STADTBIBLIOTHEK
    WINTERTHUR. Winterthur 1810-   .

N38
NEUJAHRSBLATT. ZÜRCHER KUNSTGESELL-
    SCHAFT. Zurich 1805-   . Soci-
    ety's name varies slightly.

N39
NEUPHILOLOGISCHE MITTEILUNGEN.
    Helsinki 1899-   .

N40
NEUSUMERISCHEN GERICHTSURKUNDEN /
    A. Falkenstein. Munich 1956-57.
    (Bayerische Akademie der Wissen-
    schaften. Philosophisch-Histor-
    ische Klasse. Abhandlungen; N.F.
    39-40, 44).

NEW CATHOLIC ENCYCLOPEDIA see
    C96.

NEW CLASSICAL FRAGMENTS and OTHER
    GREEK and LATIN PAPYRI see
    A111.

N41
NEW ENGLISH DICTIONARY on HISTOR-
    ICAL PRINCIPLES / J. A. H. Mur-
    ray. Oxford 1888-1933. Supple-
    ment 1972. (OED).

N42
NEW PALAEOGRAPHICAL SOCIETY; fac-
    similes of ancient manuscripts
    etc. / E. M. Thompson et al.
    London 1903-12 1913-30. Index
    1932. Continues the Palaeograph-
    ical Society.

N43
NEW TESTAMENT ABSTRACTS. Weston,
    Mass. 1956-   .

N44
NEW TESTAMENT STUDIES. Washington
    D.C. 1923-33.

N45
NEW TESTAMENT STUDIES. London
    etc. 1954-   . (NTS).

N46
NEW TOMBS at DENDRA near MIDEA /
    A. W. Persson. Lund 1942.
    (Skrifter utgivna av Kungl. Hu-
    manistiska Vetenskapssamfundet
    i Lund; 34).

N47
NEW YORK REVIEW of BOOKS. New
    York etc. 1963-   .

N48
NEW ZEALAND NUMISMATIC JOURNAL.
    Wellington 1944-   .

Newell, E. T. see C154, C156,
    R350.

N49
NEWS BULLETIN and CALENDAR. WOR-
    CHESTER ART MUSEUM. Worchester
    1935/6-   . Variant title:
    Worchester Museum. News Bulletin
    and Calendar.

N50
NEWSLETTER. AMERICAN SCHOOLS of
    ORIENTAL RESEARCH. Cambridge,
    Mass. 1962-   .

NEWSLETTER. APPLIED SCIENCE CEN-
    TER for ARCHAEOLOGY. UNIVERSITY
    MUSEUM (Univ. Pennsylvania)
    see M2.

N51
NEWSLETTER for UGARITIC STUDIES.
    Calgary 1972-   .

NEWSLETTER. UNIVERSITY MUSEUM.
    APPLIED SCIENCE CENTER for
    ARCHAEOLOGY (Univ. Pennsylvania)
    see M2.

Newton, C. T. see B217.

N52
NICE HISTORIQUE. Nice 1898-   .

Nickel, J.   see   E162.

Nicole, J.   see   P44.

Niebuhr, B. G.   see   C239

N53
NIEDERDEUTSCHE BEITRÄGE zur KUNST-
GESCHICHTE. Cologne 1961-   .

N54
NIEDERSÄCHSICHES JAHRBUCH für
LANDESGESCHICHTE. Hannover
1924-   .

Nies, J. B.   see   B4.

NIES BABYLONIAN COLLECTION   see
B4.

N55
NIEUWE DRENTSE VOLKSALMANAK.
Assen 1883-   .

N56
NIEUW THEOLOGISCH TIJDSCHRIFT.
Haarlem 1912-46 Suspended 1944-
45.

NIEUWS-BULLETIN. K. NEDERLANDSE
OUDHEIDKUNDIGE BOND   see   B340.

N57
NIGERIA and the CLASSICS. Ibadan
1957-63.

Nilsson, M. P.   see   G32, G107,
M165.

N58
NOMISMA; Untersuchungen auf dem
Gebiete der antiken Münzkunde.
Berlin 1907-23.

N59
NOMISMATIKA CHRONIKA. Athens
1972-   .

N60
NOMS des HITTITES / E. Laroche.
Paris 1966.

N61
NOMS PROPRES SUD-SÉMITIQUES / G.
Ryckmans. Louvain 1934-35.
(Bibliothèque du Muséon; 2).

NON-LITERARY PAPYRI   see   S72.

N62
NOORD-HOLLAND. Bergen etc.
1956?-   .

N63
NOORDGOUW; cultureel tijdschrift
van de provincie Antwerpen.
Antwerp ?-   .

N64
NORDELBINGEN; Beiträge zur Heimatforschung in Schlesweg-Holstein,
Hamburg und Lübeck. Flensburg
1923-   .

Norden, E.   see   E20.

N65
NORDHARGER JAHRBUCH (Museen der
Stadt Halberstadt). Halber-
stadt 1964-   .

NORDISK, NORSK and NORSKE are
here interfiled.

N66
NORDISK NUMISMATIK ÅRSSKRIFT =
Scandanavian Numismatic Journal.
Copenhagen 1936-   .

N67
NORDISK NUMISMATISK UNIONS MEDLEMS-
BLAD. Oslo 1936/7-   .

NORSKE SELSKABS SKRIFTER   see   S96.

N68
NORSK TEOLOGISK TIDSSKRIFT. Oslo
1900-   . Spelling of title
varies slightly.

N69
NORDISK TIDSSKRIFT for FILOLOGI.
Copenhagen 1860-   . 1860-73
title: Tidskrift for Philologi
og Paedagogik. 1874-76 title:
Nordisk Tidskrift for Philologi
og Paedagogik. 1877-92 title:
Nordisk Tidskrift for Philologi.

NORSK TIDSSKRIFT for SPROGVIDEN-
SKAP   see   N76.

NORSKE VIDENSKABERS SELSKAB MUSE-
ET. ÅRBOK see A5.

NORSKE VIDENSKABERS SELSKAB MUSE-
ET. ÅRSBERETNING see A5.

N70
NORFOLK ARCHAEOLOGY. Norwich
1847-   .

N71
NORTH AMERICAN JOURNAL of NUMIS-
MATICS. Chicago 1965-69. 1965-
66 title: The Voice of the
Turtle. 1967 title: The Turtle.

N72
NORTH STAFFORDSHIRE JOURNAL of
FIELD STUDIES. Keele, Eng.
1961-   .

N73
NORTHAMPTONSHIRE ARCHAEOLOGY.
Leicester 1966-   . 1966-72
title: Bulletin of the Northamptonshire Federation of Archaeological Societies.

N74
NORTSIIA; problemyi istorii drev-
neĭskikh klassovykh obshchectv
evropeiskogo sredizemnomor'ia.
Voronezh 1971-   .

N75
NORWEGIAN ARCHAEOLOGICAL REVIEW.
Oslo 1968-   .

N76
NORWEGIAN JOURNAL of LINGUISTICS
= Norsk Tidsskrift for Sprog-
videnskap. Oslo 1928-77. 1928-
71 title in Norwegian only.

NOS MONUMENTS d'ART et d'HISTOIRE
see U22.

NOSTRI MONUMENTI STORICI see
U22.

N77
[NOTEBOOKS for KNOSSOS] / A. J.
Evans. Manuscript in Ashmolean
Museum, Oxford.

N78
NOTES et DOCUMENTS publiée par le
DIRECTION des ANTIQUITÉS et ARTS
de TUNISIE. Tunis 1908-   .
Suspended 1914-21.

Noth, M. see B103.

N79
NOTICES d'ARCHÉOLOGIE ARMORICAINE.
Rennes 1952-   . Issued as part
of Annales de Bretagne.

N80
NOTICES et TEXTS des PAPYRUS
GRECS du MUSÉE du LOUVRE et de
la BIBLIOTHÈQUE IMPÉRIALE / J.
A. Letronne et al. Paris 1865.
(Notices et Extraits des Manuscrits de la Bibliothèque Impériale et Autre Bibliothèques;
18, 2). (PParis).

N81
NOTICIARIO ARQUEOLÓGICO HISPÁNICO.
Madrid 1952-   . (NAH).

N82
NOTIZIARIO ARCHEOLOGICO del MINIS-
TERO delle COLONIE. Milan &
Rome 1915-27.

N83
NOTIZIE degli SCAVI di ANTICHITÀ.
Rome 1876-   . (Atti della
Accademia nazionale dei Lincei).
1876-85 in and 1886-1903 part
of the Memorie, Classe di scienze
morali of the academy. (NSc, NS,
NSA, NotScavi, NotScav).

N84
NOTRE BOURBONNAIS. Moulins
1920-   . 1920-22 title: Bulletin de la Société Bourbonnaise
des Études Locales.

N85
NOTTINGHAM MEDIAEVAL STUDIES. Nottingham 1957-   .

NOUVEAU, NOUVEAUX and NOUVELLE
are here interfiled.

N86
NOUVELLES ANNALES publiées par la

SECTION FRANÇAISE de l'INSTITUT ARCHÉOLOGIQUE. Paris & Leipzig 1836-38.

NOUVELLES ARCHÉOLOGIQUES see A457.

N87
NOUVELLES ARCHIVES des MISSIONS SCIENTIFIQUES et LITTÉRAIRES. Paris 1891-1927.

N88
NOUVELLE CLIO; revue de la découverte historique. Brussels 1949-   . (NClio, NouvClio).

N89
NOUVELLES ÉTUDES d'HISTOIRE. Bucharest 1955-   .

NOUVEAU JOURNAL ASIATIQUE see J93.

NOUVEAUX MÉMOIRES de l'ACADÉMIE Royale de BELGIQUE see M95.

NOUVEAUX MÉMOIRES. ACADÉMIE des SCIENCES, ARTS et BELLES-LETTRES de DIJON see M99.

N90
NOUVELLE REVUE FRANC-COMTOISE. Dôle ?-   .

NOUVELLE REVUE HISTORIQUE de DROIT FRANÇAIS et ÉTRANGER see R176.

N91
NOUVELLE REVUE de HONGRIE. Budapest 1908-   . 1908-31 title: Revue de Hongrie. Suspended 1918-20.

N92
NOUVELLE REVUE THÉOLOGIQUE. Paris etc. 1868/9-   . (NRTh, NRT).

NOUVELLE REVUE de THÉOLOGIE see R242.

N93
NOVAE PATRUM BIBLIOTHECAE / A. Mai. Rome 1852-1905.

N94
NOVISSIMO DIGESTO ITALIANO / A. Azara. 3. ed. Turin 1957. 1st edition 1884.

N95
NOVUM GLOSSARIUM MEDIAE LATINITATIS. Copenhagen 1957-   .

N96
NOVUM TESTAMENTUM. Leiden 1956-   . Suspended 1957-58. (NT).

N97
NUMAGA; tijdschrift gewijd aan heden en verleden van Nijmegen en Omgeving. Nijmegen 1954-   .

N98
NUMARIO HISPÁNICO. Barcelona etc. 1952-   .

N99
NUMEN; international review for the history of religion. Leiden 1954-   .
--. Supplements: Studies in the history of religions. 1954-   .

NUMIS- and NUMIZ-: entries beginning with this spelling are here interfiled.

N100
NUMISMA (Sociedad Ibero-americana de Estudios Numismáticos). Madrid 1951-   .

N101
NUMISMATICA. Rome 1935-   . 1935-40 title: Numismatica e scienze affini.

N102
NUMISMATIK. Munich 1932-34.

N103
NUMISMATIKA. Zagreb 1933-   .

N104
NUMIZMATIKA. Sofia ?-   .

N105
NUMISMATICA e ANTICHITÀ CLASSICHE. Lugano 1972-   . (Quaderni Ticenesi). (NAC).

N106
NUMISMATIC CHRONICLE and JOURNAL
of the ROYAL NUMISMATIC SOCIETY.
London 1838-   . (NC, NumChron,
NumChr).

N107
NUMISMATIC CIRCULAR (Spink & Sons
Ltd). London 1892-   . 1892-
1939 title: Spinks & Sons's
(monthly) Numismatic Circular.
Suspended 1940-46 and replaced
during this time by its Numismatic Circular List of Coins.
(NCirc, NumCirc).

N108
NUMIZMATIKA i EPIGRAFIKA (Institut
Arkheologii. Akademiia Nauk
SSSR). Moscow 1960-   . (NE).

N109
NUMISMATIC JOURNAL. London
1836-38.

N110
NUMIZMATIKAI KÖZLÖNY. Budapest
1902-   . (NumKözl).

N111
NUMISMATICKÉ LISTY. Prague
1945-   .

N112
NUMISMATIC LITERATURE. New York
1947-   . (NL).

N113
NUMISMATISCHES LITERATUR-BLATT.
Stade 1880-   . Suspended
1914-19.

N114
NUMISMATIK LITERATUR OSTEUROPAS
und das BALKANS. Graz 1960-   .

N115
NUMISMATISCHES NACHRICHTENBLATT.
Hamburg 1952-   .

N116
NUMISMATIC NOTES and MONOGRAPHS
(American Numismatic Society).
New York 1920-   . (NNM).

N117
NUMISMATIC REVIEW. New York 1943-
47. (NR).

N118
NUMISMATICKÝ SBORNIK. Prague
1953-   .

N119
NUMIZMATICHESKIĬ SBORNIK. Moscow
1955-   .

NUMISMATICA e SCIENZE AFFINI
see N101.

N120
NUMIZMATIKA i SFRAGISTIKA. Kiev
1963-   .

N121
NUMISMATICA STOCKHOLMIENSIA.
Stockholm 1975/6-   .

N122
NUMISMATIC STUDIES (American Numismatic Society). New York
1938-   . (ANSNS).

N123
NUMIZMATIČKE VIJESTI. Zagreb
1954-   .

N124
NUMISMATISCHE ZEITSCHRIFT. Vienna
1869-1937 1946-   . 1938-40/1?
published as Deutsches Jahrbuch
für Numismatik. (NZ, NumZ, Num-
Zeit).

N125
NUMMUS. Pôrto 1952-   .

NUOVA, NUOVI and NUOVO are here
interfiled.

N126
NUOVA ANTOLOGIA. Florence 1866- .
1866-1926 title: Nuova Antologia
di Scienze, Lettere ed Arti
(varies slightly).

NUOVA ARCHIVIO VENETO see A557.

N127
NUOVO BULLETTINO di ARCHEOLOGIA
CRISTIANA. Rome 1895-1922.

Supersedes Bullettino di Arche-
ologia Cristiana. Superseded by
Rivista di Archeologia Cristiana.
(NuovBull).

N128
NUOVO DIDASKALEION (Centro di Studi
sull'Antico Cristianesimo). Cantania 1947-   . (ND).

N129
NUOVO DIGESTO ITALIANO / M. d'Amelio
& A. Azara. Turin 1937-40.

N130
NUOVA RIVISTA STORICA. Milan
1917-   . (NRS).

NUOVI STUDI MEDIEVALI see S213.

NY CALRSBERG GLYPTOTEKS SAMLINGEN
see F56.

NYE SAMLING. K. NORSKE VIDENSKABERS
SELSKAB see S96.

N131
NYELVTUDOMÁNYI ÉRTEKEZÉSEK. Budapest 1953-   .

NYESTE SAMLING. K. NORSKE VIDENS-
KABERS SELSKAB see S96.

N132
NYIREGYHÁZI JÓSA ANDRÁS MÚZEUM
ÉVKÖNYVE. Budapest 1958-   .

NYT HISTORISK TIDSSKRIFT see
H113.

O

Oates, J. F. see Y5.

O1
OBERBAYERISCHES ARCHIV für VATER-
  LÄNDISCHE GESCHICHTE. Munich
  1839-1939 1950-   .

O2
OBERGERMANISCH-RAETISCHE LIMES des
  RÖMERREICHES. Berlin etc. 1894-
  1937?. (ORL).

OBERÖSTERREICHISCHE BIBLIOGRA-
  PHIE see O3.

O3
OBERÖSTERREICHISCHE HEIMATBLÄTTER.
  Linz 1947-   . 1955- accompanied
  by supplement: Oberösterreichische Bibliographie.

O4
OBERPFÄLZER HEIMAT. Weiden 1968- .

OBERRHEINISCHE HEIMAT   see B8.

O5
OBZOR PRAEHISTORICKÝ. Prague 1910-
  15.

O6
OBZOR PRAEHISTORICKÝ = Revue Préhistorique. Prague 1922-   .

ÖSTERREICHISCHE JAHRESHEFTE   see
  J74.

O7
ÖSTERREICHISCHE ZEITSCHRIFT für

KUNST und DENKMALPFLEGE. Vienna
  1947-   . 1947-51 title: Österreichische Zeitschrift für Denkmalpflege.

O8
ÖSTERREICHISCHE ZEITSCHRIFT für
  VOLKSKUNDE. Vienna 1895-1944
  1947-   . 1919-44 title: Wiener
  Zeitschrift für Volkskunde.

O9
OFFA; Berichte und Mitteilungen
  aus des Schleswig-Holsteinischen
  Landesmuseum für Vor- und Frühgeschichte in Schleswig und dem Institut für Ur- und Frühgeschichte
  an der Universität Kiel. Neumünster i.H. 1936-   .

O10
OGAM (Amis de la Tradition Celtiques). Rennes 1948-   .

Ohnefalsh-Richter, M. H. see K82.

Oikonomides, N. see A54.

O11
OIKUMENE; studia ad historiam anti-
  quam classicam et orientaliam
  spectantia. Budapest 1976-   .

O12
OLDENBURGER JAHRBUCH (Verein für
  Landesgeschichte und Altertums-
  kunde). Oldenburg 1892-
  1892-1914 title: Jahrbuch für die
  Geschichte des Herzogstums Olden-

burg. 1918-21 title: Oldenburger
Jahrbuch für Altertumskunde und
Landesgeschichte, Kunst und
Kunstgewerbe.

Olivier, J. P. see R47, I14.

Olivieri, A. see F59, I58.

013
OLTENIA; studii şi comunicǎri is-
torie (Muzeul Olteniei). Craiova,
Romania ?-   .

014
OLTENIA ROMANǍ / D. Tudor. 4. ed.
Budapest 1978. 1st edition 1942.

015
OLTNER NEUJAHRSBLÄTTER. Olten
1950-   .

016
OLYMPIA: die Ergebnisse der von
dem Deutschen reich Veranstalten
Ausgrabung. Berlin 1890-97.

017
OLYMPISCHE FORSCHUNGEN. Berlin
1944-   .

018
ON the KNOSSOS TABLETS / **L. R.** Palmer & J. Boardman. Oxford 1963.

019
ONOMA (International Committee of
Onomastic Sciences). Louvain
1950-   .

020
OPUSCULA ARCHAEOLOGICA. Lund 1935-
52. (Skrifter Utgivna av Svenska
Institutet i Rome, 4°; 4, etc.).
(OpArch).

021
OPUSCULA ARCHAEOLOGICA (Radovi
Arheološkog Institutǎ. Univ. Za-
greb). Zagreb 1956-   .

022
OPUSCULA ATHENIENSIA. Lund 1953- .
(Skrifter utgivna av Svenska In-
stitutet i Athen, 4°; 2, etc.).
(OpAth).

023
OPUSCULA. ISTITUTO di GLOTTOLOGIA.
(Univ. Roma). Rome 1976-   .

024
OPUSCULA PHILOLOGICA. Linz 1926-34.

025
OPUSCULA ROMANA. Lund 1954-   .
(Skrifter utgivna av Svenska In-
stitutet i Rome, 4°; 18, etc.).
(OpRom).

026
ORATORUM ROMANORUM FRAGMENTA / H.
Meyer. Paris 1837.

027
ORATORUM ROMANORUM FRAGMENTA liberae
rei publicae / E. Malcovati. 2.
ed. Turin 1955. (Corpus Scriptorum
Latinorum Paravianum). (ORF).

Orelli, J. K. von see I81.

028
ORIENS (International Society for
Oriental Research). Leiden
1948-   .

029
ORIENS ANTIQUUS. Rome 1962-   .
(OA).

030
ORIENS ANTIQUUS; dissertationes
sociorum Societatis Hungaricae
ad Antiquitates Asiae Anterioris
Inquirendas. Budapest 1944-45?.

031
ORIENS CHRISTIANUS. Rome & Wiesbaden 1901-   . Suspended
1941-52. (OC, OrChr).

032
ORIENT (Society for Near Eastern
Studies in Japan). Tokyo
1960-   .

033
ORIENT, HELLAS und ROM in der
ARCHÄOLOGISCHEN FORSCHUNG seit
1939 / K. Schefold. Bern 1949.
(Wissenschaftliche Forschungsberichte. Geisteswissenschaft-
liche Reihe; 15).

034
ORIENT SYRIEN.   Vernon 1956-67.

ORIENTAL-: entries beginning with
   this spelling are here interfiled.

035
ORIENTALIA.   Rome 1920-30. Continued
   by 3 series: Orientalia n.s.
   1932-   ), Analecta Orientalia and
   Orientalis Christiana Analecta.
   (Or).

036
ORIENTALISCHES ARCHIV.   Leipzig
   1910-13.   (OAr).

037
ORIENTALIA et BIBLICA LOVANIENSIA.
   Louvain 1957-   .

038
ORIENTALISCHE BIBLIOGRAPHIE.   Berlin 1887-1926. 1900-10 also had
   title: Oriental bibliography.
   Suspended 1912-25.

ORIENTLIA CHRISTIANA   see   039.

039
ORIENTALIA CHRISTIANA ANALECTA.
   Rome 1923-   . Title of nos. 1-
   2: Orientalia. Series II: christi-
   ana. 1923-34 title: Orientalia
   Christiana.   (OCA).

040
ORIENTALIA CHRISTIANA PERIODICA.
   Rome 1935-   . (OCP).

ORIENTAL INSTITUTE ASSYRIOLOGICAL
   STUDIES   see   A622.

ORIENTAL INSTITUTE COMMUNICATIONS
   see   C178.

ORIENTAL INSTITUTE PUBLICATIONS
   see   P244.

ORIENTAL INSTITUTE STUDIES in
   ANCIENT ORIENTAL CIVILIZATION
   see   S160.

041
ORIENTALISTISCHE LITERATURZEITUNG.
   Berlin & Leipzig 1898-   .Sus-

pended 1944-52. Title varies
slightly. (OLZ).

042
ORIENTALIA LOVANIENSIA ANALECTA.
   Louvain 1975-   .

043
ORIENTALIA LOVANIENSIA PERIODICA.
   Louvain 1970-   .

ORIENTALISCHE RUNDSCHAU   see   K17.

044
ORIENTALIA SUECANA.   Uppsala
   1952-   .

045
ORIENTIS GRAECI INSCRIPTIONES SE-
   LECTAE / W. Dittenberger.   Leipzig 1903-05. Reprinted Hildesheim 1970. (OGIS, OGI).

ORIGIN et DÉBUTS des SLAVES   see
   V80.

046
ORPHEUS; rivista di umanità classica e cristiana.   Catania
   1954-   .

047
ORPHICORUM FRAGMENTA / O. Kern.
   Berlin 1922. Reprint Berlin 1963.

048
ORSZÁGOS MAGYAR RÉGÉZETI TÁRSULAT
   ÉVKÖNYVE = Jahrbuch des Ungarischen Archäologischen Gesellschaft.   Budapest 1878-88 1920/2-
   23/6.

049
ORSZÁGOS MAGYAR SZÉPMŰVÉSZETI MÚ-
   ZEUM ÉVKÖNYVE = Jahrbücher des
   Museums der Bildenen Künste in
   Budapest.   Budapest 1918?-   .

ORSZÁGOS ORVOSTÖRTÉNETI KÖNYVTAR
   KÖZLEMÉNYEI   see   C177.

050
ORTENAU; Mitteilungen des Histor-
   ischen Vereins für Mittelbaden.
   Offenburg i.B. 1910-41 1949-   .

051
OSJEČKI ZBORNIK (Muzej Slavonije).
Osijek 1942-   .

052
OSNABRÜCKER MITTEILUNGEN (Verein für
Geschichte und Landeskunde von
Osnabrück). Osnabrück 1848-   .
1848-1950 title: Mitteilungen.
Verein für Geschichte und Landes-
kunde von Osnabrück. Suspended
1914-15 1942-46.

053
OSTBAIRISCHE GRENZMARKEN (Institut
für Ostbairische Heimatforschung).
Passau 1912-   .

054
OSTKIRCHLICHE STUDIEN. Würzburg
1952-   . (OKS).

055
OSTRACA GRECS de la COLLECTION
CHARLES-EDWIN WILBOUR au MUSÉE
de BROOKLYN / C. Préaux. New
York 1935. Reprint Milan 1975.
(OWilb).

056
OSTRACA OSLOËNSIA; Greek ostraca
in Norwegian Collections / L.
Amundsen. Oslo 1933. (Avhand-
linger utgitt av det Norske
Videnskaps-Akademi i Oslo. II.
Hist.-filos. Klasse; 1933,2).
(OOslo).

Oswald, F. see I13, I100.

057
OTCHET IMPERATORSKOĬ ARKHEOLOGI-
CHESKOĬ KOMMISSII. Leningrad
1859-1915. 1859-88 also appeared
in a French version: Compte-
rendu de la Commission Impériale
Archéologique. (CRPetersb).

Otten, H. see H70, L89.

Otto, W. G. A. see H11.

058
OUDE LAND van LOON. Hasselt
1946-   .

OUDHEIDKUNDIG JAARBOEK see B340.

059
OUDHEIDKUNDIGE MEDEDELINGEN uit
het RIJKSMUSEUM van OUDHEDEN te
LEIDEN. Leiden 1907-13 1920-   .
(OudhMeded, OMLeiden, OMRL,
OMRO).

060
OUDTESTAMENTISCHE STUDIEN. Leiden
1942-   .

Oxe, A. see C244.

061
OXFORD BOOK of GREEK VERSE / G.
Murray et al. Oxford 1930.
Many printings available.

062
OXFORD CLASSICAL DICTIONARY / N.
G. L. Hammond et al. 2. ed.
Oxford 1970. 1st edition 1949
by M. Cary et al. (OCD).

OXFORD CLASSICAL TEXTS see S59.

063
OXFORD DICTIONARY of the CHRIS-
TIAN CHURCH / F. L. Cross & E. A.
Livingstone. 2. ed. London &
New York 1974. 1st edition 1957.
(ODCC).

064
OXFORD EDITIONS of CUNEIFORM TEXTS.
Oxford 1923-   .

OXFORD ENGLISH DICTIONARY see
N41.

065
OXFORD LATIN DICTIONARY. Oxford
1968-82.

066
OXFORD MEDIEVAL TEXTS. London
1967-   .

067
QXONIENSIA. Oxford 1936-   .

068
QXYRHYNCHUS PAPYRI / B. P. Grenfell
& A. S. Hunt et al. London
1898-   . (POxy).

P

P1
PACT: the journal of the European
Study Group on Physical, Chemical
and Mathematical Techniques
applied to Archaeology. Strasbourg 1977-   .

P2
PMLA; publications of the Modern
Language Association of America.
New York etc. 1888-   .

P3
PSR BULLETIN. Berkeley 19??-   .
Earlier title: Bulletin. Pacific
School of Religion.

P4
PADOVA. Padua 1927-   .

P5
PADUSA (Centro Polesano di Studi
Storici, Archeologici ed Etno-
grafici). Rovigo 1965-   .

P6
PAESTAN POTTERY / A. D. Trendall.
London 1936.

Page, D. L.   see P145-P146, S278,
G83, S72.

P7
PAGINE di STORIA della MEDICINA.
Rome 1957-   .

P8
PAIDEIA; rivista letteraria di in-
formazione bibliografica.
Arona 1946-   .

P9
PAIDEIA kai ZOĒ. Athens 1946-   .
1946-51 title: Paideia.

P10
PAIDEUMA; Mitteilungen zur Kultur-
kunde. Bamberg etc. 1938-   .

P11
PALACE of MINOS / A. J. Evans.
London 1921-36. Reprint London
and New York 1964. (PM, PofM).

P12
PALACE of NESTOR at PYLOS in WES-
TERN MESSENIA / C. W. Blegen et
al. Princeton, N.J. 1966-73. (PN).

P13
PALAEOGRAPHIA LATINA. New York &
London 1922-29.

P14
PALAEOGRAPHICAL SOCIETY; facsimiles
of manuscripts and inscriptions /
E. A. Bond & E. M. Thompson.
London 1873-83 1884-94. Index
1901. Continued by the New
Palaeographical Society.

P15
PALAEOHISTORIA; acta et communicationes Instituti Bio-archaeolo-
gici Universitatis Groninganae.
Groningen 1951-   .

P16
PALAEOLOGIA (Palaeological Association of Japan). Osaka 1952-   .

P17
PALÄSTINA HEFTE des Deutschen Vereins vom Heiligen Lande. Cologne
1931-37?

P18
PALÄSTINAJAHRBUCH des Deutschen
Evangelischen Instituts für
Altertumswissenschaft des Heili-
gen Landes zu Jerusalem. Berlin
1905-41. (PjB).

P19
PALAIS ROYAL d'UGARIT / C. F. A.
Schaeffer. Paris 1955-   .
(Mission de Ras Shamra; 6, etc.).
(PRU).

P20
PALESTINE EXPLORATION FUND ANNUAL.
London 1911-53? (PalEFA, PEFA).

PALESTINE EXPLORATION FUND. QUAR-
TERLY STATEMENT see P21.

P21
PALESTINE EXPLORATION QUARTERLY.
London 1869- . 1869-1936 title:
Palestine Exploration Fund. quar-
terly statement. Ceased publica-
tion? (PEQ, PalEQ, PEFQ).

P22
PALESTINSKIĬ SBORNIK. Moscow &
Leningrad 1954-   .

P23
PALETTE. Basel 1959-73.

P24
PALLADIO; rivista di storia
dell'architettura. Rome 1937-
43 1951-   .

P25
PALLAS. Toulouse 1953. Part of
series: Annales de l'Université
de Toulouse-Le Mirail (title
varies slightly).

Pallottino, M. see E26, M275,
T20.

Palmer, L. R. see O18.

P26
PAMÁTKY ARCHEOLOGICKÉ. Prague
1854-   . Former title: Památky
archeologické a místopisné.
Additional 1920-30 title: Monuments archéologique.

PAMÁTKY ARCHEOLOGICKÉ a MÍSTOPISNÉ
see P26.

P27
PAM'IATNIKI KUL'TURY : NOVYE OTKRY-
TIIA = Monuments of Culture:
new discoveries. Moscow
1974-   .

P28
PAM'IATNIKI TURKMENISTANA. Ashka-
bad 1966-   .

P29
PAMIĘTNIK SLOWIAŃSKI. Wroclaw
1949-   .

P30
PAN (Istituto di Filologia Latina
Univ. Palermo). Palermo
1973-   .

P31
PANNONHALMI SZEMLE. Pannonhalma
1926-   .

P32
PANTHEON; internationale Zeitschrift für Kunst. Munich
1928-   . Suspended 1945-59.

P33
PANTHEON; rivista di Roma. Rome
1947-   .

Papachryssanthou, D. see A79.

Papazoglou, F. see I84.

P34
PAPELES de ARQUELOGÍA (Laboratorio
di Arqueología. Univ. Valencia).
Valencia 1968-   . 1968-72 ti-
tle: Papeles de Laboratorio de
Arqueología (Univ. Valencia).

PAPELES de LABORATORIO de ARQUEOLO-
GÍA (Univ. Valencia) see P34.

P35
PAPERS of the AMERICAN SCHOOL of
   CLASSICAL STUDIES at ATHENS.
   Boston 1882/3-97. (PASAthens).

P36
PAPERS of the BRITISH SCHOOL at
   ROME. London 1902-   . (PBSR).

PAPERS. DUMBARTON OAKS see D98.

P37
PAPERS and MONOGRAPHS of the AMER-
   ICAN ACADEMY in ROME. Rome
   1919-   .

P38
PAPERS and PROCEEDINGS. HAMPSHIRE
   FIELD CLUB and ARCHAEOLOGICAL
   SOCIETY. Southampton 1885/9-   .

P39
PAPOLI e CIVILTÁ dell'ITALIA AN-
   TICA. Rome 1974-78. (Bibliotheca
   de Storia Patria).

PAPYR-: and PAPIR-: entries beginning with this spelling are here
   interfiled. See also the special
   section on papyri in the introduction.

P40
PAPYRUS BOURIANT / P. Collart.
   Paris 1926. (PBour).

P41
PAPYROLOGICA BRUXELLENSIA. Brussels 1962-   . (PapBrux).

P42
PAPYROLOGICA CASTROCTAVIANA. Barcelona 1967-   . (PapCastr).

PAPYROLOGICA COLONENSIA see W33.

PAPYRUS ERZHERZOG RAINER see
   M212.

P43
PAPYRUS FOUAD I / A. Bataille et
   al. Cairo 1939. (Publications
   de la Société Fouad I de Papyrologie. Textes et Documents; 3).
   (PFouad).

P44
PAPYRUS de GENÈVE / J. Nicole.
   Geneva 1896-1909. (PGen).

P45
PAPYRI GRAECAE HAUNIENSES. Copenhagen & Bonn 1942 1981. (PHaun).

P46
PAPYRUS GRAECUS HOLMENSIS / O.
   Lagercrantz. Uppsala etc. 1913.
   (Arbeiten utgifna med understöd
   af Vilhelm Ekmans Universitets-
   fond; 13). (PHolm).

P47
PAPYRI GRAECAE MAGICAE = Griechischen Zauberpapyri / K. Preisendanz et al. Leipzig & Berlin
   1928-31. Revised edition 1973-
   74 by A. Henrichs. (PGraecMag).

P48
PAPYRI GRAECI MUSEI ANTIQUARII
   PUBLICI LUGDUNI-BATAVI / C. Lee-
   mans. Leiden 1843-85. (PLeid).

P49
PAPYRI GRAECI REGII TAURINENSIS
   MUSEI AEGYPTII / A. Peyron.
   Turin 1827-29. (Memorie della
   R. Accademia de Torino; 31
   (1827) pp.9-188 and 33 (1829)
   pp.1-80). (PTor).

P50
PAPYRUS GRECS (Institut Papyrologique de l'Université de Lille) /
   P. Jouguet et al. Paris 1907-
   28. Title of vol. II: Papyrus
   de Magdôla. (PLille).

P51
PAPYRUS GRECS de la BIBLIOTHÈQUE
   MUNICIPALE de GOTHENBOURG / H.
   Frisk. Gothenburg 1929. (Göte-
   borgs Högskolas Årsskrift; 35,
   1). (PGot).

P52
PAPYRUS GRECS et DÉMOTIQUES RE-
   CUEILLIS en ÉGYPTE / T. Reinach
   et al. Paris 1905. Vol. 2
   appeared as Papyrus Théodore
   Reinach, tome II by P. Collart.
   Cairo 1940. (Bulletin. Institut

Français d'Archéologie Orientale; 39). (PRein).

P53
PAPIRI GRECO-EGIZII, PAPIRI FIOREN-
TINI / G. Vitelli et al. Milan
1906-15. (PFlor).

P54
PAPYRUS GRECS d'ÉPOQUE BYZANTINE /
J. Maspero. Cairo 1911-16.
(Catalogue Géneral des Antiquités
Egyptiénnes du Musée du Caire;
51 etc.). (PCairMasp).

P55
PAPIRI GRECI e LATINI; pubblicazioni della Società Italiana per la
Ricerca dei Papiri Greci e Latini in Egitto. Florence
1912-   . (PSI).

P56
PAPYRI IANDANAE / C. Kalbfleisch
et al. Leipzig 1912-38. (PIand).

P57
PAPYRI from KARANIS / E. J. Good-
speed. Chicago 1902. (Univ. of
Chicago. Studies in Classical
Philology; 3). (PKarGoodsp).

P58
PAPYROLOGICA LUGDUNO-BATAVA. Leiden 1941-   . (PapLugdBat).

P59
PAPYRUS de MAGDOLA / J. Lesquier.
Paris 1912. (Papyrus Grecs. Institut Papyrologique de l'Université de Lille; 2). (PLilleII).

P60
PAPYRI MICHAELIDAE, being a catalogue of the Greek and Latin
papyri tablets and ostraca in
the library of Mr. G. A. Micha-
ïlidis of Cairo / D. S. Crawford.
Aberdeen 1955. (PMichael).

P61
PAPIRI MILANESI / A. Calderini.
Milan 1928. 2nd edition 1967 by
S. Daris published as Pubblicazi-
oni dell'Università Cattolica del
Sacro Cuore. Contributi. Ser. 3:

Pubblicazioni di "Aegyptus" I.
Vol. 2, also by Daris, published
in 1966 as no. 2 of the series.
(PMil).

P62
PAPYRUSURKUNDEN der ÖFFENTLICHEN
BIBLIOTHEK der UNIVERSITÄT zu
BASEL / E. Rabel. Berlin 1917.
(Abhandlungen. Akademie der
Wissenschaften, Göttingen. N.F.
16,3). (PBas).

P63
PAPYRI OSLOENSES / S. Eitrem & L.
Amundsen. Oslo 1925-36. (POslo).

P64
PAPYRUS de PHILADELPHIE / J. Scherer. Cairo 1947. (Publication de
la Société Fouad I de Papyrologie. Textes et Documents; 7).
(PPhil).

P65
PAPYROLOGICAL PRIMER / M. David &
B. A. van Groningen. 4. ed.
Leiden 1965. 1st edition in
Dutch 1940.

P66
PAPYRI in the PRINCETON UNIVERSITY
COLLECTIONS / A. C. Johnson et
al. Baltimore 1931-42. Published
in two series: Johns Hopkins
Univ. Studies in Archaeology and
Princeton Univ. Studies in Papy-
rology. (PPrinc).

P67
PAPYRUS ROLL in the PRINCETON
COLLECTION/ E. H. Kase. Balti-
more 1933. Thesis, Princeton
University. (PPrincRoll).

P68
PAPYRI RUSSISCHER und GEORGISCHER
SAMMLUNGEN/ G. Tsereteli et al.
Tiflis etc. 1925-35. (PRoss-
Georg).

P69
PAPYRI SOCIETATIS ARCHAEOLOGICAE
ATHENIENSIS / G. A. Petropoulos.
Athens 1939. (Pragmateiai tēs
Akadēmias Athēnōn; 10). (PAthen).

P70
PAPYRUS de la SORBONNE / H. Cadell.
Paris 1966-   . Published in
two series: Publications de la
Faculté des Lettres et Sciences
Humaines de Paris, Série Textes
et Documents and Travaux de
l'Institut de Papyrologie de
Papyrologie de Paris. (PSorb).

P71
PAPYRI from TEBTUNIS / A. E. R.
Boak et al. Ann Arbor 1933-44.
(Univ. of Michigan Studies. Hu-
manistic series; 28, 47). These
constitute volumes 2 and 5 of
Michigan Papyri. (PMichII,
PMichV).

P72
PAPYRUS de THÉADELPHIE / P. Jouguet. Paris 1911. (PThead).

PAPYRUS THÉODORE REINACH see P52.

P73
PAPYRI der UNIVERSITÄTSBIBLIOTHEK
ERLANGEN / W. Schubart. Leipzig
1942. (Katalog der Handschriften
der Universitätsbibliothek Erlangen, Neubearb.; 3, 1). (PErl).

PAPYRUSSAMMLUNG der UNIVERSITÄTS-
BIBLIOTHEK in LUND see A684.

P74
PAPIRI della UNIVERSITÀ degli studi
di MILANO / A. Vogliano et al.
Milan 1937-   . Title changes
slightly. (PMilVogl).

P75
PAPYRI VARSOVIENSES / G. Manteuffel
etc. Warsaw 1935. (Universitas
Varsovienses: Acta Facultatis
Litterarum; I). (PVars).

P76
PARADORUM EPICORUM GRAECORUM et
ARCHESTRATI reliquiae / P.
Brandt. Leipzig 1888. (Corpus-
culum poesis epicae graecae
ludibundae; 1).

P77
PARADOXOGRAPHOI; scriptores rerum

mirabilium graeci / A. Westermann. Brunswick 1839. Reprint
Amsterdam 1963.

P78
PARADOXOGRAPHORUM GRAECORUM RELI-
QUIAE / A. Giannini. Milan
1965. (Classici Greci e Latini:
Sezione Testi e Commenti; 3).

P79
PARAGONE; rivista mensile di arte
figurativa e letteratura. Florence 1950-   .

P80
PARALIPOMENA; additions to Attic
Black Figure Vase-Painters
and to Attic Red Figure Vase-
Painters / J. D. Beazley. Oxford
1971.

P81
PARIS et ÎLE-de-FRANCE. Paris
1949-   . vols. 1-4 title: Mémoires. Sociétés Historiques et
Archéologiques de Paris et d'Île-
de-France.

Parlasca, K. see R318.

P82
PARNASSOS (Philologikos Syllogos
Parnassos). Athens 1877-1894/5.

P83
PAROLA del PASSATO; rivista di
studi antichi. Naples 1946-   .
(PP, ParPass, PdP).

P84
PAROLE d'ORIENT. Kaslik 1970-   .

Parrot, A. see A530, M178.

Pasoli, A. see A58.

P85
PAST and PRESENT. Oxford 1952-   .

Paton, W. R. see I46.

P86
PATRISTIC GREEK LEXICON / G. W. H.
Lampe. Oxford 1961.

PATROLOGIA GRAECA see P89.

PATROLOGIA LATINA see P90.

P87
PATROLOGIA ORIENTALIS / R. Graffin
et al. Paris 1907. (PO).

P88
PATROLOGIA SYRIACA / R. Graffin.
Paris 1894- .

P89
PATROLOGIAE CURSUS COMPLETUS:
SERIES GRAECA / J. P. Migne.
Paris 1857-1904. (PG).

P90
PATROLOGIAE CURSUS COMPLETUS:
SERIES LATINA / J. P. Migne.
Paris 1884-1904.
--. Supplement 1958- . (PL).

Pauly, A. F. von see R20.

Payne, H. see N15, P227.

P91
PAYS d'ARGENTAN. Argentan 1929- .

P92
PAYS d'AUGE. Lisieux 1951?- .

P93
PAYS BAS-NORMAND. Flers 1908- .

P94
PAYS de BOURGOGNE. Dijon 1953- .

P95
PAYS LORRAIN. Nancy 1904- .

Pedersen, H. see L92.

Peek, W. see G130.

Peeters, P. see B90.

P96
PEGASUS (Classical Society of Exeter University). Exeter 1964- .

P97
PELOPONNESIAKA. Athens 1956- .

Pendlebury, J. D. S. see A431.

P98
PEREDNEAZIATSKIĬ ÉTNOGRAFICHESKIĬ
SBORNIK. Moscow 1958- .

P99
PEREDNEAZIATSKIĬ SBORNIK. Moscow
1961- .

Peremans, W. see P220.

P100
PERFICIT; publicatión mensual de
estudios clásicos. Salamanca
1967/8- .

P101
PERGAMENISCHE FORSCHUNGEN. Berlin
1972- .

P102
PERIODICO della SOCIETÀ STORIA
COMENSE. Como 1878 1936- .

P103
PERISTIL; zbornik radova za histo-
riju umjetnosti i arheologiju.
Zagreb 1954- .

Perkins, J. B. Ward see I91.

Persson, A. W. see N46, R352.

Peter, H. see H109.

P104
PETERMANNS GEOGRAPHISCHE MITTEI-
LUNGEN. Gotha 1855- . 1855-78
title: Mittheilungen aus Justus
Perthes' Geographischer Anstalt.
1879-1938 title: Dr. A. Peter-
manns Mitteilungen aus Justus
Perthes' Geographischer Anstalt.
1931-37 cover title: Petermanns
Mitteilungen.

Petit, L. see A45, A75, A89.

Petrie, W. M. F. see A194, F19,
R353, T74.

Petropoulos, G. A. see P69.

P105
PEUCE; studii şi comunicări de is-
torie, etnografie şi muzeologie.
Tulcea, Romania ?- .

Peyron, A.. see P49.

P106
PFÄLZER HEIMAT. Kaiserlautern
  1950-   .

Pfuhl, E. see M26.

Philippson, A. see G111.

PHILOL-: entries beginning with
  this spelling are here interfiled.

P107
PHILOLOGUS; Zeitschrift für das
  klassiche Altertum. Berlin etc.
  1846-   . Suspended 1944-47
  1949-53.
  --. Supplementband   1859-   .
  (Philol).

P108
PHILOLOGISCHER ANZEIGER als ERGÄN-
  ZUNG des PHILOLOGUS. Göttingen
  1869-87.

P109
PHILOLOGIA CLASSICA. Leningrad
  1977-   .

P110
PHILOLOGICAL MONOGRAPHS of the
  AMERICAN PHILOLOGICAL ASSOCIA-
  TION. Middleton, Conn. etc.
  1931-   .

P111
PHILOLOGICAL MUSEUM. Cambridge
  1832-33.

P112
PHILOLOGISCHE STUDIEN. Louvain
  1929/30-   .

P113
PHILOLOGISCHE UNTERSUCHUNGEN.
  Berlin 1880-1925.

P114
PHILOLOGISCHE WOCHENSCHRIFT.
  Berlin & Leipzig 1881-1944. 1884-
  1920 title: Berliner Philolo-
  gische Wochenschrift. (PhW,
  PhilWoch, BPW).

PHILOS-: entries beginning with
  this spelling are here interfiled.

P115
PHILOSOPHIA. Athens 1971-   .

P116
PHILOSOPHY (British Institute of
  Philosophy). London 1926-   .
  1926-31 title: Journal of Philosophical Studies.

P117
PHILOSOPHIA ANTIQUA; a series of
  monographs on ancient philosophy.
  Leiden 1946-   .

P118
PHILOSOPHICAL FORUM. Boston
  1943-   .

P119
PHILOSOPHISCHES JAHRBUCH. Fulda &
  Bonn 1888-   . Suspended 1943-
  45 1952. (PhJ).

P120
PHILOSOPHISCHER LITERATURANZEIGER.
  Meisenheim etc. 1949-   .

PHILOSOPHISCHE MONATSHEFTE see
  A555.

P121
PHILOSOPHIA PATRUM. Leiden 1971- .

P122
PHILOSOPHY and PHENOMENOLOGICAL
  RESEARCH. Buffalo, N.Y. 1940- .

P123
PHILOSOPHICAL QUARTERLY. St.
  Andrews 1950-   . (PhQ,
  PhilosQ)

P124
PHILOSOPHICAL REVIEW. Boston etc.
  1892-   . (PhR, PR).

P125
PHILOSOPHY & RHETORIC. University
  Park, PA. 1968-   .

P126
PHILOSOPHISCHE RUNDSCHAU. Tübingen
  1953/4-   .

P127
PHOENIX ("Het Kompas" N. V.).
Amsterdam 1946-49.

P128
PHOENIX (Vooraziatisch-Egyptisch
Genootschap ex Oriente Lux).
Leiden 1955-   .

P129
PHOENIX; journal of the Classical
Association of Canada. Toronto
1946-   .

P130
PHOIBOS (Cercle de Philologie
Classique et Orientale de l'Université de Bruxelles). Brussels
1946/7-1958?

P131
PHOTOGRAPHISCHE EINZELAUFNAHMEN
ANTIKER SKULPTUREN / P. Arndt.
et al. Munich 1893-1940. (EA).

P132
PHRONESIS; a journal for ancient
philosophy. Assen 1955-   .

P133
PHYSICI et MEDICI GRAECI MINORES /
J. L. Ideler. Berlin 1841-42.
Reprint Amsterdam 1963.

P134
PHYSICS; rivista di storia della
scienza. Florence 1959-   .

P135
PIANTA MARMOREA di ROMA ANTICA;
Forma urbis Romae / G. Carettoni
et al. Rome 1960.

Pickard-Cambridge, A. W. see D93.

P136
PICTORAL DICTIONARY of ANCIENT
ATHENS / J. Travlos. New York
1971.

P137
PICTORAL DICTIONARY of ANCIENT
ROME / E. Nash. New York & Lon-
don 1968. 1st edition 1961.

Piercy, W. C. see D49.

Pippidi, D. M. see D66.

Piraino, M. T. Manni see I116.

P138
PIRINEOS (Instituto de Estudios
Pirenaicos). Saragosa 1945-   .

Pisani, V. see L65.

P139
PITT PRESS SERIES. Cambridge
--. [Greek authors] 1878-   .
--. [Latin authors] 1874?-   .

P140
PITTURA ELLENISTICO-ROMANA / G. E.
Rizzo. Milan 1929. (Thesaurum
Artium).

PITTURE delle CATACOMBE ROMANE
see R330.

P141
PLATON (Hetaireia Hellēniōn Philo-
logōn). Athens 1949-   .

P142
PLATO'S THEORY of KNOWLEDGE / F.
M. Cornford. London & New York
1935.

Plaumann, G. see G120.

PMLA see P2.

P143
POETAE LATINI MINORES post E. Baeh-
rens iterum rec. F. Vollmer.
Leipzig 1910-   . (Bibliotheca
Scriptorum Graecorum et Romanorum
Teubneriana). 1st edition 1879-
83. (PLM).

P144
POETAE LYRICI GRAECI / T. Bergk.
Leipzig 1914-23. (PLG).

P145
POETAE MELICI GRAECI / D. L. Page.
Oxford 1962. (PMG).

P146
POETARUM LESBIORUM FRAGMENTA / E.
Lobel & D. Page. Oxford 1955.
Corrected edition 1968. (PLF).

P147
POETARUM PHILOSOPHORUM FRAGMENTA /
H. Diels. Berlin 1901. (Poetarum
Graecorum Fragmenta; III, 1).

P148
POETARUM ROMANORUM VETERUM RELI-
QUIAE / E. Diehl. Berlin 1911.

P149
POETICA; Zeitschrift für Sprach-
und Literaturwissenschaft.
Munich 1967-   .

Pokorny, J. see I18, V16.

P150
POLEMŌN. Athens 1929-   .

P151
POLIMNIA; bollettino d'arte,
storia, archaeologia della Valdi-
chiana e delle provincie fini-
time. Rome 1924-33.

P152
POLITISCHE DOKUMENTE aus KLEINAS-
IEN / E. F. Wiedner. Leipzig
1923. (Boghazköi Studien; 8-9).
Reprint Hildesheim 1970.

P153
POLNOE SOBRANĬE RUSSKIKH LĬĒTOPI-
SEĬ. Leningrad 1922-28? (PSRL).

P154
POMPEIANARUM ANTIQUITATUM HISTORIA
/ G. Fiorelli. Naples 1860-64.

P155
POMPEJANISCHE MALEREI / K. Schefold. Basel 1952.

P156
PONTICA (Muzeul de Arheologie).
Constanta 1968-   .

Popsecu, E. see I60.

Popham, M. R. see D26, L10.

Porter, B. see T75.

P157
PORTUGALIAE MONUMENTA HISTORICA.
Olsipone 1856-1936.

Postgate, J. P. see C235.

P158
[POTTERY NOTEBOOKS for KNOSSOS] /
D. Mackenzie. Manuscript in the
library, British School of Archaeology at Athens.

P159
PÓVOA de VARZIM. Povoa de Varzim
1958-   .

Powell, J. E. see R67.

Powell, J. U. see C159.

P160
PRACE ARCHEOLOGICZNE = Schedae
Archaeologicae. Cracow 1960-   .

P161
PRACE ARCHEOLOGICZNE. Torin
1971?-   .

P162
PRACE FILOLOGICZNE. Warsaw
1884-   .

P163
PRACE i MATERIALY. SERIA ARCHEOLO-
GICZNA. Lodz 1956-   .

PRACE ZAKŁADU ARCHEOLOGII SRÓD-
ZIEMNOMORSKIEJ POLSKIEJ AKADEMII
NAUK see T107.

P164
PRAE-ITALIC DIALECTS of ITALY /
R. S. Conway, J. Whatmough & S.
E. Johnson. Cambridge 1933.
Reprint Hildesheim 1968. (PID)

P165
PRÄHISTORSICHE BLÄTTER. Munich
1889-1907.

P166
PRÄHISTORISCHE BRONZEFUNDE. Munich 1969-   . (PBF).

P167
PRAEHISTORISCHE ZEITSCHRIFT. Berlin & Leipzig 1909-   . (PZ).

P168
PRAKTIKA tēs AKADĒMIAS ATHĒNŌN.
Athens 1926-   . (PAA).

PRAKTIKA. ARCHAIOLOGIKĒ HETAIREIA
en ATHĒNAIS see P169.

P169
PRAKTIKA tēs en ATHĒNAIS ARCHAIOLO-
GIKĒS HETAIREIAS. Athens 1837-
49 1858-   . Title varies
slightly. (PAAH, PAE).

P170
PRAVOSLAVNYĬ PALESTINSKII SBORNIK.
Leningrad 1881-1917.

Préaux, C. see O55.

P171
PREHISTORIC MACEDONIA / W. A.
Heurtley. Cambridge 1939.

PREHISTORIC REVIEW see U33.

P172
PREHISTORIC THESSALY / A. J. B.
Wace & M. S. Thompson. Cambridge
1912. (Cambridge Archaeological
and Ethnological Series). Reprint
New York 1979.

P173
PREHISTORIC TOMBS at KNOSSOS / A.
J. Evans. London 1906. Also
in Archaeologia 59 (1905).

Preisendanz, K. see P47.

Preisigke, F. see S15, B56, G121,
G127, N6.

PREISTORIA seee B179.

Preller, L. see G113.

P174
PRESOCRATIC PHILOSOPHERS / G. S.
Kirk & J. E. Raven. Cambridge
1957.

P175
PREUSSICHE JAHRBÜCHER. Berlin
1858-1935.

Price, T. D. see I100.

P176
PRILOZI POVIJESTI UMJETNOSTI u DAL-
MACIJU. Split 1953-   .

PRIMITIVE MAN see A338.

P177
PRINCETON MONOGRAPHS in ART and
ARCHAEOLOGY. Princeton, N.J.
--. Folio Series. 1929-39?
--. Quarto Series. 1912-   .

P178
PRINCETON THEOLOGICAL REVIEW.
Princeton, N.J. 1903-29.

P179
PRINCIPE de VIANA. Pamplona
1940-   .

P180
PRISCAE LATINIATIS MONUMENTA
EPIGRAPHICA / F. W. Ritschl.
Berlin 1862. (Corpus Inscrip-
tionum Latinarum; voluminis
primi, tabulae, lithographae).
Reprint Berlin 1968.

Pritchard, J. B. see A196-A198.

P181
PRO ALESIA; revue trimestrielle
des fouilles d'Alise et des questions relative à Alesia. Paris
1906-32.

P182
PRO AUSTRIA ROMANA. Vienna 1951-
1951-   . (PAR).

P183
PRO NERVIA; revue historique &
archéologique du Pays des Ner-
viens. Avesnes 1923-   .

PROBLEME, PROBLEMES, PROBLEMS
and PROBLEMY are here interfiled.
See also VOPROSY.

P184
PROBLEMY ARKHEOLOGII i ĒTNOGRAFII.
Leningrad 1977-   .

PROBLEMS of HISTORY see V66.

P185
PROBLEMY ISTORII DOKAPITALISTICHES-
KIKH OBSHCHESTV. Moscow & Lenin-
grad 1926-35. 1926-32 title:
Soobshcheniia Gosudarstvennoĭ

Akademii Istorii Material'noĭ
Kultury. 1933 title: Problemy
istorii material'noĭ kultury.

PROBLEMY ISTORII MATERIAL'NOĬ
KULTURY see P185.

PROBLÈMES de LINGUISTIQUE see
V64.

P186
PROBLEME de MUZEOGRAFIE. Cluj
1960-64?

PROBLÈMES de PHILOLOGIE see V62.

PROBLÈMES de PHILOSOPHIE see V63.

PROBLEMY VOSTOKOVEDENIĨA see N9.

P187
PROCEEDINGS of the AFRICAN CLASSI-
CAL ASSOCIATIONS. Salisbury
1958-   . (PACA).
--. Supplement. 1962-   .

P188
PROCEEDINGS of the AMERICAN CATH-
OLIC PHILOSOPHICAL ASSOCIATION.
Baltimore 1926-   .

P189
PROCEEDINGS of the AMERICAN PHILO-
LOGICAL ASSOCIATION. Baltimore
104- 1974-   . Formerly included
in the Association's Transactions.
(PAPA).

P190
PROCEEDINGS of the AMERICAN PHILO-
SOPHICAL SOCIETY. Philadelphia
1838/40-   . (PAPS, PAPhS).

P191
PROCEEDINGS of the BATH NATURAL
HISTORY and ANTIQUARIAN FIELD
CLUB. Bath 1867-1909.

P192
PROCEEDINGS of the BERWICKSHIRE
NATURALISTS CLUB. Alnwick
1831-   . Variant title: History.

P193
PROCEEDINGS of the BRISTOL and

GLOUCESTERSHIRE ARCHAEOLOGICAL
SOCIETY. Gloucester 1952-   .

P194
PROCEEDINGS of the BRITISH ACADEMY.
London 1903/4-   . (PBA, Proc-
BritAcad).

PROCEEDINGS of the BURY and WEST
SUFFOLK ARCHAEOLOGICAL INSTITUTES
see P209.

P195
PROCEEDINGS. CAMBRIDGE ANTIQUARIAN
SOCIETY. Cambridge 1859-   .
1859-64 title: Antiquarian Communications ... papers presented
at the meetings of the Cambridge
Antiquarian Society. 1864-88 title: Cambridge Antiquarian Communications.

P196
PROCEEDINGS of the CAMBRIDGE PHI-
LOLOGICAL SOCIETY. Cambridge
1882-   . (PCPhS, PCPS).

P197
PROCEEDINGS of the CLASSICAL ASSO-
CIATION. London 1904/5-   .
1904-05 title: Proceedings of
the Classical Association of
England and Wales. (PCA).

PROCEEDINGS of the CLASSICAL ASSO-
CIATION of ENGLAND and WALES
see P197.

P198
PROCEEDINGS of the DEVON ARCHAEOLO-
GICAL EXPLORATION SOCIETY.
Torquay 1929-   .

P199
PROCEEDINGS of the DORSET NATURAL
HISTORY and ARCHAEOLOGICAL SOCI-
ETY. Dorchester etc. 1876/7-   .
Earlier name of the society:
Dorset Natural History and Anti-
quarian Field Club.

P200
PROCEEDINGS of the Royal GEOGRAPH-
ICAL SOCIETY. London 1855-92.

P201
PROCEEDINGS of the royal IRISH
ACADEMY. Dublin 1836-69 1889-
1902.
--. Section of polite literature
and antiquities. 1870-88.
--. Section C: Archeology, lin-
guistics and literature. 1902- .

P202
PROCEEDINGS of the royal NUMISMATIC
SOCIETY. London 1836-39. The
proceedings are continued in the
Numismatic Chronicle.

PROCEEDINGS and PAPERS of the
Royal SOCIETY of ANTIQUARIES of
IRELAND see J132.

PROCEEDINGS. PHILOLOGICAL SOCIETY,.
OXFORD see T100.

P203
PROCEEDINGS of the royal PHILOSO-
PHICAL SOCIETY of GLASGOW.
Glasgow 1841/4-1951/2.

P204
PROCEEDINGS of the PREHISTORIC SOCI-
ETY of EAST ANGLIA. Cambridge
1908- . (PPS, ProcPrSoc).

PROCEEDINGS of the ROYAL ... see
PROCEEDINGS of the ... (the word
royal is disregarded in filing,
but may have been regarded in
forming an abbreviation).

P205
PROCEEDINGS of the SOCIETY of ANTI-
QUARIES of LONDON. London 1843-
1920. (PSA).

P206
PROCEEDINGS of the SOCIETY of ANTI-
QUARIES of NEW CASTLE-UPON-TYNE..
Newcastle-upon-Tyne 1855-58
1882- .

P207
PROCEEDINGS of the SOCIETY of ANTI-
QUARIES of SCOTLAND. Edinburgh
1851- . (PSAS).

P208
PROCEEDINGS of the SOCIETY of BIB-

LICAL ARCHAEOLOGY. London 1878-
1918. (PSBA).

PROCEEDINGS of the SOMERSETSHIRE
ARCHAEOLOGICAL and NATURAL
HISTORY SOCIETY see S113.

PROCEEDINGS of the STATE SERVICE
for ARCHAEOLOGICAL INVSTIGATIONS
in the NETHERLANDS see B51.

P209
PROCEEDINGS of the SUFFOLK INSTI-
TUTE of ARCHAEOLOGY. Ipswich
1848- . 1848-58 title: Pro-
ceedings of the Bury and West
Suffolk Archaeological Insti-
tutes. Other minor changes.
Suspended 1941-46.

PROCEEDINGS and TRANSACTIONS of the
KILKENNY and SOUTHEAST of IRE-
LAND ARCHAEOLOGICAL SOCIETY see
J132.

P210
PROCEEDINGS of the VIRGIL SOCIETY.
London 1961/2- .

PROCÈS-VERBAUX. ACADÉMIE de NÎMES
see B351.

P211
PROCÈS-VERBAUX de la COMMISSION
du VIEUX. Paris ?- .

PROCÈS-VERBAUX et DOCUMENTS de la
COMMISSION HISTORIQUE et ARCHÉ-
OLOGIQUE de la MAYENNE see
B282.

P212
PROCÈS-VERBAUX et MÉMOIRES. ACA-
DÉMIE des SCIENCES, BELLES-LET-
TRES et ARTS de BESANÇON. Besan-
çon 1754- . Previous title:
Séances publiques, Mémoires,
Bulletin, Années.

PROCÈS-VERBAUX (des SÉANCES/et
NOTES SUCCINTES). SOCIÉTÉ ARCHÉ-
OLOGIQUE de BORDEAUX see B366.

PROCÈS-VERBAUX SÉANCES. SOCIÉTÉ des
ÉTUDES LITTÉRAIRES, SCIENTIFIQUES
et ARTISTIQUES du LOT see B399.

P213
PROCÈS-VERBAUX des SÉANCES de la
    SOCIÉTÉ des LETTRES, SCIENCES et
    ARTS de l'AVEYRON. Rodex
    1836/58-   .

PROCÈS-VERBAUX. SOCIÉTÉ ARCHÉOLO-
GIQUE de BORDEAUX see B366.

P214
PROCHE-ORIENT CHRÉTIEN. Jerusalem
    1951-   .

PROGRAMM zum WINCKELMANNSFEST see
    W31.

P215
PROMETHEUS; rivista quadrimestrale
    di studi classici. Florence
    1975-   .

P216
PROPYLÄEN KUNSTGESCHICHTE. Berlin
    1966-   .

P217
PROSOPOGRAPHIA ATTICA / J. E.
    Kirchner & S. Lauffer. 2. ed.
    Berlin 1966. 1st edition 1901-
    03. (PA).

P218
PROSOPOGRAPHIA IMPERII ROMANI. 2.
    ed. Berlin & Leipzig 1933-   .
    1st edition 1897-98. (PIR).

P219
PROSOPOGRAPHIA MILITIARUM EQUES-
    TRIUM quae fuerunt ab AUGUSTO
    ad GALLIENUM / H. Devijer. Lou-
    vain 1976-80. (Symbolae Facul-
    tatis Litterarum et Philosophiae
    Lovaniensis. Ser. A; 3).

P220
PROSOPOGRAPHIA PTOLEMAICA / W.
    Peremans & E. Van't Dack. Lou-
    vain 1950-   . (Studia Hellen-
    istica; 6).

P221
PROSOPOGRAPHISCHES LEXIKON der
    PALAIOLOGENZEIT / E. Trapp et
    al. Vienna 1976-   . (PLP).

P222
PROSOPOGRAPHY of the LATER ROMAN
    EMPIRE / A. H. M. Jones et al.
    Cambridge 1971-   . (PLRE).

P223
PROSPETTIVA; rivista di storia
    dell'arte antica e moderna.
    Siena 1975-   .
    --. Supplement. 1981?-   .

P224
PROSPEZIONI ARCHEOLOGICHE. Rome
    1966-   .

P225
PROTEUS; rivista di filosofia.
    Rome 1970-   .

P226
PROTOGEOMETRIC POTTERY / V. R. d'A.
    Desborough. Oxford 1952. (Ox-
    ford Monographs on Classical
    Archaeology; 2). (PGP).

P227
PROTOKORINTHISCHE VASENMALEREI /
    H. Payne. Berlin 1933. (For-
    schung zur Antiken Keramik: Reihe
    1: Bilder Griechischer Vasen; 7).
    Reprint Mainz 1974.

Prott, J. von see L23.

P228
PROVENCE HISTORIQUE. Marseille
    1950-   .

P229
PROVINCE du MAINE. Le Mans 1893-
    1914 1921-   . Title of vol. 1:
    Union historique et littéraires
    du Maine.

P230
PROVINCIA; revue d'histoire et
    d'archéologie provençales. Mar-
    seille 1921-   .

P231
PROVINCIA di LUCCA. Lucca 1962- .

P232
PRUDENTIA; a journal devoted to the
    intellectual history of the Hel-
    lenistic and Roman periods.
    Auckland, NZ 1969-   .

Pryce, F. N. see B225.

P233
PRZEGLĄD ARCHEOLOGICZNY. Poznan
   1919-   .

P234
PRZEGLAD HISTORYCZNY. Warsaw
   1905-   . Suspended 1940-45.

P235
PRZEGLĄD HUMANISTYCZNY. Lvov, Warsaw 1922-25.

P236
PRZEGLĄD HUMANISTYCZNY, Warsaw
   1957-   .

P237
PRZEGLĄD KLASYCZNY。 Lvov 1935-39。

P238
PRZEGLĄD ORIENTALISTYCZNY. Warsaw
   1952-   .

P239
PSEUDEPIGRAPHA VETERIS TESTAMENTI
   GRAECAE. Leiden 1964-   .

PSR BULLETIN see P3.

P240
PTOLEMÄISCHE KÖNIGSURKUNDEN / L.
   Koenen. Wiesbaden 1957. (Klassisch-Philologische Studien;
   19). (PKroll).

PUBBLICAZIONI, PUBLICACIONES, PUB-
   LICATION, PUBLICATIONS and PUB-
   LIKATIONEN are here interfiled.

PUBLIKATIONEN. ARCHÄOLOGISCHE
   MUSEUM (Istanbul) see A575.

PUBLICATIONS. BABYLONIAN SECTION.
   UNIVERSITY MUSEUM (Univ. Pennsylvania) see P249.

P241
PUBLICATIONS. BRITISH SCHOOL of
   ARCHAEOLOGY in EGYPT. London
   1895/6-1953. 1895/6-1904 title:
   Publications. Egyptian research
   account.

PUBLICATION in CLASSICAL ARCHAEO-
   LOGY see U16.

PUBLICATIONS in CLASSICAL PHILO-
   LOGY see U17.

PUBLICATIONS. HENRY BRADSHAW SOCI-
   ACCOUNT see P241.

P242
PUBLICATIONS. HEBRY BRADSHAW SOCI-
   ETY. Salisbury 1891-   .

P243
PUBLICATIONS of the METROPOLITAN
   MUSEUM of ART. EGYPTIAN EXPE-
   DITION. New York 1916-   .
   Title varies slightly.

PUBLICATIONS of the MODERN LANGUAGE
   ASSOCIATION of AMERICA see P2.

PUBLICATIONS du MUSÉE d'ANTHROPO-
   LOGIE et d'ETHNOGRAPHIE (Leningrad) see S30.

PUBLICATIONS des MUSÉES d'ANTIQUI-
   TÉ de STAMBOUL see A575.

PUBLICATIONS of the NEW SOCIETY
   of LETTERS at LUND see S100.

P244
PUBLICATIONS. ORIENTAL INSTITUTE.
   UNIV. of CHICAGO. Chicago
   1924-   . (OIP).

PUBLIKATIONEN. K. OSMANISCHE
   MUSEEN, ISTANBUL see A575.

P245
PUBLICATIONS of the PRINCETON UNI-
   VERSITY ARCHAEOLOGICAL EXPEDI-
   TIONS to SYRIA. Leiden 1914-49.
   At head of title: Syria.

P246
PUBLICATIONS de la SECTION HISTO-
   RIQUE de l'INSTITUT (royal)
   GRANDDUCAL de LUXEMBOURG. Luxemburg 1845/6-   . 1845-67 title:
   Puolications de la Société pour
   la Recherche et la Conservation
   des Monuments Historiques dans
   le Grande-Duché de Luxembourg.

PUBLICATIONS de la SECTION NUMIS-
   MATIQUE et ARCHÉOLOGIQUE du
   MUSÉE de TRANSSYLVANIE à KOLOZ-
   SVAR see K44.

PUBLICACIONES del SEMINARIO de ARQUEOLOGÍA y NUMISMÁTICA ARAGONESAS see C3.

P247
PUBLICATIONS du SERVICE des ANTIQUITÉS du MAROC. Rabat 1935-   .
(PSAM).

PUBLICATIONS de la SOCIÉTÉ d'ARCHÉOLOGIE dans le DUCHÉ de LIMBOURG see P248.

P248
PUBLICATIONS de la SOCIÉTÉ HISTORIQUE et ARCHÉOLOGIQUE dans le DUCHÉ de LIMOURG = Jaarboek van Limburgs Geschied- en Oudheidkundig Genootschap. Maastricht 1864-   . 1864-66 French title:
Publications de la Société d'Archéologie dans le Duché de Limbourg.

PUBLICATIONS de la SOCIÉTÉ d'HISTOIRE TURQUE see T132.

PUBBLICAZIONI della SOCIETÀ ITALIANA per al RICERCA dei PAPIRI GRECA e LATINI in EGITTO see P55.

PUBLICATIONS de la SOCIÉTÉ pour la RECHERCHE et la CONSERVATION des MONUMENTS HISTORIQUES dans le GRAND-DUCHÉ de LUXEMBOURG see P246.

PUBLICATIONS of the SZEGED CITY MUSEUM see S303.

P249
PUBLICATIONS. UNIVERSITY MUSEUM. BABYLONIAN SECTION. (Univ. Pennsylvania). Philadelphia 1911- .

Pugliese Carratelli, G. see I120, T71

Purgold, K. see I37.

P250
PUTEOLI; studi di storia antica. Naples 1977-   .

P251
PYRENAE. (Instituto de Arqueología y Prehistoria. Univ. Barcelona). Barcelona 1965-   .

P252
PYTANNIA KLASYCHNOI FILOLOGII. Lvov 1959-   .

Q

QADMONIOT see K1.

Q1
QUADERNI di ARCHEOLOGIA della
  LIBIA. Rome 1950-   . (QAL).

Q2
QUADERNI d'ARCHEOLOGIA REGGIANA.
  Bologna 1970-   .

Q3
QUADERNI CATANESI di STUDI CLASSICI
  e MEDIEVALI. Catania 1979-   .

Q4
QUADERNI di FILOLOGIA CLASSICA
  (Univ. di Trieste, Istituto di
  Filologia Classica). Rome
  1978-   .

Q5
QUADERNI dell'ISTITUTO di FILOLO-
  GIA GRECA (Univ. Cagliari). Cag-
  liari 1966-68.

Q6
QUADERNI dell'ISTITUTO di FILOLO-
  GIA GRECA (Univ. Padua). Padua
  1974-   .

Q7
QUADERNI dell'ISTITUTO di FILOLO-
  GIA LATINA (Univ. Padua). Padua
  1970-   .

Q8
QUADERNI dell'ISTITUTO di LINGUE
  e LETTERATURA CLASSICHE (Univ.
  di Lecce). Bari 1980-   .

Q9
QUADERNI dell'ISTITUTO di STORIA
  dell'ARCHITETTURA (Univ. Rome).
  Rome 1953-   .

Q10
QUADERNI dell'ISTITUTO di TOPOGRA-
  FIA ANTICA (Univ. Rome). Rome
  1964-   .

Q11
QUADERNI MEDIEVALI. Bari 1976-   .

Q12
QUADERNI del MUSEO ARCHEOLOGICO
  F. RIBEZZO di BRINDISI. Brun-
  disium ?-   .

Q13
QUADERNI "RASSEGNA degli ARCHIVI di
  STATO". Rome 1960-   .

Q14
QUADERNI di STORIA; rassegna di
  antichità. Bari 1975-   .

Q15
QUADERNI di STORIA ANTICA ed EPI-
  GRAFIA. Rome 1973-   . (Pubb-
  licazione. Univ. di Trieste.
  Istituto di Storia Antica).

QUADERNI TICINESI NUMISMATICA e
  ANTICHITÀ CLASSICHE see N105.

Q16
QUADERNI TRIESTINI per il LESSICO
  della LIRICA CORALE GRECA. Trieste 1970-   .

Q17
QUADERNI TRIESTINI sul TEATRO AN-
TICO. Trieste 1968-   .

Q18
QUADERNI dell'UMANESIMO. Rome
1973-   .

Q19
QUADERNI URBINATI di CULTURA CLAS-
SICA. Urbino 1966-   . (QUCC).

Q20
QUARTALSCHRIFT. Milwaukee
1904-   . Title of vols. 1-43:
Theologische Quartalschrift.

QUARTERLY BULLETIN of the JOHN
RYLANDS LIBRARY see B319.

Q21
QUARTERLY CHECKLIST of BIBLICAL
STUDIES. Darien, Conn. 1958-
73.

Q22
QUARTERLY CHECKLIST of CLASSICAL
STUDIES. E. Northport, N.Y.
1958-77.

Q23
QUARTERLY CHECKLIST of LINGUISTICS.
E. Northport, N.Y. 1958-   .

Q24
QUARTERLY CHECKLIST of MEDIEVALIA.
Darien, Conn. 1948-77.

Q25
QUARTERLY CHECKLIST of ORIENTAL
STUDIES. Darien, Conn. 1959-77?.

Q26
QUARTERLY CHECKLIST of RENAISSANCE
STUDIES. Darien, Conn. 1959-75.

Q27
QUARTERLY of the DEPARTMENT of
ANTIQUITIES of JORDON. Amman
1951-   .

Q28
QUARTERLY of the DEPARTMENT of
ANTIQUITIES in PALESTINE. Jeru-
salem 1931-50. (QDAP, QDPal).

QUARTERLY JOURNAL. BERKSHIRE ASHMO-
LEAN SOCIETY see B57.

QUARTERLY JOURNAL of PUBLIC SPEAK-
ING see Q29.

Q29
QUARTERLY JOURNAL of SPEECH. Chi-
cago 1915-   . 1915-17 title:
Quarterly Journal of Public
Speaking. 1918-27 title: Quart-
erly Journal of Speech Education.

QUARTERLY STATEMENT. PALESTINE
EXPLORATION FUND see P21.

Q30
QUELLEN und FORSCHUNGEN aus ITALI-
ENISCHEN ARCHIVEN und BIBLIO-
THEKEN. Rome 1898-   . Sus-
pended 1915-23 1945-53.

Q31
QUELLEN und STUDIEN zur GESCHICHTE
und KULTUR des ALTERTUMS und
des MITTELALTERS. Heidelberg
1935-39?.

Q32
QUELLEN und STUDIEN zur GESCHICHTE
der MATHEMATIK, ASTRONOMIE und
PHYSIK. Berlin
--. Abt. A: Quellen. 1930-36.
--. Abt. B: Studien. 1929-38.

Q33
QUELLEN und STUDIEN zur GESCHICHTE
der NATURWISSENSCHAFTEN und der
MEDIZIN. Berlin 1908-   . 1908-
31 title: Archiv für Geschichte
[der Mathematik] der Naturwissenschaften und der Medizin.

QUESTIONS d'HISTOIRE see V66.

QUESTIONS de PHILOLOGIE CLASSIQUE
see P252.

R

R1
RILA; répertoire international de
la littérature de l'art = International Repertory of the Literature of Art. Williamson, Mass.
1974/5-   . (RILA).

Rabel, E. see P62

R2
RAD VOJVODANSKIH MUZEJA = Travaux
des Musées de Voivodina. Novi
Sad 1952-   .

Radermacher, L. see A615.

R3
RADOVI INSTITUTA JUGOSLAVENSKE
AKADEMIJE ZNANOSTI i UMJETNOSTI
u ZADRU = Acta Instituti Academiae Jugoslavicae Scientiarum
et Artium in Zadar. Zadar
1954-   . Institute's name
varies slightly. (RadJAZU).

R4
RADOVI. ODSJEK za POVIJEST FILO-
ZOFSKI FAKULTET. UNIV. ZAGREB.
Zagreb 1959-   .

R5
RADOVI. RAZRED HISTORIJE, ARHEO-
LOGIJE i HISTORIJE UMJETNOSTI.
Zadar ?-   .

R6
RAGGI; Zeitschrift für Kunstgeschichte und Archäologie. Basel
1958-   . Suspended 1958-61.

Rahner, K. see L45.

Ramsay, W. M. see S199.

R7
RAMUS; critical studies in Greek
and Roman Literature. Clayton,
Victoria 1972-   .

R8
RANDENSCHAU; Schaffhauser Heimatblätter. Schleitheim 1951-   .

Rapp, G. K. see M163.

RAPPORT ANNUEL. MUSÉE NATIONAL
SUISSE à ZURICH see J78.

RAPPORT de l'INSTITUT d'ARCHÉOLOGIE
de l'ÉTAT TCHÉCOSLOVAQUE see
Z89.

RASSEGNA degli ARCHIVI di STATO
see Q13.

R9
RASSEGNA d'ARTE ANTICA e MODERNA.
Rome & Milan 1901-22. Variant
title: Rassegna d'arte.

R10
RASSEGNA GALLARATESE di STORIA e
d'ARTE. Gallarate 1930-37
1950-   .

R11
RASSEGNA ITALIANA di LINGUE e
LETTERATURE CLASSICHE. Naples
1918-20.

R12
RASSEGNA del LAZIO; rivista mensile
della provincia di Roma. Rome
1954-   .

R13
RASSEGNA MENSILE di ISRAEL. Rome
1925-   . Suspended 1938-48.

R14
RASSEGNA MONETARIA. Rome 1904-43?
1904-30 title: Rassegna numismatica. 1931-35 title: Rassegna
numismatica finanziaria e tecnicomonetaria.

RASSEGNA NUMISMATICA (FINANZIARIA
e TECNICOMONETARIA) see R14.

R15
RASSEGNA di SCIENZE FILOSOFICHE.
Naples & Rome 1948-   .

R16
RASSEGNA STORICA SALERNITANA. Salerno 1937-   .

R17
RAVENSBERGER BLÄTTER für GESCHICHTS-
VOLKS- und HEIMATKUNDE. Beile-
feld 1901-   .

Rawlinson, H. C. see B216.

R18
RAZKOPI i PROUCHIVANNIA = Fouilles
et Recherches (Bŭlgarska Akademiîa
na Nautike. Naroden Arkheologicheski Muzei). Sofia 1948-   .

R19
RAZPRAVE. SLOVENSKA AKADEMIJA ZNA-
NOSTI i UMETNOSTI. Ljubljana
1943-   .

R20
REAL ENCYCLOPÄDIE der K/CLASSISCHEN
ALTERTUMSWISSENSCHAFT / A. F. von
Pauly; rev. G. Wissowa. Stutt-
gart 1894-1972.
--. Supplementbände. 1903-   .
(RE, PW, PWRE).

R21
REALLEXIKON der ÄGYPTISCHEN RELI-
GIONSGESCHICHTE / H. Bonnet.
Berlin & New York 1952.

R22
REALLEXIKON für ANTIKE und CHRIS-
TENTUM / T. Klauser. Stuttgart
1950-   . (RAC, RLAC).

R23
REALLEXIKON der ASSYRIOLOGIE / E.
Ebeling & B. Meissner. Berlin
1928-38 1957-   . (RLA).

R24
REALLEXIKON der BYZANTINISTIK / P.
Wirth. Amsterdam 1968-   .

R25
REALLEXIKON zur BYZANTINISCHEN
KUNST / K. Wessel. Stuttgart
1963-   . (RBK).

R26
REALLEXIKON der GERMANISCHEN ALTER-
TUMSKUNDE / J. Hoops. 2. Aufl.
Berlin 1968. 1st edition 1911-19.

R27
REALLEXIKON der INDOGERMANISCHEN
ALTERTUMSKUNDE / O. Schrader.
2. Aufl. Berlin 1917-29. 1st
edition 1901.

R28
REALLEXIKON der VORGESCHICHTE / M.
Ebert. Berlin 1924-32. (RLV,
RV).

RECHERCHES sur l'ART see Z11.

R29
RECHERCHES AUGUSTINIENNES. Paris
1958-   . Supplement to Revue
des Études Augustiniennes.

R30
RECHERCHES sur les CULTES GRECS et
l'OCCIDENT. Naples ?-   .

RECHERCHES HISTORIQUES see C108.

R31
RECHERCHES de PAPYROLOGIE. Paris
1961-   .

R32
RECHERCHES de PHILOLOGIE et de
LINGUISTIQUE. Louvain 1967-   .

R33
RECHERCHES de SCIENCE RELIGIEUSE.
Paris 1910-   . Suspended 1915
1940-46. 1943-44 replaced by:
Science religieuse. (RecSR,
RSR).

R34
RECHERCHES de THÉOLOGIE ANCIENNE
et MÉDIÉVALE. Louvain 1929-   .
(RecTh).

R35
RECORD of the ART MUSEUM (Prince-
ton University). Princeton,
N.J. 1942-   . 1942-47 title:
Record. Museum of Historic Art.

R36
RECORDS of BUCKINGHAMSHIRE. Ayles-
bury 1858-   .

RECORD. MUSEUM of HISTORIC ART
(Princeton University) see R35.

R37
RECORDS of the PAST. Washington,
D.C. 1902-14.

RECUEIL des ACTES de l'ACADÉMIE
royale/imperiale des SCIENCES,
BELLES-LETTRES et ARTS de BOR-
DEAUX see A32.

R38
RECUEIL d'ARCHÉOLOGIE ORIENTALE.
Paris 1885-1924?

R39
RECUEIL de l'ASSOCIATION des AMIS
du VIEUX HAVRE. Le Havre 1924?-
1937/8.

R40
RECUEIL GÉNÉRAL des BAS-RELIEFS de
la GAULE ROMAINE./ E. Espérandieu.
Paris 1907-   . (Collection de
Documents Inédits sur l'Histoire
de France).

R41
RECUEIL GÉNÉRAL des MONNAIES
GRECQUES d'ASIE MINEURE / W. H.
Waddington, E. Babelon & T.
Reinach. Paris 1904-25. Fasc. 1
revised in 1925.

R42
RECUEIL GÉNÉRAL des MOSAÏQUES de la
GAULE. Paris 1957-   . (Supple-
ment à "Gallia"; 10).

R43
RECUEIL d'INSCRIPTIONS GRECQUES /
C. Michel. Brussels & Paris
1900.
--. Supplement. 1912-27. Reprint
Hildesheim 1976.

R44
RECUEIL des INSCRIPTIONS GRECQUES-
CHRÉTIENNES d'ASIE MINEURE / H.
Grégoire. Paris 1922. Reprint
Chicago 1980 and Amsterdam 1968.

R45
RECUEIL des INSCRIPTIONS JURIDIQUES
GRECQUES / R. Dareste. Paris
1891-1904. Reprint Rome 1965 in
series: Studia Juridica; 6.

R46
RECUEIL des INSCRIPTIONS LIBYQUES /
J. B. Chabot. Paris 1940-41.

R47
RECUEIL des INSCRIPTIONS en LINÉ-
AIRE A / L. Godart & J. P. Oli-
vier. Paris 1976-   . (Études
Crétoises 21). (GORILA).

R48
RECUEIL de MÉMOIRES et TRAVAUX de
la SOCIÉTÉ d'HISTOIRE du DROIT et
des INSTITUTIONS de ANCIENS PAYS
de DROIT ÉCRIT. Montpellier
1948-   .

R49
RECUEIL des NOTICES et MÉMOIRES de
la SOCIÉTÉ ARCHÉOLOGIQUES, HIS-
TORIQUE et GÉOGRAPHIQUE du DÉ-
PARTEMENT de CONSTANTINE. Con-
stantine 1853-   . 1853-62
title: Annuaire de la Société
Archéologique de la Province de
Constantine. (RSAC, RecConst).

R50
RECUEIL des PUBLICATIONS de la
SOCIÉTÉ HAVRAISE d'ÉTUDES DIVER-
SES. Le Havre 1834-   . 1834
title: Compte-rendu. 1835-37

title: Resumé analytique des
travaux. Society's name changes
slightly.

R51
RECUEIL de la SOCIÉTÉ d'ARCHÉOLOGIE
et d'HISTOIRE de la CHARENTE
MARITIME. Saintes ?-   .

R52
RECUEIL de la SOCIÉTÉ JEAN BODIN
pour l'HISTOIRE COMPARATIVE des
INSTITUTIONS. Brussels 1936-   .

RECUEIL des TRAVAUX de la FACULTÉ
de DROIT de l'UNIVERSITÉ de ZA-
GREB see Z13.

RECUEIL de TRAVAUX de la FACULTÉ
des LETTRES de LJUBLJANA see Z9.

RECUEIL des TRAVAUX de la FACULTÉ
de PHILOSOPHIE (Univ. Belgrad)
see Z8.

RECUEIL des TRAVAUX de l'INSTITUT
d'ÉTUDES BYZANTINES see Z14.

RECUEIL des TRAVAUX du MUSÉE
ARCHÉOLOGIQUE du MACEDOINE see
Z7.

RECUEIL des TRAVAUX du MUSÉE
ARCHÉOLOGIQUE, SKOPJE see Z7.

RECUEIL des TRAVAUX du MUSÉE National, BELGRAD see Z12.

R53
RECUEIL de TRAVAUX RELATIFS à la
PHILOLOGIE et à l'ARCHÉOLOGIE
ÉGYPTIENNES et ASSYRIENNES. Paris
1870-1923. (RevTrav, RT).

R54
RED-FIGURED VASES of APULIA / A. D.
Trendall & A. Cambitoglou. Oxford 1978-   . (Oxford Monographs on Classical Archaeology).

R55
RED-FIGURES VASES of LUCANIA, CAM-
PANIA and SICILY / A. D. Trendall.
Oxford 1967. (Oxford Monographs
on Classical Archaeology). (LCS).
--. Supplement. London 1970.

(Supplement. Bulletin of the Institute of Classical Studies;
26).

Regel, W. see A91.

R56
RÉGÉSZETI DOLOGOZATOK (az EÖTVÖS
LORÁND TUDOMÁNYEGYETEM RÉGÉSZETI
INTERETÉBÜL) = Dissertationes
Archaeologicae (ex Instituto
Archaeologico Universitatis de
Rolando Eötvös Nominata). Buda-
pest 1958-   .

R57
RÉGÉSZETI FÜZETEK (Magyar Nemzeti
Múzeum). Budapest 1955-   .
Variant title: Régészeti Kutatá-
sai. (RF, RégFüz).

RÉGÉSZETI KUTATÁSAI see R57.

R58
RÉGÉSZETI TANULMÁNYOK. Budapest
1962-   .

R59
REGULAE BENEDICTI STUDIA. Hildesheim 1972-   .

Rehkopf, F. see G80.

Rehm, A. see I32.

REI CRETARIAE ROMANAE FAUTORUM see
A80, C179.

Reichhold, K. see G129.

Reinach, S. see R77, R79-R81,
C119, A639, V75.

Reinach, T. see R41, P52.

RELAZIONE INTORNO degli ATTI
dell'ACCADEMIA di UDINE see
A647.

RELIGIO see R261.

R60
RELIGION; a journal of religion and
religions. Newcastle-upon-Tyne
1971-   .

R61
RELIGION in GESCHICHTE und GEGEN-
WART; Handwörterbuch für Theologie und Religionswissenschaft.
3. Aufl. Tübingen 1957-65. 1st
edition 1908-13. (RGG).

R62
RELIGION und KULTUS der RÖMER / G.
Wissowa. 2. Aufl. Munich 1912.
1st edition 1902.

RELIGIONI e CIVILTÀ see S212.

R63
RELIGIONSGESCHICHTLICHE VERSUCHE
und VORARBEITEN. Giessen 1903- .
(RGVV, RVV).

R64
RELIGIOUS STUDIES. London 1965- .

RENAISSANCE NEWS see R65.

R65
RENAISSANCE QUARTERLY. New York
1948- . 1948-66 title: Renaissance News.

R66
RENAISSANCE TEXT SERIES. New York
1967- .

Renaudot, E. see L75.

R67
RENDEL HARRIS PAPYRI of WOOD-
BROOKE COLLEGE, BIRMINGHAM / J.
E. Powell. Cambridge 1936.
(PHarr).

R68
RENDICONTI della ACCADEMIA di ARCH-
EOLOGIA, LETTERE e BELLE ARTI di
NAPOLI. Naples 1865-1908 1910- .
1865-1935 title: Atti della Reale
Accademia di Archeologia, Lettere
e Belle Arti. Academy's name
changes slightly.

RENDICONTO della Reale ACCADEMIA di
ARCHEOLOGIA, LETTERE e BELLE ARTI
(Naples 1862-64 1887-1934)
see R72.

RENDICONTI. ACCADEMIA d'ITALIA
see R69.

R69
RENDICONTI. ACCADEMIA nazionale
dei LINCEI. Rome 1884/5-91.
Supersedes the Academy's Trans-
uniti.
--. Classe di scienze morali,
storiche, critiche e filologiche.
1892- . Published as part of
the Academy's continuing Atti
series. Academy's name 1939-43:
Accademia d'Italia.

R70
RENDICONTO. ACCADEMIA delle SCI-
ENZE dell'ISTITUTO di BOLOGNA.
Bologna 1829-1909.
--. Classe di Scienze Morali.
1906- .

RENDICONTI. ACCADEMIA di SCIENZE,
LETTERE ed ARTI degli ZELANTI
see M133.

RENDICONTI. ACIREALE see M133.

RENDICONTO. BOLOGNA see R70.

RENDICONTI. CLASSE di LETTERE e
SCIENZE MORALI e POLITICHE.
ISTITUTO LOMBARDO di SCIENZE e
LETTERE see R71.

RENDICONTO. CLASSE di SCIENZE
MORALI. ACCADEMIA dell'ISTITUTO
di BOLOGNA see R70.

R71
RENDICONTI dell'ISTITUTO LOMBARDO
di SCIENZE e LETTERE. CLASSE di
LETTERE e SCIENZE MORALI e POLI-
TICHE. Milan 1864- . Until
1936 not classified.

RENDICONTI e MEMORIE, ACCADEMIA di
SCIENZE, LETTERE ed ARTI degli
ZELANTI see M133.

RENDICONTI e MEMORIE. ACIREALE
see M133.

RENDICONTI. MILANO see R71.

RENDICONTO. NAPOLI (1862-64 1887-
1934) see R72.

RENDICONTI. NAPOLI (1865-1908
1910-) see R68.

RENDICONTI. PONTIFICIA ACCADEMIA
ROMANA di ARCHEOLOGIA see A668.

RENDICONTO delle SESSIONI della
ACCADEMIA dell'ISTITUTO di BOLO-
GNA see R70.

R72
RENDICONTO delle TORNATE e dei LA-
VORI della R. ACCADEMIA di ARCHE-
OLOGIA, LETTERE e BELLE ARTI.
Naples 1862-64 ns. 1887-1934.
1862-64 title: Rendiconto della
Reale Accademia di Archeologia,
Lettere e Belle Arti.

Renier, L. see I89.

RÉPERTOIRE and REPERTORIUM are
here interfiled.

R73
RÉPERTOIRE d'ART et d'ARCHÉOLOGIE.
Paris 1910-   .

R74
RÉPERTOIRE CHRONOLOGIQUE d'ÉPIGRA-
PHIE ARABE. Cairo 1931-   .

R75
RÉPERTOIRE d'ÉPIGRAPHIE SÉMITIQUE.
Paris 1900-   .

RÉPERTOIRE INTERNATIONAL de la LIT-
TÉRATURE de l'ART see R1.

R76
REPERTORIUM für KUNSTWISSENSCHAFT
Berlin & Stuttgart 1876-1931.
(RepKunstW).

R77
RÉPERTOIRE de PEINTURES GRECQUES
et ROMAINES / S. Reinach. Paris
1922. Reprint Rome 1970. (RPGR).

R78
RÉPERTOIRE de PRÉHISTOIRE et
d'ARCHÉOLOGIE de la SUISSE. Basel 1958-   . Also published in
German as: Repertorium der Ur-
und Frühgeschichte der Schweiz.
(Zurich 1955-61).

R79
RÉPERTOIRE de RELIEFS GRECS et RO-

MAINS / S. Reinach. Paris 1902-
12. (RRGR).

R80
RÉPERTOIRE de la STATUAIRE GRECQUE
et ROMAINE/ S. Reinach. Reprint
Rome 1965. Appeared in numerous
Paris editions ca. 1897-1910.
(RSGR).

REPERTORIUM der UR- und FRÜHGE-
SCHICHTE der SCHWEIZ see R78.

R81
RÉPERTOIRE des VASES PEINTS GRECS
et ÉTRUSQUES / S. Reinach. 2.
ed. Paris 1922-29. Reprint of
1st edition (1899-1900) Nandeln
1979.

REPORT. ARCHAEOLOGICAL MUSEUMS of
ISTANBUL see I128.

R82
REPORT of the COUNCIL for BRITISH
ARCHAEOLOGY. London 1950/1-   .

R83
REPORT of the DEPARTMENT of ANTI-
QUITIES, CYPRUS. Nicosia 1934-
48 1963-   . Supplements and
at times replaced by the Annual
Report of the Director of the
Department of Antiquities.
(RDAC).

R84
REPORT. EGYPT EXPLORATION SOCIETY.
London 1882-   . Earlier title:
Report of the Ordinary Meetings.

R85
REPORTS and PAPERS. LINCOLNSHIRE
ARCHITECTURAL and ARCHAEOLOGICAL
SOCIETY. Lincoln 1936/7-   .
Reports prior to 1936 were published as the Reports and Papers
of the Architectural and Archaeological Societies of the Counties of Lincoln and Northampton.

R86
REPORTS of the RESEARCH COMMITTEE
of the SOCIETY of ANTIQUARIES of
LONDON. London 1913-   .

REPORTS of the STATE HERMITAGE
MUSEUM see S117.

REPORTS and TRANSACTIONS. CARDIFF
NATURALIST'S SOCIETY see T92.

R87
REPORT and TRANSACTIONS. DEVON-
SHIRE ASSOCIATION for the ADVANCE-
MENT of SCIENCE, LITERATURE and
ART. Plymouth 1862-   .

R88
REPORT on the WORKING of the MUSEUM
DEPARTMENT of the YEAR ... (Malta
National Museum). Valetta
1903/4-   . Some only have title:
Malta.

R89
RERUM ITALICARUM SCRIPTORES ab
anno aerae Christianae 500 ad
1500 / L. A. Muratore. Milan
1723-70.   .
--. Supplement. 1748-70.
--. Nuova ed. / G. Carducci et
al. Citta di Castello 1900-   .

R90
RERUM NATURALIUM SCRIPTORES GRAECI
MINORES / O. Keller. Leipzig
1877. (Bibliotheca Scriptorum
Graecorum et Romanorum Teubner-
iana).

R91
RÉSEAUX; revue interdisciplinaire
de philosophie morale et politique. Mons 18/19- 1972-   .
Continues Revue universitaire de
science morale.

R92
RESTAURO; quaderni di restauro dei
monumenti e di urbanistica dei
Centri Antichi. Naples 1972-   .

RESUMÉ ANALYTIQUES des TRAVAUX.
SOCIÉTÉ nationale HAVRAISE d'É-
TUDES DIVERSES see R50.

Revett, N. see A375.

REV-: entries beginning with this
spelling are here interfiled.
See also RIVISTA.

R93
REVUE de l'ACADÉMIE du CENTRE.
Châteauroux 1895-   . 1895 title: Revue du Centre. 1896-1901
title: Revue Archéologique, Historique et Scientifique du Barry.
1902-05 title: Revue du Berry et
du Centre.

R94
REVUE AFRICAINE. Algiers 1856-   .
(RAf, RAfr).

R95
REVUE de l'AFRIQUE FRANÇAISE. Paris 1882-88. 1882-85 title: Bulletin Trimestriel des Antiquités
Africaines.

R96
REVUE de l'AGENAIS et des ANCIENNES
PROVINCES du SUD-OUEST. Agen
1874-   .

R97
REVUE d'ANTHROPOLOGIE. Paris
1872-89.

R98
REVUE ANTHROPOLOGIQUE. Paris
1891-   . 1891-1910 title: Revue
de l'École d'Anthropologie de
Paris. Suspended 1943-54.

R99
REVUE ARCHÉOLOGIQUE. Paris 1844- .
(RA, RevArch).

REVUE ARCHÉOLOGIQUE (Alep 1931)
see R104.

REVUE d'ARCHÉOLOGIE et d'ART IRAN-
IENS see B21.

R100
REVUE ARCHÉOLOGIQUE du CENTRE.
Vichy 1962-   .

R101
REVUE ARCHÉOLOGIQUE de l'EST et
du CENTRE-EST. Dijon 1950-   .
(RAE).

R102
REVUE des ARCHÉOLOGUES et HISTORI-
ENS d'ART de LOUVAIN. Louvain
1968-   .

REVUE ARCHÉOLOGIQUE, HISTORIQUE
et SCIENTIFIQUE du BERRY see
R93.

R103
REVUE ARCHÉOLOGIQUE de NARBONNAISE.
Paris 1968- . (RAN).

R104
REVUE ARCHÉOLOGIQUE SYRIENNE. Alep
1931-35. 1931 title: Revue Archéologique. (RASyr).

R105
REVISTA de ARCHIVOS, BIBLIOTECAS y
MUSEOS. Madrid 1871-78 1883
1897-1931 1947- . 1896 title:
Boletín de Archivos, Bibliotecarios y Museos. 1934-35 replaced
by Anuario del Cuerpo Facultativo
de Archiveros, Bibliotecarios y
Arqueólogos. (RABM).

R106
REVISTA ARHIVELOR. Bucharest
1924/6-1946/7 1958- .

R107
REVUE des ARTS. Musées de France.
Paris 1951-60. Superseded by
Revue du Louvre et des Musées de
France.

R108
REVUE de l'ART; revue de l'art ancien et moderne. Paris 1897-
1937. Variant title: La revue de
l'Art Ancien et Moderne. Suspended 1914-19.

REVUE de l'ART ANCIEN et MODERNE
see R108.

R109
REVUE des ARTS ASIATIQUES. Paris
1924-42.

R110
REVUE de l'ART CHRÉTIEN. Lille
1857-1914.

REVUE d'ASCÉTIQUE et de MYSTIQUE
see R185.

REVUE de l'ASSOCIATION CANADIENNE
de LINGUISTIQUE see C52.

REVUE de l'ASSOCIATION SUISSE pour
CHÂTEAUX et RUINES see N5.

R111
REVUE d'ASSYRIOLOGIE et d'ARCHÉO-
LOGIE ORIENTALE. Paris 1884- .
(RA, RAss, RAssyr).

R112
REVUE d'AUVERGNE. Clermont-Ferrand 1884- .

R113
REVUE de l'AVRANCHIN. Avranches,
France 1882- . 1882-84 title:
Revue trimestrielle de la Société
d'Archéologie, de Littérature,
Sciences et Arts d'Avranches et
de Mortain.

R114
REVUE du BAS-POITOU. Fontenay-le-
Compte, Paris 1888- .

R115
REVUE BELGE d'ARCHÉLOGIE et d'HIS-
TOIRE de l'ART = Belgisch Tijd-
schrift voor Oudheidkunde en
Kunstgeschiedenis. Brussels
1931- . (RBA).

R116
REVUE BELGE de NUMISMATIQUE et de
SIGILLOGRAPHIE. Brussels
1842- . 1842-74 title: Revue
de la Numismatique Belge. (RBN,
RBNum).

R117
REVUE BELGE de PHILOLOGIE et d'HIS-
TOIRE = Belgisch Tijdschrift voor
Philologie en Geschiedenis.
Brussels & Paris 1922- .
(RBPh, RBPhil, RBPhH).

R118
REVUE BÉNÉDICTINE. Abbaye de Mar-
edsous, Belgium 1884- . 1884-
89 title: Messager des Fidèles.
(RB, RBen).

REVUE du BERRY et du CENTRE see
R93.

R119
REVUE BIBLIQUE. Paris 1892- .

1892-94 title: Revue Biblique
Trimestrielle. 1895-1914 title:
Revue Biblique Internationale.
Suspended 1940-46, but replaced
by Vivre et Penser. (RB, RBibl,
RBi, RevBibl).

REVUE BIBLIQUE (INTERNATIONALE/TRI-
MESTRIELLE) see R119.

R120
REVUE de BOULOGNE. Boulogne
1926-   . 1926-27 title: Revue
du Porte et de la Ville de Boulogne-sur-Mer.

R121
REVUE BYZANTINE = Vizantiĭskoe
Obozrĭenie. Dorpat 1915-17.

REVUE CANADIENNE de LINGUISTIQUE
see C52.

REVUE du CENTRE   see R93.

R122
REVISTA CLASICĂ. Bucharest
192?-   .

R123
REVUE de COMMINGES-PYRÉNÉES CEN-
TRALES. St. Gauden 1885-   .
Title varies slightly.

R124
REVUE des COURS et CONFÉRENCES.
Paris 1892-1940.

R125
REVUE CRITIQUE d'HISTOIRE et de
LITTÉRATURE. Paris 1866-1935.

R126
REVUE du DÉPARTEMENT de la MANCHE.
Saint-Lô ?-   .

R127
REVUE de DROIT CANONIQUE. Strasburg 1951-   .

R128
REVUE DROMOISE. Valence 1866-   .
1866-73 title: Bulletin d'Archéologie et Statistique de la
Drôme.

REVUE de l'ÉCOLE d'ANTHROPOLOGIE
de PARIS see R98.

R129
REVUE d'ÉGYPTOLOGIE. Paris
1933-   . Suspended 1934-35
1939 1941-45. (RdE, REg).

R130
REVUE de l'ÉGYPTE ANCIENNE. Paris
1925-31. Suspended 1926-27.

R131
REVUE de l'ENSEIGNEMENT PHILOSO-
PHIQUE. Paris 1950-   .

R132
REVUE ÉPIGRAPHIQUE. Paris 1878-
1908 1913-14. 1878-1914 title:
Revue Épigraphique du Midi de
la France. (RevEp, REpigr, REp).

R133
REVISTA ESPAÑOLA de DERECHO CANÓ-
NICO. Madrid 1946-   .

R134
REVISTA ESPAÑOLA de TEOLOGÍA.
Madrid 1940-   .

R135
REVUE d'ESTHÉTIQUE. Paris 1948-   .

R136
REVISTA de ESTUDIOS CLÁSICOS. Men-
doza 1944-   . (REC).

R137
REVISTA de ESTUDIOS EXTREMEÑOS; revista historica, literaria y artistica. Badajoz, Spain ?-   .

R138
REVUE d'ETHNOGRAPHIE. Paris 1882-
89.

R139
REVISTA de ETNOGRAFIA. Oporto
1963-   .

R140
REVUE des ÉTUDES ANCIENNES. Bordeaux 1899-   . (REA, RevEtAnc).

R141
REVUE des ÉTUDES ARMÉNIENNES. Paris 1920-33 1964-   .

R142
REVUE des ÉTUDES AUGUSTINIENNES.
Paris 1955-   . (REAug).

REVUE des ÉTUDES AUGUSTINIENNES.
SUPPLEMENT see R29.

R143
REVUE des ÉTUDES BYZANTINES. Bucharest & Paris 1943-   . 1943-45
title: Études Byzantines. (REByz,
REB, EtByz).

REVUE d'ÉTUDES CORSES, HISTORIQUES,
LITTÉRAIRES et SCIENTIFIQUES see
C247.

R144
REVUES des ÉTUDES GRECQUES. Paris
1888-   . Includes the Bulletin
Archéologique, Bulletin Épigraphique, and Bulletin Papyrologique. (REG, RevEtGr).

R145
REVUE des ÉTUDES HISTORIQUES. Paris
1834-1944. 1834-40 title: Journal.
Institut Historique. 1841-82 title: L'Investigateur. 1883-98 title: Revue de la Société des É-
tudes Historiques. (REH).

REVUE d'ÉTUDES HISTORIQUES, LIT-
TÉRAIRES et SCIENTIFIQUES CORSES
see C247.

R146
REVUE des ÉTUDES HOMÉRIQUES. Monoco
1931-35. (REHom).

R147
REVUE des ÉTUDES INDO-EUROPÉENNES.
Bucharest 1938-47. Published
irregularly. (REIE).

R148
REVUE des ÉTUDES ISLAMIQUES. Paris
1927-   . (REI).

R149
REVUE des ÉTUDES ITALIENNES. Paris
1936-38 1954-   .

R150
REVUE des ÉTUDES JUIVES. Paris
1880-   . Suspended 1915-18.
(REJ).

R151
REVUE des ÉTUDES LATINES. Paris
1923-   . (REL).

REVUE des ÉTUDES LIGURES see
R301.

R152
REVUE des ÉTUDES ROUMAINES. Paris
1953-   .

R153
REVUE des ÉTUDES SÉMITIQUES et BA-
BYLONIACA. Paris 1934-45. 1934
title: Revue des Études Sémitiques.

R154
REVUE des ÉTUDES SLAVES. Paris
1921-   .

R155
REVUE des ÉTUDES SUD-EST EUROPÉEN-
NES. Bucharest 1963-   .
(RESEE, RESE).

REVUE de FACULTÉ de LANGUES, d'HIS-
TOIRE et de GÉOGRAPHIE. UNIV.
ANKARA see D65.

R156
REVISTA de FACULDADE de LETRAS.
UNIV. LISBOA. Lisbon 1933-   .

R157
REVISTA de FACULDADE de LETRAS.
UNIV. PORTO. Oporto
--. Serie de historia. 1970-   .
--. Serie de filosofia. 1970-   .

R158
REVUE de la FACULTÉ des LETTRES.
UNIV. TEHERAN. Tehran 1953-   .

R159
REVISTA di FILOLOGÍA ESPAÑOLA.
Madrid 1914-   .

R160
REVISTA de FILOZOFIE. Bucharest
?-   . Title until 1963: Cerce-
tări Filozofice.

R161
REVUE GÉOGRAPHIQUE de l'EST. Nancy
1961-   .

R162
REVUE de GÉOGRAPHIE de LYON. Lyons 1925-   . 1925 title: Études
et Travaux. Institut des Études
Rhodaniennes (Univ. Lyons).
1926-48 title: Études Rhodaniennes.

R163
REVISTA de GERONA. Gerona 1876- .

R164
REVUE du GÉVAUDAN, des CAUSSES et
des CÉVENNES. Mende ?-   .

R165
REVISTA de GUIMARÃES. Oporto
1884-   .

R166
REVUE de la HAUTE AUVERGNE. Au-
rillac 1899-   .

R167
REVISTA de HISTORIA. Lisbon 1912-
28.

R168
REVUE HISTORIQUE. Paris 1876-   .
(RH, RHist).

REVUE HISTORIQUE (Sofia 1945-   )
see I133.

REVUE HISTORIQUE (Belgrad 1948-)
see I138.

REVUE d'HISTOIRE ANCIENNE see
V33.

R169
REVUE HISTORIQUE et ARCHÉOLOGIQUE
du LIBOURNAIS. Libourne
1933-   .

R170
REVUE HISTORIQUE et ARCHÉOLOGIQUE
du MAINE. Le Mans etc. 1876-   .

R171
REVUE HISTORIQUE ARDENNAISE. Char-
levillemeziers, France 1969-   .

R172
REVUE HISTORIQUE de BORDEAUX et du
DÉPARTEMENT de la GIRONDE. Bor-
deaux etc. 1908-45 1952-   .

R173
REVUE d'HISTOIRE et de CIVILISATION
du MAGHREB = Majallat Tārīkh wa-
ḥaḍārat al-Maghrib. Algiers
1966-   .

R174
REVUE d'HISTORIE COMPARÉE. Paris
1923-48.

REVUE d'HISTOIRE des DOCTRINES
ÉCONOMIQUES et SOCIALES see
R178.

R175
REVUE d'HISTOIRE du DROIT = Tijdschrift voor Rechtsgeschiedenis.
Haarlem 1918-   . Suspended
1941-45. (RHD, Tijdschr).

R176
REVUE HISTORIQUE de DROIT FRANÇAIS
et ÉTRANGER. Paris 1855-   .
1870-76 title: Revue de Législation Ancienne et Moderne, Française et étrangère. 1877-1921
title: Nouvelle Revue Historique
de Droit Français et Étranger.
(RHD, RD, RHDFE, NRH, NRHD).

R177
REVUE d'HISTORIE ECCLÉSIASTIQUE.
Louvain 1900-   . (RHE).

REVUE d'HISTOIRE ECCLÉSIASTIQUE
SUISSE see Z63.

R178
REVUE d'HISTORIE ÉCONOMIQUE et
SOCIALE. Paris 1908-   . 1908-
12 title: Revue d'histoire des
doctrines économiques et sociales. Suspended 1914-19.

R179
REVUE d'HISTOIRE de l'ÉGLISE de
FRANCE. Paris 1910-   .

R180
REVUE d'HISTOIRE et de LITTÉRATURE
RELIGIEUSES. Paris 1896-1922.
Suspended 1908-09 1915-19.
(RHLR).

R181
REVUE d'HISTOIRE des MINES et de la
MÉTALLURGIE. Geneva 1969-   .

REVUE d'HISTOIRE de la PHILOSOPHIE
(et d'Histoire Générale della
Civilisation) see R234.

R182
REVUE d'HISTOIRE et de PHILOSOPHIE
RELIGIEUSE. Strasbourg 1921-   .
(RHPHR, RHPR).

R183
REVUE de l'HISTOIRE des RELIGIONS.
Paris 1880-   . (RHR, RevHist-
Rel).

R184
REVUE d'HISTOIRE des SCIENCES et
de leurs APPLICATIONS. Paris
1947-   .

R185
REVUE d'HISTOIRE de la SPIRITUA-
LITÉ. Paris & Toulouse 1920-   .
1920-72 title: Revue d'Ascétique
et de Mystique. Suspended 1940-
46.

R186
REVUE HISTORIQUE du SUD-EST EURO-
PÉEN. Bucharest 1924-46.
(RHSEE, RHSE).

R187
REVUE d'HISTOIRE des TEXTES.
Paris 1971-   .

R188
REVUE HISTORIQUE VAUDOISE. Lausanne 1893-   . (RHV).

REVUE HISTORIQUE YOUGOSLAVE see
J142.

R189
REVUE HITTITE et ASIANIQUE. Paris
1930-   . (RHA).

REVUE HONGRIE see N91.

REVUE de l'INSTITUT ARCHÉOLOGIQUE
ACADÉMIE SERBE des SCIENCES
see S145.

REVISTA del INSTITUTO EGIPCIO de
ESTUDIOS ISLÁMICOS see R190.

R190
REVISTA del INSTITUTO de ESTUDIOS

ISLÁMICOS. Madrid 1953-   .
1953-56 title: Revista del Instituto Egipcio de Estudios Islámicos.

R191
REVUE INTERNATIONALE des DROITS
de l'ANTIQUITÉ. Brussels 1948-
51 1954-   . In 1952-53 this
journal combined with Archives
d'Histoire du Droit Oriental and
was issued under that title, with
Revue Internationale des Droits
de l'Antiquité as a subtitle. In
1954 it resumed publication under
the title Revue etc. (RIDA).

R192
REVUE INTERNATIONALE des ÉTUDES
BALKANIQUES. Belgrad 1934/5-   .
(RIEB).

R193
REVUE INTERNATIONALE d'HISTOIRE
MILITAIRE = International Review
of Military History, Paris
1939-   .

R194
REVUE INTERNATIONALE d'ONOMASTIQUE.
Paris 1949-   . (RIO).

R195
REVUE. INTERNATIONAL ORGANIZATION
for ANCIENT LANGUAGES ANALYSIS
by COMPUTER = Revue. Organisation
Internationale pour l'Étude des
Langues Anciennes par Ordinateur.
Leige 1966-   . Vol. 1 published
in 1968.

R196
REVUE INTERNATIONALE de PHILOSO-
PHIE. Brussels 1938-   . Sus-
pended 1939-48. (RIPh).

R197
REVISTĂ de ISTORIE. Bucharest
1958-   . 1958-63 title: Studii;
revistă de istorie.

REVISTĂ pentru ISTORIE ARHEOLOGIE
şi FILOLOGIE see R216.

R198
REVISTA ISTORICĂ ROMÂNĂ. Bucharest
1931-47. (RIR).

R199
REVUE JURIDIQUE et ÉCONOMIQUE du
  SUD-OUEST. Bordeaux 1950-55.
  --. Série Juridique. 3- 1952-   .
  --. Série Economique. 1952-   .

R200
  REVISTA LATINO AMERICANA de FILO-
  SOFÍA. Buenas Aires 1975-   .

R201
REVENUE LAWS of PTOLEMY PHILADEL-
  PHUS / B. P. Grenfell. Oxford
  1896. (PRev).

REVUE de LÉGISLATION ANCIENNE et
  MODERNE, FRANÇAISE et ÉTRANGÈRE
  see R176.

R202
REVISTA de LETRAS. (Faculdade de
  Filosofia, Ciencias e Letras
  Univ. Asses). Assiz 1960-   .

REVUE de LINGUISTIQUE see R232.

R203
REVUE de LINGUISTIQUE ROMANE.
  Paris 1925-   .

R204
REVUE du LOUVRE et des MUSÉES de
  FRANCE. Paris 1961-   . Super-
  sedes Revue des Arts.

R205
REVIEW of METAPHYSICS. New Haven
  1947-   .

R206
REVUE de MÉTAPHYSIQUE et de MORALE.
  Paris 1893-   . Suspended 1942-
  44, but 1944 issue replaced by
  Études de Métaphysique et de Mo-
  rale. (RMM).

R207
  REVUE du MOYEN ÂGE LATIN. Lyons
  1945-   .

R208
REVUE des MUSÉES de BORDEAUX.
  Bordeaux ?-   .

R209
REVISTA MUZEELOR. Bucharest 1964-

73. Continues Buletinul Comisiunii Monumentelor Istorice?
  (RevMuz).

R210
REVISTA MUZEELOR şi MONUMENTELOR.
  Bucharest.
  --. Seria Muzee. 11- 1974-   .
  Numbering continues that of Re-
  vista Muzeelor.
  --. Seria Monumente, Istorice şi
  Arta. 1975?-   .

REVUE NÉO-SCOLASTIQUE (de Philosophie) see R220.

R211
REVUE du NORD. Lille 1910-   .

R212
REVUE NUMISMATIQUE. Paris 1836-77
  1883-   . 1836-37 title: Revue
  de la numismatique française.
  (RN, RevNum).

REVUE de la NUMISMATIQUE BELGE
  see R116.

REVUE de la NUMISMATIQUE FRANÇAISE
  see R212.

R213
REVISTA de OCCIDENTE. Madrid
  1980-   . Supersedes journal by
  the same name (1923-77).

REVUE. ORGANISATION INTERNATIONALE
  pour l'ÉTUDE des LANGUES ANCIEN-
  NES par ORDINATEUR see R195.

REVUE ORIENTALE see K17.

R214
REVUE de l'ORIENT CHRÉTIEN. Paris
  1896-1946. (ROC).

R215
REVUE de l'ORIENT LATIN. Brussels
  1893-1911. (ROL).

R216
REVISTA PENTRU ISTORIE, ARHEOLOGIE
  şi FILOLOGIE. Bucharest 1882-94.

REVUE de PHILOSOPHIE et d'HISTOIRE
  ANCIENNE see E89.

R217
REVUE de PHILOLOGIE de LITTÉRATURE
et d'HISTOIRE ANCIENNES. Paris
1845-47 1877-   . (RPh, Rev-
Phil).

R218
REVUE de PHILOSOPHIE. Paris 1900-
14 1919-39.

R219
REVUE PHILOSOPHIQUE de la FRANCE
et de l'ÉTRANGER. Paris 1876- .
(RPhilos).

R220
REVUE PHILOSOPHIQUE de LOUVAIN.
Louvain 1894-   . 1894-1909 title: Revue Néo-scolastique.
1910-45 title: Revue Néo-scolastique de Philosophie. Suspended
1914-19 and 1940-45. (RPhL).

REVUE du PORTE et de la VILLE de
BOULOGNE-sur-MER see R120.

R221
REVISTA PORTUGUESA de FILOLOGIA.
Coimbra etc. 1947-   .

R222
REVISTA PORTUGUESA de HISTÓRIA.
Coimbra 1940/1-   .

R223
REVUE PRÉHISTORIQUE. Paris 1906-11.

REVUE PRÉHISTORIQUE (Prague 1922-)
see 06.

R224
REVISTA de PREISTORIE şi ANTICHITĂŢI
NAŢIONALE. Bucharest 1937-40?

R225
REVUE des QUESTIONS HISTORIQUES.
Paris 1866-1939.

R226
REVUE des QUESTIONS SCIENTIFIQUES.
Namur & Louvain 1877-   . Sus-
pended 1915-19 and 1940-45.

R227
REVUE de QUMRÂN. Paris 1958-   .
(RQ).

R228
REVIEW of RELIGION. New York
1936-58. (RR).

R229
REVUE du ROUERGUE. Rodez 1947-   .

R230
REVUE ROUMAINE d'HISTOIRE. Bucharest 1962-   . (RRH).

R231
REVUE ROUMAINE d'HISTOIRE de l'ART.
Bucharest 1964-   .

R232
REVUE ROUMAINE de LINGUISTIQUE.
Bucharest 1956-   . 1956-63
title: Revue de Linguistique.

R233
REVUE SAVOISIENNE. Annecy 1860-   .

R234
REVUE des SCIENCES HUMAINES. Paris
1927-   . 1927-31 title: Revue
d'Histoire de la Philosophie.
1933-46 title: Revue d'Histoire
de la Philosophie et d'Histoire
Générale de la Civilisation.

REVUE des SCIENCES et des LETTRES
see M293.

R235
REVUE des SCIENCES PHILOSOPHIQUES
et THÉOLOGIQUES. Paris etc.
1907-   . Suspended 1941-46, but
replaced in 1941-42 by Sciences
Philosophiques et Théologiques.
(RSPh).

R236
REVUE des SCIENCES RELIGIEUSES.
Paris & Strasburg 1921-   . Sus-
pended 1940-47. (RSR).

R237
REVUE SÉMITIQUE d'ÉPIGRAPHIE et
d'HISTOIRE ANCIENNE. Paris 1893-
1914.

REVUE trimestrielle de la SOCIÉTÉ
d'ARCHÉOLOGIE, de LITTÉRATURE,
SCIENCES et ARTS d'AVRANCHES et
de MORTAIN see R113.

REVUE de la SOCIÉTÉ des ÉTUDES HIS-
TORIQUES see R145.

REVUE de SOCIÉTÉ de MUSÉE SLOVAQUE
see Z16.

R238
REVUE des SOCIÉTÉS SAVANTES de
HAUTE NORMANDIE. Rouen 1956-   .

REVUE SUISSE d'ART et d'ARCHÉOLOGIE
see Z62.

REVUE SUISSE d'HISTOIRE see S50.

R239
REVUE SUISSE de NUMISMATIQUE =
Schweizerische Numismatische
Rundschau. Geneva etc. 1891-   .
(SNR, RSN).

R240
REVUE de SYNTHÈSE. Paris 1931-   .
(RS).

R241
REVUE du TARN. Albi 1921-   .
1921-34 title: Bulletin. Société
des Science, Arts et Belles-Lettres du Tarn.

R242
REVUE de THÉOLOGIE. Paris etc.
1850-69. 1850-57 title: Revue de
Théologie et de Philosophie Chré-
tienne. 1858-62 title: Nouvelle
Revue de Théologie.

R243
REVUE THÉOLOGIQUE de LOUVAIN. Louvain 1970-   .

R244
REVUE de THÉOLOGIE et de PHILOSO-
PHIE. Geneva etc. 1868-   .
1868-72 title: Théologie et philosophie. (RThPh).

REVUE de THÉOLOGIE et de PHILOSOPHIE
CHRÉTIENNE see R242.

R245
REVUE THOMISTE. Paris 1893-   .
Suspended 1939-46.

REVUE TRIMESTRIELLE ... see

REVUE ... (the word the word
trimestriel is disregarded in
filing, but may have been regarded in forming an abbreviation).

R246
REVUE TUNISIENNE. Tunis 1894-1927
1930-   .

R247
REVUE de l'UNIVERSITÉ de BRUXEL-
LES. Brussels 1895-   . Sus-
pended 1941-47. (RUB).

R248
REVISTA da UNIVERSIDADE de COIMBRA.
Coimbra 1912-   .

R249
REVISTA de la UNIVERSIDAD COM-
PLUTENSE de MADRID. Madrid
1940-43 1952-   .

REVISTA de la UNIVERSIDAD de MA-
DRID see R249.

REVISTA UNIVERSIDADE de PORTO.
FACULTADE de LETRAS see R157.

REVUE de l'UNIVERSITÉ de TEHERAN.
FACULTÉ des LETTRES see R158.

R250
REVISTA VENEZOLANA de FILOSOFIA.
Caracas 1973-   .

R251
REVUE du VIVARAIS. Lagentière
?-   .

Revett, N. see A375.

Reynolds, J. M. see I91.

R252
RHEINFELDER NEUJAHRSBLÄTTER
Rheinfelden 1956-   .

R253
RHEINISCHE LANDESMUSEUM. Bonn
1966-   .

R254
RHEINISCHES MUSEUM für PHILOLOGIE.
Bonn & Frankfurt 1827-29 1833-39
1842-   . Suspended 1920-24

1944-48. Title varies slightly.
(RhM, RhMus, RheinMus).

R255
RHEINISCHE VIERTELJAHRSBLÄTTER.
Bonn 1931-   .

R256
RHEINISCHE ZEITSCHRIFT für ZIVIL-
und PROZESSRECHT des IN- und
AUSLANDES. Mannheim & Leipzig
1908-25.

R257
RHETORES GRAECI / L. von Spengel.
Leipzig 1853-56. Revised edi-
tions of some volumes 1874-   .
(Bibliotheca Scriptorum Graecorum
et Romanorum Teubneriana).

R258
RHETORES LATINI MINORES / K. F.
Halm. Leipzig 1863.

R259
RHODANIA. Vienne 1919-   .

Ribbeck, O. see C170, T85.

Riccobono, S. see F31.

R260
RICERCHE MEDIEVALI. Pavia 1966- .

R261
RICERCHE RELIGIOSE; rivista di
studi storico-religiosi. Rome
1925-   . 1934-44 title: Religio.
Suspended 1940-42 1945-56.
(RicRel).

R262
RICERCHE e STUDI (Museo Provinciale
Francesco Ribezzo). Brindisi
?-   .

Riese, A. see G22.

RILA see R1.

R263
RILIEVI delle URNE ETRUSCHE / H.
von Brunn & G. Körte. Rome
1870-1916.

R264
RINASCIMENTO; rivista dell'Istituto
Nazionale di Studi sul Rinas-
cimento. Florence 1950-   .

R265
RISCONTRI; rivista trimestrale di
cultura e di attualità. Avel-
lino 1979-   .

Ritschl, F. W. see P180.

RIVISTA see also REVISTA.

R266
RIVISTA di ANTROPOLOGIA. Rome
1891/2-   . 1891-1910 title:
Atti. Società Romana di Antropologia.

R267
RIVISTA di ARCHEOLOGIA. Rome
1977-   . (RdA).

R268
RIVISTA di ARCHEOLOGIA CRISTIANA.
Rome 1924-   . Supersedes
Nuovo Bullettino di Archeologia
Cristiana. (RAC, RACr).

R269
RIVISTA ARCHEOLOGICA della PROVIN-
CIA e DIOCESI di COMO. Milan
1872-   . 1872 title: Studii
Archeologici su la Provincia di
Como. Variant title: Rivista
Archeologica della Provincia e
Antica Diocesi di Como.

R270
RIVISTA d'ARTE. Florence 1903- .
Title of vol. 1: Miscellanea
d'arte. Suspended 1908-11 1913-
16 1918-28 1943-49.

R271
RIVISTA BIBLICA. Rome 1953-   .
1953-56 title: Rivista Biblica
Italiana.

RIVISTA BIBLICA ITALIANA see R271.

RIVISTA CALABRESE di STORIA e
GEOGRAFIA see R292.

R272
RIVISTA CRITICA di STORIA della
   FILOSOFIA. Milan & Florence
   1946-   . 1946-49 title: Rivista
   di Storia della Filosofia. (RSF).

R273
RIVISTA di CULTURA CLASSICA e MEDI-
   OEVALE. Rome 1959-   . (RCCM).

R274
RIVISTA di DIRITTO CIVILE. Padua
   1955-   .

R275
RIVISTA di DIRITTO COMMERCIALE e
   del DIRITTO GENERALE delle OBBLI-
   GAZIONE. Milan 1903-   . Title
   varies slightly.

R276
RIVISTA di DIRITTO INTERNAZIONALE.
   Milan 1906-   .

R277
RIVISTA di EPIGRAFIA ETRUSCA.
   Florence 1927-   . Issued as
   part of Studi Etruschi.

R278
RIVISTA di EPIGRAFIA ITALICA.
   Florence 1973-   . Issued as
   part of Studi Etruschi.

R279
RIVISTA di ESTETICA. Padua etc.
   1956-   .

RIVISTA di FILOLOGIA CLASSICA   see
   R280.

R280
RIVISTA di FILOLOGIA e d'ISTRUZIONE
   CLASSICA. Turin 1873-   .
   1944/5-49 title: Rivista di Filo-
   logia Classica. (RFic, RivFil,
   RFC, RivFC).

R281
RIVISTA di FILOSOFIA. Modena
   1909-   .

R282
RIVISTA INDO-GRECO-ITALICA di FILO-
   LOGIA, LINGUA, ANTICHITÀ. Naples
   1916-37. (RIGI, RivIGI).

R283
RIVISTA INGAUNA e INTEMELIA N.S.
   Bordighera 1946-   . [For the
   publication with this title that
   appeared 1937-41 see Rivista di
   Studi Liguri.]

RIVISTA INGAUNA e INTEMELIA   see
   R301.

R284
RIVISTA INTERNAZIONALE di FILOSOFIA
   del DIRITTO. Genoa & Rome
   1921-   .

R285
RIVISTA dell'ISTITUTO NAZIONALE
   d'ARCHEOLOGIA e STORIA dell'ARTE.
   Rome 1929-42 1952-   . Name of
   Institute varies slightly.
   (RIA, RIASA, RivIstArch).

R286
RIVISTA ITALIANA di NUMISMATICA e
   SCIENZE AFFINI. Milan 1888-
   1928/9 1941-   . 1888-97 title:
   Rivista Italiana di Numismatica.
   (RIN, RivNum, RivItNum, RINum).

R287
RIVISTA ITALIANA per la SCIENZE
   GIURIDICHE. Rome & Turin 1886-
   1921 1926-39. (RISG).

R288
RIVISTA di SCIENZE PREISTORICHE.
   Florence 1946-   . (RScPr,
   RivScPr).

R289
RIVISTA di STORIA ANTICA. Padua &
   Messina 1895-1910. 1895-99 title:
   Rivista di Storia Antica e Sci-
   enze Affini. (RSA).

R290
RIVISTA STORICA dell'ANTICHITÀ.
   Bologna 1971-   . (RSA).

RIVISTA di STORIA ANTICA e SCIENZE
   AFFINI   see   R289.

R291
RIVISTA di STORIA, ARTE, ARCHEOLO-
   GIA per la PROVINCIA di ALESSAN-
   DRIA e ASTI. Alessandria, Italy
   1892-   .

R292
RIVISTA STORICA CALABRESE. Con-
    tanzara, Sienna 1893-1906. 1893
    title: Rivista Calabrese di Sto-
    ria e Geografia.

R293
RIVISTA di STORIA della CHIESA in
    ITALIA. Rome 1947-   .

R294
RIVISTA di STORIA del DIRITTO ITA-
    LIANO. Rome etc. 1928-   .
    --. Biblioteca. 1928-41.

RIVISTA di STORIA della FILOSOFIA.
    see R272.

R295
RIVISTA STORICA ITALIANA. Turin
    etc. 1884-   . Suspended 1943-
    47. (RSI).

R296
RIVISTA di STORIA e LETTERATURA
    RELIGIOSA. Florence 1965-   .

RIVISTA STORICA SVIZZERA see S50.

R297
RIVISTA STORICA TICENESE; archeo-
    logia, storia, belle arti. Bel-
    linzona 1938-46?

R298
RIVISTA di STUDI BIZANTINI e NEO-
    ELLENICI. Rome 1924-   . 1924-
    27 title: Studi Bizantini. 1927-
    63 title: Studi Bizantini e Neo-
    ellenici. (RSBN).

R299
RIVISTA di STUDI CLASSICI. Turin
    1952-79. (RSC).

R300
RIVISTA di STUDI FENICI. Rome
    1973-   .

R301
RIVISTA di STUDI LIGURI = Revue
    des Études Ligures. Bordighera
    1934/5-   . 1934 title: Bollet-
    tino della Società Storico-Arch-
    eologica Ingauna e Intemelia.
    1935 title: Bollettino della R.

Deputazione di Storia Patria per
    la Liguria. Sezione Ingauna e
    Intemelia. 1937-41 title: Rivista
    Ingauna e Intemelia. [See also
    Rivista Ingauna e Intemelia. N.
    S.] (RStLig, RSL, RivStLig).

R302
RIVISTA degli STUDI ORIENTALI.
    Rome 1907-   . (RSO, RStO).

R303
RIVISTA di STUDI POMPEIANI. Naples
    1934-46.

RIVISTA SVIZZERA d'ARTE e d'ARCHE-
    OLOGIA see Z62.

RIVISTA UNIV. LISBON. FACULDADE
    de LETRAS see R156.

Rizzo, G. E. see P140.

Robert, C. see A364, G113.

Robert, J. see B290.

Robert, L. see B290, E130, H45.

Roberts, C. H. see A367.

Robertson, A. S. see R334.

Robinson, D. M. see G91.

R304
ROČENKA NÁRDOPISNÉHO a PRŮMYSLO-
    VÉHO MUSEA MĚSKA PROSTĚJOVA a
    HANÉ. Prostějov 1924-40 1948-   .

R305
ROCZNIK BIALOSTOCKI. Bialystok
    1961-   .

R306
ROCZNIKI HISTORYCZNE. Poznan
    1925-   . Vol. 15 constitutes
    1939/46. Suspended 1939-45.

R307
ROCZNIK MUZEUM NARODOWEGO W WARS-
    ZAWIE = Annuaire du Musée Nation-
    al de Varsovie. Warsaw 2-
    1957-   . Numbered in continua-
    tion of another Rocznik issued
    in 1938.

R308
ROCZNIK ORJENTALISTYCZNY. Krakow
    1914/15-   . Spelling of title
    varies slightly. Suspended
    1940-48.

ROCZNIK PAPIROLOGII PRAWNICZEJ
    see J119.

Rodenwaldt, C. see A364.

Rodriguez Adrados, F. see D40.

Röhl, H. see I53, I10.

R309
RÖMISCH-GERMANISCHE FORSCHUNGEN.
    Berlin 1928-   . (RGF).

R310
RÖMISCH-GERMANISCHES KORRESPONDENZ-
    BLATT. Trier 1908-16.

R311
RÖMISCHE HISTORISCHE MITTEILUNGEN.
    Graz 1956/7-   .

R312
RÖMISCHEN INSCHRIFTEN und BILD-
    WERKE WÜRTTEMBERGS / F. Haug &
    P. Gössler. 2. Aufl. Stuttgart ⌐
    1914. 1st edition 1900 by Haug ⌐
    G. Sixt.

R313
RÖMISCHEN INSCHRIFTEN von TARRACO /
    G. Alföldy. Berlin 1975. (Mad-
    rider Forschungen; 10).

R314
RÖMISCHEN INSCHRIFTEN UNGARNS /
    L. Barkóczi & A. Móscy. Amster-
    dam 1972-   . (RIU).

R315
RÖMISCHES JAHRBUCH für KUNSTGE-
    SCHICHTE. Rome ètc. 1937-   .
    1937-38 title: Kunstgeschicht-
    liches Jahrbuch des Bibliotheca
    Hertziana. Suspended 1945-54.

R316
RÖMISCHE LIMES in ÖSTERREICH.
    Vienna etc. 1900-   . (RLiO,
    RLÖ).

R317
RÖMISCHE LIMES in UNGARN / J.
    Fitz. Székesfehérvár 1976. (Az
    István Király Múzeum Közlemén-
    yei).

RÖMISCHE MITTEILUNGEN   see M193.

R318
RÖMISCHEN MOSAIKEN in DEUTSCHLAND /
    K. Parlasca. Berlin 1959.

R319
RÖMISCHEN MOSAIKEN und MALEREIEN
    der KIRCHLICHEN BAUTEN von IV bis
    XIII Jahrhundert / J. Wilpert.
    Freiburg i.B. 1916.

R320
RÖMISCHES ÖSTERREICH; Jahresschrift
    der Österreichischen Gesellschaft
    für Archäologie. Vienna 1973-   .

R321
RÖMISCHE PRIVATRECHT / M. Kaser.
    11. Aufl. Munich 1979. (Handbuch
    der Altertumswissenschaft; X, 3,
    3). (RPR).

R322
RÖMISCHE QUARTALSCHRIFT für CHRIST-
    LICHE ALTERTUMSKUNDE und für
    KIRCHENGESCHICHTE. Rome
    1887-   . Suspended 1943-52.
    (RQ, RQA, RömQ).

R323
RÖMISCHE RECHTSGESCHICHTE / W. Kun-
    kel. 6. Aufl. Cologne 1971. 1st
    edition 1948. English edition in
    2nd edition Oxford 1975.

R324
RÖMISCHE RELIGIONSGESCHICHTE / K.
    Latte. 2. Aufl. Munich 1967. 1st
    edition 1960. (Handbuch der Al-
    tertumswissenschaft; V, 4).
    (RRG).

R325
RÖMISCHES STAATSRECHT / T. Mommsen.
    3. Aufl. Leipzig 1887-88. (Hand-
    buch der römischen Alterthumer;
    1-3). 1st edition 1871. French
    edition (1887) with title: Le
    droit public romain (Manuel des
    antiquités romaines; 1-3).

R326
RÖMISCHE STFARECHT / T. Mommsen.
Leipzig 1899. (Systematische
Hanbuch der deutschen Rechts-
wissenschaft; I, 4). Reprint
Graz 1955.

R327
RÖMISCHE ZIVILPROZESSRECHT / M.
Kaser. Munich 1966. (Handbuch
der Altertumswissenschaft; X, 3,
4).

R328
ROERSTREEK; jaarboek heemkunde Vereniging Roerstreek. Roermond
?-   .

Röhl, H. ssee I53, I10.

RÖM-: entries beginning with this
spelling are filed as if spelled
.ROEM-.

Roller, M. see D83.

R329
ROMA; rivista di studi e vita
romana. Rome 1923-44.

R330
ROMA SOTTERRANEA; le pitture delle
catacombe romane / J. Wilpert.
Rome 1903. Also issued under
title: Malereien der Katakomben
Roms. Planned to accompany G. B.
de Rossi's La Roma Sotterranea
Cristiana.

R331
ROMA SOTTERANEA CRISTIANA / G. B.
de Rossi. Rome 1864-77.
--. Nuova serie / O. Marucchi.
1909-14.

R332
ROMAN DOCUMENTS from the GREEK
EAST / R. K. Sherk. Baltimore
1969.

R333
ROMAN IMPERIAL COINAGE / H. Mat-
tingly et al. London 1923-   .
(RIC).

R334
ROMAN IMPERIAL COINS in the HUNTER
COIN CABINET, Univ. of Glasgow /
A. S. Robertson. London, Glasgow
& New York 1962-67.

R335
ROMAN INSCRIPTIONS of BRITAIN / R.
G. Collingwood & R. P. Wright.
Oxford 1965-   . (RIB).

R336
ROMAN POLITICS and the CRIMINAL
COURTS, 149-78 B.C. / E. S.
Gruen. Cambridge 1968. (RPCC).

R337
ROMAN REPUBLICAN COIN HOARDS / M.
H. Crawford. London 1969. (Royal
Numismatics Society. Special
Publications; 4).

R338
ROMAN REPUBLICAN COINAGE / M. H.
Crawford. London & New York
1974-   .

R339
ROMAN REVOLUTION / R. Syme. Oxford
1939. Appeared in many printings.

R340
ROMAN RULE in ASIA MINOR to the
end of third century after Christ
/ D. Magie. Princeton 1950.
(RRAM).

R341
ROMANA (Associazione Archeologica
Romana). Rome 1911-30. 1919-22
never published. 1911-28 title:
Bollettino.

R342
ROMANA CONTACT. Braine l'Alleud
1958?-   .

R343
ROMANIA; recueil trimestriel con-
sacré à l'étude des langues et
des littératures romanes. Paris
1872-   .

R344
ROMANIC REVIEW. New York 1910-   .

R345
ROMANISCHES ETYMOLOGISCHES WÖRTER-
BUCH / W. Meyer-Lübke. 3. Aufl.
Heidelberg 1935. 1st edition
1911-20.

R346
ROMANISCHE FORSCHUNGEN. Frankfurt
a.M. 1883-   .

R347
ROMANITAS; revista de cultura romana. Rio de Janeiro 1958-   .

R348
ROMANOBARBARICA. Rome 1976-   .

Roscher, W. H. see A688.

Rossi, G. B. de see I44, R331.

Rostovtsev, M. see S107-S108.

Rotondi, G. see L24.

Rowe, A. see C74.

ROYAL CENTRAL ASIAN JOURNAL   see
J97.

R349
ROYAL CORRESPONDENCE in the HELLEN-
ISTIC PERIOD / C. B. Wells. New
Haven 1934. Reprint Chicago 1974.
(RC).

R350
ROYAL GREEK PORTRAIT COINS / E. T.
Newell. New York 1937. Reprint
Racine, Wisc. 1968.

R351
ROYAL INSCRIPTIONS from SUMER and
AKKAD / G. A. Barton. New Haven
1929. (Library of Ancient Sem-
tic Inscriptions; 1). (RISA).

R352
ROYAL TOMBS at DENDRA near MEDEA /
A. W. Persson. Lund 1931. (Humanistiska Vetenskaps-samfundet
i Lund Skrifter; 15).

R353
ROYAL TOMBS of the FIRST DYNASTY /
W. F. Petrie. London & Boston

1900-01. (Egypt Exploration Fund;
Memoir; 18, 21).

R354
ROZPRAVY ČESKOSLOSLOVENSKÉ AKADEMIE
věd a UMĚNÍ = Abhandlungen der
Tschechoslowakischen Akademie
der Wissenschaften.
--. 1. Třída: pro vědy, filosofické, právní a historické
(Klasse für Philosophie, Rechts-
und Historische Wissenschaft).
1891-1942 1946-52?
--. 3. Třída. Filologická
(Philologische Klasse). 1892-
1941.
--. Řada S[polečenských] V[ěd]
= Sozialwissenschaftliche Reihe.
1953-   .

Rubensohn, O. see E27.

Rüstow, W. see G110.

Ruggiero, E. de see D78.

Rumpf, A. see M27.

R355
RUSSIE et CHRÉTIENTÉ. Boulogne-
sur-Seine 1934-50. 1946-48 title:
Cahiers de Russie et Chrétienté.

Russu, I. I. see I50.

Rüstow, W. see G110.

Ryckmans, G. see N61.

S

S1
SAN; journal of the Society for
Ancient Numismatics. Granada
Hills, CA. etc. 1969-   .

S2
STK; Svensk teologisk kvartalsskrift. Lund 1925-   . Until
1971 STK not part of the title.

S3
SAALBURG JAHRBUCH (Saalburg-Muse-
um). Saalburg 1910-   . (SJ).

S4
SAARBRÜCKER HEFTE (Saarbrücken
Kultur und Schulamt). Saar-
brücken 1955-   .

Sacconi, A. see 187.

SACRA SCRIPTURA ANTIQUITATIBUS
ORIENTALIBUS ILLUSTRATA see
B73.

S5
SACRIS ERUDIRI; jaarboek voor
godsdienstwetenschappen.
Brugge etc. 1948-   .

S6
SÄCHISCHE HEIMATBLÄTTER. Leipzig
1955?-   .

S7
SAECULUM; Jahrbuch für Universalgeschichte. Freiburg i.B.
1950-   .

SAGGI di DISSERTAZIONI dell'ACCAD-
EMIA PALERMITANA del BUON GUSTO
see A646.

S8
SAGGI e MEMORIE di STORIA dell'
ARTE. Venice 1957-   .

Saglio, E. see D41.

S9
SAISONS d'ALSACE. Strasbourg
1948-   .

S10
SAITABI; noticiario de historia,
arte y arqueología de Levante.
Valencia 1940-   .

S11
SALESIANUM; theologiae, iuris
canonici, philosophiae. Rome
& Turin 1939-   .

S12
SALMANTICENSIS; commentarius de
sacris disciplinis cura Facul-
tatum Pontificae Universitatis
Ecclesiasticae editus. Salamanca 1954-   .

S13
SAMLINGAR utgivna av SVENSKA FORN-
SKRIFT-SÄLLSKAPET. Ser. 2: La-
tinska skrifta. Stockholm
1924/31-   .

S14
SAMMELBLATT des HISTORISCHEN VER-
EINS INGOLSTADT (und Umgebung).
Ingolstadt 1870-   . Title var-
ies slightly. Suspended 1941-49.

S15
SAMMELBUCH GRIECHISCHER URKUNDEN
aus AEGYPTEN / F. Preisigke et al.
Strasbourg 1915-   .
--. Beiheft 1952-61. (SB).

SAMMELWERK der SLOWAKISCHEN MUZEUMS
GESELLSCHAFT see Z16.

S16
SAMMLUNG AUSGEWÄHLTER KIRCHEN- und
DOGMENGESCHICHTLICHER QUELLEN-
SCHRIFTEN. Tübingen etc.
1891-   . Publication suspended
during WW II period.

S17
SAMMLUNG der GRIECHISCHEN DIALEK-
INSCHRIFTEN / F. Bechtel, H.
Collitz et al. Göttingen 1884-
1915. (SGDI, GDI).

S18
SAMMLUNG GRIECHISCHER und LATEIN-
ISCHER GRAMMATIKER. Berlin & New
York 1974-   .

S19
SAMMLUNG WISSENSCHAFTLICHER C/KOM-
MENTARE (zu griechischen und
römischen Schriftstellen). Leipzig 1897?-   .

S20
SAMNIUM; pubblicazione trimestrale
di studi storici. Naples & Bene-
vento 1928-   .

SAN see S1.

S21
SANAT TARIHI YILLIGI. Istanbul
1964/5?-   .

S22
SANDALION; quaderni di cultura classica, cristiana e medievale. Genoa 1978-   .

Sanmartin, J. see K9.

Santos, F. Diego see E72.

S23
SARCOFAGI CRISTIANI ANTICHI / J.
Wilpert. Rome 1929-36. (Monumenti dell'Antichità Cristiana;
ser. 1,1).

S24
SARGETIA; acta Musei Regioñalis
Devensis = Buletinul Muzeului
Judetului hunedoora. Deva
1937-   .

Saria, B. see A359.

Šašel, A. and J. see I77.

Sathas. K. N. see M153.

S25
SAVARIA; a vas megyei múzeumok
értesitöje. Szombathely
1963-   .

SBORNIK see also SPOMENIK, ZBOR-
NIK.

S26
SBORNIK ČESKOSLOVENSKÁ AKADEMIE
VĚD. ARCHEOLOGICKÝ USTAV. Pobo-
čka v Brne. Brno 1960-   .

S27
SBORNIK. ČESKOSLOVENSKÁ SPOLEČNOSŤ
ARCHEOLOGICKÁ. Brno 1961-   .

S28
SBORNIK FILOLOGICKÝ. Prague
1910-   .

S29
SBORNIK FILOZOFICKEJ FAKULTY UNI-
VERZITY KOMENSKEHO. Bratislava
1922-32.
--. Historia. 9- 1958-   .
--. Philologica. 9- 1950-   .
--. Philosophica. 10- 1960-   .

S30
SBORNIK MUZEÍA ANTROPOLOGII i ET-
NOGRAFII. Leningrad 1900-   .
Early volumes also had French
title: Publications du Musée
d'Anthropologie et d'Ethnographie.

SBORNÍK MUZEÁLNEJ SLOVENSKEJ SPO-
LOČNOSTI see Z16.

S31
SBORNÍK NÁRODNÍHO MUZEA v PRAVE
RADA A: HISTORICKÝ = Acta Musei
Nationalis Pragae. Series A: His-
toria. Prague 1938/9-   . Sus-
pended 1940-47.

S32
SBORNIK za NARODNI UMOTVORENIĪA i
NARODOPIS. Sofia 1889-. .
1889-1901 title: Sbornik za Narodnu Umotvoreniia, nauka i
knizhnina.

SBORNIK za NARODNU UMOTVORENIIA
NAUKA i KNIZHNINA see S32.

S33
SBORNIK NAUCHNYKH RABOT ASPIRANTOV.
(Univ. Druzhby Narodov). Moscow
1965?-   .

S34
SBORNÍK PRACI FILOSOFICKÉ FAKULTY
BRNĚNSKÉ UNIVERSITY. Brno
--. A. Rada Jazykovedná.
1952-   .
--. B. Rada Filosoficka.
1953-   .
--. C. Rada Historicka. 1954- .
--. E. Rada Archeologiko-Klasic-
ká. 1956-   .

SBORNÍK PRACÍ HISTORICKÝCH see
H83.

SBORNIK SLOVENSKÉHO NÁRODNÉHO MÚ-
ZEA see Z15.

SBORNIK. UNIVERZITY KOMENSKEHO.
FILOZOFICKÁ FAKULTA see S29.

S35
SBORNIK VELEHRADSKÝ (Archeologický
Spolek Starý Velehrad se Sidlem
na Velehradě). Velehradě 1880-
1948. Suspended 1943-45.

S36
SCAENICORUM ROMANORUM FRAGMENTA /
A. Klotz. Monachii 1953-   .

SCANDANAVIAN JOURNAL of THEOLOGY
see S254.

SCANDANAVIAN NUMISMATIC JOURNAL
see N66.

S37
SCANDIA; tidskrift för historisk
forskning. Stockholm 1928-   .

S38
SCHACHTGRÄBER von MYKENAE / G.
Karo. Munich 1930-33.

Schaeffer, C. F. A. see E47,
M179, S153.

S39
SCHAFFHAUSER BEITRÄGE zur VATER-
LÄNDISCHEN GESCHICHTE. Schaff-
hausen etc. 1863-   . Variant
title: Beiträge zur vaterländischen Geschichte.

Schanz, M. von see G34.

S40
SCHAU-in's-LAND; Zeitschrift des
Breisgau-Geschichtsvereins.
Freiburg i.B. 1873/4-   .

SCHEDAE ARCHAEOLOGICAE see P160.

Schefold, K. see F71, M85, O33,
P155, U25, V12, W1.

Scherer, A. see H14.

Scherer, J. see P64.

S41
SCHILD von STEIER: Beiträge zur
steirischen Vor- und Frühgeschichte (und Münzkunde). Graz
1945-   .

S42
SCHLERN; Monatsschrift für Heimat-
und Volkskunde. Bolzano 1920- .

S43
SCHLESIENS VORZEIT in BILD und
SCHRIFT. Breslau 1859-1933.

Schliemann, H. see H41.

SCHLIEMANNS SAMMLUNG TROJANISCHER
ALTERTÜMER see H41.

Schmid, W. see G31.

Schmidt, C. see V24.

Schmidt, H. see H41.

S44
SCHMOLLERS JAHRBUCH für GESETZGE-
    BUNG, VERWALTUNG und VOLKWISSEN-
    SCHAFT im DEUTSCHEN REICH. Leip-
    zig 1877-   . 1877-1912 title
    did not include Schmollers.

Schneider, F. see J83.

Schneider, R. see G78.

Schneidewin, F. G. see C234.

Schoell, R. see A214.

Schrader, E. see K10.

Schrader, O. see R27.

S45
SCHRIFTEN. AKADEMIE der WISSEN-
    SCHAFTEN zu BERLIN. Berlin
    --. Sektion für Altertumswissen-
    schaft. 1956-   .
    --. Sektion für Vor- und Frühge-
    schichte. 1953-   .

SCHRIFTEN. BERLIN see S45.

S46
SCHRIFTEN der Königsberger GELEHRTEN
    GESELLSCHAFT GEISTESWISSENSCHAFT-
    LICHE KLASSE. Berlin 1924-   .

SCHRIFTEN. SEKTION für ALTERTUMSWIS-
    SENSCHAFT. AKADEMIE der WISSEN-
    SCHAFTEN zu BERLIN see S45.

SCHRIFTEN. SEKTION für VOR- und
    FRÜHGESCHICHTE. AKADEMIE der
    WISSENSCHAFTEN zu BERLIN see
    S45.

S47
SCHRIFTEN zur UR- und FRÜHGESCHICHTE
    der SCHWEIZ. Basel 1950?-   .

S48
SCHRIFTEN des VEREINS für GESCHICHTE
    des BODENSEES. Lindau i.B.
    1869-   .

Schroeder, O. see K14.

Schubart, W. see P73.

Schullen, A. see F29.

Schulz, F. see C145.

Schulze, W. see Z95.

Schwartz, E. see A49, E4.

Schwartz, J. see G121.

S49
SCHWEIZER MÜNZBLÄTTER = Gazette
    Numismatique Suisse. Basel
    1949-   . (SM, GNS, SchwMbII).

SCHWEIZERISCHE NUMISMATISCHE RUND-
    SCHAU see R239.

S50
SCHWEIZERISCHE ZEITSCHRIFT für
    GESCHICHTE = Revue Suisse
    d'Histoire = Rivista Storica
    Svizzera. Zurich 1951-   .
    (SZG).

Schwyzer, E. see D36, G108.

SCIENCES ECCLÉSIASTIQUES see
    S51.

S51
SCIENCE et ESPRIT. Montreal
    1948-   . 1948-67 title: Sci-
    ences ecclésiastiques.

SCIENCES PHILOSOPHIQUES et THÉOLO-
    GIQUES see R235.

SCIENCE RELIGIEUSE (Paris 1910- .)
    see R33.

SCIENCES RELIGIEUSES (Toronto
    1971-   .) see S237.

S52
SCIENTIA. Milan & Bologna etc.
    1907?-   .

S53
SCIENTIFIC AMERICAN. New York
    1845-   .

Scott, R. see G87.

S54
SCOTTISH ARCHAEOLOGICAL FORUM.
  Edinburgh 1969-   .

S55
SCOTTISH HISTORICAL REVIEW. Glasgow 1903-   . Suspended 1928-47.

S56
SCOTTISH JOURNAL of THEOLOGY.
  Edinburgh 1948-   .

SCRIPT-: <u>entries beginning with
  this spelling are here interfiled.</u>

S57
SCRIPTORIUM; revue internationale
  des études relatives aux manuscrits. Brussels 1946/7-   .

S58
SCRIPTA CLASSICA ISRAELICA. Jerusalem 1974-   .

S59
SCRIPTORUM CLASSICORUM BIBLIOTHECA
  OXONIENSIA. (OCT).
  --. Scriptores Graeci. Oxford
  1890-   .
  --. Scriptores Latini. Oxford
  1898-   .

S60
SCRIPTA HIEROSOLYMITANA. Jerusalem
  1954-   .

S61
SCRIPTA MINORA / A. J. Evans. Oxford 1909-52.

S62
SCRIPTA MINORES (Kungl, Humanistis-
  ka Vetenskapssamfundt i Lund).
  Lund 1957/8-   .

S63
SCRIPTORES RERUM HUNGARICARUM / E.
  Szentpétery <u>et al</u>. Budapest
  1937-   .

S64
SCRIPTORES RERUM MYTHICARUM LATINI
  TRES ROMAE nuper reperti / G. H.

Bode. Cellis 1834. Reprint
  Hildesheim 1968.

S65
SCRIPTORES RERUM SUECIARUM MEDII
  AEVI. Uppsala 1818-76.

S66
SCRITTURA e CIVILTÀ. Turin .
  1977-   .

S67
SEABY'S COIN and MEDAL BULLETIN.
  London 1917-   .

S68
SÉANCES GÉNÉRALES. CONGRÈS ARCHÉ-
  OLOGIQUE de FRANCE. Paris
  1834-   .

SÉANCE GÉNÉRALE. SOCIÉTÉ des LET-
  TRES, SCIENCES et ARTS (et d'AG-
  RICULTURE) de METZ see M98.

SÉANCE PUBLIQUE. ACADÉMIE des
  SCIENCES, ARTS et BELLES-LETTRES
  de DIJON see M99.

SÉANCES PUBLIQUES. ACADÉMIE des
  SCIENCES, BELLES-LETTRES et ARTS
  de BESANÇON see P212.

S69
SEFARAD (Instituto "Arias Montano"
  de Estudios Hebraícos y Oriente
  Próximo). Madrid 1941-   .

S70
SEFUNIM (Haifa Maritime Museum).
  Haifa 1966-   .

Segre, M. see T70, T71, T77.

Seidel, J. see F4.

S71
SELECT DOCUMENTS of the PRINCIPATES
  of the FLAVIAN EMPERORS / M. Mc-
  Crum & A. G. Woodhead. Cambridge 1961.

S72
SELECT PAPYRI. Cambridge, Mass. &
  London 1932-42. (Loeb Classical
  Library). Consists of Non-liter-
  ary papyri by A. S. Hunt and C.

C. Edgar and Greek Literary Papyri by D. L. Page. (SelPap).

S73
SELECTED PAPYRI from the ARCHIVES of ZENON / C. C. Edgar. Appeared in Annales du Service des Antiquités de l'Egypte 1918-24. (PEdg).

S74
SELECTION of GREEK HISTORICAL INSCRIPTIONS to the END of the FIFTH CENTURY B.C. / M. N. Tod. 2. ed. Oxford 1946-68. 1st edition 1933. (GHI).

S75
SELECTION of GREEK HISTORICAL INSCRIPTIONS to the END of the FIFTH CENTURY B.C. / R. Meiggs & D. Lewis. Oxford 1969. Based in part on Tod's work of the same name. (ML).

S76
SEMANTISCHE HEFTE. Hamburg 1974- .

SEMINARIUM KONDAKOVIANUM see A273.

S77
SEMITICA. Paris 1948- .

S78
SEMITISKIE IAZYKI (Akademiia nauk SSSR. Institut Narodov Azii). Moscow 1963- .

S79
SEPTENTRION: revue archéologique. Calais 1969- .

SERBSKI LIETOPIS see L34.

Sethe, K. H. see U34.

S80
SHEKEL (American Israel Numismatic Association). New York 1968- .

SHENATON. MU'SEON HA-ARETS see B334.

Sherk, R. K. see R332.

Short, C. see L17.

S81
SIBRIUM (Centro di Studi Preistorici e Archeologici). Varese 1953/4- .

S82
SICILIA ARCHEOLOGICA. Trapani 1968- .

S83
SICILIA ARTISTICA ed ARCHEOLOGICA. Palermo 1887-89.

S84
SICULORUM GYMNASIUM. Catania 1948- .

S85
SIEBENBÜRGISCHE VIERTELJAHRSSCHRIFT. Sibiu 1878- . 1878-1930 title: Korrespondenzblatt des Vereins für Siebenbürgische Landeskunde. (KVSL).

S86
SIEGEL aus BOĞAZKÖY / H. G. Güterbock. Berlin 1940-42. (Archiv für Orientforschung. Beiheft; 5 & 7). Reprint Osnabrück 1967.

Sijpesteijn, P. J. see E19.

S87
SILENO; rivista di studi classici e cristiani. Modica 1975- .

Simpson, G. see C103.

S88
SINAI. Jerusalem 1937- .

S89
SITULA (Narodni Muzej). Ljubljana 1960- .

SITZUNGSBERICHTE. AKADEMIE der WISSENSCHAFTEN, HEIDELBERG. PHILOSOPHISCHE-HISTORISCHE KLASSE see S92.

SITZUNGSBERICHTE. AKADEMIE der
WISSENSCHAFTEN zu LEIPZIG see
S94.

SITZUNGSBERICHTE. AKADEMIE der
WISSENSCHAFTEN, MUNICH. PHILOSO-
PHISCH-HISTORISCHE KLASSE see
S90.

SITZUNGSBERICHTE der AKADEMIE der
WISSENSCHAFTEN in WIEN. PHILOSO-
PHISCH-HISTORISCHE KLASSE see
S93.

S90
SITZUNGSBERICHTE der BAYERISCHEN
AKADEMIE der WISSENSCHAFTEN.
Munich 1860-70.
--. Philosophisch-historische
Klasse. 1871-   . Name of the
section varies; until 1909:
Philosophisch-philologische
Klasse. 1910-28: Philosophisch-
philologische und Historische
Klasse. 1928-45: Philosophisch-
historische Abteilungen. (SBAW,
SbMünchen).

SITZUNGSBERICHTE. BERLIN see S91.

S91
SITZUNGSBERICHTE der DEUTSCHEN AKA-
DEMIE der WISSENSCHAFTEN zu
BERLIN. Berlin 1882-1921. Issued
under the Academy's earlier name:
(K.) Preussischen Akademie der
Wissenschaften.
--. Philosophisch-historische
Klasse. 1922-44. (Issued as part
of the Jahrbuch 1939-42). Also
appeared under the Academy's
earlier name.
--. Klasse für Sprachen, Litera-
tur und Kunst. 1950-   .
--. Klasse für Gesellschaftswis-
senschaften. 1950-54.
--. Klasse für Philosophie,
Geschichte, Staats-, Rechts-
und Wirtschaftwissenschaften.
1955-   .

S92
SITZUNGSBERICHTE der HEIDELBERGER
AKADEMIE der WISSENSCHAFTEN.
PHILOSOPHISCH-HISTORISCHE
KLASSE. Heidelberg 1910-   .
(SHAW, SbHeidelberg).

SITZUNGSBERICHTE. KLASSE für GE-
SELLSCHAFTWISSENSCHAFTEN. AKADE-
MIE der WISSENSCHAFTEN zu BER-
LIN see S91.

SITZUNGSBERICHTE. KLASSE für PHIL-
OSOPHIE, GESCHICHTE, STAATS-,
RECHTS-,und WIRTSCHAFTSWISSEN-
SCHAFTEN see S91.

SITZUNGSBERICHTE. KLASSE für SPRA-
CHEN, LITERATUR und KUNST. AKA-
DEMIE der WISSENSCHAFTEN zu
BERLIN see S91.

SITZUNGSBERICHTE. KÖNIGLICHE
AKADEMIE ... see SITZUNGSBER-
ICHTE AKADEMIE (the word königliche is disregarded in filing,
but may have been regarded in
forming an abbreviation).

SITZUNGSBERICHTE. LEIPZIG see
S94.

SITZUNGSBERICHTE. MÜNCHEN see
S90.

S93
SITZUNGSBERICHTE der ÖSTERREICH-
ISCHEN AKADEMIE der WISSENSCHAF-
TEN. PHILOSOPHISCH-HISTORISCHE
KLASSE. Vienna 1848-   . Var-
iant name of the Academy: Aka-
demie der Wissenschaften in
Wien. (SbWien, SAWW).

SITZUNGSBERICHTE. PHILOLOGISCH-
HISTORISCHE KLASSE. SÄCHSISCHE
AKADEMIE der WISSENSCHAFTEN see
S94.

SITZUNGSBERICHTE. PHILOSOPHISCH-
HISTORISCHE KLASSE. AKADEMIE
der WISSENSCHAFTEN zu BERLIN
see S91.

SITZUNGSBERICHTE. PHILOSOPHISCH-
HISTORISCHE KLASSE. AKADEMIE der
WISSENSCHAFTEN, HEIDELBERG see
S92.

SITZUNGSBERICHTE. PHILOSOPHISCH-
HISTORISCHE KLASSE. BAYERISCHE
AKADEMIE der WISSENSCHAFTEN
see S90.

SITZUNGSBERICHTE. PHILOSOPHISCH-
HISTORISCHE KLASSE. ÖSTERREICH-
ISCHE AKADEMIE in WIEN see
S93.

SITZUNGSBERICHTE. PREUSSISCHE AKA-
DEMIE der WISSENSCHAFTEN see
S91.

S94
SITZUNGSBERICHTE der SÄCHSISCHEN
AKADEMIE der WISSENSCHAFTEN zu
LEIPZIG. PHILOLOGISCH-HISTORISCHE
KLASSE. Leipzig 1849-   . 1849-
61 title: Berichte über die Verhandlungen der Sächsischen Akademie (until 1920: Gesellschaft)
der Wissenschaften. Suspended
1944-47.

SITZUNGSBERICHTE. WIEN see S93.

Sixt, G. see R312.

SKRIFTER, BERGENS MUSEUMS see
U14.

SKRIFTER. HISTORISK-FILOSOFISK
KLASSE. NORSKE VIDENSKAPS-AKADEMI
i OSLO see S97.

S95
SKRIFTER utgivna av K. HUMANISTISKA
VETENSKAPSSAMFUNDET i UPPSALA.
Uppsala 1890-   .

SKRIFTER. K. NORSKE SELSKAB see
S96.

S96
SKRIFTER. K. NORSKE VIDENSKABERS
SELSKAB. Trondheim & Copenhagen
1761-   . Title varies: 1761-65:
Skrifter. Trondhjemske Selskab.
1784-88: Nye Samling. 1798: Nyeste samling. 1813/17-74/7: Det
k. norske selskabs skrifter.

S97
SKRIFTER utgitt av det NORSKE VID-
ENSKAPS-AKADEMI i OSLO. HISTOR-
ISK-FILOSOFISK KLASSE. Oslo
1894-   .

S98
SKRIFTER utgivna av SVENSKA INSTI-

TUTET i ATHEN = Acta Instituti
Atheniensis Regni Sueciae. Lund
--. 4° = Series prima. 1951-   .
--. 8° = Series altera. 1951-71.

SKRIFTER utgivna av SVENSKA INSTI-
TUTET i ATHEN see also 022.

S99
SKRIFTER utgivna av SVENSKA INSTI-
TUTET i ROM = Acta Institutis
Romani Regni Sueciae. Lund
--. 4° = Series prima. 1932-   .
--. 8° = Series altera. 1939-   .

SKRIFTER utgivna av SVENSKA INSTI-
TUTET i ROM see also 020, 025.

SKRIFTER. TRONDHJEMSKE SELSKAB see
S96.

SKRIFTER. UNIVERSITETET i BERGEN
see U14.

SKRIFTER. UNIVERSITETETS OLDSAK-
SAMMLING see U15.

S100
SKRIFTER av VETENSKAPS-SOCIETETEN
i LUND = Publications of the
New Society of Letters at Lund.
Lund 1921-   .

S101
SLAVIA ANTIQUA. Posnań 1948-   .

S102
SLAVIA OCCIDENTALIS. Posnań
1921-   .

S103
SLAVISTIČNA REVIJA. Ljubljana
1948-   .

S104
SLOVENSKÁ ARCHEOLÓGIA. Bratislava
1953-   . (SlovArch).

S105
SLOVENSKA NUMIZMATIKA. Bratislava
1970-   .

Smith, A. H. see B225.

Smith, W. see D48-D49.

Smith, W. S.   see   I93.

Smyly, J. G.   see   F19, G96.

Snell, B.   see   L41, T83-T84.

Snodgrass, A.   see   El.

Snyder, J. W.   see   S271.

S106
SOCIAL and ECONOMIC COMMENTARIES
  on CLASSICAL TEXTS.   Leiden
  1959-   .

S107
SOCIAL and ECONOMIC HISTORY of the
  HELLENISTIC WORLD / M. Rostov-
  tsev.   Oxford 1941. Reprinted
  Oxford 1972.   (SEHHW).

S108
SOCIAL and ECONOMIC HISTORY of the
  ROMAN EMPIRE / M. Rostovtsev.
  Oxford 1926. 2nd   revised edition
  by P. M. Fraser.   Oxford 1957.
  (SEHRE).

SOCIETY for ANCIENT NUMISMATICS
  see   S1.

S109
SODALITAS (Sociedad Española de
  Estudios Clásicos).   Granada
  1980-   .

Soden, W. von   see   A105, G134.

S110
SOESTER ZEITSCHRIFT.   Soest
  1881/2-   . Title of vols. 1-
  64: Zeitschrift. Verein für die
  Geschichte von Soest und der
  Börde.

Sokolowski, F.   see   L82-83.

S111
SOKRATES.   Berlin 1847-1924. 1847-
  1912 title: Zeitschrift für das
  Gymnasialwesen.

Solmsen, F.   see   I55.

S112
SOME OXFORD PAPYRI / E. P. Wegener.

Leiden 1942-48. (Papyrologica
  Lugduno-Batava; 3). (POxf).

S113
SOMERSET ARCHAEOLOGY and NATURAL
  HISTORY. Dorcester etc. 1849- .
  Title varies slightly.

Sommer, F.   see   H64, H66.

S114
SOMOGYI MÚZEUMOK KÖZLEMÉNYEI.
  Kaposvár 1973-   .

S115
SONDERSCHRIFTEN. ÖSTERREICHISCHES
  ARCHÄOLOGISCHES INSTITUT in
  WIEN. Vienna 1901-   .

S116
SOOBSHCHENIIA AKADEMII NAUK GRUZIN-
  SKOĬ SSR = Bulletin of the Acade-
  my of Science of the Georgian SSR.
  Ḟiflis 1940-   .

SOOBSHCHENIIA GOSUDARSTVENNOĬ
  AKADEMII ISTORII MATERIAL'NOĬ
  KULTURY   see   P185.

S117
SOOBSHCHENIIA GOSUDARSTVENNOGO ĖR-
  MITAZHA = Reports of the State
  Hermitage Museum. Leningrad
  1940-   .

S118
SOOBSHCHENIIA. GOSUDARSTVENNYĬ
  MUZEĬ IZOBRAZITEL'NYKH ISKUSSTV
  im. A. S. PUSHKINA. Moscow
  1960-   .

S119
SOOBSHCHENIIA KHERSONNESSKOGO MU-
  ZEĬA. Simferopol 19?-   .

S120
SOPHIA; rivista internazionale di
  fonti e studi di storia della
  filosofia. Naples & Palermo
  1933-   .

S121
SOPRONI SZEMLE. Sopron 1957-   .

Sotgiu, G.   see   I119.

S122
SOURCES from the ANCIENT NEAR EAST.
  Malibu, Ca. 1974-   . (SANE).

S123
SOURCES BIBLIQUES. Paris 1971?-   .

S124
SOURCES CHRÉTIENNES. Paris 1941- .
  Some volumes in 2nd editions.
  (SC).

S125
SOUTH ITALIAN VASE PAINTING / A. D.
  Trendall. 2. ed. London 1976. 1st
  edition 1966.

S126
SOVETSKAĨA ARKHEOLOGIIA = Soviet
  Archaeology. Moscow 1936-   .
  French title 1975-78: Archéologie
  Sovietique. (SA, SovArch, Sov-
  Arkh).

S127
SOVETSKAĨA ETNOGRAFIIA. Moscow
  etc. 1931-   . 1946-47 also had
  French title: L'ethnographie so-
  vietiques.

S128
SOVETSKOE VOSTOKOVEDENIE [Sbornik],
  Moscow & Leningrad 1940-58. Sus-
  pended 1950-54.

S129
SOVIET ANTHROPOLOGY and ARCHAEOLOGY.
  White Plains, N. Y. 1962-   .

SOVIET ARCHAEOLOGY see S126.

S130
SPECULUM; journal of medieval studies. Cambridge, Mass. 1926-   .

SPEECH MONOGRAPHS see C176.

Spengel, L. von see R257.

S131
SPICILEGIUM SACRUM LOVANIENSIS.
  Louvain 1922-   .

S132
SPIEGEL HISTORIAEL; maandblad voor
  geschiedenis en archaeologie.
  Bussum 1966-   .

Spiegelberg, W. see V23.

SPINKS and SON'S (MONTHLY) NUMIS-
  MATIC CIRCULAR see N107.

S133
SPISANIE na BULGARSKATA AKADEMIĨA
  na NAUKITE i IZKUSTVATA. Sofia
  1911-45? Name of the Academy
  varies slightly.

S134
SPOLETIUM; rivista di arte, storia,
  cultura. Spoleto 1954-   .

SPOMENIK se also SBORNIK, ZBORNIK.

S135
SPOMENIK. SRPSKA AKADEMIJA NAUKA
  i UMJETNOSTI. Belgrade 1888- .
  Name of the Academy varies
  slightly.

S136
SPRACHE. Vienna & Wiesbaden
  1949-   .

S137
SPRACHE der HETHITER / B. Hrozný.
  Leipzig 1917. (Boghazköi-Stu-
  dien; 1-2).

S138
SPRAWOZDANIA ARCHEOLOGICZNE. Wroclaw etc. 1955-   .

S139
SPRAWOZDANIA P.M.A. (Pánstwowe
  Museum Arzheologiczne) = Comptes
  Rendus M.A.P. Warsaw 1945/7- .

S140
SPUDASMATA; Studien zur klassischen
  Philologie und ihren Grenzge-
  bieten. Hildesheim 1964-   .

SRBSKI LETOPIS see L34.

S141
SREDNIE VEKA; sbornik. Moscow
  1942-   .

STADER ARCHIV see S142.

S142
STADER JAHRBUCH (Stader Geschichts-

und Heimatverein).   Stade 1911-   .
1911-42 title: Stader Archiv.
Suspended 1943-46.

S143
STADION; Zeitschrift für Geschichte
des Sports und der Körperkultur.
Leiden 1975-   . Variant title:
Arena.

S144
STÄDEL JAHRBUCH.   Frankfurt a.M.
1921-   .

Stählin, O. see G31.

Stanfield, J. A. see C103.

S145
STARINAR; organ Arheološkog Instituta Srpska Akademija Nauk. Belgrad 1884-1895 1906-11 1922-40
1950-   .

S146
STAROHRVATSKA PROSVJETA (Muzej
Hrvatskih Starina Jugoslovenske
Akademije Znanosti i Umjetnosti).
Zagreb 1895-1904 1927-28 1949-   .

S147
STAVANGER MUSEUMS ÅRBOK. Stavanger
1882-   . Title varies; 1882-99:
Aarsberetning; 1901-45: Årshefte.

STAVANGER MUSEUMS (AARSBERETNING/
ÅRSHEFTE) see S147.

STEIRISCHE ZEITSCHRIFT für GE-
SCHICHTE see Z44.

Stephanus, H. see T54.

Sterrett, J. R. S see E80, W51.

STK see S2.

S148
STOCKHOLM STUDIES in CLASSICAL
ARCHAEOLOGY. Stockholm 1961-   .
1961 title: Studies in Classical
Archaeology. At head of title:
Acta Universitatis Stockholmien-
sis.

S149
STOICORUM VETERUM FRAGMENTA / H.
von Arnim. Leipzig 1903-24.
(SVF).

S150
STORIA dell'ARTE. Florence
1969-   .

S151
STORIA dell'ARTE ETRUSCA / P.
Ducati. Florence 1927.

S152
STORIA e LITTERATURA. Rome
1943-   .

S153
STRATIGRAPHIE COMPARÉE et CHRONO-
LOGIE de l'ASIE OCCIDENTALE / C.
F. A. Schaeffer. London 1948.

Straub, J. see A49.

Struve, V. V. see K41.

Stuart, J. see A375.

Studemund, W. F. A. see A214.

S154
STUDENCHESKIE NAUCHN'IE RABOT'I
KAZAKHSKOGO UN-TA. Alma-Ata ?-   .

STUDI, STUDIA, STUDIEN, STUDIES,
STUDII, STUDIME are here interfiled. See also STUDIJME.

STUDII; revistă di istorie see
R197.

S155
STUDIA et ACTA ORIENTALIA. Bucharest 1957-   .

S156
STUDIA ALBANICA. Tirana 1964-   .

S157
STUDIEN zur ALTÄGYPTISCHEN KUL-
TUR. Hamburg 1974-   .

S158
STUDIEN zum ALTEN und NEUEN TESTA-
MENT. Munich 1960-   .

S159
STUDIA AMSTELODAMENSIA ad EPIGRA-
PHICAM, IUS ANTIQUUM et PAPYRO-
LOGICAM PERTINENTIA.   Amsterdam
etc. 1972-   . (StudAmst).

S160
STUDIES in ANCIENT ORIENTAL CIVI-
LIZATION (Oriental Institute).
Chicago 1931-   . (SAOC).

S161
STUDI di ANTICHITÀ CRISTIANA.
Rome 1929-   .

S162
STUDIES in the ANTIQUITIES of STO-
BI. Austin, Texas 1973-   .

S163
STUDIA ARCHAEOLOGICA.   Rome 1961- .

S164
STUDIA ARCHAEOLOGICA.   Budapest
1963-   . (Publicationes Instituti Archaeologica Academiae
Scientiarum Hungarica).

STUDII ARCHEOLOGICI su la PROVINCIA
di COMO see R269.

S165
STUDII și ARTICOLE de ISTORIE.
Bucharest 1956-   .

S166
STUDIA BALCANICA.   Sofia 1970?-   .

S167
STUDII BIBLICI FRANCISCANI. LIBER
ANNUS. Jerusalem 1950/1?-   .

STUDI BIZANTINI (e NEOELLENICI)
see R298.

S168
STUDIEN zu den BOĞAZKÖY-TEXTEN.
Wiesbaden 1965-   .

S169
STUDIA CATHOLICA.   Nijmegen 1842-
1960. 1842-1923 title: Katholieke Utrecht.

S170
STUDII și CERCETĂRI de ISTORIE.

Cluj 7- 1956-   . Supersedes
Studii si cercetări științifice.
Ser. III.

S171
STUDII și CERETĂRI de ISTORIA AR-
TEI. Bucharest 1954-63. (SCIA).

S172
STUDII și CERCETĂRI de ISTORIA AR-
TEI. SERIA ARTA PLASTICA. Bucharest 11- 1964-   . Supersedes
in part Studii și Cercetări de
Istoria artei (1954-63) and
continues its numbering.

S173
STUDII și CERCETĂRI de ISTORIE
VECHE și di ARHEOLOGIE. Buch-
arest 1950-   . Variant title:
Studii și Cercetări de Istorie
Veche. Title also appeared with
French and Russian titles: É-
tudes et Recherches d'Histoire
Ancienne and Trudy i Issledo-
vaniia po Drevnei istorii.
(SCIV, SCIVA).

S174
STUDII și CERCETĂRI LINGVISTICE =
Lingvisticheskie Ocherki i Issle-
dovaniia = Études et Recherches
Linguistiques. Bucharest
1950-   .

S175
STUDII și CERCETĂRI de NUMISMATICĂ.
Bucharest 1957-   . (SCN).

S176
STUDII și CERCETĂRI ȘTIINȚIFICE
(Filiala Cluj. Academia Republicii Populare Romîne).   Cluj
1-5 1949?-54. Publication continued in series:
--. Series III. Științe sociale.
6 1955. Superseded by Studii și
Cercetări de Istorie. (SCSCluj).

S177
STUDII CLASICE. Bucharest 1959- .
(StudClas, StCl, SC).

STUDIES in CLASSICAL ARCHAEOLOGY
see S148.

S178
STUDI CLASSICI e ORIENTALI. Pisa
  1951-   . (SCO).

S179
STUDIES in CLASSICAL PHILOLOGY.
  Chicago 1895-1907.

S180
STUDIA COMITATENSIA; Tanulmányok
  Pest Magye Múzeumalbád. Szenten-
  dre 1972-   .

S181
STUDII şi COMUNICĂRI (Muzeul Bruk-
  enthal) = Untersuchungen und
  Mitteilungen des Museums Bruken-
  thal. Sibiu 1956-   . (StCom-
  Sibiu).

S182
STUDII şi COMUNICĂRI: istorie,
  stinţele naturii. Piteşti ?-   .

S183
STUDIES in CONSERVATION = Études
  de Conservation. Aberdeen &
  London 1952-   .

S184
STUDIA et DOCUMENTA HISTORIAE et
  IURIS. Rome 1935-   . (SDHI).

S185
STUDIA et DOCUMENTA ad IURA ORIEN-
  TIS ANTIQUI PERTINENTIA. Leiden
  1936-   .

S186
STUDI e DOCUMENTI di STORIA e
  DIRITTO. Rome 1880-1904.

S187
STUDIES of the DUTCH ARCHAEOLOGICAL
  and HISTORICAL SOCIETY. Groningen 1969-   .

S188
STUDI ETRUSCHI. Florence 1927-   .
  (SE, StEtr).

S189
STUDIES in FIFTH-CENTURY ATTIC
  EPIGRAPHY / D. W. Bradeen & M. F.
  McGregor. Norman. Ok. 1973.
  (Univ. of Cincinnati Classical
  Studies; 4).

S190
STUDIME FILOLOGJIKE. Tirana
  1964-   .

S191
STUDIEN zu den FUNDMÜNZEN der
  ANTIKE. Berlin 1979-   .

S192
STUDIUM GENERALE; Zeitschrift für
  die Einheit der Wissenschaften
  in Zusammenhang ihrer Begriffs-
  bildung und Forschungsmethoden.
  Berlin 1947-   .

S193
STUDI GENUENSI. Genoa 1957-   .

S194
STUDIEN zur GESCHICHTE und KULTUR
  des ALTERTUMS. Paderborn 1907-
  42.
  --. Ergänzungsbände. 1912-32.

STUDIEN zur GESCHICHTE der STADT
  BUDAPEST see T6.

S195
STUDIEN zur GRIECHISCHEN und LA-
  TEINISCHEN GRAMMATIK. Leipzig
  1868-78.

S196
STUDIA HELLENISTICA. Louvain
  1942-   .

S197
STUDIA HISTORICA; acta Societatis
  Historiae Oulouensis. Oulu
  ?-   .

S198
STUDIME HISTORIKE. Tirana 1964-   .

S199
STUDIES in the HISTORY and ART of
  the EASTERN PROVINCES of the
  ROMAN EMPIRE / W. M. Ramsay.
  Aberdeen 1906.

STUDIES in the HISTORY of RELIGIONS
  see N99.

STUDI INTERNAZIONALE di FILOSOFIA
  see I98.

S200
STUDII de ISTORIE BANATULUI. Timişoara 1969?-   .

S201
STUDI ITALIANI di FILOLOGIA CLAS-
SICA. Florence 1893-1915 1920- .
(SIFC, StIt, StudIt).

S202
STUDI ITALIANI di LINGUISTICA TEO-
RICA ed APPLICATA. Padua 1972- .

S203
STUDIES in JUDAISM in LATE ANTIQUI-
TY. Leiden 1973-   .

S204
STUDIES in LANGUAGE and LITERATURE.
Urbana, Ill. 1915-33. Title of
vol. 1: University of Illinois
Studies in Language and Liter-
ature.

STUDIES in LANGUAGE and LITERATURE
(Madison 1918-36) see U19.

S205
STUDIA LINGUISTICA. Copenhagen
& Lund 1947-   .

S206
STUDI MAGREBINI. Naples 1966-   .

S207
STUDII şi MATERIALE (Muzeul Judetean). Târgu-Mures ?-   .

STUDII si MATERIALE: archeologie,
istorie, etnografie see M38.

S208
STUDI e MATERIALI di ARCHEOLOGIA e
NUMISMATICA. Florence 1899-1905.

S209
STUDII şi MATERIALI de ISTORIE
MEDIE. Bucharest 1956-   .
(SMIM).

S210
STUDII şi MATERIALE de MUZEOGRAFIE
si ISTORIE MILITARĂ. Bucharest
?-   .

S211
STUDII şi MATERIALE PRIVITOARE la
TRECUTUL ISTORIE al JUDETULUI:
prahova, istorie, etnografie.
Ploieşti ?-   .

S212
STUDI e MATERIALI de STORIA delle
RELIGIONI. Bari etc. 1925-76.
1975-76 also had title: Religioni
e civiltà. Continued by Studi
Storico Religiosi. (SMSR, Ste-
Mat).

S213
STUDI MEDIEVALI. Turin 1904/5-
12/3 1923-52? 1923-27 title:
Nuovi studi medievali.

S214
STUDI MEDIEVALI. Spoleto 1960-   .

S215
STUDIES in MEDITERRANEAN ARCHAEO-
LOGY. Lund 1962-   . (SIMA).

S216
STUDI MICENEI ed EGEO-ANATOLICI.
Rome 1966-   . (Incunabula
Graeca; 11, etc.). (SMEA).

S217
STUDI MISCELLANEI (Seminario di
Archeologia e Storia dell'Arte
Greca e Romana. Univ. Roma).
Rome 1958/9-   .

S218
STUDIA MONÁSTICA. Barcelona
1959-   .

S219
STUDIES in MYCENAEAN INSCRIPTIONS
and DIALECT. Cambridge 1953/5-
(SMID).

S220
STUDIA NEOTESTAMENTICA.
--. Studia. Bruges 1963-   .
--. Subsidia. Paris 1961-   .

S221
STUDIA OLIVERIANA. Pesaro 1953-   .

S222
STUDIA ORIENTALIA. Helsinki
1925-   . (StOr).

S223
STUDIEN zur PALÄOGRAPHIE und PA-
PYRUSKUNDE. Leipzig 1901-24.
(StudPal, SPP).

S224
STUDIA PALMYREŃSKIE = Études Palmyréniennes. Warsaw 1966-   .

S225
STUDIA PAPYROLOGICA. Barcelona
1962-   .

S226
STUDIA PATAVINA; rivista di scienze
religiose. Padua 1954-   .

S227
STUDIA PATRISTICA; papers delivered
to the International Conferences
on Patristic Studies. Berlin 2-
1955-   .

S228
STUDIA PATRISTICA et BYZANTINA.
Ettal 1953-   .

S229
STUDIES in PHILOLOGY. Chapel Hill,
N.C. 1906-   .

S230
STUDIA PHILOLOGICA SALMANTICENSIA.
Salamanca 1977-   . Part of the
series: Acta Salmanticensia. Filosofía y Letras.

S231
STUDIA PHILONICA. Chicago 1972- .

S232
STUDIA PHILOSOPHICA. Basel
1941-   . Vols. 1-5 published
as Jahrbuch. Schweizerische Philosophische Gesellschaft = Annuaire. Société Suisse de Philosophie.

S233
STUDIA PICENA. Fano 1925-   .
(Pubblicazioni del Pontificio
Seminario Marchigiano Pius XI).

S234
STUDIA POHL (Pontificio Istituto
Biblico). Rome 1967-   .

S235
STUDIA PONTICA. Brussels 1903-10.

STUDIA i PRACE. ZAKŁADU ARCHEOLOGII
ŚRÓDZIEMNOMORSKIEJ (Polska Akademia Nauk) see E151.

S236
STUDIEN zur PROBLEMGESCHICHTE der
ANTIKEN und MITTELALTERLICHEN
PHILOSOPHIE. Leiden 1966-   .

S237
STUDIES in RELIGION = Sciences Religieuses. Toronto 1971-   .

S238
STUDI e RICHERCHE dell'ISTITUTO
di LATINO (Univ. Genova). Genoa
1977-   .

S239
STUDI ROMAGNOLI. Faenza 1950-   .

S240
STUDI ROMANI (Istituto di Studi Romani). Rome 1953-   .

S241
STUDI ROMANI; rivista di archeologia e storia. Rome 1913-22.

S242
STUDI e SAGGI LINGUISTICI. Pisa
1961-   . Supplement to Italia
Dialettale.

S243
STUDI SALENTI. Lecce 1956-   .

S244
STUDI SARDI. Sassari 1934-   .

S245
STUDI della SCUOLA PAPIROLOGICA
(R. Accademia Scientifico-Let-
teraria). Milan 1915-26.

S246
STUDIA SEMITICA NEERLANDICA. Assen 1955-   .

S247
STUDIA SLAVICA. Budapest 1955-   .

S248
STUDI STORICI. Rome 1959-   .

S249
STUDI STORICI per l'ANTICHITÀ
    CLASSICA. Pisa 1908-13. Contin-
    eud by Historia (Milan).

S250
STUDI STORICO RELIGIOSI. L'Aquila
    1977-   . Continues Studi e
    Materiali di Storia delle
    Religioni.

S251
STUDII TEOLOGICE. Bucharest
    1929/30-40 1949-   .

S252
STUDI e TESTI (Biblioteca Aposto-
    lica Vaticana). Rome 1900-   .

S253
STUDIEN und TEXTE zur GEISTESGE-
    SCHICHTE des MITTELALTERS. Lei-
    den 1950-   .

S254
STUDIA THEOLOGICA. Lund etc.
    1947-   . 1966-73? title: Scan-
    danavian journal of theology.

S255
STUDIA THEOLOGICA LUNDENSIA. Lund
    1952-   .

S256
STUDI TRENTINI di SCIENZE STORICHE.
    Trento 7- 1926-   . Suspended
    1944-45. Supersedes in part
    Studi Trentini (1920-25) and
    continues its numbering.

S257
STUDIA UNIVERSITATIS BABES-BOLYAI.
    Cluj
    --. Series 4. 3-6. 1958-61.
    --. Series historia. 7- 1962-   .
    --. Series philologica. 7-
    1962-   .
    --. Series philosophia. 11-
    1966-   .

S258
STUDI URBINATI di STORIA FILOSOFIA
    e LETTERATURA. Urbino 24-

1950-   . Supersedes Studi Ur-
    binati di Scienze Giuridiche.
    Ser. B which appeared as v. 12-16
    (1938-42); v. 17-23 for 1943-49
    never appeared. That was the
    successor to Studi Urbinati
    (1927-37).

S259
STUDI VENEZIANI. Venice 1959-   .
    1959-64 title: Bollettino dell'
    Istituto per la Storia della
    Società e dello Stato Veneziano.

S260
STUDIES of the WARBURG INSTITUTE.
    London 1936-   .

S261
STUDIJNÉ ZVESTI ARCHEOLOGICKÉHO
    ÚSTAVU SLOVENSKEJ AKADÉMIE v
    NITRA. Nitra 1956-   .

ŠTUDIJNÉ ZVESTI AÚSAV see S261.

S262
STUDIO; an illustrated magazine of
    fine and applied art. London
    1893-   .

S263
STUTTGARTER BIBELSTUDIEN. Stutt-
    gart 1965-   .

S264
STUTTGARTER BIBLISCHE MONOGRAPHIEN.
    Stuttgart 1967-   .

S265
SUBSIDIA HAGIOGRAPHICA. Brussels
    1886-   . Most of the early
    vols. appeared as supplements to
    Analecta Bollandiana.

S266
SUDETENLAND. Munich 1958/9-   .

S267
SUDHOFFS ARCHIV. Wiesbaden etc.
    1907-   . 1907-28 title: Archiv
    für Geschichte der Medizin.
    1929-65 title: Sudhoffs Archiv
    für Geschichte der Medizin und
    der Naturwissenschaft. Suspended
    1943-52. (AGM).
    --. Beihefte. 1961-   .

SUDHOFFS ARCHIV für GESCHICHTE der
MEDIZIN und der NATURWISSEN-
SCHAFT see S267.

S268
SÜDOSTDEUTSCHES ARCHIV. Munich
1958-   .

SÜDOSTDEUTSCHE FORSCHUNGEN see
S269.

S269
SÜDOSTFORSCHUNGEN; internationale
Zeitschrift für Geschichte, Kultur und Landeskunde südosteuro
pas. Munich & Leipzig 1936-   .
1936-39 title: Südostdeutsche
Forschungen.

SUISSE PRIMITIVE see U31.

S270
SUMER. Bagdad 1945-   .

S271
SUMERIAN ECONOMIC TEXTS from the
THIRD UR DYNASTY / T. B. Jones &
J. W. Snyder. Minneapolis 1961.
Reprint Westport, Conn. 1974.

S272
SUMERISCHEN und AKKADISCHEN KÖN-
IGSINSCHRIFTEN / F. Thureau-
Dangin. Leipzig 1907. (Vorder-
asiatische Bibliothek; 1 Bd.,
Abt. 1). Reprint Berlin 1972.
(SAK).

S273
ŠUMERISCHES LEXIKON / A. Deimel.
Rome 1928-50. Vol. 1 in 3rd
edition (1947).

SUOMALAINEN TIEDEAKATEMIAN TOIMIT-
UKSIA see A219.

S274
SUOMEN MUINAISMUISTOYHDISTYKSEN AI-
KAKAUSKIRJA = Finska Fornminnesföreningens Tidskrift = Zeitschrift der Finnischen Altertums-
gesellschaft. Helsinki 1874-   .

SUOMEN MUSEO see F18.

SUPPLEMENT/SUPPLEMENTUM ... look
under the name of the journal.

S275
SUPPLEMENTARY PAPERS of the AMERI-
CAN SCHOOL of CLASSICAL STUDIES
in ROME. New York 1905-08.

S276
SUPPLEMENTUM COMICUM; commoediae
Graecae fragmenta post editiones
Kockianam et Kaibelianam / J.
Demiańczuk. Cracow 1912. Re-
print Hildesheim 1967.

S277
SUPPLEMENTUM EPIGRAPHICUM GRAECUM.
Leiden etc. 1923-   . Suspended
between v. 25 (1971) and v. 26
(1976-77 published in 1979).
(SEG).

S278
SUPPLEMENTUM LYRICIS GRAECIS / D.
Page. Oxford 1974.

S279
SURREY ARCHAEOLOGICAL COLLECTIONS
London 1854-   . Title of vols.
1-2: Collections of the Survey
Archaeological Society. Also
known as the Surrey collections.

SURREY COLLECTIONS see S279.

S280
SURVEY of EASTERN PALESTINE / C. R.
Conder. London 1889.

S281
SURVEY of WESTERN PALESTINE / C. R.
Conder & H. H. Kitchener. Lon-
don 1881-83.

S282
SUSSEX ARCHAEOLOGICAL COLLECTIONS.
Oxford 1848-   . (SussexArch-
Coll).

S283
SUSSIDI ERUDITI. Rome 1950-   .

SVENSKA CYPERNEXPEDITIONEN see
S286.

S284
SVENSK EXEGETISK ÅRSBOK. Uppsala
1936-   .

S285
SVENSKA FORNMINNESFÖRENINGENS.
TIDSKRIFT. Stockholm 1871-1905.

SVENSK TEOLOGISK KVARTALSSKRIFT
see S2.

S286
SWEDISH CYPRESS EXPEDITION. Stockholm 1934-   . (SCE).

Sydenham, E. A. see C155.

S287
SYLLOGE INSCRIPTIONUM CHRISTIAN-
ARUM VETERUM MUSEI VATICANI / H.
Zilliacus. Helsinki 1963. (Acta
Instituti Romani Findlandiae; 1,
1-2).

S288
SYLLOGE INSCRIPTIONUM GRAECARUM /
W. Dittenberger. 3. ed. Leipzig
1915-24. 1st edition 1883. Re-
print Hildesheim 1960. (SIG,
Syll).

S289
SYLLOGE INSCRIPTIONUM OSCARUM / J.
Zuetaieff. Leningrad & Leipzig
1878.

S290
SYLLOGE INSCRIPTIONUM RELIGIONIS
ISIACAE et SERAPICAE / L. Vidman.
Berlin 1969. (Religionsgeschicht-
liche Versuche und Vorarbeiten;
28).

S291
SYLLOGE NUMMORUM GRAECORUM [by
country, place or collection].
place varies 1931-   . (SNG).

SYMBOLAE ARCTOAE see S292.

S292
SYMBOLAE OSLOENSES. Oslo 1922- .
1922 title: Symbolae arctoae.
(SO, SymbOsl, (SOsl).

S293
SYMBOLAE PHILOLOGORUM POSNANIENSIUM
GRAECAE et LATINAE. Posnań
1973-   .

S294
SYMBOLON; Jahrbuch für Symbolfor-
schung. Basel etc. 1960-   .

Syme, R. see R339.

S295
SYMMEIKTA (Kenton Vyzantinon Ereunōn). Athens 1966-   .

S296
SYMPOSIUM de PREHISTORIA de la PEN-
INSULA IBÉRICA. Ponencias
1959-   .

S297
SYNAXARIUM ECCLESIAE CONSTANTINO-
POLITANAE / H. Delehaye. Brus-
sels 1902. Reprint Louvain 1954.

S298
SYNODICON ORIENTAL ou recueil des
synodes Nestoriéns / J. B Chabot. Paris 1902.

S299
SYNTAX of CLASSICAL GREEK / B.
L. Gildersleeve & C. W. E. Miller. New York & Cincinnati.
1900. Reprint Groningen 1980.

S300
SYRIA. Paris 1920-   .

S301
SYRO-MESOPOTAMIAN STUDIES. Mali-
bu, CA. 1977-   . (Monographic
Journals of the Near East).
(SMS).

Szantyr, A. see L15.

S302
SZÁZADOK. Budapest 1867-   .

S303
SZEGEDI VÁROSI MÚZEUM KIADVÁNYAI =
Veröffentlichungen des Städtischen Museums in Szeged = Publications of the Szeged City
Muzeum. Szeged 1931-44. Title
changes slightly.

S304
SZEKSZÁRDI BÉRI BALOGH ÁDÁM MÚZEUM
ÉVKÖNYVE = Annales Musei Szekszár-

diensis de Béri Balogh Ádam Nominati. Szekszárd 1973/4?-   .

Szentpetery, E. see S63.

S305
SZÉPHALOM. Szeged 1927-   .

SZÉPMŰVÉSZETI MÚZEUM KÖZLEMÉNYEI
   see B336.

T

T1
T.L.S.; the TIMES LITERARY SUPPLE-
MENT. London 1902-   . 1902-
68 initials did not appear as
part of the title. (TLS).

T2
TABLETTES CAPPADOCIENNES / G. Contenau. Paris 1920-   . (Museé
du Louvre. Département des Antiquités Orientales, Textes Cuneiformes; 4 etc.). Reprint 1973.

T3
TABULA IMPERII BYZANTINI. Vienna
1976-   . (Österreichisches
Akademie der Wissenschaften;
Philosophisch-Historische Klasse.
Denkschriften; 125).
--. Beiheft. 1976-   .

T4
TABULA IMPERII ROMANI [by city or
province]. place varies
1954?-   . (TIR).

Tait, J. G. see G93.

T5
TALANTA; proceedings of the Dutch
Archaeological and Historical
Society. Groningen etc.
1969-   .

T6
TANULMÁNYOK BUDAPEST MÚLTJÁBÓL.
Budapest 1932-   . (Budapest
várostörténeti monográfiái; 37
etc.).

T7
TAPHIKOS KYKLOS B´ ton MYKENŌN /
G. E. Mylonas. Athens 1971-73.

T8
TARBIZ; a quarterly for Jewish
studies. Jerusalem 1929-   .

TARTU. ÜLIKOOL. ACTA et COMMENTATI-
ONES see A48.

T9
TAXANDRIA; tijdschrift voor noord-
brabantsche geschiedenis en volkskunde. Turnhout 1894-   .

Tcherikover, V. A. see C231.

T10
TEBTUNIS PAPYRI / B. P. Grenfell
et al. London etc. 1902-   .
Published in two series: Graeco-
Roman Memoirs of the Egypt Ex-
ploration Society and the Uni-
versity of California's Graeco-
Roman Archaeology. (PTebt).

T11
TECHNOLOGY and CULTURE. Detroit
1959-   .

T12
TEHERANER FORSCHUNGEN (Deutsches
Archäologisches Institut. Abteilung Teheran). Berlin
1961-   .

T13
TEIRESIAS; a review and continuing

bibliography of Boiotian studies.
Montreal 1971-   .
--. Supplement. 1972-   .
--. Appendex Epigraphica.
1976-
--. Appendex Archeologica.
1978-   .

T14
TEL AVIV; journal of the Tel Aviv
University Institute of Archae-
ology. Tel Aviv 1974-   .

T15
TELL EDFOU (1937-39) [papyri and
greek ostraca] / B. Bruyère, K.
Michalowski et al. Cairo 1937-
50. (Fouilles Franco-Polonaises).
(PEdfou).

T16
TEMENOS; studies in comparative
religion. Helsinki 1965-   .

T17
TEMPLE UNIVERSITY AEGEAN SYMPOSIUM.
Philadelphia 1976-   .

Temporini, H. see A678.

T18
TEOLOGINEN AIKAKAUSKIRJA = Teologisk Tidskrift. Helsinki etc.
1896-   .

TEOLOGISK TIDSKRIFT see T18.

T19
TERUEL (Instituto de Estudios Turo-
lenses). Teruel 1949-   .

T20
TESTIMONIA LINGUAE ETRUSCAE / M.
Pallottino. 2. ed. Florence 1968.
(Biblioteca di Studi Superiore;
24). 1st edition 1954. (TLE).

TEUBNER TEXTS see B100.

T21
TEV'A VA-ARETS. Tel Aviv 1959-   .

T22
TEXTE und FORSCHUNGEN zur BYZANTIN-
ISCH-NEUGRIECHISCHEN PHILOLOGIE.
Athens etc. 1922-56. Supplement

to Byzantinisch-neugriechische
Jahrbücher.

T23
TEXTE der HETHITER. Heidelberg
1971-   .

T24
TEXTE und UNTERSUCHUNGEN zur GE-
SCHICHTE der ALTCHRISTLICHEN
LITERATUR. Berlin 1883-   .
(TU).

T25
TEXTES CUNÉIFORMES (Musée du Lou-
vre. Département des Antiquités
Orientales et de la Céramique
Antique). Paris 1910-   .
(TCL).

T26
TEXTES et MONUMENTS FIGURÉS RELA-
LIFS aux MYSTÈRES de MITHRA /
F. Cumont. Brussels 1896-99.
(MMM).

T27
TEXTES OUGARITIQUES; introduction,
traduction, commentaire / A.
Caquot. Paris 1974-   . (Litteraires Anciennes du Proche Orient; 7. Textes Sémetiques de
l'Ouest).

T28
TEXTILE MUSEUM JOURNAL. Washington D.C. 1962-   .

T29
TEXTS from CUNEIFORM SOURCES.
Locust Valley, New York 1966-   .

T30
TEXTS and STUDIES; contributions
to Biblical and patristic literature. Cambridge 1891-   .

T31
TEXTUS; annual of the Hebrew University Bible Project. Jerusalem 1960-   .

T32
TEXTUS MINORES in USUM ACADEMICUM
SUMPTIBUS. Leiden 1948-   .

T33
THEBAN OSTRACA / A. H. Gardiner et
  al. Toronto & London 1913. (Univ.
  of Toronto Studies; Papyrological
  Series; 1). (OTheb).

T34
THEOKRATIA; Jahrbuch des Institutum
  Judaicum Delitzschianum. Leiden
  1967/9- .

THEOL-: entries beginning with this
  spelling are here interfiled.

T35
THEOLOGISCHE BLÄTTER. Leipzig
  1922-42.

THEOLOGICAL DICTIONARY of the NEW
  TESTAMENT see T50.

T36
THEOLOGIE und GLAUBE. Paderborn
  1909- . Suspended 1945-46.

T37
THEOLOGISCHE JAHRBÜCHER. Tübingen
  1842-57.

T38
THEOLOGISCHES LITERATURBLATT.
  Leipzig 1880-1943.

T39
THEOLOGISCHE LITERATURZEITUNG.
  Leipzig, Berlin 1876-   . Sus-
  pended 1945-47. (ThLZ, TLZ).
  --. Bibliographisches Beiblatt.
  1922- .

T40
THEOLOGIE und PHILOSOPHIE. Freiburg i.B. 1926- .

THÉOLOGIE et PHILOSOPHIE (Geneva
  1868-72) see R244.

T41
THEOLOGISCH-PRAKTISCHE QUARTAL-
  SCHRIFT. Linz 1848-   . Sus-
  pended 1941-47.

T42
THEOLOGISCHE QUARTALSCHRIFT.
  Tübingen etc. 1819-   . Sus-
  pended 1945. (ThQ).

THEOLOGISCHE QUARTALSCHRIFT (Milwaukee, Wisc. 1904-47?) see
  Q20.

T43
THEOLOGISCHE REVUE. Münster
  1902- . Suspended 1945-47.

T44
THEOLOGISCHE RUNDSCHAU. Freiburg
  i.B. & Tübingen 1897-1917
  1929- . Suspended 1944-47.

T45
THEOLOGICAL STUDIES. Baltimore
  1940- . (TS).

T46
THEOLOGISCHE STUDIEN und KRITIKEN;
  eine Zeitschrift für das gesamte
  Gebeit der Theologie. Hamburg
  1828- . Suspended 1942-46.

T47
THEOLOGIAI SZEMLE. Debrecen
  1925- . Suspended 1949?-57.

T48
THEOLOGISCH TIJDSCHRIFT. Leiden
  & Amsterdam 1867-1911.

T49
THEOLOGISCHES WÖRTERBUCH zum ALTEN
  TESTAMENT / G.J. Botterweck.
  Stuttgart 1973-77. Also avail-
  able in English translation.

T50
THEOLOGISCHES WÖRTERBUCH zum NEUEN
  TESTAMENT / G. Kittel et al.
  Stuttgart 1933-   . Also avail-
  able in English translation.

T51
THEOLOGISCHE ZEITSCHRIFT. Basel
  1945- . (ThZ, TZ).

T52
THEORIA; tidskrift for filosofi och
  psykologi = Swedish journal of
  philosophy and psychology. Gö-
  tenburg 1935- .
                                ○

T53
THESAURISMATA; periodikon tou Hellēnikou Institutou Vyzantinōn

kai Metavyzantinōn Spoudōn.
Venice 1962-   .

T54
THESAURUS GRAECAE LINGUAE = Thēsau-
rus tēs Hellēnikēs Glōssēs / H.
Stephanus. Geneva 1572. Appeared
in several editions and printings.

THESAURUS tēs HELLĒNIKĒS GLŌSSĒS
see T54.

T55
THESAURUS. INSCRIPTIONUM AEGYPTIA-
CARUM / H. K. Brugsch. Leipzig
1883-91. Reprint Graz 1968.

T56
THESAURUS LINGUAE LATINAE. Leipzig
1900-   . (ThLL, TLL).

T57
THESKEUTIKĒ kai ĒTHIKĒ ENKYKLO-
PAIDEIA. Athens 1962-68.

T58
THESSALIKA. Volos 1958-   .

T59
THOMIST; a speculative quarterly
review. Washington D.C. 1939-   .

Thompson, E. M. see N42, P14.

Thompson, M. see I105.

Thompson, M. S. see P172.

T60
THRAKIKA. Athens 1928-75 1978-   .

Thumb, A. see H14.

Thureau-Dangin, F. see S272.

T61
THURGAUISCHE BEITRÄGE zur VATER-
LÄNDISCHEN GESCHICHTE. Frauen-
feld 1861-   . Suspended 1920,
22-23.

T62
TIBISCUS (Muzeul Banatului). Timişoara 1970?-   .

T63
TIDSKRIFT för KONSTVETENSKAP. Lund
1916-   . (TfK).

TIDSKRIFT for PHILOLOGI og PAEDAGO-
GIK see N69.

TIDSKRIFT. UPPLANDS FORNMINNESFÖR-
ENINGS see U27.

T64
TIJDSCHRIFT voor FILOSOFIE. Lou-
vain 1939-   . 1939-61 title:
Tijdschrift voor filosofie.

T65
TIJDSCHRIFT voor GESCHIEDENIS. Amsterdam etc. 1886-   . 1892-93
title: Geschiedenis en aardrijks-
kunde. (TG).

TIJDSCHRIFT voor PHILOSOPHIE see
T64.

TIJDSCHRIFT voor RECHTSGESCHIED-
ENIS see R175.

TIMES LITERARY SUPPLEMENT see T1.

T66
TIROLER HEIMAT; Jahrbuch für Ge-
schichte und Volkskunde de Tirois.
Innsbruck etc. 1925-   .

T67
TIROLER HEIMATBLÄTTER. Innsbruck
1923-   . Title of vol 1: Heimatblätter; title of vols. 20-
21: Heimatblätter für den Reichsgau Tirol und Vorarlberg.

T68
TITULI (Istituto di Epigrafia e
Antichità Greche e Romane. Univ.
di Roma). Rome 1980-   .

T69
TITULI ASIAE MINORIS. Vienna
1901-   . (TAM).
--. Ergänzungsbände. 1966-   .

T70
TITULI CALYMNII / M. Segre. Bergamo 1952. (Annuario della Scuola
Archeologica di Atene; n.s. 6-7
for 1944-45).

T71
TITULI CAMIRENSES / M. Serge & I.
Pugliese Carratelli. Rome 1952.
Originally published in n.s. 11-
13 (1949-51) of the Annuario della
Scuola Archeologica di Atene, pp.
141-318. Supplement in n.s. 14-16
(1952-54), pp. 211-46.

TLS see T1.

Tod, M. N. see S74, C84.

T72
TOIMETISED TARTU ULIKOOL = Uchenye
Zapiski Tartu Universitatea.
Tartu 1941-   . Suspended 1942-
45.

TOIMITUKSIA. SUOMALAINEN TIEDEAKA-
TEMIA see A219.

T73
TOMB of the DOUBLE AXES and ASSOCI-
ATED GROUP / A. J. Evans. London
1914. Originally published as pp.
1-94 of Archaeologia 65 (1914).
(TDA).

T74
TOOLS and WEAPONS ILLUSTRATED by
the EGYPTIAN COLLECTION UNIVERSI-
TY COLLEGE, LONDON / W. M. F.
Petrie. London 1917. Reprint
Warminster 1974.

T75
TOPOGRAPHICAL BIBLIOGRAPHY of
ANCIENT EGYPTIAN HIEROGLYPHIC
TEXTS, RELIEFS and PAINTINGS /
B. Porter & R. L. B. Moss.
2. ed. Oxford 1960-   . 1st
edition 1927.

T76
TOR; meddelanden från Institutionem
för Nordisk Fornkunskap vid Uppsala Universitet. Uppsala
1948-   .

T77
TÖRTÉNELMI és RÉGÉSZETI ÉRTESITÖ;
a Délmagyarorszagi Történelmi
és Régészeti Múzeumtársulat Közlönye. Timişoara 1872-1917?.

T78
TÖRTÉNELMI SZEMLE = Historische
Rundschau. Budapest 1958-   .

T79
TOTIUS LATINITATIS LEXICON / E.
Forcellini. Padua 1771. Variant
title: Lexicon totius latinitatis.
Appeared in several editions and
printings.

T80
TRABAJOS de PREHISTORIA. Madrid
1960-   .

T81
TRABALHOS de ANTROPOLGÍA e ETNOLO-
GÍA. Oporto 1919-   . 1919-42/4
title: Trabalhos de Sociedade
Portuguesa de Antropología e Et-
nología.

TRABALHOS de SOCIEDADE PORTUGUESA
de ANTROPOLOGÍA e ETNOLOGÍA see
T81.

T82
TRADITIO; studies in ancient and
medieval history, thought and
religion. New York 1943-   .

T83
TRAGICORUM GRAECORUM FRAGMENTA / A.
Nauck. 2. ed. Leipzig & Lenin-
grad 1889-92. 1st edition 1856.
(TGF).
--. Supplement / B. Snell. Hil-
desheim 1964.

T84
TRAGICORUM GRAECORUM FRAGMENTA /
B. Snell. Göttingen 1971-   .

T85
TRAGICORUM ROMANORUM FRAGMENTA /
O. Ribbeck. 2. Aufl. Leipzig 1871.
1st edition 1852-55. (Scaenicae
Romanorum Poesis Fragmenta; 1).
(TRF).

T86
TRAITÉ des MONNAIES GRECQUES et
ROMAINES / E. Babelon. Paris
1903-33.

T87
TRANSACTIONS of the AMERICAN PHI-
LOLOGICAL ASSOCIATION. Baltimore
1869-   . 1897-1972 title: Trans-
actions and Proceedings. (TAPhA,
TAPA).

T88
TRANSACTIONS of the AMERICAN PHI-
LOSOPHICAL SOCIETY. Philadelphia
1769-1809 1816-   . (TAPS).

T89
TRANSACTIONS and ANNUAL REPORT of
the NORTH STAFFORDSHIRE FIELD
CLUB and ARCHAEOLOGICAL SOCIETY.
Stafford 1965-   . Title varies
slightly.

T90
TRANSACTIONS of the BIRMINGHAM and
WARWICKSHIRE ARCHAEOLOGICAL SOCI-
ETY. Birmingham 1870-   . 1870-
97 name of the society: Birmingham and Midland Institute. Archaeological Section. 1898-1968 name
of society: Birmingham Archaeological Society.

T91
TRANSACTIONS of the BRISTOL and
GLOUCESTERSHIRE ARCHAEOLOGICAL
SOCIETY. Gloucester 1876-   .

T92
TRANSACTIONS of the CARDIFF NATURA-
LIST'S SOCIETY. Cardiff
1867/8-   . 1867/8 title: First
Annual Report. 1868-1945 title:
Reports and Transactions.

T93
TRANSACTIONS of the CARMARTHEN-
SHIRE ANTIQUARIAN SOCIETY and
FIELD CLUB. Carmarthen 1905-39.

T94
TRANSACTIONS of the CUMBERLAND and
WESTMORLAND ANTIQUARIAN and ARCH-
AEOLOGICAL SOCIETY. Kendal
1866-   . (CW, C&W).

TRANSACTIONS of the DEPARTMENT of
ARCHAEOLOGY, FREE MUSEUM of
SCIENCE and ART see T97.

T95
TRANSACTIONS of the DUMFRIESSHIRE
and GALLOWAY NATURAL HISTORY and
ANTIQUARIAN SOCIETY. Edinburgh
1862/3-67/8 1876-   . Variant
name: Transactions and Journal of
Proceedings.

T96
TRANSACTIONS of the DURHAM and
NORTHUMBERLAND ARCHITECTURAL
and ARCHAEOLOGICAL SOCIETY. n.p.
1862-   .

TRANSACTIONS of the ESSEX ARCHAE-
OLOGICAL SOCIETY see E102.

T97
TRANSACTIONS of the FREE MUSEUM of
SCIENCE and ART (Univ. Pennsyl-
vania). Philadelphia 1904-07.
1904-05 title: Transactions of
the Department of Archaeology,
Free Museum of Science and Art.
(TFMSA).

TRANSACTIONS and JOURNAL of PRO-
CEEDINGS of the DUMFRIESSHIRE
and GALLOWAY NATURAL HISTORY and
ANTIQUARIANS SOCIETY see T95.

T98
TRANSACTIONS of the LANCASHIRE and
CHESHIRE ANTIQUARIAN SOCIETY.
Manchester 1883-   .

TRANSACTIONS of the LICHFIELD ARCH-
AEOLOGICAL and HISTORICAL SOCIETY
see T104.

TRANSACTIONS of the LICHFIELD and
SOUTH STAFFORDSHIRE ARCHAEOLO-
GICAL and HISTORICAL SOCIETY
see T104.

T99
TRANSACTIONS of the LONDON and
MIDDLESEX ARCHAEOLOGICAL SOCIETY.
London 1856-90 1905-   .

TRANSACTIONS. NORTH STAFFORDSHIRE
FIELD CLUB see T89.

T100
TRANSACTIONS of the PHILOLOGICAL
SOCIETY, OXFORD. Oxford 1842-   .

1842-54 title: Proceedings.
(TPhS, TPS).

TRANSACTIONS and PROCEEDINGS of the
AMERICAN PHILOLOGICAL ASSOCIATION
see T87.

TRANSACTIONS of the ROYAL ... see
Transactions of the ... (the word
royal is disregarded in filing,
but may have been regarded in
forming an abbreviation).

T101
TRANSACTIONS of the SHROPSHIRE
ARCHAEOLOGICAL and NATURAL HIS-
TORY SOCIETY. Shrewsbury 1878-
Society's name varies slightly.

T102
TRANSACTIONS of the SOCIETY of BIB-
LICAL ARCHAEOLOGY. London 1872-
93. (TSBA).

T103
TRANSACTIONS of the royal SOCIETY
of LITERATURE of the UNITED
KINGDOM. London 1823-38 1840-
1919.

T104
TRANSACTIONS of the SOUTH STAFFORD-
SHIRE ARCHAEOLOGICAL and HISTOR-
ICAL SOCIETY. Bloxwich
1959/60-   . Vols. 1-2 issued
by the Lichfield Archaeological
and Historical Society; vols. 3-
9 issued by the Lichfield and
South Staffordshire Archaeological
and Historical Society.

T105
TRANSACTIONS of the WORCESTERSHIRE
ARCHAEOLOGICAL SOCIETY. Worces-
ter 1923/4-   .

T106
TRANSUNTI. ACCADEMIA nazionale dei
LINCEI. Rome 1876/7-83/4. Supersedes in part the Atti of the
academy. Superseded by its Rendiconti. Published as part of the
continuing Atti series of the
academy.

Trapp, E. see P221.

Traulos, I. see P136.

TRAVAUX see also TRUDY.

T107
TRAVAUX du CENTRE d'ARCHÉOLOGIE
MÉDITERRANÉENNE de l'ACADÉMIE
POLONAISE des SCIENCES = Prace
Zakładu Archeologii Śródziem-
nomorskiej Polskiej Akademii
Nauk. Warsaw 1959-   .

TRAVAUX du DÉPARTEMENT de l'HIS-
TOIRE de l'ART et de la CULTURE
ANTIQUE see T124.

TRAVAUX du DÉPARTEMENT NUMISMA-
TIQUE. MUSÉE de l'ERMITAGE see
T125.

TRAVAUX du DÉPARTEMENT ORIENTAL,
MUSÉE de l'ERMITAGE see T126.

TRAVAUX de l'EXPEDITION ARCHÉO-
LOGIQUE de TURKMÉNISTAN MÉR-
IODIONAL see T123.

TRAVAUX de l'INSTITUT ARCHÉOLOGIQUE
de l'UNIVERSITÉ FRANCOIS-JOSEPH
see D88.

T108
TRAVAUX et MÉMOIRES. CENTRE de
RECHERCHE d'HISTOIRE et de CIVI-
LISATION BYZANTINES. Paris
1965-   . (TM).

T109
TRAVAUX MÉMOIRES de l'ÉCOLE FRAN-
ÇAISE d'ATHÈNES. Paris 1929-   .

TRAVAUX. MUSÉE de l'ERMITAGE see
T117, T124-T126.

TRAVAUX du MUSÉE d'ÉTAT de l'ERMI-
TAGE see T117.

TRAVAUX des MUSÉES de VOIVODINA
see R2.

T110
TRAVAUX et RECHERCHES. FÉDÉRATION
TARNAISE de SPÉLÉO-ARCHÉOLOGIE.
Albi ?-   .

TRAVAUX de la SECTION NUMISMATIQUE
et ARCHÉOLOGIQUE du MUSÉE NATIONAL
de TRANSYLVANIE à KOLOZSVÁR   see
D87.

Travlos, J.   see   P136.

Trendall, A. D.   see   I7, P6, R54-
R55.

T111
TRIBUS (Linden Museums, Heidelberg).
Stuttgart 1951-   . 1951 title:
Jahrbuch des Linden-Museums.

T112
TRIERER JAHRESBERICHTE. Trier 1850-
1922. 1850- 1905 title: Jahresbericht der Gesellschaft für Nützliche Forschungen zu Trier.

T113
TRIERER THEOLOGISCHE ZEITSCHRIFT.
Trier 1947-   .

T114
TRIER ZEITSCHRIFT für GESCHICHTE
und KUNST des TRIERER LANDES und
seiner NACHBARGEBIETE. Trier
1926-   . Title varies slightly.
Suspended 1941/2-49. (TrZ, TZ).

T115
TROMSØ MUSEUMS ÅRSBERETNING.
Tromsø 1873-   .

TRUDY see also TRAVAUX.

TRUDY. AKADEMIIA NAUK GRUZINSKOI
SSR see T121.

TRUDY. ALMA-ATA see T122.

TRUDY. BAKU see T120.

T116
TRUDY CHOREZMSKOĬ ARKHEOLOGO-ÉTNO
GRAFISCHESKOI ÉKSPEDICHII. Mos-
cow 1952-   .

TRUDY. ÉRMITAZHA see T117, T124-
T126.

T117
TRUDY GOSUDARSTVENNOGO ÉRMITAZHA.
Leningrad 1956-   .

T118
TRUDY GOSUDARSTVENNOGO ISTORISCHES-
KOGO MUZEIIA. Moscow 1926-   .
Name of issuing body changes
slightly.

T119
TRUDY INSTITUTA IAZYKOZNANIIA
(Akademiia Nauk SSSR). Moscow
1952-   .

T120
TRUDY INSTITUTA ISTORII. (Akademiia
nauk Azerbaidzhanskoi SSR). Baku 195?-   .

T121
TRUDY INSTITUTA ISTORII. (Akademiia
nauk Gruzinskoi SSR). Tiflis
1955-   .

T122
TRUDY INSTITUTA ISTORII, ARKHEOLO-
GII i ÉTNOGRAFII (Akademiia Nauk
Kasachskoi SSR). Alma-Ata
1956-   .

TRUDY i ISLEDOVANIIA po DREVNEI
ISTORII see S173.

T123
TRUDY IUZHNO-TURKMENISTANSKOI
ARKHEOLOGICHESKOI KOMPLEKSNOI
ÉKPEDITSII. Moscow 1946-   .

T124
TRUDY OTDELA ISTORII ISKUSSTVA i
KUL'TURY ANTICHNOGO MIRA GOSUD-
ARSTVENNOGO ÉRMITAZHA = Travaux
du Département de l'Histoire
de l'Art de la Culture Antique,
Musée de l'Ermitage. Leningrad
1945.

T125
TRUDY OTDELA NUMISMATIKI GOSUDARS-
TVENNOGO ÉRMITAZHA = Travaux du
Département Numismatique, Musée
de l'Ermitage. Leningrad 1945.

T126
TRUDY OTDELA VOSTOKA GOSUDARSTVEN-
NOGO ÉRMITAZHA = Travaux du Département Orientale, Musée du
l'Ermitage. Leningrad 1940.

TRUDY. TIFLIS   see   T121.

T127
TRUDY. TOMSK. UNIVERSITET = Arbei-
ten der Tomsker Staatsuniversität.
Tomsk 1889-   . 1889-1929 title:
Izvestiſa = Bericht = Bulletin.

Tsereteli, G.   see   P68.

TSIYON   see   Z84.

TSvetaev, I. V.   see   I69.

Tudor, D.   see   O14.

T128
TÜBINGER ATLAS der VORDERORIENTS.
Wiesbaden 1972-   .
--. Arbeitsheft. 1975-   .
--. Beihefte.
--.--. Reihe A. 1977-   .
--.--. Reihe B. 1972-   . .

T129
TÜRK ARKEOLOJI DERGISI = Turkish
Review of Archaeology. Ankara
6- 1956-   . In part continues
Türk Tarih, Arkeologya ve Et-
nografya Dergisi. (TAD,
TürkArkDerg).

T130
TÜRK ETNOĞRAFYA DERGISI = Turkish
Review of Ethnography. Ankara
1956-   .

T131
TÜRK TARIH ARKEOLOGYA ve ETNOĞRA-
FYA DERGISI. Istanbul 1933-49.
(TTAED, TürkTarDerg).

TÜRK TARIH KURUMU. BELLETEN   see
B45.

TÜRK TARIH KURUMU RAPORLARI   see
K8.

T132
TÜRK TARIH KURUMU YALINLARININ =
Publications de la Société d'His-
toire Turque. Istanbul 1932-   .
Issued in 20 series. (TTKY).

TURKISH REVIEW of ARCHAEOLOGY   see
T129.

TURKISH REVIEW of ETNOGRAPHY   see
T130.

Turner, C. H.   see   E4.

Turner, G.   see   C77.

TURTLE   see   N71.

T133
TUSCULUM BÜCHER. Munich 1923-   .

T134
TVORCHESTVO; zhurnal literatury,
iskusstva, nauki. Moscow &
Leningrad 1918-   .

T135
TWAYNES WORLD AUTHOR SERIES. New
York 1966-   .

U

U1
UCHENYE ZAPISKI. GOSUDARSTVENNYĬ
PEDAGOGICHESKIĬ INSTITUT, PENZA.
Penza 1953-   .

U2
UCHENYE ZAPISKI. LENINGRADSKIĬ
GOSUDARSTVENNIĬ PEDAGOGISCHESKIĬ
INSTITUT Imini A. I. Gercena.
Leningrad 1935-   .

U3
UCHENYE ZAPISKI. MOSKOVSKIĬ GOSU-
DARSTVENNYĬ PEDAGOGICHESKIĬ IN-
STITUT. Moscow 1940-   .

U4
UCHENYE ZAPISKI PERMSKOGO GOSU-
DARSTVENNOGO UNIVERSITETA. Perm
1929-   .

U5
UCHENYE ZAPISKI SVERDLOVSKOGO GO-
SUDARSTVENNOGO PEDAGOGICHESKOGO
INSTITUTA. Sverdlovsk 1938-   .

UCHENYE ZAPISKI. TARTU. ULIKOOL
see T72.

U6
UDINE; bollettino delle biblioteca e dei musei civici. Udine
1962-   .

U7
UGARIT FORSCHUNGEN. Kevelaer
1969-   . (UF).

U8
UGARITIC HANDBOOK / C. J. Gordon.
Rome 1947. (Analecta Orientalia;
25).

U9
UGARITIC MANUAL/ C. J. Gordon.
Rome 1955. (Analecta Orientalia;
35).

U10
UGARITIC TEXTBOOK / C. J. Gordon.
Rome 1965. (Analecta Orientalia;
38). Revision of the author's
Ugaritic manual. Reprint pub-
lished 1967 with supplement.

U11
UKRAINS'KYI ISTORYCHNYI ZHURNAL.
Kiev 1957-   .

U12
ULM und OBERSCHWABEN; Zeitschrift
für Geschichte und Kunst. Ulm
1891-   . 1891-1937 title: Mitteilungen des Vereins für Kunst
und Altertum in Ulm und Oberschwaben.

U13
ULSTER JOURNAL of ARCHAEOLOGY.
Belfast 1853-61/2 1894-1911
1938-   .

Ungnad, A. see A625, B5.

UNION HISTORIQUE et LITTÉRAIRE du
MAINE see P229.

UNIVERSITETET i BERGEN. ÅRBOK
see A6.

U14
UNIVERSITETET i BERGEN SKRIFTER.
Bergen 1878-   . 1878-1943
title: Bergens Museums Skrifter.

UNIVERSITETET OLDSAKSAMLINGS ÅRBOK
see A7.

U15
UNIVERSITETET OLDSAKSAMLINGS
SKRIFTER. Oslo 1929-53? Published irregularly; vol. 1:
1938; vol. 2: 1929; vol. 3:
1946; vol. 4: 1953.

U16
UNIVERSITY of CALIFORNIA PUBLICA-
TIONS in CLASSICAL ARCHAEOLOGY.
Berkeley 1929-63.

U17
UNIVERSITY of CALIFORNIA PUBLICA-
TIONS in CLASSICAL PHILOLOGY.
Berkeley & Los Angeles 1904-   .

UNIVERSITY of CINCINNATI CLASSICAL
STUDIES see C124.

UNIVERSITY of ILLINOIS STUDIES in
LANGUAGE and LITERATURE see
S204.

U18
UNIVERSITY MUSEUM BULLETIN (Univ.
Pennsylvania). Phi..adelphia
1930-58.

U19
UNIVERSITY of WISCONSIN STUDIES in
LANGUAGE and LITERATURE. Madi-
son 1918-36.

U20
UNPUBLISHED OBJECTS from PALAI-
KASTRO EXCAVATIONS, 1902-09 / R.
C. Bosanquet & R. M. Dawkins.
London 1923. (British School
at Athens. Supplementary Paper;
1).

U21
UNSERE HEIMAT (Verein für Landes-
kunde von Niederösterreich und
Wien). Vienna 1902-   .

U22
UNSERE KUNSTDENKMÄLER = Nos Monuments d'Art et d'Histoire =
Nostri Monumenti Storici. Bern
1950-   .

Untermann, J. see M266.

U23
UNTERSUCHUNGEN zur ANTIKEN LITERA-
TUR und GESCHICHTE. Berlin
1968-   .

U24
UNTERSUCHUNGEN zur ASSYRIOLOGIE
und VORDERASIATISCHEN ARCHÄOLO-
GIE. Berlin 1960-   . (UAVA).

U25
UNTERSUCHUNGEN zu den KERTSCHEN
VASEN / K. Schefold. Berlin &
Leipzig 1934. (Archäologische
Mitteilungen aus Russischen
Sammlungen; 4).

UNTERSUCHUNGEN und MITTEILUNGEN
des MUSEUMS BRUCKENTHAL (Sibiu)
see S181.

U26
UNTERSUCHUNGEN der ZWEIGSTELLE
KAIRO des ÖSTERREICHISCHEN ARCH-
ÄOLOGISCHEN INSTITUTES. Vienna
1975-   . (Denkschriften. Österreichischen Akademie der Wissenschaften).

U27
UPPLANDS FORNMINNESFÖRENINGS
TIDSKRIFT. Uppsala 1871/6-   .

U28
UPSALA UNIVERSITETS ÅRSSKRIFT.
Uppsala 1861-   .

U29
UR EXCAVATIONS. London 1927-   .
(UE).

U30
UR- und FRÜHGESCHICHTE ARCHÄOLOGIE
der SCHWEIZ. Basel 1968-79.

U31
UR-SCHWEIZ = Suisse Primitive.
Basel 1937-   . (US).

U32
URBE; rivista romana. Rome
  1936-   .

Urech, Ê. see D43.

U33
URGESCHICHTLICHER ANZEIGER = Pre-
  historic Review = Indicateur
  Préhistorique = Monitore Preis-
  torico = Indicador Prehistorico.
  Vienna 1924-25.

U34
URKUNDEN des 18. DYNASTIE: histo-
  risch-biographische Urkunden / K.
  H. Sethe. Leipzig 1906-09.

U35
URKUNDEN der PTOLEMÄERZEIT / U.
  Wilcken. Berlin 1927-57. (UPZ).

V

Vacant, A. see D61.

V1
VALLESIA; bulletin annuel de la
  Bibliothèque et des archives
  Cantonales du Valais, des Musées
  de Valère et de la Majorie.
  Sion 1946-   . Subtitle also in
  German.

van Groningen, B. A. see F3, P65.

van Orelli, J. see I81.

Vandier, J. see M29.

V2
VARIA BIO-ARCHAEOLOGICA. Groningen
  1955-   .

V3
VARSTVO SPOMENIKOV. Ljubljana
  1949-   .

V4
VASENLISTEN zur GRIECHISCHEN HELD-
  ENSAGE / F. Brommer. 3. Aufl.
  Marburg 1973. 1st edition 1956.

V5
VASES SICYONIENS / K. Friis
  Johansen. Copenhagen & Paris
  1923. Reprint Rome 1966.

V6
VASI ITALIOLI ed ETRUSCHI a FIGURE
  ROSSE / A. D. Trendall. Vatican
  City 1953-55. (Vasi antichi di-
  pinti del Vaticano; 2, suppl.).

VASI SZEMLE see D101.

V7
VAULTED TOMBS of the MESARA / S.
  A. Xanthoudides. Liverpool
  1924. Reprint Farnborough 1971.

V8
VELTRO; rivista della civiltà
  italiana. Rome 1957-

Ventris, M. see D82, K32.

V9
VERBUM CARO. Neuchâtel 1947-69.

V10
VERBUM DOMINI. Rome 1921-69.
  Suspended 1944-47.

V11
VERGANGENHEIT und GEGENWART. Leipzig & Berlin 1911-44?.

V12
VERGESSENES POMPEJI / K. Schefold.
  Bern & Munich 1962. (Schriften
  der Schweizerischen Geisteswis-
  senschaftlichen Gesellschaft;
  4).

VERGILIAN DIGEST see V14.

V13
VERGILIUS. Evanston, Ill. 1938-40.

V14
VERGILIUS (Vergilian Society of
  America). Atlanta, Ga. etc.

1955?-   . Title until 1958
Vergilian Digest.

V15
VERGLEICHENDE LAUT- und FORMEN-
LEHRE des HETHITISCHEN / H. Kron-
asser. Heidelberg 1956.

V16
VERGLEICHENDES WÖRTERBUCH der IN-
DOGERMANISCHE SPRACHE / A. Walde
& J. Pokorny. Berlin & Leipzig
1927-32. Reprint Berlin 1973.

VERHANDELINGEN and VERHANDLUNGEN are
here interfiled. See also VERÖF-
FENTLICHUNGEN.

VERHANDELINGEN. Koninklijke ACADE-
MIE van BELGE see M95.

VERHANDELINGEN. Koninklijke AKADE-
MIE van WETENSCHAPPEN, AMSTERDAM
see V20.

V17
VERHANDLUNGEN. BERLINER GESELL-
SCHAFT für ANTHROPOLOGIE, ETH-
NOLOGIE und URGESCHICHTE. Ber-
lin 1869-1902. Issued as part
of the Zeitschrift für Ethnologie.

V18
VERHANDLUNGEN des HISTORISCHEN VER-
EINS für NIEDERBAYERN. Landshut
1846/7.

V19
VERHANDLUNGEN des HISTORISCHEN VER-
EINS für den REGENKREIS der OBER-
PFALZ und von REGENSBURG. Regens-
burg 1831-   .

VERHANDELINGEN KONINKLIJKE ... see
VERHANDELINGEN ... (the word koninklijke is disregarded in filing,
though it may have been regarded
in the formation of an abbreviation).

V20
VERHANDELINGEN der koninklijke
NEDERLANDSE AKADEMIE van WETEN-
SCHAPPEN. AFDELING LETTERKUNDE.
Amsterdam 1858-   . Also is-
sued under the earlier names of

the Academy: Koninklijke Akademie van Wetenschappen, Nederlandse Akademie van Wetenschappen, and Koninklijke Nederlandse Akademie van Wetenschappen.

V21
VERHANDLUNGEN der VERSAMMLUNGEN
DEUTSCHER PHILOLOGEN und SCHUL-
MÄNNER. Nürnberg etc. 1838-   .

V22
VERHANDLUNGEN van de koninklijke
VLAAMSE ACADEMIE voor WETEN-
SCHAPPEN LETTEREN en SCHONE
KUNSTEN van BELGIË. KLASSE der
LETTEREN. Antwerp 1941-   .

Vermaseren, M. J. see C206, C221.

VERÖFFENTLICHUNGEN see also VER-
HANDELINGEN and VERHANDLUNGEN.

V23
VERÖFFENTLICHUNGEN aus der BAD-
ISCHEN PAPYRUS-SAMMLUNGEN / W.
Spiegelberg. Heidelberg 1923-
38. (PBad).

VERÖFFENTLICHUNGEN. BAYERISCHE
AKADEMIE der WISSENSCHAFTEN.
KOMMISSION zur ARCHÄOLOGISCHEN
ERFORSCHUNG des SPÄTRÖMISCHEN
RÄTIEN see V26.

VERÖFFENTLICHUNGEN des HANAUER
GESCHICHTSVEREINS see H8.

V24
VERÖFFENTLICHUNGEN aus der HEIDEL-
BERGER PAPYRUSSAMMLUNG / C.
Schmidt et al. Heidelberg &
Leipzig 1904-64. (PHeid).

V25
VERÖFFENTLICHUNGEN des INSTITUTS
für ORIENTFORSCHUNG der DEUTSCHEN
AKADEMIE der WISSENSCHAFTEN.
Berlin 1950-   .

V26
VERÖFFENTLICHUNGEN. KOMMISSION zur
ARCHÄOLOGISCHEN ERFORSCHUNG des
SPÄTRÖMISCHEN RÄTIEN (Akademie
der Wissenschaften). Munich
1964-   .

VERÖFFENTLICHUNGEN. LANDESANSTALDT
für VOLKHEITSKUNDE zu HALLE   see
V27.

VERÖFFENTLICHUNGEN. LANDESANSTALDT
für VORGESCHICHTE, HALLE see
V27

V27
VERÖFFENTLICHUNGEN des LANDESMU-
SEUMS für VORGESCHICHTE in HALLE.
Halle 1918-   . Also published
under the Museum's earlier names:
Landesanstaldt für Vorgeschichte,
Landesanstaldt für Volkheits-
kunde zu Halle, and Provinzial
Museum zu Halle.

VERÖFFENTLICHUNGEN. MÜNCHEN see
V26.

V28
VERÖFFENTLICHUNGEN des MUSEUMS für
UR- und FRÜHGESCHICHTE, POTSDAM.
Potsdam 1962-   .

VERÖFFENTLICHUNGEN des PROVINZIAL
MUSEUMS zu HALLE see V27.

VERÖFFENTLICHUNGEN des STÄDTISCHEN
MUSEUMS in SZEGED see S303.

V29
VERSLAG van de COMMISSIE van BES-
TUUR van het PROVINCIAAL MUSEUM
van OUDHEIDEN en GESCHIEDKUNDIGE
VOORWERPEN in DRENTHE van de GE-
DEPUTEERDE STALEN. Assen 1939-
48?

VERSLAGEN en MEDEDELINGEN van de
LEIEGOUW see L25.

VERSLAGEN en MEDEDEELINGEN. Koninklijke NEDERLANDSE AKADEMIE van
WETENSCHAPPEN see M69.

VERSLAGEN en MEDEDEELINGEN van de
Koninklijke VLAAMSE ACADEMIE
van BELGIE see M76.

V30
VERSTREUTE BOGHAZKÖI-TEXTE / A.
Götze. Marburg a. d. Lahn 1930.

VESNIK, VESTI, VESTNIK, VIESTNIK,
VISNIK, VISNYK and VISTNYK are
here interfiled. See also VI-
JESTI and VJESNIK.

V31
VESTI. AKADEMIIA NAVUK BSSR.
Minsk 1943-   .

V32
VESTNIK AKADEMII NAUK SSSR.
Moscow 1931-   .

V33
VESTNIK DREVNEÏ ISTORII = Journal
of Ancient History. Moscow
1937-   . Previously also had
French title: Revue d'Histoire
Ancienne. (VDI).

V34
VESTNIK GOSUDARSTVENNOGO MUZEIA
GRUZII = Bulletin du Musée de
Géorgie. Tiflis 1922-   .
Title also in Georgian.

VIESTNIK HRVATSKOGA ARHEOLOŠKOGA
DRUŠTVA u ZAGREBU see V59.

V35
VISNIK KHARKIVS'KCHO UNIVERSYTETU.
Kharkiv 1964-   . Russian ti-
tle: Vestnik.

V36
VISNYK KYIVS'KOHO UNIVERSYTETU.
Kiev 1924-34.
--. Seriia Istorii ta Filosofii.
1958-   .
--. Seriia Filolohii ta Zhurnal-
istyky. 1958-66.
--. Seriia Filolohii. 1967-   .

V37
VESTNIK LENINGRADSKOGO GOSUDARST-
VENNOGO UNIVERSITETA. Leningrad
1947-55? Name of institution
varies slightly.
--. Seriia Istorii. IAzyka i
Literatury. 1956?-   .

V38
VISNYK L'VIVS'KOHO DERZHAVNAGO
UNIVERSYTETU im I. FRANKA. SERIIA
ISTORIIA, EKONOMIKA, PRAVO.
Lvov 1968-   .

V39
VESTNIK MOSKOVSKOGO UNIVERSITETA.
  Moscow
  --. Ser. 7 Filosofiia. 1977-   .
  --. Ser. 8 Istoriia. 1977-   .
  --. Ser. 9 Filologiia. 1977-   .
  Continue earlier numbered series
  which combine the disciplines
  differently.

VESTNIK OBSHCHESTVENNYKH NAUK
  (Erevan) see I167.

V40
VISTNYK ODES'KOĬ KOMISIĬ KRAEZNAV-
  STVA (Ukraĭns'kiĭ Akademii Nauk).
  Odessa 1924-30?.

V41
VESTNIK. RUSSKOGO ZAPADNO-EVROPEIS-
  KOGO PATRIARSHEGO EKZARKHATA =
  Messager de l'Exarchat du Patri-
  arche Russe en Europe Occidentale.
  Paris 1950-   .

V42
VESNIK VOJNOG MUZEJA u BEOGRADU =
  Bulletin du Musée Militaire à
  Belgrade. Belgrad 1954-   .

V43
VESTNIK VYSSHEĬ SHKOLY. Moscow
  1940-   .

V44
VESZPRÉM MEGYEI MŰZEUMOK KÖZLE-
  MÉNYEI. Veszprém 1963-   .

V45
VETERA CHRISTIANORUM. Bari 1964-   .

V46
VETUS TESTAMENTUM. Leiden 1951-   .
  --. Supplement. 1953-   . (VT).

V47
VIATOR; medieval and renaissance
  studies. Berkeley 1970-   .

V48
VICHIANA: rassegna di studi classici. Naples 1964-   . Subtitle varies.

VICTORIA COUNTY HISTORY see V49.

V49
VICTORIA HISTORY of the COUNTIES
  of ENGLAND. London 1901-   .
  (VCH).

Vidman, L. see S290.

V50
VIE SPIRITUELLE. Paris 1919-   .
  --. Supplement. 1947-69.

Viereck, P. see G109.

V51
VIERTELJAHRESSCHRIFT für SOZIAL-
  und WIRTSCHAFTSGESCHICHTE.
  Leipzig 1903-   .

V52
VIERZEHN BERLINER GRIECHISCHE PA-
  PYRI / H. Zilliacus. Helsingör
  1941. (Societatis Scientiarum
  Fennica. Commentationes Human-
  arum Litterarum; 11, 4).
  (PBerlZill).

V53
VIGILIAE CHRISTIANAE. Amsterdam
  1947-   . (VChr, VigChr).

Vigouroux, F. G. see D46.

VIJESTI see also VESNIK and VJES-
  NIK.

VIJESTI DRUŠTVA MUZEJSKO-KONZERVA-
  TORSKIH RADNIKA N.R. HRVATSKE
  see V54.

V54
VIJESTI MUZEALACA i KONZERVATORA
  N.R. HRVASTKE. Zagreb 1952-   .
  1952-58 title: Vijesti Društva
  Muzejsko-Konzervatorskih Rad-
  nika N.R. Hrvatske.

Viller, M. see D60.

VISNIK and VISNYK see VESNIK
  (the words are interfiled).

V55
VITA LATINA. Avignon 1957-   .

Vitelli, G. see P53.

Kungl. VITTERHETS HISTORIE- och
ANTIKVITETSAKADEMIENS ÅRSBOK
see A9.

V56
VIVARIUM; a journal for mediaeval
philosophy and the intellectual
life of the Middle Ages. Assen,
1963-   .

Vives, J. see I48, I75.

VIVRE et PENSER see R119.

V57
VIZANTIĬSKIĬ VREMENNIK. Leningrad
& Moscow 1894-1927 1947-   .
1st series also had Greek title:
Byzantina Chronika. (VV, Viz-
Vrem).

 VIZANTIĬSKIĬ VREMENNIK. PRILOZHE-
NIE see A75, A77, A89, A91.

VIZANTIĬSKOE OBOZRĬENIE see R121.

VJESNIK see also VIJESTI and VES-
NIK.

V58
VJESNIK za ARHEOLOGIJU i HISTORIJU
DALMATINSKU = Bulletin d'Arché-
ologie et d'Histoire Dalmate.
Split etc. 1878-   . 1878 ti-
tle: Bullettino di archeologia e
storia patria. 1879-1919 title:
Bullettino di archeologia e sto-
ria Dalmata. Suspended 1936-52.
(VAHD).

V59
VJESNIK ARHEOLOŠKOG MUZEJA u ZAGRE-
BU. Zagreb 1879-92 1895-1942?.
1958-   . 1879-95 title: Viestnik Hrvatskoga Arkeološkoga
Društva u Zagrebu. 1896-1942
title: Vjesnik Hrvatskoga Arheološkoga Društva u Zagrebu.

VJESNIK HRVATSKOGA ARHEOLOŠKOGA
DRUŠTVA u ZAGREBU see V59.

V60
VOENNO-ISTORICHESKIĬ ZHURNAL. Moscow 1959-   .

Vogliano, A. see P74.

Vogt, J. see A678.

VOICE of the TURTLE see N71.

V61
VOKRUG SVETA. Moscow 1860-   .
Suspended 1869-84 1918-26
1942?-45 ?-   .

Vollmer, F. see I41, P143.

von Arnim, H. see S149.

von Gaertringen, F. Hiller see
I39.

von Soden, W. see A105, G134.

V62
VOPROSY FILOLOGII. Leningrad
1970-   .

V63
VOPROSY FILOSOFII. Moscow
1947-   .

V64
VOPROSY IAZYKOZNANIIA (Akademiia
Nauk SSSR). Moscow 1952-   .

V65
VOPROSY ISTORII. Minsk 1974-   .

V66
VOPROSY ISTORII = Problems of
History = Questions d'Histoire
= Cuadernos de Historia. Mos-
cow 1945-   .

V67
VOPROSY ISTORIOGRAFII VSEOBSHCHEI
ISTORII. Kazan 1964-   .

VOPROSY JAZYKOZNANIJA see V64.

V68
VOPROSY KLASSICHESKOI FILOLOGII.
Moscow 1965-   .

V69
VORDERASIATISCHE BIBLIOTHEK.
Leipzig 1907-16. (VAB).

V70
VORDERASIATISCHE ROLLSIEGEL / A.
Moortgat. 2. Aufl. Berlin 1966.
1st edition 1940.

V71
VORDERASIATISCHE SCHRIFTDENKMÄLER
der KÖNIGLICHEN MUSEEN zu BERLIN.
Berlin 1907-17. (VS).

V72
VORGESCHICHTLICHES JAHRBUCH für die
GESELLSCHAFT für VORGESCHICHT-
LICHE FORSCHUNG. Berlin & Leip-
zig 1924-27.

V73
VORTRÄGE der BIBLIOTHEK WARBURG.
Leipzig & Berlin 1921/2-30/1.

VOSTOCHNYĬ SBORNIK see K7.

V74
VOX ROMANICA. Paris & Zurich
1936-   .

V75
VOYAGE ARCHÉOLOGIQUE en GRÈCE et en
ASIE MINEURE / P. LeBas, W. H.
Waddington & P. Foucart. Paris
1847-77. Vol. 3 also published
separately as: Inscriptions
grecques et latins recueilles en
Asie Mineure.
--. Supplement / S. Reinach.
1898.

V76
VRANJSKI GLASNIK (Narodni Muzej,
Vranje). Vranje 1965-   .

V77
VRIJE FRIES (Friesch Genootschap
van Geschied-, Oudheid- en Taal-
kunde). Leeuwarden 1837-   .

V78
VSPOMOGATEL'NYE ISTORICHESKIE
DISTSIPLINY (Akademiia Nauk SSSR.
Arkheograficheskaĩa. Kommissiĩa.
Leningradskoe Otdelenie).
Leningrad 1968-   .

V79
VYZANTINA. Thessalonike 1969-   .

VYZANTINA CHRONIKA see V57.

VYZANTINA kai NEOELLĒNIKA CHRONIKA
see B458.

V80
VZNIK a POČÁTKY SLOVANU = Origin
et Débuts des Slaves. Prague
1956-   .

W

Wace, A. J. B. see C84, C110, P172.

Wace, H. see D49.

Wachsmuth, C. see C246.

Wackernagel, J. see A128.

Waddington, W. H. see V75, I61, I63, I103, R41.

Wade-Gery, H. T. see A635, E101.

W1
WÄNDE POMPEJIS; topographisches Verzeichnis der Bildmotive / K. Schefold. Berlin 1957.

Wagner, R. see M330.

Walde, A. see L14, V16.

Walstein, C. see A564.

W2
WALLRAF-RICHARTZ-JAHRBUCH; Westdeutsches Jahrbuch für Kunstgeschichte. Cologne 1924- . 1936-43 title: Westdeutsches Jahrbuch für Kunstgeschichte: Wallraf-Richartz Jahrbuch.

Walters, H. B. see B209, B214, B219, B226.

Ward Perkins, J. B. see I91.

W3
WARREN PAPYRI. Leiden 1941. (Pa-pyrologica Lugduno-Batava; 1). (PWarr).

W4
WAVRIENSIA; bulletin du Cercle Historique et Archéologique de Wavre et de la Region. Wavre 1952- .

Weber, H. see D24.

Weber, O. see B120.

Webster, T. B. L. see I7, M261-M263.

W5
WEGE der FORSCHUNGEN. Darmstadt 1956?- .

Wegener, E. P. see S112.

Weidner, E. F. see P152.

Wells, C. B. see R349.

Wells, V. see C174.

W6
WELT als GESCHICHTE; eine Zeitschrift für Universalgeschichte. Stuttgart 1935- . (WG).

W7
WELT des ISLAMS = World of Islam = Monde d'Islam. Berlin & Leiden 1913-43 1951- .

W8
WELT des ORIENTS. Wuppertal
   1947-   . (WO).

Wenger, L. see B459.

Wessel, K. see R25.

Wessely, C. see C230, C233, G118.

West, M.L. see I2.

WESTDEUTSCHES JAHRBUCH für KUNST-
   GESCHICHTE see W2.

W9
WESTDEUTSCHE ZEITSCHRIFT für GE-
   SCHICHTE und KUNST. Trier 1882-
   1913.
   --. Ergänzungsheft 1884-1912.

W10
WESTERHEEM. (Archaeologische Werk-
   gemeenschap voor Westelijk Ne-
   derland). Leiden 1952-   .

Westermann, W. L. see B112, G97,
   P77, Z76.

W11
WESTFÄLISCHE FORSCHUNGEN. Münster
   1938-   .

W12
WESTFÄLISCHE ZEITSCHRIFT. Münster
   1838-   . 1838-1930 title: Zeitschrift für Vaterländische Geschichte und Alterthumskunde. Suspended 1941-46.

W13
WESTFALEN. Münster 1909-   .

W14
WESTFALENSPIEGEL (Westfälischer
   Heimatbund). Dortmund 1952-   .

W15
WEST-FRIESLANDS "OUD en NIEUW".
   Hoorn 1926-   .

W16
WETTERAUER GESCHICHTSBLÄTTER.
   Freidberg 1952-   .

Whatmough, J. see D37, P164.

Whittemore, T. see C71.

W17
WIADOMOŚCI ARCHEOLOGICZNE = Bul-
   letin Archéologique Polonais.
   Warsaw 1873-   .

W18
WIADOMOŚCI NUMIZMATYCZNE. Warsaw
   1957-   . (WN).

W19
WIADOMOŚCI NUMIZMATYCZNO-ARCHE-
   OLOGICZNE. Cracow 1892-1940/8.

WIENER ... (e.g. Wiener Jahrbuch,
   Wiener Zeitschrift) see also
   JAHRBUCH ..., ZEITSCHRIFT ...

W20
WIENER BEITRÄGE zur KUNST und
   KULTURGESCHICHT ASIENS. Vienna
   1926-37? (WB).

W21
WIENER BLÄTTER für die FREUNDE der
   ANTIKE. Vienna 1923-33.

W22
WIENER BYZANTINISTISCHE STUDIEN.
   Vienna 1964-   .

W23
WIENER GESCHICHTSBLÄTTER. Vienna
   1939-43 1946-   . 1939-43 title: Nachrichtenblatt des Vereins für Geschichte der Stadt
   Wien.

W24
WIENER HUMANISTISCHE BLÄTTER.
   Graz 1956-   .

W25
WIENER JAHRBUCH für KUNSTGE-
   SCHICHTE. Vienna 1856-60 1903-
   35. Title varies; 1856-60: Jahrbuch der K. K. Central Commission zur Erforschung und Erhaltung der Baudenkmale; 1903-06:
   Jahrbuch der K. K. Zentral Kommission für Erforschung und Erhaltung der Kunst- und Historischen Denkmale; 1907-10: Kunstgeschichtliches Jahrbuch der K.
   K. Zentral Kommission für Erfor-

schung und... 1911-17: Jahrbuch
des Kunsthistorischen Institutes
der K. K. Zentral-Kommission für
Denkmalpflege; 1918-19: Jahrbuch
des Kunsthistorischen Institutes;
1921-22: Jahrbuch für Kunstgeschichte. (JZK).

WIENER JAHRBÜCHER der LITERATUR
see J39.

WIENER JAHRESHEFTE see J74.

WIENER NUMISMATISCHE ZEITSCHRIFT
see N124.

W26
WIENER PRÄHISTORISCHE ZEITSCHRIFT.
Vienna 1914-43. (WPZ).

W27
WIENER STUDIEN; Zeitschrift für
klassische Philologie. Vienna
1879- . (WS, WSt, WienStud).

W28
WIENER VORLEGEBLÄTTER für ARCHÄOLO-
GISCHE ÜBUNGEN. Vienna 1888-
1890/1.

W29
WIENER ZEITSCHRIFT für die KUNDE
des MORGENLANDES. Vienna 1887- .
(WZKM).

WIENER ZEITSCHRIFT für VOLKSKUNDE
see O8.

Wilamowitz-Moellendorff, U. von
see G131.

Wilbour, C. E. see O55.

Wilcken, U. see G114, M222, U35.

Wilpert, J. see R319, R330, S23.

W30
WILTSHIRE ARCHAEOLOGICAL and NATURAL
HISTORY MAGAZINE. Devizes
1854- .

W31
WINCKELMANNSPROGRAMM der ARCHÄOLO-
GISCHEN GESELLSCHAFT zu BERLIN.
Berlin 1841- . 1841-1919 title:
Programm zum Winckelmannsfest.

Winter, F. see K71.

W32
WINTERTHUR JAHRBUCH. Winterthur
1954- .

Wirth, P. see R24.

WISCONSIN STUDIES in LANGUAGE and
LITERATURE see U19.

Wiseman, D. J. see A107.

W33
WISSENSCHAFTLICHE ABTEILUNGEN der
ARBEITSGEMEINSCHAFT für FOR-
SCHUNG des LANDES NORDRHEIN-
WESTFALEN. Cologne 1958- .
--. Sonderreihe: Papyrologica
Coloniensia. 1964- . (Pap-
Colon).

W34
WISSENSCHAFTLICHE KOMMENTARE zu
GRIECHISCHEN und LATEINISCHEN
SCHRIFTSTELLERN. Heidelberg
195?- .

W35
WISSENSCHAFTLICHER LITERATURAN-
ZEIGER. Freiburg 1962- .
1962-63 title: Neuer Literaturanzeiger.

W36
WISSENSCHAFTLICHE MITTHEILUNGEN
aus BOSNIEN und der HERZEGOWINA.
Vienna 1893-1916. (WMBH).

W37
WISSENSCHAFTLICHE MONOGRAPHIEN
zum ALTEN und NEUEN TESTAMENT.
Neukirchen-Vluyn 1959- .

W38
WISSENSCHAFTLICHE UNTERSUCHUNGEN
zum NEUEN TESTAMENT. Tübingen
1950- .

W39
WISSENSCHAFTLICHE VERÖFFENTLICHUN-
GEN der DEUTSCHEN ORIENTGESELL-
SCHAFT. Leipzig 1900?- .
(WVDOG).

W40
WISSENSCHAFTLICHE ZEITSCHRIT der
 ERNST-MORITZ-ARNDT-UNIVERSITÄT
 GREIFSWALD. REIHE GESELLSCHAFTS
 und SPRACHWISSENSCHAFTEN.
 Greifswald 1951/2-   .

W41
WISSENSCHAFTLICHE ZEITSCHRIFT der
 FRIEDRICH-SCHILLER-UNIVERSITÄT.
 REIHE GESELLSCHAFT und SPRACH-
 WISSENSCHAFTEN. Jena 1951/2-   .

W42
WISSENSCHAFTLICHE ZEITSCHRIFT der
 HUMBOLDT-UNIVERSITÄT zu BERLIN.
 REIHE GESELLSCHAFT und SPRACHWIS-
 SENSCHAFT. Berlin 1951/2-   .

W43
WISSENSCHAFTLICHE ZEITSCHRIFT der
 KARL-MARX-UNIVERSITÄT, LEIPZIG.
 REIHE GESELLSCHAFT und SPRACHWIS-
 SENSCHAFTEN. Leipzig 1951/2-   .

W44
WISSENSCHAFTLICHE ZEITSCHRIFT der
 MARTIN-LUTHER-UNIVERSITÄT HALLE-
 WITTENBERG. REIHE GESELLSCHAFTS
 und SPRACHWISSENSCHAFTEN. Halle-
 Wittenberg 1951/2-   . (WZHalle).

W45
WISSENSCHAFLICHE ZEITSCHRIFT der
 UNIVERSITÄT ROSTOCK. REIHE GE-
 SELLSCHAFTS und SPRACHWISSEN-
 SCHAFTEN. Rostock 1951/2-   .

W46
WOCHENSCHRIFT für KLASSISCHE PHIL-
 OLOGIE. Berlin 1884-1920. United
 with Berliner Philologische Woch-
 enschrift to form Philologische
 Wochenschrift.

W47
WÖRTER und SACHEN; Zeitschrift für
 indogermanische Sprachenwissen-
 schaft. Heidelberg 1909-43/4.

W48
WÖRTERBUCH der ÄGYPTISCHEN SPRACHE /
 A. Erman & H. Grapow. Leipzig
 1926-50.

W49
WÖRTERBUCH der MYTHOLOGIE / H. W.
 Haussig. Stuttgart 1965-   .

W50
WÖRTERBUCH der UGARITISCHE SPRACHE
 / J. Aistleitner. 4. Aufl. Berlin 1974. (Sächsische Akademie
 der Wissenschaften. Philologisch-
 historische Klasse. Sitzungsberichte: 160, 3).

W51
WOLF EXPEDITION to ASIA MINOR / J.
 R. S. Sterrett. Boston 1888.
 (Papers of the American School
 of Classical Studies at Athens;
 3).

Woodhead, A. G. see S71.

W52
WORD (Linguistic Circle of New
 York). New York 1945-   .
 --. Supplement; monograph.
 1951-   .

W53
WORLD ARCHAEOLOGY. London 1969-   .

WORLD of ISLAM see W7.

W54
WORMSGAU. Worms 1926-   . Suspended 1944-50.

W55
WORT und DIENST; Jahrbuch der
 Theologischen Schule Bethel.
 Bethel bei Bielefeld 1950?-   .

WÖRTERBUCH see W48-W50.

Wright, R. P. see R335.

Wroth, W. see B210.

Wuensch, R. see D8.

W56
WÜRTTEMBERGISCH-FRANKEN (Historischer Verein für Württembergisch Franken). Hall am Kocher
 1859-73 1882-1915?

W57
WÜRZBURGER JAHRBÜCHER für die
  ALTERTUMSWISSENSCHAFT. Würzburg
  1946-50 1975-   . (WüJbb, WJA).

Wuilleumier, P. see I82.

X-Y

Xanthoudides, S. A.   see V7.

YALE ART GALLERY BULLETIN   see
  B445.

YALE CLASSICAL SERIES   see Y1.

Y1
YALE CLASSICAL STUDIES. New Haven
  1920-23. 1920 title: Yale Classical Series.

Y2
YALE CLASSICAL STUDIES. New Haven
  1928-   . (YC1S, YCS).

Y3
YALE NEAR EASTERN RESEARCHES. New
  Haven 1967-   .

Y4
YALE ORIENTAL SERIES. New Haven
  --. Babylonian Texts. 1915-   .
  --. Researches. 1912-   .
  (YOS).

Y5
YALE PAPYRI in the BEINECKE RARE
  BOOK and MANUSCRIPT LIBRARY /
  J. F. Oates et al. New Haven
  1967-   . (American Studies in
  Papyrology; 2). (PYale).

Y6
YALE UNIVERSITY LIBRARY GAZETTE.
  New Haven 1926-   .

YAYINLARI. ARKEOLOJI MÜZELERI
  see A575.

YAYINLARININ. TÜRK TARIH KURUMU
  see T132.

YEARBOOK of the BRITISH ASSOCIA-
  TION of NUMISMATIC SOCIETIES see
  C279.

YEARBOOK of the JÁSZMÚZEUM see
  J82.

Y7
YEAR'S WORK in CLASSICAL STUDIES.
  Bristol, Eng. 1906-47. (YWCS).

YEDI'OT (Israel Exploration Society) see B318.

YILLIGI. AYASOFYA MÜZESI see
  A696.

YILLIGI. ISTANBUL (ARKEOLOJI) MÜZE-
  LERI see I128.

Y8
YORKSHIRE ARCHAEOLOGICAL JOURNAL.
  London 1870-   . 1870-91 title:
  Yorkshire Archaeological and
  Topographical Journal. (YAJ).

YORKSHIRE ARCHAEOLOGICAL and TOP-
  OGRAPHICAL JOURNAL see Y8.

Youtie, H. C.   see A486.

YUGOSLAV HISTORICAL REVIEW see
  J142.

Z

ZAK   see   Z62.

Z1
ZALMOXIS; revue des études religieuses. Paris 1938-42.

ZAPISKI ARKHEOLOGO-NUMIZMATICHES-KAGO OBSHCHESTVA   see   Z2.

ZAPISKI IMPERATORSKAGO ODESSKAGO OBSHCHESTVA ISTORII i DREVNOSTEĬ see   Z6.

Z2
ZAPISKI IMPERATORSKAGO RUSSKAGO ARKHEOLOGICHESKAGO OBSHCHESTVA. Leiningrad 1849-1916. 1849-50 name of Society: Sanktpeterburg-skoe Arkheologichesko-numizma-ticheskoe Obshchestvo. Other slight changes.

Z3
ZAPISKI KOLLEGII VOSTOKOVEDOV pri AZIATSKOM MUZEE = Mémoires du Comité des Orientalistes. (Akademiĭa Nauk SSSR). Leningrad 1925-30?

Z4
ZAPISKI NUMISMATICHESKAGO OTDELENI-ĬA IMPERATORSKAGO RUSSKAGO ARKHE-OLOGICHESKAGO OBSHCHESTVA. Leningrad 1906/9-1910/3?

Z5
ZAPISKI ODESSKAGO ARKHEOLOGICHES-KAGO OBSHCHESTVA. Odessa 1960-   . Also numbered in con-tinuation of the Zapiski Odess-kago Obshchestva Istorii i Drev-nosteĭ (1844-1919?).

Z6
ZAPISKI ODESSKAGO OBSHCHESTVA ISTORII i DREVNOSTEĬ. Odessa 1844-1919? Title varies slightly. Continued by the Zapiski Odesskago Arkheologicheskago Obshchestva (1960-   ).

ZAPISKI RUSSKAGO ARKHEOLOGICHES-KAGO OBSHCHESTVA   see   Z2.

ZAPISKI. SANKTPETERBURGSKOE ARK-HEOLOGICHESKO-NUMIZMATICHESKOE OBSHCHESTVO   see   Z2.

ZBORNIK see also SBORNIK and SPOME-NIK.

Z7
ZBORNIK. ARHEOLOŠKI MUZEJ na MAKE-DONIJA = Recueil des Travaux du Musée Archéologique de Mace-doine. Skopje 1955/6-   . Earlier title: Zbornik. Arheolo-ški Muzej, Skopje = Recueil des Travaux du Musée Archéologique, Skopje.

ZBORNIK. ARHEOLOŠKI MUZEJ, SKOPJE see   Z7.

Z8
ZBORNIK FILOZOFSKOG FAKULTETA, BELGRAD = Recueil des Travaux de la Faculté de Philosophie (Univ. Belgrad). Belgrad 1948-   .

Z9
ZBORNIK FILOZOFSKE FAKULTETE LJUB-
LJANA = Recueil de Travaux de la
Faculté des Lettres de Ljubljana.
Ljubljana 1950-   .

Z10
ZBORNIK INSTITUTA za HISTORIJSKE
NAUKE u ZADRU = Mélanges de
l'Institut des Sciences Historique à Zadar. Zadar 1955-   .

Z11
ZBORNIK za LIKOVNE UMETNOSTI MATICE
SRPSKE = Recherches sur l'Art;
Matica Srpska: Section des Arts.
Novi Sad 1965?-   .

Z12
ZBORNIK NARODNOG MUZEJA (Belgrad)
= Revueil des Travaux du Musée
National. Belgrad 1956/7-   .
1956-61 title: Zbornik radova.

Z13
ZBORNIK PRAVNOG FAKULTETA u ZAGREBA
= Recueil des Travaux de la Facul-
té de Droit de l'Université de
Zagreb = Collected Papers of the
Zagreb Law School. Zagreb
1948?-   .

ZBORNIK RADOVA NARODNOG MUZEJA (Belgrad) see Z12.

Z14
ZBORNIK RADOVA VIZANTOLOŠKOG INSTI-
TUTA = Recueil des Travaux de
l'Institut d'Études Byzantines.
Belgrad 1952-   . (ZRVI).

Z15
ZBORNIK SLOVENSKÉHO NÁRODNÉHO
MÚZEA. Bratislava 1961-   .
Earlier title: Historický Sbornik
Variant title: Sbornik.

Z16
ZBORNIK SLOVENSKÉHO NÁRODNÉHO
MÚZEA = Historia; Annales Musei
Nationalis Slovaci. Turčiansky
Sv. Martin 1896-1951 1960-   .
1896-1951 title: Sbornik Muzeálnej
Slovenskej Spoločnosti = Revue de
Société de Musée Slovaque = Sam-
melwerk des Slowakischen Museums

Gesellschaft; 1960-61 title:
Sbornik Slovenského Národného
Muzéa.

Z17
ZBORNIK. SRPSKA AKADEMIJA NAUK i
UMETNOSTI. ODELJENJE DRUŠTVENIH
NAUKA = Bulletin de l'Académie
Serbe des Sciences. Classe des
Sciences Sociales. Belgrad
1951-   . Name of society
varies slightly.

Z18
ZEITSCHRIFT des AACHENER GESCHICHTS-
VEREINS. Aachen 1879-   . Sus-
pended 1941-48.

Z19
ZEITSCHRIFT für ÄGYPTISCHE SPRACHE
und ALTERTUMSKUNDE. Leipzig
1863-   . (ZÄS, ÄZ, ZAS, ZAeS,
AegZ).

Z20
ZEITSCHRIFT für ÄSTHETIK und ALLGE-
MEINE KUNSTWISSENSCHAFT. Stuttgart 1905/6-   . 1951-65 title:
Jahrbuch für Ästhetik und Allgemeine Kunstwissenschaft. Suspended 1944-50.

ZEITSCHRIFT für ALTER PHILOLOGIE
und GESCHICHTE see E89.

Z21
ZEITSCHRIFT für die ALTERTHUMSWIS-
SENSCHAFT. Giessen etc. 1834-57.

Z22
ZEITSCHRIFT für die ALTTESTAMENT-
LICHE WISSENSCHAFT. Berlin etc.
1881-   . (ZATW, ZAW).
--. Beihefte. 1896-   .

Z23
ZEITSCHRIFT für ARCHÄOLOGIE. Berlin 1967-   . (ZfA).

Z24
ZEITSCHRIFT für ARCHÄOLOGIE des
MITTELALTERS. Bonn 1973-   .

ZEITSCHRIFT für ASSYRIOLOGIE und
VERWANDTE GEBIETE see Z25.

Z25
ZEITSCHRIFT für ASSYRIOLOGIE und
    VORDERASIATISCHE ARCHÄOLOGIE.
    Leipzig 1886- . 1886-1922
    title: Zeitschrift für Assyrio-
    logie und verwandte Gebiete.
    (ZA).

ZEITSCHRIFT für ASZESE und MYSTIK
    see Z45, G9.

Z26
ZEITSCHRIFT für BAYERISCHE LANDES-
    GESCHICHTE. Munich 1928- .

Z27
ZEITSCHRIFT für BILDENDE KUNST.
    Leipzig 1866-1932.

ZEITSCHRIFT für CELTISCHE PHILO-
    LOGIE see Z47.

Z28
ZEITSCHRIFT für CHRISTLICHE KUNST.
    Düsseldorf 1888-1921. (ZChrK).

Z29
ZEITSCHRIFT für DEUTSCHES ALTERTUM
    und DEUTSCHE LITERATUR. Leipzig
    etc. 1841- . Suspended 1944-
    48.

Z30
ZEITSCHRIFT der DEUTSCHEN MORGEN-
    LÄNDISCHEN GESELLSCHAFT. Leipzig
    & Wiesbaden 1847- .
    --. Supplément. Wiesbaden
    1969- . (ZDMG).

Z31
ZEITSCHRIFT für die DEUTSCHE-ÖSTER-
    REICHISCHEN GYMNASIEN. Vienna
    1850-1920. 1850-1919 title:
    Zeitschrift für die Österreich-
    ischen Gymnasien. (ZöG).

Z32
ZEITSCHRIFT für DEUTSCHEN PALÄS-
    TINAVEREINS. Wiesbaden 1878- .
    Variant title: Beiträge zur
    biblischen Landes- und Altertums-
    kunde. Suspended 1946-49. (ZDPV,
    ZPal).

Z33
ZEITSCHRIFT für DEUTSCHE PHILOLOGIE.
    Berlin 1869- .

Z34
ZEITSCHRIFT des DEUTSCHEN VEREINES
    für die GESCHICHTE MÄHRENS und
    SCHLESIENS. Brno 1897-1940.
    Suspended 1920-21.

Z35
ZEITSCHRIFT des DEUTSCHEN VEREINS
    für KUNSTWISSENSCHAFT. Berlin
    1934-43.

Z36
ZEITSCHRIFT des DEUTSCHEN VEREINS
    für KUNSTWISSENSCHAFT. Berlin
    1947- . 1947-62 title: Zeit-
    schrift für Kunstwissenschaft.

Z37
ZEITSCHRIFT für ETHNOLOGIE. Berlin
    1869- . Includes the Verhand-
    lungen of the Berliner Gesell-
    schaft für Anthropologie, Ethno-
    logie und Urgeschichte 1869-1902.
    Suspended 1945-49. (ZE).

ZEITSCHRIFT der FINNISCHEN ALTER-
    TUMSGESELLSCHAFT see S274.

Z38
ZEITSCHRIFT für GESCHICHTE der
    ARCHITEKTUR. Heidelberg 1907/8-
    1924/8.

Z39
ZEITSCHRIFT für die GESCHICHTE des
    OBERRHEINS. Karlsruhe, Heidel-
    berg 1850- .

Z40
ZEITSCHRIFT für die GESCHICHTE der
    SAARGEGEND. Saarbrücken 1951- .
    1951-55 title: Zeitschrift für
    Saarländische Heimatkunde.

Z41
ZEITSCHRIFT des GESCHICHTSVEREINS.
    MÜLHEIM an der RUHR. Mülheim a.
    R. 1906- .

Z42
ZEITSCHRIFT für GESCHICHTSWISSEN-
    SCHAFT. Berlin 1953- .

Z43
ZEITSCHRIFT der GESELLSCHAFT für
    SCHLESWIGHALSTEINISCHE GESCHICHTE.

Neumünster etc. 1870-   .
--. Ergänzungsband. 1931-   .

ZEITSCHRIFT für das GYMNASIALSWESEN
see S111.

Z44
ZEITSCHRIFT des HISTORISCHEN VER-
EINS für STEIERMARK. Graz
1903-   . 1903-05 title: Steir-
ische Zeitschrift für Geschichte.
(ZHVst).

Z45
ZEITSCHRIFT für KATHOLISCHE THEO-
LOGIE. Innsbruck 1876-   . Vols.
67 (no. 3/4) and 68 (no. 3/4)
merged into Zeitschrift für
Aszese und Mystik; independent
publication resumed in 1947.
(ZKTh, ZKT).

Z46
ZEITSCHRIFT für KEILSCHRIFTFOR-
SCHUNG und VERWANDTE GEBIETE.
Leipzig 1884-85.

Z47
ZEITSCHRIFT für KELTISCHE PHILOLO-
GIE und VOLKSFORSCHUNG. Halle
1896-1943. 1896-1939 title had
spelling celtische.

Z48
ZEITSCHRIFT für KIRCHENGESCHICHTE.
Gotha & Tübingen 1876-   .
(ZKG).

Z49
ZEITSCHRIFT für KIRCHLICHE WISSEN-
SCHAFT und KIRCHLICHEN LEBEN.
Leipzig 1880-89

Z50
ZEITSCHRIFT für KUNSTGESCHICHTE.
Leipzig etc. 1932-   . Suspended
1944-49.

ZEITSCHRIFT für KUNSTWISSENSCHAFT
see Z36.

ZEITSCHRIFT des MÄHRISCHEN LANDES-
MUSEUMS see C63.

Z51
ZEITSCHRIFT für NAMENFORSCHUNG.

Munich 1925-43. 1925-37 title:
Zeitschrift für Ortsnamenforschung. (ZONF).

Z52
ZEITSCHRIFT für die NEUTESTATMENT-
LICHE WISSENSCHAFT und die KUNDE
der ÄLTEREN KIRCHE. Berlin
1900-   . Title varies slightly.
Suspended 1943-48. (ZNTW, ZNW,
BZNW).
--. Beihefte. 1923-   ?

Z53
ZEITSCHRIFT für NUMISMATIK. Berlin
1874-1935. (ZfN, ZNum, ZfNum).

ZEITSCHRIFT für die ÖSTERREICH-
ISCHEN GYMNASIEN see Z31.

ZEITSCHRIFT für ORTSNAMENFORSCHUNG
see Z51.

Z54
ZEITSCHRIFT für OSTFORSCHUNG. Marburg 1952-   .

Z55
ZEITSCHRIFT für PAPYROLOGIE und
EPIGRAPHIK. Bonn 1967-   .
(ZPE).

Z56
ZEITSCHRIFT für PHILOSOPHISCHE
FORSCHUNG. Wurzbach, Ger.
1946-   . (ZPhF).

Z57
ZEITSCHRIFT für PHILOSOPHIE und
PHILOSOPHISCHE KRITIK. Leipzig
etc. 1837-1918. 1837-46 title:
Zeitschrift für Philosophie und
Spekulative Theologie. Suspended
1849-52.

ZEITSCHRIFT für PHILOSOPHIE und
SPEKULATIVE THEOLOGIE see Z57.

ZEITSCHRIFT für PRAKTISCHE THEO-
LOGIE see E156.

Z58
ZEITSCHRIFT für RECHTSGESCHICHTE.
Weimar 1861-78.

Z59
ZEITSCHRIFT für RELIGIONS- und
   GEISTESGESCHICHTE. Marburg
   1948-   . (ZRGG).

Z60
ZEITSCHRIFT für ROMANISCHE PHILO-
   LOGIE. Halle & Tübingen 1877-   .
   Suspended 1945-48. (ZRPh).
   --. Beihefte. 1905-   .

ZEITSCHRIFT für SAARLÄNDISCHE
   HEIMATKUNDE see Z40.

Z61
ZEITSCHRIFT der SAVIGNY-STIFTUNG
   für RECHTSGESCHICHTE. ROMANIS-
   TISCHE ABTEILUNG. Weimar 1880-   .
   Suspended 1945-47. (ZRG, ZSav,
   ZSS).

Z62
ZEITSCHRIFT für SCHWEIZERISCHE
   ARCHÄOLOGIE und KUNSTGESCHICHTE
   = Revue Suisse d'Art et d'Arch-
   éologie = Rivista Svizzera d'Arte
   e d'Archeologia. Basel 1939-   .
   Supersedes Anzeiger für Schweiz-
   erische Altertumskunde (1868-
   1939). 1982-   calls itself ZAK;
   Zeitschrift etc. (ZAK, RSAA,
   ZSchwAkg).

Z63
ZEITSCHRIFT für SCHWEIZERISCHE
   KIRCHENGESCHICHTE = Revue d'His-
   toire Ecclésiastique Suisse.
   Fribourg 1907-   .

Z64
ZEITSCHRIFT für SEMITISTIK und VER-
   WANDTE GEBIETE. Leipzig 1922-25.

ZEITSCHRIFT für SYSTEMATISCHE
   THEOLOGIE see N33.

Z65
ZEITSCHRIFT für THEOLOGIE und
   KIRCHE. Tübingen etc. 1891-   .
   Suspended 1939-50. (ZThK).
   --. Beiheft. 1959-   .

ZEITSCHRIFT für VATERLÄNDISCHE GE-
   SCHICHTE und ALTERTHUMSKUNDE
   see W12.

ZEITSCHRIFT. VEREIN für die GE-
   SCHICHTE von SOEST und der BÖRDE
   see S110.

Z66
ZEITSCHRIFT des VEREINS für HAM-
   BURGISCHE GESCHICHTE. Hamburg
   1841-   .

Z67
ZEITSCHRIFT des VEREINS für HES-
   SISCHE GESCHICHTE und LANDES-
   KUNDE. Kassel 1837-   .
   --. Supplement. 1940-   .

Z68
ZEITSCHRIFT des VEREINS für LÜ-
   BECKISCHE GESCHICHTE und ALTER-
   TUMSKUNDE. Lübeck 1885-   .
   Vol. 31 covers 1942-49.

Z69
ZEITSCHRIFT des VEREINS für VOLKS-
   KUNDE. Berlin etc. 1860-1928.
   1860-90 title: Zeitschrift für
   Völkerpsychologie und Sprach-
   wissenschaft.

Z70
ZEITSCHRIFT für VERGLEICHENDE LI-
   TERATURGESCHICHTE. Berlin etc.
   1887?-1910. 1889-91 title: Zeitschrift für Vergleichende Literaturgeschichte und Renaissance-
   Literatur.

ZEITSCHRIFT für VERGLEICHENDE LI-
   TERATURGESCHICHTE und RENAIS-
   SANCE-LITERATUR see Z70.

Z71
ZEITSCHRIFT für VERGLEICHENDE
   RECHTSWISSENSCHAFT. Stuttgart
   1878-   . Suspended 1945-52.

Z72
ZEITSCHRIFT für VERGLEICHENDE
   SPRACHFORSCHUNG auf dem GEBIETE
   der INDOGERMANISCHEN SPRACHEN.
   Göttingen 1852-   . Title varies
   slightly. For many years edited
   by A. Kuhn. (ZVS).

ZEITSCHRIFT für VÖLKERPSYCHOLOGIE
   und SPRACHWISSENSCHAFT see Z69.

Z73
ZEITSCHRIFT für WISSENSCHAFTLICHE
  THEOLOGIE. Frankfurt a.M. 1858-
  1914.

ZEITSCHRIFT für WISSENSCHAFTGE-
  SCHICHTE see S267.

Z74
ZEITSCHRIFT für WÜRTTEMBERGISCHE
  LANDESGESCHICHTE. Stuttgart
  1937-   . Vol. 8 covers 1944-48.

Z75
ZENON PAPYRI / C. C. Edgar et al.
  Cairo 1925-40. (Catalogue Général
  des Antiquités Égyptiennes du Mu-
  sée du Caire; 79, etc.). Vol. 5
  appeared as Publications de la
  Société Fouad de Papyrologie; 5.
  (PCairZen).

Z76
ZENON PAPYRI; business papers of
  the third century B.C. dealing
  with Palestine and Egypt / W. L.
  Westermann et al. New York
  1934-40. (Columbia Papyri. Greek
  Series; 3 & 4). (PColZen).

Z77
ZENON PAPRI in the UNIVERSITY of
  MICHIGAN COLLECTION./ C. C. Ed-
  gar. Ann Arbor 1931. (Univ. of
  Michigan Studies. Humanistic
  Series; 24). Constitutes vol. 1
  of Michigan Papyri. (PMichI).

Z78
ZENTRALBLATT für BIBLIOTHEKSWESEN.
  Leipzig 1884-   . 1884-1903
  title: Centralblatt. Suspended
  1944-46.
  --. Beihefte. 1888-   . None
  published 1943-47.

Z79
ZEPHYRUS (Seminario de Arqueología y de la Sección Arqueoló-
  gica del Centro de Estudios Sal-
  mantinos). Salamanca 1950-   .

Zereteli, G. see P68.

Z80
ZETEMATA; Monographien zur Klas-

sischen Altertumswissenschaft.
  Munich 1951-   .

Z81
ZGODOVINSKI ČASOPIS = Istoricheskiĭ
  Zhurnal = Historical Review.
  Ljubljana 1947-   .

Zgusta, L. see A188, K27.

Z82
ZHURNAL MINISTERSTVA NARODNOGO
  PROSVĨESHCHENIĨA. Leningrad
  1834-1917. (ZMNP).

Z83
ZHURNAL MOSKOVSKOI PATRIARCHII.
  Moscow 1931-34 1943-   .

Ziehen, L. see L23.

Zilliacus, H. see S287, V52.

Z84
ZION; a quarterly for research in
  Jewish history. Jerusalem
  1949-   .

Z85
ŽIVA ANTIKA = Antiquité Vivante.
  Skopje 1951-   .

Z86
ZOFINGER NEUJAHRSBLATT. Zofingen
  1905-   . Suspended 1909-19.

Z87
ZOGRAF. Belgrade 1966-   .

Z88
ZOTCHŁANI WIEKOW (Polskie Towarzystwo Archeologiczne). Wroclaw
  1926-   . Suspended 1939-45 and
  1954-56. 1954-56 replaced by
  Dawna Kultura.

Z89
ZPRÁVY ČESKOSLOVENSKÉHO STÁTNIHO
  ARCHEOLOGICKÉHO ÚSTAVU = Rapport
  de l'Institut d'Archéologie
  del'État Tchécoslovaque. Prague
  1919/28-31?

Z90
ZPRÁVY JEDNOTY KLASICKÝCH FILOLOGU.
  Prague 1959-   .

Zucker, F. see J83.

Z91
ZÜRCHER-CHRONIK. Zurich ?-   .

Z92
ZÜRCHER DENKMALPFLEGE. Zurich
  1958/9-   .

Z93
ZÜRCHER TASCHENBUCH. Zurich 1858-
  59 1862 1878-   .

Zuetaieff, J. see S289.

Z94
ZUGER NEUJAHRSBLATT. Zug 1842-46
  1882-   .

Z95
ZUR GESCHICHTE LATEINISCHER EIGEN-
  NAMEN / W. Schulze. Berlin 1904.
  (Abhandlungen der Köninglichen
  Gesellschaft der Wissenschaften
  zu Göttingen. Philologisch-his-
  torische Klasse; N.F. 5, 5).

Zvetaieff, J. see I69.

About the Compiler

JEAN SUSORNEY WELLINGTON is head of the Classics Library at the University of Cincinnati. She holds masters degrees in both Library Science and Ancient History.